What Others S

Alan Hoenig makes learning and remembering Chinese ... secrets to mastering 2,000 of the most common Chinese characters, Hoenig has produced ... he best books I have come across for learning the language spoken by more than a billion people around the world.

Dr. Choon Fong Shih, *President, National University of Singapore*

Love the book! For the first time I think I could realize my teenage dream of learning Chinese—I am now 67. It's time.

Cherry, August 2013, via Internet

I just wanted to say "thank you." I'd decided not to bother learning to write characters but to focus on the other skills, when a trip to China made me question my decision. The only characters I found I could read with confidence out of context were those few I'd learnt to write. I found your book—and suddenly it gave me the key to the door. I now can write about 1000 characters, *and counting*. Big thank you.

Helen (March, 2012), via Internet

I recently purchased the Chinese Characters dictionary by Alan Hoenig. ... I have several Chinese/English dictionaries but have been very dissatisfied with them. I found [that] Alan Hoenig's Chinese Characters dictionary ... is far better than the other character dictionaries I have. I followed the link to MDBG on the web and was even more excited. I must commend Doctor Hoenig for his work. I love your website and ... am sure I will be returning to your website many times. Thank you,

David Spence (October, 2013), via Internet

Hi Dr. Alan, Thank you for writing a very practical book. It's quite perfect. Ciao,

Roderick, via Internet

Congratulations. "Chinese Characters" has given me hope that some day I might be able make myself understood in Chinese. Besides, the book is most entertaining. "Chinese Characters" has been my favourite reading during the last couple of months.

Dr. L. V., Kokkola, Finland, via Internet

I live in Cape Town, South Africa and recently purchased your book. I am a 3rd year University of South Africa student, majoring in Chinese. My pinyin is good....but I can't read or recognize characters *at all*! Now I want to do my Honours degree in Translation Studies: Chinese–English, so I have to learn a LOT of characters, like yesterday. Your book is making is so easy!!! I've already learned 38 characters from your book—I can remember them very well, and I am ecstatic!!! Thank you so much!! A huge thank you from a very happy reader!!

Blair, December 2011

I just bought this book a couple weeks ago and I was surprised at how easy it is to pick up your learning system. I am using it to extend my knowledge of the Chinese language. ... Thank you for writing this book on learning the meanings of the characters. I have found it significantly more helpful than the various books by Sam Song and Rita Mei-Wah Choy and the several Tuttle books.

Jennifer F., via Internet

...let me express my regard for the creativity you have shown in creating Chinese Characters and providing a set of core building blocks (rather like the old radicals) that link subsets of the basic characters in ways that are unconventional and ahistorical but are mnemonically useful. ... Even more kudos to you, though, for taking a step that I have often thought about but – given my focus on classroom materials rather that self-study materials – never actually put into practice; that is, grasping the graph (or glyph) by the horns and treating the problem of learning the graphs independently from other aspects of the language. ...You have certainly thought the presentation through, with useful visuals – the little boxes – and notes, as well as providing flashcards online, and even detailed instructions on how to produce them. I wish I could provide such good support for my own materials!

Professor Julian Wheatley

Prof. Wheatley is visiting Assoc. Prof. of Chinese, Nat'l Inst. of Education, Nanyang Tech. Univ. of Singapore; former Senior Lecturer in Foreign Languages and Literatures at the Massachusetts Institute of Technology, and Director of the MIT China Program.

Your present project "Chinese Characters" has more eye appeal than any others in the marketplace. It's a beautiful volume with bright yellow background and rich red Han characters. The pages themselves are formatted and laid out in an inviting fashion. The material is presented in small digestible increments.

Dr. M. S., via Internet

Fantastic material if you want to memorize Chinese characters. This is an under-publicized, unique system for memorizing characters quickly.

Derek

Anyway—great book! I passed my Japanese first level proficiency test last year so together with some supercharging from your book I am hoping to pass intermediate HSK this year. ... Thanks very much for your reply—I am flattered that the author of such an excellent book should respond so generously and comprehensively as well. Very best regards and look forward to your next work!

Malcolm L., via Internet

I've been enjoying working my way through the sample PDF of your book. It's brilliant! Kudos ... I really prefer your explanations; it's as if you're talking to me directly, explaining tricks on how to remember each character.

Matthew, via Internet

Your book is terrific. I have been unable to put it down which is actually a problem as I have other things to get done. But I wanted to send you a quick email. I couldn't resist the challenge you put into your preface.

Judith

I just received your book. I've always been puzzled by why I can't remember the simple Chinese characters. This book provides a very creative and fun approach to learning the easy and the complicated characters!

John, via Internet

I would like to thank you for your excellent book on learning Chinese. It is a great help and, after only a few months of study, I am progressing far beyond what I would have thought possible. ... I just find the methods I have seen thus far so useful! And could I quickly take the opportunity to thank you for loading the flashcard deck onto Anki; this has been absolutely essential for me.

Toby Tricks, via Internet

David Martin's blog at MandarinFromScratch.com describes "One man's quest to learn Mandarin Chinese from scratch to fluency as quickly as possible using Automatic Language Growth." On December 2, 2009 (modified on May 27, 2011), he describes his efforts at "Learning the Mandarin Characters (Hanzi)." Here is an excerpt:

"Once you've got a good listening base in Mandarin, and not before, you'll want to get started on learning the Hanzi. I've found the following combination quite good for learning the characters:

"Alan Hoenig's *Learn and Remember 2,178 Characters and Their Meanings* - builds up your character knowledge systematically going from least to most complex by introducing the components first

and showing how they're combined to form more complicated characters. An explanation appears at www.EZChinesey.com.

First of all, let me thank you for the book preview and free material on your website. It's really motivating! Also, your method seems to work realllly well :-)

Andy

First of all, let me thank you for the great book and the excellent characters memorization method. I've been waiting for someone to come up with this for a long time! ...I already got the files from your site to complement the book. Thanks for putting them up for free! I'm eagerly waiting for more books from you, especially the ones helping memorization of character's pronunciation and tone. I find it one of the most challenging aspects in studying Chinese.

Val

Thank you for such a great book. I'm a Malaysian Chinese who was brought up speaking Chinese but has no formal education reading or writing Chinese. This is a great book which I'm sure will benefit my learning.

NGIM

I have just starting reading your delightful book. ... I am very impressed with usefulness of the unit review pdf file that has the characters, pinyin, and meanings with "the shuffles." ... In closing I would say that I am looking forward to your forthcoming books, especially the one to speak and remember names of characters.

Gerald

This (EZChinesey.com) is a really well-designed site. It would tempt me to learn Chinese! That's saying quite a bit. The checkerboard logo has a nice punch—it works to tie together all the disparate picture and text elements.

Joyce, via Internet

What a scholarly publication! I am very impressed! I look forward to reading it and sharing it with my middle school students as well. Perhaps it will give me some insights as to how I can make the learning and memorization of characters more interesting to my students. It is the one aspect of Chinese they all quite dread.

Elizabeth

I love your program, it's the best I've found and I've tried everything.

Derek M. in Taiwan

I just purchased your "Chinese Characters" and then accessed your web site and the supporting materials. Thank you! Your support of learning in this way makes your product even more valuable. I've recommended it already to a colleague who is also studying Chinese.

Barry H. from Canada

Hi there, I have been using your book for some time now and it is the absolute best way to learn Chinese I have come across! I was wondering, though, as I am interested in going to Taiwan: do you have any kind of traditional character study guides available or are you planning to make a version of your book that includes traditional chinese characters? That would be so helpful. Thank you.

Justin, via Internet

Firstly, I'd like to say I think your book is great, and so too are the free resources on your website. I'm at unit 13 at the moment, and very much enjoying learning the characters, and remembering them! I can't believe I can learn and retain 50+ characters in a week. Thank you very much. ...generally your stories to remember each character are very good, and they have inspired me to create my own for the the pinyin pronunciation, and also to create my own for any new characters I come across elsewhere. ... I forgot to mention how useful I find your jpg flashcards (I use them on my Blackberry) - great revision. Thanks again for your hard work. Best wishes for your new book.

Martin H., Norwich, England, via Internet

First of all, I want to thank you for this book! I've been living & teaching English in China for 5 years and kept hitting a brick wall when it came to learning to read Chinese. I've just started using the book and the online PDFs and I feel it's a very well rounded system. I've been expounding its virtues to all my friends that are also studying Chinese!

Rich Robertson, via Internet

Love the Chinese Characters book. After years of just dabbling, some characters are finally starting to come together for me.

Grant Remer, via Internet

I recently purchased your EZChinesey book and have been very impressed with it and its organization and how I can use it as a reference as well as for reading straight through. ... My next request is that you do a traditional character version of your book. In the meantime, thank you for your wonderful book... I really enjoy your simplified book and the ease of reference and how you indicate which part of the character is the radical and where that radical is introduced in your book. I have actually used other books that offer various mnemonic strategies for learning Chinese but yours is my favorite. Thank you once again.

Holly

I have found your 2000 characters book to be excellent and the Anki deck too. Kind regards.

Martin Donegan, via Internet

I like your progressive approach to character development that results in a memory link to similar characters. At the moment your book has the advantage because of the pinyin included with each character.

Garth Lane, via Internet

Your wonderful book has made it easier for me to study and memorize Chinese characters easier. It still takes a long time, but a lot less time than before. ...I just checked out Anki. It is quite a good learning aid as well. ...If you have a mailing list, please put me in the list for future product announcements.

David Yoon, via Internet

Read Me First! (An Overview)

See How Our Method Works for You!

Here is an actual demonstration of the **EZChinesey** method, which proves that it *will* work for you. In this overview, you will learn eight Chinese characters.

We begin with the three simplest characters; they are:

一 one   二 two   三 three

These three characters so clearly convey their meaning that you can easily remember them as long as you know how to count!

We move forward by introducing a non-freestanding component that will give us the flexibility to construct new characters. This one looks like an upright stick: ' | '. It is *not* a freestanding character and will only be used as an element in constructing other characters. This stick-like vertical stroke resembles many things—a primitive tool, a fence post, or the scepters that kings and emperors wielded as symbols of their authority. We have chosen to call this component a **scepter c**. The 'c' emphasizes the 'scepter' as a **c**omponent that will always be used to build other characters, and will never be a freestanding character itself. Whenever we form a new character by combining, say, a scepter with other elements, we will incorporate the meaning of the new character with its components into a unique 'memory story' that will help you tie them all together—visually and mentally. Sometimes these stories are very imaginative, at times even comparable to nursery rhymes—all in order to provide you with the most memorable story possible.

Now, back to learning characters, and the next one on our list is:

十 ten

You can easily remember the meaning of this character if you imagine the '*scepter c*' crossing the '*one*' to form the letter 't', the first letter of the character's meaning, '**ten**'.

The next Chinese character is formed by placing '*ten*' on top of '*one*':

士 knight

Formerly, someone who was smart enough to count backwards from '*ten*' to '*one*' might qualify to be a **knight**. That's a story to help you remember this character.

We form the next character by combining '*scepter c*' with 二, '*two*'.

工 work, labor

Imagine how much **work** it takes to pry apart and insert a *stick* between *two* heavy bars.

The *scepter* can combine with 二, '*two*', in another way. Here the scepter is a stick or a hoe, and the bars of 'two' represent the top and bottom of the layer the hoe passes through. Layer of what? Why, layers of **earth**, of course—and this character often means **earth** or **soil**.

土 **earth, soil**

In the final character, 干, imagine that sometimes, perhaps in time of drought, the earth is so soft and powdery that the hoe slips all the way through the earth until only its top is at the surface. This happens when the soil is thirsty and **dry**, and that's what this character often means.

干 **dry**

Okay, now don't look back.

We just introduced eight Chinese characters and their meanings to you:

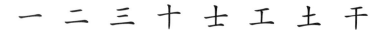

Can you remember their meanings? I bet you surprised yourself with how well you did! Our method really is that EZ!

Character Line-up

To help you appreciate the 'big picture' of what you will learn, we compiled this virtual line-up of all the characters and components in this book. Components (which are used like building blocks to construct characters) appear in white set in a gray square. Since we could not possibly display over 2,200 characters and components on a single line, you need to imagine the single line-up cut into equal pieces and stacked vertically to form the very long display you see below and that extends onto the next page.

Take some time to examine these forms. Notice how they become increasingly more complex from left to right, and from top to bottom. When a new component is introduced, the forms become briefly simpler, only to resume their rightward march toward complexity!

一二三山非十士土圭击工五互王丰干丁于手拜了子排打托挂聿彗丑扭扫口中甲里哩理埋押吐吾吉呈扣回串品古固叶咕申由抽可哥呵田日早晶旦昌唱旦坦量担旧目耳冒而面峀瑞喘看且直盯菲苦草苗描卉甘曲曹革鞋皿孟置罪司羽习韦围韩卫节再同册巾吊帽帛七匕旨指比批昆毕北也地世己巳巴把吧弓引弗弱岂孔乙瓦艺电龟扎巨臣拒匪出屯吨画事幅印叫丽刊副班帅师归玉国主午缶竹血毛斗抖卜占上止址扯正是提此些卸下卡吓卓掉單卧临监蓝扑生年星牛制牲寸封耐寻寺持特时导白百皇皆拍帛帕自咱告靠兆挑吕雨雪需雷门问闻间闰币书市闹高搞亭言詈罚亡芒亨享哼笔等简营带宜宇宫宙宣它富守害割向响牢字宁宝审宅儿先宪兄克元玩完冠园四西酉酷醒配牺见现觅宽览儿匹水沓益泉永求球派承录剥隶江汪油河洞池混浩注茫酒洗泄温洁汗汇润津范冰冲况计订语词许证讨诗记让谨勾匀均旬询句苟勺的白鼠与举誉写丐喝葛揭渴包抱泡马玛吗骂驻冯鸟岛鸣鸿乌原源岸斤丘折哲誓斥诉听岳匠氏氐抵昏厚爪抓畏喂爬厅压厂厄广店底广扩庄庙症疗癌卑乒乓兵宾川荒训乍昨才牙呀在存闭团者署诸著勿物易易场扬汤荡吻刀切力功助男勒加驾另别历为劳勃召招昭刃片牌方芳访不否坏环老孝尸居据剧届刷尾尿尺局民眠尽尼呢泥眉户声扁卢乃扔石碧碍础码岩矿身射谢九丸孰执势人坐座全拖企齿大因咽太天吴误笑矢知智疑凝医疾乔毫吞木杜植查呆果课棵困操某谋桃柏桌村耗宋末抹未味朱珠本相箱湘束策刺禾租和程香科稿兼廉乘剩利莉秀诱季种菌林森麻摩嘛磨桥析床材杨架梁杯李染术荣柜桂闲柱柴棍柯棉奇寄骑椅莫摸幕模漠墓弋式试戈找战戍咸喊减成城盛诚我哦或域戋浅尧晓臧藏划武犬哭器厌央映英唤立端站辛辟壁拉啦音暗章竟境童撞帝膏滴蒂竞旁产竭契牵夺奋头买卖读实奔庆奄掩沃夫替潜失秩规庚唐康扶巫足捉走捷赶越超起赴楚兔免晚勉挽欠吹歌旡次盗茨歇欣肉背肚胞膀肠脉肝肤膜两满寅演千重董舌括甜舍啥活阔话辞乱插垂睡它入内丙病商黎女娃姑如姐耍妇她姓要腰媒妹委矮嫌威姿安按案毌毒妻凄妾接母姆每梅海舟舰盘妨奶好婚妈奸妖娇久危脆乞吃气汽色六亦赤赫弯湾仓抢苍创枪舱闪鱼鲁渔认个众从丛茸争净睁挣仑论抛翰盐乾刍趋夕名外多移够歹死殊残列殖歼梦将蒋奖宛碗罗岁几机亮沿船凡讯巩筑朵躲兀抗航虎虚壳冗沉凯肌万厉励长帐套张涨勹卯留溜聊柳昂抑隔骨滑夹缺决块阻院阿啊障阳防陷队萨陆陶邦帮邮耶邪都郭厶私瓜孤云层会坛动去法劫丢却脚罢摆至到室屋握予野舒序矛柔台抬治始允充矣埃幺幻幽玄兹滋磁畜蓄幼么鬼魔魂魏以拟虫属蛋虽强蛇县勾构沟灬然烈庶席照熟点杰热燕纟组红素累细结纯系紫绕纳线绿约药统丝绪绍纪绝纸纵续绘乡纽绳衤衣哀表裁裂袁卒醉碎农浓衰初补袖袍犭狂猫犯貌狱狗猛猪犹获独心闷必宓密秘瑟悲慧忠思惠息媳忘惑想意慈恋忌怨志恩嗯意怎忽忍急稳隐愿态恐虑患悬忄悟懂怕性忙快悔恒怀忆怔慌距跳跌踏跑跃践亻仁仙什伍佳值估仲伸但侵他仰件伯住任凭信似促休保堡例们倒依何荷化花

华佰宿缩佳堆推唯售集谁维翟准焦瞧雁鹰雅崔催霍惟隽携截付符府腐附咐代
袋侯候位亿作伤仍佛低仔仇体伦伟佩侍仆俩伐俄伏仿储伪 彳往行街律征惩待
得徒德彻御 八小尖慕示奈禁欸宗崇综踪票漂标余茶除徐涂斜亲新尉慰杂际
东陈练车辈辑军挥浑斩暂渐库软辆载阵轮辖轨乐肖稍消削悄京景凉惊琼掠雀
你您少省吵妙沙莎步涉劣尘当挡档尔弥称添孙其基斯欺甚堪穴窝突探深空控
腔穿奂换穷挖究兑脱税说阅悦谷容裕俗欲公松衮滚讼具俱真填惧慎州洲分芬
纷份扮介界价阶贝贡贵溃质则测侧贴责绩债贾赞页项顶顷倾颠题硕颗预顾顺
频颤员损圆赢贾惯资贞侦货财赌贺费负赖赋购贲喷愤贷赔贸贫只职识织积函
豕豪蒙象缘家象像豫率办胁协苏飞肃萧啸兰拦南献喃酋尊拳半胖伴判禹融隔
羊善鲜美洋样详辛弟第梯差羞养氧着平评革萍乎呼曾增僧火烧烟灭燃伙光耀
晃辉秋愁炎淡谈烂灾炸烦灯煤炮灵炼米粗糟料粉类粒粹糖来莱娄楼继断金针
锦钱锐镇锁镜锁鉴业亚晋恶严显湿尚堂掌常尝偿赏党躺倘黑墨默兴总聪墙丧
券单弹兽夹侠峡盖关联郑 豆短首前箭 喜嘻嘉 部倍培陪 彡须彭影趁穆诊
珍参惨 昔措籍惜借错腊猎共翼典塞赛洪寒供恭巷港暴爆展黄横董勤 奥
噢澳悉番播翻 安采菜彩浮俘乳摇应 奏凑秦泰春卷圈奉寿春 合拿拾哈答
塔停搭给恰俞输愈愉偷金剑签险验检盒今琴吟含贪令玲零龄冷铃领命邻怜念
轻经径劲 辨辩 沈肱雄宏左佐右若诺惹布怖尤就忧扰优龙庞袭笼灰恢无
抚 开 丌 卉 鼻异戴弄井讲耕升戒械算 伊君群 川 丹月霸肯望脸期有郁青晴睛清
请猜情精静明盟朝潮那哪娜能熊朕腾胜朋鹏用甫捕博溥薄浦蒲傅甬痛勇涌角
嘴触衡确拥胃谓胡湖糊胎肥臂肿胆阴脏周调雕 丈仗艾哎希稀又坚贤紧怪
双蠢聂摄报祭察擦友爱发拔废服桑支技枝鼓皮坡颇被彼破波婆皱玻疲敲叟搜
瘦艘取最趣聚娶曼漫慢奴怒努反板版叛度渡叔督寂受授爱缓援暖拔变戏叟投
段股设役毅般搬毁殿疫没叙邓圣叹汉难欢权劝观仅择泽译对树释鸡史驶吏使
更便鞭硬艮眼根痕限狠恨跟很银爵良浪娘狼朗食餐郎粮辰振震雇晨唇既概即
艰凶胸脑恼文彦颜齐挤济剂纹刘夜液父爷爸交咬较校风疯飘凤杀刹区欧驱网
赵义议仪冈刚纲钢岗 开 开形研刑型并拼屏瓶普碰舛舞 饰饮饱饭饲饿 攵峰
夏凌酸俊窗陵锋傻冬疼终图复复覆腹履麦各略客额格阁络洛落路露降隆处蜂
后户扁篇骗编偏房雇护启炉所盾循扇肩 攻玫收牧政微败救数致改敌散撒
敦教效故做敕整敏繁敬警攸修条放敖傲缴激施旋族旅旗斿游务敢枚备 迪
遭近逃迎逼迫造这远过遗速述迁遥迟遍迈运还进逻适迷途达选逊巡边逐透递
违通随逢缝邀迅之乏泛连莲避道退腿送返递遵迹 建健廷挺庭蜓艇延诞及吸
级极 禺愚偶遇离璃 流疏弃亥刻核该孩育撤 祖社神福视祝祥祸礼 追官
管馆薛遣 假 亏 巧号考夸跨污专转传 状壮装 登 纠 钻铜铺铅铁钟键
觉学

Learn to Read Chinese *Fast!*

Simplified Characters

Master 2,197 Characters
In No Time

Learn to
Read Chinese *Fast!*
Simplified Characters

Master 2,197 Characters
In No Time

Second Edition

Alan Hoenig, Ph.D.

Use this Innovative Memory Method
and Put the *Ease* into *Learning Chinese...*
You *Will* Learn *and* Remember
Simplified Mandarin Chinese Characters

An EZChinesey™ *Guide*

EZChinesey.com
21 GLENVIEW PLACE, HUNTINGTON, NEW YORK 11743

2 0 1 4

About the cover. The cover photo shows a portion of the China Central Television Headquarters, Beijing; photo courtesy castelfranco, via wikipedia.org. This striking structure was designed by Rem Koolhaas and Ole Scheeren. The main building is not a traditional tower, but a loop of six horizontal and vertical sections covering 473,000 square meters (5,090,000 sq ft) of floor space. It was fully completed on May 16, 2012.

The pumpkin-colored Chinese characters on the left are symbols of good luck and fortune. Reading from top to bottom, here are their meanings and official pinyin transliterations: beautiful (měi), longevity (shòu), lucky (jí), wealth (cái), good fortune (fú), harmonious (hé), love (aì), virtue (dé), happiness (xǐ), and emolument (lù). The character on the spine is hóng (large, vast), the author's Chinese surname.

The interior body types are drawn from the family of Baskerville Ten Pro fonts, designed by František Štorm. The typesetting was done by means of the XeTeX program of Jonathan Kew, itself an extension of Donald Knuth's TeX typesetting program.

Copyright © 2014 by Alan Hoenig

All rights reserved
Printed in the United States of America
Second Edition

Library of Congress Cataloging-in-Publication Data

Hoenig, Alan.
Learn to Read Chinese *Fast!* (Simplified Characters): Master 2,197 Characters in No Time / Alan Hoenig —2nd ed.
    p. cm.
Includes indices.

ISBN 978-0-9822324-4-6
1. Chinese language. 2. Mandarin language. 3. Chinese characters. 4. Chinese language study. 5. Hanzi characters. 6. Chinese simplified characters

EZChinesey.com
21 Glenview Pl, Huntington, Long Island, NY 11743
631–385–0736

www.EZChinesey.com

1 2 3 4 5 6 7 8 9 0

2008912226

美梦成真

To Maddy

望女成凤

Contents

Preface to the Second Edition

The existence of this second edition is a tribute to the many readers who have encouraged this project with their generous and gracious comments. Many thanks!

I've taken advantage of this opportunity to correct errors, re-write *many* stories, and make other revisions to the narratives that seemed appropriate. Readers will notice the larger page size, so there's more of the white space that many people requested (now it's easy to make notes). The layout of each character panel has changed quite a bit. The most noticeable new feature is the addition of stroke order diagrams. With these, students can learn how Chinese speakers create these remarkable characters. References to other characters in the diagrams which illustrate each character's decomposition now include page numbers. Marginal notes provide additional meanings and pronunciations for a character (if there are any). Finally, I've included the traditional form of a character if it differs from the simplified form.

You can find additional review files at www.EZChinesey.com, and they are still free. They have been revised to include the changes we described above.

It is my great pleasure to dedicate this second edition to my granddaughter Madison. I hope she finds all her wishes fulfilled, and that she grows and matures into a truly special person.

Lastly, let it continue to be known that I welcome comments, questions, and even criticism. Contact me at EZChinesey@gmail.com. I look forward to hearing from you.

Preface to the First Edition

Chinese characters have been in use for 3200 years, and despite arguments that have probably raged for about the same amount of time, the Chinese people have never bothered to reform these characters in any meaningful way. The so-called *simplified characters* promulgated in the nineteen-fifties provided a reform which is substantial (many characters were changed), but not meaningful (no attempt, for example, to design an alphabetic system comparable to ours or to the phonetic system they use in Taiwan). This book deals with this reformed, *simplified* character set. (The original, *traditional* character set is the subject of a separate guide, *Traditional Chinese Characters: Learn & Remember 2,193 Character Meanings*, by Alan Hoenig, ISBN 978-0-9822324-3-9, and published by EZChinesey.com.)

The very fact that these characters have persevered for such a long time must mean something. I've never encountered a person brought up in China who complained about all the work it took to learn them. That's cold comfort for us non-native speakers, and the purpose of this book is to present a method which makes this task much easier for us. For a far more expansive discussion of this innovative method, please see the 'Read Me First!' overview.

I will conclude this section with a plethora of acknowledgments. First off, I am pleased to point out that many of the ideas in this presentation drew upon the earlier work of James W. Heisig and Michael Rowley on Japanese kanji.

I relied heavily on a small handful of remarkable reference works, though they were not always in agreement! The list of books in my personal canon begins with the "Oxford Concise English-Chinese Chinese-English Dictionary" (I used the second edition). Alas, this trusty volume is now out-of-print, but appears to have been superseded by the "Pocket Oxford Chinese Dictionary (4th ed.)" (Oxford Univ. Press, ISBN 978-0198005940). This dictionary contains both English-Chinese and Chinese-English sections, but at 8x5x2 inches and 2 pounds, I can't help but wonder whose pocket it will fit into!

The next two are Rick Harbaugh's "Chinese Characters: A Genealogy and Dictionary" (1998, published by Zhongwen.com; I used the fourteenth printing; ISBN 978-0966075007); and the "Chinese-English Comprehensive Dictionary," ed. John DeFrancis (2003, University of Hawai'i Press; ISBN 978-0824827663).

Finally, I recommend the magisterial "New Age Chinese-English Dictionary" (2009, Commercial Press, Beijing; ISBN 978-7-100-04345-8). At almost 2200 pages, it contains everything you'll ever need to know about Chinese words, idioms, expressions, and their meanings. (And, yes, there is a companion volume, "New Age English-Chinese Dictionary;" ISBN 978-7-100-04564-3.) The titles of these volumes might make you think that they cater to the incense-and-crystal crowd; not so. These are very fine and worthwhile works. Every serious student of Chinese should have these books.

With the sheer volume of material in this book—and occasionally contradictory source materials—I fear that errors remain in this book, despite scrupulous care. I hope that I can rely on you, gentle reader, to assist me in ruthlessly rooting them out. If you find any errors or have any suggestions for improvement, please share them! If you include permission for me to use this material in any and all subsequent editions and printings, then I will cheerfully list the name of the first person who finds an error, and the names of all readers whose suggestions are incorporated into the volume. (Drop a line to me at info@EZChinesey.com.) Many thanks in advance.

This book would have been written in half the time without the gentle ministrations of Hannah, Sam, and Madison! Thanks, kids. Hey, Max, Cody, and Rosie—thank you, too! My wife, Jozefa, has been, as always, my bulwark against stupor, discouragement, crankiness, and lassitude— the four horsemen of the authorial apocalypse. She has supported and encouraged this venture with good cheer, great advice, and unstinting love.

—Alan Hoenig
Huntington, Long Island, New York
Summer 2013, Year of the Snake

Our Method: An Introduction

This book exists for a single purpose—to teach you the meanings of more than two thousand common *simplified* Chinese characters, to teach these meanings to you *fast*, and to teach them to you in a way so that you *will* remember them! This method makes learning characters EZ!

With knowledge of these two thousand characters, you will be prepared to read almost 96% of an average general purpose piece of modern Chinese literary text. Even better, you will be able to extend the **EZChinesey** method to apply to other characters you encounter.

This volume deals *solely* with **simplified characters**. The designation *simplified* refers to the simplifications applied to the original set of characters. By the nineteen-fifties, the mainland government ordered a few hundred traditional characters to be replaced with these *simplified* forms. The original traditional characters are typically used in Chinese communities outside of mainland China, in many Chinese language courses, and on certain formal occasions. This volume deals *only* with simplified character forms. (Other **EZChinesey** guides teach the same method for the traditional forms.)

We'll lay out the complete details later, but here's the gist of our method. Think about learning words in a typical English language course for foreigners. In this class, we surely expect to learn words like 'restaurant' or 'computer' before the word 'ewe', even though the latter word is shorter and easier to say—because when learning to *speak* a language, it's frequency of use, and hence relative importance, that matter.

But learning to read the characters comprising the unique Chinese writing system presents some challenges not found in European language courses. You might think it makes sense to learn the characters of the Chinese *writing* system in their approximate order of frequency, since that ensures that we learn the most common, and therefore the most important, characters first—that is, the same strategy we might use to learn the *spoken* language. But if you tried that, you would often have to learn complex-looking glyphs early on just because they possess simple or common meanings. Moreover, such an approach ignores any relationships between constituent parts that might exist between characters.

So instead of this apparently sensible method, let's imagine what would happen if we listed the characters in order of writing ease, and learned them *this* way—that is, learning easy-to-write characters in advance of complicated ones, as if we choose to learn 'ewe' before 'restaurant'. There's more merit here than you might think, by virtue of another crucial fact—Chinese characters are built up from simpler building blocks. As a result, we can create simple *mnemonic* memory stories that make it easy for us to remember the meanings of the two thousand most frequent traditional characters in terms of characters that have simpler structures. Since the simpler characters have already been learned, these memory stories relate the meanings and forms of any character in terms of the meaning and structures of simpler characters. This is the essence of our **EZChinesey** method, and the many hundreds of testimonials we've received from our readers show that it works.

This executive summary of **EZChinesey** omits or simplifies a wide variety of details, details that are really important, at least once you start on our method in earnest. It seems best to keep this and other additional information encapsulated in special sections so you can peruse them conveniently without the distractions of the remainder of the book, which is devoted to detailing this method.

Several of these sections are so important that they precede the rest of this book. Encapsulated in a section entitled 'Read Me First!' are two discussions. The first is a proof—yes, a *proof!*—that this method will work for you. The second shows the characters in this book lined up in the order in which we present them. You can clearly see (I hope!) how the characters proceed from simple to involved structure, and how each character incorporates bits and pieces from characters that have come before it.

Five additional sections occur interspersed among the units, each of which is a grouping of panels. These interludes treat various topics that expand or supplement the methods of this book. The first interlude, for example, explains the conventions and significance of all the items in a character panel. Others discuss the marginal notes in the right margin, flashcards (because ultimately, you want to master character recognition so that you immediately recognize meaning, with no reliance on the intermediate memory story to slow you down), effective study tips, and other resources available from the EZChinesey website.

Many new students find that studying the Chinese language is somehow addictive in ways that other foreign languages are not, perhaps because its structure is so intriguing and so different from Western languages. As many people have learned, China's writing system can seem like a brick wall—a Great Brick Wall, if you will—very effective at deterring all but the most persistent students. The **EZChinesey** method will provide you with a ladder over this brick wall, so that learning China's writing system will be much easier for you. With this book, you will master a method to easily remember the meanings of traditional Chinese characters, a method that will put the 'ease' into learning 'Chinese'.

Abbreviations Listing

Sentence endings ('s-end') are characters that appear at the ends of sentences or clauses to alter the sentence or clause in some way. Traditional grammar refers to them as 'particles'. The most well-known example of a sentence ending is the s-end 'ma'. It changes a direct statement into a question requiring a yes-or-no answer. For example, adding the s-end 'ma' to the Chinese sentence "He bought a dog" will change it to the question "Did he buy a dog?"

The EZChinesey Method *Prelude 1*

The ideas behind our **EZChinesey** method are different from other memory techniques you may have tried.

Imagine staring at some Chinese text. The only way you can differentiate the characters is by the variations in complexity among them, such as the most simple

一 and 二

versus the more complex

猿 and 俊.

You might also notice that the same elements often appear in many different characters. Sometimes, a complete freestanding character is dropped like a module into others, such as the character 古 (meaning 'ancient') which is an element of many other characters, including 咕, 估, 沽, and many, many more.

The key to the **EZChinesey** method is to sort all the characters based on their complexity—beginning with the simplest up to the most complex. Imagine placing these characters on a line—a *character line-up*, similar to a line-up of possible crime suspects—with the simplest on the far left, and the most complex on the far right. If you focus on any specific character on this line, the characters to its left are simpler in structure, and the ones to its right are more complex.

Specific character
⇓
⇐======= less complex 俊 more complex =======⇒

Depiction of a "character line-up." The full character line-up for all the characters in this book appears in the 'Read Me First!' overview.

The very first character in this line-up is special, because there is no character to its left—none is simpler than it. The first such character is

一

which means '**one**'. We are fairly confident that anyone can remember this character and its meaning without relying on any special system.

So now you can assume that there is at least one character in our list that you can remember. Each character to the right of '**one**' is slightly more complex. In general, the next character will be made up of characters that you previously learned (because they are located to its left). The heart of our method is to create a 'memory story' for each character, to help you remember how and why the elements of the current character, drawn from those to the left, come together.

We perform this process for each character in our character line-up. From time to time, we'll introduce elements that are not freestanding characters, but are needed to construct characters further to the right on our list.

The individual memory stories make it easy for you to keep track of the hundreds of characters you need when studying and reading Chinese. The 'Read Me First!' overview presents examples to prove that this method will work for you.

In this book, the term *character* refers to independent, free-standing, honest-to-God characters. We'll use the term *component* for parts of a character that cannot stand on their own. (Strictly speaking, there are two types of components, those known to students as 'radicals', and others that we've created solely for use in our memory method and have no special significance otherwise. The distinction between the two is not critical, which is why we use the term 'component' for both. Further discussion appears in Interlude 1 on 'Names'.)

There is one striking disadvantage to using our method. The order in which you learn characters in the **EZChinesey** method is different from that used in any other Chinese language course curriculum. Why? Because Chinese *language* courses introduce the most frequently used characters first, regardless of their graphic complexity. Our method, on the contrary, introduces characters beginning with the *visually* simple and moving up to the *visually* complex. So the two methods will never match. Although this difference may make using our method more difficult in a traditional classroom setting, it is our hope that the ease and speed with which the new learner can commit meanings to memory will convince students to use the **EZChinesey** method along with their course material.

If you're interested in memory and mnemonics, we recommend Joshua Foer's *Moonwalking with Einstein: The Art and Science of Remembering Everything* (2011, Penguin Press, New York; ISBN 978-1-59420-229-2). Packed with anecdotes and facts, and very well written, this book will teach you virtually everything there is to know about memorization, plus where to turn to learn more.

The Panels *Prelude 2*

As you leaf through this book, you'll notice that the main central portion consists of a series of units, each of which is divided into numbered panels. Each panel contains a great deal of information about a particular character or component, and this prelude is a guide to that information.

All panels are numbered consecutively, and all retain the same general structure. For character panels, directly to the right of the panel number, is the outsize character itself printed on a gray field. Although this guide deals exclusively with the so-called simplified character set (which includes the several hundred characters which the mainland government simplified in the 1950s and 60s), it's helpful to be aware of a character's traditional ancestry. Thus, if one or more distinct traditional forms correspond to a given character, you'll see it or them printed in a slightly smaller font to the character's left, beneath the panel number. Labels provide gentle reminders. Whenever the character is the same for both conventions, it's labeled 'SIMP & TRAD' (for 'simplified and traditional'); otherwise, the distinct characters are captioned 'SIMPLIFIED' and 'TRAD'.

To the character's right is a columnar portion, headed by the character definition. Directly underneath is the pinyin pronunciation and its frequency ranking. A rank, for example, of 372 means the character is the 372nd most common character in Modern Chinese. A rank of 1 means it's the most common. A rank of 9999 means the character is too rare to possess a meaningful frequency ranking. You should interpret this rank to mean 'extremely rare'.

This bottom part of this portion provides information on how to write or draw this character. After a phrase indicating the number of strokes in the character is a row of 'stroke order diagrams', which show readers how to build up the characters stroke by stroke. When reviewing characters, it's helpful to be able to draw characters when given the definition and pinyin, and you should get in the habit of drawing them correctly. I use these diagrams myself, using the index finger of my left hand (I'm a lefty) to 'draw' them on the palm of my right hand.

Moving to the right are the component decompositions of the character. As you know, we've presented characters in a particular order so that a given character is built up from simpler characters and components that have been previously presented; let's call these character building blocks— which may either be independent characters or portions of characters that are re-used over and over in different characters—'**decomponents**'. For each of the decomponents, you see the definition, panel number, and page number of the decomponent, as well as the decomponent itself. Partially blackened squares suggest where in the character the decomponent building block occurs. So, for example, consider the character 中, zhōng, 'middle', built up from the character 口, kǒu, 'mouth', and a vertical stroke | component which we liken to a king's scepter. Hopefully, the graphs '■' and '□' suggest how the ancient scribes placed 口 and | together to create 中.

The material in the right margin is the subject of its own interlude, titled 'Marginal Examples'.

The narrative that forms the bottom portion of a panel is a key part of our **EZChinesey** method, for it provides the mnemonics—the memory links—that connect the meanings of each 'decomponent' to the meaning of the panel's character.

All but eighty-three of the panels pertain to independent characters. These eighty-three deal with character building blocks that I've termed components, and they are never independent, free-standing characters. Typically, components appear over and over in different characters, and so therefore it makes sense to ascribe a meaning to them so they can participate in our memory method. However, since components don't have an independent existence in Chinese, they don't possess pronunciations, frequency ranks, or stroke order diagrams of their own. Therefore, their panels possess a much simpler structure—you'll just see the panel number (but grayed-out to provide a visual cue), the meaning, a memory story, and possibly a decomposition into simpler components. A grayed-out COMPONENT identifier replaces the pinyin, rank, and stroke information present in a character panel.

Unit 1

1

SIMP & TRAD

This character with the definition:

one

Pinyin **yī** *and Frequency Rank* **2**

Contains **1 stroke**:

Contains these components:

With all these meanings & readings:

yī [一] **1** one **2** 1 **3** single **4** a (article) **5** as soon as **6** entire **7** whole **8** all **9** throughout **10** "one" radical in Chinese characters (Kangxi radical 1)

Chinese tally marks are written horizontally rather than vertically. **One** such horizontal stroke stands for the number **one.** • This character frequently appears as an element in more complex characters. In order to create a story linking all elements together to remember a character's meaning, we'll often use this character to stand for 'horizontal', 'straight', 'bar', 'line', and other comparable concepts, as well as **one**.

2

SIMP & TRAD

This character with the definition:

two

Pinyin **èr** *and Frequency Rank* **157**

Contains **2 strokes** in the following order:

Contains these components:

one (×2) — 1, p.10

With all these meanings & readings:

èr [二] **1** two **2** 2 **3** stupid (Beijing dialect)

One tally drawn twice equals the number **two**.

3

SIMP & TRAD

This character with the definition:

three

Pinyin **sān** *and Frequency Rank* **125**

Contains **3 strokes** in the following order:

Contains these components:

one — 1, p.10

two 二 2, p.10

With all these meanings & readings:

sān [三] **1** three **2** 3

Three horizontal bars signify the number **three**. Since the middle stroke is the shortest, it's natural to interpret this symbol as *two* plus *one*.

4

SIMP & TRAD

This character with the definition:

mountain

Pinyin **shān** *and Frequency Rank* **259**

Contains **3 strokes** in the following order:

Contains these components:

three 三 (altered) 3, p.10

one — 1, p.10

With all these meanings & readings:

shān [山] **1** mountain **2** hill **3** m 座[zuò] **4** surname Shan

Three vertical peaks form *one* **mountain**.

5

This component has the meaning:

scepter c

COMPONENT

This vertical staff represents a **scepter**-like symbol of authority, a simple tool, or just a long stick.

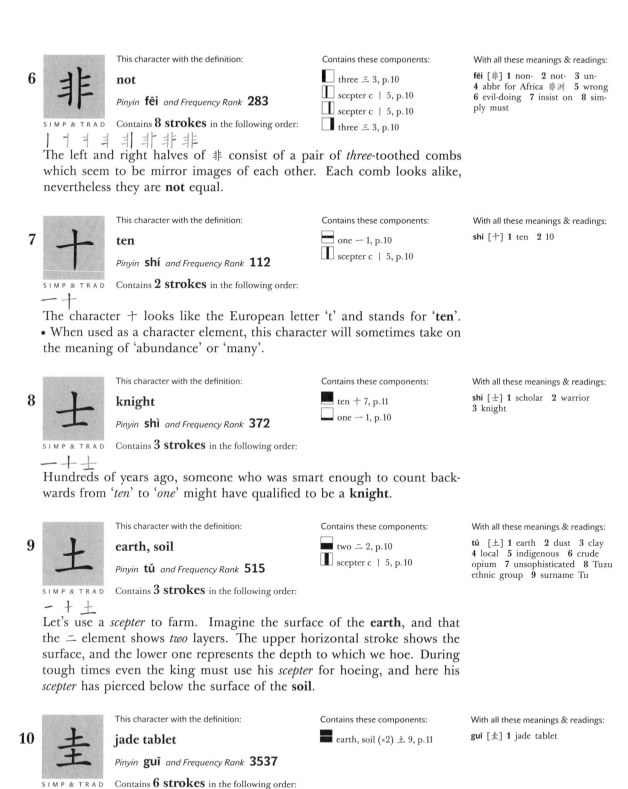

6 非

not

Pinyin **fēi** *and Frequency Rank* **283**

SIMP & TRAD Contains **8 strokes** in the following order:

| 丨 刁 丬 ヺ 习 刲 非 非 非

Contains these components:

▌ three 三 3, p.10

▌ scepter c 丨 5, p.10

▐ scepter c 丨 5, p.10

▌ three 三 3, p.10

With all these meanings & readings:

fēi [非] **1** non- **2** not- **3** un- **4** abbr for Africa 非洲 **5** wrong **6** evil-doing **7** insist on **8** simply must

The left and right halves of 非 consist of a pair of *three*-toothed combs which seem to be mirror images of each other. Each comb looks alike, nevertheless they are **not** equal.

7 十

ten

Pinyin **shí** *and Frequency Rank* **112**

SIMP & TRAD Contains **2 strokes** in the following order:

一 十

Contains these components:

▭ one 一 1, p.10

▐ scepter c 丨 5, p.10

With all these meanings & readings:

shí [十] **1** ten **2** 10

The character 十 looks like the European letter 't' and stands for '**ten**'. • When used as a character element, this character will sometimes take on the meaning of 'abundance' or 'many'.

8 士

knight

Pinyin **shì** *and Frequency Rank* **372**

SIMP & TRAD Contains **3 strokes** in the following order:

一 十 士

Contains these components:

▮ ten 十 7, p.11

▭ one 一 1, p.10

With all these meanings & readings:

shì [士] **1** scholar **2** warrior **3** knight

Hundreds of years ago, someone who was smart enough to count backwards from '*ten*' to '*one*' might have qualified to be a **knight**.

9 土

earth, soil

Pinyin **tǔ** *and Frequency Rank* **515**

SIMP & TRAD Contains **3 strokes** in the following order:

一 十 土

Contains these components:

▭ two 二 2, p.10

▐ scepter c 丨 5, p.10

With all these meanings & readings:

tǔ [土] **1** earth **2** dust **3** clay **4** local **5** indigenous **6** crude opium **7** unsophisticated **8** Tuzu ethnic group **9** surname Tu

Let's use a *scepter* to farm. Imagine the surface of the **earth**, and that the 二 element shows *two* layers. The upper horizontal stroke shows the surface, and the lower one represents the depth to which we hoe. During tough times even the king must use his *scepter* for hoeing, and here his *scepter* has pierced below the surface of the **soil**.

10 圭

jade tablet

Pinyin **guī** *and Frequency Rank* **3537**

SIMP & TRAD Contains **6 strokes** in the following order:

一 十 土 圭 圭 圭

Contains these components:

▮ earth, soil (×2) 土 9, p.11

With all these meanings & readings:

guī [圭] **1** jade tablet

A **jade tablet** symbolizes authority and possesses great value. You safeguard it by digging a hole in several layers of *earth* to hide it—and only the tribal leader, you, knows where.

Unit 2

11

撃
TRAD   SIMPLIFIED

This character with the definition:

beat, knock

Pinyin **jī** *and Frequency Rank* **395**

Contains **5 strokes** in the following order:

Contains these components:

■ earth, soil 土 9, p.11

▬ mountain 山 4, p.10

With all these meanings & readings:

jī [撃] **1** to hit **2** to strike **3** to break **4** Taiwan pr jí

Earth viewed from the bottom of a *mountain* appears as a landslide—it **beats** down with great force.

12

工

SIMP & TRAD

This character with the definition:

labor, work

Pinyin **gōng** *and Frequency Rank* **118**

Contains **3 strokes** in the following order:

一 丁 工

Contains these components:

■ two 二 2, p.10

▯ scepter c ｜ 5, p.10

With all these meanings & readings:

gōng [工] **1** work **2** worker **3** skill **4** profession **5** trade **6** craft **7** labor

The elements of 工 are 二 and ｜. Normally, though, the horizontal strokes of *two* are close together. If we pry these *two* strokes apart and keep them separated by inserting our *scepter* in between them, then we have done some useful **work**.

13

五
SIMP & TRAD

This character with the definition:

five

Pinyin **wǔ** *and Frequency Rank* **279**

Contains **4 strokes** in the following order:

Contains these components:

■ labor, work 工 12, p.12

▬ one 一 (altered) 1, p.10

With all these meanings & readings:

wǔ [五] **1** five **2** 5

One laborer suffered an unexpected stroke after working like a slave for **five** hours. This *one* worker's abilities were forever after altered.

14

互
SIMP & TRAD

This character with the definition:

mutual

Pinyin **hù** *and Frequency Rank* **819**

Contains **4 strokes** in the following order:

一 工 五 互

Contains these components:

■ five 五 (altered) 13, p.12

With all these meanings & readings:

hù [互] **1** mutual

Look carefully and see a bent arm reaching down to grab an identical arm reaching up to grab the first. They are providing each other with some **mutual** assistance.

15

王
SIMP & TRAD

This character with the definition:

king

Pinyin **wáng** *and Frequency Rank* **299**

Contains **4 strokes** in the following order:

一 二 千 王

Contains these components:

■ three 三 3, p.10

▯ scepter c ｜ 5, p.10

With all these meanings & readings:

Wáng [王] **1** king **2** surname Wang

Traditionally, kingdoms possessed *three domains*: that of air, land, and water. The **king** *ruled* all *three*.

16
豐
丰
TRAD SIMPLIFIED

丰

This character with the definition:

plentiful

Pinyin **fēng** *and Frequency Rank* **1189**

Contains **4 strokes** in the following order:

一 二 三 丰

Contains these components:

■ king 王 (altered) 15, p.12

With all these meanings & readings:

fēng [丰] **1** buxom **2** good-looking **3** appearance and carriage of a person
fēng [豐] **1** surname Feng **2** abundant **3** plentiful **4** great

In times of abundance and **plentiful** resources, a *king*'s authority grows and expands. In this character, his scepter is overflowing beyond the bounds of the horizontal elements, emphasizing this abundance.

17
乾
TRAD SIMPLIFIED

干

This character with the definition:

dry

Pinyin **gān** *and Frequency Rank* **353**

Contains **3 strokes** in the following order:

一 二 干

Contains these components:

▭ two 二 2, p.10

▌ scepter c ｜ 5, p.10

With all these meanings & readings:

gān [乾] **1** dry **2** clean **3** surname Gan
gān [干] **1** to concern **2** to interfere **3** shield **4** stem
gàn [干] **1** to work **2** to do **3** to manage
gàn [幹] **1** tree trunk **2** main part of sth **3** to manage **4** to work **5** to do **6** capable **7** cadre (in communist party) **8** to kill (slang) **9** to have sex (taboo word)

If soil is exceptionally **dry**, as happens during a drought, a hoe or other *stick* might well plunge through the *two* top layers so the tip of the *stick* is level with the soil.

18

亅

This component has the meaning:

hooked stick c

COMPONENT

A *scepter* with a hook can be made into a (much more useful) **hooked stick** tool.

19

SIMP & TRAD

丁

This character with the definition:

fourth (in a series)

Pinyin **dīng** *and Frequency Rank* **1168**

Contains **2 strokes** in the following order:

一 丁

Contains these components:

▭ one 一 1, p.10

▌ hooked stick c 亅 18, p.13

With all these meanings & readings:

dīng [丁] **1** fourth of 10 heavenly stems 十天干 **2** fourth in order **3** letter "D" or roman "IV" in list "A, B, C", or "I, II, III" etc **4** butyl **5** surname Ding **6** cubes (of food)

(The definition here refers to 'fourth in a series of items' or 'fourth item in a list', but not the 'fourth grade', 'fourth day of the week', etc.) This shape reminds me of the special *hook*-like tool you use to open *one* can of sardines. Once the cramped fish are finally exposed, they are free to go 'forth' (sounds like **fourth**) toward your tasting pleasure. • Sometimes we will use this shape to refer to a platform or table, because it resembles a tabletop and leg.

20

SIMP & TRAD

于

This character with the definition:

in, at, to

Pinyin **yú** *and Frequency Rank* **40**

Contains **3 strokes** in the following order:

一 二 于

Contains these components:

▭ two 二 2, p.10

▌ hooked stick c 亅 18, p.13

With all these meanings & readings:

Yú [于] **1** surname Yu
Yú [於] **1** surname Yu
yú [於] **1** in **2** at **3** to **4** from **5** by **6** than **7** out of

The *hook* is well and truly entangled in the *two* (sounds like 'to'); it's so far **in** that it will be hard to extract.

21

This character with the definition:

hand

Pinyin **shǒu** *and Frequency Rank* **143**

SIMP & TRAD   Contains **4 strokes** in the following order:

一 二 三 手

Contains these components:

▬ three 三 3, p.10

❘ hooked stick c ⌡ 18, p.13

With all these meanings & readings:

shǒu [手] **1** hand **2** (formal) to hold **3** person engaged in certain types of work **4** person skilled in certain types of work **5** personal(ly) **6** convenient **7** m 双 [雙][shuāng], 只 [雙][zhī]

The *hooked stick* is shorthand for an entire arm; the hook is the elbow, but only the forearm is explicitly drawn. The *three* horizontal strokes are the stylized fingers of the **hand**, so stylized that no one cares that we show six fingers!

Unit 3

22

This character with the definition:

do obeisance, salute

Pinyin **bài** *and Frequency Rank* **1218**

Contains these components:

▮ hand 手 (altered) 21, p.14
▮ king 王 (altered) 15, p.12

With all these meanings & readings:

bài [拜] **1** to pay respect **2** worship **3** visit **4** salute

SIMP & TRAD Contains **9 strokes** in the following order:

丿 二 三 手 手⁻ 手⁼ 手⁼ 拜 拜

Is this character evidence for subtle subversion on the part of ancient scribes? Observe a slightly disfigured left *hand* performing a **salute** to a trumped-up *king*, one with too many stripes and a too-long scepter.

23
了
瞭
TRAD

This character with the definition:

s-end le

Pinyin **le** *and Frequency Rank* **5**

Contains these components:

丁 hooked stick c (×2, altered) 亅18, p.13

With all these meanings & readings:

le [了] **1** (modal particle intensifying preceding clause) **2** (completed action marker)
liǎo [了] **1** to know **2** to understand
liǎo [了] **1** clear
liào [瞭] **1** to look afar from a high place

SIMPLIFIED Contains **2 strokes** in the following order:

⼁ 了

了 is the supreme example of an important Chinese 'word' which defies easy translation. This common character often signifies a sudden significant 'change of state'—suggested by its squiggly turns made from two *hooked sticks* (the top one is turned on its side). We'll use it to signify a sudden, significant change.

24

This character with the definition:

son, child

Pinyin **zǐ** *and Frequency Rank* **37**

Contains these components:

▮ s-end le 了 23, p.15
▭ one 一 1, p.10

With all these meanings & readings:

zǐ [子] **1** son **2** child **3** seed **4** egg **5** small thing **6** 1st earthly branch: 11 p.m.-1 a.m., midnight, 11th solar month (7th December to 5th January), year of the Rat **7** Viscount, fourth of five orders of nobility 五等爵位[wǔ děng jué wèi]
zi [子] **1** (noun suffix)

SIMP & TRAD Contains **3 strokes** in the following order:

乛 了 子

Our **son's** birth was just *one sudden change* we enjoyed last year.

25
才

This component has the meaning:

hand r

COMPONENT

And contains these subcomponents:

▮ hand 手 (abbrev) 21, 14

This component is a truncated **hand**, used as an element in other characters when space is tight.

26
排

This character with the definition:

put in order

Pinyin **pái** *and Frequency Rank* **682**

Contains these components:

▮ hand r 扌 25, p.15
▮ not 非 6, p.11

With all these meanings & readings:

pái [排] **1** a row **2** a line **3** to set in order **4** to arrange **5** to line up **6** to eliminate **7** to drain **8** to push open **9** platoon **10** raft **11** m for lines, rows etc

SIMP & TRAD Contains **11 strokes** in the following order:

一 十 扌 扫 扫 扫 扫 捐 排 排 排

Imagine a young boy using his *hand* to **put** his toy soldiers **in order**. The straight lines of '*not*' suggest the ordered arrangement of soldiers in formation. (A second meaning for 'pái' is **platoon**.)

27 打

This character with the definition:

hit

Pinyin **dǎ** *and Frequency Rank* **223**

SIMP & TRAD   Contains **5 strokes** in the following order:

一 十 才 扌 打

Contains these components:
- hand r 扌 25, p.15
- fourth (in a series) 丁 19, p.13

With all these meanings & readings:

dá [打] **1** dozen
dǎ [打] **1** to beat **2** to strike **3** to hit **4** to break **5** to type **6** to mix up **7** to build **8** to fight **9** to fetch **10** to make **11** to tie up **12** to issue **13** to shoot **14** to calculate **15** since **16** from **17** m 顿 [顿][dùn]

My friend decided to hire a contractor after he **hit** his *hand* for the *fourth* time trying to hammer a nail.

28
託
托
TRAD   SIMPLIFIED

托

This character with the definition:

hold (in palm)

Pinyin **tuō** *and Frequency Rank* **799**

Contains **6 strokes** in the following order:

一 十 才 扌 扗 托

Contains these components:
- hand r 扌 25, p.15
- hand 手 (altered) 21, p.14

With all these meanings & readings:

tuō [托] **1** prop **2** support (for weight) **3** rest (e.g. arm rest) **4** thanks to **5** to hold in one's hand **6** to support in one's palm **7** to give **8** to base **9** to commit **10** to set
tuō [託] **1** to trust **2** to entrust **3** to be entrusted with **4** to act as trustee

Two *hands* suggest **holding** something **in the palm** of your hand. The rightmost '*hand*' has been altered to better look like a palm-shaped gesture (and, in the process, has lost a couple of fingers).

29
掛
TRAD   SIMPLIFIED

挂

This character with the definition:

hang

Pinyin **guà** *and Frequency Rank* **1232**

Contains **9 strokes** in the following order:

一 十 才 扌 扗 垆 挂 挂 挂

Contains these components:
- hand r 扌 25, p.15
- jade tablet 圭 10, p.11

With all these meanings & readings:

guà [掛] **1** to hang **2** to put up **3** to suspend

It's a good idea to get your *hand* to **hang** the valuable *jade tablet* and keep it out of harm's way.

---

30 彐

This component has the meaning:

boar's head r

COMPONENT

While this component does not resemble the head of anything, the three horizontals can be seen as the stiff bristles that surround a feral pig's or **boar's head**.

---

31 聿

This character with the definition:

writing instrument, pen

Pinyin **yù** *and Frequency Rank* **3526**

SIMP & TRAD   Contains **6 strokes** in the following order:

コ ヲ ヨ 彐 聿 聿

Contains these components:
- boar's head r 彐 30, p.16
- scepter c | 5, p.10
- two 二 2, p.10

With all these meanings & readings:

yù [聿] **1** (arch. introductory particle) **2** then **3** and then

There are a total of five horizontal strokes in this rare character, representing five fingers holding a vertical **writing instrument**. The first and third fingers are linked, emphasizing that the first three fingers of the hand are the strongest and most dexterous.

32

彗

SIMP & TRAD

This character with the definition:

comet

Pinyin **huì** *and Frequency Rank* **3591**

Contains **11 strokes** in the following order:

一 彐 彐 彗 彗 彗 彗 彗 彗 彗 彗

Contains these components:

plentiful (×2) 丰 16, p.13

boar's head r 彐 30, p.16

With all these meanings & readings:

huì [彗] **1** comet

You can see the path of this **comet** by the *boar's head* bristles lined up horizontally, as the **comet** speeds past a *plentiful* array of stars (represented here by two eight-pointed ones).

33

醜
丑

TRAD SIMPLIFIED

This character with the definition:

clown

Pinyin **chǒu** *and Frequency Rank* **1901**

Contains **4 strokes** in the following order:

フ 刀 丑 丑

Contains these components:

boar's head r 彐 (altered) 30, p.16

scepter c | 5, p.10

With all these meanings & readings:

chǒu [丑] **1** clown **2** surname Chou **3** 2nd earthly branch: 1-3 a.m., 12th solar month (6th January to 3rd February), year of the Ox
chǒu [醜] **1** shameful **2** ugly **3** disgraceful

Part of the **clown's** routine was to balance a *boar's head* on a *scepter*-like pole while wheeling around the circus ring on a unicycle.

34

扭

SIMP & TRAD

This character with the definition:

twist, wrench

Pinyin **niǔ** *and Frequency Rank* **1805**

Contains **7 strokes** in the following order:

一 十 扌 扌 扣 扭 扭

Contains these components:

hand r 扌 25, p.15

clown 丑 33, p.17

With all these meanings & readings:

niǔ [扭] **1** to turn **2** to twist **3** to grab **4** to wring

The *clown* enchanted the crowd as he **twisted** long colorful balloons with his *hands* into many fantastic shapes.

35

掃
TRAD SIMPLIFIED

This character with the definition:

sweep

Pinyin **sǎo** *and Frequency Rank* **1435**

Contains **6 strokes** in the following order:

一 十 扌 扫 扫 扫

Contains these components:

hand r 扌 25, p.15

boar's head r 彐 30, p.16

With all these meanings & readings:

sǎo [掃] **1** to sweep
sào [掃] **1** broom

Someone's *hand* holds a broom—its bristles are from a *boar's head* and are particularly effective for gathering dust—and gets ready to **sweep**.

36

This component has the meaning:

enclosure r

COMPONENT

The symbol says it all!

37

口

SIMP & TRAD

This character with the definition:

mouth

Pinyin **kǒu** *and Frequency Rank* **212**

Contains **3 strokes** in the following order:

丨 冂 口

Contains these components:

enclosure r 口 36, p.17

With all these meanings & readings:

kǒu [口] **1** mouth **2** (classifier for things with mouths such as people, domestic animals, cannons, wells etc)

Think of this stylized representation as a **mouth** that's square shaped rather than round (historically, Chinese was written with a calligraphy brush and circular curves are difficult to execute with a calligraphy brush), but it actually represents a small *enclosure*. It's useful to imagine 口 as representing a person speaking or sometimes just a person. The characters 囗 and 口 closely resemble each other, and it's only possible to reliably distinguish between the two when they're placed next to each other.

38 中

SIMP & TRAD

This character with the definition: **middle**

Pinyin **zhōng** *and Frequency Rank* **14**

Contains **4 strokes** in the following order:

丨 ⺆ 口 中

Contains these components:

mouth 口 37, p.17

scepter c 丨 5, p.10

With all these meanings & readings:

zhōng [中] **1** within **2** among **3** in **4** middle **5** center **6** wh (doing sth) **7** during **8** China **9** Chinese

zhòng [中] **1** hit (the mark)

A *mouth* with the lips pierced through the **middle** by a *scepter*-like stud visually describes this character.

39 甲

SIMP & TRAD

This character with the definition: **first (in a series)**

Pinyin **jiǎ** *and Frequency Rank* **1106**

Contains **5 strokes** in the following order:

丨 ⺆ 日 日 甲

Contains these components:

mouth 口 37, p.17

ten 十 7, p.11

With all these meanings & readings:

jiǎ [甲] **1** armor **2** first of 10 heavenly stems 十天干 **3** first in order **4** letter "A" or roman "I" in list "A, B, C", or "I, II, III" etc **5** first party (in legal contract, usually 甲方[jiǎ fāng], as opposed to 乙方[yǐ fāng]) **6** methyl

At the protest rally, I stood **first** in a line of *ten* marchers, shouting with my *mouth* open and carrying a sign that resembles this character!

40 里

裡 裏

TRAD

SIMPLIFIED

This character with the definition: **neighborhood**

Pinyin **lǐ** *and Frequency Rank* **50**

Contains **7 strokes** in the following order:

丨 ⺆ 日 日 甲 甲 里

Contains these components:

first (in a series) 甲 39, p.18

two 二 2, p.10

With all these meanings & readings:

lǐ [裏] **1** lining **2** interior **3** side **4** internal **5** also written [裡] [lǐ]

lǐ [裡] **1** lining **2** interior **3** side **4** internal **5** also written [裏] [lǐ]

lǐ [里] **1** Li (surname)

lǐ [里] **1** li (Chinese mile) **2** 500 meters (modern) **3** hom **4** hometown **5** village **6** neigh borhood **7** administrative unit

My **neighborhood** means so much to me that during the holidays, I'm always the *first in a series* of neighbors who return after spending only *two* days with my family.

Unit 4

41 **哩**

This character with the definition:

mile

Pinyin **lǐ** *and Frequency Rank* **1949**

SIMP & TRAD   Contains **10 strokes** in the following order:

丨 冂 口 叮 叮 吧 吧 呷 哩 哩

Contains these components:

☐ mouth 口 37, p.17
☐ neighborhood 里 40, p.18

With all these meanings & readings:

li [哩] **1** this (Cantonese) **2** see also 呢 [呢][ni] **3** see also 哩哩罗罗 [~~羅羅][li li luō luō]
lǐ [哩] **1** mile **2** old form of modern 英里 [yīng lǐ]
li [哩] **1** (modal final particle similar to 呢 [呢][ne] or 啦 [啦][la])

My old *neighborhood* is in the shape of a square, similar to the 'mouth' element. The *neighborhood* is small, only about a **mile** square in size.

42 **理**

This character with the definition:

rational

Pinyin **lǐ** *and Frequency Rank* **89**

SIMP & TRAD   Contains **11 strokes** in the following order:

一 二 丅 王 尹 尹 玾 玾 珇 理 理

Contains these components:

☐ king 王 15, p.12
☐ neighborhood 里 40, p.18

With all these meanings & readings:

lǐ [理] **1** texture **2** grain (of wood) **3** inner essence **4** intrinsic order **5** reason **6** logic **7** truth **8** science **9** natural science (especially physics) **10** to manage **11** to pay attention to **12** to run (affairs) **13** to handle **14** to put in order **15** to tidy up

The *king* was no fool, so he made sure that only **rational** people such as himself lived in the *neighborhood* surrounding his palace.

43 **埋**

This character with the definition:

bury

Pinyin **mái** *and Frequency Rank* **1640**

SIMP & TRAD   Contains **10 strokes** in the following order:

一 十 土 圵 坤 坤 坦 押 埋 埋

Contains these components:

☐ earth, soil 土 9, p.11
☐ neighborhood 里 40, p.18

With all these meanings & readings:

mái [埋] **1** to bury
mán [埋] **1** to blame

When they **bury** you, the *earth* becomes your entire *neighborhood*.

44 **押**

This character with the definition:

mortgage, pawn, give as security

Pinyin **yā** *and Frequency Rank* **1775**

SIMP & TRAD   Contains **8 strokes** in the following order:

一 十 才 扌 扣 扣 押 押

Contains these components:

☐ hand r 扌 25, p.15
☐ first (in a series) 甲 39, p.18

With all these meanings & readings:

yā [押] **1** mortgage **2** to pawn **3** to detain in custody

Before I can get a bank loan, I must *hand* over the item that's *first* in my possessions—my house, as a guarantee to the bank it will get its money back. This is the essence of **pledging** collateral or **mortgaging** your house.

45 **吐**

This character with the definition:

spit

Pinyin **tǔ** *and Frequency Rank* **1653**

SIMP & TRAD   Contains **6 strokes** in the following order:

丨 冂 口 口一 吐 吐

Contains these components:

☐ mouth 口 37, p.17
☐ earth, soil 土 9, p.11

With all these meanings & readings:

tǔ [吐] **1** to spit **2** to put **3** to say
tù [吐] **1** to vomit **2** to throw up

Spit releases germs into the air as it travels from the *mouth* to the *soil*.

46 吾

This character with the definition:

me

Pinyin **wú** *and Frequency Rank* **1649**

SIMP & TRAD Contains **7 strokes** in the following order:

一 丁 五 五 五 吾 吾

Contains these components:

five 五 13, p.12

mouth 口 37, p.17

With all these meanings & readings:

wú [吾] **1** I **2** my

My head, the center of consciousness, with its *five* orifices or *'mouths'* (two ears, two nostrils, and a mouth) is considered to be the essence of **me**.

47 吉

This character with the definition:

lucky

Pinyin **jí** *and Frequency Rank* **856**

SIMP & TRAD Contains **6 strokes** in the following order:

一 十 士 吉 吉 吉

Contains these components:

knight 士 8, p.11

mouth 口 37, p.17

With all these meanings & readings:

jí [吉] **1** lucky **2** abbr for Jilin 吉林 province in northeast China **3** giga- (meaning billion or 1,000,000,000) **4** surname Ji

Words of praise spoken from a *knight*'s *mouth* are thought to be **lucky**.

48 呈

This character with the definition:

appear

Pinyin **chéng** *and Frequency Rank* **1563**

SIMP & TRAD Contains **7 strokes** in the following order:

丨 冂 口 呂 呈 早 呈

Contains these components:

mouth 口 37, p.17

king 王 15, p.12

With all these meanings & readings:

chéng [呈] **1** to assume (a form) **2** to submit **3** to petition **4** to show **5** to present **6** to offer

In ancient societies, *kings* were often isolated from their subjects. When the *king* did **appear** in public for ceremonial or ritual purposes, his **appearance** would have been a key event in his subjects' lives. The *mouth* represents the facial features of the *king*.

49 扣 釦

This character with the definition:

to button, to buckle

Pinyin **kòu** *and Frequency Rank* **1625**

TRAD SIMPLIFIED Contains **6 strokes** in the following order:

一 十 扌 扣 扣 扣

Contains these components:

hand r 扌 25, p.15

mouth 口 37, p.17

With all these meanings & readings:

kòu [扣] **1** 10 percent **2** button **3** detain
kòu [釦] **1** to fasten, button, buckle, latch **2** to invert a hollowed object **3** to cover with the hollowed part of an object **4** button **5** knot **6** to knock **7** to smash **8** to spike (a ball) **9** to arrest, detain **10** to set right **11** to deduct **12** to intercept **13** to request advice **14** (after numeral) reduced to (90% etc) **15** fig. to tag unfair label onto sb **16** to besmirch

I use my *hand* **to button** the decorative clasp, which eerily resembles a doll's *mouth*.

50 回

This character with the definition:

return

Pinyin **huí** *and Frequency Rank* **172**

SIMP & TRAD Contains **6 strokes** in the following order:

丨 冂 冂 冋 回 回

Contains these components:

enclosure r 囗 36, p.17

mouth 口 37, p.17

huí [回] **1** to circle **2** to go back **3** to turn around **4** to answer **5** to return **6** to revolve **7** Hui ethnic group (Chinese Muslims) **8** time **9** m for acts of a play **10** section or chapter (of a classic book)

Imagine this character as a lonely man imprisoned in an *enclosure*, using his *mouth* to signal his desire to **return** home to friends and family.

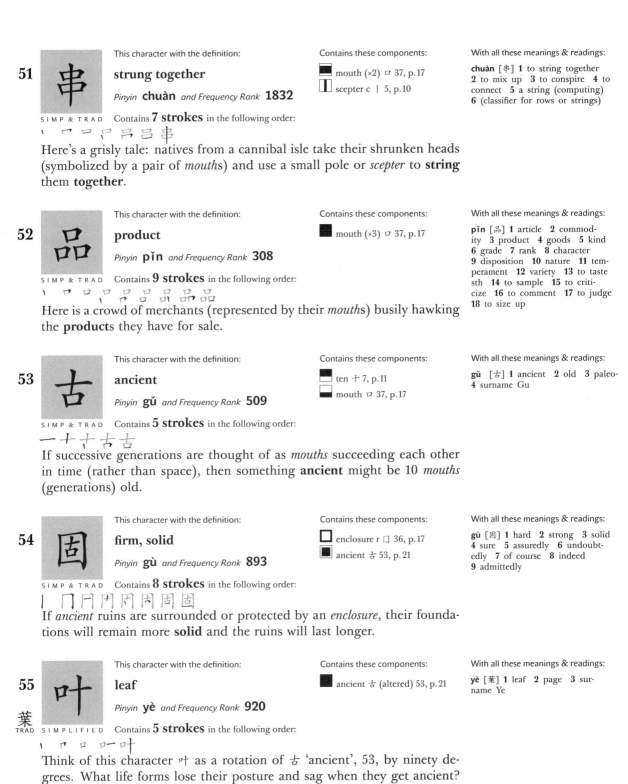

51 **串**

SIMP & TRAD

This character with the definition: **strung together**

Pinyin **chuàn** *and Frequency Rank* **1832**

Contains **7 strokes** in the following order:

Contains these components:

- mouth (×2) 口 37, p.17
- scepter c 丨 5, p.10

With all these meanings & readings:

chuàn [串] **1** to string together **2** to mix up **3** to conspire **4** to connect **5** a string (computing) **6** (classifier for rows or strings)

Here's a grisly tale: natives from a cannibal isle take their shrunken heads (symbolized by a pair of *mouth*s) and use a small pole or *scepter* to **string** them **together**.

52 **品**

SIMP & TRAD

This character with the definition: **product**

Pinyin **pǐn** *and Frequency Rank* **308**

Contains **9 strokes** in the following order:

Contains these components:

- mouth (×3) 口 37, p.17

With all these meanings & readings:

pǐn [品] **1** article **2** commodity **3** product **4** goods **5** kind **6** grade **7** rank **8** character **9** disposition **10** nature **11** temperament **12** variety **13** to taste sth **14** to sample **15** to criticize **16** to comment **17** to judge **18** to size up

Here is a crowd of merchants (represented by their *mouth*s) busily hawking the **product**s they have for sale.

53 **古**

SIMP & TRAD

This character with the definition: **ancient**

Pinyin **gǔ** *and Frequency Rank* **509**

Contains **5 strokes** in the following order:

Contains these components:

- ten 十 7, p.11
- mouth 口 37, p.17

With all these meanings & readings:

gǔ [古] **1** ancient **2** old **3** paleo- **4** surname Gu

If successive generations are thought of as *mouths* succeeding each other in time (rather than space), then something **ancient** might be 10 *mouths* (generations) old.

54 **固**

SIMP & TRAD

This character with the definition: **firm, solid**

Pinyin **gù** *and Frequency Rank* **893**

Contains **8 strokes** in the following order:

Contains these components:

- enclosure r 囗 36, p.17
- ancient 古 53, p.21

With all these meanings & readings:

gù [固] **1** hard **2** strong **3** solid **4** sure **5** assuredly **6** undoubtedly **7** of course **8** indeed **9** admittedly

If *ancient* ruins are surrounded or protected by an *enclosure*, their foundations will remain more **solid** and the ruins will last longer.

55 **叶**

葉 TRAD

SIMPLIFIED

This character with the definition: **leaf**

Pinyin **yè** *and Frequency Rank* **920**

Contains **5 strokes** in the following order:

Contains these components:

- ancient 古 (altered) 53, p.21

With all these meanings & readings:

yè [葉] **1** leaf **2** page **3** surname Ye

Think of this character 叶 as a rotation of 古 'ancient', 53, by ninety degrees. What life forms lose their posture and sag when they get ancient? Why, **leaves** do!

56

This character with the definition:

cluck

Pinyin **gū** *and Frequency Rank* **2418**

Contains these components:

mouth 口 37, p.17
ancient 古 53, p.21

With all these meanings & readings:

gū [咕] **1** mutter

SIMP & TRAD   Contains **8 strokes** in the following order:

丨 冂 口 口一 叶 吐 咕 咕

For some *ancient* people, the sounds from their *mouths* resembled the **clucks** of chickens.

57

This character with the definition:

express

Pinyin **shēn** *and Frequency Rank* **1110**

Contains these components:

mouth 口 37, p.17
ten 十 7, p.11

With all these meanings & readings:

shēn [申] **1** to extend **2** to state
3 to explain **4** surname Shen
5 9th earthly branch: 3-5 p.m.,
7th solar month (7th August-7th
September), year of the Monkey

SIMP & TRAD   Contains **5 strokes** in the following order:

丨 冂 曰 曰 申

A skilled orator can **express** herself eloquently on any subject, allowing more than *ten* words to flow effortlessly from her *mouth*.

58

This character with the definition:

reason, by means of

Pinyin **yóu** *and Frequency Rank* **136**

Contains these components:

mouth 口 37, p.17
ten 十 7, p.11

With all these meanings & readings:

yóu [由] **1** to follow **2** from
3 it is for...to **4** reason **5** cause
6 because of **7** due to **8** to
9 to leave it (to sb) **10** by (introduces passive verb)

SIMP & TRAD   Contains **5 strokes** in the following order:

丨 冂 曰 由 由

He's got *ten* stones in his *mouth*, which is the **reason** why it's difficult to make sense of what he is saying. Still, **by means of** constant practice speaking with the *mouth*ful of pebbles, he will become a skilled orator.

59

This character with the definition:

take out

Pinyin **chōu** *and Frequency Rank* **1178**

Contains these components:

hand r 扌 25, p.15
reason, by means of 由 58, p.22

With all these meanings & readings:

chōu [抽] **1** to draw out **2** to smoke (cigarettes) **3** to pump

SIMP & TRAD   Contains **8 strokes** in the following order:

一 十 才 扎 扣 扣 抽 抽

The doctor was able to find and **take out** the splinter from my *hand by means of* special tweezers and a magnifier.

Unit 5

60

SIMP & TRAD

This character with the definition:

can, may

Pinyin **kě** *and Frequency Rank* **30**

Contains **5 strokes** in the following order:

一 丁 丆 口 可

Contains these components:

◻ fourth (in a series) 丁 19, p. 13
◼ mouth 口 37, p. 17

With all these meanings & readings:

kě ［可］ **1** can **2** may **3** able to **4** to approve **5** to permit **6** certain(ly) **7** to suit **8** very (particle used for emphasis)

In the children's tale of Little Red Riding Hood, the Big Bad Wolf needs to huff and puff over and over to blow the house down. Only after the *fourth* mighty puff from his *mouth* **can** the wolf succeed in his demolition work. • This character 可 often appears as part of another character; it then takes on the meaning of '**ability**', the related noun form of '**can**' and '**may**'.

61

SIMP & TRAD

This character with the definition:

elder brother

Pinyin **gē** *and Frequency Rank* **804**

Contains **10 strokes** in the following order:

一 丆 丆 可 可 哥 哥 哥 哥 哥

Contains these components:

◼ can, may (×2) 可 60, p. 23

With all these meanings & readings:

gē ［哥］ **1** elder brother

If you have an **elder brother**, life is not easy, especially when you're young; you really need a thick skin and a *double dose* of *ability* to survive. His rank as **elder brother** means he *can* get away with twice as many things as you can.

62

SIMP & TRAD

This character with the definition:

breathe out

Pinyin **hē** *and Frequency Rank* **1861**

Contains **8 strokes** in the following order:

丨 丆 口 口 叮 呵 呵 呵

Contains these components:

◻ mouth 口 37, p. 17
◼ can, may 可 60, p. 23

With all these meanings & readings:

ā ［呵］ **1** variant of 啊［啊］[ā]
hē ［呵］ **1** expel breath **2** my goodness

Exhaling, or **breathing out**, is one very useful *activity* that a *mouth can* do.

63

SIMP & TRAD

This character with the definition:

field

Pinyin **tián** *and Frequency Rank* **778**

Contains **5 strokes** in the following order:

丨 冂 日 用 田

Contains these components:

◻ enclosure r 囗 36, p. 17
◼ ten 十 7, p. 11

With all these meanings & readings:

tián ［田］ **1** field **2** farm **3** surname Tian **4** m 片［piàn］

Traditionally, this pictograph represents a **field** with irrigation ditches. However, it's better to think of it as a cultivated **field** with *ten* different crops surrounded by an *enclosure*.

64

日

SIMP & TRAD

This character with the definition:

day, sun

Pinyin **rì** *and Frequency Rank* **101**

Contains **4 strokes** in the following order:

丨 冂 冂 日

Contains these components:

■ enclosure r 囗 36, p.17

▭ one 一 1, p.10

With all these meanings & reading

rì [日] **1** sun **2** day **3** date, d of the month **4** abbr for 日本 Japan

A stylized pictograph of the **sun**. A **day** *encloses one* major time period.

65

早

SIMP & TRAD

This character with the definition:

morning

Pinyin **zǎo** *and Frequency Rank* **462**

Contains **6 strokes** in the following order:

丨 冂 冃 日 旦 早

Contains these components:

▭ day, sun 日 64, p.24

■ ten 十 7, p.11

With all these meanings & reading

zǎo [早] **1** early **2** morning

The *sun* is jauntily perched on *ten* o'clock, a great time to begin the **morning**.

66

晶

SIMP & TRAD

This character with the definition:

crystal

Pinyin **jīng** *and Frequency Rank* **1725**

Contains **12 strokes** in the following order:

丨 冂 冃 日 日 日 日 日 日 昂 晶 晶

Contains these components:

■ day, sun (×3) 日 64, p.24

With all these meanings & reading

jīng [晶] **1** crystal

Light shining through a multi-faceted **crystal** can appear as bright and brilliant as several *suns*.

67

曰

SIMP & TRAD

This character with the definition:

speak

Pinyin **yuē** *and Frequency Rank* **1656**

Contains **4 strokes** in the following order:

丨 冂 冃 曰

Contains these components:

■ day, sun 日 64, p.24

With all these meanings & reading

yuē [曰] **1** to speak **2** to say

A *day* hasn't truly begun until you first **speak** with your friends and family, including your 'son' (sounds like *sun*).

68

昌

SIMP & TRAD

This character with the definition:

flourishing

Pinyin **chāng** *and Frequency Rank* **1606**

Contains **8 strokes** in the following order:

丨 冂 冃 日 曰 昌 昌 昌

Contains these components:

■ speak (×2) 曰 67, p.24

With all these meanings & reading

chāng [昌] **1** prosperous **2** flo ish **3** surname Chang

Repeating the element for *speak* emphasizes the importance of merchants *speaking* with customers in order for their businesses to flourish—the more sales pitches they deliver, the more deals they will strike.

69

唱

SIMP & TRAD

This character with the definition:

sing

Pinyin **chàng** *and Frequency Rank* **1252**

Contains **11 strokes** in the following order:

丶 丷 口 口¹ 叩 叩 叩 唱 唱 唱 唱

Contains these components:

▮ mouth 口 37, p.17

▮ flourishing 昌 68, p.24

With all these meanings & readings:

chàng [唱] **1** sing **2** to call loudly **3** to chant

It's possible to think of a song as a melodious speech, that is, the expressive nature of the **singing** *mouth* gives way to powers that have *flourished* beyond normal impact.

70

旦

SIMP & TRAD

This character with the definition:

dawn

Pinyin **dàn** *and Frequency Rank* **1300**

Contains **5 strokes** in the following order:

丨 冂 冃 日 旦

Contains these components:

▮ day, sun 日 64, p.24

▬ one 一 1, p.10

With all these meanings & readings:

dàn [旦] **1** dawn **2** morning **3** day-break **4** day

Can you help but see the *sun* rise above the horizon *line* at **dawn**?

71

坦

SIMP & TRAD

This character with the definition:

flat

Pinyin **tǎn** *and Frequency Rank* **1017**

Contains **8 strokes** in the following order:

一 十 土 圠 坦 坦 坦 坦

Contains these components:

▮ earth, soil 土 9, p.11

▮ dawn 旦 70, p.25

With all these meanings & readings:

tǎn [坦] **1** flat **2** open-hearted **3** level **4** smooth

No matter what, *earth* at *dawn* appears **flat**.

72

量

SIMP & TRAD

This character with the definition:

measure

Pinyin **liàng** *and Frequency Rank* **241**

Contains **12 strokes** in the following order:

丨 冂 冃 日 旦 旦 昊 昌 昌 昌 量 量

Contains these components:

▮ dawn 旦 70, p.25

▮ neighborhood 里 40, p.18

With all these meanings & readings:

liáng [量] **1** to measure
liàng [量] **1** capacity **2** quantity **3** amount **4** to estimate **5** abbr for 量词 [~词][liàng cí], classifier (in Chinese grammar) **6** measure word

At the break of *dawn*, visibility improves all over the *neighborhood*; the light makes it easy to **measure** the distance between things.

73

担

TRAD   SIMPLIFIED

This character with the definition:

undertake

Pinyin **dān** *and Frequency Rank* **720**

Contains **8 strokes** in the following order:

一 十 扌 扣 扣 担 担 担

Contains these components:

▮ hand r 扌 25, p.15

▮ dawn 旦 70, p.25

With all these meanings & readings:

dān [擔] **1** to undertake **2** to carry **3** to shoulder **4** to take responsibility
dàn [擔] **1** a picul (100 catties, 50 kg.) **2** two buckets full **3** carrying pole and it's load

Undertaking the tasks of daily life begins early. At *dawn*, people begin using their *hands* to perform their various chores.

74

舊
TRAD

旧
SIMPLIFIED

This character with the definition:

antiquated, outdated

Pinyin **jiù** and Frequency Rank **915**

Contains these components:

☐ scepter c ｜5, p.10

▣ day, sun 日 64, p.24

With all these meanings & readings

jiù [舊] **1** old **2** opposite: new 新 **3** former

Contains **5 strokes** in the following order:

｜ ｜｜ ｜刀 ｜日 旧

An aged leader, with her *scepter* as symbol of authority, has seen many *days* and reflects on **bygone** times.

75

目

SIMP & TRAD

This character with the definition:

eye

Pinyin **mù** and Frequency Rank **239**

Contains these components:

☐ enclosure r 囗 36, p.17

▣ two 二 2, p.10

With all these meanings & readings

mù [目] **1** eye **2** item **3** section **4** list **5** catalogue **6** table of contents **7** order (taxonomy) **8** goal **9** name **10** title

Contains **5 strokes** in the following order:

｜ 冂 月 目 目

The *two* **eye** sockets in the upper half of your head function as *enclosures* for your **eye**balls. Also, imagine turning an open **eye** on its end, and simplifying its curves to horizontal and vertical segments to resemble this character, 目.

76

耳

SIMP & TRAD

This character with the definition:

ear

Pinyin **ěr** and Frequency Rank **887**

Contains these components:

▣ eye 目 (altered) 75, p.26

With all these meanings & readings

ěr [耳] **1** ear **2** handle (archaeology) **3** and that is all (classical Chinese)

Contains **6 strokes** in the following order:

一 丆 丌 F 耳 耳

Ears and eyes are a person's main sensory. The **ear** is shown here as a slightly deformed *eye*. The horizontal extensions emphasize the external structures that surround our **ears**. The extended vertical stroke on the right side is the earlobe of the right **ear**.

77

冒

SIMP & TRAD

This character with the definition:

brave

Pinyin **mào** and Frequency Rank **1222**

Contains these components:

▢ enclosure r 囗 (altered) 36, p.17

▣ two 二 2, p.10

▣ eye 目 75, p.26

With all these meanings & readings

mào [冒] **1** to emit **2** to give off **3** to send out (or up, forth) **4** brave **5** bold **6** to cover

Contains **9 strokes** in the following order:

丨 冂 冃 日 冒 冒 冒 冒 冒

A soldier feels more **brave** when his head is protected by a helmet that acts as a small *enclosure* around his face in such a way that it protects his *two eyes*.

78

而

SIMP & TRAD

This character with the definition:

but, yet (contrast)

Pinyin **ér** and Frequency Rank **36**

Contains these components:

☐ one 一, p.10

▣ eye 目 (altered) 75, p.26

With all these meanings & readings

ér [而] **1** and **2** as well as **3** and so **4** but (not) **5** yet (not) **6** (indicates causal relation) **7** (indicates change of state) **8** (indicates contrast)

Contains **6 strokes** in the following order:

一 丆 厂 而 而 而

If you see this glyph (with your *eye*) as a sketch with the little 'dab' connecting the upper smooth *horizontal* line with the lower rough, beard-like frame, then you'll see that this character shows **contrast**.

79
面
面
麵
TRAD   SIMPLIFIED

This character with the definition:

face, aspect

Pinyin **miàn** *and Frequency Rank* **74**

Contains **9 strokes** in the following order:

一 ブ プ 丌 丌 币 而 面 面

Contains these components:

■ but, yet (contrast) 而 78, p. 26

▣ eye 目 75, p. 26

▢ one 一 1, p. 10

With all these meanings & readings:

miàn [面] **1** fade **2** side **3** surface **4** aspect **5** top **6** face **7** m for flat surfaces such as drums, mirrors, flags etc
miàn [麵] **1** flour **2** noodles

My dog has a **face** with *contrasting* features—*one eye* is blue and the other is brown.

80
耑
SIMP & TRAD

This character with the definition:

concentrate on, specialize in

Pinyin **zhuān** *and Frequency Rank* **9047**

Contains **9 strokes** in the following order:

` 凵 山 屮 屮 屵 屵 耑 耑

Contains these components:

▢ mountain 山 4, p. 10

■ but, yet (contrast) 而 78, p. 26

With all these meanings & readings:

zhuān [耑] **1** variant of 专 [專], concentrated **2** specialized

The *mountain's* great majesty projects such a *contrast* to the environment of my everyday life that I have trouble **concentrating on** mundane matters.

81
瑞
SIMP & TRAD

This character with the definition:

auspicious

Pinyin **ruì** *and Frequency Rank* **1332**

Contains **13 strokes** in the following order:

一 三 F 王 王' 玔 玑 玭 珆 玥 瑞 瑞 瑞

Contains these components:

■ king 王 15, p. 12

▣ concentrate on, specialize in 耑 80, p. 27

With all these meanings & readings:

ruì [瑞] **1** lucky **2** auspicious **3** propitious **4** rayl (acoustical unit)

During my brief audience with the *king*, his words *concentrated on* my achievements. It was an **auspicious** moment for me.

82
喘
SIMP & TRAD

This character with the definition:

gasp for breath

Pinyin **chuǎn** *and Frequency Rank* **1977**

Contains **12 strokes** in the following order:

丨 冂 口 口' 叫 叫 哯 哯 喘 喘 喘 喘

Contains these components:

■ mouth 口 37, p. 17

▢ mountain 山 4, p. 10

■ but, yet (contrast) 而 78, p. 26

With all these meanings & readings:

chuǎn [喘] **1** to gasp **2** to pant **3** asthma

Consider a *mountain* and its *contrast*, the valley down below, and suppose you run like the wind from the top of the *mountain* down to the bottom of the valley. You'll be **gasping for breath** through your *mouth*.

83
看
SIMP & TRAD

This character with the definition:

see, look at

Pinyin **kàn** *and Frequency Rank* **76**

Contains **9 strokes** in the following order:

一 二 三 チ 手 看 看 看 看

Contains these components:

■ hand 手 (altered) 21, p. 14

▢ eye 目 75, p. 26

With all these meanings & readings:

kān [看] **1** to look after **2** to take care of **3** to watch **4** to guard
kàn [看] **1** to see, look at, watch **2** to read **3** to consider **4** to regard as **5** to view as **6** to treat as **7** to judge **8** (after repeated verb) to give it a try **9** depending on (how you're judging) **10** to visit **11** to call on **12** to treat (an illness) **13** to look after **14** Watch out! (for a danger)

In this character, my *hand* shades my light-sensitive *eyes* so that I am better able to **see** into the distance.

84

且

SIMP & TRAD

This character with the definition:

moreover

Pinyin **qiě** *and Frequency Rank* **296**

Contains **5 strokes** in the following order:

丨 冂 冃 日 且

Contains these components:

■ eye 日 75, p. 26

☐ one 一 1, p. 10

With all these meanings & readings

qiě [且] **1** further **2** moreover

Do you like this small system of bookshelves? Well, 'I won' (sounds like '*eye one*') it at the fair! I use it to stack **more** things **over** other things. • This character frequently appears as a component, and it's often convenient to apply the 'bookcase' or 'bookshelf' metaphor to it in those cases.

Unit 6

85

This character with the definition:

straight, vertical

Pinyin **zhí** *and Frequency Rank* **255**

SIMP & TRAD   Contains **8 strokes** in the following order:

一 十 广 方 方 有 首 直

Contains these components:

☐ ten 十 7, p.11

■ moreover 且 (altered) 84, p.28

With all these meanings & readings:

zhí [直] **1** straight **2** vertical **3** frank **4** directly **5** straightly **6** upright

If we stack *ten* bookshelves (from the definition of *moreover*) on top of each other, they will need to be as **straight** and **vertical** as possible so that they don't topple over. *Moreover*, we will need to add an extra horizontal 'shelf' for additional strength and support. As if to tempt fate, the vertical shaft of 十 is written a bit to the right in this character—look closely!

86

This character with the definition:

stare

Pinyin **dīng** *and Frequency Rank* **1906**

SIMP & TRAD   Contains **7 strokes** in the following order:

丨 冂 冂 月 目 盯 盯

Contains these components:

■ eye 目 75, p.26

■ fourth (in a series) 丁 19, p.13

With all these meanings & readings:

dīng [盯] **1** to watch attentively **2** to fix attention on **3** to stare **4** to gaze **5** to follow **6** to shadow sb

A **stare** is a fixed gaze, in which *one* person *hooks* you with his *eye*. (Here, we are deconstructing the 丁 component of panel 19 into its components.)

87

This component has the meaning:

grass r

COMPONENT

The horizontal ground surface marks the boundary between the shoots extending up to the sky and the roots reaching into the earth.

88

This character with the definition:

luxuriant

Pinyin **fēi** *and Frequency Rank* **1418**

SIMP & TRAD   Contains **11 strokes** in the following order:

一 十 艹 艹 芋 芋 菲 菲 菲 菲 菲

Contains these components:

☐ grass r 艹 87, p.29

■ not 非 6, p.11

With all these meanings & readings:

fēi [菲] **1** rich **2** luxurious **3** phenanthrene (chemistry) **4** abbr for the Philippines 菲律宾 [~~賓][fēi bin]

Think of the parts of '*not*' (panel 6) as two *combs* stuck in the hair of a royal princess. She further affixes a costly gold hair clip at the top of her head with a clasp that is designed to make the clip look like a tuft of golden *grass* in her hair. How **luxurious**!

89 苦

This character with the definition:

bitter

Pinyin **kǔ** *and Frequency Rank* **634**

SIMP & TRAD   Contains **8 strokes** in the following order:

一 十 艹 艹 苎 芐 苦 苦

Contains these components:

☐ grass r 艹 87, p.29

■ ancient 古 53, p.21

With all these meanings & readings:

kǔ [苦] **1** bitter **2** hardship **3** pain **4** to suffer **5** painstaking

Experience soon teaches you that *ancient grass* tastes the most **bitter**.

90 This character with the definition:

grass

Pinyin **cǎo** *and Frequency Rank* **789**

Contains these components:

☐ grass r ⻆ 87, p. 29
■ morning 早 65, p. 24

With all these meanings & reading

cǎo [草] **1** grass **2** straw **3** m
4 draft (of a document) **5** car
less **6** rough **7** m 稞[kē],
攃[zuǒ], 株[zhū], 根[gēn]

SIMP & TRAD Contains **9 strokes** in the following order:

一 十 艹 艹 艹 芦 苔 苩 草

1 If you consider the small '*grass*' component at the top of this character as actual **grass**, you can remember the whole character by imagining a gardener cutting that **grass** in the *morning*. 2 Glowing in the *morning* light and refreshed by drops of dew, **grass** appears even *grassier* in the *morning*.

91 This character with the definition:

seedling

Pinyin **miáo** *and Frequency Rank* **1920**

Contains these components:

☐ grass r ⻆ 87, p. 29
■ field 田 63, p. 23

With all these meanings & reading

miáo [苗] **1** Hmong or Miao
ethnic group of southwest Chir
2 surname Miao
miáo [苗] **1** sprout

SIMP & TRAD Contains **8 strokes** in the following order:

一 十 艹 艹 苦 苗 苗 苗

Soon after the **seedlings** begin to sprout, the *field* quickly gets populated with *grass*-like plants.

92 This character with the definition:

to trace

Pinyin **miáo** *and Frequency Rank* **1246**

Contains these components:

■ hand r 扌 25, p. 15
☐ seedling 苗 91, p. 30

With all these meanings & reading

miáo [描] **1** depict **2** to trace
drawing) **3** to copy **4** to tou
up

SIMP & TRAD Contains **11 strokes** in the following order:

一 十 扌 扌 扩 扩 扩 描 描 描 描

Sometimes tiny seeds are planted close together in shallow flatbeds of soil. As soon as a *seedling* sprouts a few leaves, it is time for the farmer to use his *hand* **to trace** a small hole in the field, into which he plants the tender *seedling*, hoping it will grow to maturity.

93 This character with the definition:

decorative grasses

Pinyin **huì** *and Frequency Rank* **3341**

Contains these components:

☐ ten 十 7, p. 11
■ grass r ⻆ (altered) 87, p. 29

With all these meanings & reading

huì [卉] **1** plants

SIMP & TRAD Contains **5 strokes** in the following order:

一 十 土 芋 卉

Over the centuries, many—at least *ten*—types of *grass* have been selected for beauty and have been bred to be **decorative grasses**.

94 This component has the meaning:

horned animal c

COMPONENT

An example of a **horned animal** is a cow or an ox. The verticals represent the horns and the sides of the head. The upper horizontal stroke represents the top of its head and ears, and the lower one the base of its head.

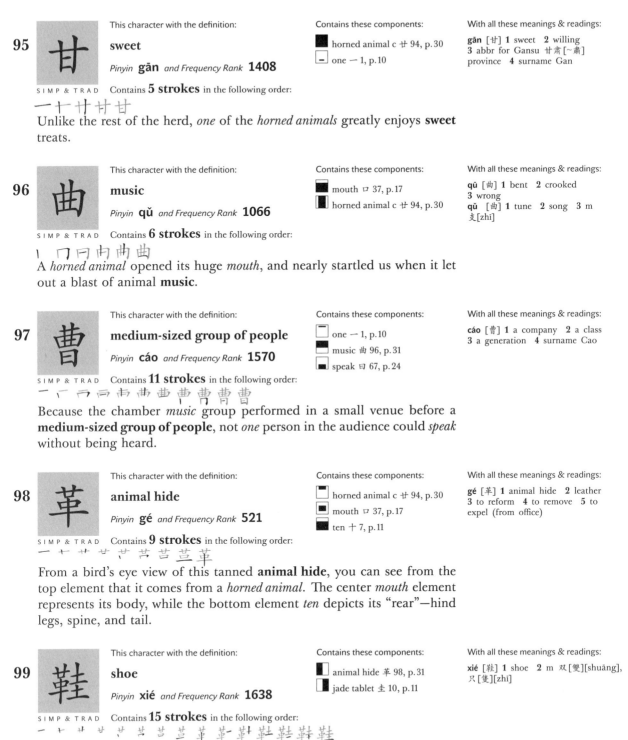

95

甘

SIMP & TRAD

This character with the definition:

sweet

Pinyin **gān** and Frequency Rank **1408**

Contains **5 strokes** in the following order:

一 十 廿 甘 甘

Contains these components:

■ horned animal c 廿 94, p. 30

━ one 一 1, p. 10

With all these meanings & readings:

gān [甘] **1** sweet **2** willing
3 abbr for Gansu 甘肃 [~肅]
province **4** surname Gan

Unlike the rest of the herd, *one* of the *horned animals* greatly enjoys **sweet** treats.

96

曲

SIMP & TRAD

This character with the definition:

music

Pinyin **qǔ** and Frequency Rank **1066**

Contains **6 strokes** in the following order:

丨 冂 日 内 曲 曲

Contains these components:

■ mouth 口 37, p. 17

■ horned animal c 廿 94, p. 30

With all these meanings & readings:

qū [曲] **1** bent **2** crooked
3 wrong
qǔ [曲] **1** tune **2** song **3** m
支 [zhī]

A *horned animal* opened its huge *mouth*, and nearly startled us when it let out a blast of animal **music**.

97

曹

SIMP & TRAD

This character with the definition:

medium-sized group of people

Pinyin **cáo** and Frequency Rank **1570**

Contains **11 strokes** in the following order:

一 厂 冖 冃 声 曲 曹 曹 曹 曹 曹

Contains these components:

□ one 一 1, p. 10

■ music 曲 96, p. 31

■ speak 曰 67, p. 24

With all these meanings & readings:

cáo [曹] **1** a company **2** a class
3 a generation **4** surname Cao

Because the chamber *music* group performed in a small venue before a **medium-sized group of people**, not *one* person in the audience could *speak* without being heard.

98

革

SIMP & TRAD

This character with the definition:

animal hide

Pinyin **gé** and Frequency Rank **521**

Contains **9 strokes** in the following order:

一 十 廿 甘 芇 苗 莒 莒 革

Contains these components:

□ horned animal c 廿 94, p. 30

■ mouth 口 37, p. 17

■ ten 十 7, p. 11

With all these meanings & readings:

gé [革] **1** animal hide **2** leather
3 to reform **4** to remove **5** to
expel (from office)

From a bird's eye view of this tanned **animal hide**, you can see from the top element that it comes from a *horned animal*. The center *mouth* element represents its body, while the bottom element *ten* depicts its "rear"—hind legs, spine, and tail.

99

鞋

SIMP & TRAD

This character with the definition:

shoe

Pinyin **xié** and Frequency Rank **1638**

Contains **15 strokes** in the following order:

一 十 廿 甘 芇 苗 莒 莒 革 革 革 鞋 鞋 鞋 鞋

Contains these components:

■ animal hide 革 98, p. 31

□ jade tablet 圭 10, p. 11

With all these meanings & readings:

xié [鞋] **1** shoe **2** m 双 [雙][shuāng],
只 [隻][zhī]

With limited technology in the past, it must have been difficult to create durable and useful **shoes**. The '*animal hide*' component emphasizes the raw material used, while the '*jade tablet*' reminds us of its exorbitant price.

100

This component has the meaning:

net r

COMPONENT

This radical is derived from the character whose traditional form is 網 (simplified 网), wǎng, '**net**', often used today for '**Internet**'. Interpret this component as a small portion of a tennis **net** containing three adjacent openings framed by the **net**'s cords.

101

This character with the definition:

vessel, container

Pinyin **mǐn** *and Frequency Rank* **3763**

SIMP & TRAD　Contains **5 strokes** in the following order:

丶　丆　冂　冂　皿

Contains these components:

■ net r ﾛ 100, p. 32
□ one 一 1, p. 10

With all these meanings & readings

mǐn [皿] **1** dish **2** vessel **3** shallow container **4** rad. no. 108

Imagine the profile of a fancy bowl, resting on a *horizontal surface*. The scribes have sketched vertical lines to represent *net*-like designs on the outside of the **vessel**.

102

This character with the definition:

eldest brother

Pinyin **mèng** *and Frequency Rank* **1575**

SIMP & TRAD　Contains **8 strokes** in the following order:

乛　了　子　孟　孟　孟　孟　孟

Contains these components:

□ son, child 子 24, p. 15
■ vessel, container 皿 101, p. 32

With all these meanings & readings

Mèng [孟] **1** first month **2** eldest brother **3** surname Meng

Any family acts like a *vessel* that contains parents and children; however, in Chinese culture the **eldest brother** was always the *child* destined to be captain of the *vessel* should anything happen to the father.

103

This character with the definition:

place, put

Pinyin **zhì** *and Frequency Rank* **677**

SIMP & TRAD　Contains **13 strokes** in the following order:

丶　丆　冂　冂　罒　罒　罗　罘　罟　置　置　置　置

Contains these components:

□ net r ﾛ 100, p. 32
■ straight, vertical 直 85, p. 29

With all these meanings & readings

zhì [置] **1** to install **2** to place **3** to put

Pictographically, here is a *net* emptying its catch of fish into a *vertical* storage container resting on a horizontal platform. Once this is done, the fish will have been **placed** securely in storage. At the end of the day, we clean the *net* carefully, before *straightening it out* and hanging it *vertically* on the wall. We've **put** it in **place** afterwards, ready for tomorrow.

104

This character with the definition:

crime, guilt

Pinyin **zuì** *and Frequency Rank* **718**

SIMP & TRAD　Contains **13 strokes** in the following order:

丶　丆　冂　罒　罒　罪　罪　罪　罪　罪　罪　罪　罪

Contains these components:

□ net r ﾛ 100, p. 32
■ not 非 6, p. 11

With all these meanings & readings

zuì [罪] **1** guilt **2** crime **3** fault **4** blame **5** sin

Getting mixed up in **crime** and becoming awash with **guilt** feels like being entangled in a *net* that has *not* been laid out properly.

105

This component has the meaning:

place of refuge c

COMPONENT

This land form, shaped like an arm that is encircling and protecting a loved one, signifies a **place of refuge**, where people come together for mutual assistance and help.

106

This character with the definition:

company

Pinyin **sī** and Frequency Rank **278**

SIMP & TRAD   Contains **5 strokes** in the following order:

丁 丆 刁 司 司

Contains these components:

▢ place of refuge c 丁 105, p.33
▬ one 一 1, p.10
▪ mouth 口 37, p.17

With all these meanings & readings:

sī [司] **1** company **2** control **3** surname Si

A **company** is a *place of refuge* (so to speak) for people who have been brought together to work toward the **company**'s goals. In a sense, the employees speak out of *one mouth*—that of the **company**.

107

This character with the definition:

feather, wing

Pinyin **yǔ** and Frequency Rank **1865**

SIMP & TRAD   Contains **6 strokes** in the following order:

丁 丬 刁 羽 羽 羽

Contains these components:

▪ place of refuge c 丁 105, p.33
▪ two 二 (altered) 2, p.10
▪ place of refuge c 丁 105, p.33
▪ two 二 (altered) 2, p.10

With all these meanings & readings:

yǔ [羽] **1** feather **2** 6th note in pentatonic scale

The ancient scribes sketched the *two* **wings** of a bird. Each wing can provide a *place of refuge*. Each inner *two* (somewhat misaligned) suggests how each **feather** can become ruffled during flight.

108

習
TRAD   SIMPLIFIED

This character with the definition:

practice, study

Pinyin **xí** and Frequency Rank **676**

Contains **3 strokes** in the following order:

丁 丬 刁

Contains these components:

▪ feather, wing 羽 (abbrev) 107, 33

With all these meanings & readings:

xí [習] **1** to practice **2** to study **3** habit

Half a feather or *half of a wing* suggests that we have to **practice** more in order to earn a complete set of *wings*!

109

韋
TRAD   SIMPLIFIED

This character with the definition:

leather

Pinyin **wéi** and Frequency Rank **1667**

Contains **4 strokes** in the following order:

一 二 弓 韦

Contains these components:

▪ plentiful 丰 16, p.13
▪ place of refuge c 丁 105, p.33

With all these meanings & readings:

wéi [韋] **1** soft leather **2** surname Wei

(Note how the horizontal part of '*place of refuge*' coincides with the bottom horizontal of '*plentiful*'.) **Leather** clothes are the strongest, and are a *plentiful* source of warmth. Encasing your body in **leather** ensures that you are in your own portable *place of refuge*.

Unit 7

110

围

圍 TRAD   SIMPLIFIED

This character with the definition:

surround, enclose

Pinyin **wéi** *and Frequency Rank* **576**

Contains **7 strokes** in the following order:

丨 冂 冂 冃 冃 围 围

Contains these components:

☐ enclosure r 囗 36, p.17

■ leather 韦 109, p.33

With all these meanings & readings

wéi [圍] **1** to encircle **2** to surround **3** all around **4** to wear by wrapping around (scarf shawl) **5** a surname

The farmer built a barbed-wire, electrified *enclosure* to **surround** his valuable cattle. Still, thieves wearing thick *leather* clothing and gloves were successful in stealing his entire herd.

111

韩

韓 TRAD   SIMPLIFIED

This character with the definition:

South Korea

Pinyin **hán** *and Frequency Rank* **1221**

Contains **12 strokes** in the following order:

一 十 ナ 古 古 查 查 卓 卓 卓 韩 韩

Contains these components:

■ ten 十 7, p.11

■ morning 早 65, p.24

■ leather 韦 109, p.33

With all these meanings & readings

Hán [韓] **1** Han, one of the Seven Hero States of the Warring States 战国七雄 [戰國~~] **2** Korea from the fall of the Joseon dynasty in 1897 **3** Korea especially South Korea 大韩民国 [~韓~國] **4** surname Han

Those businessmen from **South Korea** are too canny for me! Despite meeting with them every *morning* for the past *ten* days, I still have no contract to import their *leather* chopsticks!

112

卫

衛 TRAD   SIMPLIFIED

This character with the definition:

protect*

Pinyin **wèi** *and Frequency Rank* **669**

Contains **3 strokes** in the following order:

フ 卫 卫

Contains these components:

■ place of refuge c ㄱ 105, p.33

▮ scepter c 丨 5, p.10

☐ one 一 1, p.10

With all these meanings & readings

wèi [衛] **1** to guard **2** to prote **3** to defend **4** abbr for 卫生间 [衛~間], toilet **5** surname Wei

At the *place of refuge* for the clans, the leader wields his *scepter* of authority as if to **guard** and **protect** his people from the danger just over the *horizon*.

113

节

節 TRAD   SIMPLIFIED

This character with the definition:

festival

Pinyin **jié** *and Frequency Rank* **514**

Contains **5 strokes** in the following order:

一 十 艹 艼 节

Contains these components:

☐ grass r 艹 87, p.29

■ protect* 卫 (abbrev) 112, 34

With all these meanings & readings

jié [節] **1** festival **2** holiday **3** node **4** joint **5** section **6** se ment **7** part **8** to economize **9** to save **10** to abridge **11** m integrity **12** m for segments, e. lessons, train wagons, biblical verses **13** m 个 [個][gè]

The earliest **festivals** were celebrations that followed the successful *guarding* of a tribe during an attack. Fronds of *grass* were hung everywhere to serve as convenient (and cheap) decorations.

114

冂

This component has the meaning:

borders r

COMPONENT

And contains these subcomponents:

☐ scepter c 丨 5, p.10

■ place of refuge c ㄱ 105, p.33

The **borders** of a country mark the boundaries of a distinct region in which the government (signified by the *scepter*-like stroke on the left side) provides a *place of refuge* to the citizens living within it.

115

再

SIMP & TRAD

This character with the definition:

again

Pinyin **zài**   *and Frequency Rank* **242**

Contains **6 strokes** in the following order:

一 丆 丏 丙 币 再

Contains these components:

king 王 15, p.12

borders r 冂 114, p.34

With all these meanings & readings:

zài [再] **1** again **2** once more **3** re- **4** second **5** another **6** then (after sth, and not until then)

The *king* and his court have an uncontrollable urge to extend their reach beyond the country's *borders*; as such, they will continue to do so **again** and **again**.

116

同

SIMP & TRAD

This character with the definition:

same, similar

Pinyin **tóng**   *and Frequency Rank* **69**

Contains **6 strokes** in the following order:

丨 冂 冋 同 同 同

Contains these components:

borders r 冂 114, p.34

one 一 1, p.10

mouth 口 37, p.17

With all these meanings & readings:

tóng [同] **1** like **2** same **3** similar **4** together **5** alike **6** with

People who live within the **same** set of *borders* usually speak the **same** language. You can think of them as one unified group speaking with *one mouth.*

117

册

册
TRAD   SIMPLIFIED

This character with the definition:

book, booklet

Pinyin **cè**   *and Frequency Rank* **1525**

Contains **5 strokes** in the following order:

丿 几 凡 刑 册

Contains these components:

borders r (×2) 冂 114, p.34

one 一 1, p.10

With all these meanings & readings:

cè [册] **1** book **2** booklet **3** m for books

This character depicts a pair of **booklets** bound together to form *one* large **book**. You can think of the hard binding as the **book**'s *borders.*

118

巾

SIMP & TRAD

This character with the definition:

towel

Pinyin **jīn**   *and Frequency Rank* **2281**

Contains **3 strokes** in the following order:

丨 冂 巾

Contains these components:

borders r 冂 114, p.34

scepter c 丨 5, p.10

With all these meanings & readings:

jīn [巾] **1** towel **2** kerchief **3** turban

The neighboring king (symbolized here by his royal *scepter*) has successfully invaded our *borders*. Is it time to throw in the **towel**? • By extension, since a **towel** is a piece of cloth that serves a special function, when this character appears as an element within a character, we will often interpret it as a special purpose fabric.

119

吊
吊
TRAD   SIMPLIFIED

This character with the definition:

suspend, hang

Pinyin **diào**   *and Frequency Rank* **2050**

Contains **6 strokes** in the following order:

丨 口 口 吊 吊 吊

Contains these components:

mouth 口 37, p.17

towel 巾 118, p.35

With all these meanings & readings:

diào [吊] **1** to suspend **2** to hang up **3** to hang a person
diào [吊] **1** a string of 100 cash (arch.) **2** to lament **3** to condole with

What *special fabric* (see panel 118) is worn **suspended** below a man's *mouth*? A necktie.

120

This character with the definition:

hat

Pinyin **mào** *and Frequency Rank* **1750**

Contains these components:

▯ towel 巾 118, p. 35
▮ brave 冒 77, p. 26

With all these meanings & readings:

mào [帽] **1** hat **2** cap

SIMP & TRAD Contains **12 strokes** in the following order:

丨 冂 巾 帄 帄 帄 帄 帽 帽 帽 帽 帽

Some men need fancy clothes as accessories to bolster their self-esteem. For many, the *special fabric* that makes them feel *brave* is a **hat** (much like the helmet of a warrior).

121

This character with the definition:

broom

Pinyin **zhǒu** *and Frequency Rank* **3630**

Contains these components:

▭ boar's head r ⇒ 30, p. 16
▭ borders r 冂 (altered) 114, p. 34
▬ towel 巾 118, p. 35

With all these meanings & readings:

zhǒu [帚] **1** broom

SIMP & TRAD Contains **8 strokes** in the following order:

⁊ ⁼ ⁼ ⁼ ⁼ ⁼ ⁼ 帚

The *boar's head* bristles on the **broom** have been wrapped with *towels* to mop the floor within the *borders* of the large room.

122

This component has the meaning:

mineshaft c

COMPONENT

If the component in panel 105 is a place of refuge, then this component represents the opposite: trouble, or a **place of danger**! Think of it as a mineshaft you fell into. • This **place of danger** is a place of refuge (panel 105) that's been turned upside-down.

123

This character with the definition:

seven

Pinyin **qī** *and Frequency Rank* **530**

Contains these components:

▮ mineshaft c ∟ 122, p. 36
▬ one 一 1, p. 10

With all these meanings & readings:

qī [七] **1** seven **2** 7

SIMP & TRAD Contains **2 strokes** in the following order:

一 七

Rotate this character half-way around, so that its horizontal bottom is at the top. You'll see the number 'seven', written with a horizontal stroke in the European fashion.

124

This character with the definition:

ancient ladle

Pinyin **bǐ** *and Frequency Rank* **3252**

Contains these components:

▮ seven 七 (altered) 123, p. 36

With all these meanings & readings:

bǐ [匕] **1** dagger **2** ladle **3** ancient type of spoon

SIMP & TRAD Contains **2 strokes** in the following order:

丿 匕

Ancient ladles were not only sturdier but much larger in size. With an **ancient ladle**, you could fill *seven* bowls and serve *seven* guests from a single scoop. The bottom curve represents the 'scoop' that holds the soup.

125 旨

This character with the definition:

intention, meaning

Pinyin **zhǐ** *and Frequency Rank* **1685**

SIMP & TRAD Contains **6 strokes** in the following order:

Contains these components:
- ancient ladle 匕 124, p. 36
- day, sun 日 64, p. 24

With all these meanings & readings:
zhǐ [旨] **1** imperial decree **2** purport **3** aim **4** purpose

Whenever the ancient leaders wanted to signal a special **intention** or **meaning** during their meetings, they would position the polished bottom of an *ancient ladle* and align it with the rays of the *sun* on a particular spot.

126 指

This character with the definition:

finger

Pinyin **zhǐ** *and Frequency Rank* **261**

SIMP & TRAD Contains **9 strokes** in the following order:

Contains these components:
- hand r 扌 25, p. 15
- intention, meaning 旨 125, p. 37

With all these meanings & readings:
zhǐ [指] **1** finger **2** to point **3** to direct **4** to indicate **5** to refer to **6** to rely on **7** to count on **8** (hair) stands stiffly on end

It's rude to point with one's **finger**! So I try to use my *hand* to communicate my *intentions* and *meanings* as much as possible.

127 比

This character with the definition:

compared with

Pinyin **bǐ** *and Frequency Rank* **199**

SIMP & TRAD Contains **4 strokes** in the following order:

Contains these components:
- ancient ladle 匕 (altered) 124, p. 36
- ancient ladle 匕 124, p. 36

With all these meanings & readings:
bǐ [比] **1** (particle used for comparison and "-er than") **2** to compare **3** to contrast **4** to gesture (with hands) **5** ratio **6** abbr for Belgium 比利时 [~~時]
bì [比] **1** associate with **2** be near

When the two *ancient ladles* are **compared with** each other side by side, the one on the right seems more elegant.

128 批

This character with the definition:

criticize, annotate

Pinyin **pī** *and Frequency Rank* **569**

SIMP & TRAD Contains **7 strokes** in the following order:

Contains these components:
- hand r 扌 25, p. 15
- compared with 比 127, p. 37

With all these meanings & readings:
pī [批] **1** to ascertain **2** to act on **3** to criticize **4** to pass on **5** m for batches, lots, military flights **6** tier (for the ranking of universities and colleges)

If ancient *hand*-made Chinese vases are *compared with* present-day manufactured counterparts, the mass-produced forms will inevitably receive **criticism** over the decline in quality of these vases.

129 昆

昆
崑

This character with the definition:

elder brother**

Pinyin **kūn** *and Frequency Rank* **1759**

TRAD SIMPLIFIED Contains **8 strokes** in the following order:

Contains these components:
- day, sun 日 64, p. 24
- compared with 比 127, p. 37

With all these meanings & readings:
kūn [崑] **1** Kunlun mountains
kūn [昆] **1** descendant **2** elder brother **3** a style of Chinese poetry

The man is the **elder brother** because he saw the *sun* first, at least when *compared with* his younger brothers.

130

畢
TRAD   SIMPLIFIED

This character with the definition:

finish, conclude

Pinyin **bì** *and Frequency Rank* **1093**

Contains **6 strokes** in the following order:

一 ト ㅏ 比 比 毕

Contains these components:

▭ compared with 比 127, p. 37

▬ ten 十 7, p. 11

With all these meanings & readings

bì [畢] **1** the whole of **2** to finish **3** to complete **4** compl **5** full **6** finished **7** surname F

Finishing a task, *compared with* completing only *ten* percent of it, is better.

131

SIMP & TRAD

This character with the definition:

north

Pinyin **běi** *and Frequency Rank* **315**

Contains **5 strokes** in the following order:

丨 丄 ㅓ 扎 北

Contains these components:

▮ ancient ladle ヒ (altered) 124, p. 36

▮ ancient ladle ヒ 124, p. 36

With all these meanings & readings

běi [北] **1** north

We see *two ladles* above, with the one on the left almost a mirror image of the one on the right. Consider the long vertical strokes of each as levees that are channeling the flow of a river traveling from the **north** (the top part of the picture) down to the farmlands in the south. Think of the short horizontal strokes as support structures to keep the levees from toppling.

132

SIMP & TRAD

This character with the definition:

also, too*

Pinyin **yě** *and Frequency Rank* **31**

Contains **3 strokes** in the following order:

乛 ㇇ 也

Contains these components:

▬ mineshaft c ㄴ 122, p. 36

▮ scepter c 丨 5, p. 10

▭ place of refuge c ㄱ (altered) 105, p. 33

With all these meanings & readings

yě [也] **1** also **2** too **3** (in classical Chinese) final particle serving as copula

The central *scepter* represents the court of a powerful king. His court can be a *place of refuge* but **also** a *place of danger*, a potential mineshaft, depending on how well you play politics.

133

SIMP & TRAD

This character with the definition:

earth, ground

Pinyin **dì** *and Frequency Rank* **21**

Contains **6 strokes** in the following order:

一 十 土 圠 圠 地

Contains these components:

▮ earth, soil 土 9, p. 11

▮ also, too* 也 132, p. 38

With all these meanings & readings

de [地] **1** -ly **2** structural particle: used before a verb or adjective, linking it to preceding modifying adverbial adjunct
dì [地] **1** earth **2** ground **3** fi **4** place **5** land **6** m 片[piàn]

This character is more descriptive for '**earth**' than the one we saw back in panel 9. In addition to containing the *soil* itself, the character reminds us that our planet can be dangerous—watch out for mineshafts!—but *also* a secure place of refuge.

134

SIMP & TRAD

This character with the definition:

generation

Pinyin **shì** *and Frequency Rank* **181**

Contains **5 strokes** in the following order:

一 十 卅 卋 世

Contains these components:

▮ mineshaft c ㄴ 122, p. 36

▯ horned animal c 卄 94, p. 30

With all these meanings & readings

shì [世] **1** life **2** age **3** generation **4** era **5** world **6** lifetime

There's a new breed of *horned animals* that can survive and thrive in a *mineshaft*. Look, a new **generation** is marching out.

Unit 8

135

己

SIMP & TRAD

This character with the definition:

self*

Pinyin **jǐ**   and Frequency Rank **162**

Contains **3 strokes** in the following order:

フ コ己

Contains these components:

▭ place of refuge c ㇆ 105, p. 33
▭ one 一 1, p. 10
▭ mineshaft c ㄴ 122, p. 36

With all these meanings & readings:

jǐ [己] **1** self **2** oneself **3** sixth of 10 heavenly stems 十天干 **4** sixth in order **5** letter "F" or roman "VI" in list "A, B, C", or "I, II, III" etc **6** hexa

The life story of one**self** consists of a series of happy events symbolized by *places of refuge* punctuated by unfortunate and desperate circumstances (illustrated by *mineshafts*). The *horizontal bar* reminds us of the connection between successive events. • This character also looks like a backwards 's', which stands for '**self**'.

136

已

SIMP & TRAD

This character with the definition:

already

Pinyin **yǐ**   and Frequency Rank **117**

Contains **3 strokes** in the following order:

フ コ已

Contains these components:

▪ self* 己 (altered) 135, p. 39

With all these meanings & readings:

yǐ [已] **1** already **2** to stop **3** then **4** afterwards

Compared to panel 135, the topmost open space in this character appears about to close up as if the development of one's *self* has **already** been charted or predetermined.

137

巴

SIMP & TRAD

This character with the definition:

cling to, stick to

Pinyin **bā**   and Frequency Rank **546**

Contains **4 strokes** in the following order:

フ コ コ 巴

Contains these components:

▪ already 已 (altered) 136, p. 39
▭ scepter c | 5, p. 10

With all these meanings & readings:

bā [巴] **1** Ba state during Zhou dynasty (east of modern Sichuan) **2** abbr for east Sichuan or Chongqing **3** surname Ba **4** abbr Palestine **5** abbr Pakistan
bā [巴] **1** to long for **2** to wish **3** to cling to **4** to stick to **5** sth that sticks **6** close to **7** next to **8** spread open **9** informal abbr for bus 巴士 **10** bar (unit of pressure) **11** nominalizing suffix on certain nouns, such as 尾巴, tail

The emperor's young son has *already* started imitating his father—he even knows the proper way to **cling to** the heavy imperial *scepter*!

138

把

SIMP & TRAD

This character with the definition:

grip

Pinyin **bǎ**   and Frequency Rank **110**

Contains **7 strokes** in the following order:

一 十 扌 扫 扣 扣 把

Contains these components:

▪ hand r 扌 25, p. 15
▭ cling to, stick to 巴 137, p. 39

With all these meanings & readings:

bǎ [把] **1** to hold **2** to contain **3** to grasp **4** to take hold of **5** a handle **6** particle marking the following noun as a direct object **7** m for objects with handle
bà [把] **1** handle

Athletes who rely on their *hand* skills often wear special gloves during games to help them **grip** a bat more firmly or to catch and *cling to* a moving ball more effectively.

139

This character with the definition:

s-end: suggestion, request

Pinyin **ba** *and Frequency Rank* **470**

SIMP & TRAD   Contains **7 strokes** in the following order:

丨 丨フ 口 口フ 口フ 口ヱ 吧

Contains these components:

■ mouth 口 37, p. 17

▯ cling to, stick to 巴 137, p. 39

With all these meanings & readings

bā [吧] **1** (onomat.)   **2** dumb
ba [吧] **1** (modal particle indicating polite suggestion)   **2** ...right
3 ...OK?

Even though I wanted to order my young son to stop *clinging to* me, I forced my *mouth* to frame my desire as a **suggestion** and asked him to "Please go outside and gather some flowers for me." • Chinese people consider it impolite to make a direct command; this character is used at the end of a direct statement to make it seem like a suggestion or request.

140

This character with the definition:

bow (weapon)

Pinyin **gōng** *and Frequency Rank* **2229**

SIMP & TRAD   Contains **3 strokes** in the following order:

フ ㄱ 弓

Contains these components:

■ self* 己 (altered) 135, p. 39

With all these meanings & readings

gōng [弓] **1** a bow (weapon)
2 surname Gong   **3** m 张 [張][z

One of the few **weapons** in ancient times that could be handled independently by the soldier him*self* was the **bow**. The twisty stroke of this character resembles the two knuckles he would use to grab and pull the bowstring.

141

This character with the definition:

lead, guide

Pinyin **yǐn** *and Frequency Rank* **479**

SIMP & TRAD   Contains **4 strokes** in the following order:

フ ㄱ 弓 引

Contains these components:

■ bow (weapon) 弓 140, p. 40

▯ scepter c 丨 5, p. 10

With all these meanings & readings

yǐn [引] **1** to draw (a bow)   **2** pull   **3** to stretch sth   **4** to extend   **5** to lengthen   **6** to involve in   **7** to attract   **8** to lead   **9** to guide   **10** to divert (water)   **11** unit of distance equal to 10 丈 [zhāng], now one-thirtieth km or 33.33 meters

Great kings rule by **leading** during times of war and peace, and are as skillful with the *bow* as with the *scepter*.

142

This character with the definition:

not (literary works)

Pinyin **fú** *and Frequency Rank* **1257**

SIMP & TRAD   Contains **5 strokes** in the following order:

フ ㄱ 弓 弗 弗

Contains these components:

■ bow (weapon) 弓 140, p. 40

▮ scepter c 丨 (altered) 5, p. 10

▯ scepter c 丨 5, p. 10

With all these meanings & readings

fú [弗] **1** not

Use a *bow*string to tie two *scepters* together. A secure 'knot' (sounds like 'not') will hold everything together.

143

This character with the definition:

weak, feeble, inferior

Pinyin **ruò** *and Frequency Rank* **1038**

SIMP & TRAD   Contains **10 strokes** in the following order:

フ ㄱ 弓 弓 弔 弔ˊ 弔ˇ 弱 弱 弱

Contains these components:

■ bow (weapon) (×2) 弓 140, p. 40

⬚ two (×2) 二 2, p. 10

With all these meanings & readings

ruò [弱] **1** weak   **2** feeble   **3** yo
4 inferior

Even though *two bows* can appear as a strong defense system, the *two* notches on each bow render them **weak** and **feeble**.

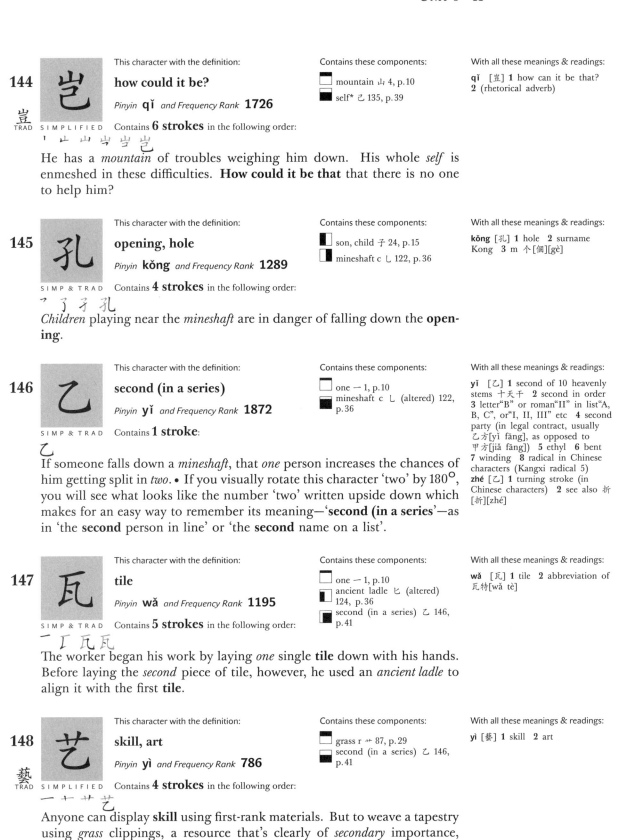

144

岂

岂
TRAD　SIMPLIFIED

This character with the definition:

how could it be?

Pinyin **qǐ** *and Frequency Rank* **1726**

Contains **6 strokes** in the following order:

Contains these components:

☐ mountain 山 4, p. 10
■ self* 己 135, p. 39

With all these meanings & readings:

qǐ [岂] **1** how can it be that? **2** (rhetorical adverb)

He has a *mountain* of troubles weighing him down. His whole *self* is enmeshed in these difficulties. **How could it be that** that there is no one to help him?

145

孔

SIMP & TRAD

This character with the definition:

opening, hole

Pinyin **kǒng** *and Frequency Rank* **1289**

Contains **4 strokes** in the following order:

Contains these components:

■ son, child 子 24, p. 15
■ mineshaft c ㄥ 122, p. 36

With all these meanings & readings:

kǒng [孔] **1** hole **2** surname Kong **3** m 个[個][gè]

Children playing near the *mineshaft* are in danger of falling down the **opening**.

146

乙

SIMP & TRAD

This character with the definition:

second (in a series)

Pinyin **yǐ** *and Frequency Rank* **1872**

Contains **1 stroke**:

乙

Contains these components:

☐ one 一 1, p. 10
■ mineshaft c ㄥ (altered) 122, p. 36

With all these meanings & readings:

yǐ [乙] **1** second of 10 heavenly stems 十天干 **2** second in order **3** letter "B" or roman "II" in list "A, B, C", or "I, II, III" etc **4** second party (in legal contract, usually 乙方[yǐ fāng], as opposed to 甲方[jiǎ fāng]) **5** ethyl **6** bent **7** winding **8** radical in Chinese characters (Kangxi radical 5) **zhé** [乙] **1** turning stroke (in Chinese characters) **2** see also 折 [折][zhé]

If someone falls down a *mineshaft*, that *one* person increases the chances of him getting split in *two*. • If you visually rotate this character 'two' by 180°, you will see what looks like the number 'two' written upside down which makes for an easy way to remember its meaning—'**second (in a series)**'—as in 'the **second** person in line' or 'the **second** name on a list'.

147

瓦

SIMP & TRAD

This character with the definition:

tile

Pinyin **wǎ** *and Frequency Rank* **1195**

Contains **5 strokes** in the following order:

Contains these components:

☐ one 一 1, p. 10
■ ancient ladle 匕 (altered) 124, p. 36
■ second (in a series) 乙 146, p. 41

With all these meanings & readings:

wǎ [瓦] **1** tile **2** abbreviation of 瓦特[wǎ tè]

The worker began his work by laying *one* single **tile** down with his hands. Before laying the *second* piece of tile, however, he used an *ancient ladle* to align it with the first **tile**.

148

艺

藝
TRAD　SIMPLIFIED

This character with the definition:

skill, art

Pinyin **yì** *and Frequency Rank* **786**

Contains **4 strokes** in the following order:

Contains these components:

■ grass r 艹 87, p. 29
■ second (in a series) 乙 146, p. 41

With all these meanings & readings:

yì [藝] **1** skill **2** art

Anyone can display **skill** using first-rank materials. But to weave a tapestry using *grass* clippings, a resource that's clearly of *secondary* importance, shows real **skill**, real **art**.

149

電
TRAD   SIMPLIFIED

This character with the definition:

electric current

Pinyin **diàn** *and Frequency Rank* **230**

Contains **5 strokes** in the following order:

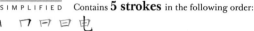

Contains these components:

■ day, sun 日 64, p. 24
▌ mineshaft c ∟ 122, p. 36

With all these meanings & readings:

diàn [電] **1** electric **2** electricity **3** electrical

Look closely at this portion of an **electric** grid. The current runs through the *mineshaft*-shaped wire and disperses through the network in a regular pattern resembling the *sun*. • For readers with some background in physics, a moving current gives rise to an **electro**magnetic field, nicely symbolized by the '*sun*' component. The *sun* itself has a massive **electro**magnetic field associated with it.

150

黽
TRAD   SIMPLIFIED

This character with the definition:

tadpole

Pinyin **mǐn** *and Frequency Rank* **5223**

Contains **8 strokes** in the following order:

Contains these components:

□ mouth 口 37, p. 17
▌ mineshaft c ∟ 122, p. 36
■ day, sun 日 64, p. 24

With all these meanings & readings:

mǐn [黽] **1** toad

Here's a scribe's eye view of a **tadpole**. A giant *mouth*-head is attached to a wiggling, wriggling *mineshaft*-shaped body. A round, *sun*-shaped stomach provides nourishment until this little creature achieves self-sufficiency.

151

扎
紮

TRAD   SIMPLIFIED

This character with the definition:

pierce, prick

Pinyin **zhā** *and Frequency Rank* **1411**

Contains **4 strokes** in the following order:

Contains these components:

▌ hand r 扌 25, p. 15
▌ mineshaft c ∟ 122, p. 36

With all these meanings & readings:

zā [扎] **1** to tie **2** to bind
zhā [扎] **1** to prick **2** to run or stick (a needle etc) into **3** jug (a classifier for liquids such as beer)
zhá [扎] **1** penetrating (as of cold) **2** struggle
zā [紮] **1** tie with string or ribbon **2** bind with rope or cord **3** to stop

The *hand* grabs the *wire* (the shape of a *mineshaft* suggests a segment of a live wire) in a careless manner. The sharp end **pierces** his *hand* and causes it to bleed a bit.

152

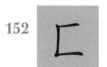

This component has the meaning:

basket, box r

COMPONENT

And contains these subcomponents:

□ one 一 1, p. 10
■ mineshaft c ∟ (altered) 122, p. 36

One way to **box** up a *mineshaft* securely is to put a *lid* on it.

153

SIMP & TRAD

This character with the definition:

huge

Pinyin **jù** *and Frequency Rank* **913**

Contains **4 strokes** in the following order:

Contains these components:

□ basket, box r ⼕ 152, p. 42
■ basket, box r ⼕ (altered) 152, p. 42

With all these meanings & readings:

jù [巨] **1** very large **2** huge **3** tremendous **4** gigantic

The outer *box* contains the inner *box*, but only because it is **huge**.

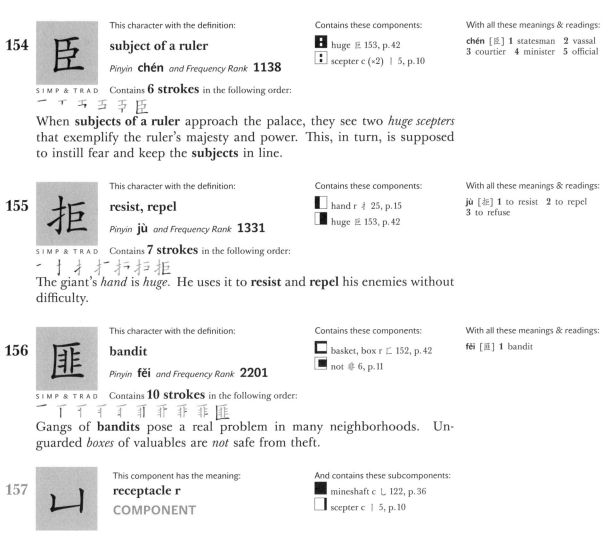

154

臣

SIMP & TRAD

This character with the definition:

subject of a ruler

Pinyin **chén** *and Frequency Rank* **1138**

Contains **6 strokes** in the following order:

Contains these components:

huge 巨 153, p. 42

scepter c (×2) | 5, p. 10

With all these meanings & readings:

chén [臣] **1** statesman **2** vassal **3** courtier **4** minister **5** official

When **subjects of a ruler** approach the palace, they see two *huge scepters* that exemplify the ruler's majesty and power. This, in turn, is supposed to instill fear and keep the **subjects** in line.

155

拒

SIMP & TRAD

This character with the definition:

resist, repel

Pinyin **jù** *and Frequency Rank* **1331**

Contains **7 strokes** in the following order:

Contains these components:

hand r 扌 25, p. 15

huge 巨 153, p. 42

With all these meanings & readings:

jù [拒] **1** to resist **2** to repel **3** to refuse

The giant's *hand* is *huge*. He uses it to **resist** and **repel** his enemies without difficulty.

156

匪

SIMP & TRAD

This character with the definition:

bandit

Pinyin **fěi** *and Frequency Rank* **2201**

Contains **10 strokes** in the following order:

Contains these components:

basket, box r 匚 152, p. 42

not 非 6, p. 11

With all these meanings & readings:

fěi [匪] **1** bandit

Gangs of **bandits** pose a real problem in many neighborhoods. Unguarded *boxes* of valuables are *not* safe from theft.

157

凵

This component has the meaning:

receptacle r

COMPONENT

And contains these subcomponents:

mineshaft c ㄴ 122, p. 36

scepter c | 5, p. 10

When a second *mineshaft* is drilled, the image of the two *mineshafts* connected by a tunnel resembles a **receptacle**.

158

出

SIMP & TRAD

This character with the definition:

exit

Pinyin **chū** *and Frequency Rank* **28**

Contains **5 strokes** in the following order:

Contains these components:

mountain 屮 (altered) 4, p. 10

receptacle r 凵 157, p. 43

With all these meanings & readings:

chū [出] **1** to go out **2** to come out **3** to occur **4** to produce **5** to go beyond **6** to rise **7** to put forth **8** to happen **9** m for dramas, plays, operas etc

A *mountain* pass resembles a *receptacle*-like passage through a *mountain* range. Because it is at a much lower altitude, the pass allows people to enter and **exit** the *mountain* range without having to climb over the high peaks. *Mountain* passes are well-known throughout history for assisting migrating populations, invading armies, and merchants to travel to distant new lands.

159

SIMP & TRAD

This character with the definition:

stockpile, store up

Pinyin **tún** *and Frequency Rank* **2864**

Contains **4 strokes** in the following order:

一 匸 屯 屯

Contains these components:

▬ one 一 1, p.10

▬ receptacle r ⊔ 157, p.43

▮ mineshaft c L 122, p.36

With all these meanings & readings

tún [屯] **1** to station (soldiers) **2** to store up

zhūn [屯] **1** difficult **2** stingy

Abandoned *mineshafts* and *receptacles* with *horizontal* covers make great places to **stockpile** and **store** surplus stuff.

Unit 9

160

This character with the definition:

ton

Pinyin **dūn** *and Frequency Rank* **1700**

Contains **7 strokes** in the following order:

Contains these components:

▮ mouth 口 37, p.17

▮ stockpile, store up 屯 159, p.44

With all these meanings & readings:

dūn [頓] **1** ton **2** Taiwan pr
dùn

Here's how to identify a pretentious nobody at a party: look for the person who, when he opens his *mouth*, pours out a **ton** of worthless trivia that he's *stockpiled* over the years.

161
畫
TRAD SIMPLIFIED

This character with the definition:

draw, drawing

Pinyin **huà** *and Frequency Rank* **883**

Contains **8 strokes** in the following order:

Contains these components:

▯ one 一 1, p.10

▮ field 田 63, p.23

▮ receptacle r 凵 157, p.43

With all these meanings & readings:

huà [畫] **1** to draw **2** picture **3** painting **4** m 幅[fú], 张 [張][zhāng]

Discerning critics have always said your paintings are larger than life, and look how the **drawing** explodes out of the frame formed by '*one*' plus '*receptacle*'. You're a great artist in general, but it seems that the *field* you truly excel in is **drawing**.

162
畐

This component has the meaning:

size range c

COMPONENT

And contains these subcomponents:

▯ one 一 1, p.10

▮ mouth 口 37, p.17

▮ field 田 63, p.23

Even though the **size** of American farms **ranges** from tens to tens of thousands acres, all of them include at least *one field* that is surrounded by a fence-like *enclosure*.

163
事
SIMP & TRAD

This character with the definition:

matter, affair

Pinyin **shì** *and Frequency Rank* **58**

Contains **8 strokes** in the following order:

Contains these components:

▮ size range c 畐 (altered) 162, p.45

▮ hooked stick c 亅 18, p.13

With all these meanings & readings:

shì [事] **1** matter **2** thing **3** item **4** work **5** affair **6** m 件[jiàn], 桩[樁][zhuāng]

Thousands of years ago, Chinese people were so advanced in agriculture that they required a king with a *scepter* to manage their growing *range in the size* and scope of social and economic **affairs**.

164
幅
SIMP & TRAD

This character with the definition:

width (cloth)

Pinyin **fú** *and Frequency Rank* **1444**

Contains **12 strokes** in the following order:

Contains these components:

▮ towel 巾 118, p.35

▮ size range c 畐 162, p.45

With all these meanings & readings:

fú [幅] **1** width **2** roll **3** m for textiles or pictures

Towels are made in a wide *range of sizes* in varying lengths and **widths**—from a hand *towel* to a beach *towel*.

165

This component has the meaning:

single ear r

COMPONENT

He has **one ear** that sticks out a bit more from the side of his head than the other, so try not to laugh when you see him.

166

SIMP & TRAD

This character with the definition:

seal, stamp

Pinyin **yìn** *and Frequency Rank* **640**

Contains **6 strokes** in the following order:

Contains these components:

■ boar's head r ⇒ (altered) 30, p.16

■ single ear r 卩 165, p.46

With all these meanings & readings

yìn [印] **1** surname Yin **2** abbr for 印度[yìn dù]

yìn [印] **1** to print **2** to mark **3** to engrave **4** a seal **5** a prir **6** a stamp **7** a mark **8** a trace **9** image

A **stamp** or **seal** makes a mark that's uniquely yours. Stick *one ear* to the back of a *boar's head* (that's how it has been altered) and use the *single ear* as a handle. Now, add ink to the head and press it to paper for a unique and memorable mark. The component *single ear* is drawn on the right of a *boar's head* so one can imagine the *single ear* as the handle of an old-fashioned wax **seal** or ink **stamp**.

167

SIMP & TRAD

This character with the definition:

be called

Pinyin **jiào** *and Frequency Rank* **387**

Contains **5 strokes** in the following order:

Contains these components:

■ mouth 口 37, p.17

■ single ear r 卩 (altered) 165, p.46

With all these meanings & readings

jiào [叫] **1** to shout **2** to call **3** to order **4** to ask **5** to be called **6** by (indicates agent in the passive mood)

The child knows he's **been called** by his mom. The words coming out of her *mouth* have reached a *single ear*.

168

TRAD SIMPLIFIED

This character with the definition:

elegant*

Pinyin **lì** *and Frequency Rank* **834**

Contains **7 strokes** in the following order:

Contains these components:

□ one — 1, p.10

■ single ear r (×2, altered) 卩 165, p.46

With all these meanings & readings

lì [麗] **1** Korea

lì [麗] **1** beautiful

Here are two *ears*, each wearing *one* earring, which together makes up a *single* pair. The jewelry is exquisite and very **elegant**.

169

This component has the meaning:

knife r

COMPONENT

It looks like a multi-purpose pen-**knife**.

170

刊

SIMP & TRAD

This character with the definition:

publish

Pinyin **kān** *and Frequency Rank* **1241**

Contains **5 strokes** in the following order:

一 二 千 刊 刊

Contains these components:

■ dry 干 17, p.13
□ knife r 刂 169, p.46

With all these meanings & readings:

kān [刊] **1** to print **2** to publish **3** publication **4** periodical

At the 'Publish or Perish **Publishing** Company', we **publish** books written by professors. The subject matter is often *dry—dry* as dust—and the pages are trimmed using extremely sharp *knives*.

171

副

SIMP & TRAD

This character with the definition:

vice-

Pinyin **fù** *and Frequency Rank* **764**

Contains **11 strokes** in the following order:

一 尸 币 币 尸 吊 吊 畐 畐 副 副

Contains these components:

■ size range c 畐 162, p.45
□ knife r 刂 169, p.46

With all these meanings & readings:

fù [副] **1** secondary **2** auxiliary **3** deputy **4** assistant **5** vice- **6** abbr for 副词 [~词] adverb **7** m for pairs

Since a **vice**-president earns the second largest compensation in a company's *size range* of salaries, an ambitious employee will use every 'tool' short of a *knife* to become one.

172

班

SIMP & TRAD

This character with the definition:

team, class

Pinyin **bān** *and Frequency Rank* **884**

Contains **10 strokes** in the following order:

一 二 千 王 王 玑 玔 班 班 班

Contains these components:

■ king 王 15, p.12
■ knife r 刂 (altered) 169, p.46
■ king 王 15, p.12

With all these meanings & readings:

bān [班] **1** team **2** class **3** squad **4** work shift **5** m for groups **6** ranking **7** surname Ban **8** m 个 [個][gè]

The two grids on either side represent organized groups of people, perhaps sitting in rows as in a **team** or **class**, with a divider as thin as a *knife* separating them.

173

帅

TRAD SIMPLIFIED

This character with the definition:

good-looking, attractive

Pinyin **shuài** *and Frequency Rank* **1888**

Contains **5 strokes** in the following order:

丿 刀 小 师 帅

Contains these components:

■ knife r 刂 (altered) 169, p.46
□ towel 巾 118, p.35

With all these meanings & readings:

shuài [帥] **1** handsome **2** graceful **3** smart **4** commander in chief

The craftsman skillfully cut the *towel* with a *knife* and then fashioned the pieces into a cunning doll, which somehow looked very **handsome**.

174

师

TRAD SIMPLIFIED

This character with the definition:

teacher, master

Pinyin **shī** *and Frequency Rank* **333**

Contains **6 strokes** in the following order:

丿 刀 师 师 师 师

Contains these components:

■ good-looking, attractive 帅 173, p.47
□ one 一 1, p.10

With all these meanings & readings:

shī [師] **1** a division (military) **2** teacher **3** master **4** expert **5** model

The most *attractive* student in class usually becomes *one* of the '**teacher's** pets'.

175

归

归
TRAD SIMPLIFIED

This character with the definition:

go back, return

Pinyin **guī** *and Frequency Rank* **933**

Contains **5 strokes** in the following order:

丿 刂 刂ㄱ 刂彐 归

Contains these components:

■ knife r 刂 (altered) 169, p.46
□ boar's head r 彐 30, p.16

With all these meanings & readings:

guī [歸] **1** to go back **2** to return

We killed a wild pig that was destroying crops and livestock. We removed the *boar's head* with a *knife*, and, with this proof of our success, were then ready to **go back** to the farm.

176

This component has the meaning:

dab r

COMPONENT

This little dab of ink appears in many characters, often at or near the top of the character (for example, 主). Sometimes we'll see it with an opposite slant (for example, the little topknot in 白. At still other times, it takes on an elongated form, as on the top stroke of 丢; look closely at these cases, for the **dabs** are barely distinguishable from a true horizontal stroke. • When used as a component, it's useful to let the **dab** represent '**a drop**' or '**a little bit**' of a larger quantity.

177

玉
SIMP & TRAD

This character with the definition:

jade

Pinyin **yù** *and Frequency Rank* **1001**

Contains **5 strokes** in the following order:

一 二 千 王 玉

Contains these components:

■ king 王 15, p.12
□ dab r 丶 176, p.48

With all these meanings & readings:

yù [玉] **1** jade

Jade is almost as valuable as the the *king*'s scepter because it is such a precious stone. Owning **jade** is almost like owning a *dab* of the *king* himself. '**Jade**' will often be used to represent something precious and valuable. • The ancient scribes often used this character as an element, without the *dab*, making it appear as 王 (king, panel 15). Our guide will alert you when this shape means 'king' and when it means '**jade**'.

178

国

國
TRAD SIMPLIFIED

This character with the definition:

country

Pinyin **guó** *and Frequency Rank* **20**

Contains **8 strokes** in the following order:

丨 冂 冂 冃 囯 国 国 国

Contains these components:

□ enclosure r 囗 36, p.17
■ jade 玉 177, p.48

With all these meanings & readings:

guó [國] **1** country **2** nation **3** state **4** national **5** surname Guo **6** m 个 [個][gè]

Here, *jade* symbolically represents all the king's possessions—everything inside his country. 国 represents the *enclosure* that contains everything belonging to the king, that is, the **country**.

179

SIMP & TRAD

This character with the definition:

master

Pinyin **zhǔ** and Frequency Rank **87**

Contains **5 strokes** in the following order:

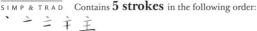

Contains these components:

▫ dab r ⟍ 176, p. 48

■ king 王 15, p. 12

With all these meanings & readings:

zhǔ [主] **1** to own **2** to host **3** master **4** lord **5** primary

Just as the ruler of a country is the king, so too is the **master** of a house a *little bit* of a *king* in his own domain.

180

SIMP & TRAD

This character with the definition:

noonish

Pinyin **wǔ** and Frequency Rank **1004**

Contains **4 strokes** in the following order:

Contains these components:

■ dry 干 17, p. 13

▫ dab r ⟍ 176, p. 48

With all these meanings & readings:

wǔ [午] **1** 7th earthly branch: 11 a.m.-1 p.m., noon, 5th solar month (6th June-6th July), year of the Horse

I tend to get a *little bit dry* around **noonish**—much time has passed since my morning coffee. • This character can refer either to 'noon' exactly or to 'noonish'—the time period roughly between 11 am and 1 pm.

181

SIMP & TRAD

This character with the definition:

archaeological vessel

Pinyin **fǒu** and Frequency Rank **5328**

Contains **6 strokes** in the following order:

Contains these components:

▫ noonish 午 180, p. 49

■ receptacle r ㇄ 157, p. 43

With all these meanings & readings:

fǒu [缶] **1** pottery

The experts determined that the **archaeological vessel** had functioned as a *receptacle* for tribal religious rites that were performed *at noon*.

182

SIMP & TRAD

This character with the definition:

bamboo

Pinyin **zhú** and Frequency Rank **1588**

Contains **6 strokes** in the following order:

Contains these components:

▫ dab r (×2) ⟍ 176, p. 48

■ fourth (in a series) (×2) 丁 19, p. 13

With all these meanings & readings:

zhú [竹] **1** bamboo **2** m 棵[kē], 支[zhī], 根[gēn]

Young **bamboo** shoots might be the fastest growing plants on the planet, growing an inch or two per hour! Since it grows so fast, ancient Chinese artists adapted their calligraphic painting methods to depict a young **bamboo** plant having split in two, as seen here, with plant parts growing next to each other, and one *dab*-like leaf at the top of each section.

183

SIMP & TRAD

This character with the definition:

blood

Pinyin **xiě** and Frequency Rank **658**

Contains **6 strokes** in the following order:

Contains these components:

▫ dab r ⟍ 176, p. 48

■ vessel, container 皿 101, p. 32

With all these meanings & readings:

xuè [血] **1** blood **2** informal colloquial and Taiwan pr xiě **3** also pr xuě **4** m 滴[dī], 片[piàn]

After ancient societies performed animal sacrifices, they would collect the **blood** in *vessels* for easy disposal. The only clues about each *vessel*'s contents are the rich, dark *drops* of red along their rims.

184

SIMP & TRAD

This character with the definition:

hair

Pinyin **máo** *and Frequency Rank* **623**

Contains **4 strokes** in the following order:

ノ ニ 三 毛

Contains these components:

■ mineshaft c ㄴ 122, p. 36

▢ dab r ヽ 176, p. 48

▬ two 二 2, p. 10

With all these meanings & readings

máo [毛] **1** hair **2** fur **3** pore **4** dime (classifier for jiao 角, one tenth of yuan) **5** surname Mao **6** m 根[gēn]

Consider the *mineshaft* element as the chin of a young teenage boy, with a *dab*-like whisker growing above *two* genuine strands of facial **hair**. He can't wait to start shaving!

Unit 10

185
鬥
斗
TRAD SIMPLIFIED

This character with the definition:

cup-shaped

Pinyin **dǒu** *and Frequency Rank* **580**

Contains **4 strokes** in the following order:

丶 ⼆ 三 斗

Contains these components:

⬛ dab r (×2) 丶 176, p. 48

✚ ten 十 7, p. 11

With all these meanings & readings:

dǒu [斗] **1** decaliter **2** peck **3** dry measure for grain equal to ten sheng 升 or one-tenth dan 石
dòu [鬥] **1** to fight **2** to struggle **3** to condemn **4** to censure **5** to contend **6** to put together **7** coming together

A **cup-shaped** object holds coffee, which is sometimes so hot that you need to grip the cup with all *ten* of your fingers—here depicted as the horizontal line on each side of the vertical **cup** handle with the two *dabs* representing your knuckles.

186

SIMP & TRAD

This character with the definition:

tremble

Pinyin **dǒu** *and Frequency Rank* **1757**

Contains **7 strokes** in the following order:

一 十 扌 扌 扌 抖 抖

Contains these components:

⬛ hand r 扌 25, p. 15

⬛ cup-shaped 斗 185, p. 51

With all these meanings & readings:

dǒu [抖] **1** shake out **2** tremble

The cup we saw in panel 185 is too heavy for me. My *hand*, from the effort of holding the *cup*, gets weak and starts **trembling**.

187
卜
蔔
TRAD SIMPLIFIED

This character with the definition:

foretell

Pinyin **bǔ** *and Frequency Rank* **1979**

Contains **2 strokes** in the following order:

丨 卜

Contains these components:

⬛ scepter c 丨 5, p. 10

⬛ dab r 丶 176, p. 48

With all these meanings & readings:

bo [卜] **1** turnip
bǔ [卜] **1** to divine **2** foretell **3** surname Bu
bo [蔔] **1** turnip

Which way will the stick fall? We may **foretell** the answer by noting that there's the extra *dab* of weight on the right side of the *scepter*-like stick. (Historically, this glyph referred to the cracks in a tortoise shell which ancient priests would "read" to **foretell** future events.) By virtue of its connection with **foretelling**, we will often apply a '**magic wand**' meaning to this element.

188
佔
占
TRAD SIMPLIFIED

This character with the definition:

practice divination

Pinyin **zhān** *and Frequency Rank* **737**

Contains **5 strokes** in the following order:

卜 卜 占 占 占

Contains these components:

⬛ foretell 卜 187, p. 51

⬛ mouth 口 37, p. 17

With all these meanings & readings:

zhàn [佔] **1** to take possession of **2** to occupy **3** to constitute **4** to make up **5** to account for **6** ⊠ sometimes used as traditional character
zhān [占] **1** to observe **2** to divine
zhàn [占] **1** to take possession of **2** to occupy **3** to constitute **4** to make up **5** to account for **6** ⊠ sometimes used as traditional character

When you **practice divination**, you rely on two main tools—your **magic wand**, with which you use to *foretell* the future, and your *mouth*, with which you use to woo credulous followers.

189 上

This character with the definition:

on

Pinyin **shàng** *and Frequency Rank* **16**

SIMP & TRAD   Contains **3 strokes** in the following order:

丨 卜 上

Contains these components:

foretell 卜 187, p. 51
one 一 1, p. 10

With all these meanings & readings:

shǎng [上] **1** see 上声 [~聲][shǎng, shēng]
shàng [上] **1** on **2** on top **3** upon **4** first (of multiple parts) **5** previous **6** last **7** upper **8** higher **9** above **10** to climb **11** to go into **12** to go up **13** to attend (class or university)

We erect the *magic wand* **on** *one* single surface to mark the most interesting side; in this case, it is the side **on** top.

190 止

This character with the definition:

stop!

Pinyin **zhǐ** *and Frequency Rank* **596**

SIMP & TRAD   Contains **4 strokes** in the following order:

丨 卜 止 止

Contains these components:

on 上 189, p. 52
scepter c 丨 5, p. 10

With all these meanings & readings:

zhǐ [止] **1** to stop **2** to prohibit **3** until

As we ice skate *on* the surface of a pond, we need to grab onto a *scepter*-like pole that's anchored in the ice to **stop** ourselves.

191 址

This character with the definition:

foundation, site

Pinyin **zhǐ** *and Frequency Rank* **1848**

SIMP & TRAD   Contains **7 strokes** in the following order:

一 十 土 址 圵 圵 址

Contains these components:

earth, soil 土 9, p. 11
stop! 止 190, p. 52

With all these meanings & readings:

zhǐ [址] **1** location **2** site

The purpose of building a strong **foundation** is to *stop* the structure above it from sinking into the *earth*.

192 扯

This character with the definition:

pull

Pinyin **chě** *and Frequency Rank* **2084**

SIMP & TRAD   Contains **7 strokes** in the following order:

一 十 扌 扯 扯 扯 扯

Contains these components:

hand r 扌 25, p. 15
stop! 止 190, p. 52

With all these meanings & readings:

chě [扯] **1** pull **2** tear **3** to talk casually

The driver of a subway train has learned to react quickly whenever he sees a red light or a *stop* sign by using his *hand* to **pull** on the brakes.

193 正

This character with the definition:

to correct, rectify

Pinyin **zhèng** *and Frequency Rank* **129**

SIMP & TRAD   Contains **5 strokes** in the following order:

一 丁 下 正 正

Contains these components:

one 一 1, p. 10
stop! 止 190, p. 52

With all these meanings & readings:

zhēng [正] **1** Chinese 1st month of year
zhèng [正] **1** just (right) **2** main **3** upright **4** straight **5** to correct, rectify **6** positive **7** greater than zero **8** principle

New drivers often fail to fully *stop* right at the *line* before the *stop* sign. Instructors and parents must be careful **to correct** this behavior.

194

是

is

Pinyin **shì** *and Frequency Rank* **3**

SIMP & TRAD   Contains **9 strokes** in the following order:

丶 丨 冂 曰 旦 早 昙 昰 是

This character with the definition:

Contains these components:

■ day, sun 日 64, p. 24
□ to correct, rectify 正 (altered) 193, p. 52

With all these meanings & readings:

shì [是] **1** is **2** are **3** am **4** yes **5** to be

When the *sun* **is** shining, all **is** proper and *correct* in the world.

195

提

lift

Pinyin **tí** *and Frequency Rank* **196**

SIMP & TRAD   Contains **12 strokes** in the following order:

一 十 扌 扌 扩 押 押 担 捍 捍 捍 提

This character with the definition:

Contains these components:

■ hand r 扌 25, p. 15
■ is 是 194, p. 53

With all these meanings & readings:

dī [提] **1** carry (suspended)
tí [提] **1** to carry (hanging down from the hand) **2** to lift **3** to put forward **4** to mention **5** to raise (an issue) **6** upwards character stroke **7** lifting brush stroke (in painting) **8** scoop for measuring liquid

Use your *hands* to **lift** something that *is* on the floor and place it on the table.

196

此

this

Pinyin **cǐ** *and Frequency Rank* **116**

SIMP & TRAD   Contains **6 strokes** in the following order:

丨 卜 ⺊ 止 此 此

This character with the definition:

Contains these components:

■ stop! 止 190, p. 52
■ ancient ladle ヒ 124, p. 36

With all these meanings & readings:

cǐ [此] **1** this **2** these

I can't put up with **this** noise! *Stop* banging the *old ladle* against the sidewalk.

197

些

some

Pinyin **xiē** *and Frequency Rank* **86**

SIMP & TRAD   Contains **8 strokes** in the following order:

丨 卜 ⺊ 止 此 此 此 些

This character with the definition:

Contains these components:

■ this 此 196, p. 53
□ two 二 2, p. 10

With all these meanings & readings:

xiē [些] **1** some **2** few **3** several **4** (a measure word)

I am looking forward to having **some** fun *this* weekend—my *two* best friends are getting married to each other!

198

卸

unload, take sth off

Pinyin **xiè** *and Frequency Rank* **2479**

SIMP & TRAD   Contains **9 strokes** in the following order:

丿 ⺊ 上 午 午 缶 缶 卸 卸

This character with the definition:

Contains these components:

■ noonish 午 180, p. 49
■ stop! 止 190, p. 52
■ single ear r ⻏ 165, p. 46

With all these meanings & readings:

xiè [卸] **1** unload **2** take off

This summer job as an airport baggage handler is brutal. Everyone looks forward to the break at *noon* so we can **unload** the bags for a bit. In fact, we all keep a *single ear* cocked for the whistle announcing the time to *stop* working.

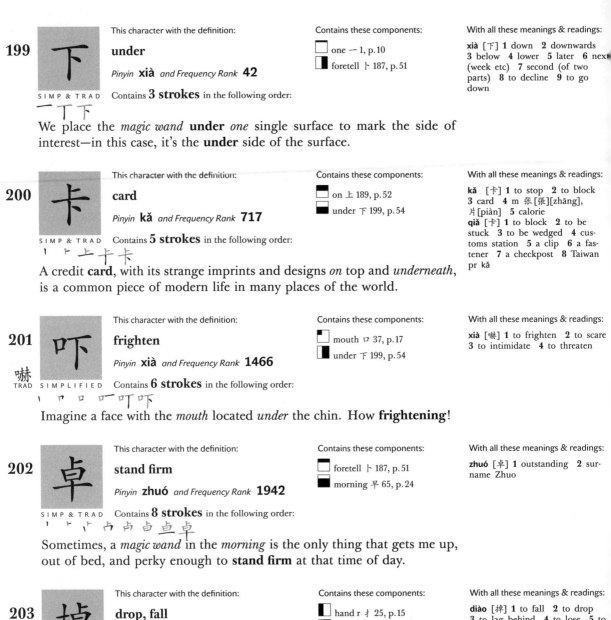

199　下

SIMP & TRAD

This character with the definition:

under

Pinyin **xià** *and Frequency Rank* **42**

Contains **3 strokes** in the following order:

一 丁 下

Contains these components:

☐ one 一 1, p.10
☐ foretell 卜 187, p.51

With all these meanings & readings:

xià [下] **1** down **2** downwards **3** below **4** lower **5** later **6** next (week etc) **7** second (of two parts) **8** to decline **9** to go down

We place the *magic wand* **under** *one* single surface to mark the side of interest—in this case, it's the **under** side of the surface.

200　卡

SIMP & TRAD

This character with the definition:

card

Pinyin **kǎ** *and Frequency Rank* **717**

Contains **5 strokes** in the following order:

丨 卜 上 卡 卡

Contains these components:

☐ on 上 189, p.52
☐ under 下 199, p.54

With all these meanings & readings:

kǎ [卡] **1** to stop **2** to block **3** card **4** m 张[張][zhāng], 片[piàn] **5** calorie
qiǎ [卡] **1** to block **2** to be stuck **3** to be wedged **4** customs station **5** a clip **6** a fastener **7** a checkpost **8** Taiwan pr kǎ

A credit **card**, with its strange imprints and designs *on* top and *underneath*, is a common piece of modern life in many places of the world.

201　吓

嚇　　　吓
TRAD　SIMPLIFIED

This character with the definition:

frighten

Pinyin **xià** *and Frequency Rank* **1466**

Contains **6 strokes** in the following order:

丨 冂 口 口一 吓 吓

Contains these components:

☐ mouth 口 37, p.17
☐ under 下 199, p.54

With all these meanings & readings:

xià [嚇] **1** to frighten **2** to scare **3** to intimidate **4** to threaten

Imagine a face with the *mouth* located *under* the chin. How **frightening**!

202　卓

SIMP & TRAD

This character with the definition:

stand firm

Pinyin **zhuó** *and Frequency Rank* **1942**

Contains **8 strokes** in the following order:

丨 卜 卜 占 占 卣 卓 卓

Contains these components:

☐ foretell 卜 187, p.51
☐ morning 早 65, p.24

With all these meanings & readings:

zhuó [卓] **1** outstanding **2** surname Zhuo

Sometimes, a *magic wand* in the *morning* is the only thing that gets me up, out of bed, and perky enough to **stand firm** at that time of day.

203　掉

SIMP & TRAD

This character with the definition:

drop, fall

Pinyin **diào** *and Frequency Rank* **849**

Contains **11 strokes** in the following order:

一 十 才 扌 扩 扩 护 捾 捾 掉 掉

Contains these components:

☐ hand r 扌 25, p.15
☐ stand firm 卓 202, p.54

With all these meanings & readings:

diào [掉] **1** to fall **2** to drop **3** to lag behind **4** to lose **5** to go missing **6** to reduce **7** fall (in prices) **8** to lose (value, weight etc) **9** to wag **10** to swing **11** to turn **12** to change **13** to exchange **14** to swap **15** to show off **16** to shed (hair)

The element on the right appears to *stand firm*. But if I push it with my *hand*, it will **fall** over.

204

SIMP & TRAD

This character with the definition:

bamboo fish trap

Pinyin **zhào** *and Frequency Rank* **1978**

Contains **13 strokes** in the following order:

丶 冖 冖 ⺲ ⺳ 甲 甲 罖 罘 罩 罩 置 罩

Contains these components:

☐ net r ⺲ 100, p. 32

■ stand firm 卓 202, p. 54

With all these meanings & readings:

zhào [罩] **1** cover **2** fish trap (basket) **3** shade

Rope *nets* are notoriously floppy things. If we make *nets* out of bamboo, the strands of the net *stand firm* and the resulting **bamboo fish trap** is very effective.

205

卧
TRAD

SIMPLIFIED

This character with the definition:

lie down, crouch (animals)

Pinyin **wò** *and Frequency Rank* **1944**

Contains **8 strokes** in the following order:

一 丆 丆 王 卫 臣 臤 卧

Contains these components:

■ subject of a ruler 臣 154, p. 43

☐ foretell 卜 187, p. 51

With all these meanings & readings:

wò [臥] **1** to lie **2** to crouch

Animals are good at hiding. They **crouch down** low and keep out of sight when the king's loyal *subjects* are on the hunt for fresh meat for the royal supper. But the hunters have been *foretold* where to locate and how to subdue the well-concealed animals.

206

臨
TRAD

SIMPLIFIED

This character with the definition:

face, overlook

Pinyin **lín** *and Frequency Rank* **839**

Contains **9 strokes** in the following order:

丨 丨 丨' 丬⺊ 临 临 临 临 临

Contains these components:

■ lie down, crouch (animals) 卧 (altered) 205, p. 55

■ product 品 (altered) 52, p. 21

With all these meanings & readings:

lín [臨] **1** to face **2** to overlook **3** to arrive **4** to be (just) about to **5** just before

As the warehouse boss **overlooked** his stacks of *products*, my girlfriend and I *crouched down like animals* and hid behind a pile of his *products*, quiet as mice until he passed by.

207

監
TRAD

SIMPLIFIED

This character with the definition:

inspect, supervise

Pinyin **jiān** *and Frequency Rank* **838**

Contains **10 strokes** in the following order:

丨 丨 丨' 丬⺊ 怀 吆 吆 监 监 监

Contains these components:

■ lie down, crouch (animals) 卧 (altered) 205, p. 55

■ blood 血 (altered) 183, p. 49

With all these meanings & readings:

jiān [監] **1** hard **2** strong **3** solid **4** firm **5** to supervise **6** to inspect **7** jail **8** prison
jiàn [監] **1** supervisor

The courtier *crouched* over the bowl of *blood*, **inspecting** its contents to decide if they were suitable for the ritual. • Note the altered 'blood' component's 'drop of blood' has been moved to its right side (血, panel 183).

208

藍
TRAD

藍

SIMPLIFIED

This character with the definition:

blue

Pinyin **lán** *and Frequency Rank* **1190**

Contains **13 strokes** in the following order:

一 艹 艹 芗 艻 莎 莎 莎 莎 蓝 蓝 蓝 蓝

Contains these components:

☐ grass r ⺿ 87, p. 29

■ inspect, supervise 监 207, p. 55

With all these meanings & readings:

lán [藍] **1** blue **2** cabbage **3** surname Lan

The landscaper was glad to see clear **blue** skies that day since he had to *supervise* five different crews mow the *grass* of dozens of lawns.

209

撲
扑

TRAD   SIMPLIFIED

This character with the definition:

dedicate oneself

Pinyin **pū** *and Frequency Rank* **1509**

Contains **5 strokes** in the following order:

Contains these components:

■ hand r 扌 25, p.15

■ foretell 卜 187, p.51

With all these meanings & readings:

pū [撲] **1** to assault   **2** to pound
3 to rush at sth   **4** to throw
oneself on

一 十 才 扩 扑

With his magic *wand* in *hand*, the sorcerer is ready to **dedicate himself** to good works.

Unit 11

210

生

SIMP & TRAD

This character with the definition:

give birth to

Pinyin **shēng** *and Frequency Rank* **34**

Contains **5 strokes** in the following order:

ノ ノ ヒ 牛 生

Contains these components:

■ plentiful ‡ (altered) 16, p. 13

□ dab r ﹨ 176, p. 48

With all these meanings & readings:

shēng [生] **1** to be born **2** to give birth **3** life **4** to grow **5** raw, uncooked

Population increase is the result of *plenty* during earlier times. The woman who will **give birth** to a baby hopes that this *dab* of humanity will contribute to society's *plenty*.

211

年

SIMP & TRAD

This character with the definition:

year

Pinyin **nián** *and Frequency Rank* **45**

Contains **6 strokes** in the following order:

ノ ヒ ニ ヒ 乍 年

Contains these components:

■ give birth to 生 (altered) 210, p. 57

With all these meanings & readings:

nián [年] **1** year **2** m 个[個][gè]

Here 生, 'to give birth' has been slightly altered in two ways. The horizontal stroke points down instead of up, because as the **years** pass, we journey away from *birth* and (down) towards death. An unexpected short stroke of ink suggests that the years themselves are full of unexpected events.

212

星

SIMP & TRAD

This character with the definition:

star

Pinyin **xīng** *and Frequency Rank* **537**

Contains **9 strokes** in the following order:

丶 ⼏ ⼞ 日 旦 旦 旦 星 星

Contains these components:

□ day, sun 日 64, p. 24

■ give birth to 生 210, p. 57

With all these meanings & readings:

xīng [星] **1** star **2** satellite **3** small amount

An ancient storyteller described how sparks released from the *sun* generated the material compounds that *gave birth* to the **stars**.

213

牛

SIMP & TRAD

This character with the definition:

ox

Pinyin **niú** *and Frequency Rank* **1018**

Contains **4 strokes** in the following order:

ノ ノ ニ 牛

Contains these components:

■ dab r ﹨ 176, p. 48

■ two 二 2, p. 10

▮ scepter c ｜ 5, p. 10

With all these meanings & readings:

niú [牛] **1** ox **2** cow **3** bull **4** m 条[條][tiáo], 头[頭][tóu]

Think of this pictograph as a top-down view of a "stylized **ox** or **cow**" positioned to sit upright. The vertical *scepter* depicts the central spine, the *two* horizontals are the legs, and the *dab* of ink shows its left horn. • The character 'noonish' 午 (panel 180) is often confused with this one for 'ox' 牛. The only difference between them is the horn-like extension in the top center of 'ox'. Remember this single 'horn' and associate that character with 'ox', while the flat top of 'noonish' calls to mind a flat surface that people can lie on for a 'noonish' siesta!

214
制
製
TRAD SIMPLIFIED

This character with the definition:

manufacture, system

Pinyin **zhì** *and Frequency Rank* **163**

Contains **8 strokes** in the following order:

丿 ㇀ ㇒ ㇒ 𠂤 𠂤 制 制

Contains these components:

⬛ ox 牛 213, p. 57
⬛ towel 巾 118, p. 35
⬛ knife r 刂 169, p. 46

With all these meanings & readings:

zhì [制] **1** system **2** to make **3** to manufacture **4** to control **5** to regulate
zhì [製] **1** manufacture

These items were needed for a production **system** to **manufacture** things in pre-modern societies: The *cow* or *ox* provided power; the *cloth* polished and cleaned the finished products; and the *knife* symbolized the instruments used for cutting and fine detailing.

215

SIMP & TRAD

This character with the definition:

domestic animal

Pinyin **shēng** *and Frequency Rank* **1582**

Contains **9 strokes** in the following order:

丿 ㇀ 牛 牛 牜 牲 牲 牲 牲

Contains these components:

⬛ ox 牛 213, p. 57
⬛ give birth to 生 210, p. 57

With all these meanings & readings:

shēng [牲] **1** domestic animal

It's easy for **domesticated animals**, such as *oxen* and *cows*, to *give birth* in captivity, but that's not the case for their wild cousins.

216

SIMP & TRAD

This character with the definition:

inch

Pinyin **cùn** *and Frequency Rank* **1904**

Contains **3 strokes** in the following order:

一 十 寸

Contains these components:

⬛ hand 手 (altered) 21, p. 14
⬛ dab r 丶 176, p. 48

With all these meanings & readings:

cùn [寸] **1** a unit of length **2** inch **3** thumb

Hand? Where do you see a *hand*, or anything remotely like the image in panel 21? Some artistic license is in order. The fact that the 'hook' of panel 18 extends above the horizontal 'one' indicates that some other strokes are missing, namely the top two horizontals. The little *dab* of ink marks a special point on the wrist—the point where you can feel your pulse, about an **inch** below the heel of the hand. Side note: A 'Chinese inch' is approximately 1.3 American **inches**. • We will sometimes use this character as an element representing something 'little' or 'small'.

217

封

SIMP & TRAD

This character with the definition:

confer, grant, seal (off)

Pinyin **fēng** *and Frequency Rank* **871**

Contains **9 strokes** in the following order:

一 十 土 圭 圭 圭 圭 封 封

Contains these components:

⬛ jade tablet 圭 10, p. 11
⬛ inch 寸 216, p. 58

With all these meanings & readings:

fēng [封] **1** to confer **2** to grant **3** to bestow a title **4** to seal **5** m for sealed objects, especially letters **6** surname Feng

In recognition of your notable achievements, we **confer** upon you this honorary degree. The inscription appears on a *jade tablet*, in *inch*-high letters.

218

SIMP & TRAD

This character with the definition:

endure, bear

Pinyin **nài** *and Frequency Rank* **1409**

Contains **9 strokes** in the following order:

一 一 厂 丙 丙 而 而 耐 耐

Contains these components:

☐ but, yet (contrast) 而 78, p. 26
☐ inch 寸 216, p. 58

With all these meanings & readings:

nài [耐] **1** capable of enduring **2** able to tolerate **3** patient **4** durable **5** hardy **6** resistant

The heavy snowstorm arrived after the first flowers of spring had begun to bloom—seeing their bright colors get buried gradually under *inches* of snow was an image of *contrasting* seasons that was difficult to **endure**.

219

寻
TRAD SIMPLIFIED

This character with the definition:

search, seek

Pinyin **xún** *and Frequency Rank* **962**

Contains **6 strokes** in the following order:

ㄱ ㄹ ㅋ ㅋ 寻 寻

Contains these components:

☐ boar's head r ⼹ 30, p. 16
☐ inch 寸 216, p. 58

With all these meanings & readings:

xún [寻] **1** to search **2** to look for **3** to seek

As you **search** high and low for your missing possessions, ask anyone you meet whether they have seen the special whisk broom that's made of one-*inch boar's head* bristles.

220

SIMP & TRAD

This character with the definition:

Buddhist temple

Pinyin **sì** *and Frequency Rank* **1892**

Contains **6 strokes** in the following order:

一 十 土 士 寺 寺

Contains these components:

☐ earth, soil 土 9, p. 11
☐ inch 寸 216, p. 58

With all these meanings & readings:

sì [寺] **1** Buddhist temple

In the very old days, **Buddhist temples** were not much grander than any other house. This one is made of *earth* and only stands a few *inches* taller than any other nearby buildings.

221

SIMP & TRAD

This character with the definition:

control, handle (under duress)

Pinyin **chí** *and Frequency Rank* **357**

Contains **9 strokes** in the following order:

一 十 扌 扌 扩 扗 扶 持 持

Contains these components:

☐ hand r 扌 25, p. 15
☐ Buddhist temple 寺 220, p. 59

With all these meanings & readings:

chí [持] **1** to hold **2** to grasp **3** to support **4** to maintain **5** to persevere **6** to manage **7** to run (i.e. administer) **8** to control

During the long famine, many people would visit the local *Buddhist temple*. The sight of Buddha's open *hands* gave them the spiritual comfort and inner strength they needed to **handle** long periods of starvation.

222

特

SIMP & TRAD

This character with the definition:

special, unusual

Pinyin **tè** *and Frequency Rank* **173**

Contains **10 strokes** in the following order:

丿 ㄟ 牛 牛 牛 牜 牜 特 特 特

Contains these components:

☐ ox 牛 213, p. 57
☐ Buddhist temple 寺 220, p. 59

With all these meanings & readings:

tè [特] **1** special **2** unique **3** distinguished **4** especially **5** unusual **6** very

Buddhists don't eat meat. Only on rare, **special** occasions will you find *cow* meat in a *Buddhist temple*.

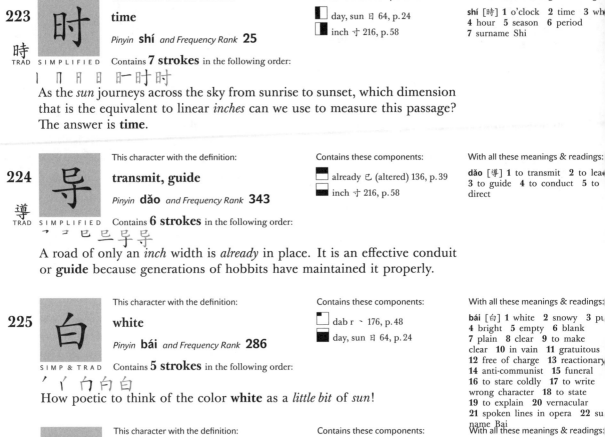

223

時
TRAD   SIMPLIFIED

时

This character with the definition:

time

Pinyin **shí** and Frequency Rank **25**

Contains **7 strokes** in the following order:

Contains these components:

▪ day, sun 日 64, p. 24
▪ inch 寸 216, p. 58

With all these meanings & readings:

shí [時] **1** o'clock **2** time **3** wh▪
4 hour **5** season **6** period
7 surname Shi

As the *sun* journeys across the sky from sunrise to sunset, which dimension that is the equivalent to linear *inches* can we use to measure this passage? The answer is **time**.

224

導
TRAD   SIMPLIFIED

导

This character with the definition:

transmit, guide

Pinyin **dǎo** and Frequency Rank **343**

Contains **6 strokes** in the following order:

Contains these components:

▪ already 巳 (altered) 136, p. 39
▪ inch 寸 216, p. 58

With all these meanings & readings:

dǎo [導] **1** to transmit **2** to lea▪
3 to guide **4** to conduct **5** to direct

A road of only an *inch* width is *already* in place. It is an effective conduit or **guide** because generations of hobbits have maintained it properly.

225

白

SIMP & TRAD

This character with the definition:

white

Pinyin **bái** and Frequency Rank **286**

Contains **5 strokes** in the following order:

Contains these components:

▪ dab r ` 176, p. 48
▪ day, sun 日 64, p. 24

With all these meanings & readings:

bái [白] **1** white **2** snowy **3** pu▪
4 bright **5** empty **6** blank
7 plain **8** clear **9** to make
clear **10** in vain **11** gratuitous
12 free of charge **13** reactionar▪
14 anti-communist **15** funeral
16 to stare coldly **17** to write
wrong character **18** to state
19 to explain **20** vernacular
21 spoken lines in opera **22** su▪
name Bai

How poetic to think of the color **white** as a *little bit* of *sun*!

226

百

SIMP & TRAD

This character with the definition:

hundred

Pinyin **bǎi** and Frequency Rank **407**

Contains **6 strokes** in the following order:

Contains these components:

▪ one 一 1, p. 10
▪ white 白 225, p. 60

With all these meanings & readings:

bǎi [百] **1** hundred **2** numerous
3 all kinds of **4** surname Bai

After trying to sell our old house for months, we finally figured out that *one* coat of *white*wash would make all the difference. It looked a **hundred** times better, and was quickly snapped up by a buyer.

227

皇

SIMP & TRAD

This character with the definition:

emperor

Pinyin **huáng** and Frequency Rank **759**

Contains **9 strokes** in the following order:

Contains these components:

▪ white 白 225, p. 60
▪ king 王 15, p. 12

With all these meanings & readings:

Huáng [皇] **1** emperor **2** surname Huang

Since 'white' is suggestinve of purity and even superiority, the Chinese portrayed the **emperor** as a *white king*, the *king-above-all-kings*.

228

This character with the definition:

each and every

Pinyin **jiē** *and Frequency Rank* **1419**

SIMP & TRAD　Contains **9 strokes** in the following order:

一 上 上' 比 比 毕 毕 皆 皆

Contains these components:

☐ compared with 比 127, p.37

■ white 白 225, p.60

With all these meanings & readings:

jiē [皆] **1** all **2** each and every **3** in all cases

Since *white* light is said to include the light rays of all colors, the individual color of **each and every** ray could be *compared to* the color *white*.

229

This character with the definition:

clap

Pinyin **pāi** *and Frequency Rank* **1167**

SIMP & TRAD　Contains **8 strokes** in the following order:

一 十 扌 扌' 扌' 拍 拍 拍

Contains these components:

☐ hand r 扌 25, p.15

■ white 白 225, p.60

With all these meanings & readings:

pāi [拍] **1** to pat **2** to clap **3** to slap **4** fly-swatter **5** racket **6** to take (a photograph)

If you **clap** your *hands* together especially hard, your palms will turn *white* briefly as blood is forced out by the pressure of the clap. Try it!

230

This character with the definition:

silk

Pinyin **bó** *and Frequency Rank* **3682**

SIMP & TRAD　Contains **8 strokes** in the following order:

丿 亻 白 白 白 自 帛 帛

Contains these components:

☐ white 白 225, p.60

■ towel 巾 118, p.35

With all these meanings & readings:

bó [帛] **1** silk

Combining *special fabric* with a *white towel* clearly symbolizes the unique quality of **silk**.

231

This character with the definition:

handkerchief

Pinyin **pà** *and Frequency Rank* **1519**

SIMP & TRAD　Contains **8 strokes** in the following order:

丿 口 巾 巾' 帕' 帕 帕 帕

Contains these components:

■ towel 巾 118, p.35

■ white 白 225, p.60

With all these meanings & readings:

pà [帕] **1** to wrap **2** kerchief **3** handkerchief **4** headscarf **5** (used as phonetic, e.g. 帕米尔 Pamir)

A **handkerchief** is a special *towel* which is *white*.

232 自

This character with the definition:

self

Pinyin **zì** *and Frequency Rank* **43**

SIMP & TRAD　Contains **6 strokes** in the following order:

丿 亻 口 白 白 自

Contains these components:

☐ dab r 丶 176, p.48

■ eye 目 75, p.26

With all these meanings & readings:

zì [自] **1** from **2** self **3** oneself **4** since

The *eye* is the gateway for all visual information to enter into our brains, where a *small portion* is retained and processed, allowing us to visualize our core **self** as a *dab* among our surroundings.

233

This character with the definition:

you and me

Pinyin **zán** *and Frequency Rank* **1265**

Contains these components:

■ mouth 口 37, p. 17
■ self 自 232, p. 61

With all these meanings & readings:

zá [咱] **1** see 咱 [咱][zán]
zán [咱] **1** we (including the person spoken to)

SIMP & TRAD   Contains **9 strokes** in the following order:

丿 丿 口 口 口 咋 咋 咱 咱

This is the inclusive we—that is, it includes the speaker. Think of these two elements as two companions. The *mouth* refers to the speaker ('you'), and *self* refers to 'me'. Both of us together make up this special form of 'we'—**you and me**.

234

This character with the definition:

tell

Pinyin **gào** *and Frequency Rank* **310**

Contains these components:

■ earth, soil 土 9, p. 11
■ dab r ⟋ 176, p. 48
■ mouth 口 37, p. 17

With all these meanings & readings:

gào [告] **1** to tell **2** to inform **3** to say

SIMP & TRAD   Contains **7 strokes** in the following order:

丿 ㇄ 屮 生 生 告 告

As you open your *mouth* to **tell** your buddy some crucial bit of news on a very windy day, the wind will blow *little bits* of *earth* into your *mouth*.

Unit 12

235

靠

SIMP & TRAD

This character with the definition:

depend on

Pinyin **kào** *and Frequency Rank* **808**

Contains **15 strokes** in the following order:

Contains these components:

■□ tell 告 234, p. 62

■■ not 非 6, p. 11

With all these meanings & readings:

kào [靠] **1** depend upon **2** lean on **3** near **4** by **5** against **6** to support

I know I can **depend on** my son's good behavior, and do *not* have to *tell* him to do his homework or clean his room.

236

兆

SIMP & TRAD

This character with the definition:

omen

Pinyin **zhào** *and Frequency Rank* **2246**

Contains **6 strokes** in the following order:

Contains these components:

■ north 北 (altered) 131, p. 38

■□ dab r 、 176, p. 48

With all these meanings & readings:

zhào [兆] **1** omen **2** million **3** million million, trillion

In the far *north*, the native people interpret the colorful *dabs* of flashing lights in the night sky as bright **omens** for the future.

237

挑

SIMP & TRAD

This character with the definition:

select, pick

Pinyin **tiāo** *and Frequency Rank* **1309**

Contains **9 strokes** in the following order:

Contains these components:

■ hand r 扌 25, p. 15

■ omen 兆 236, p. 63

With all these meanings & readings:

tiāo [挑] **1** carry on a pole **2** choose
tiǎo [挑] **1** incite

When my wife asked what happened to our food money, I told her an *omen* appeared and told the little finger on my *hand* to take the money and use it to buy a lottery ticket based on the 'lucky' numbers I **picked**.

238

呂

TRAD SIMPLIFIED

This character with the definition:

bamboo pitch pipes

Pinyin **lǚ** *and Frequency Rank* **1716**

Contains **6 strokes** in the following order:

Contains these components:

■ mouth (×2) 口 37, p. 17

■ dab r 、 176, p. 48

With all these meanings & readings:

lǚ [呂] **1** surname Lü
lǚ [呂] **1** pitchpipe, pitch standard, one of the twelve semitones in the traditional tone system

We produce pure musical tones with **bamboo pitch pipes** by blowing through a series of holes, designed to resemble several mini-*mouths* bound together with *small amounts* of string.

239

雨

SIMP & TRAD

This character with the definition:

rain

Pinyin **yǔ** *and Frequency Rank* **928**

Contains **8 strokes** in the following order:

一 ㄧ 一 一 雨 雨 雨 雨

Contains these components:

■ but, yet (contrast) 而 (altered) 78, p. 26

■■ dab r (×4) 、 176, p. 48

With all these meanings & readings:

yǔ [雨] **1** rain **2** m 阵 [陣][zhèn], 场 [場][cháng]

Today's weather is such a *contrast* with yesterday! Yesterday it was sunny *but* today it's pouring big *dabs* of water—also known as **rain**!

240

SIMP & TRAD

This character with the definition:

snow

Pinyin **xuě** *and Frequency Rank* **1003**

Contains these components:

▢ rain 雨 239, p.63
▢ boar's head r ⼹ 30, p.16

With all these meanings & readings:

xuě [雪] **1** snow **2** m 场[場][cł

Contains **11 strokes** in the following order:

一 ⼀ ⼅ 币 币 雨 零 雨 雪 雪 雪

Precipitation can fall as either *rain* or **snow**. You can be certain it is **snow** when the precipitate appears white and accumulates to such a high level that you need a broom made from a *boar's head* to sweep it away!

241

SIMP & TRAD

This character with the definition:

needs, requirements

Pinyin **xū** *and Frequency Rank* **408**

Contains these components:

▢ rain 雨 239, p.63
▢ but, yet (contrast) 而 78, p.26

With all these meanings & readings:

xū [需] **1** to require **2** to need **3** to want **4** necessity **5** need

Contains **14 strokes** in the following order:

一 ⼀ ⼅ 币 币 雨 雷 雨 需 需 需 需 需 需

Rain produces a *contrast* with previous weather conditions and previous personal **needs**—by creating **requirements** for protective gear such as umbrellas, raincoats, and hats.

242

SIMP & TRAD

This character with the definition:

thunder

Pinyin **léi** *and Frequency Rank* **686**

Contains these components:

▢ rain 雨 239, p.63
▢ field 田 63, p.23

With all these meanings & readings:

léi [雷] **1** surname Lei
léi [雷] **1** thunder **2** (internet slang) terrifying **3** terrific

Contains **13 strokes** in the following order:

一 ⼀ ⼅ 币 币 雷 雷 雷 雷 雷 雷 雷 雷

Long steady *rain* showers which deeply soak the *fields* are ideal for growing healthy crops. Intense storms which produce very heavy *rain* in a short period of time, flood the *fields*, damage the crops, and are often accompanied by the frightening sound of **thunder**.

243

門
TRAD   SIMPLIFIED

This character with the definition:

doorway

Pinyin **mén** *and Frequency Rank* **185**

Contains these components:

▢ scepter c ｜ 5, p.10
▢ dab r ⼂ 176, p.48
▢ place of refuge c ⼁ 105, p.33

With all these meanings & readings:

mén [門] **1** gate **2** door **3** m 扇[shàn] **4** gateway **5** doorway **6** m 个[個][gè] **7** opening **8** valve **9** switch **10** way to do something **11** knack **12** family **13** house **14** (religious) sect **15** school (of thought) **16** class **17** category **18** phylum or division (taxonomy) **19** m for large guns **20** m for lessons, subjects branches of technology

Contains **3 strokes** in the following order:

⼂ ｢ 门

Here are the parts of a **doorway**. The *scepter* represents the left doorpost, which supports the rest of the frame. The *dab* of ink up top at the left is the hinge around which the actual door—the right-angle '*place of refuge*' stroke on the right—swings. • 门 can also symbolize a 'place of gathering' or 'gate'. People often do socialize around entrances and exits.

244

問
TRAD   SIMPLIFIED

This character with the definition:

ask

Pinyin **wèn** *and Frequency Rank* **137**

Contains these components:

▢ doorway 门 243, p.64
▢ mouth 口 37, p.17

With all these meanings & readings:

wèn [問] **1** to ask

Contains **6 strokes** in the following order:

⼂ ｢ 门 门 问 问

As a group of friends gathers together near the *doorway*, the 'gossip' of the group opens his *mouth* to **ask** a prying question.

245

聞
TRAD SIMPLIFIED

This character with the definition:

hear, smell

Pinyin **wén** *and Frequency Rank* **825**

Contains **9 strokes** in the following order:

丶 丨 门 门 门 门 闫 闻 闻

Contains these components:

doorway 门 243, p. 64

ear 耳 76, p. 26

With all these meanings & readings:

wén [聞] **1** to hear **2** news **3** well-known **4** famous **5** reputation **6** fame **7** to smell **8** to sniff at **9** surname Wen

With your *ear* and nose properly placed close to a *doorway*, you can both **hear** and **smell** everything going on inside.

246

間
TRAD SIMPLIFIED

This character with the definition:

room

Pinyin **jiān** *and Frequency Rank* **135**

Contains **7 strokes** in the following order:

丶 丨 门 门 闩 间 间

Contains these components:

doorway 门 243, p. 64

day, sun 日 64, p. 24

With all these meanings & readings:

jiān [間] **1** between **2** among **3** space **4** m for rooms **5** time (duration)
jiàn [間] **1** interstice **2** separate

On a hot summer day, air conditioning makes it tempting to retreat from the *sun* and go through the *doorway* into your **room**.

247

閏
TRAD SIMPLIFIED

This character with the definition:

intercalary month

Pinyin **rùn** *and Frequency Rank* **4183**

Contains **7 strokes** in the following order:

丶 丨 门 门 闩 闰 闰

Contains these components:

doorway 门 243, p. 64

king 王 15, p. 12

With all these meanings & readings:

rùn [閏] **1** intercalary **2** extra day or month inserted into the lunar or solar calendar (such as Feb 29)

In ancient China, the *king* did in fact sit at the *gate* during the special **intercalary months** that were added to the lunar calendar.

248

幣
TRAD SIMPLIFIED

This character with the definition:

money, currency

Pinyin **bì** *and Frequency Rank* **1188**

Contains **4 strokes** in the following order:

丿 丆 币 币

Contains these components:

dab r 丶 176, p. 48

towel 巾 118, p. 35

With all these meanings & readings:

bì [幣] **1** money **2** coins **3** currency

A little *bit* of *towel*, perhaps a small strip, was a forerunner to the system of money that would become **currency**.

249

書
TRAD SIMPLIFIED

This character with the definition:

book

Pinyin **shū** *and Frequency Rank* **282**

Contains **4 strokes** in the following order:

乛 乙 书 书

Contains these components:

place of refuge c (×2) 乛 105, p. 33

dab r 丶 176, p. 48

scepter c 丨 5, p. 10

With all these meanings & readings:

shū [書] **1** book **2** letter **3** same as 书经 [書經] Book of History **4** m 本[běn], 册 [冊][cè], 部[bù], 丛 [叢][cóng]

A good **book** is the ultimate *place of refuge*, perhaps why this component appears twice. Moreover, **books** extend their grace to all and sundry, from those with riches, wealth and material trappings (the '*scepter*') to those with *very little* to their names.

250

This component has the meaning:

cover r

COMPONENT

And contains these subcomponents:

☐ dab r ⟍ 176, p. 48

☐ one 一 1, p. 10

A *dab* of material on a *horizontal* surface functions as a handy knob on the top of a **cover**.

251

SIMP & TRAD

This character with the definition:

market

Pinyin **shì** *and Frequency Rank* **254**

Contains **5 strokes** in the following order:

、 一 亠 市 市

Contains these components:

☐ cover r 亠 250, p. 66

■ towel 巾 118, p. 35

With all these meanings & readings

shì [市] **1** market **2** city **3** m
[個][gè]

Crowded open-air Chinese **markets** generate lots of filth, dust, and soot! Nearby residents need to *cover* their white linens and *towels* to keep them clean.

252

鬧
TRAD SIMPLIFIED

This character with the definition:

make a noise

Pinyin **nào** *and Frequency Rank* **1336**

Contains **8 strokes** in the following order:

、 丨 门 门 门 闹 闹 闹

Contains these components:

☐ doorway 门 243, p. 64

■ market 市 251, p. 66

With all these meanings & readings

nào [鬧] **1** noisy **2** cacophono
3 to make noise **4** to disturb
5 to vent (feelings) **6** to fall i
7 to have an attack (of sickness
8 to go in (for some activity)
9 to joke

Today is *market* day. Since you live right on the main square of the town the *market* vendors set up right outside your *doorway*, and their customers **make a noise** so loud that you can barely think.

253

SIMP & TRAD

This character with the definition:

high

Pinyin **gāo** *and Frequency Rank* **134**

Contains **10 strokes** in the following order:

、 一 亠 宁 亨 高 高 高 高 高

Contains these components:

☐ cover r 亠 250, p. 66

■ mouth (×2) 口 37, p. 17

■ borders r 冂 114, p. 34

With all these meanings & readings

gāo [高] **1** high **2** tall **3** abov
average **4** loud **5** your (hon-
orific) **6** surname Gao

Nothing is built as **high** as a modern skyscraper. Here, the two 'mouths' represent the building blocks, which are piled higher and higher. The *borders* support the lower portion and help reinforce the foundation. The *cover* is appropriately placed on top, providing the final architectural feature.

254

SIMP & TRAD

This character with the definition:

make, do

Pinyin **gǎo** *and Frequency Rank* **1146**

Contains **13 strokes** in the following order:

一 十 才 扩 扩 扩 护 护 护 搞 搞 搞 搞

Contains these components:

■ hand r 扌 25, p. 15

■ high 高 253, p. 66

With all these meanings & reading

gǎo [搞] **1** to do **2** to make
3 to go in for **4** to set up **5**
get hold of **6** to take care of

Even young children can **make** creative 'sculptures' with sand by stacking their *hands* on top of a *high* pile of sand and positioning their fingers in a creative form.

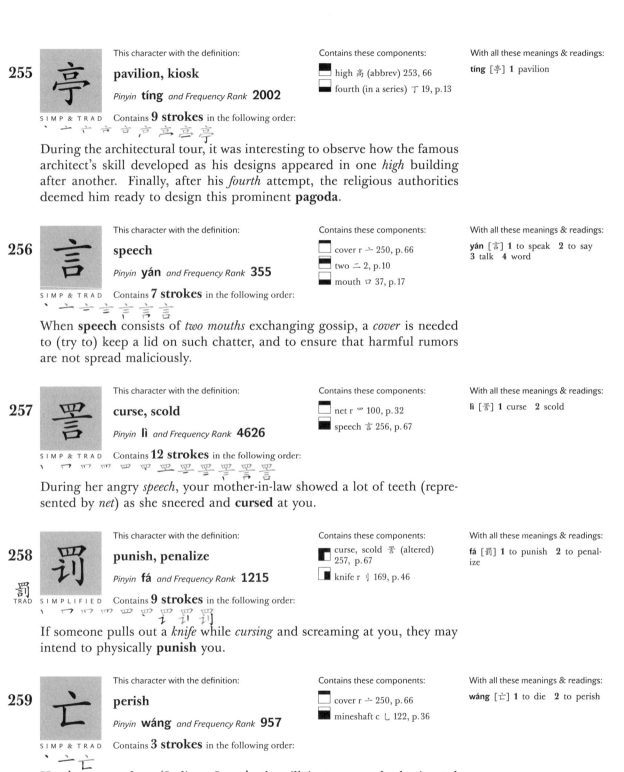

255 亭

SIMP & TRAD

This character with the definition:

pavilion, kiosk

Pinyin **tíng** *and Frequency Rank* **2002**

Contains **9 strokes** in the following order:

Contains these components:

☐ high 高 (abbrev) 253, 66
☐ fourth (in a series) 丁 19, p.13

With all these meanings & readings:

tíng [亭] **1** pavilion

During the architectural tour, it was interesting to observe how the famous architect's skill developed as his designs appeared in one *high* building after another. Finally, after his *fourth* attempt, the religious authorities deemed him ready to design this prominent **pagoda**.

256 言

SIMP & TRAD

This character with the definition:

speech

Pinyin **yán** *and Frequency Rank* **355**

Contains **7 strokes** in the following order:

Contains these components:

☐ cover r ⼍ 250, p.66
☐ two ⼆ 2, p.10
☐ mouth ⼝ 37, p.17

With all these meanings & readings:

yán [言] **1** to speak **2** to say **3** talk **4** word

When **speech** consists of *two mouths* exchanging gossip, a *cover* is needed to (try to) keep a lid on such chatter, and to ensure that harmful rumors are not spread maliciously.

257 詈

SIMP & TRAD

This character with the definition:

curse, scold

Pinyin **lì** *and Frequency Rank* **4626**

Contains **12 strokes** in the following order:

Contains these components:

☐ net r ⽹ 100, p.32
☐ speech 言 256, p.67

With all these meanings & readings:

lì [詈] **1** curse **2** scold

During her angry *speech*, your mother-in-law showed a lot of teeth (represented by *net*) as she sneered and **cursed** at you.

258 罚

TRAD 罰   SIMPLIFIED

This character with the definition:

punish, penalize

Pinyin **fá** *and Frequency Rank* **1215**

Contains **9 strokes** in the following order:

Contains these components:

☐ curse, scold 詈 (altered) 257, p.67
☐ knife r ⼑ 169, p.46

With all these meanings & readings:

fá [罰] **1** to punish **2** to penalize

If someone pulls out a *knife* while *cursing* and screaming at you, they may intend to physically **punish** you.

259 亡

SIMP & TRAD

This character with the definition:

perish

Pinyin **wáng** *and Frequency Rank* **957**

Contains **3 strokes** in the following order:

Contains these components:

☐ cover r ⼍ 250, p.66
☐ mineshaft c ⼃ 122, p.36

With all these meanings & readings:

wáng [亡] **1** to die **2** to perish

Here's a scene from 'Indiana Jones': the villain removes the horizontal *cover*, throws you down the *mineshaft*, and leaves you there to **perish**.

Unit 13

260

芒

SIMP & TRAD

This character with the definition:

spike, sharp point

Pinyin **máng** *and Frequency Rank* **2251**

Contains **6 strokes** in the following order:

一 十 十 艹 芒 芒 芒

Contains these components:

☐ grass r 艹 87, p. 29

☐ perish 亡 259, p. 67

With all these meanings & readings:

máng [芒] **1** awn (of cereals) **2** arista (of grain) **3** tip (of a blade)Miscanthus sinensis (a type of grass) **4** variant of 邙

Don't be fooled by the smooth and soft texture of grass—bamboo and other tough *grasses* make for potent weapons. Unwary travelers have *perished* in traps created by using long pieces of these *grasses* for **sharp spikes**.

261

亨

SIMP & TRAD

This character with the definition:

smooth

Pinyin **hēng** *and Frequency Rank* **2146**

Contains **7 strokes** in the following order:

丶 亠 亠 吂 吂 亨 亨

Contains these components:

☐ cover r 宀 250, p. 66

▬ mouth 口 37, p. 17

▬ s-end le 了 23, p. 15

With all these meanings & readings:

hēng [亨] **1** prosperous

A roof (*cover*) over your head, food for your *mouth*, and several lifestyle *changes* for the better indicate that the journey of life has finally become **smooth** for you.

262

享

SIMP & TRAD

This character with the definition:

enjoy

Pinyin **xiǎng** *and Frequency Rank* **1227**

Contains **8 strokes** in the following order:

丶 亠 亠 吂 吂 亨 享 享

Contains these components:

■ smooth 亨 261, p. 68

▬ one 一 1, p. 10

With all these meanings & readings:

xiǎng [享] **1** to enjoy **2** to benefit **3** to have the use of

This main character very closely resembles the *'smooth'* element, with only *one* additional stroke that transforms a merely *smooth* situation into one that is truly **enjoyable**.

263

哼

SIMP & TRAD

This character with the definition:

hum, croon

Pinyin **hēng** *and Frequency Rank* **1966**

Contains **10 strokes** in the following order:

丨 口 口 口 口丶 哼 哼 哼 哼 哼

Contains these components:

▌ mouth 口 37, p. 17

▐ smooth 亨 261, p. 68

With all these meanings & readings:

hēng [哼] **1** hum **2** (interjection of contempt)

The sound your *mouth* makes when things go *smoothly* is described by a contented **humming**.

264

𥫗

This component has the meaning:

bamboo r

COMPONENT

And contains these subcomponents:

☐ bamboo 竹 (altered) 182, p. 49

Taking a knife and slicing off the bottom stems of **bamboo** shoots creates the **bamboo radical** that frequently appears in Chinese characters.

265

筆
TRAD SIMPLIFIED

This character with the definition:

pen

Pinyin **bǐ** *and Frequency Rank* **956**

Contains **10 strokes** in the following order:

丿 𠂊 𠂉 竺 竹 竺 笔 笔 笔 笔

Contains these components:

☐ bamboo r ⺮ 264, p. 68

■ hair 毛 184, p. 50

With all these meanings & readings:

bǐ ［筆］ **1** pen **2** pencil **3** writing brush **4** to write or compose **5** the strokes of Chinese characters **6** m for sums of money, deals **7** m 支[zhī], 枝[zhī]

Ancient **pens** were made of *bamboo*, which provided the shell to hold and *hair* fibers for the nib.

266

等
SIMP & TRAD

This character with the definition:

wait

Pinyin **děng** *and Frequency Rank* **158**

Contains **12 strokes** in the following order:

丿 𠂊 𠂉 竺 竹 竺 竺 笁 笁 竺 等 等

Contains these components:

☐ bamboo r ⺮ 264, p. 68

■ Buddhist temple 寺 220, p. 59

With all these meanings & readings:

děng ［等］ **1** class **2** rank **3** grade **4** equal to **5** same as **6** to wait for **7** to await **8** et cetera **9** and so on **10** et al. (and other authors) **11** after **12** as soon as **13** once

Since I am not a particularly pious person, I envision myself attending a religious service in a *Buddhist temple* out of curiosity, but then staring at the *bamboo* walls and **waiting** for the service to end.

267

簡
TRAD SIMPLIFIED

This character with the definition:

simple, simplified

Pinyin **jiǎn** *and Frequency Rank* **716**

Contains **13 strokes** in the following order:

丿 𠂊 𠂉 竺 竹 竺 笁 笂 简 简 简 简 简

Contains these components:

☐ bamboo r ⺮ 264, p. 68

■ room 间 246, p. 65

With all these meanings & readings:

jiǎn ［簡］ **1** simple

The **simple** elegance of the *room* is so stunning because everything in it is made from *bamboo*.

268

冖
COMPONENT

This component has the meaning:

smooth cover r

It's a **smooth cover** because there's no handle on top (compared with the 'regular' cover in panel 250).

269

營
TRAD SIMPLIFIED

This character with the definition:

battalion

Pinyin **yíng** *and Frequency Rank* **536**

Contains **11 strokes** in the following order:

一 十 艹 芦 芦 带 带 营 营 营 营

Contains these components:

☐ grass r ⺿ 87, p. 29

☐ smooth cover r 冖 268, p. 69

▭ mouth 口 37, p. 17

▭ mouth 口 37, p. 17

With all these meanings & readings:

yíng ［營］ **1** army **2** to deal in **3** to trade **4** to operate **5** to run **6** camp **7** nourishment **8** to manage

A multitude of *mouths*—here there's only two, because that's all there's room for—symbolizes all the men that form a **battalion**. We know this is a battalion because battalions require food, symbolized by a vegetable (*grass*), and by a shelter (*cover*).

270

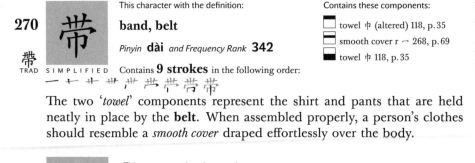

帯
TRAD

This character with the definition:

band, belt

Pinyin **dài** *and Frequency Rank* **342**

SIMPLIFIED   Contains **9 strokes** in the following order:

一 十 卄 世 带 芾 带 带 带

Contains these components:

☐ towel 巾 (altered) 118, p. 35

▤ smooth cover r ⌐ 268, p. 69

■ towel 巾 118, p. 35

With all these meanings & readings:

dài [带] **1** band **2** belt **3** girdl **4** ribbon **5** tire **6** area **7** zone **8** region **9** to wear **10** to carry **11** to lead **12** to bring **13** to look after **14** to raise **15** m 条 [條][tiáo]

The two '*towel*' components represent the shirt and pants that are held neatly in place by the **belt**. When assembled properly, a person's clothes should resemble a *smooth cover* draped effortlessly over the body.

271

This component has the meaning:

roof r

COMPONENT

This stylized **roof** includes a *dab* at the top to represent the pitch line of traditional Chinese houses.

272

SIMP & TRAD

This character with the definition:

fitting

Pinyin **yí** *and Frequency Rank* **1290**

Contains **8 strokes** in the following order:

丶 丷 宀 宀 宀 官 官 宜

Contains these components:

☐ roof r ⌐ 271, p. 70

■ moreover 且 84, p. 28

With all these meanings & readings:

yí [宜] **1** surname Yi
yí [宜] **1** proper **2** should **3** suitable **4** appropriate

It is **fitting** to be sitting under our own *roof* in our cozy den, surrounded by *bookcases* lining the walls, on this cold and rainy night.

273

SIMP & TRAD

This character with the definition:

building, house

Pinyin **yǔ** *and Frequency Rank* **1156**

Contains **6 strokes** in the following order:

丶 丷 宀 宀 宇 宇

Contains these components:

☐ roof r ⌐ 271, p. 70

■ in, at, to 于 20, p. 13

With all these meanings & readings:

yǔ [宇] **1** room **2** universe

This *roof* spreads over the place that you go home *to*, that you stay *at*, and that you're always happy to be *in*: your own **house**.

274

宫

宫
TRAD

This character with the definition:

palace

Pinyin **gōng** *and Frequency Rank* **982**

SIMPLIFIED   Contains **9 strokes** in the following order:

丶 丷 宀 宀 宫 宫 宫 宫 宫

Contains these components:

☐ roof r ⌐ 271, p. 70

■ bamboo pitch pipes 吕 238, p. 63

With all these meanings & readings:

gōng [宫] **1** palace **2** surname Gong **3** castration (as corporal punishment) **4** first note in pentatonic scale

If you think of the openings in the *bamboo pitch pipes* as a series of rooms protected by a *roof*, you have the elements of a royal **palace**.

275

宙

SIMP & TRAD

This character with the definition:

for all time

Pinyin **zhòu** *and Frequency Rank* **1421**

Contains **8 strokes** in the following order:

丶 丶 宀 宀 宀 宙 宙 宙

Contains these components:

roof r ⼧ 271, p. 70

reason, by means of 由 58, p. 22

With all these meanings & readings:

zhòu [宙] **1** universe

Despite the cost, people choose to build a *roof* made of copper for the sole *reason* that they believe this roof will last **for all time**.

276

宣

SIMP & TRAD

This character with the definition:

proclaim, declare

Pinyin **xuān** *and Frequency Rank* **770**

Contains **9 strokes** in the following order:

丶 丶 宀 宀 宀 宫 宫 宣 宣

Contains these components:

roof r ⼧ 271, p. 70

two 二 (altered) 2, p. 10

speak 日 (altered) 67, p. 24

With all these meanings & readings:

xuān [宣] **1** to declare (publicly) **2** to announce **3** surname Xuan

The '*roof*' is really a decorated handle, attached to the upper of the *two* horizontal rods; between them is a scroll, on which the words of the **proclamation** are written, and from which the emperor will soon find inspiration to *speak* to his subjects.

277

它

SIMP & TRAD

This character with the definition:

it

Pinyin **tā** *and Frequency Rank* **107**

Contains **5 strokes** in the following order:

丶 丶 宀 宀 它

Contains these components:

roof r ⼧ 271, p. 70

ancient ladle 匕 124, p. 36

With all these meanings & readings:

tā [它] **1** it (used for things)

It takes hard work to build a functional home. Here the *roof* covers the *ladle*, which represents all the **i**nternal **t**asks that must be done. Remember these **i**nternal **t**asks by their acronym, **it**.

278

富

SIMP & TRAD

This character with the definition:

rich, wealthy

Pinyin **fù** *and Frequency Rank* **733**

Contains **12 strokes** in the following order:

丶 丶 宀 宀 宀 宫 宫 宫 富 富 富 富

Contains these components:

roof r ⼧ 271, p. 70

size range c 畐 162, p. 45

With all these meanings & readings:

fù [富] **1** rich **2** surname Fu

The **wealthy** art collector hired security guards to protect his collection of expensive paintings, which span a wide *range of sizes* and styles, that is currently on display under his *roof*.

279

守

SIMP & TRAD

This character with the definition:

defend

Pinyin **shǒu** *and Frequency Rank* **796**

Contains **6 strokes** in the following order:

丶 丶 宀 宀 守 守

Contains these components:

roof r ⼧ 271, p. 70

inch 寸 216, p. 58

With all these meanings & readings:

shǒu [守] **1** to guard **2** to defend **3** to keep watch **4** to abide by the law **5** to observe (rules or ritual) **6** nearby **7** adjoining

The *inch* resembles a martial arts expert with the horizontal representing his extended leg, ready to inflict serious damage on an intruder. He is in this special position underneath the *roof* to **defend** the entire building.

280

SIMP & TRAD

This character with the definition:

harm, injure

Pinyin **hài** *and Frequency Rank* **579**

Contains these components:

☐ roof r 宀 271, p.70

▤ plentiful 丯 16, p.13

▤ mouth 口 37, p.17

With all these meanings & reading

hài [害] **1** to do harm to **2** to cause trouble to **3** harm **4** e **5** calamity

Contains **10 strokes** in the following order:

丶 丷 宀 宀 宀 宀 宔 宔 害 害

So-called friends whose *mouths* are *plentiful* with gossip, exchanged under the security of one's *roof*, can inflict the worst **harm** toward people.

281

SIMP & TRAD

This character with the definition:

cut apart, sever

Pinyin **gē** *and Frequency Rank* **1665**

Contains these components:

▤ harm, injure 害 280, p.72

☐ knife r 刂 169, p.46

With all these meanings & reading

gē [割] **1** to cut **2** to cut apa

Contains **12 strokes** in the following order:

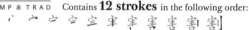

Even though the bad guy in a Hollywood movie uses a *knife* to *injure* the hero, and even tries to **sever** or **cut** a major blood vessel with it, he invariably fails to complete this mission.

282

向

SIMP & TRAD

This character with the definition:

to face

Pinyin **xiàng** *and Frequency Rank* **146**

Contains these components:

■ roof r 宀 (altered) 271, p.70

▫ mouth 口 37, p.17

With all these meanings & reading

xiàng [向] **1** direction **2** orien tion **3** to face **4** to turn towa **5** to **6** towards **7** shortly be fore **8** formerly **9** to side wit **10** to be partial to **11** all alon (previously) **12** surname Xiang

Contains **6 strokes** in the following order:

丿 亻 冂 向 向 向

If you are **facing** someone when you cough or sneeze, it's important to thoroughly cover your *mouth*, so thoroughly that it seems like a *roof* around your **face**. The exaggerated verticals emphasize this thoroughness.

283

響
TRAD

SIMPLIFIED

This character with the definition:

make a sound

Pinyin **xiǎng** *and Frequency Rank* **503**

Contains these components:

■ mouth 口 37, p.17

▤ to face 向 282, p.72

With all these meanings & reading

xiǎng [響] **1** to make a sound **2** to sound **3** to ring **4** loud **5** m for noises

Contains **9 strokes** in the following order:

丨 口 口 口' 吖 吶 响 响 响

To **make a sound** that's easily heard, talk with your *mouth* while *facing* the direction you want to be heard.

284

SIMP & TRAD

This character with the definition:

pen, cage

Pinyin **láo** *and Frequency Rank* **1696**

Contains these components:

☐ roof r 宀 271, p.70

▤ ox 牛 213, p.57

With all these meanings & reading

láo [牢] **1** firm **2** sturdy **3** fo (for animals) **4** sacrifice **5** pri

Contains **7 strokes** in the following order:

丶 丷 宀 宀 宝 宝 牢

The *ox* was kept in a **pen**, while the smaller animals were kept in a **cage**, both of which were sheltered by a *roof*.

Names *Interlude 1*

All of our panels concern written glyphs called either characters or components. It's important to remember the distinction between the two, and to bear in mind the conventions by which we've named them.

There are eighty-three **components** in all, and exactly fifty of them—about seventy-two percent—have a second life as components in traditional Chinese orthography. For obscure reasons English grammarians and linguists have termed them *radicals*. Actually, they serve as category heads, into which characters are slotted. (Most readers know by now that this categorization plays a major role in dictionary lookups.) For example, all characters containing the 'hand' radical ⺘ supposedly have something to do with hand movements or other handy things, just as characters including the 'grass' radical ⺿ pertain to things grassy or at least vegetational in nature. This system is far from 100% consistent, but is very helpful in reminding you of a character's meaning.

When any of our components appeared as one of these radicals, we took care to use its traditional title, and to append the suffix 'r' as a further reminder that this particular radical has an alternative existence in dictionaries and other Chinese reference works. That is why our official names for the two radicals above are 'hand **r**' and 'grass **r**'.

That leaves thirty-three components which appear recognizably in the written forms of other characters. It's important that you keep in mind at all times that these components are not independent characters and, to this end, their definitions include a 'c' at the end as a gentle but constant reminder. Thus, the components we've identified, for example, as 'wound' and 'contented cows' are actually 'wound **c**' and 'contented cows **c**'.

Why this emphasis on the distinction between components and characters? The crucial difference between them lies in their status as independent entities. Components can *never* appear independently as a character, but if there was nothing in their naming conventions to indicate this, you might imagine that the 'wound c' component ⽧ could be used anywhere in a text when you need the word 'wound' or 'injury'. Similarly, you might think that an author could use ⺿ for grass but that is never correct!

The naming convention for independent characters is more clear-cut, for we just use its meaning as its panel heading. Chinese characters often possess several meanings, sometimes related, but often not. Our policy has been to keep, whenever possible, the 'main' meaning for each character. The only time this strategy fails is when a character has a meaning similar to that of a completely distinct character. In this case, in an attempt to eliminate confusion to the reader—you!—we've adopted a secondary meaning for one of the characters.

Sometimes, though, this helpful strategy is simply not available. For example, the concept of 'elder brother' is an important one to the Chinese, as made evident in the three distinct characters with this meaning. Moreover, these characters do not possess any secondary meanings! In this case, we insert an asterisk at the end of the word to indicate the variant. So, you'll find characters in this book with the meaning 'elder brother', 'elder brother*', and 'elder brother**'.

Unit 14

285

字

SIMP & TRAD

This character with the definition:

character, word

Pinyin **zì** *and Frequency Rank* **393**

Contains **6 strokes** in the following order:

丶 丶 宀 宁 宁 字

Contains these components:

roof r 宀 271, p. 70

son, child 子 24, p. 15

With all these meanings & readings

zì [字] **1** letter **2** symbol **3** character **4** word **5** m 个 [個][gè]

Our *son* is a very calm and quiet *child*; he hardly speaks a **word**, so much so that sometimes we forget he lives under our *roof*!

286

宁

寧

TRAD SIMPLIFIED

This character with the definition:

rather, would rather

Pinyin **nìng** *and Frequency Rank* **1019**

Contains **5 strokes** in the following order:

丶 丶 宀 宁 宁

Contains these components:

roof r 宀 271, p. 70

fourth (in a series) 丁 19, p. 13

With all these meanings & readings

níng [寧] **1** peaceful **2** rather **3** Ningxia (abbr.) **4** Nanjing (abbr.) **5** surname Ning
nìng [寧] **1** rather **2** to prefer

Help! The *roof* is collapsing for the *fourth* time. I **would rather** that this didn't happen. Next time, I'm making the roof supports out of **wood** (sounds like '**would**').

287

宝

寶

TRAD SIMPLIFIED

This character with the definition:

treasure

Pinyin **bǎo** *and Frequency Rank* **811**

Contains **8 strokes** in the following order:

丶 丶 宀 宁 宁 宇 宝 宝

Contains these components:

roof r 宀 271, p. 70

jade 玉 177, p. 48

With all these meanings & readings

bǎo [寶] **1** a jewel or gem **2** a treasure **3** precious

1 People hide their **treasures** under their own *roof*. Scribes use the symbol for '*jade*' to represent these valuables. 2 This character shows a *house* made of *jade*. What a precious **treasure**!

288

审

審

TRAD SIMPLIFIED

This character with the definition:

examine, go over

Pinyin **shěn** *and Frequency Rank* **746**

Contains **8 strokes** in the following order:

丶 丶 宀 宁 宁 宙 宙 审

Contains these components:

roof r 宀 271, p. 70

express 申 57, p. 22

With all these meanings & readings

shěn [審] **1** to examine **2** to investigate **3** carefully **4** to try (in court)

When I study for a test, I need to **go over** all the material out loud. I feel comfortable doing this under my own *roof*, where I can *express myself* out loud with no one giving me funny looks.

289

宅

SIMP & TRAD

This character with the definition:

residence, house

Pinyin **zhái** *and Frequency Rank* **1858**

Contains **6 strokes** in the following order:

丶 丶 宀 宁 宅 宅

Contains these components:

roof r 宀 271, p. 70

hair 毛 (abbrev) 184, 50

With all these meanings & readings

zhái [宅] **1** residence

I've been living at this same *residence* since childhood. The *roof* has seen my *hair* grow in and, as of late, fall out.

290

This component has the meaning:

walking man r

COMPONENT

Imagine a very clumsy amateur photographer trying to take a candid shot of a **walking man**. Unfortunately, all he has managed to capture are what appears here: the **walking man**'s legs.

291

This character with the definition:

first

Pinyin **xiān** *and Frequency Rank* **188**

SIMP & TRAD   Contains **6 strokes** in the following order:

ノ ト 山 生 キ 先

Contains these components:

◻ dab r ヽ 176, p. 48

◻ earth, soil 土 9, p. 11

◼ walking man r 儿 290, p. 75

With all these meanings & readings:

xiān [先] **1** early **2** prior **3** former **4** in advance **5** first

The *man walked* through unpaved back alleys in order to become the **first** person in line. Along the way, he acquired a *bit* of muddy *soil* on his pants.

292

憲
TRAD

This character with the definition:

constitution, statute, law

Pinyin **xiàn** *and Frequency Rank* **1484**

SIMPLIFIED   Contains **9 strokes** in the following order:

ヽ 丷 宀 宀 宀 宋 宔 宲 宪

Contains these components:

◻ roof r 宀 271, p. 70

◼ first 先 291, p. 75

With all these meanings & readings:

xiàn [憲] **1** statute **2** constitution

The experience of the United States is salutary in the following respect: drafting a **constitution** was the *first* responsibility of the country's founders. Done properly, it served as a *roof*, protecting and nurturing the infant nation as it matures.

293

This character with the definition:

elder brother*

Pinyin **xiōng** *and Frequency Rank* **1089**

SIMP & TRAD   Contains **5 strokes** in the following order:

ヽ 丷 口 尸 兄

Contains these components:

◻ mouth 口 37, p. 17

◼ walking man r 儿 290, p. 75

With all these meanings & readings:

xiōng [兄] **1** elder brother

This character shows a *walking man* whose *mouth* does all the talking. Sometimes, younger siblings view their **elder brothers** this way!

294

克
尅
TRAD

This character with the definition:

subdue

Pinyin **kè** *and Frequency Rank* **262**

SIMPLIFIED   Contains **7 strokes** in the following order:

一 十 キ 古 古 声 克

Contains these components:

◻ elder brother* 兄 293, p. 75

◼ ten 十 7, p. 11

With all these meanings & readings:

kè [克] **1** to be able to **2** to subdue **3** to restrain **4** to overcome **5** gram
kè [尅] **1** to subdue **2** to overthrow

The original 'Band of Brothers' consisted of a group of *ten elder brothers*, capable of **subduing** anyone who got in their way.

295

This character with the definition:

dollar

Pinyin **yuán** *and Frequency Rank* **370**

SIMP & TRAD   Contains **4 strokes** in the following order:

一 二 亍 元

Contains these components:

☐ two 二 2, p.10
☐ walking man r 儿 290, p.75

With all these meanings & readings:

yuán [元] **1** Chinese monetary unit **2** dollar **3** primary **4** first **5** the Yuan or Mongol dynasty (1279-1368) **6** surname Yuan

The *man walking* slowly around the park is lost deep in his thoughts, thinking about ways to add to the *two* **dollars** he has in his pocket. • This character also refers to the unit of currency in the People's Republic of China.

296

This character with the definition:

have fun, amuse oneself

Pinyin **wán** *and Frequency Rank* **1072**

SIMP & TRAD   Contains **8 strokes** in the following order:

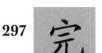

Contains these components:

☐ king 王 15, p.12
☐ dollar 元 295, p.76

With all these meanings & readings:

wán [玩] **1** toy **2** sth used for amusement **3** curio or antique (Taiwan pr wàn) **4** to play **5** have fun **6** to trifle with **7** to keep sth for entertainment

With a few *dollars* in your pocket, you can certainly **have fun**—but not as much as the *king*, who could easily **amuse himself** with or without money.

297

This character with the definition:

to complete, finish

Pinyin **wán** *and Frequency Rank* **301**

SIMP & TRAD   Contains **7 strokes** in the following order:

丶 宀 宀 宁 宇 宇 完

Contains these components:

☐ roof r 宀 271, p.70
☐ dollar 元 295, p.76

With all these meanings & readings:

wán [完] **1** to finish **2** to be over **3** whole **4** complete **5** entire

The *roof* on top of a *dollar* is the Chinese way of reminding shoppers that they need to have a spending "cap"—the time or dollar amount in which they need **to finish** shopping and call it a day.

298

This character with the definition:

crest, topmost part

Pinyin **guān** *and Frequency Rank* **1713**

SIMP & TRAD   Contains **9 strokes** in the following order:

丶 宀 宀 宁 宇 完 完 冠 冠

Contains these components:

☐ defend 守 (altered) 279, p.71
☐ dollar 元 (altered) 295, p.76

With all these meanings & readings:

guān [冠] **1** hat **2** crown **3** crest **4** cap
guàn [冠] **1** to head

The champion reached a **crest** of popular adulation when he offered to *defend* the emperor for a *dollar* a day.

299

TRAD 園   SIMPLIFIED

This character with the definition:

garden

Pinyin **yuán** *and Frequency Rank* **988**

Contains **7 strokes** in the following order:

丨 冂 冂 冃 冋 园 园

Contains these components:

☐ enclosure r 囗 36, p.17
☐ dollar 元 295, p.76

With all these meanings & readings:

yuán [園] **1** garden

Gardens and parks demand huge amounts of labor to keep them looking attractive. Vast infusions of *dollars* keep the lands inside the park's *boundaries* looking tip-top.

300

四

four

Pinyin **sì** *and Frequency Rank* **226**

SIMP & TRAD   Contains **5 strokes** in the following order:

丨 冂 冂 冈 四

This character with the definition:

Contains these components:

■ enclosure r 囗 36, p.17
■ walking man r 儿 290, p.75

With all these meanings & readings:

sì [四] **1** four **2** 4

The *walking man* who completes endless circuits around his **four**-walled room is really a restless prisoner desperately seeking a way out of this *enclosure*.

301

西

west

Pinyin **xī** *and Frequency Rank* **167**

SIMP & TRAD   Contains **6 strokes** in the following order:

一 丆 丆 丙 西 西

This character with the definition:

Contains these components:

□ one 一 1, p.10
■ four 四 (altered) 300, p.77

With all these meanings & readings:

xī [西] **1** west **2** the West **3** Spain (abbr.)   **4** Spanish

This is another vignette of the poor prisoner trapped in '*four*' (panel 300), this time depicted with his two legs and lower torso. The prisoner has succeeded in breaking through the **west** side of his *four*-walled enclosure— only to be stopped by *one* more barrier.

302

酉

five to seven pm

Pinyin **yǒu** *and Frequency Rank* **3839**

SIMP & TRAD   Contains **7 strokes** in the following order:

一 丆 丆 丙 西 酉 酉

This character with the definition:

Contains these components:

□ west 西 301, p.77
□ one 一 1, p.10

With all these meanings & readings:

yǒu [酉] **1** 10th earthly branch: 5-7 p.m., 8th solar month (8th September-7th October), year of the Rooster

It's best to think of the '*one*' as the horizon. In turn, this should make us think of the sun setting in the *west*, an event that occurs daily between **five to seven pm**, or during the **early evening.** • Since this is the earliest time that you can, in good conscience, open a bottle of **wine** for responsible refreshment, we frequently use this character to refer to '**wine**'.

303

酷

cruel

Pinyin **kù** *and Frequency Rank* **1867**

SIMP & TRAD   Contains **14 strokes** in the following order:

一 丆 丆 丙 酉 酉 酉′ 酉⌐ 酉⌐ 酷 酷 酷 酷

This character with the definition:

Contains these components:

■ five to seven pm 酉 302, p.77
■ tell 告 234, p.62

With all these meanings & readings:

kù [酷] **1** ruthless **2** strong (as of wine) **3** cool (loanword)

In the *early evening*, people tend to relax and *tell* a friend things that they normally wouldn't think of mentioning during the full light of day. Such unguarded revelations can be unintentionally **cruel.** • The Chinese have adopted the English word 'cool'—meaning great, nifty, way to go!—and use this character and pronunciation for it.

304

SIMP & TRAD

This character with the definition:

wake up

Pinyin **xǐng** *and Frequency Rank* **1075**

Contains these components:

■ five to seven pm 酉 302, p. 77
■ star 星 212, p. 57

With all these meanings & readings

xǐng [醒] **1** to wake up **2** to awaken **3** to be awake

Contains **16 strokes** in the following order:

一 丆 丌 襾 襾 酉 酉 酉` 酉⌐ 酉⌐ 酉⌐ 酉⌐ 醒 醒 醒 醒

It's *early evening*, and the *stars* have started to appear. Most adults are thinking of going to sleep, but many teenagers and college students are just beginning to **wake up**.

305

SIMP & TRAD

This character with the definition:

join together

Pinyin **pèi** *and Frequency Rank* **738**

Contains these components:

■ five to seven pm 酉 302, p. 77
■ self* 己 135, p. 39

With all these meanings & readings

pèi [配] **1** to join **2** to fit **3** mate **4** to mix **5** to match **6** to deserve **7** to make up (a prescription)

Contains **10 strokes** in the following order:

一 丆 丌 襾 襾 酉 酉 酉` 酉⌐ 配

The tradition of having the bride and groom sip *wine* out of glasses during the wedding celebrations demonstrates the willingness of each individual '*self*' to commit to and **join together** in a new life as one married couple.

306

犧
TRAD   SIMPLIFIED

This character with the definition:

sacrificial animal

Pinyin **xī** *and Frequency Rank* **1814**

Contains these components:

■ ox 牛 213, p. 57
■ west 西 301, p. 77

With all these meanings & readings

xī [犧] **1** sacrifice

Contains **10 strokes** in the following order:

丿 ⺧ 午 牛 牛 牜 牜 牺 牺 牺

An *ox* facing the setting sun in the *west* makes a picture perfect **sacrificial animal**.

307

見
TRAD   SIMPLIFIED

This character with the definition:

see

Pinyin **jiàn** *and Frequency Rank* **153**

Contains these components:

▢ borders r 冂 114, p. 34
■ walking man r 儿 290, p. 75

With all these meanings & readings

jiàn [見] **1** to see **2** to meet **3** to appear (to be sth) **4** to interview
xiàn [見] **1** appear

Contains **4 strokes** in the following order:

丨 冂 见 见

Here's a *guy walking around* with a paper bag over his head. Look, you can even see its *borders* whereas he can't **see** a thing. • Alternatively, the *borders* represent the shape of his head, so as he *walks around*, he can **see** where he's going.

308

現
TRAD   SIMPLIFIED

This character with the definition:

now

Pinyin **xiàn** *and Frequency Rank* **70**

Contains these components:

■ king 王 15, p. 12
■ see 见 307, p. 78

With all these meanings & readings

xiàn [現] **1** appear **2** present **3** now **4** existing **5** current

Contains **8 strokes** in the following order:

一 二 丅 王 玑 珋 现 现

The *king* is the *king*, and he can look at whatever he wants whenever he wants—and he wants to *see* it right **now**!

309

苋
TRAD   SIMPLIFIED

This character with the definition:

amaranth

Pinyin **xiàn** *and Frequency Rank* **4820**

Contains **7 strokes** in the following order:

一 十 艹 艹 芦 苋 苋

Contains these components:

☐ grass r 艹 87, p. 29

■ see 见 307, p. 78

With all these meanings & readings:

xiàn [苋] **1** amaranth (genus Amaranthus) **2** Joseph's coat (Amaranthus tricolor) **3** Chinese spinach (Amaranth mangostanus)

Amaranth is an ancient grain that was recently rediscovered; its seeds, when roasted, pop like popcorn. The ancient Chinese treated it as a leafy *vegetable*, which they would stir fry. They believed eating this grain would helped one to *see* better.

Unit 15

310

寛
TRAD | SIMPLIFIED

This character with the definition:

wide, broad

Pinyin **kuān** *and Frequency Rank* **1155**

Contains **10 strokes** in the following order:

Contains these components:

- roof r ⼧ 271, p. 70
- amaranth 苋 309, p. 79

With all these meanings & readings

kuān [寬] **1** lenient **2** wide **3** broad

Amaranth kernels are tiny but numerous. Imagine someone making a carpet from the seeds of a single *amaranth* plant. They are so plentiful that the house and the *roof* that covers it would have to be both **wide and broad** to encompass them all.

311

覽
TRAD | SIMPLIFIED

This character with the definition:

view, look at

Pinyin **lǎn** *and Frequency Rank* **1886**

Contains **9 strokes** in the following order:

Contains these components:

- inspect, supervise 监 (altered) 207, p. 55
- see 见 307, p. 78

With all these meanings & readings

lǎn [覽] **1** look over **2** to view

Curators *supervise* the display of museum paintings so that visitors can clearly *see* the paintings they paid to **view**.

312

兒
TRAD | SIMPLIFIED

This character with the definition:

son

Pinyin **ér** *and Frequency Rank* **192**

Contains **2 strokes** in the following order:

丿 儿

Contains these components:

- walking man r 儿 290, p. 75

With all these meanings & readings

ér [兒] **1** son
ér [兒] **1** non-syllabic diminutive suffix **2** retroflex final

Here are the *legs of a man*, but the rest of him is missing—he has no head or other limbs! It's actually an undeveloped man—a **son**.

313

匹

SIMP & TRAD

This character with the definition:

be a match for

Pinyin **pǐ** *and Frequency Rank* **1908**

Contains **4 strokes** in the following order:

一 丆 兀 匹

Contains these components:

- basket, box r 匚 152, p. 42
- walking man r 儿 290, p. 75

With all these meanings & readings

pǐ [匹] **1** mate **2** one of a pair
pǐ [匹] **1** ordinary person **2** m for horses, mules etc **3** m for cloth: bolt

The *man walking* all around the flea market has lost one of the cufflinks left to him by his father, and he is devastated. He is opening every *box* he can find, searching **for a match** to the one he lost.

314

氵

This component has the meaning:

water r

COMPONENT

Drop a stone into a pool. The drops of water that splash out feel good on a hot summer day. Here are three of those drops.

315 水

This character with the definition:

water

Pinyin **shuǐ** *and Frequency Rank* **202**

SIMP & TRAD   Contains **4 strokes** in the following order:

亅 刀 水 水

Contains these components:

■ water r 氵 (altered) 314, p. 80

With all these meanings & readings:

shuǐ [水] **1** water **2** river **3** liquid **4** beverage **5** molten (metal) **6** surname Shui **7** m 杯[bēi], 筒[tǒng], 瓶[píng] **8** see also 氵[氵][shuǐ]

The graceful lines of 水 suggest a river delta—the coming together of several streams of **water**.

---

316 沓

This character with the definition:

repeat sth numerous times

Pinyin **tà** *and Frequency Rank* **3806**

SIMP & TRAD   Contains **8 strokes** in the following order:

亅 刀 水 水 水 沓 沓 沓

Contains these components:

□ water 水 315, p. 81

■ speak 曰 67, p. 24

With all these meanings & readings:

tà [沓] **1** again and again **2** many **3** surname Ta

The gurgling noises of swift streams, like tones **repeated numerous times**, sound like *water speaking*.

---

317 益

This character with the definition:

benefit, advantage

Pinyin **yì** *and Frequency Rank* **649**

SIMP & TRAD   Contains **10 strokes** in the following order:

丶 丷 二 产 兯 苎 芐 谷 益 益

Contains these components:

□ water 水 (altered) 315, p. 81

■ vessel, container 皿 101, p. 32

With all these meanings & readings:

yì [益] **1** benefit **2** profit **3** advantage **4** beneficial **5** to increase **6** to add **7** all the more **8** surname Yì

A *vessel* of fresh *water* is an invaluable **benefit** to the parched traveler.

---

318 泉

This character with the definition:

spring, fountain

Pinyin **quán** *and Frequency Rank* **1641**

SIMP & TRAD   Contains **9 strokes** in the following order:

丿 亻 白 白 白 身 身 泉 泉

Contains these components:

□ white 白 225, p. 60

■ water 水 315, p. 81

With all these meanings & readings:

quán [泉] **1** fountain **2** spring **3** money (archaic)

White water is the image used for a clear mountain **spring**.

---

319 永

This character with the definition:

forever, always

Pinyin **yǒng** *and Frequency Rank* **842**

SIMP & TRAD   Contains **5 strokes** in the following order:

丶 丁 刀 水 永

Contains these components:

■ water 水 (altered) 315, p. 81

□ dab r 丶 176, p. 48

With all these meanings & readings:

yǒng [永] **1** forever **2** always **3** perpetual

A marooned desert traveler could live **forever** if he only has a *bit* of *water*.

---

320 求

This character with the definition:

request, entreat

Pinyin **qiú** *and Frequency Rank* **312**

SIMP & TRAD   Contains **7 strokes** in the following order:

一 十 寸 寸 求 求 求

Contains these components:

□ dab r 丶 176, p. 48

□ one 一 1, p. 10

■ water 水 (altered) 315, p. 81

With all these meanings & readings:

qiú [求] **1** to seek **2** to look for **3** to request **4** to demand **5** to beseech

After *one* gust of wind blew my hat into the *water*, my friend refused my **request** to turn his boat around to go back and retrieve it. Soon, my hat was only a white *dab* floating on the *water's* vast blue surface.

321

SIMP & TRAD

This character with the definition:

ball, sphere

Pinyin **qiú** *and Frequency Rank* **628**

Contains **11 strokes** in the following order:

一 二 于 王 玎 玎 玗 玮 玮 球 球

Contains these components:

king 王 15, p.12

request, entreat 求 320, p.81

With all these meanings & readings

qiú [球] **1** ball **2** sphere **3** m [個][gè], 场 [場][chǎng]

Whenever our *king* needs to make a decision, he *requests* that his psychic look into the 'Magic **Ball**' to find the answer for what he should do.

322

SIMP & TRAD

This character with the definition:

faction, clique

Pinyin **pài** *and Frequency Rank* **532**

Contains **9 strokes** in the following order:

丶 丿 氵 汀 沪 浐 派 派 派

Contains these components:

water r 氵 314, p.80

water 水 (altered) 315, p.81

With all these meanings & readings

pài [派] **1** clique **2** school **3** group **4** faction **5** to dispatch **6** to send **7** to assign **8** to appoint **9** pi (Greek letter π) **10** the circular ratio pi = 3.1415926...

This character is composed of the '*water*' component written in two different ways, perhaps symbolizing a group of people splitting into two different **factions**.

323

SIMP & TRAD

This character with the definition:

carry, hold

Pinyin **chéng** *and Frequency Rank* **639**

Contains **8 strokes** in the following order:

フ 了 孑 承 承 承 承 承

Contains these components:

water 水 (altered) 315, p.81

son, child 子 (altered) 24, p.15

two 二 (altered) 2, p.10

With all these meanings & readings

chéng [承] **1** to bear **2** to carry **3** to hold **4** to continue **5** to undertake **6** to take charge **7** owing to **8** due to **9** to receive

When I am in the *water*, I can **hold** *two children* in my arms at once because they are more buoyant in *water*.

324

錄
TRAD SIMPLIFIED

This character with the definition:

record, write down

Pinyin **lù** *and Frequency Rank* **919**

Contains **8 strokes** in the following order:

フ ヨ ヨ 寻 寻 寻 录 录

Contains these components:

boar's head r ⺕ (altered) 30, p.16

water 水 (altered) 315, p.81

With all these meanings & readings

lù [錄] **1** diary **2** record **3** to hit **4** to copy **5** surname Lu

The ancients wasted nothing! They steeped a *boar's head* in *water* for several weeks to create an ink that didn't fade. Moreover, they removed bristles from the skin and used these 'pens' to **record** tribal history.

325

剝
TRAD SIMPLIFIED

This character with the definition:

to peel, shell, skin

Pinyin **bāo** *and Frequency Rank* **1959**

Contains **10 strokes** in the following order:

フ ヨ ヨ 寻 寻 寻 录 录 剥 剥

Contains these components:

record, write down 录 324, p.82

knife r 刂 169, p.46

With all these meanings & readings

bāo [剝] **1** to peel **2** to skin **3** to shell **4** to shuck
bō [剝] **1** to peel **2** to skin **3** to flay **4** to shuck

In medieval times, parchment was too valuable to discard after a single use. Instead, scribes would **peel** with a *knife* what had been *written down* to create new space to write on.

326

This character with the definition:

belong to

Pinyin **lì** *and Frequency Rank* **1801**

Contains these components:

▬ boar's head r ⸺ (altered) 30, p.16
▬ water 水 (altered) 315, p.81

With all these meanings & readings:

lì [隶] **1** attached to **2** scribe

SIMPLIFIED   Contains **8 strokes** in the following order:

The face of a *boar* **belongs to** the *boar*, but (being only a *boar*) he can only see it by glimpsing his *altered* reflection in the *water*.

327

江

This character with the definition:

river, Yangtze

Pinyin **jiāng** *and Frequency Rank* **577**

Contains these components:

▬ water r 氵 314, p.80
▬ labor, work 工 12, p.12

With all these meanings & readings:

jiāng [江] **1** river **2** surname Jiang **3** m 条[條][tiáo], 道[dào]

SIMP & TRAD   Contains **6 strokes** in the following order:

丶 丶 氵 汀 江 江

A good **river** system helps a civilization accomplish *work*—transport goods, maintain communications, move people, and so on. It's no wonder that the learned scribes early combined the components of *water* and *labor* to form this character for **river**. Nowadays, you may see '**Yangtze**' spelled according to pinyin rules as '**Yangzi**', for traditional 揚子 or simplified 扬子, Yángzǐ.

328

汪

This character with the definition:

expanse of water

Pinyin **wāng** *and Frequency Rank* **1876**

Contains these components:

▬ water r 氵 314, p.80
▬ king 王 15, p.12

With all these meanings & readings:

wāng [汪] **1** expanse of water **2** ooze **3** surname Wang

SIMP & TRAD   Contains **7 strokes** in the following order:

A large **expanse of water** surrounding the king's palace impressed ancient scribes as nature's expression of a *king* of *waters*.

329

油

This character with the definition:

oil

Pinyin **yóu** *and Frequency Rank* **948**

Contains these components:

▬ water r 氵 314, p.80
▬ reason, by means of 由 58, p.22

With all these meanings & readings:

yóu [油] **1** oil **2** sly

SIMP & TRAD   Contains **8 strokes** in the following order:

Using very light **oil**, near the consistency of *water*, is the *reason* we can do things like quiet noisy hinges.

330

河

This character with the definition:

river*

Pinyin **hé** *and Frequency Rank* **574**

Contains these components:

▬ water r 氵 314, p.80
▬ can, may 可 60, p.23

With all these meanings & readings:

hé [河] **1** river **2** m 条[條][tiáo], 道[dào]

SIMP & TRAD   Contains **8 strokes** in the following order:

One benefit of a **river** with its fast-flowing *water* is that it *can* help develop so many activities that provide recreation and productivity—such as sailing, fishing, water power, irrigation.

331

SIMP & TRAD

This character with the definition:

hole, cavity

Pinyin **dòng** *and Frequency Rank* **1015**

Contains **9 strokes** in the following order:

丶 丶 氵 氵 汩 洞 洞 洞 洞

Contains these components:

■ water r 氵 314, p. 80
■ same, similar 同 116, p. 35

With all these meanings & readings

dòng [洞] **1** cave **2** hole **3** ze (unambiguous spoken form whe spelling out numbers) **4** m 个 [個][gè]

Drop by drop, *water* has the *same* effect on any stone surface; it eventually produces a **cavity** on it.

332

SIMP & TRAD

This character with the definition:

pool, pond

Pinyin **chí** *and Frequency Rank* **1709**

Contains **6 strokes** in the following order:

丶 丶 氵 汋 沝 池

Contains these components:

■ water r 氵 314, p. 80
■ also, too* 也 132, p. 38

With all these meanings & readings

chí [池] **1** surname Chi
chí [池] **1** pond **2** reservoir

What kind of body of *water* supports this odd-shaped vessel with a curved bottom, tall mast, and other things on the deck? The 'also' element helps us visualize a small boat on a **pond**.

333

SIMP & TRAD

This character with the definition:

confuse, mix up

Pinyin **hùn** *and Frequency Rank* **1137**

Contains **11 strokes** in the following order:

丶 丶 氵 氵 汩 沪 沪 混 混 混 混

Contains these components:

■ water r 氵 314, p. 80
■ elder brother** 昆 129, p. 37

With all these meanings & readings

hún [混] **1** confused **2** dirty **3** to mix **4** muddy **5** also wri ten 浑 [渾]
hùn [混] **1** to mix **2** to mingle **3** muddled **4** to drift alor **5** to muddle along **6** to pass for **7** to get along with sb **8** thoughtless **9** reckless

It's too **confusing** to tell which *brother* is the *elder* when the two boys are thrashing around in the *water*, with their hair plastered all over their faces.

334

SIMP & TRAD

This character with the definition:

vast, grand

Pinyin **hào** *and Frequency Rank* **1864**

Contains **10 strokes** in the following order:

丶 丶 氵 氵 汇 汁 浩 浩 浩 浩

Contains these components:

■ water r 氵 314, p. 80
■ tell 告 234, p. 62

With all these meanings & readings

hào [浩] **1** grand **2** vast (water

The lake was a **vast** but shallow body of *water*. Any large-hulled boat required special equipment to *tell* how deep the *water* level was at any location before they could move towards it.

Unit 16

335

注

注
註
TRAD SIMPLIFIED

This character with the definition:

pour

Pinyin **zhù** *and Frequency Rank* **492**

Contains **8 strokes** in the following order:

丶 丶 氵 汀 注 注 注 注

Contains these components:

water r 氵 314, p.80

master 主 179, p.49

With all these meanings & readings:

zhù [注] **1** to inject **2** to pour into **3** to concentrate **4** to pay attention **5** to note **6** to comment on **7** to record **8** to register **9** to annotate
zhù [註] **1** annotate

Pouring *water* with what appears to be effortless grace and style is harder than it looks. The successful bartender rightly deserves his title as *master* of serving drinks.

336

茫

SIMP & TRAD

This character with the definition:

boundless, vast

Pinyin **máng** *and Frequency Rank* **1951**

Contains **9 strokes** in the following order:

一 十 艹 艹 艹 艹 茫 茫 茫

Contains these components:

water r 氵 314, p.80

spike, sharp point 芒 (altered) 260, p.68

With all these meanings & readings:

máng [茫] **1** vague **2** vast

The ocean is **vast** and **boundless**—a discouraging thought for the shipwrecked sailor who is floating on calm *waters*, until his thirst pierces him like a *sharp spike*.

337

酒

SIMP & TRAD

This character with the definition:

wine, liquor

Pinyin **jiǔ** *and Frequency Rank* **797**

Contains **10 strokes** in the following order:

丶 丶 氵 汀 汀 沂 酒 酒 酒 酒

Contains these components:

water r 氵 314, p.80

five to seven pm 酉 302, p.77

With all these meanings & readings:

jiǔ [酒] **1** wine (especially rice wine) **2** liquor **3** spirits **4** alcoholic beverage **5** m 杯[bēi], 瓶[píng], 罐[guàn], 桶[tǒng], 缸[gāng]

My work days are long and draining. The **wine** I drink by early evening, say from *five to seven pm*, is as necessary to me as *water* to a stranded traveler.

338

洗

SIMP & TRAD

This character with the definition:

wash, bathe

Pinyin **xǐ** *and Frequency Rank* **1247**

Contains **9 strokes** in the following order:

丶 丶 氵 汀 汇 汁 泮 洗 洗

Contains these components:

water r 氵 314, p.80

first 先 291, p.75

With all these meanings & readings:

xǐ [洗] **1** to wash **2** to bathe

You use *water* to **wash** and **bathe** the *first* thing in the morning.

339

泄

洩
TRAD SIMPLIFIED

This character with the definition:

drain, vent, leak

Pinyin **xiè** *and Frequency Rank* **2010**

Contains **8 strokes** in the following order:

丶 丶 氵 一 汁 泄 泄 泄

Contains these components:

water r 氵 314, p.80

generation 世 134, p.38

With all these meanings & readings:

xiè [泄] **1** to leak (of water or gas) **2** to drip **3** to drain **4** to discharge **5** to leak out **6** to divulge (secrets) **7** to give vent (to anger, spite etc) **8** to disperse **9** to reduce

It looks like *water* flows through this complex mechanism on the right, one of our *generation's* most impressive inventions. Even so, it's so complicated that the *water* will **leak out** for sure.

340

溫
TRAD SIMPLIFIED

This character with the definition:

lukewarm, to warm up

Pinyin **wēn** *and Frequency Rank* **867**

Contains **12 strokes** in the following order:

丶 丶 氵 氵 沪 沪 沪 沪 渭 渭 温 温 温

Contains these components:

■ water r 氵 314, p. 80

■ day, sun 日 64, p. 24

■ vessel, container 皿 101, p. 32

With all these meanings & reading

wēn [溫] **1** warm **2** lukewarm **3** temperature **4** to warm up **5** mild **6** soft **7** tender **8** to review **9** to revise **10** epidem **11** surname Wen

Cold *water* in a *dish* sitting under the summer *sun* all day will be **warmed up** by evening.

341

淚
TRAD SIMPLIFIED

This character with the definition:

tears

Pinyin **lèi** *and Frequency Rank* **1271**

Contains **8 strokes** in the following order:

丶 丶 氵 氵 沪 沪 泪 泪

Contains these components:

■ water r 氵 314, p. 80

■ eye 目 75, p. 26

With all these meanings & reading

lèi [淚] **1** tears

Tears are *water* that flows from the *eyes*.

342

潔
TRAD SIMPLIFIED

洁

This character with the definition:

clean

Pinyin **jié** *and Frequency Rank* **1531**

Contains **9 strokes** in the following order:

丶 丶 氵 氵 一 汁 注 洁 洁 洁

Contains these components:

■ water r 氵 314, p. 80

■ lucky 吉 47, p. 20

With all these meanings & reading

jié [潔] **1** clean

Water has feelings about what it is used for. It doesn't care to water plants or to flush toilets, but it feels *lucky* when people use it to **clean** with.

343

SIMP & TRAD

This character with the definition:

sweat

Pinyin **hàn** *and Frequency Rank* **1490**

Contains **6 strokes** in the following order:

丶 丶 氵 氵 汗 汗

Contains these components:

■ water r 氵 314, p. 80

■ dry 干 17, p. 13

With all these meanings & reading

hàn [汗] **1** perspiration **2** swea **3** m 滴[dī], 头[頭][tóu], 身[shē **4** Khan (Persian or Mongol kir or emperor) **5** Khan (name) **6** to be speechless (out of help lessness, embarrassment, etc.) (Internet slang used as an inter jection)

Sweat is *water* released from our skin and, as it *dries*, keeps you cool.

344

匯
匯
彙
TRAD SIMPLIFIED

汇

This character with the definition:

gather together

Pinyin **huì** *and Frequency Rank* **1187**

Contains **5 strokes** in the following order:

丶 丶 氵 氵 汇

Contains these components:

■ water r 氵 314, p. 80

■ basket, box r 匚 152, p. 42

With all these meanings & reading

huì [匯] **1** remit **2** to converge (of rivers) **3** to exchange **huì** [彙] **1** class **2** collection

There are some chips of wood in the bottom of the basket that are so small they fit between the basket reeds and are hard to **gather together**. But all I need to do is to pour *water* into the *basket*. The water floats the chips to the surface, where they will clump together for easy **gathering**.

345

润

润 TRAD SIMPLIFIED

This character with the definition:

moist, soft

Pinyin **rùn** *and Frequency Rank* **1369**

Contains **10 strokes** in the following order:

丶 丶 氵 氵 汀 汩 润 润 润 润

Contains these components:

☐ water r 氵 314, p. 80
☐ intercalary month 闰 247, p. 65

With all these meanings & readings:

rùn [润] **1** smooth **2** moist

The ancients believed that the *intercalary months*, the extra months added to the lunar calendar to keep the length of the year more-or-less constant, were particularly auspicious. For farmers, this meant a promise of additional *water* to keep their crops **moist** and healthy.

346

津

SIMP & TRAD

This character with the definition:

ferry crossing

Pinyin **jīn** *and Frequency Rank* **1353**

Contains **9 strokes** in the following order:

丶 丶 氵 汀 沪 浄 津 津 津

Contains these components:

☐ water r 氵 314, p. 80
☐ writing instrument, pen 聿 31, p. 16

With all these meanings & readings:

jīn [津] **1** saliva **2** sweat **3** a ferry crossing **4** a ford (river crossing) **5** abbr for Tianjin 天津

People put **ferry crossings** where the river is narrowest. Here's one crossing so convenient that it takes only a giant *pen* floating on the calm *waters* to **ferry** people across. Of course, pens are messy, but better 'ink' than 'sink'.

347

范

範 TRAD SIMPLIFIED

This character with the definition:

pattern, model, example

Pinyin **fàn** *and Frequency Rank* **705**

Contains **8 strokes** in the following order:

一 艹 艹 艹 艻 艻 芀 范

Contains these components:

☐ grass r 艹 87, p. 29
☐ water r 氵 314, p. 80
☐ single ear r 卩 (altered) 165, p. 46

With all these meanings & readings:

fàn [范] **1** pattern **2** model **3** example
fàn [範] **1** surname Fan

The famous *one-eared* painter Vincent van Gogh sliced one ear off in a fit of pique. And yet, even today, his techniques continue to inspire; he is a powerful role **model**. His colored areas, in which bits of colored *grass* swirls in *watery* backgrounds, radiate energy that others try to replicate.

348

冫

This component has the meaning:

ice r

COMPONENT

Think of these two strokes as chips of **ice** flying into the air as you struggle to scrape off the sheet of **ice** from your car windshield.

349

冰

SIMP & TRAD

This character with the definition:

ice

Pinyin **bīng** *and Frequency Rank* **1070**

Contains **6 strokes** in the following order:

丶 冫 冫 汀 沙 冰 冰

Contains these components:

☐ ice r 冫 348, p. 87
☐ water 水 315, p. 81

With all these meanings & readings:

bīng [冰] **1** ice **2** m 块 [塊][kuài] **3** see also 冫 [冫][bīng]

If enough *ice* is added to *water*, the *water* will convert to **ice**.

350

冲
TRAD SIMPLIFIED

This character with the definition:

rinse, flush, wash away

Pinyin **chōng** *and Frequency Rank* **702**

Contains **6 strokes** in the following order:

丶 冫 氵 氵 冲 冲

Contains these components:

■ ice r 冫 348, p.87
■ middle 中 38, p.18

With all these meanings & readings:

chōng [冲] **1** (of water) to dash against **2** to mix with water **3** to infuse **4** to rinse **5** to flush **6** to develop (a film) **7** rise in the air **8** to clash **9** to collide with
chōng [衝] **1** thoroughfare **2** to go straight ahead **3** to rush **4** to clash
chòng [衝] **1** powerful **2** vigorous **3** pungent **4** towards **5** in view of

Water, good soap, and hard scrubbing can **wash away** stains that have penetrated deep into the *middle* of a fabric. In this character, we've scrubbed so hard that we've deleted a dot on the 'water r' component (氵, panel 314). With only two dots, water becomes '*ice*'.

351

况
TRAD SIMPLIFIED

This character with the definition:

situation

Pinyin **kuàng** *and Frequency Rank* **419**

Contains **7 strokes** in the following order:

丶 冫 氵 氵 氵 汜 况

Contains these components:

■ ice r 冫 348, p.87
■ elder brother* 兄 293, p.75

With all these meanings & readings:

kuàng [況] **1** moreover **2** situation

My *elder brother* was in a difficult **situation** because he broke through the *ice* on a pond, and drifted away from the water's edge before he could come back up through the hole.

352

This component has the meaning:

speech r

COMPONENT

Chinese scribes have derived this component from the character for 'speech', panel 256, so when we use it as an element in another character, it will appear in this form.

353

计
TRAD SIMPLIFIED

This character with the definition:

compute, calculate

Pinyin **jì** *and Frequency Rank* **251**

Contains **4 strokes** in the following order:

丶 讠 讠 计

Contains these components:

■ speech r 讠 352, p.88
■ ten 十 7, p.11

With all these meanings & readings:

jì [計] **1** to calculate **2** to compute **3** to count **4** reckon **5** ruse **6** to plan **7** surname Ji

Making a *speech* to help you count up to *ten* is a primitive way to **calculate**.

354

订
TRAD SIMPLIFIED

This character with the definition:

draw up, agree on

Pinyin **dìng** *and Frequency Rank* **1176**

Contains **4 strokes** in the following order:

丶 讠 订 订

Contains these components:

■ speech r 讠 352, p.88
■ fourth (in a series) 丁 19, p.13

With all these meanings & readings:

dìng [訂] **1** to agree **2** to conclude **3** to draw up **4** to subscribe to (a newspaper etc) **5** to order

Imagine the *'fourth'* element on the right as a table on which two opponents will **draw up** a truce and give a *speech* to affirm that he **agrees on** the terms to end hostilities.

355

语

語
TRAD   SIMPLIFIED

This character with the definition:

language

Pinyin **yǔ** *and Frequency Rank* **493**

Contains **9 strokes** in the following order:

` 讠 讠 訮 评 语 语 语 语

Contains these components:

▪ speech r 讠 352, p. 88

▪ me 吾 46, p. 20

With all these meanings & readings:

yǔ [语] **1** dialect **2** language **3** speech

yù [語] **1** to tell to

Speak to *me* in *my* own native **language** if you want *me* to understand you.

356

词

詞
TRAD   SIMPLIFIED

This character with the definition:

word, term

Pinyin **cí** *and Frequency Rank* **959**

Contains **7 strokes** in the following order:

` 讠 订 词 词 词 词

Contains these components:

▪ speech r 讠 352, p. 88

▪ company 司 106, p. 33

With all these meanings & readings:

cí [词] **1** works **2** phrases **3** classical Chinese poem **4** word **5** diction **6** m 组[組][zǔ], 个 [個][gè]

A *company speech* often includes special **words** and **terms** that only its employees and other insiders understand.

357

许

許
TRAD   SIMPLIFIED

This character with the definition:

praise, commend

Pinyin **xǔ** *and Frequency Rank* **263**

Contains **6 strokes** in the following order:

` 讠 订 计 许 许

Contains these components:

▪ speech r 讠 352, p. 88

▪ noonish 午 180, p. 49

With all these meanings & readings:

xǔ [許] **1** surname Xu

xǔ [許] **1** to allow **2** to permit **3** to praise **4** somewhat **5** perhaps

Our boss plans to give a company-wide *speech around noon-time* so that he can personally **praise** and award all employees who have perfect attendance records.

358

证

證
TRAD   SIMPLIFIED

This character with the definition:

evidence

Pinyin **zhèng** *and Frequency Rank* **373**

Contains **7 strokes** in the following order:

` 讠 讠 订 讵 证 证

Contains these components:

▪ speech r 讠 352, p. 88

▪ to correct, rectify 正 193, p. 52

With all these meanings & readings:

zhèng [證] **1** certificate **2** proof **3** to prove **4** to demonstrate **5** to confirm

In courtroom trials, a witness's *speech* can go a long way toward *correcting* faulty impressions and nothing persuades a jury as effectively as solid **evidence**.

359

讨

討
TRAD   SIMPLIFIED

This character with the definition:

discourse, discuss

Pinyin **tǎo** *and Frequency Rank* **833**

Contains **5 strokes** in the following order:

` 讠 订 计 讨

Contains these components:

▪ speech r 讠 352, p. 88

▪ inch 寸 216, p. 58

With all these meanings & readings:

tǎo [討] **1** to demand **2** to ask for **3** to send punitive expedition against **4** to marry (of man) **5** to provoke **6** to attract attention **7** to discuss

The scientist was willing to enter **discourse** about the life cycles of *inch*worms during one of his *speeches* at the annual conference of *inch*-size lifeforms.

Unit 17

360

詩
TRAD   SIMPLIFIED

This character with the definition:

poem, poetry

Pinyin **shī** *and Frequency Rank* **906**

Contains **8 strokes** in the following order:

丶 讠 讠 讠⁺ 讠⁺ 诗 诗

Contains these components:

■ speech r 讠 352, p. 88
■ Buddhist temple 寺 220, p. 59

With all these meanings & readings

shī [詩] **1** poem **2** m 首[shǒu]
3 poetry **4** verse **5** abbr for
Book of Songs 诗经[詩經][shī
jīng]

Buddhist temples are so special that using ordinary *speech* to describe them is inadequate. Instead, devotees compose inspired **poetry**.

361

記
TRAD   SIMPLIFIED

This character with the definition:

remember

Pinyin **jì** *and Frequency Rank* **306**

Contains **5 strokes** in the following order:

丶 讠 讠⁺ 讠⁺ 记

Contains these components:

■ speech r 讠 352, p. 88
■ self* 己 135, p. 39

With all these meanings & readings

jì [記] **1** to remember **2** to note
3 mark **4** sign **5** to record

The best way to **remember** a list of items is by making a 'mental *speech*' for one*self* that repeats the items over and over in one's brain.

362

讓
TRAD   SIMPLIFIED

This character with the definition:

give way, yield

Pinyin **ràng** *and Frequency Rank* **339**

Contains **5 strokes** in the following order:

丶 讠 讠⁺ 讠⁺ 让

Contains these components:

■ speech r 讠 352, p. 88
■ on 上 189, p. 52

With all these meanings & readings

ràng [讓] **1** to yield **2** to permit
3 to let sb do sth **4** to have sb
do sth

In a heated discussion, you initially might disagree with a friend. But after a short, impassioned *speech* convinces you that he's *on* target, you **yield** to the force of his argument.

363

謹
TRAD   SIMPLIFIED

This character with the definition:

careful, cautious

Pinyin **jǐn** *and Frequency Rank* **1917**

Contains **13 strokes** in the following order:

丶 讠 讠⁺ 讠⁺ 讲 讲 讲 谨 谨 谨 谨 谨 谨

Contains these components:

■ speech r 讠 352, p. 88
□ animal hide 革 98, p. 31
■ earth, soil 土 9, p. 11

With all these meanings & readings

jǐn [謹] **1** cautious

Chinese people behaved **carefully** and **cautiously** during the Cultural Revolution. One wrong or misunderstood *speech* might have forced them to *hide* (different word, but the same sound as in '*animal hide*') in the *earth* to escape the fury of the Red Guards!

364

勹

wrap r

COMPONENT

And contains these subcomponents:
■ smooth cover r ⌒ (altered)
268, p. 69

The latch at the upper left of the radical has come undone; lay your things inside the strap while you fix the latch—now it's a **wrap**!

365

勺
TRAD   SIMPLIFIED

This character with the definition:

evenly divided

Pinyin **yún** *and Frequency Rank* **2692**

Contains **4 strokes** in the following order:

Contains these components:

■ wrap r 勹 364, p.90
■ two 二 2, p.10

With all these meanings & readings:

yún [勻] **1** even **2** well-distributed **3** uniform **4** to distribute evenly **5** to share

The bundle was **evenly divided** into *two* parts and each part was *wrapped* up as a single unit.

366

This character with the definition:

equal, even

Pinyin **jūn** *and Frequency Rank* **903**

SIMP & TRAD   Contains **7 strokes** in the following order:

Contains these components:

 earth, soil 土 9, p.11
 evenly divided 勻 365, p.91

With all these meanings & readings:

jūn [均] **1** equal **2** even **3** all **4** uniform

If you plant seeds in the *soil* in *evenly divided* sections, then the crops in each section will grow to approximately **equal** heights.

367

This character with the definition:

period of ten days, years

Pinyin **xún** *and Frequency Rank* **2332**

SIMP & TRAD   Contains **6 strokes** in the following order:

Contains these components:

■ wrap r 勹 364, p.90
■ day, sun 日 64, p.24

With all these meanings & readings:

xún [旬] **1** ten days **2** ten years **3** full period

'*Sun*' is a metaphor for a period of time, often a day. Here, the **period of time—either ten days or ten year—**is *wrapped up* in one character.

368

詢
TRAD   SIMPLIFIED

This character with the definition:

inquire

Pinyin **xún** *and Frequency Rank* **1617**

Contains **8 strokes** in the following order:

Contains these components:

 speech r 讠 352, p.88
 period of ten days, years 旬 367, p.91

With all these meanings & readings:

xún [詢] **1** inquire

My neighbor stopped me and pretended to **inquire** about the weather, but, in actuality, really wanted to deliver an annoying *speech* about politics. It was so boring that it seemed to last *ten days*!

369

This character with the definition:

sentence

Pinyin **jù** *and Frequency Rank* **707**

SIMP & TRAD   Contains **5 strokes** in the following order:

Contains these components:

 wrap r 勹 364, p.90
 mouth 口 37, p.17

With all these meanings & readings:

jù [句] **1** sentence **2** clause **3** phrase **4** m for phrases or lines of verse

Your *mouth* is used to producing words, and the *mouth* element here represents a sequence of words. If you *wrap* them up grammatically, you will have a complete **sentence**.

370

This character with the definition:

thoughtless, careless

Pinyin **gǒu**   and Frequency Rank **2886**

SIMP & TRAD   Contains **8 strokes** in the following order:

一 十 艹 艹 芍 芍 苟 苟

Contains these components:

grass r 艹 87, p. 29

sentence 句 369, p. 91

With all these meanings & reading

gǒu [苟] **1** surname Gou   **2** if indeed   **3** thoughtless

My son received a *sentence* of thirty hours of 'community service' after a policeman observed his **careless** act of dropping a candy-wrapper on the *grass* in the town park.

371

This character with the definition:

spoon

Pinyin **sháo**   and Frequency Rank **3275**

SIMP & TRAD   Contains **3 strokes** in the following order:

丿 勹 勺

Contains these components:

wrap r 勹 364, p. 90

dab r 丶 176, p. 48

With all these meanings & reading

sháo [勺] **1** spoon   **2** m 把[bǎ]

Think of the '*wrapper*' as a **spoon**, with the latch as a distorted handle, and an exaggerated bowl so small that it could only contain a single *drop* of Grandma's chicken soup.

372

This character with the definition:

of

Pinyin **de**   and Frequency Rank **1**

SIMP & TRAD   Contains **8 strokes** in the following order:

丿 亻 白 白 白 白 的 的

Contains these components:

white 白 225, p. 60

spoon 勺 371, p. 92

With all these meanings & reading

de [的] **1** of   **2** structural parti used before a noun, linking it preceding possessive or descriptive attributive
dí [的] **1** really and truly
dì [的] **1** aim   **2** clear

'**Of**' appears in quotes, because that brief definition grossly simplifies the role that 的 plays in Chinese grammar. This glyph appears more frequently than any other character, as signified by its rank of 1. • Chinese people themselves often refer to this 'de' as the bái sháo (*white spoon*) 'de'—believe it or not, there are a few other "de"s in the language and each plays a different grammatical role.

373

This character with the definition:

mortar

Pinyin **jiù**   and Frequency Rank **4066**

SIMP & TRAD   Contains **6 strokes** in the following order:

丿 亻 亻 臼 臼 臼

Contains these components:

three 三 (altered) 3, p. 10

scepter c 丨 5, p. 10

spoon 勺 (altered) 371, p. 92

With all these meanings & reading

jiù [臼] **1** mortar

When the Crown Prince reached the age of *three*, he was gifted with a silver *spoon* embedded in **mortar** that resembled the Royal *Scepter* he would carry one day.

374

This character with the definition:

mouse, rat

Pinyin **shǔ**   and Frequency Rank **1693**

SIMP & TRAD   Contains **13 strokes** in the following order:

丿 亻 亻 臼 臼 白 臼 臼 臼 鼠 鼠 鼠 鼠

Contains these components:

mortar 臼 373, p. 92

compared with 比 (altered) 127, p. 37

dab r (×2) 丶 176, p. 48

mineshaft c ㄥ (altered) 122, p. 36

With all these meanings & reading

shǔ [鼠] **1** rat   **2** mouse   **3** m 只[隻][zhi]

After I trapped a **mouse** in my house last week, my house still felt like a place of danger, a *mineshaft*, so I decided it would be easier to buy a cat that hunts mice *compared with* trying to find *tiny* **mouse** holes and cover them with *mortar*.

375

与

與
TRAD   SIMPLIFIED

This character with the definition:

offer, present

Pinyin **yǔ** *and Frequency Rank* **108**

Contains **3 strokes** in the following order:

一 与 与

Contains these components:

 spoon 勹 (altered) 371, p. 92
一 one 一 1, p. 10

With all these meanings & readings:

yú [與] **1** (same as 欤 [歟], final particle expression doubt or surprise, similar to 吗 or 呢)
yǔ [與] **1** and   **2** to give   **3** together with
yù [與] **1** take part in

When I ask my young children to raise a *spoon*ful of vegetables and **offer** it to *one* another, they forget that they are eating a food they dislike.

376

举

舉
TRAD   SIMPLIFIED

This character with the definition:

hold up, raise

Pinyin **jǔ** *and Frequency Rank* **586**

Contains **9 strokes** in the following order:

丶 丶 ⺍ ⺍ 产 兴 举 举 举

Contains these components:

 offer, present 与 375, p. 93
hand 手 (altered) 21, p. 14

With all these meanings & readings:

jǔ [舉] **1** to lift   **2** to hold up   **3** to cite   **4** to enumerate   **5** to act   **6** to raise   **7** to choose   **8** to elect

When using your *hand* to *present* an award, you often **raise** your *hand* to do it.

377

誉

譽
TRAD   SIMPLIFIED

This character with the definition:

reputation, fame

Pinyin **yù** *and Frequency Rank* **1676**

Contains **13 strokes** in the following order:

丶 丶 ⺍ ⺍ 产 兴 兴 誉 誉 誉 誉 誉 誉

Contains these components:

 offer, present 与 (altered) 375, p. 93
speech 言 256, p. 67

With all these meanings & readings:

yù [譽] **1** reputation

Offering to deliver a *speech* is a great way to enhance your **reputation**.

378

写

寫
TRAD   SIMPLIFIED

This character with the definition:

write

Pinyin **xiě** *and Frequency Rank* **448**

Contains **5 strokes** in the following order:

丶 冖 冖 写 写

Contains these components:

smooth cover r 冖 268, p. 69
offer, present 与 375, p. 93

With all these meanings & readings:

xiě [寫] **1** to write

The constant rain inspired me to **write** you a tender note. Before I *present* it to you, I will *cover* it to protect it from the downpour.

379

丐

SIMP & TRAD

This character with the definition:

beg

Pinyin **gài** *and Frequency Rank* **2606**

Contains **4 strokes** in the following order:

一 丅 丆 丐

Contains these components:

under 下 199, p. 54
wrap r 勹 364, p. 90

With all these meanings & readings:

gài [丐] **1** beg for alms   **2** beggar

People who **beg** are often quite successful, though you'd never know it because they keep their gains *wrapped* securely *under* layers of tattered clothes.

380

This character with the definition:

how, why, when

Pinyin **hé** *and Frequency Rank* **5256**

Contains these components:

☐ speak 曰 67, p. 24
▬ beg 丐 (altered) 379, p. 93

With all these meanings & readings:

hé [曷] **1** why **2** how **3** when **4** what **5** where

SIMP & TRAD   Contains **9 strokes** in the following order:

丶 口 曰 日 尸 早 另 易 曷

The *speech* of *beggars* can be wildly creative; elaborate stories about **how, why,** and **when** they became beggars flow naturally out of their mouths.
• We'll use this element to represent **a number of causes or sources**.

381

This character with the definition:

drink

Pinyin **hē** *and Frequency Rank* **983**

Contains these components:

▮ mouth 口 37, p. 17
▬ how, why, when 曷 380, p. 94

With all these meanings & readings:

hē [喝] **1** to drink **2** (interj.) My goodness!
hè [喝] **1** shout applause

SIMP & TRAD   Contains **12 strokes** in the following order:

丶 口 口 口` 口ㄱ 口ㅋ 呷 呷 喝 喝 喝 喝

I need a **drink**, and I don't care *how* I get it. I don't know *why* but I can't wait to feel it in my *mouth*.

382

This character with the definition:

kudzu vine

Pinyin **gé** *and Frequency Rank* **1919**

Contains these components:

☐ grass r 艹 87, p. 29
▬ how, why, when 曷 380, p. 94

With all these meanings & readings:

gé [葛] **1** surname Ge
gé [葛] **1** hemp cloth **2** arrowroot **3** Pueraria lobata (lobed kudzu vine (a legume with starchy roots used in traditional Chinese medicine)

SIMP & TRAD   Contains **12 strokes** in the following order:

一 十 艹 艹 芐 苔 苔 苜 苜 葛 葛 葛 葛

Kudzu is the voracious *grass*-like vine that grew so rapidly that it devoured the native plants of the American South. Experts still wrestle with the *how, why,* and *when* of its conquest.

383

This character with the definition:

tear off, take off

Pinyin **jiē** *and Frequency Rank* **1666**

Contains these components:

▮ hand r 扌 25, p. 15
▮ how, why, when 曷 380, p. 94

With all these meanings & readings:

jiē [揭] **1** lift off (a cover) **2** divulge

SIMP & TRAD   Contains **12 strokes** in the following order:

一 十 扌 扌 护 护 护 护 捐 揭 揭 揭

The '*how, why, when*' component looks like an ornate bottle, and the 'sun' at the top is a cork stuffed in to keep the many ingredients from evaporating. But someone's *hand* is already on the cork, ready to **tear it off**.

384

This character with the definition:

thirsty

Pinyin **kě** *and Frequency Rank* **1972**

Contains these components:

▮ water r 氵 314, p. 80
▮ how, why, when 曷 380, p. 94

With all these meanings & readings:

kě [渴] **1** thirsty

SIMP & TRAD   Contains **12 strokes** in the following order:

丶 丶 氵 氵 沪 沪 沪 渇 渇 渇 渴 渴

The thought of ice cold *water* splish-splashing *all over the place* drives me mad with **thirst** as I stand stranded in the desert, contemplating *how, why, and when* I will be rescued.

Unit 18

385

SIMP & TRAD

This character with the definition:

wrap, bag

Pinyin **bāo** *and Frequency Rank* **454**

Contains **5 strokes** in the following order:

ノ 勹 匀 匇 包

Contains these components:

■ wrap r 勹 364, p. 90

■ self* 己 (altered) 135, p. 39

With all these meanings & readings:

bāo [包] **1** to cover **2** to wrap **3** to hold **4** to include **5** to take charge of **6** package **7** wrapper **8** container **9** bag **10** to hold or embrace **11** bundle **12** packet **13** to contract (to or for) **14** surname Bao **15** m 个[個][gè], 只[隻][zhi]

Wrapping a warm winter cloak tightly tightly around one*self* demonstrates the concept of **wrapping**.

386

SIMP & TRAD

This character with the definition:

hold, carry (in arms)

Pinyin **bào** *and Frequency Rank* **1122**

Contains **8 strokes** in the following order:

一 十 扌 扌 扚 抅 抱 抱

Contains these components:

■ hand r 扌 25, p. 15

■ wrap, bag 包 385, p. 95

With all these meanings & readings:

bào [抱] **1** to hold **2** to carry (in one's arms) **3** to hug or embrace **4** surround **5** cherish

I bought too many items and could not carry them all by *hand* in a *bag*; the store had to *wrap* them in a bundle so that I could **carry** out all the items **in my arms**.

387

SIMP & TRAD

This character with the definition:

blister, bubble

Pinyin **pào** *and Frequency Rank* **2000**

Contains **8 strokes** in the following order:

丶 冫 氵 氵 汋 泃 泡 泡

Contains these components:

■ water r 氵 314, p. 80

■ wrap, bag 包 385, p. 95

pāo [泡] **1** puffed **2** swollen **3** spongy **4** small lake (especially in place names) **5** m for urine or feces

pào [泡] **1** bubble **2** foam **3** blister (i.e. skin bubble) **4** to soak **5** to steep **6** to infuse **7** to dawdle **8** to shilly-shally **9** to hang about **10** to pick up (a girl) **11** to get off with (a sexual partner)

A **blister** looks like a **bubble** of *water wrapped* in your skin.

388

TRAD SIMPLIFIED

This character with the definition:

horse

Pinyin **mǎ** *and Frequency Rank* **276**

Contains **3 strokes** in the following order:

フ 马 马

Contains these components:

■ place of refuge c 丁 105, p. 33

■ wrap r 勹 (altered) 364, p. 90

■ one 一 1, p. 10

With all these meanings & readings:

mǎ [馬] **1** surname Ma **2** abbr for Malaysia 马来西亚[馬來~亞]

mǎ [馬] **1** horse **2** horse or cavalry piece in Chinese chess **3** knight in Western chess

In a romantic novel, the hero *wraps* his legs around the **horse** and rides like the wind to deliver his *one* true love to a *place of refuge*.

389

TRAD SIMPLIFIED

This character with the definition:

agate

Pinyin **mǎ** *and Frequency Rank* **1248**

Contains **7 strokes** in the following order:

一 二 干 王 珏 玛 玛

Contains these components:

■ jade 玉 (altered) 177, p. 48

■ horse 马 388, p. 95

With all these meanings & readings:

mǎ [瑪] **1** agate **2** cornelian

Agates are *jade*-like gemstones with flowing bands of color that resemble the mane of a *horse* at full gallop.

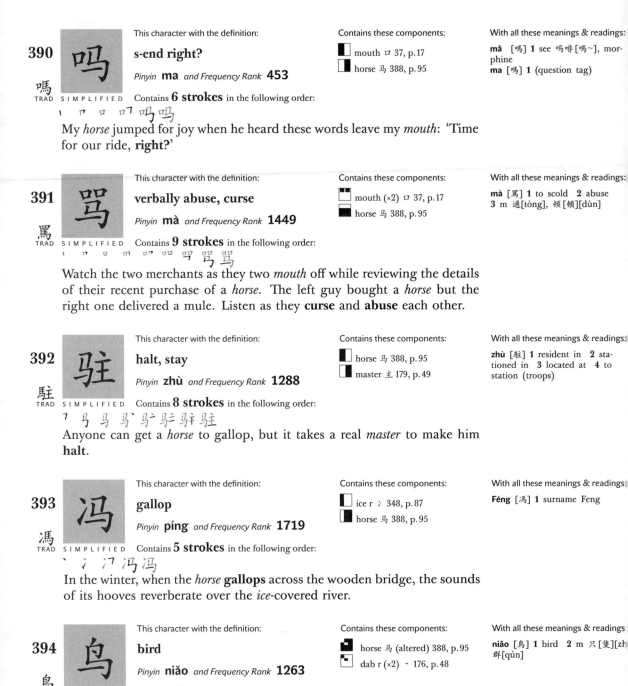

390

吗

嗎
TRAD   SIMPLIFIED

This character with the definition:

s-end right?

Pinyin **ma** *and Frequency Rank* **453**

Contains **6 strokes** in the following order:

丶 丨 口 口丨 吗 吗

Contains these components:

mouth 口 37, p.17

horse 马 388, p.95

With all these meanings & readings:

mǎ [吗] **1** see 吗啡[吗~], mor-
phine
ma [吗] **1** (question tag)

My *horse* jumped for joy when he heard these words leave my *mouth*: 'Time
for our ride, **right?**'

391

骂

罵
TRAD   SIMPLIFIED

This character with the definition:

verbally abuse, curse

Pinyin **mà** *and Frequency Rank* **1449**

Contains **9 strokes** in the following order:

丨 口 口 口 口广 口口 骂 骂 骂

Contains these components:

mouth (×2) 口 37, p.17

horse 马 388, p.95

With all these meanings & readings:

mà [罵] **1** to scold **2** abuse
3 m 通[tòng], 顿[頓][dùn]

Watch the two merchants as they two *mouth* off while reviewing the details
of their recent purchase of a *horse*. The left guy bought a *horse* but the
right one delivered a mule. Listen as they **curse** and **abuse** each other.

392

驻

駐
TRAD   SIMPLIFIED

This character with the definition:

halt, stay

Pinyin **zhù** *and Frequency Rank* **1288**

Contains **8 strokes** in the following order:

丁 马 马 马丶 马亠 驻 驻 驻

Contains these components:

horse 马 388, p.95

master 主 179, p.49

With all these meanings & readings:

zhù [駐] **1** resident in **2** stationed in **3** located at **4** to
station (troops)

Anyone can get a *horse* to gallop, but it takes a real *master* to make him
halt.

393

冯

馮
TRAD   SIMPLIFIED

This character with the definition:

gallop

Pinyin **píng** *and Frequency Rank* **1719**

Contains **5 strokes** in the following order:

丶 冫 冫丨 冯 冯

Contains these components:

ice r 冫 348, p.87

horse 马 388, p.95

With all these meanings & readings:

Féng [馮] **1** surname Feng

In the winter, when the *horse* **gallops** across the wooden bridge, the sounds
of its hooves reverberate over the *ice*-covered river.

394

鸟

鳥
TRAD   SIMPLIFIED

This character with the definition:

bird

Pinyin **niǎo** *and Frequency Rank* **1263**

Contains **5 strokes** in the following order:

丿 勹 勹 鸟 鸟

Contains these components:

horse 马 (altered) 388, p.95

dab r (×2) 丶 176, p.48

With all these meanings & readings

niǎo [鳥] **1** bird **2** m 只[隻][zh
群[qún]

Bird-like, flying *horses* feature in the folklore of many cultures; think of
winged Pegasus of Greek myth. The small *dabs* call attention to the bird's
beady eyes and decorative tufts of feathers.

395

岛

島
TRAD   SIMPLIFIED

This character with the definition:

island

Pinyin **dǎo** *and Frequency Rank* **798**

Contains **7 strokes** in the following order:

丿 勹 勺 鸟 鸟 岛 岛

Contains these components:

bird 鸟 (abbrev) 394, 96

mountain 山 4, p. 10

With all these meanings & readings:

dǎo [島] **1** island **2** m 个[個][gè], 座[zuò]

When scribes first designed this character, an **island** was recognized as the peak of an undersea *mountain* that only had *birds* for inhabitants.

396

鸣

鳴
TRAD   SIMPLIFIED

This character with the definition:

bird or animal cry

Pinyin **míng** *and Frequency Rank* **1680**

Contains **8 strokes** in the following order:

丨 口 口 口丿 口勹 口勺 鸣 鸣

Contains these components:

mouth 口 37, p. 17

bird 鸟 394, p. 96

With all these meanings & readings:

míng [鳴] **1** to cry (of birds)

A **bird call** is emitted through the *mouth* of a *bird*.

397

鸿

鴻
TRAD   SIMPLIFIED

This character with the definition:

wild swan

Pinyin **hóng** *and Frequency Rank* **1924**

Contains **11 strokes** in the following order:

丶 冫 氵 广 汀 江 汀丿 汋 泋 鸿 鸿

Contains these components:

river, Yangtze 江 327, p. 83

bird 鸟 394, p. 96

With all these meanings & readings:

hóng [鴻] **1** eastern bean goose **2** great **3** large

The **wild swan** is one of the most elegant *river birds*.

398

乌

烏
TRAD   SIMPLIFIED

This character with the definition:

dark

Pinyin **wū** *and Frequency Rank* **1244**

Contains **4 strokes** in the following order:

丿 勹 乌 乌

Contains these components:

bird 鸟 (abbrev) 394, 96

With all these meanings & readings:

wū [烏] **1** a crow **2** black **3** surname Wu **4** abbr for Ukraine 乌克兰[烏～蘭][wū kè lán]

A crow appears to be an eyeless *bird* because its eyes are as **dark** as its head and beak, with little color differentiation among the parts.

399

厂

COMPONENT

This component has the meaning:

cliff r

The ledge of a **cliff** would look just like this image.

400

原

SIMP & TRAD

This character with the definition:

original, unprocessed

Pinyin **yuán** *and Frequency Rank* **193**

Contains **10 strokes** in the following order:

一 厂 厂 厂 厒 原 原 原 原 原

Contains these components:

cliff r 厂 399, p. 97

spring, fountain 泉 (altered) 318, p. 81

With all these meanings & readings:

yuán [原] **1** former **2** original **3** primary **4** raw **5** level **6** cause **7** source

Imagine the *'cliff'* element on the left as the profile of a pristine mountain *spring* gracefully flowing over a *cliff*—the tranquil image of nature in its **original** undisturbed state.

401

This character with the definition:

source of river, fountainhead

Pinyin **yuán** *and Frequency Rank* **670**

SIMP & TRAD　Contains **13 strokes** in the following order:

丶 丶 氵 汀 汀 沪 沪 沥 沥 沥 源 源 源

The **source of a river** is the *original* point at which *water* flows out.

Contains these components:

water r 氵 314, p.80
original, unprocessed 原 400, p.97

With all these meanings & readings

yuán [源] **1** root **2** source **3** origin

402

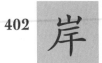

This character with the definition:

shore, coast

Pinyin **àn** *and Frequency Rank* **971**

SIMP & TRAD　Contains **8 strokes** in the following order:

丨 凵 屮 屵 屵 岸 岸 岸

Cliffs and *mountains* stay *dry* even though they are often near the **coast**. Their high elevation protects them from the moisture found in lower altitudes.

Contains these components:

mountain 山 4, p.10
cliff r 厂 399, p.97
dry 干 17, p.13

With all these meanings & readings

àn [岸] **1** bank **2** shore **3** beach **4** coast **5** m 个[個][gè]

403

This character with the definition:

catty

Pinyin **jīn** *and Frequency Rank* **1866**

SIMP & TRAD　Contains **4 strokes** in the following order:

丿 厂 斤 斤

By itself, this character looks like the left half of a table that's covered by half a table cloth which here stands somewhat upright. Because it's so unstable, the table will topple over if you **pound** on it too hard. • When this character serves as element, it takes on the meaning '**unstable**' or '**unbalanced**'. Other times, it is interpreted in its '**pound**' or weight-related sense. • **Catty** is a noun, a Chinese unit of weight. It's about one-half kilogram or 1.1 pounds.

Contains these components:

cliff r 厂 (altered) 399, p.97
fourth (in a series) 丁 (altered) 19, p.13

With all these meanings & readings

jīn [斤] **1** catty **2** weight equal to 0.5 kg

404

This character with the definition:

mound, little hill

Pinyin **qiū** *and Frequency Rank* **1929**

SIMP & TRAD　Contains **5 strokes** in the following order:

丿 亻 斤 斤 丘

The vagrant is a little *unbalanced*. As he looks toward the distant *horizon*, he believes that a mountain in the distance is only a **little hill**.

Contains these components:

catty 斤 403, p.98
one 一 1, p.10

With all these meanings & readings

qiū [丘] **1** surname Qiu
qiū [丘] **1** mound **2** hillock **3** grave

405

This character with the definition:

discount

Pinyin **zhé** *and Frequency Rank* **1131**

SIMP & TRAD　Contains **7 strokes** in the following order:

一 十 扌 扩 折 折 折

Contains these components:

hand r 扌 25, p.15
catty 斤 403, p.98

With all these meanings & readings

shé [折] **1** to break (e.g. stick or bone) **2** a loss
zhē [折] **1** to turn sth over **2** to turn upside-down **3** to tip sth out (of a container)
zhé [折] **1** to break **2** to fracture **3** to snap **4** to suffer loss **5** to bend **6** to twist **7** to turn **8** change direction **9** convinced **10** to convert into (currency) **11** discount **12** rebate **13** tenth (in price) **14** m for theatrical scenes **15** to fold **16** accounts book
zhé [摺] **1** to fold (a document) **2** to turn **3** to bend

The store gave us such a big **discount** on the table we bought today that, for the same price under normal circumstances, it would cost the same as only *half a table* (see panel 403). We quickly grabbed the table with our *hands* before anyone else could reach for it—or before the salesman changed his mind!

406

SIMP & TRAD

This character with the definition:

wise, sagacious

Pinyin **zhé** *and Frequency Rank* **1117**

Contains **10 strokes** in the following order:

一 十 扌 扩 扩 折 折 折 哲 哲

Contains these components:

discount 折 405, p.98

mouth 口 37, p.17

With all these meanings & readings:

zhé [哲] **1** philosophy **2** wise

The scholar bought a new *mouth* that makes him sound more **sagacious** than his old one—and he got it at a *discount*!

407

SIMP & TRAD

This character with the definition:

vow, pledge

Pinyin **shì** *and Frequency Rank* **2095**

Contains **14 strokes** in the following order:

一 十 扌 扩 扩 护 折 折 折 折 誓 誓 誓 誓

Contains these components:

discount 折 405, p.98

speech 言 256, p.67

With all these meanings & readings:

shì [誓] **1** oath **2** vow **3** to swear **4** to pledge

The price you paid to watch that *speech* includes no *discount*. I **vow** to keep every transaction between us honest.

408

SIMP & TRAD

This character with the definition:

scold, reprimand

Pinyin **chì** *and Frequency Rank* **1857**

Contains **5 strokes** in the following order:

´ 厂 斤 斤 斥

Contains these components:

catty 斤 403, p.98

dab r ˋ 176, p.48

With all these meanings & readings:

chì [斥] **1** to blame **2** to reprove **3** to reprimand **4** to expel **5** to oust

When you tried to reduce the *instability* of the table (see panel 403) by adding a *dab* of support, it still fell down—so the boss **scolded** you, yet again.

409

TRAD SIMPLIFIED

This character with the definition:

speak one's mind, tell

Pinyin **sù** *and Frequency Rank* **595**

Contains **7 strokes** in the following order:

` 讠 讠 订 诉 诉 诉

Contains these components:

speech r 讠 352, p.88

scold, reprimand 斥 408, p.99

With all these meanings & readings:

sù [訴] **1** complain **2** sue **3** tell

Constantly **speaking your mind** to your family will degenerate the conversation into a *speech* of *reprimand*.

Unit 19

410

听

聴
TRAD SIMPLIFIED

This character with the definition:

hear, listen

Pinyin **tīng** *and Frequency Rank* **285**

Contains **7 strokes** in the following order:

丨 ﾉ 口 口 ᅡ 听 听 听

Contains these components:

☐ mouth 口 37, p.17
☐ catty 斤 403, p.98

With all these meanings & readings:

tīng [聽] **1** to listen **2** to hear **3** to obey **4** a can (loanword from English"tin") **5** m for canned beverages
tìng [聽] **1** to let **2** to allow

That guy is talking really crazy. Whenever someone *mouths* off in an *unbalanced* manner, I **listen** very carefully to see whether an intervention is necessary.

411

岳

嶽
TRAD SIMPLIFIED

This character with the definition:

high mountain peak

Pinyin **yuè** *and Frequency Rank* **1844**

Contains **8 strokes** in the following order:

ﾉ ᅡ ᅡ ᅡ 丘 乒 岳 岳

Contains these components:

☐ catty 斤 403, p.98
☐ one 一 1, p.10
☐ mountain 山 4, p.10

With all these meanings & readings:

Yuè [岳] **1** surname Yue
yuè [岳] **1** wife's parents and paternal uncles
yuè [嶽] **1** surname Yue
yuè [嶽] **1** high mountain

You will feel *unbalanced* when you reach *one* high *mountain's* **peak**.

412

匠

SIMP & TRAD

This character with the definition:

craftsman

Pinyin **jiàng** *and Frequency Rank* **2110**

Contains **6 strokes** in the following order:

一 二 厂 匚 斤 匠

Contains these components:

☐ basket, box r 匚 152, p.42
☐ catty 斤 403, p.98

With all these meanings & readings:

jiàng [匠] **1** craftsman

Give a true **craftsman** scrap materials, such as an old *box* and *an unbalanced table*, and soon you will receive a creative work of art.

413

氏

SIMP & TRAD

This character with the definition:

surname

Pinyin **shì** *and Frequency Rank* **1500**

Contains **4 strokes** in the following order:

ﾉ 厂 斤 氏

Contains these components:

☐ cliff r 厂 (altered) 399, p.97
☐ one 一 1, p.10
☐ mineshaft c L (altered) 122, p.36

With all these meanings & readings:

shì [氏] **1** clan name **2** maiden name

After capturing our soldiers, the enemy separated them by **surname** into two groups. They forced *one* group to jump into a *mineshaft* and the other off a high *cliff*.

414

氐

SIMP & TRAD

This character with the definition:

basic

Pinyin **dǐ** *and Frequency Rank* **4355**

Contains **5 strokes** in the following order:

ﾉ 厂 斤 氏 氐

Contains these components:

☐ surname 氏 413, p.100
☐ dab r 丶 176, p.48

With all these meanings & readings:

dī [氐] **1** name of an ancient tribe
dǐ [氐] **1** foundation **2** on the whole

In Russian, a *few* letters are added to the end of the **basic** *surname* of a woman's father to indicate that she is his daughter.

415

抵

SIMP & TRAD

This character with the definition:

support, sustain

Pinyin **dǐ**   and Frequency Rank **1119**

Contains **8 strokes** in the following order:

Contains these components:

hand r 扌 25, p.15

basic 氐 414, p.100

With all these meanings & readings:

dǐ [抵] **1** to hold up **2** to support **3** to prop up **4** to resist **5** to compensate **6** to make up for **7** to mortgage **8** to offset **9** to counterbalance **10** to balance **11** to set against **12** on the whole **13** to push against **14** to reach **15** to arrive

Knowing how to use of one's *hands* is a *basic* survival skill that is necessary to **support** oneself.

416

昏

SIMP & TRAD

This character with the definition:

dusk

Pinyin **hūn**   and Frequency Rank **1561**

Contains **8 strokes** in the following order:

Contains these components:

surname 氏 413, p.100

day, sun 日 64, p.24

With all these meanings & readings:

hūn [昏] **1** muddle-headed **2** twilight **3** to faint **4** to lose consciousness

In Western languages, the *surname* appears at the end of one's name just as **dusk** occurs at the end of every *day*.

417

厚

SIMP & TRAD

This character with the definition:

thick, deep, profound

Pinyin **hòu**   and Frequency Rank **1235**

Contains **9 strokes** in the following order:

Contains these components:

cliff r 厂 399, p.97

day, sun 日 64, p.24

son, child 子 24, p.15

With all these meanings & readings:

hòu [厚] **1** generous **2** thick (for flat things)

The student philosopher is lost in **deep** and **profound** thought on the *cliff*, pondering how words such as '*son*' and '*sun*' can sound alike yet have completely unrelated meanings. This student is rather **thick** with knowledge!

418

爪

SIMP & TRAD

This character with the definition:

claw

Pinyin **zhuǎ**   and Frequency Rank **2363**

Contains **4 strokes** in the following order:

Contains these components:

cliff r 厂 399, p.97

scepter c 丨 5, p.10

mineshaft c ㇄ (altered) 122, p.36

With all these meanings & readings:

zhuǎ [爪] **1** claw

Using only a *scepter*-shaped staff, the mountain climber was so skilled that he scaled the steep rocky *cliffs* so swiftly and perilous *mineshafts* so deftly. He seemed to have animal **claws** instead of human fingers.

419

抓

SIMP & TRAD

This character with the definition:

seize, arrest

Pinyin **zhuā**   and Frequency Rank **992**

Contains **7 strokes** in the following order:

Contains these components:

hand r 扌 25, p.15

claw 爪 418, p.101

With all these meanings & readings:

zhuā [抓] **1** to grab **2** to catch **3** to arrest **4** to snatch

Humans use their *hands* while animals use their *claws* to **seize** moving objects.

420

SIMP & TRAD

This character with the definition:

fear, dread*

Pinyin **wèi** *and Frequency Rank* **2039**

Contains **9 strokes** in the following order:

Contains these components:

☐ field 田 63, p. 23
☐ claw 爪 (altered) 418, p. 101

With all these meanings & readings:

wèi [畏] **1** to fear

丶 冂 口 甲 田 里 甲 畀 畏

I began to **fear** for the safety of my children when I saw animal tracks with large *claws* in the *field* behind my house.

421

喂
餵

TRAD   SIMPLIFIED

This character with the definition:

to feed

Pinyin **wèi** *and Frequency Rank* **1988**

Contains **12 strokes** in the following order:

Contains these components:

☐ mouth 口 37, p. 17
☐ fear, dread* 畏 420, p. 102

With all these meanings & readings:

wèi [喂] **1** hello (interjection, especially on telephone) **2** hey **3** to feed (sb or some animal)
wèi [餵] **1** to feed

丨 冂 口 口¹ 口¹ 吖 呷 呷 咀 哩 喂 喂

Every visitor that enters the nature park is warned not **to feed** the wild animals. If they get used to receiving food from visitors, they will no longer *fear* humans and a visitor may find himself in a wild animal's *mouth*!

422

SIMP & TRAD

This character with the definition:

crawl, creep

Pinyin **pá** *and Frequency Rank* **1426**

Contains **8 strokes** in the following order:

Contains these components:

☐ claw 爪 418, p. 101
☐ cling to, stick to 巴 137, p. 39

With all these meanings & readings:

pá [爬] **1** to crawl **2** to climb

丿 厂 爫 爪 爬 爬 爬 爬

Animals and insects use their *claws* to *cling to* and **crawl** up steep, smooth surfaces.

423

厅
廳

TRAD   SIMPLIFIED

This character with the definition:

public room

Pinyin **tīng** *and Frequency Rank* **1217**

Contains **4 strokes** in the following order:

Contains these components:

☐ cliff r 厂 399, p. 97
☐ fourth (in a series) 丁 19, p. 13

With all these meanings & readings:

tīng [廳] **1** (reception) hall **2** office

一 厂 厅 厅

The diabolical warlord built a special **hall** to receive his enemies. If found wanting, they were ushered *forth* (sounds like *fourth*) to the rear exit, which opened out onto the edge of a high *cliff*.

424

压
壓

TRAD   SIMPLIFIED

This character with the definition:

press down

Pinyin **yā** *and Frequency Rank* **756**

Contains **6 strokes** in the following order:

Contains these components:

☐ cliff r 厂 399, p. 97
☐ earth, soil 土 9, p. 11
☐ dab r 丶 176, p. 48

With all these meanings & readings:

yā [壓] **1** to press **2** to push down **3** to keep under (control) **4** pressure
yà [壓] **1** in the first place **2** to crush

一 厂 厂 厇 压 压

A huge load of *earth* fell from the top of the *cliff* and landed with a loud thud on the *little* man who happened to be standing below. The fallen earth **pressed down** on him and he remained trapped forever.

425

廠
TRAD

SIMPLIFIED

一 厂

This character with the definition:

factory

Pinyin **chǎng** *and Frequency Rank* **963**

Contains **2 strokes** in the following order:

Contains these components:

■ cliff r 厂 399, p. 97

With all these meanings & readings:

chǎng [厂] **1** "roof" radical in Chinese characters (Kangxi radical 27), occurring in 原, 历, 压, etc. **2** see also 厂字旁[廠~~][chǎng zì páng]
chǎng [廠] **1** cliff **2** slope **3** factory **4** yard **5** depot **6** workhouse **7** works **8** (industrial) plant

Imagine working in a nineteenth century **factory**—long hours, demeaning work, and negligible pay. Exhausted workers would climb on the **factory**'s roof and fling themselves off this man-made *cliff* hoping to end life once and for all.

426

SIMP & TRAD

一 厂 厃 厄

This character with the definition:

trapped in a difficult situation

Pinyin **è** *and Frequency Rank* **2407**

Contains **4 strokes** in the following order:

Contains these components:

■ cliff r 厂 399, p. 97

■ self* 己 (altered) 135, p. 39

With all these meanings & readings:

è [厄] **1** distressed

Here *I* am, near the edge of a high *cliff*, **trapped** as a maniac tries to push me off. • The '*self*' part resembles the end of a tight fist, while the whole character looks like a fist enclosed within a glove. I'm ready to throw my flying fists to get out of this mess so I will not be **trapped in a difficult situation**.

427

COMPONENT

This component has the meaning:

shelter r

And contains these subcomponents:

■ cliff r 厂 (altered) 399, p. 97

■ dab r 丶 176, p. 48

The *dab* at the top of the *cliff* represents a small overhang, where a grateful traveler can find protective **shelter**.

428

SIMP & TRAD

丶 亠 广 广 庐 店 店 店

This character with the definition:

shop

Pinyin **diàn** *and Frequency Rank* **1041**

Contains **8 strokes** in the following order:

Contains these components:

■ shelter r 广 427, p. 103

■ practice divination 占 188, p. 51

With all these meanings & readings:

diàn [店] **1** inn **2** shop **3** store **4** m 家[jiā]

Originally, a **shop** functioned as a special *shelter* for shamans to *practice divination*. Bit by bit, the fortune teller would start to supplement his income by furnishing items to sell, until one day the retail operation overshadowed the original one.

429

SIMP & TRAD

丶 亠 广 庐 庐 庐 底 底

This character with the definition:

bottom, base

Pinyin **dǐ** *and Frequency Rank* **543**

Contains **8 strokes** in the following order:

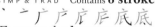

Contains these components:

■ shelter r 广 427, p. 103

■ basic 氐 414, p. 100

With all these meanings & readings:

de [底] **1** (equivalent to 的 as possessive particle)
dǐ [底] **1** background **2** bottom **3** base **4** the end of a period of time **5** towards the end of (last month)

Those at the **bottom** rung of society survive on only the *basic* elements of life—food, *shelter*, and clothing.

430

广

廣
TRAD SIMPLIFIED

This character with the definition:

extensive

Pinyin **guǎng** *and Frequency Rank* **468**

Contains **3 strokes** in the following order:

丶 一 广

Contains these components:

shelter r 广 427, p. 103

With all these meanings & readings

guǎng [廣] **1** wide **2** numerous **3** to spread **4** surname Guang

The good thing about proper *shelter* is that it keeps you protected against the elements during harsh weather. The most primitive cave can feel like an **extensive** castle to a person in need.

431

扩

擴
TRAD SIMPLIFIED

This character with the definition:

enlarge

Pinyin **kuò** *and Frequency Rank* **1051**

Contains **6 strokes** in the following order:

一 十 扌 扩 扩 扩

Contains these components:

hand r 扌 25, p. 15

extensive 广 430, p. 104

With all these meanings & readings

kuò [擴] **1** enlarge

The hired laborers' *hands* are busy working on an *extensive* project to **enlarge** our house.

432

庄

莊
TRAD SIMPLIFIED

This character with the definition:

village

Pinyin **zhuāng** *and Frequency Rank* **1024**

Contains **6 strokes** in the following order:

丶 一 广 广 庄 庄

Contains these components:

extensive 广 430, p. 104

earth, soil 土 9, p. 11

With all these meanings & readings

zhuāng [莊] **1** farm **2** village **3** manor

When a cluster of houses are spread out *extensively* over the *earth*, we call that a **village**.

433

庙

廟
TRAD SIMPLIFIED

This character with the definition:

temple

Pinyin **miào** *and Frequency Rank* **1889**

Contains **8 strokes** in the following order:

丶 一 广 广 庐 庐 庙 庙

Contains these components:

shelter r 广 427, p. 103
reason, by means of 由 58, p. 22

With all these meanings & readings

miào [廟] **1** temple **2** monaster **3** m 座[zuò]

A **temple** provides a special kind of *shelter*. It offers such an uplifting and enlightening experience that that *reason* alone is enough to be there.

434

疒

COMPONENT

This component has the meaning:

sick r

And contains these subcomponents:

dab r (×2) 丶 176, p. 48

shelter r 广 427, p. 103

While the **sick** person is recovering in the comforting *shelter* of home, he is also coughing, sneezing, and expelling *dabs* of disgusting matter from his system.

Unit 20

435

SIMP & TRAD

This character with the definition:

disease

Pinyin **zhèng** *and Frequency Rank* **1258**

Contains these components:

☐ sick r 疒 434, p.104

◧ to correct, rectify 正 193, p.52

With all these meanings & readings:

zhèng [症] **1** disease **2** illness
zhēng [癥] **1** abdominal tumor

Contains **10 strokes** in the following order:

丶 一 广 广 广 疒 疒 疒 疒 症

Disease makes you *sick*. Proper diagnosis and treatment are necessary *to correct* your ill health.

436

療
TRAD   SIMPLIFIED

This character with the definition:

cure, treat illness

Pinyin **liáo** *and Frequency Rank* **949**

Contains these components:

☐ sick r 疒 434, p.104

◧ s-end le 了 23, p.15

With all these meanings & readings:

liáo [療] **1** to treat **2** to cure
3 therapy

Contains **7 strokes** in the following order:

丶 一 广 广 疒 疗 疗

One of the functions of the '*le*' character is to signal a change of state. Thus, if someone starts out *sick* and then experiences a *change in the state* of their health, they must be **cured**!

437

SIMP & TRAD

This character with the definition:

cancer

Pinyin **ái** *and Frequency Rank* **1799**

Contains these components:

☐ sick r 疒 434, p.104

◧ product 品 52, p.21

◼ mountain 山 4, p.10

With all these meanings & readings:

ái [癌] **1** cancer **2** carcinoma

Contains **17 strokes** in the following order:

丶 一 广 广 疒 疒 疒 疒 疒 癌 癌 癌 癌 癌 癌 癌

A beloved mother has become *sick* and the *three mouths* symbolize how closely her family huddles together around her for support. Little do they know, they have a *mountain* of trouble to contend with, and will need many medicinal *products* before they're through the ordeal, for the news is not good—their mother has **cancer**.

438

丿

This component has the meaning:

action path c

COMPONENT

The presence of this element suggests a **path** along which something important happened. Sometimes, it suggests just the **action** itself.

439

SIMP & TRAD

This character with the definition:

low, inferior

Pinyin **bēi** *and Frequency Rank* **2059**

Contains these components:

◼ white 白 225, p.60

◻ action path c 丿 438, p.105

◼ ten 十 7, p.11

With all these meanings & readings:

bēi [卑] **1** low **2** base **3** vulgar
4 inferior **5** humble

Contains **8 strokes** in the following order:

  丿 亻 白 白 白 皀 鱼 卑

An *action* sequence: you're using a *white*-tipped hammer to pound a spike (in the shape of the Chinese numeral *ten*) until it's **low** in the ground.

440

SIMP & TRAD

This character with the definition:

ping-pong

Pinyin **pīng** *and Frequency Rank* **3447**

Contains these components:

◻ mound, little hill 丘 404, p. 98
◻ action path c 丿 438, p. 105

With all these meanings & readings:

pīng [乒] **1** onomat. ping **2** bing

Contains **6 strokes** in the following order:

丿 厂 乒 乒 乒 乒

The most common type of **ping-pong** paddle is that which is covered with a rubber surface made from *mounds* of material. Players say that this increases the *action* of a game. In fact, the '*action*' stroke resembles the handle on the paddle. Holding it this way seems to suggest that the play happens on the right side of the racket. Both pinyin 'pīng' and 'right' contain the letter 'i'.

441

SIMP & TRAD

This character with the definition:

ping-pong*

Pinyin **pāng** *and Frequency Rank* **3502**

Contains these components:

◻ mound, little hill 丘 404, p. 98
◻ action path c 丿 (altered) 438, p. 105

With all these meanings & readings:

pāng [乓] **1** onomat. bang

Contains **6 strokes** in the following order:

丿 厂 乒 乒 乓 乓

This character re-uses all the elements from the previous panel. Here, though, a mirror image of the *action path* appears under the *mounds* of rubber, but on the right, to suggest play on the character's left. These characters taken separately (乒, 乓) look unstable and seem ready to fall to the right and left. But together (乒乓), we form a stable ping-pong table.

442

SIMP & TRAD

This character with the definition:

soldier

Pinyin **bīng** *and Frequency Rank* **398**

Contains these components:

◻ ping-pong 乒 440, p. 106
◻ ping-pong* 乓 441, p. 106

With all these meanings & readings:

bīng [兵] **1** soldiers **2** a force **3** an army **4** weapons **5** arms **6** military **7** warlike **8** m 个 [個][gè]

Contains **7 strokes** in the following order:

丿 厂 乒 乒 乓 兵 兵

Chinese *ping-pong* champions play with an unrivaled intensity. The players approach each match as if they are **soldiers** engaged in a critical military campaign.

443

TRAD SIMPLIFIED

This character with the definition:

guest, visitor

Pinyin **bīn** *and Frequency Rank* **1534**

Contains these components:

◻ roof r 宀 271, p. 70
◻ soldier 兵 442, p. 106

With all these meanings & readings:

bīn [賓] **1** visitor **2** guest **3** object (in grammar)

Contains **10 strokes** in the following order:

丶 丷 宀 宀 宀 宀 宀 宾 宾 宾

In the old days, the most notorious **guests** were *soldiers* that the government forced you to shelter under your *roof*.

444

SIMP & TRAD

This character with the definition:

river

Pinyin **chuān** *and Frequency Rank* **1109**

Contains **3 strokes** in the following order:

丿 刂 川

Contains these components:

☐ action path c ╱ 438, p.105

☐ scepter c (×2) ｜ 5, p.10

With all these meanings & readings:

chuān [川] **1** river **2** creek **3** plain **4** an area of level country **5** abbr for Sichuan Province 四川 in southwest China

The flowing water runs between the two banks of the river. Here, the left bank has a curved path that's not present on the right.

445

SIMP & TRAD

This character with the definition:

barren, desolate

Pinyin **huāng** *and Frequency Rank* **1328**

Contains **9 strokes** in the following order:

一 十 卝 艹 艹 芒 芢 芋 荒

Contains these components:

☐ spike, sharp point 芒 260, p.68

☐ river 川 444, p.107

With all these meanings & readings:

huāng [荒] **1** out of practice **2** uncultivated

Desolation can result from natural causes—*rivers* which overflow onto their banks—or man-made carnage—such as *spikes* and other weapons used to destroy villages.

446

TRAD SIMPLIFIED

This character with the definition:

lecture, train, teach

Pinyin **xùn** *and Frequency Rank* **1022**

Contains **5 strokes** in the following order:

丶 讠 训 训 训

Contains these components:

☐ speech r 讠 352, p.88

☐ river 川 444, p.107

With all these meanings & readings:

xùn [训] **1** example **2** pattern **3** to teach **4** to train **5** instruction

In order to **teach** effectively, it's helpful to make your *speech* flow like a *river*.

447

SIMP & TRAD

This character with the definition:

abruptly

Pinyin **zhà** *and Frequency Rank* **2914**

Contains **5 strokes** in the following order:

丿 ㇂ 乍 乍 乍

Contains these components:

☐ action path c ╱ 438, p.105

☐ scepter c ｜ 5, p.10

☐ three 三 (altered) 3, p.10

With all these meanings & readings:

zhà [乍] **1** for the first time **2** suddenly

You should think of the misaligned horizontals of '*three*' as crude steps in a ladder formed by nailing several planks together; the '*scepter*' is an equally-crude stair rail. Imagine yourself climbing this ladder, and as you reach the top you **abruptly** slip and fall—your descent toward the ground is captured by the '*action path*' stroke.

448

SIMP & TRAD

This character with the definition:

yesterday

Pinyin **zúo** *and Frequency Rank* **1475**

Contains **9 strokes** in the following order:

丨 冂 日 日 日' 昨 昨 昨 昨

Contains these components:

☐ day, sun 日 64, p.24

☐ abruptly 乍 447, p.107

With all these meanings & readings:

zúo [昨] **1** yesterday

You've been having such a good time with your old college friends that you hardly noticed the *sun* has long since gone down. This great day has *abruptly* ended and turned into another **yesterday**.

449
才 繳
TRAD SIMPLIFIED

This character with the definition:

sth just happened

Pinyin **cái** *and Frequency Rank* **235**

Contains **3 strokes** in the following order:

一 十 才

Contains these components:

hand 手 (altered) 21, p.14

action path c ⟍ 438, p.105

With all these meanings & readings:

cái [才] **1** ability **2** talent **3** endowment **4** gift **5** an expert **6** only (then) **7** only if **8** just
cái [繳] **1** just **2** not until

Top of the ninth and it's a tie score. A fly ball was headed out of the park and we watched the *path it takes*. But wait—**something** surprising **just happened**! The rookie outfielder stuck his *hand* up, caught the fly, and the batter is out! Notice that the scribes used an abbreviated form of '*hand*', quite appropriate as it was the *hand* that interrupted the *action path* of the baseball.

450

This character with the definition:

tooth*

Pinyin **yá** *and Frequency Rank* **997**

SIMP & TRAD Contains **4 strokes** in the following order:

一 二 于 牙

Contains these components:

sth just happened 才 (altered) 449, p.108

one 一 1, p.10

With all these meanings & readings:

yá [牙] **1** tooth **2** ivory **3** m 颗 [颗][kē]

The 'action path' (panel 438) shows the inner surface of *one* sharp canine **tooth** pointing up; the hooked vertical forms the outer surface of the tooth, but the root of the tooth, anchored in the animal's jaw, is not drawn. The point of the **tooth** has *just* penetrated a juicy slab of meat, representing the layer drawn at the top.

451

This character with the definition:

ah!, oh!

Pinyin **yā** *and Frequency Rank* **929**

SIMP & TRAD Contains **7 strokes** in the following order:

丨 冂 口 口⁻ 吁 呀 呀

Contains these components:

mouth 口 37, p.17

tooth* 牙 450, p.108

With all these meanings & readings:

ya [呀] **1** (particle equivalent to 啊 after a vowel, expressing surprise or doubt)

It is not surprising to hear expletives such as **Oh!** come out of your *mouth* when there is a dog's *tooth* embedded in your flesh.

452

This character with the definition:

located at

Pinyin **zài** *and Frequency Rank* **6**

SIMP & TRAD Contains **6 strokes** in the following order:

一 ナ 才 右 存 在

Contains these components:

sth just happened 才 (altered) 449, p.108

earth, soil 土 9, p.11

With all these meanings & readings:

zài [在] **1** (located) at **2** (to be) in **3** to exist **4** in the middle doing sth **5** (indicating an action in progress)

Something just happened after the heavy downpour—the mound of *earth* that was **located at** the construction site shrunk to a muddy mess.

453

This character with the definition:

store, preserve

Pinyin **cún** *and Frequency Rank* **384**

SIMP & TRAD Contains **6 strokes** in the following order:

一 ナ 才 存 存 存

Contains these components:

sth just happened 才 (altered) 449, p.108

son, child 子 24, p.15

With all these meanings & readings:

cún [存] **1** exist **2** deposit **3** store **4** keep **5** survive

The long-awaited birth of our neighbor's *child just happened*, and her family has already begun to **preserve** mementos from the event.

454

闭

閉
TRAD   SIMPLIFIED

This character with the definition:

shut, close*

Pinyin **bì** *and Frequency Rank* **1267**

Contains **6 strokes** in the following order:

`丶 丨 门 冂 闭 闭`

Contains these components:

☐ doorway 门 243, p.64

☐ sth just happened 才 449, p.108

With all these meanings & readings:

bì [閉] **1** to close **2** stop up
3 shut **4** obstruct

A sudden gust of wind *just blew* the door **shut** with such force that it caused the *doorway* to crack.

455

团

團
TRAD   SIMPLIFIED

This character with the definition:

round, circular

Pinyin **tuán** *and Frequency Rank* **405**

Contains **6 strokes** in the following order:

`丨 冂 冂 用 闭 团`

Contains these components:

☐ enclosure r 囗 36, p.17

☐ sth just happened 才 449, p.108

With all these meanings & readings:

tuán [團] **1** regiment **2** round
3 circular **4** group **5** society
tuán [糰] **1** dumpling

Remember, the surrounding *enclosure* is really **round**—it just looks square because writing brushes don't form actual **circles** well! The prisoner in the **round** enclosure hears a sharp noise and knows *something just happened*. Yet, when he looks in all directions, all parts look the same because he's in a **round** cell.

456

者

SIMP & TRAD

This character with the definition:

-er

Pinyin **zhě** *and Frequency Rank* **103**

Contains **8 strokes** in the following order:

Contains these components:

☐ earth, soil 土 9, p.11

☐ day, sun 日 64, p.24

☐ action path c ノ 438, p.105

With all these meanings & readings:

zhě [者] **1** -ist, -er (person)
2 person (who does sth)

'**-Er**' is the same thing as 'one who…' and this character describes the objective of **someone who performs an activity**, a perform-**er**. One needs to apply *action* to bring something up from under the *earth* to the light of *day*—a metaphor for a fully finished activity.

457

署

SIMP & TRAD

This character with the definition:

government office

Pinyin **shǔ** *and Frequency Rank* **1379**

Contains **13 strokes** in the following order:

`丶 冖 罒 罒 四 罒 罖 里 罗 罘 署 署 署`

Contains these components:

☐ net r 罒 100, p.32

☐ -er 者 456, p.109

With all these meanings & readings:

shǔ [署] **1** office **2** bureau
3 to sign

Despite his best efforts working in the **government office**, the civil servant finds himself and his *actions* trapped in a *net* of red tape.

458

诸

諸
TRAD   SIMPLIFIED

This character with the definition:

all, various

Pinyin **zhū** *and Frequency Rank* **1021**

Contains **10 strokes** in the following order:

Contains these components:

☐ speech r 讠 352, p.88

☐ -er 者 456, p.109

With all these meanings & readings:

zhū [諸] **1** surname Zhu **2** all
3 many **4** various

Speech is so important because you can *use it* to express **all** kinds of meanings.

459

著

SIMP & TRAD

This character with the definition:

write, compose

Pinyin **zhù** *and Frequency Rank* **777**

Contains **11 strokes** in the following order:

一 十 サ 芏 芏 苎 莎 莑 著 著 著

Contains these components:

☐ grass r ⺾ 87, p. 29
■ -er 者 456, p.109

With all these meanings & readings:

zhù [著] **1** to make known **2** to show **3** to prove **4** to write **5** book **6** outstanding

Paper, one of the great discoveries of ancient China, was developed in the East long before its production began in the West. Made from *grass* and other vegetable matter, the components in 著 refer to an *active process* which uses this vegetable matter invention, namely **writing** on paper.

Unit 21

460 **勿**

SIMP & TRAD

This character with the definition:

do not

Pinyin **wù** *and Frequency Rank* **2563**

Contains **4 strokes** in the following order:

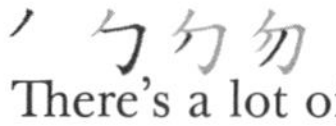

Contains these components:

- action path c (×3) ㇒ 438, p. 105
- place of refuge c ㇆ 105, p. 33

With all these meanings & readings:

wù [勿] **1** do not

There's a lot of *activity* happening—but all of it is **not permitted**. To limit the amount of ongoing *activity*, everyone should be directed to the *place of refuge*.

461 **物**

SIMP & TRAD

This character with the definition:

thing, matter

Pinyin **wù** *and Frequency Rank* **142**

Contains **8 strokes** in the following order:

Contains these components:

- ox 牛 213, p. 57
- do not 勿 460, p. 111

With all these meanings & readings:

wù [物] **1** thing **2** object **3** matter **4** abbr for physics 物理

Many foreigners pronounce 'ask' like '*ox*', as in "No**thing**'s the **matter**—*do not ox* me again!"

462 **易**

SIMP & TRAD

This character with the definition:

easy

Pinyin **yì** *and Frequency Rank* **461**

Contains **8 strokes** in the following order:

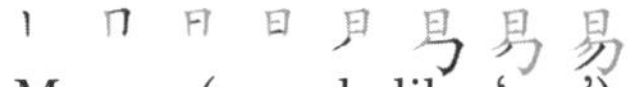

Contains these components:

- day, sun 日 64, p. 24
- do not 勿 460, p. 111

With all these meanings & readings:

yì [易] **1** change **2** easy **3** simple **4** surname Yi

My *son* (sounds like '*sun*') *does not* do anything all day long but lounge around the house! Life is too **easy** for him!

463 **昜**

SIMP & TRAD

This character with the definition:

glorious, bright

Pinyin **yáng** *and Frequency Rank* **9999**

Contains **9 strokes** in the following order:

Contains these components:

- dawn 旦 70, p. 25
- do not 勿 460, p. 111

With all these meanings & readings:

yáng [昜] **1** to open out, to expand **2** bright, glorious

A plague of bad thoughts often precedes a sleepless night. However, with the arrival of a **bright** and **glorious** new day, the *dawn* washes away any negative memories that you *do not* want or need. The diagonal curves of the *do not* element represent the **glorious** rays of a *dawning* sun.

464 **场**

場 TRAD

SIMPLIFIED

This character with the definition:

gathering place, field

Pinyin **chǎng** *and Frequency Rank* **249**

Contains **6 strokes** in the following order:

Contains these components:

- earth, soil 土 9, p. 11
- glorious, bright 昜 463, p. 111

With all these meanings & readings:

cháng [場] **1** threshing floor **2** m for events and happenings
chǎng [場] **1** a place **2** an open space **3** a field **4** a courtyard **5** m for events such as sports matches, concerts, or cultural events **6** m for number of exams

Open-air fairs on expanses of *earth* draw customers in with their *glorious* decoration. Such **fields** became **gathering places** that evolved into towns.

465

扬

揚
TRAD SIMPLIFIED

This character with the definition:

publicize, make known

Pinyin **yáng** *and Frequency Rank* **1084**

Contains **6 strokes** in the following order:

一 丁 扌 扔 扬 扬

Contains these components:

▯ hand r 扌 25, p. 15

▯ glorious, bright 昜 463, p. 111

With all these meanings & readings:

yáng [揚] **1** to raise **2** to hoist **3** the action of tossing or winnowing **4** scattering (in the wind) **5** to flutter **6** to propagate

In order to **publicize** his new bakery, my father wrote, by *hand* in *bright* colors, 'Open for Business!' on a big sign that he then placed in the front window.

466

汤

湯
TRAD SIMPLIFIED

This character with the definition:

soup

Pinyin **tāng** *and Frequency Rank* **1618**

Contains **6 strokes** in the following order:

丶 冫 氵 汚 汤 汤

Contains these components:

▯ water r 氵 314, p. 80

▯ glorious, bright 昜 463, p. 111

With all these meanings & readings:

tāng [湯] **1** soup **2** surname Tang **3** m 碗[wǎn]

Soup is a *glorious liquid* to eat, especially on cold days.

467

荡

盪
蕩
TRAD SIMPLIFIED

This character with the definition:

swing, shake, wash away

Pinyin **dàng** *and Frequency Rank* **1424**

Contains **9 strokes** in the following order:

一 十 艹 艹 艹 芗 荡 荡 荡

Contains these components:

▯ grass r 艹 87, p. 29

▯ soup 汤 466, p. 112

With all these meanings & readings:

dàng [盪] **1** variant of 荡 [蕩][dà

tàng [盪] **1** variant of 烫 [燙][tàŋ **2** variant of 趟 [趟][tàng]

dàng [蕩] **1** to wash **2** to squa der **3** to sweep away **4** to mo **5** to shake **6** dissolute **7** pond

By accident, the chef put ordinary *grass* clippings in the *soup* instead of parsley and dill. The resulting brew tasted bitter, and the whole batch had to be **washed away**.

468

吻

SIMP & TRAD

This character with the definition:

kiss

Pinyin **wěn** *and Frequency Rank* **1973**

Contains **7 strokes** in the following order:

丿 冂 口 口' 吻 吻 吻

Contains these components:

▯ mouth 口 37, p. 17

▯ do not 勿 460, p. 111

With all these meanings & readings:

wěn [吻] **1** kiss **2** mouth

A **kiss** is sometimes an unwanted overture so *do not* bring your lips near your beloved's *mouth* unless you're given a clear signal.

469

刀

SIMP & TRAD

This character with the definition:

knife

Pinyin **dāo** *and Frequency Rank* **1067**

Contains **2 strokes** in the following order:

刁 刀

Contains these components:

▯ place of refuge c 丁 105, p. 33

▯ action path c 丿 438, p. 105

With all these meanings & readings:

dāo [刀] **1** knife **2** m 把[bǎ] **3** see also 刂 [刂][dāo]

Our *place of refuge* was disturbed by the *actions* of an intruder. Luckily, we had a brave hero who used his **knife** to save us all. • This character expands the slim **knife** of panel 169, but it's still the same **knife**.

470

切

SIMP & TRAD

This character with the definition:

cut, slice

Pinyin **qiē** *and Frequency Rank* **337**

Contains **4 strokes** in the following order:

Contains these components:

■ seven 七 123, p. 36
■ knife 刀 469, p. 112

With all these meanings & readings:

qiē [切] **1** to cut **2** to slice **qiè** [切] **1** definitely **2** absolutely (not) **3** to grind **4** close to **5** eager **6** to correspond to **7** see also 反切[fǎn qiè]

That expensive set of *seven knives* makes precision **slicing** and **cutting** a breeze.

471

力

SIMP & TRAD

This character with the definition:

strength

Pinyin **lì** *and Frequency Rank* **106**

Contains **2 strokes** in the following order:

Contains these components:

■ knife 刀 (altered) 469, p. 112

With all these meanings & readings:

lì [力] **1** power **2** force **3** strength

The handle of the *knife* has been altered to emphasize the **strength** you will need to force the blade deep into the bowels of... well, you fill in the rest. • Take care not confuse this character with 刀, *knife*, panel 469.

472

功

SIMP & TRAD

This character with the definition:

meritorious service, deed

Pinyin **gōng** *and Frequency Rank* **452**

Contains **5 strokes** in the following order:

Contains these components:

■ labor, work 工 12, p. 12
■ strength 力 471, p. 113

With all these meanings & readings:

gōng [功] **1** merit **2** achievement **3** result **4** service **5** accomplishment **6** work (physics)

The most prosperous societies define **meritorious service** as the combination of *strength* of character and hard *work*.

473

助

SIMP & TRAD

This character with the definition:

help*

Pinyin **zhù** *and Frequency Rank* **607**

Contains **7 strokes** in the following order:

Contains these components:

■ moreover 且 84, p. 28
■ strength 力 471, p. 113

With all these meanings & readings:

zhù [助] **1** to help **2** to assist

丨 冂 冂 日 且 助 助

I lost my way in the forest, wandered around all day, and did not feel I had the *strength* to survive the night. Fortunately, a search team arrived just in time to **help** me; *moreover*, they gave me food and water!

474

男

SIMP & TRAD

This character with the definition:

male

Pinyin **nán** *and Frequency Rank* **602**

Contains **7 strokes** in the following order:

Contains these components:

■ field 田 63, p. 23
■ strength 力 471, p. 113

With all these meanings & readings:

nán [男] **1** male **2** Baron, lowest of five orders of nobility 五等爵位[wǔ děng jué wèi] **3** m 个 [個][gè]

丨 冂 冂 田 田 甼 男

In the entire *field* of human endeavors, only those enterprises that require great physical *strength* are considered to be 'exclusively **male**' activities.

475

勒

SIMP & TRAD

This character with the definition:

rein in

Pinyin **lè** *and Frequency Rank* **966**

Contains **11 strokes** in the following order:

一 十 卄 艹 艹 芏 苎 苎 革 靪 勒

Contains these components:

animal hide 革 98, p. 31

strength 力 471, p. 113

With all these meanings & readings

lè [勒] **1** rein in
lēi [勒] **1** to choke **2** to throttl
3 to strangle

The only way to **rein in** a high-strung horse is to exert human *strength* on the bridle made of *animal hide.*

476

加

SIMP & TRAD

This character with the definition:

add, increase

Pinyin **jiā** *and Frequency Rank* **166**

Contains **5 strokes** in the following order:

フ 力 加 加 加

Contains these components:

strength 力 471, p. 113

mouth 口 37, p. 17

With all these meanings & readings

jiā [加] **1** to add **2** plus **3** abb
for Canada 加拿大

The *strength* of the vocal cords in all those *mouths* will determine the volume of noise the kids **add** to the child's birthday party.

477

駕

TRAD   SIMPLIFIED

This character with the definition:

harness, draw a cart

Pinyin **jià** *and Frequency Rank* **1567**

Contains **8 strokes** in the following order:

フ 力 加 加 加 驾 驾 驾

Contains these components:

add, increase 加 476, p. 114

horse 马 388, p. 95

With all these meanings & readings

jià [驾] **1** to harness **2** to draw
(a cart etc) **3** to drive **4** to pi
lot **5** to sail **6** to ride **7** your
good self **8** surname Jia **9** pre
fixed word denoting respect (po
lite 敬辞)

If you *add* some special equipment, such as a **harness**, to the *horse* you can use it to **draw a cart**.

478

另

SIMP & TRAD

This character with the definition:

other, another

Pinyin **lìng** *and Frequency Rank* **489**

Contains **5 strokes** in the following order:

丶 冖 口 另 另

Contains these components:

mouth 口 37, p. 17

strength 力 471, p. 113

With all these meanings & readings

lìng [另] **1** other **2** another
3 separate **4** separately

Poor people often curse the existence of destitute relatives: "**Another** *mouth* to feed! I'll need all my *strength* to earn more money."

479

別

TRAD   SIMPLIFIED

This character with the definition:

do not, must not

Pinyin **bié** *and Frequency Rank* **222**

Contains **7 strokes** in the following order:

丶 冖 口 另 另 别 别

Contains these components:

other, another 另 (altered) 478, p. 114

knife r 刂 169, p. 46

With all these meanings & readings

bié [别] **1** to leave **2** to depart
3 to separate **4** to distinguish
5 to classify **6** other **7** anothe
8 do not **9** must not **10** to
pin
biè [彆] **1** see 别扭[彆~], contra
2 difficult **3** awkward

There are two kitchen *knives* on the counter. One is dull and the *other* is deadly sharp. Whatever you do, **do not** play around with the sharp *knife*.

480

歷
TRAD   SIMPLIFIED

This character with the definition:

experience

Pinyin **lì** *and Frequency Rank* **480**

Contains **4 strokes** in the following order:

一 厂 厉 历

Contains these components:

□ cliff r 厂 399, p. 97

■ strength 力 471, p. 113

With all these meanings & readings:

lì [曆] **1** calendar
lì [歷] **1** to experience **2** to undergo **3** to pass through **4** all **5** each **6** every **7** calendar **8** history

The terrorists almost succeeded in throwing me off the *cliff*. Luckily, I held on by my fingertips and used all my *strength* to pull myself up to safety. What an **experience**!

481

為
TRAD   SIMPLIFIED

This character with the definition:

do, accomplish

Pinyin **wéi** *and Frequency Rank* **18**

Contains **4 strokes** in the following order:

丶 ソ 为 为

Contains these components:

■ strength 力 471, p. 113

□ dab r (×2) 丶 176, p. 48

With all these meanings & readings:

wéi [為] **1** as (in the capacity of) **2** to take sth as **3** to act as **4** to serve as **5** to behave as **6** to become **7** to be **8** to do
wèi [為] **1** because of **2** for **3** to

With the *strength* of his arms, the thug made *little* cutting marks with his knife, and realized that he had **accomplished** the killing deed quicker than he anticipated.

482

勞
TRAD   SIMPLIFIED

This character with the definition:

toil

Pinyin **láo** *and Frequency Rank* **679**

Contains **7 strokes** in the following order:

一 十 艹 艹 艹 劳 劳

Contains these components:

□ grass r 艹 87, p. 29

□ cover r 冖 250, p. 66

■ strength 力 471, p. 113

With all these meanings & readings:

láo [勞] **1** toil

One needs great *strength* to haul dried *grass* into the hut and construct a thatched *covering*. All in all, too much **toil** is required.

483

SIMP & TRAD

This character with the definition:

flourishing, thriving

Pinyin **bó** *and Frequency Rank* **1533**

Contains **9 strokes** in the following order:

一 十 ナ 古 ち 孛 孛 勃 勃

Contains these components:

■ ancient 古 (altered) 53, p. 21

■ son, child 子 24, p. 15

■ strength 力 471, p. 113

With all these meanings & readings:

bó [勃] **1** flourishing **2** prosperous **3** suddenly **4** abruptly

If the family environment is *strong*, *children* will reach *old* age in **thriving** health.

484

SIMP & TRAD

This character with the definition:

call, convene

Pinyin **zhào** *and Frequency Rank* **1214**

Contains **5 strokes** in the following order:

フ 刀 刀 召 召

Contains these components:

□ knife 刀 469, p. 112

■ mouth 口 37, p. 17

With all these meanings & readings:

zhào [召] **1** surname Shao **2** name of an ancient state
zhào [召] **1** to call together **2** to summon **3** to convene

The leader **convenes** the meeting of his followers with a *verbal* shout. For those who don't respond, the leader brandishes his *knife* and threatens to inflict a dire punishment on them.

Unit 22

485

招

SIMP & TRAD

This character with the definition:

beckon, enlist

Pinyin **zhāo** *and Frequency Rank* **941**

Contains **8 strokes** in the following order:

Contains these components:

☐ hand r 扌 25, p.15
☐ call, convene 召 484, p.115

With all these meanings & readings

zhāo [招] **1** to recruit **2** to provoke **3** to beckon **4** to incur **5** to infect **6** contagious **7** a move (chess) **8** a maneuver **9** device **10** trick **11** to confes

The recruiter waves his *hand* at you to get your attention. He wants you to heed the *call* of duty to serve your country and **enlist** in the military.

486

昭

SIMP & TRAD

This character with the definition:

clear, obvious

Pinyin **zhāo** *and Frequency Rank* **2190**

Contains **9 strokes** in the following order:

Contains these components:

☐ day, sun 日 64, p.24
☐ call, convene 召 484, p.115

With all these meanings & readings

zhāo [昭] **1** bright **2** clear **3** manifest **4** to show clearly

They *convened* the meeting early in the *day* because the bright light would make **clear** who the troublemakers were.

487

刃

SIMP & TRAD

This character with the definition:

blade edge

Pinyin **rèn** *and Frequency Rank* **2700**

Contains **3 strokes** in the following order:

刁 刀 刃

Contains these components:

■ knife 刀 469, p.112
☐ dab r 丶 (altered) 176, p.48

With all these meanings & readings

rèn [刃] **1** edge of blade

Ow! I just cut myself on the **blade edge** of that *knife*. Look at that *dab* of blood if you don't believe me!

488

片

SIMP & TRAD

This character with the definition:

slice, flake

Pinyin **piàn** *and Frequency Rank* **455**

Contains **4 strokes** in the following order:

丿 丿' 片' 片

Contains these components:

☐ action path c 丿 438, p.105
☐ on 上 (abbrev) 189, 52
☐ place of refuge c 丁 (altered) 105, p.33

With all these meanings & readings

piàn [片] **1** disc **2** sheet
piàn [片] **1** thin piece **2** flake **3** a slice **4** film **5** TV play **6** to slice **7** to carve thin **8** p tial **9** incomplete **10** one-side **11** m for slices, tablets, tract of land, area of water **12** m for CDs, movies, DVDs etc **13** use with numeral 一[yī]: classifier for scenario, scene, feeling, atm sphere, sound etc

After working *actively* and strenuously outside, it feels good to come inside to a warm *place of refuge* where the people pile stacks of hot food *on* your plate. My favorite are **slices** of roast beef.

489

牌

SIMP & TRAD

This character with the definition:

plate, tablet

Pinyin **pái** *and Frequency Rank* **1261**

Contains **12 strokes** in the following order:

Contains these components:

☐ slice, flake 片 488, p.116
☐ low, inferior 卑 439, p.105

With all these meanings & readings

pái [牌] **1** mahjong tile **2** play ing card **3** game pieces **4** sig board **5** plate **6** tablet **7** me **8** m 片[piàn], 个[個][gè], 块 [塊][kuài]

The *slice* of metal close to the surface looks *low* because the surface itself is so flat and horizontal; it is a **tablet** inscribed with important information.

490

方

SIMP & TRAD

This character with the definition:

square; direction

Pinyin **fāng** *and Frequency Rank* **60**

Contains **4 strokes** in the following order:

Contains these components:

☐ cover r 冖 250, p. 66

■ action path c 丿 438, p. 105

☐ place of refuge c 乛 105, p. 33

With all these meanings & readings:

fāng [方] **1** square **2** quadri-lateral **3** power (such as cube 立方) **4** m for square things **5** upright **6** honest **7** fair and square **8** surname Fang **9** direction **10** party (to a dispute) **11** one side **12** place **13** method **14** prescription **15** just **16** then **17** only then

This stylized plow emphasizes the importance of this tool to the ancient economy. The strokes depict how the furrows of the plow precisely change **direction**, with the result being an outline of a **square** field. Moreover, can you see how the *action* extends at its upper end, past the *place of refuge*? Only the *cover* provides the restraint to ensure that the **direction** of motion stays within the defined **square**.

491

芳

SIMP & TRAD

This character with the definition:

aromatic

Pinyin **fāng** *and Frequency Rank* **1586**

Contains **7 strokes** in the following order:

Contains these components:

☐ grass r 艹 87, p. 29

■ square; direction 方 490, p. 117

With all these meanings & readings:

fāng [芳] **1** fragrant

The town residents decided to add **fragrant** flowers as a colorful and scent-filled border to the rather boring plot of *grass* in the town *square*.

492

访

TRAD   SIMPLIFIED

This character with the definition:

visit, call on, seek

Pinyin **fǎng** *and Frequency Rank* **1037**

Contains **6 strokes** in the following order:

Contains these components:

■ speech r 讠 352, p. 88

☐ square; direction 方 490, p. 117

With all these meanings & readings:

fǎng [访] **1** to visit **2** to call on **3** to seek **4** to inquire **5** to investigate

On my way to **visit** my cousin, I stopped and *spoke* to an old man sitting in the *square* to make sure I was headed in the right *direction*.

493

不

SIMP & TRAD

This character with the definition:

no!

Pinyin **bù** *and Frequency Rank* **4**

Contains **4 strokes** in the following order:

Contains these components:

■ under 下 199, p. 54

☐ action path c 丿 438, p. 105

With all these meanings & readings:

bù [不] **1** (negative prefix) **2** not **3** no

1 One way to make sure an *action* will **not** be completed is to halt its progress by forcing it 'under ground', or 'under the radar'. 2 Think of a martini glass, complete with its stirrer that's turned upside-down! That's definitely **not** the way to get drunk!

494

否

SIMP & TRAD

This character with the definition:

negate

Pinyin **fǒu** *and Frequency Rank* **620**

Contains **7 strokes** in the following order:

Contains these components:

☐ no! 不 493, p. 117

■ mouth 口 37, p. 17

With all these meanings & readings:

fǒu [否] **1** to negate **2** to deny **3** not

pǐ [否] **1** clogged **2** evil

When you use your *mouth* to say *no*, you **negate** an opinion.

495

壞
TRAD SIMPLIFIED

This character with the definition:

bad

Pinyin **huài** *and Frequency Rank* **832**

Contains **7 strokes** in the following order:

一 十 土 圵 坏 坏 坏

Contains these components:

■ earth, soil 土 9, p.11
■ no! 不 493, p.117

With all these meanings & readings

huài [壞] **1** bad **2** spoiled **3** broken **4** to break down

In ancient days, people thought that vapors emanating from the *earth* had a **bad** and harmful effect, rendering everything that grew too close to the soil *not* good.

496

環
TRAD SIMPLIFIED

This character with the definition:

encircle

Pinyin **huán** *and Frequency Rank* **681**

Contains **8 strokes** in the following order:

一 二 干 王 玎 玎 珩 环

Contains these components:

■ king 王 15, p.12
■ no! 不 493, p.117

With all these meanings & readings

huán [環] **1** bracelet **2** ring (no for finger) **3** to surround **4** to loop **5** loop

The *king* slammed his fist so hard on the table when he shouted *"No!"* that it caused his cup to fall over. Soon his cup was **encircled** by the wine that had been in it. • It's easy to mistake the two characters in panels 495, 496 for each other—坏 versus this panel's 环. If you've ever bought food and stored it for later use, you know that you have to keep it off the ground, for ground contact promotes spoilage. In olden times, the circle was considered to be the most perfect of geometric forms, so much so that it sometimes received holy or royal status, so it's easy therefore to associate '*king*' with '**encircling**'.

497

SIMP & TRAD

This character with the definition:

old

Pinyin **lǎo** *and Frequency Rank* **179**

Contains **6 strokes** in the following order:

一 十 土 少 老 老

Contains these components:

■ earth, soil 土 9, p.11
■ action path c ノ 438, p.105
■ hair 毛 (abbrev) 184, 50

With all these meanings & readings

lǎo [老] **1** prefix used before the surname of a person or a numeral indicating the order of birth of the children in a family or to indicate affection or familiarity **2** old (of people) **3** venerable (person) **4** experienced **5** of long standing **6** always **7** all the time **8** of the past **9** very **10** outdated **11** (of mea etc) tough

On the natural *path* of the human life cycle, a person becomes **old** and his hair turns *gray* before he returns to the *earth*.

498

孝

SIMP & TRAD

This character with the definition:

filial

Pinyin **xiào** *and Frequency Rank* **2116**

Contains **7 strokes** in the following order:

一 十 土 少 耂 孝 孝

Contains these components:

■ old 老 (abbrev) 497, 118
■ son, child 子 24, p.15

With all these meanings & readings

xiào [孝] **1** filial

The position of these elements—with the '*son*' supporting the '*old*' element— illustrates the meaning of **filial** responsibility.

499

屍
尸
TRAD   SIMPLIFIED

This character with the definition:

corpse

Pinyin **shī** *and Frequency Rank* **1517**

Contains **3 strokes** in the following order:

一 コ 尸

Contains these components:

■ action path c ノ 438, p.105
□ enclosure r 囗 (altered) 36, p.17

With all these meanings & readings:

shī [尸] **1** person representing the dead (during burial ceremonies) **2** to put a corpse on display (after execution) **3** variant of ⊠ **4** corpse
shī [屍] **1** corpse

The body acts as an *enclosure* for the vital spirit and *actions* of a living person. Upon reaching death, the *action* departs (is it leaking out from the left of the character in that *path*-like trail?), and all that remains is a shell, or the **corpse**.

500

SIMP & TRAD

This character with the definition:

reside

Pinyin **jū** *and Frequency Rank* **678**

Contains **8 strokes** in the following order:

一 コ 尸 尸 尸 居 居 居

Contains these components:

□ corpse 尸 499, p.119
■ ancient 古 53, p.21

With all these meanings & readings:

jū [居] **1** reside

The emperor's *corpse* still **resides** in the splendor of his highly decorated *ancient* tomb.

501

據
TRAD   SIMPLIFIED

This character with the definition:

hold, occupy, seize

Pinyin **jù** *and Frequency Rank* **313**

Contains **11 strokes** in the following order:

一 十 扌 扩 护 护 护 捉 捉 据 据

Contains these components:

■ hand r 扌 25, p.15
□ reside 居 500, p.119

With all these meanings & readings:

jū [据] **1** see 拮据 [~據][jié jū]
jù [據] **1** according to **2** to act in accordance with **3** to depend on **4** to seize **5** to occupy

The *hand* represents the enemy occupier, come to your *residence* to **seize** and **occupy** the premises.

502

劇
TRAD   SIMPLIFIED

This character with the definition:

drama, play

Pinyin **jù** *and Frequency Rank* **909**

Contains **10 strokes** in the following order:

一 コ 尸 尸 尸 居 居 居 剧 剧

Contains these components:

■ reside 居 500, p.119
□ knife r 刂 169, p.46

With all these meanings & readings:

jù [劇] **1** drama **2** play **3** show **4** severe

The set resembles the interior of a charming nineteenth century *residence*. When the curtain goes up, a hooded figure enters silently from stage right, holding a wicked *knife* that gleams in the footlights, and so the suspense and **drama** begin. The audience will be on the edge of their seats throughout the entire show!

503

屆
TRAD   SIMPLIFIED

This character with the definition:

a year's graduates

Pinyin **jiè** *and Frequency Rank* **1522**

Contains **8 strokes** in the following order:

一 コ 尸 尸 尺 屈 屈 届

Contains these components:

□ corpse 尸 499, p.119
■ reason, by means of 由 58, p.22

With all these meanings & readings:

jiè [届] **1** to arrive at (place or time) **2** period **3** to become due **4** m for events, meetings, elections, sporting fixtures etc

I worked so hard and ate so little at university that I thought I would become a *corpse*. Four years later, *they let me* **graduate**.

504

SIMP & TRAD

This character with the definition:

brush, scrub

Pinyin **shuā** *and Frequency Rank* **1824**

Contains **8 strokes** in the following order:

丶 ｺ 尸 尸 启 吊 刷 刷

Contains these components:

corpse 尸 499, p.119

towel 巾 118, p.35

knife r 刂 169, p.46

With all these meanings & readings

shuā [刷] **1** to brush **2** to paint **3** to daub **4** to paste up **5** to skip class (of students) **6** to fire from a job
shuà [刷] **1** to select

The proper cleaning of a *corpse* is a delicate art. The most important of the artist's tools are his *towels* to **scrub** the corpse and *knife* to remove evidence of violence.

505

SIMP & TRAD

This character with the definition:

tail

Pinyin **wěi** *and Frequency Rank* **1282**

Contains **7 strokes** in the following order:

丶 ｺ 尸 尸 尼 屋 尾

Contains these components:

corpse 尸 499, p.119

hair 毛 184, p.50

With all these meanings & readings

wěi [尾] **1** tail **2** m for fish

The roadkill was the *corpse* of a fine raccoon. Even though the body was intact, all the fur had been stripped off of the raccoon with the exception of its **tail** with *hair* still on it.

506

SIMP & TRAD

This character with the definition:

urine

Pinyin **suī** *and Frequency Rank* **1877**

Contains **7 strokes** in the following order:

丶 ｺ 尸 尸 戸 尿 尿

Contains these components:

corpse 尸 499, p.119

water 水 315, p.81

With all these meanings & readings

niào [尿] **1** to urinate **2** urine **3** m 泡[pāo]
suī [尿] **1** (less common reading) to urinate **2** urine

Your kidneys remove harmful *fluids* from your body by producing **urine**. Without normal kidney function, these *fluids* would become toxic and your body would transform into a *corpse*.

507

SIMP & TRAD

This character with the definition:

ruler (length)

Pinyin **chǐ** *and Frequency Rank* **1474**

Contains **4 strokes** in the following order:

丶 ｺ 尸 尺

Contains these components:

corpse 尸 499, p.119

mineshaft c ㄴ (altered) 122, p.36

With all these meanings & readings

chě [尺] **1** one of the notes in the gongchepu
chǐ [尺] **1** a Chinese foot **2** one-third of a meter **3** a ruler **4** a tape-measure **5** one of the three acupoints for measuring pulse in Chinese medicine **6** m 支[zhī], 把[bǎ]

They found a *corpse* in the bottom of a *mineshaft*. It was so old that all the flesh had decayed off the bones. All that was left on the bones were black marks that made each one look like a **ruler**.

508
局
偏
TRAD

SIMPLIFIED

This character with the definition:

bureau, office

Pinyin **jú** *and Frequency Rank* **483**

Contains **7 strokes** in the following order:

丶 ｺ 尸 吊 局 局 局

Contains these components:

ruler (length) 尺 (altered) 507, p.120

mouth 口 37, p.17

With all these meanings & readings

jú [偏] **1** narrow
jú [局] **1** office **2** situation **3** m for games: match, set, round e

A government **office** is a place where far too many *rules* are issued from the *mouths* of officials.

509 民

SIMP & TRAD

This character with the definition:

people, masses

Pinyin **mín** *and Frequency Rank* **113**

Contains **5 strokes** in the following order:

Contains these components:

ruler (length) 尺 507, p.120

one 一 1, p.10

With all these meanings & readings:

mín [民] **1** the people **2** nationality **3** citizen

The **masses** usually find themselves serving *one ruler*.

Unit 23

510

This character with the definition:

state of sleep, dormancy

Pinyin **mián** *and Frequency Rank* **1986**

SIMP & TRAD   Contains **10 strokes** in the following order:

丨 刀 月 日 日 日 日 肝 肝 眠 眠

Contains these components:

◻ eye 目 75, p. 26

◻ people, masses 民 509, p. 121

With all these meanings & reading

mián [眠] **1** sleep

The *eyes* of the *people* are always alert and never display fatigue or the need for the **state of sleep**!

---

511 盡
TRAD SIMPLIFIED

This character with the definition:

utmost, to the greatest extent

Pinyin **jǐn** *and Frequency Rank* **488**

Contains **6 strokes** in the following order:

フ コ ア 尺 尽 尽

Contains these components:

◼ ruler (length) 尺 507, p. 120

◻ two 二 2, p. 10

With all these meanings & reading

jǐn [盡] **1** to the utmost
jìn [盡] **1** to use up **2** to exhaust **3** to end **4** to finish **5** to the utmost **6** exhausted **7** finished **8** to the limit (of sth)

The *two* marks underneath the *ruler* represent the **greatest extent** we are willing to go to achieve our goals.

512

This character with the definition:

nun

Pinyin **ní** *and Frequency Rank* **654**

SIMP & TRAD   Contains **5 strokes** in the following order:

フ コ ア 尸 尼

Contains these components:

◻ corpse 尸 499, p. 119

◼ seven 七 (altered) 123, p. 36

With all these meanings & reading

ní [尼] **1** Buddhist nun **2** (oft used in phonetic spellings)

In ancient times, **nuns** would prepare the *dead* for burial and each **nun** had to fulfill a quota of *seven corpses* per day.

513

This character with the definition:

s-end with many uses

Pinyin **ne** *and Frequency Rank* **383**

SIMP & TRAD   Contains **8 strokes** in the following order:

丨 𠃌 口 口 口 呎 呢 呢

Contains these components:

◻ mouth 口 37, p. 17

◼ nun 尼 512, p. 122

With all these meanings & reading

ne [呢] **1** (question particle for subjects already mentioned)
ní [呢] **1** this (Cantonese) **2** s also 哩 [哩][li]
ní [呢] **1** woolen material

Nuns take vows of poverty, so for all practical purposes the only things they own are very special objects that are created **with many uses**, such as multi-purpose tools. The '*mouth*' element reminds us that the *mouth* **has many uses**—to speak, eat, and kiss.

514

This character with the definition:

mud, clay

Pinyin **ní** *and Frequency Rank* **1499**

SIMP & TRAD   Contains **8 strokes** in the following order:

丶 丶 氵 氵 汋 沪 沪 泥

Contains these components:

◻ water r 氵 314, p. 80

◼ nun 尼 512, p. 122

With all these meanings & reading

ní [泥] **1** mud **2** clay **3** paste **4** pulp
nì [泥] **1** restrained

When the *nun* fell in the *water*, **mud** coated her habit. Because it was black, no one could tell that the *nun*'s habit was so dirty.

515 眉

eyebrow

Pinyin **méi** *and Frequency Rank* **1460**

SIMP & TRAD   Contains **9 strokes** in the following order:

一 宀 コ 尸 尸 尸 厈 眉 眉

Contains these components:

■ corpse 尸 (altered) 499, p.119
■ eye 目 75, p. 26

With all these meanings & readings:

méi [眉] **1** eyebrow   **2** upper margin

The form of the altered *corpse* is supposed to suggest the appearance of unruly hair and hair hanging over an *eye* makes an **eyebrow**! Perhaps a little farfetched, but it may help to remember that hair represents the growth of dead cells (*corpse*-like).

516 户

door of house

Pinyin **hù** *and Frequency Rank* **1073**

SIMP & TRAD   Contains **4 strokes** in the following order:

丶 宀 宀 户

Contains these components:

■ corpse 尸 (altered) 499, p.119
□ one 一 1, p.10

With all these meanings & readings:

hù [户] **1** a household   **2** door **3** family

1 The **doorway** to life is closed forever when *one* becomes a *corpse*. 2 Also, think of the top left corner as a door hinge. The rectangle depicts the **door** itself, and the downward, not-quite-horizontal stroke represents the limits of its swing.

517 声

聲
TRAD

sound, voice

Pinyin **shēng** *and Frequency Rank* **195**

SIMPLIFIED   Contains **7 strokes** in the following order:

一 十 士 吉 吉 吉 声

Contains these components:

□ knight 士 8, p.11
■ corpse 尸 (altered) 499, p.119

With all these meanings & readings:

shēng [聲] **1** sound   **2** voice **3** tone   **4** noise   **5** m for sounds

Imagine a frenzied *knight* jumping on a *corpse*, leaving a mark, and causing a bizarre **sound** to issue forth from the body's mouth.

518 屈

bend

Pinyin **qū** *and Frequency Rank* **1684**

SIMP & TRAD   Contains **8 strokes** in the following order:

一 コ 尸 尸 居 屈 屈 屈

Contains these components:

□ corpse 尸 499, p.119
■ exit 出 158, p.43

With all these meanings & readings:

qū [屈] **1** bent   **2** feel wronged **3** surname Qu

The *dead body* is being carried through the narrow *exit* to the hearse. (See how scrunched up the '*exit*' appears in this character.) The person in life was quite fat, so the only way it can fit through the *exit* is if you **bend** it.

519 卢

盧
TRAD

gourd

Pinyin **lú** *and Frequency Rank* **1711**

SIMPLIFIED   Contains **5 strokes** in the following order:

丨 卜 上 占 卢

Contains these components:

□ foretell 卜 187, p.51
■ corpse 尸 499, p.119

With all these meanings & readings:

Lú [盧] **1** surname Lu   **2** abbr for Luxembourg 卢森堡[盧~~]

With their eccentric, colorful, and entrancing appearance, **gourds** are ideal decorations for religious ceremonies. When dried and preserved, they symbolize the *corpses* of vegetables and can be used to *foretell* the future.

520 乃

This character with the definition:

so, therefore

Pinyin **nǎi** *and Frequency Rank* **1165**

SIMP & TRAD   Contains **2 strokes** in the following order:

Contains these components:

■ action path c ノ 438, p.105
□ bow (weapon) 弓 (altered) 140, p.40

With all these meanings & readings

nǎi [乃] **1** to be **2** thus **3** so **4** therefore **5** then **6** only **7** thereupon

乃 乃

The hunter was an expert at catching game, **so** once an arrow flew out of his *bow*, the arrow's *action path* always led to the intended target.

521 扔

This character with the definition:

throw, toss

Pinyin **rēng** *and Frequency Rank* **1905**

SIMP & TRAD   Contains **5 strokes** in the following order:

Contains these components:

■ hand r 扌 25, p.15
■ so, therefore 乃 520, p.124

With all these meanings & readings

rēng [扔] **1** to throw **2** to throw away

一 十 扌 扔 扔

One of the easiest ways to get *results* is to use your *hand* to **throw** something at your professor!

522 石

This character with the definition:

stone, rock

Pinyin **shí** *and Frequency Rank* **414**

SIMP & TRAD   Contains **5 strokes** in the following order:

Contains these components:

□ one 一 1, p.10
■ action path c ノ 438, p.105
□ mouth 口 37, p.17

With all these meanings & readings

dàn [石] **1** dry measure for grain equal to ten dou 斗 **2** ten peck **3** one hundred liters
shí [石] **1** rock **2** stone **3** surname Shi

一 丆 丆 石 石

This simple design by the scribes makes it fairly easy to visualize *one* large **stone** falling off a cliff and traveling in a downward *action path* until it comes to rest at the base of the cliff. Here the "*mouth*" represents the '**stone**' at the base.

523 碧

This character with the definition:

green jade

Pinyin **bì** *and Frequency Rank* **2165**

SIMP & TRAD   Contains **14 strokes** in the following order:

Contains these components:

□ emperor 皇 (altered) 227, p.60
■ stone, rock 石 522, p.124

With all these meanings & readings

bì [碧] **1** green jade **2** bluish green **3** blue **4** jade

一 二 干 王 王' 珇 珀 珀 珀 碧 碧 碧 碧 碧

Which precious *stone* would be most appealing to the *emperor*? **Green jade**, of course—it is China's royal gem.

524 碍

碍
TRAD   SIMPLIFIED

This character with the definition:

in the way of

Pinyin **ài** *and Frequency Rank* **1437**

Contains **13 strokes** in the following order:

Contains these components:

■ stone, rock 石 522, p.124
□ day, sun 日 64, p.24
□ one 一 1, p.10
■ inch 寸 216, p.58

With all these meanings & readings

ài [碍] **1** to hinder **2** to obstruct **3** to block

一 丆 丆 石 石 石 矼 矼 砠 碍 碍 碍 碍

We're trapped at the bottom of the mine! Peering up, we can only see *one inch* of the *sun* because a huge *stone* is **in the way of** our escape.

525

础

礎

TRAD SIMPLIFIED

This character with the definition:

base, foundation*

Pinyin **chǔ** *and Frequency Rank* **1014**

Contains **10 strokes** in the following order:

一 丆 丆 石 石 石⌐ 矿 砒 础 础

Contains these components:

■ stone, rock 石 522, p.124

▯ exit 出 158, p.43

With all these meanings & readings:

chǔ ［礎］ **1** foundation **2** base

The component that means '*exit*' has a structural appearance that looks like it could hold something up. In fact, it holds up large sheets of *stone*, which serve as a strong and solid **base** for this building.

526

码

碼

TRAD SIMPLIFIED

This character with the definition:

number

Pinyin **mǎ** *and Frequency Rank* **1345**

Contains **8 strokes** in the following order:

一 丆 丆 石 石 石⌐ 码 码

Contains these components:

▯ stone, rock 石 522, p.124

■ horse 马 388, p.95

With all these meanings & readings:

mǎ ［碼］ **1** weight **2** number **3** code **4** to pile **5** to stack **6** m for length or distance (yard), happenings, etc.

The large **number** of loose *stones* on the steep canyon trail made it difficult for my *horse* to maintain his footing.

527

岩

岩
巖

TRAD SIMPLIFIED

This character with the definition:

cliff, crag

Pinyin **yán** *and Frequency Rank* **1423**

Contains **8 strokes** in the following order:

丨 屮 山 屵 屵 屵 岩 岩

Contains these components:

▭ mountain 山 4, p.10

▭ stone, rock 石 522, p.124

With all these meanings & readings:

yán ［岩］ **1** cliff **2** rock
yán ［巖］ **1** cliff

The salient quality of a **cliff** is the abrupt and sudden contrast between the high ground on one side of the cliff and the low ground on the other. This character emphasizes the contrast in terrain—the high *mountain* on top next to the big *rock* resting on the ground below.

528

矿

礦

TRAD SIMPLIFIED

This character with the definition:

ore

Pinyin **kuàng** *and Frequency Rank* **1385**

Contains **8 strokes** in the following order:

一 丆 丆 石 石 石` 石⌐ 矿

Contains these components:

■ stone, rock 石 522, p.124

▯ extensive 广 430, p.104

With all these meanings & readings:

kuàng ［礦］ **1** ore **2** mine

Ore is composed of *extensive* supplies of an important kind of mineral or *stone*.

529

身

SIMP & TRAD

This character with the definition:

body

Pinyin **shēn** *and Frequency Rank* **164**

Contains **7 strokes** in the following order:

丿 亻 竹 白 自 身 身

Contains these components:

▭ self 自 (altered) 232, p.61

■ action path c ノ 438, p.105

▯ hooked stick c 亅 18, p.13

With all these meanings & readings:

shēn ［身］ **1** body **2** torso **3** person **4** life **5** status **6** pregnancy **7** m for clothes: suit

The *self* can prepare its **body** for constant *action* by equipping it*self* with *hooked sticks* and other useful tools.

530

This character with the definition:

shoot

Pinyin **shè** *and Frequency Rank* **703**

SIMP & TRAD   Contains **10 strokes** in the following order:

Contains these components:

◨ body 身 529, p. 125
◨ inch 寸 216, p. 58

With all these meanings & reading

shè [射] **1** to shoot **2** to laun
3 to allude to **4** radio- (chemistry)

During her first attempt at learning how to **shoot** a gun, she was shocked to find out that the force of the gun's recoil would make her *body* feel as if it had jumped an *inch*.

531

謝
TRAD   SIMPLIFIED

This character with the definition:

thank

Pinyin **xiè** *and Frequency Rank* **897**

Contains **12 strokes** in the following order:

Contains these components:

◨ speech r 讠 352, p. 88
◨ shoot 射 530, p. 126

With all these meanings & reading

xiè [謝] **1** to thank **2** to apolo
gize **3** to wither (flowers, leav
etc) **4** to decline **5** surname
Xie

Since it was tradition that a prisoner facing a firing squad be allowed to *speak* before the squad begins to *shoot*, this prisoner chose to **thank** each member of the firing squad in his *speech*.

532

This character with the definition:

nine

Pinyin **jiǔ** *and Frequency Rank* **445**

SIMP & TRAD   Contains **2 strokes** in the following order:

Contains these components:

◨ action path c 丿 438, p. 105
◨ second (in a series) 乙 146, p. 41

With all these meanings & reading

jiǔ [九] **1** nine **2** 9

Since the worker was the *second* employee to volunteer for overtime, he became upset when he saw his name listed as 'Number **Nine**' for eligibility benefits. He immediately ran an *action path* straight to his supervisor's office to protest his position.

533

This character with the definition:

pill

Pinyin **wán** *and Frequency Rank* **2462**

SIMP & TRAD   Contains **3 strokes** in the following order:

Contains these components:

◨ nine 九 532, p. 126
◨ dab r 丶 176, p. 48

With all these meanings & reading

wán [丸] **1** pill

Some nutritionists say it is healthier to eat *nine* servings of fruits and vegetables per day, and allow yourself a *dab* of your favorite 'treat', than to take a vitamin **pill** everyday.

534

This character with the definition:

who? what? which? (literary)

Pinyin **shú** *and Frequency Rank* **3568**

SIMP & TRAD   Contains **11 strokes** in the following order:

Contains these components:

◨ enjoy 享 262, p. 68
◨ pill 丸 533, p. 126

With all these meanings & reading

shú [孰] **1** who **2** which **3** w

Many people want to know, "**Which** *pill* will help me to *enjoy* a perfectly happy life?"

Unit 24

535

執
TRAD　SIMPLIFIED

执

This character with the definition:

take charge of

Pinyin **zhí** and Frequency Rank **763**

Contains **6 strokes** in the following order:

一 十 才 扎 执 执

Contains these components:

■ hand r 扌 25, p.15
■ pill 丸 533, p.126

With all these meanings & readings:

zhí [執] **1** to execute (a plan) **2** to grasp

Medicine is expensive, and the *hand* here is holding the *pill* tightly. Someone seriously wants to **take charge of** healthcare!

536

勢
TRAD　SIMPLIFIED

势

This character with the definition:

power, force, influence

Pinyin **shì** and Frequency Rank **506**

Contains **8 strokes** in the following order:

一 十 才 扎 执 执 势 势

Contains these components:

■ take charge of 执 535, p.127
■ strength 力 471, p.113

With all these meanings & readings:

shì [勢] **1** power **2** influence **3** potential **4** momentum **5** tendency **6** trend **7** situation **8** conditions **9** outward appearance **10** sign **11** gesture **12** male genitals

Mao Zedong showed great *strength* in *taking charge of* the central government. The **power** he accumulated during his lifetime and the **influence** he had on China after his death were and remain noteworthy.

537

人
SIMP & TRAD

This character with the definition:

man

Pinyin **rén** and Frequency Rank **7**

Contains **2 strokes** in the following order:

丿 人

Contains these components:

■ action path c 丿 438, p.105
■ mineshaft c ㄥ (altered) 122, p.36

With all these meanings & readings:

rén [人] **1** man **2** person **3** people **4** m 个[個][gè], 位[wèi]

Men are different from animals. They have the ability to make decisions and to choose which *action paths* they want to take. Sometimes they take the wrong path and find themselves in *trouble*.

538

坐
SIMP & TRAD

This character with the definition:

sit

Pinyin **zuò** and Frequency Rank **611**

Contains **7 strokes** in the following order:

丿 人 亻丿 从 丛 坐 坐

Contains these components:

■ earth, soil 土 9, p.11
■ man (×2) 人 537, p.127

With all these meanings & readings:

zuò [坐] **1** to sit **2** to take a seat **3** to take (a bus, airplane etc) **4** to bear fruit **5** surname Zuo

Two men **sit** back-to-back on a bench, with their spines resting up against the central backrest divider. Each man is drawn small to show that the bench he **sits** on is close to the *ground*.

539

座
SIMP & TRAD

This character with the definition:

seat

Pinyin **zuò** and Frequency Rank **812**

Contains **10 strokes** in the following order:

丶 二 广 广 庐 庐 庐 座 座

Contains these components:

■ shelter r 广 427, p.103
■ sit 坐 538, p.127

With all these meanings & readings:

zuò [座] **1** seat **2** base **3** stand **4** (classifier for buildings, mountains, large solid things etc) **5** m 个[個][gè]

For the outdoor concert, we will need a venue that has a large *sheltered* area so we can set up about a thousand **seats**—enough so that everyone in the audience will have a place to *sit* down, without worrying about inclement weather or strong sun rays.

540

SIMP & TRAD

This character with the definition:

entire

Pinyin **quán** *and Frequency Rank* **124**

Contains **6 strokes** in the following order:

ノ 人 へ 今 今 全

Contains these components:

man 人 537, p.127

king 王 15, p.12

With all these meanings & readings

quán [全] **1** all **2** whole **3** en tire **4** every **5** complete **6** s name Quan

According to the more enlightened theories of governance, the *king* serves the **entire** population of *people,* and not vice versa. Having the *king* underneath *man* helps visualize this relationship.

541

SIMP & TRAD

This character with the definition:

pull, drag, haul

Pinyin **tuō** *and Frequency Rank* **1492**

Contains **8 strokes** in the following order:

一 十 才 扌 扩 拐 拐 拖

Contains these components:

hand r 扌 25, p.15

man 人 (altered) 537, p.127

also, too* 也 132, p.38

With all these meanings & reading

tuō [拖] **1** dragging (brush str in painting) **2** to drag along

This *man* uses his *two* (sounds like '*too*') *hands* to **pull** the rickshaw.

542

This character with the definition:

look forward to

Pinyin **qǐ** *and Frequency Rank* **450**

Contains **6 strokes** in the following order:

ノ 人 个 仐 仚 企

Contains these components:

man 人 537, p.127

stop! 止 190, p.52

With all these meanings & reading

qǐ [企] **1** to plan a project **2** stand on tiptoe **3** Taiwan pr **4** abbr for 企业, enterprise or company

SIMP & TRAD

I so **looked forward to** having my house painted that I waited eagerly on my front porch for the painters to arrive. When I saw a *man* drive 'my' painters' truck onto the neighbor's driveway, I immediately shouted "*Stop!* Wrong house!"

543

齒
TRAD   SIMPLIFIED

This character with the definition:

tooth

Pinyin **chǐ** *and Frequency Rank* **1773**

Contains **8 strokes** in the following order:

丨 卜 止 止 步 步 齿 齿

Contains these components:

stop! 止 190, p.52

man (×4) 人 537, p.127

mouth 口 37, p.17

With all these meanings & reading

chǐ [齒] **1** tooth **2** m 颗 [顆][kē]

Consider this character as depicting a molar **tooth** in your upper jaw. The top part represents the root of the **tooth**, which *stops* your tooth from moving as you chew. The actual **tooth** is located at the bottom of your *mouth*. The **tooth**'s surface is not completely flat; rather, the exterior has several facets on it and their outlines resemble the character 人, '*man*'.

544

大

big

Pinyin **dà** *and Frequency Rank* **17**

SIMP & TRAD   Contains **3 strokes** in the following order:

一 ナ 大

Contains these components:

■ man 人 537, p.127
▭ one 一 1, p.10

With all these meanings & readings:

dà [大] **1** big **2** huge **3** large **4** major **5** great **6** wide **7** deep **8** oldest **9** eldest
dài [大] **1** doctor

A *man* with outstretched arms, depicted by the long *horizontal*, emphasizes the concept of **big**.

545

因

because

Pinyin **yīn** *and Frequency Rank* **96**

SIMP & TRAD   Contains **6 strokes** in the following order:

丨 冂 冂 団 因 因

Contains these components:

▢ enclosure r 囗 36, p.17
■ big 大 544, p.129

With all these meanings & readings:

yīn [因] **1** cause **2** reason **3** because

Because he has a *big mouth*, everyone always hears his side of the argument first.

546

咽

throat

Pinyin **yān** *and Frequency Rank* **2031**

SIMP & TRAD   Contains **9 strokes** in the following order:

丨 口 口 叮 叼 叼 咽 咽 咽

Contains these components:

▢ mouth 口 37, p.17
■ because 因 545, p.129

With all these meanings & readings:

yān [咽] **1** narrow pass **2** throat **3** pharynx
yàn [咽] **1** to swallow
yè [咽] **1** to choke (in crying)

Because animals need nourishment, they put food in their *mouth* and send it down their **throat** to their stomach.

547

太

too (much)

Pinyin **tài** *and Frequency Rank* **240**

SIMP & TRAD   Contains **4 strokes** in the following order:

一 ナ 大 太

Contains these components:

■ big 大 544, p.129
▢ dab r 丶 176, p.48

With all these meanings & readings:

tài [太] **1** highest **2** greatest **3** too (much) **4** very **5** extremely

The '*dab*' is so much smaller than the *big* element above it that the *dab* can serve as a **marker of excess**—compared to it, its neighbor is **too** *big*.

548

天

heaven

Pinyin **tiān** *and Frequency Rank* **78**

SIMP & TRAD   Contains **4 strokes** in the following order:

一 二 于 天

Contains these components:

▢ one 一 1, p.10
■ big 大 544, p.129

With all these meanings & readings:

tiān [天] **1** day **2** sky **3** heaven

Heaven is often imagined as *one* lofty expanse above the great, *big* world.

549

吴

吳
TRAD   SIMPLIFIED

This character with the definition:

Kingdom of Wu

Pinyin **wú** *and Frequency Rank* **1135**

Contains **7 strokes** in the following order:

丶 一 ㇆ 口 吕 旦 吴 吴

Contains these components:

mouth 口 37, p.17

heaven 天 (altered) 548, p.129

With all these meanings & readings

Wú [吴] **1** surname Wu **2** prov of Jiangsu **3** name of Southern China states at different historic periods

The ancient Wu Kingdom was located in the south of what has become modern China, started in the year 222 AD, and lasted for about 60 years. Chinese historians regard the ability to rule effectively as a divine gift, a mandate from *heaven*. Here, the central location of the *mouth* acts as a divine signpost, indicating that *heaven*'s mandate lies to the south—the location of the **Kingdom of Wu**.

550

误

誤
TRAD   SIMPLIFIED

This character with the definition:

miss (due to delay)

Pinyin **wù** *and Frequency Rank* **854**

Contains **9 strokes** in the following order:

Contains these components:

speech r 讠 352, p.88

Kingdom of Wu 吴 (altered) 549, p.130

With all these meanings & readings

wù [误] **1** mistake **2** error **3** t miss **4** to harm **5** to delay **6** to neglect

We **missed** the last bus home because we were so enthralled by *King Wu's speech*, which sounded as if the words fell directly from 'heaven' into his 'mouth'. The element '*Kingdom of Wu*' itself uses *mouth* and *heaven* (panels 37 and 548).

551

笑

SIMP & TRAD

This character with the definition:

laugh, smile

Pinyin **xiào** *and Frequency Rank* **346**

Contains **10 strokes** in the following order:

丿 𠂆 𠂇 𥫗 竺 笑 竺 笑 笑

Contains these components:

bamboo r ⺮ 264, p.68

heaven 天 548, p.129

With all these meanings & readings:

xiào [笑] **1** laugh **2** smile **3** m 个 [個][gè]

At the very top of this character, the 'bamboo' element resembles two eyes twinkling in **laughter**. Perhaps the scribes combined it with the '*heaven*' element to depict the ancient belief that the gods in *heaven* had a sense of humor and loved to **laugh**.

552

矢

SIMP & TRAD

This character with the definition:

arrow

Pinyin **shǐ** *and Frequency Rank* **2811**

Contains **5 strokes** in the following order:

Contains these components:

dab r 丶 176, p.48

heaven 天 548, p.129

With all these meanings & readings:

shǐ [矢] **1** arrow **2** dart

The heavenly paths of **arrows** shot aloft by skilled archers inspired the ancient scribes to combine '*dabs*' and '*heaven*' to symbolize an **arrow** in flight.

553

知

SIMP & TRAD

This character with the definition:

know

Pinyin **zhī** *and Frequency Rank* **123**

Contains **8 strokes** in the following order:

丿 𠂉 𠂉 午 矢 知 知 知

Contains these components:

▪ arrow 矢 552, p.130

▫ mouth 口 37, p.17

With all these meanings & readings:

zhī [知] **1** to know **2** to be aware

Knowledge is power: sharing something about a subject that you **know** well feels similar to letting an *arrow* fly out of your *mouth*.

554

智

SIMP & TRAD

This character with the definition:

wit

Pinyin **zhì** *and Frequency Rank* **885**

Contains **12 strokes** in the following order:

丿 𠂉 𠂉 午 矢 知 知 知 知 智 智 智

Contains these components:

▫ know 知 553, p.131

▪ day, sun 日 64, p.24

With all these meanings & readings:

zhì [智] **1** wisdom **2** knowledge

When your friends find broadcasts of your *knowledge* as sparkling as the *sun*, that's when you *know* that you have been granted the gift of **wit**.

555

疑

SIMP & TRAD

This character with the definition:

doubt, suspect

Pinyin **yí** *and Frequency Rank* **698**

Contains **14 strokes** in the following order:

𠂆 匕 𠤏 𠤏 𠤏 𢀓 𢀓 𢀓 𢀓 𢀓 疑 疑 疑 疑

Contains these components:

▪ ancient ladle 匕 124, p.36

▪ arrow 矢 552, p.130

▫ son, child 子 (abbrev) 24, 15

▫ under 下 199, p.54

▫ man 人 537, p.127

With all these meanings & readings:

yí [疑] **1** to doubt **2** to misbelieve **3** to suspect

As the *man* hunted for food with his bow and *arrow*, he did not **suspect** to find his *son* playing *under* the kitchen table with his mother's *ancient ladle* when he returned home.

556

凝

SIMP & TRAD

This character with the definition:

congeal, curdle

Pinyin **níng** *and Frequency Rank* **1631**

Contains **16 strokes** in the following order:

丶 冫 冫 𠀎 𠀎 𠀎 𠀎 𠀎 凝 凝 凝 凝 凝 凝 凝 凝

Contains these components:

▪ ice r 冫 348, p.87

▫ doubt, suspect 疑 555, p.131

With all these meanings & readings:

níng [凝] **1** to congeal **2** to concentrate attention **3** to stare

The children have *doubts* about their grandmother's claims that, when she was a little girl, her family had to use blocks of *ice* to keep their milk from **curdling** and turning sour.

557

医

醫
TRAD   SIMPLIFIED

This character with the definition:

medical

Pinyin **yī** *and Frequency Rank* **482**

Contains **7 strokes** in the following order:

一 丆 匸 匸 医 医 医

Contains these components:

▫ basket, box r 匚 152, p.42

▪ arrow 矢 552, p.130

With all these meanings & readings:

yī [醫] **1** medical **2** medicine **3** doctor **4** to cure **5** to treat

Medical products in a doctor's *basket* are like *arrows* aimed at a disease.

558

SIMP & TRAD

This character with the definition:

disease*

Pinyin **jí** *and Frequency Rank* **1273**

Contains **10 strokes** in the following order:

丶 一 广 广 疒 疒 疒 疒 疾 疾

Contains these components:

■ sick r 疒 434, p.104
■ arrow 矢 552, p.130

With all these meanings & readings:

jí [疾] **1** sickness **2** disease **3** hate **4** envy **5** swift

Perhaps for the ancient scribes, **disease** seemed like a dart or *arrow* that appeared out of nowhere to strike you *sick* when you least expected it.

559

喬
TRAD   SIMPLIFIED

This character with the definition:

tall

Pinyin **qiáo** *and Frequency Rank* **1488**

Contains **6 strokes** in the following order:

一 二 干 天 乔 乔

Contains these components:

■ heaven 天 548, p.129
■ son 儿 (altered) 312, p.80

With all these meanings & readings:

qiáo [喬] **1** surname Qiao
qiáo [喬] **1** tall

The **tall** *son* seems closer to *heaven* than the rest of us.

Unit 25

560 毫

This character with the definition:

long, fine hair

Pinyin **háo** *and Frequency Rank* **879**

SIMP & TRAD   Contains **11 strokes** in the following order:

Contains these components:

☐ tall 亳 (abbrev) 559, 132

▬ hair 毛 184, p. 50

With all these meanings & readings:

háo [毫] **1** hair **2** drawing brush **3** (in the) least **4** one thousandth

The calligraphy brushes used by Chinese scribes had tips made from strands of **long, fine hair** that were specifically selected from human *hair* or animal fur. The long wood section was elongated to resemble an artist's '*tall*' paint brush.

561 吞

This character with the definition:

swallow, gulp down

Pinyin **tūn** *and Frequency Rank* **1797**

SIMP & TRAD   Contains **7 strokes** in the following order:

Contains these components:

▬ heaven 天 (altered) 548, p. 129

☐ mouth 口 37, p. 17

With all these meanings & readings:

tūn [吞] **1** to swallow **2** to take

He was very thirsty when he gulped down all that water. He opened his *mouth* so wide, I thought he would **swallow** *heaven* itself.

562 木

This character with the definition:

tree

Pinyin **mù** *and Frequency Rank* **694**

SIMP & TRAD   Contains **4 strokes** in the following order:

Contains these components:

▪ big 大 544, p. 129

❚ scepter c 丨 5, p. 10

With all these meanings & readings:

mù [木] **1** tree **2** wood

The Chinese have taken some artistic license by depicting the *big* **tree** roots directly adjacent to several branches at the top. There's not a leaf in sight—only the *scepter*-like trunk, roots, and branches indicate that this is a **tree**.

563 杜

This character with the definition:

prevent

Pinyin **dù** *and Frequency Rank* **1277**

SIMP & TRAD   Contains **7 strokes** in the following order:

Contains these components:

▪ tree 木 562, p. 133

▪ earth, soil 土 9, p. 11

With all these meanings & readings:

dù [杜] **1** birchleaf pear (tree) **2** to stop **3** to prevent **4** to restrict **5** fabricate **6** surname Du

Trees planted in the hillsides of the *earth* act as natural barricades—they **prevent** erosion, water runoff, and mudslides.

564

This character with the definition:

plant, grow

Pinyin **zhí** *and Frequency Rank* **1124**

Contains these components:

☐ tree 木 562, p.133

☐ straight, vertical 直 85, p.29

With all these meanings & readings

zhí [植] **1** to plant

SIMP & TRAD   Contains **12 strokes** in the following order:

一 十 才 木 朩 朾 杧 柿 柿 植 植 植

Look at these *trees*—they're standing all so *straight* and *vertical*. Since *trees* in a forest are never found in such a grid-like array, these *trees* must have been **planted** by a farmer.

565

This character with the definition:

investigate, check

Pinyin **chá** *and Frequency Rank* **459**

Contains these components:

☐ tree 木 562, p.133

☐ dawn 旦 70, p.25

With all these meanings & readings

chá [查] **1** surname Zha
chá [查] **1** to research **2** to check **3** to investigate **4** to examine **5** to refer to **6** to search

SIMP & TRAD   Contains **9 strokes** in the following order:

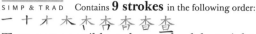

There was a terrible racket out back last night near our *tree*! Unfortunately, we have to wait for until we see the light of *dawn* before we can **investigate** into the cause.

566

This character with the definition:

dull-witted

Pinyin **dāi** *and Frequency Rank* **1338**

Contains these components:

☐ mouth 口 37, p.17

☐ tree 木 562, p.133

With all these meanings & readings

dāi [呆] **1** foolish **2** stupid **3** expression **4** to stay

SIMP & TRAD   Contains **7 strokes** in the following order:

丶 丷 口 므 무 呆 呆

The *mouth* on top of the *tree* looks like a child's puppet—head, arms, leg, and a vertical handle for holding. Because of their **stupid** and **foolish** appearance, puppets are appealing, amusing, and even endearing to most adults and children.

567

This character with the definition:

fruit

Pinyin **guǒ** *and Frequency Rank* **165**

Contains these components:

☐ field 田 63, p.23

☐ tree 木 562, p.133

With all these meanings & readings

guǒ [果] **1** fruit **2** result

SIMP & TRAD   Contains **8 strokes** in the following order:

丨 冂 冂 日 旦 甲 果 果

The *field*-like shape attached to the top of the *tree* resembles a ripe piece of **fruit** with odd stripes on its skin. The large piece of **fruit** requires a root system that's strong enough to supply the fruit with sufficient nutrients until it's ripe enough to harvest.

568

課
TRAD

This character with the definition:

subject, course, class

Pinyin **kè** *and Frequency Rank* **1208**

Contains these components:

☐ speech r 讠 352, p.88

☐ fruit 果 567, p.134

With all these meanings & readings

kè [课] **1** subject **2** course **3** class **4** lesson **5** m 堂[táng] 節 [节][jié], 门 [門][mén]

SIMPLIFIED   Contains **10 strokes** in the following order:

丶 讠 订 沪 迥 评 评 评 课 课

Naive professors believe that well-prepared *speeches* delivered to students will produce *fruitful* results for their **course** or **class**.

569

棵

SIMP & TRAD

This character with the definition:

m for trees, cabbages, etc

Pinyin **kē** *and Frequency Rank* **2108**

Contains **12 strokes** in the following order:

一 十 十 木 木 杧 杧 柙 椠 椠 椠 棵

Contains these components:

☐ tree 木 562, p.133
☐ fruit 果 567, p.134

With all these meanings & readings:

kē [棵] **1** m for trees, cabbages, plants etc

A *tree* brought forth a bountiful harvest this year. There was so much *fruit* it was hard to **count it** all.

570

困

困
困 絪
TRAD   SIMPLIFIED

This character with the definition:

hard pressed

Pinyin **kùn** *and Frequency Rank* **868**

Contains **7 strokes** in the following order:

丨 冂 冂 用 用 用 困

Contains these components:

☐ enclosure r 囗 36, p.17
■ tree 木 562, p.133

With all these meanings & readings:

kùn [困] **1** to trap **2** to surround **3** hard-pressed **4** stranded **5** destitute
kùn [睏] **1** sleepy **2** tired
kǔn [綑] **1** a bunch **2** tie together

Even though the farmer has only one *tree* on his farm and he and his family are **hard pressed** to survive, he still feels the need to build an *enclosure* around his small farm.

571

操

SIMP & TRAD

This character with the definition:

act, do

Pinyin **cāo** *and Frequency Rank* **1173**

Contains **16 strokes** in the following order:

一 十 十 扌 扩 护 护 押 押 揔 揔 撰 撰 撻 操 操

Contains these components:

■ hand r 扌 25, p.15
☐ product 品 52, p.21
■ tree 木 562, p.133

With all these meanings & readings:

cāo [操] **1** to grasp **2** to hold **3** to operate **4** to manage **5** to control **6** to steer **7** to exercise **8** to drill (practice) **9** to play **10** to speak (a language)
cào [操] **1** to have sex (vulgar) **2** also written 肏[肏][cào]

After my wife asked me to **do** something special for her birthday, I made a *hand*-carved *wood product* for her.

572

某

SIMP & TRAD

This character with the definition:

certain, some

Pinyin **mǒu** *and Frequency Rank* **517**

Contains **9 strokes** in the following order:

一 十 廿 廿 甘 甘 芇 芇 某

Contains these components:

☐ sweet 甘 95, p.31
☐ tree 木 562, p.133

With all these meanings & readings:

mǒu [某] **1** some **2** a certain **3** sb or sth indefinite **4** such-and-such

Although most *tree* parts taste bitter—sap, leaves, root—**certain** *tree* parts, such as fruits, are *sweet* and nutritious and have especially benefited mankind.

573

谋

谋
TRAD   SIMPLIFIED

This character with the definition:

work for, strive

Pinyin **móu** *and Frequency Rank* **989**

Contains **11 strokes** in the following order:

` 讠 讠 计 讲 诽 讲 谋 谋 谋 谋

Contains these components:

☐ speech r 讠 352, p.88
☐ certain, some 某 572, p.135

With all these meanings & readings:

móu [謀] **1** to plan **2** seek **3** scheme

I will **work for** my next promotion with great dedication, but I'll also need to write a *speech* and act in a *certain* way to earn it.

574

This character with the definition:

peach

Pinyin **táo** *and Frequency Rank* **1839**

SIMP & TRAD   Contains **10 strokes** in the following order:

一 十 才 才 杁 杁 朴 机 桃 桃

Contains these components:

■ tree 木 562, p. 133
■ omen 兆 236, p. 63

With all these meanings & readings:

táo [桃] **1** peach

My father feared it was a very bad *omen* when a lightning bolt struck down his only **peach** *tree*.

575

This character with the definition:

cypress

Pinyin **bǎi** *and Frequency Rank* **1596**

SIMP & TRAD   Contains **9 strokes** in the following order:

一 十 才 木 杧 柏 柏 柏 柏

Contains these components:

■ tree 木 562, p. 133
■ white 白 225, p. 60

With all these meanings & readings:

bǎi [柏] **1** surname Bai
bǎi [柏] **1** cedar **2** cypress
bó [柏] **1** (used for transcribing names)
bò [柏] **1** cypress **2** cedar **3** Taiwan pr bó

Cypress wood is valued for its resistance to inclement weather and termites. Varieties of **cypress** *trees* include *White*, Red, Yellow, and Bald; they all thrive in both tropical and temperate climates.

576

This character with the definition:

table

Pinyin **zhuō** *and Frequency Rank* **1193**

SIMP & TRAD   Contains **10 strokes** in the following order:

丨 ⺊ ⺊ 占 占 卓 卓 卓 桌 桌

Contains these components:

▭ stand firm 卓 (abbrev) 202, 54
▭ tree 木 562, p. 133

With all these meanings & readings:

zhuō [桌] **1** table

A **table** is made from a *tree* and must *stand firm*.

577

This character with the definition:

hamlet

Pinyin **cūn** *and Frequency Rank* **712**

SIMP & TRAD   Contains **7 strokes** in the following order:

一 十 才 木 朾 村 村

Contains these components:

■ tree 木 562, p. 133
■ inch 寸 216, p. 58

With all these meanings & readings:

cūn [村] **1** village

A **hamlet** compares to an urban city as an *inch*-long twig compares to a forest full of *trees*.

578

This character with the definition:

consume, cost, dawdle

Pinyin **hào** *and Frequency Rank* **1730**

SIMP & TRAD   Contains **10 strokes** in the following order:

一 二 三 丰 耒 耒 耒 耗 耗 耗

Contains these components:

■ tree 木 562, p. 133
▭ two 二 (altered) 2, p. 10
■ hair 毛 184, p. 50

With all these meanings & readings:

hào [耗] **1** mouse **2** new **3** waste **4** to spend **5** to consume **6** to squander

Two hares (sounds like *hairs*) got caught in the *tree*, and re-capturing them **cost** me lots of time.

579 宋

SIMP & TRAD

This character with the definition:

Song dynasty

Pinyin **sòng** and Frequency Rank **990**

Contains **7 strokes** in the following order:

丶 丶 宀 宀 宀 宋 宋

Contains these components:

▢ roof r 宀 271, p.70

▣ tree 木 562, p.133

With all these meanings & readings:

Sòng [宋] **1** surname Song **2** the Song dynasty (960-1279) **3** also Song of the Southern dynasties 南朝宋 (420-479)

This character, built up from an architectural element (*roof*) and from material (*tree*), serves as a historical reminder that the births of architecture and structural engineering were among the most important achievements of the **Song dynasty**.

580 末

SIMP & TRAD

This character with the definition:

end, tip

Pinyin **mò** and Frequency Rank **1164**

Contains **5 strokes** in the following order:

一 二 十 才 末

Contains these components:

▣ tree 木 (altered) 562, p.133

▢ one 一 1, p.10

With all these meanings & readings:

mò [末] **1** tip **2** end **3** final stage **4** latter part **5** inessential detail **6** powder **7** dust **8** opera role of old man

The *one* extra horizontal stroke is wider than its mate to emphasize that the higher part of the *tree*—the upper **end**, the tip of the **tip**—is the focus of the design of this character.

581 抹

SIMP & TRAD

This character with the definition:

put on, apply, smear

Pinyin **mǒ** and Frequency Rank **2087**

Contains **8 strokes** in the following order:

一 十 才 扌 扗 抃 抺 抹

Contains these components:

▣ hand r 扌 25, p.15

▣ end, tip 末 580, p.137

With all these meanings & readings:

mǒ [抹] **1** to smear **2** to wipe **3** to erase **4** (classifier for wisps of cloud, light-beams etc) **mò** [抹] **1** girdle **2** brassiere **3** to plaster

The *tip* of your *hand* is used to **apply** make-up.

582 未

SIMP & TRAD

This character with the definition:

have not yet

Pinyin **wèi** and Frequency Rank **385**

Contains **5 strokes** in the following order:

一 二 十 才 未

Contains these components:

▣ tree 木 562, p.133

▢ one 一 1, p.10

With all these meanings & readings:

wèi [未] **1** not yet **2** did not **3** have not **4** not **5** 8th earthly branch: 1-3 p.m., 6th solar month (7th July-6th August), year of the Sheep

The forest elf **has not yet** climbed to the top of the *tree*. That shorter horizontal stroke in the form of '*one*' shows exactly where he stopped. • A few comments are in order regarding the characters 未 (this panel 582) and 末 (panel 580). How do we tell them apart? They differ only in the relative lengths of the two horizontal strokes. The top of 未 looks like the character 土, 'earth' (panel 9) and the tree is still in the soil—it 'has not yet' been chopped down, while the top of 末 (panel 580) looks like 士, 'knight' (panel 8). The ancient scribes would have regarded knighthood as the the ultimate human achievement—the 'tip' top achievement!

583

SIMP & TRAD

This character with the definition:

flavor

Pinyin **wèi** *and Frequency Rank* **844**

Contains **8 strokes** in the following order:

丨 丿 口 口 口一 口二 咔 吽 味

Contains these components:

mouth 口 37, p.17

have not yet 未 582, p.137

With all these meanings & readings

wèi [味] **1** taste **2** smell

As the food critic for a major newspaper, you follow specific guidelines when reviewing a new restaurant. Before evaluating the **flavor** of an entrée, you place a morsel of it in your *mouth*. You *have not yet* swallowed because you need to chew thoroughly to make sure all the component **flavors** of the dish are properly identified.

584
朱
硃
TRAD

SIMPLIFIED

This character with the definition:

bright red

Pinyin **zhū** *and Frequency Rank* **1120**

Contains **6 strokes** in the following order:

丿 一 二 牛 牛 朱

Contains these components:

dab r 、 176, p.48

have not yet 未 582, p.137

With all these meanings & readings

zhū [硃] **1** vermilion **2** surname Zhu

Since I *have not yet* been inoculated, the doctor had to insert a *dab* of serum under my skin, which soon turned **bright red**.

Unit 26

585

珠

SIMP & TRAD

This character with the definition:

pearl

Pinyin **zhū** *and Frequency Rank* **1286**

Contains **10 strokes** in the following order:

Contains these components:

■ jade 玉 (altered) 177, p.48

□ bright red 朱 584, p.138

With all these meanings & readings:

zhū [珠] **1** bead **2** pearl **3** m 粒[lì], 颗[顆][kē]

In ancient times, *bright red jade* reminded people of **pearls**.

586

本

SIMP & TRAD

This character with the definition:

root or stem of plant

Pinyin **běn** *and Frequency Rank* **92**

Contains **5 strokes** in the following order:

Contains these components:

■ tree 木 562, p.133

▬ one 一 1, p.10

With all these meanings & readings:

běn [本] **1** roots or stems of plants **2** origin **3** source **4** this **5** the current **6** root **7** foundation **8** basis **9** (classifier for books, periodicals, files etc)

The '*one*' marks the spot where the **root** starts to grow and the **stem** (or trunk) of the *tree* emerges from the soil.

587

相

SIMP & TRAD

This character with the definition:

appearance

Pinyin **xiàng** *and Frequency Rank* **152**

Contains **9 strokes** in the following order:

Contains these components:

■ tree 木 562, p.133

◧ eye 目 75, p.26

With all these meanings & readings:

xiāng [相] **1** each other **2** one another **3** mutually
xiàng [相] **1** appearance **2** portrait **3** picture

Examine the **appearance** of this picturesque *tree* more closely with the naked *eye*.

588

箱

SIMP & TRAD

This character with the definition:

box, trunk, chest

Pinyin **xiāng** *and Frequency Rank* **1453**

Contains **15 strokes** in the following order:

ノ ト ト 竹 竹 竹 竹 竹 竹 竹 箱 箱 箱 箱 箱

Contains these components:

▢ bamboo r ⺮ 264, p.68

■ appearance 相 587, p.139

With all these meanings & readings:

xiāng [箱] **1** box **2** trunk **3** chest

The linen **chest** was designed cunningly so that the outside had the *appearance* of *bamboo*.

589

湘

SIMP & TRAD

This character with the definition:

Hunan province (abbrev)

Pinyin **xiāng** *and Frequency Rank* **2245**

Contains **12 strokes** in the following order:

丶 丶 氵 汁 汁 汁 沐 沐 湘 湘 湘 湘

Contains these components:

◧ water r 氵 314, p.80

■ appearance 相 587, p.139

With all these meanings & readings:

Xiāng [湘] **1** abbr for Hunan 湖南 province in south central China **2** abbr for Xiangjiang river in Hunan province

The food in **Hunan province** is well-known for its spiciness. There is enough sweat running down your face after taking one bite of their authentic meals that you develop a *watery appearance*.

590

This character with the definition:

bundle, bunch

Pinyin **shù** *and Frequency Rank* **998**

Contains these components:

■ tree 木 (altered) 562, p.133
▣ mouth 口 37, p.17

With all these meanings & readings

shù [束] **1** to bind **2** bunch **3** bundle **4** m for bunches, bundles, beams of light etc **5** to control **6** surname Shu

SIMP & TRAD   Contains **7 strokes** in the following order:

一　丆　丅　口　申　束　束

It's time to cut down our evergreen *tree* and sell it for the holidays. The strokes of the '*mouth*' suggest the twine with which we bind up the branches so that the tree will be a more convenient **bundle** for us to carry.

591

This character with the definition:

policy, plan, scheme

Pinyin **cè** *and Frequency Rank* **714**

Contains these components:

■ bamboo r 竹 264, p.68
■ bundle, bunch 束 (altered) 590, p.140

With all these meanings & readings

cè [策] **1** method **2** plan **3** policy **4** scheme

SIMP & TRAD   Contains **12 strokes** in the following order:

丿　𠂉　𠂉　𠂉　𥫗　𥫗　竿　竿　竿　第　第　策

The **plan** to rebuild the town's bridge was outlined on a *bundle* of *bamboo* scrolls.

592

This character with the definition:

thorn, splinter

Pinyin **cì** *and Frequency Rank* **1058**

Contains these components:

■ bundle, bunch 束 (altered) 590, p.140
■ knife r 刂 169, p.46

With all these meanings & readings

cì [刺] **1** thorn **2** sting **3** thru **4** to prick **5** to pierce **6** to sta **7** to assassinate **8** to murder

SIMP & TRAD   Contains **8 strokes** in the following order:

一　丆　丅　申　束　束　剌　刺

Because someone used a *knife* to cut the binding cords, the tree branches burst open. Watch out for the **thorns** and **splinters** as you try to gather them up!

593

This character with the definition:

rice, grain (crop)

Pinyin **hé** *and Frequency Rank* **3587**

Contains these components:

□ dab r 丶 176, p.48
■ tree 木 562, p.133

With all these meanings & readings

hé [禾] **1** cereal **2** grain

SIMP & TRAD   Contains **5 strokes** in the following order:

丿　二　千　禾　禾

The *dab* at the top of the *tree* serves to contrast the sizes of the large plant to the tiny **grain**.

594

This character with the definition:

rent

Pinyin **zū** *and Frequency Rank* **1397**

Contains these components:

■ rice, grain (crop) 禾 593, p.140
■ moreover 且 84, p.28

With all these meanings & readings

zū [租] **1** rent **2** taxes

SIMP & TRAD   Contains **10 strokes** in the following order:

丿　二　千　禾　禾　和　租　租　租　租

Centuries ago, tenant farmers paid their **rent** in quantities of *grain* from their harvest. Imagine the '*moreover*' element in this character as a stack of shelves on which landlords would store '**rent**' payments.

595

SIMP & TRAD

This character with the definition:

harmony

Pinyin **hé** *and Frequency Rank* **19**

Contains **8 strokes** in the following order:

ノ 二 千 矛 禾 禾 和 和

Contains these components:

■ rice, grain (crop) 禾 593, p.140

■ mouth 口 37, p.17

hé [和] 1 and   2 together with   3 with   4 sum   5 union   6 peace   7 harmony   8 surname He   9 Japanese related   10 Taiwan pr hàn
hè [和] 1 cap (a poem)   2 to respond in singing
hú [和] 1 to complete a set in mahjong or playing cards
huó [和] 1 soft   2 warm
huò [和] 1 to mix together   2 to blend

Harmony at the end of the day is chewing *rice* in my *mouth* to fill and still my rumbling and empty stomach.

596

SIMP & TRAD

This character with the definition:

rule, order

Pinyin **chéng** *and Frequency Rank* **314**

Contains **12 strokes** in the following order:

ノ 二 千 矛 禾 禾 和 和 和 程 程 程

Contains these components:

■ rice, grain (crop) 禾 593, p.140

■ appear 呈 48, p.20

With all these meanings & readings:

chéng [程] 1 rule   2 order   3 regulations   4 formula   5 journey   6 procedure   7 sequence   8 surname Cheng

When *rice* crops *appear* abundant at harvest time, everyone prospers and both **order** and the **rule** of law prevail.

597

SIMP & TRAD

This character with the definition:

fragrant

Pinyin **xiāng** *and Frequency Rank* **776**

Contains **9 strokes** in the following order:

ノ 二 千 矛 禾 禾 香 香 香

Contains these components:

☐ rice, grain (crop) 禾 593, p.140

☐ day, sun 日 64, p.24

With all these meanings & readings:

xiāng [香] 1 fragrant   2 incense   3 (of food) savory   4 appetizing   5 sweet   6 scented   7 popular   8 m 根[gēn]

Under the heat of the strong morning *sun*, there's an unmistakable *rice* **fragrance** wafting in the air as the grains are harvested in the field.

598

SIMP & TRAD

This character with the definition:

branch of study

Pinyin **kē** *and Frequency Rank* **277**

Contains **9 strokes** in the following order:

ノ 二 千 矛 禾 禾 禾 科 科

Contains these components:

■ rice, grain (crop) 禾 593, p.140

■ cup-shaped 斗 185, p.51

With all these meanings & readings:

kē [科] 1 branch of study   2 administrative section   3 division   4 field   5 branch   6 stage directions   7 family (taxonomy)   8 rules   9 laws   10 to mete out (punishment)   11 to levy (taxes etc)   12 to fine sb   13 m 个 [個][gè]

Grains of *rice* in a *cup* can form interesting patterns—so interesting that they could start a distinctly new **branch of study**.

599

SIMP & TRAD

This character with the definition:

draft, manuscript

Pinyin **gǎo** *and Frequency Rank* **1587**

Contains **15 strokes** in the following order:

ノ 二 千 矛 禾 禾 利 禾 秆 稿 稿 稿 稿 稿 稿

Contains these components:

■ rice, grain (crop) 禾 593, p.140

■ high 高 253, p.66

With all these meanings & readings:

gǎo [稿] 1 manuscript   2 draft   3 stalk of grain

The most common use for *rice* and other *grain* crops is as the raw materials for *high* quality **manuscript** and **draft** paper.

600

This character with the definition:

double, twice

Pinyin **jiān** *and Frequency Rank* **1515**

SIMP & TRAD   Contains **10 strokes** in the following order:

丶 丷 ⺌ 兰 ⺗ 半 半 兼 兼 兼

Contains these components:

■ rice, grain (crop) (×2) 禾 593, p.140

■ boar's head r ⺕ 30, p.16

With all these meanings & readings:

jiān [兼] **1** double **2** twice **3** simultaneous **4** holding two or more (official) posts at the same time

He thought of a clever way to use a *boar's head* to join two sheaves of *rice* together. Now we can harvest **twice** as much as before.

601

This character with the definition:

honest, upright

Pinyin **lián** *and Frequency Rank* **1818**

SIMP & TRAD   Contains **13 strokes** in the following order:

丶 亠 广 广 产 产 庐 庐 庐 库 廉 廉 廉

Contains these components:

■ shelter r 广 427, p.103

■ double, twice 兼 600, p.142

With all these meanings & readings:

lián [廉] **1** incorrupt **2** inexpensive **3** surname Lian

This contractor is one of the most **honest** workmen I've ever hired. The *house* he built for us is super-strong and sturdy because he *double* reinforced all of its supports.

602

This character with the definition:

multiply, ride

Pinyin **chéng** *and Frequency Rank* **1231**

SIMP & TRAD   Contains **10 strokes** in the following order:

丿 二 千 千 千 乖 乖 乖 乘 乘

Contains these components:

■ rice, grain (crop) 禾 (altered) 593, p.140

■■ north 北 (altered) 131, p.38

With all these meanings & readings:

chéng [乘] **1** to ride **2** to mount **3** to make use of **4** to avail oneself of **5** to take advantage of **6** to multiply **7** Buddhist teaching

In the *north* of China, people plant *rice* as a *crop*. In a year with a good yield, the crop will have **multiplied** the *grain* seeds by many times.

603

This character with the definition:

remain, be left over

Pinyin **shèng** *and Frequency Rank* **1446**

SIMP & TRAD   Contains **12 strokes** in the following order:

丿 二 千 千 千 乖 乖 乖 乘 乘 剩 剩

Contains these components:

■ multiply, ride 乘 602, p.142

■ knife r 刂 169, p.46

With all these meanings & readings:

shèng [剩] **1** have as remainder

When things are allowed to *multiply* without restraint, the result may be an excessive amount. At that point, it would be prudent to use a *knife* to cut off the excess. Whatever is **left over** is the **remainder**.

604

This character with the definition:

sharp

Pinyin **lì** *and Frequency Rank* **155**

SIMP & TRAD   Contains **7 strokes** in the following order:

丿 二 千 千 禾 利 利

Contains these components:

■ rice, grain (crop) 禾 593, p.140

■ knife r 刂 169, p.46

With all these meanings & readings:

lì [利] **1** advantage **2** benefit **3** profit **4** sharp

Rice grains are so small and slippery that you need a *knife* with a razor **sharp** lade to cut one in half.

605 莉

jasmine

Pinyin **lì** *and Frequency Rank* **1878**

SIMP & TRAD Contains **10 strokes** in the following order:

一十艹艹芓芊芓茉莉莉

This character with the definition:

Contains these components:

□ grass r 艹 87, p.29
■ sharp 利 604, p.142

With all these meanings & readings:

lì [莉] **1** jasmine

If you use a *sharp* knife to cut *grass*, wonderful fragrance, similar to **jasmine**, will be released.

---

606 秀

put forth ears of grain

Pinyin **xiù** *and Frequency Rank* **1136**

SIMP & TRAD Contains **7 strokes** in the following order:

一二千千禾秀秀

This character with the definition:

Contains these components:

□ rice, grain (crop) 禾 593, p.140
■ so, therefore 乃 520, p.124

With all these meanings & readings:

xiù [秀] **1** handsome **2** refined **3** elegant **4** graceful **5** performance **6** ear of grain **7** show (loanword) **8** m 场 [場][cháng]

Spring is the best time of year to sow seeds of *grain so that*, come Fall, the earth will **put forth ears of grain** to harvest.

---

607 诱

guide, lead, induce

Pinyin **yòu** *and Frequency Rank* **1707**

TRAD SIMPLIFIED Contains **9 strokes** in the following order:

丶讠讠讠讠讠诱诱诱

This character with the definition:

Contains these components:

□ speech r 讠 352, p.88
□ put forth ears of grain 秀 606, p.143

With all these meanings & readings:

yòu [誘] **1** to entice **2** to tempt

To **guide** the electorate, the politician assumes that *ears of grain* grow from the ears of his audience when he gives his *speeches* so he must speak very slowly and carefully at every rally.

---

608 季

season

Pinyin **jì** *and Frequency Rank* **1279**

SIMP & TRAD Contains **8 strokes** in the following order:

一二千千禾禾季季

This character with the definition:

Contains these components:

□ rice, grain (crop) 禾 593, p.140
■ son, child 子 24, p.15

With all these meanings & readings:

jì [季] **1** surname Ji
jì [季] **1** season **2** period **3** end **4** youngest among the brothers **5** surname Ji

At the start of planting **season**, the farmer employs every one of his *sons*—even the youngest—to help him sow the fields with *grain*.

---

609 种

plant, sow

Pinyin **zhòng** *and Frequency Rank* **57**

TRAD SIMPLIFIED Contains **9 strokes** in the following order:

丿二千千禾禾和和种

This character with the definition:

Contains these components:

■ rice, grain (crop) 禾 593, p.140
□ middle 中 38, p.18

With all these meanings & readings:

zhǒng [種] **1** abbr for 物种 [~種], genus **2** race **3** seed **4** breed **5** species **6** strain **7** kind **8** type **9** has guts (i.e. courage) **10** nerve **11** m for types: kind, sort **12** m for languages
zhòng [種] **1** to plant **2** to grow **3** to cultivate

Ancient scribes regarded China as the *Middle* Kingdom. People have **planted** *rice* in the *Middle* Kingdom for thousands of years.

Marginal Examples *Interlude 2*

One unfortunate shortcoming in guides such as this one has to do with—dare I say it—imperfections in the Chinese character system itself. I refer to the fact that not only do characters possess different meanings, but they also possess different pronunciations. Moreover, it will often be true that one simplified character corresponds to several traditional characters. (But the converse is false: each traditional character always corresponds to a single simplified character, which might be the traditional character itself.) As a result, we use the space in the large margin to the right of each character panel to list these alternative meanings and pronunciations belonging to each antecedent character.

For example, the panel for the character 亚 ('inferior') has this set of marginal notes

yà [亞] **1** Asia **2** Asian **3** second
4 next to **5** inferior **6** sub-
7 Taiwan pr yǎ

which informs us that the traditional form of the character is 亞, (but with the standard pronunciation yà), and it has a total of seven (reasonably) distinct meanings, although the last 'meaning' merely provides useful information comparing the Taiwanese pronunciation with that of the mainland standard.

Other character panels provide more information, such as the notes for 头 'head'. This character has two different pronunciations, and both correspond to the same traditional character form 頭.

tóu [頭] **1** head **2** hair style
3 the top **4** end **5** beginning
or end **6** a stub **7** remnant
8 chief **9** boss **10** side **11** aspect **12** first **13** leading **14** m
for pigs or livestock **15** m 个
[個][gè]
tou [頭] **1** suff. for nouns

Some of the numbered items are informative, such as the item pertaining to tóu regarding the appropriate measure word for the noun form of 头 (this measure word itself has a distinct pair of forms, one each for the simplified and traditional contexts) and the fact that when tone-free, 头 acts as a noun suffix.

Two more examples explain other issues:

le [了] **1** (modal particle intensifying preceding clause) **2** (completed action marker)
liǎo [了] **1** to know **2** to understand
liǎo [瞭] **1** clear
liào [瞭] **1** to look afar from a
high place

The simplified character 了 corresponds to a several pronunciations associated with two very distinct traditional characters.

Finally, the character 乐 generates these notes:

lè [樂] **1** happy **2** laugh **3** cheerful **4** surname Le
yuè [樂] **1** surname Yue **2** music

Here, the simplified character never matches a traditional letterform.

The information for these notes was gathered from CC-CEDICT, a publicly available dictionary database. I am grateful to the members of the project team for their Herculean efforts and for making this material publicly available. Some of their defining conventions may differ from some of the ones we've adhered to in the main parts of the panels.

Unit 27

610

菌

SIMP & TRAD

This character with the definition:

mushroom

Pinyin **jùn** *and Frequency Rank* **1733**

Contains **11 strokes** in the following order:

Contains these components:

▢ grass r ⺿ 87, p. 29

◼ enclosure r 囗 36, p. 17

◼ rice, grain (crop) 禾 593, p. 140

With all these meanings & readings:

jūn [菌] **1** germ **2** bacteria
jùn [菌] **1** bacteria **2** mold
3 mushroom

Inside the experimental *enclosure*, we sprinkle raw *grain* amongst the *grass*, just to see what will happen. But nothing sprouts—the environment's so moist that giant **mushrooms** grow instead.

611

林

SIMP & TRAD

This character with the definition:

forest

Pinyin **lín** *and Frequency Rank* **364**

Contains **8 strokes** in the following order:

Contains these components:

◼◼ tree (×2) 木 562, p. 133

With all these meanings & readings:

lín [林] **1** woods **2** forest **3** surname Lin **4** m 片[piàn]

Several *trees* form a **forest**.

612

森

SIMP & TRAD

This character with the definition:

full of trees

Pinyin **sēn** *and Frequency Rank* **1029**

Contains **12 strokes** in the following order:

Contains these components:

◼ tree 木 562, p. 133

◻ forest 林 611, p. 146

With all these meanings & readings:

sēn [森] **1** forest

The beauty of a single *tree* can be lost in a *forest* that is **full of trees**.

613

麻

SIMP & TRAD

This character with the definition:

hemp

Pinyin **má** *and Frequency Rank* **1108**

Contains **11 strokes** in the following order:

Contains these components:

▢ shelter r 广 427, p. 103

◼ forest 林 611, p. 146

With all these meanings & readings:

má [麻] **1** (to have) pins and needles **2** tingling **3** hemp **4** sesame **5** numb **6** to bother **7** surname Ma **8** m 缕[缕][lǚ]

The drying *shed* contains a virtual *forest* of raw material; it will emerge as flax and **hemp** that we will then spin into clothes.

614

摩

SIMP & TRAD

This character with the definition:

rub

Pinyin **mó** *and Frequency Rank* **1162**

Contains **15 strokes** in the following order:

Contains these components:

◼ hemp 麻 (altered) 613, p. 146

◻ hand 手 21, p. 14

With all these meanings & readings:

mó [摩] **1** rub

Please slip that *hemp* glove on your *hand* and **rub** my back!

615 嘛

This character with the definition:

s-end: persuasion

Pinyin **ma** *and Frequency Rank* **1628**

SIMP & TRAD   Contains **14 strokes** in the following order:

丨 冂 口 口 一 口一 吓 吓 吓 呀 嘛 嘛 嘛 嘛

Contains these components:

◻ mouth 口 37, p.17

◼ hemp 麻 613, p.146

With all these meanings & readings:

ma [嘛] **1** (a modal particle)

You need a strong *verbal* argument that will convince people to wear clothes fashioned from *hemp* because the fabric feels very itchy against the skin.

---

616 磨

This character with the definition:

polish, wear down, pester

Pinyin **mó** *and Frequency Rank* **1537**

SIMP & TRAD   Contains **16 strokes** in the following order:

丶 一 广 广 庁 庐 庐 庐 府 麻 麻 麻 麿 磨 磨 磨

Contains these components:

◼ hemp 麻 (altered) 613, p.146

◼ stone, rock 石 522, p.124

With all these meanings & readings:

mó [磨] **1** to sharpen **2** to delay **3** hardship **4** to grind **5** to rub

mò [磨] **1** grindstone

Primitive peoples were known to use large pieces of *hemp* to **polish** *stone*.

---

617 桥

橋
TRAD   SIMPLIFIED

This character with the definition:

bridge

Pinyin **qiáo** *and Frequency Rank* **1292**

Contains **10 strokes** in the following order:

一 十 才 木 木' 杧 杧 杯 桥 桥

Contains these components:

◻ tree 木 562, p.133

◼ tall 乔 559, p.132

With all these meanings & readings:

qiáo [橋] **1** bridge **2** m 座[zuò]

It was only a few centuries ago, that it was essential for people to find several *tall* straight *trees* to construct a **bridge** of sufficient strength and durability.

---

618 析

This character with the definition:

analyze

Pinyin **xī** *and Frequency Rank* **1073**

SIMP & TRAD   Contains **8 strokes** in the following order:

一 十 才 木 木' 杧 析 析

Contains these components:

◻ tree 木 562, p.133

◼ catty 斤 403, p.98

With all these meanings & readings:

xī [析] **1** to separate **2** to divide **3** to analyze

Wooden furniture that is *unbalanced* is apt to crash to the ground and smash into pieces. Afterwards, call in skilled carpenters to **analyze** what went wrong during construction.

---

619 床

This character with the definition:

bed

Pinyin **chuáng** *and Frequency Rank* **1068**

SIMP & TRAD   Contains **7 strokes** in the following order:

丶 一 广 广 庁 床 床

Contains these components:

◻ shelter r 广 427, p.103

◼ tree 木 562, p.133

With all these meanings & readings:

chuáng [床] **1** bed **2** couch **3** m for beds **4** m 张 [張][zhāng]

The first use for *wood* inside human *shelters* was for frames of **beds**.

620

This character with the definition:

timber

Pinyin **cái** *and Frequency Rank* **952**

SIMP & TRAD   Contains **7 strokes** in the following order:

一 十 十 才 木 木 村 材

Contains these components:

■ tree 木 562, p.133
■ sth just happened 才 449, p.108

With all these meanings & readings:

cái [材] **1** material **2** timber **3** variant of 才, ability **4** talent **5** aptitude **6** man or woman of talent

I could tell by the crashing sound that *something just happened* outside during the violent thunderstorm; the next day I saw that the majestic old maple *tree* had fallen to the ground. Now, it's a mere candidate for processing at the local **timber** mill.

621
楊
TRAD SIMPLIFIED

This character with the definition:

poplar

Pinyin **yáng** *and Frequency Rank* **1062**

Contains **7 strokes** in the following order:

一 十 十 木 杇 杨 杨

Contains these components:

■ tree 木 562, p.133
■ glorious, bright 昜 463, p.111

With all these meanings & readings:

yáng [楊] **1** poplar **2** surname Yang

Poplars are *glorious trees* to cultivate. In fact, the **poplar** has become quite **pop**ular!

622

This character with the definition:

put up, prop up

Pinyin **jià** *and Frequency Rank* **846**

SIMP & TRAD   Contains **9 strokes** in the following order:

フ 力 加 加 加 加 架 架 架

Contains these components:

□ add, increase 加 476, p.114
□ tree 木 (altered) 562, p.133

With all these meanings & readings:

jià [架] **1** to support **2** frame **3** rack **4** framework **5** m for planes, large vehicles, radios etc

You can **prop up** something heavy by *adding* pieces of *wood* to reinforce the base of the object.

623
梁
樑
TRAD SIMPLIFIED

This character with the definition:

beam

Pinyin **liáng** *and Frequency Rank* **1416**

Contains **11 strokes** in the following order:

丶 丶 氵 氵 汈 汈 沙 沙 梁 梁 梁

Contains these components:

■ water r 氵 314, p.80
■ blade edge 刃 487, p.116
■ dab r 丶 176, p.48
■ tree 木 562, p.133

With all these meanings & readings:

liáng [梁] **1** name of Kingdoms and Dynasties at different periods **2** surname Liang
liáng [梁] **1** beam of roof **2** bric

liáng [樑] **1** beam of roof

A few centuries ago, a bridge was built across a body of *water* by first using a two-man saw with a very sharp *blade edge* to cut down a few tall hardwood *trees*. Then a sawmill would cut the *trees* into thick **beams** and men would add *dabs* of sturdy connectors to erect the bridge over the water!

624

This character with the definition:

cup

Pinyin **bēi** *and Frequency Rank* **1396**

SIMP & TRAD   Contains **8 strokes** in the following order:

一 十 十 木 木 杯 杯 杯

Contains these components:

■ tree 木 562, p.133
■ no! 不 493, p.117

With all these meanings & readings:

bēi [杯] **1** cup **2** m for drinks; glass, cup

The crafts person should *not* have used *wood* to create this upside-down **cup**.

625

李

SIMP & TRAD

This character with the definition:

plum

Pinyin **lǐ** *and Frequency Rank* **472**

Contains **7 strokes** in the following order:

一 十 才 木 杏 杏 李

Contains these components:

☐ tree 木 562, p.133

■ son, child 子 24, p.15

With all these meanings & readings:

lǐ [李] **1** plum **2** surname Li

The ancient Chinese considered **plums** to be the most important of fruits; coincidentally, the *offspring* of many fruit *trees* back then were **plums**.

626

染

SIMP & TRAD

This character with the definition:

dye

Pinyin **rǎn** *and Frequency Rank* **1141**

Contains **9 strokes** in the following order:

丶 冫 氵 汈 汈 洰 染 染 染

Contains these components:

◨ water r 氵 314, p.80

☐ nine 九 532, p.126

■ tree 木 562, p.133

With all these meanings & readings:

rǎn [染] **1** to catch (a disease) **2** dye

Before the creation of modern synthetic dyes, the colors **to dye** clothing all came from natural sources. As many as *nine* chemicals, obtained from plants and *trees*, were crushed into a fine powder and mixed with *water*. An expert mixologist, with the skills of an artist and a chemist, could produce a rainbow of colors from his secret formulas.

627

术
術
TRAD SIMPLIFIED

This character with the definition:

art, skill

Pinyin **shù** *and Frequency Rank* **328**

Contains **5 strokes** in the following order:

一 十 才 木 术

Contains these components:

■ tree 木 562, p.133

☐ dab r 丶 176, p.48

With all these meanings & readings:

shù [術] **1** method **2** technique

It takes a skillful **artist** to attack a big *tree*, carve away all the surplus wood (so to speak), and just leave a *small amount* of material in the shape of a beautiful statue and a stunning work of **art**.

628

荣
榮
TRAD SIMPLIFIED

This character with the definition:

honorable

Pinyin **róng** *and Frequency Rank* **993**

Contains **9 strokes** in the following order:

一 十 艹 芦 芦 荧 荣 荣 荣

Contains these components:

☐ grass r 艹 87, p.29

☐ smooth cover r 宀 268, p.69

■ tree 木 562, p.133

With all these meanings & readings:

róng [榮] **1** surname Rong
róng [榮] **1** glory **2** honor **3** thriving

The components suggest a *tree covered* in *grass* or other decorative vegetation, a form of ornamentation that is appropriate to celebrate the guest of **honor**.

629

柜
櫃
柜
TRAD SIMPLIFIED

This character with the definition:

cupboard

Pinyin **guì** *and Frequency Rank* **1994**

Contains **8 strokes** in the following order:

一 十 才 木 杧 杧 柜 柜

Contains these components:

◧ tree 木 562, p.133

☐ huge 巨 153, p.42

With all these meanings & readings:

jǔ [柜] **1** Salix multinervis
guì [櫃] **1** cupboard **2** cabinet **3** wardrobe

A **cupboard** is a *huge* piece of furniture made from a *tree*.

630

SIMP & TRAD

This character with the definition:

cinnamon

Pinyin **guì** *and Frequency Rank* **1930**

Contains these components:
- tree 木 562, p.133
- jade tablet 圭 10, p.11

With all these meanings & readings:
guì [桂] **1** Cinnamonum cassia **2** abbr for Guangxi autonomous region in south China 广西壮族自治区 [廣~壯~~~區]

Contains **10 strokes** in the following order:

一 十 十 木 术 杧 杧 杜 桂 桂 桂

Cinnamon is a spice derived from a small evergreen *tree*. Historically, trading it was as valuable as trading in *jade tablets*.

631

閑
TRAD   SIMPLIFIED

This character with the definition:

idle

Pinyin **xián** *and Frequency Rank* **1529**

Contains these components:
- doorway 门 243, p.64
- tree 木 562, p.133

With all these meanings & readings:
xián [閑] **1** to stay idle **2** to be unoccupied **3** not busy **4** leisure **5** enclosure r

Contains **7 strokes** in the following order:

丶 丷 门 门 闲 闲 闲

I had work today, but the *tree* blocked my exit through the *doorway*. I was forced to stay home and sit **idly** all day! When my wife returned, she saw me so entranced by the TV that she thought I was a *tree*.

632

SIMP & TRAD

This character with the definition:

pillar, column

Pinyin **zhù** *and Frequency Rank* **1691**

Contains these components:
- tree 木 562, p.133
- master 主 179, p.49

With all these meanings & readings:
zhù [柱] **1** pillar **2** m 根[gēn]

Contains **9 strokes** in the following order:

一 十 十 木 术 杧 柱 柱 柱

Only the straightest, tallest, and firmest of *trees* are chosen for their architectural suitability. These *master trees* are ideal to construct **pillars** and **columns**.

633

SIMP & TRAD

This character with the definition:

firewood

Pinyin **chái** *and Frequency Rank* **1981**

Contains these components:
- this 此 196, p.53
- tree 木 562, p.133

With all these meanings & readings:
chái [柴] **1** firewood **2** surname Chai

Contains **10 strokes** in the following order:

丨 ⺊ ⺊ 止 ⺧ 此 此 柴 柴 柴

This tree has been chopped down to a small size, perfect to use for **firewood** this winter. The vertical strokes in '*this*' look like tongues of flame.

634

SIMP & TRAD

This character with the definition:

rod, stick

Pinyin **gùn** *and Frequency Rank* **2255**

Contains these components:
- tree 木 562, p.133
- elder brother** 昆 129, p.37

With all these meanings & readings:
gùn [棍] **1** stick **2** rod **3** truncheon

Contains **12 strokes** in the following order:

一 十 十 木 术 杧 柙 相 相 棍 棍 棍

The *elder brother* goes to the *tree* to find a **stick** to use to control his younger brother.

Unit 28

635

柯

SIMP & TRAD

This character with the definition:

ax handle

Pinyin **kē** *and Frequency Rank* **1903**

Contains **9 strokes** in the following order:

一 十 十 木 木 杧 柯 柯 柯

Contains these components:

☐ tree 木 562, p.133

☐ can, may 可 60, p.23

With all these meanings & readings:

kē [柯] **1** surname Ke **2** handle of ax **3** stem

The *wooden* part of the ax is called the **ax handle**. With a long, inflexible handle, I *can* do much more work than my neighbor.

636

棉

SIMP & TRAD

This character with the definition:

cotton

Pinyin **mián** *and Frequency Rank* **1967**

Contains **12 strokes** in the following order:

一 十 十 木 木 村 柏 柏 柏 棉 棉

Contains these components:

☐ tree 木 562, p.133

☐ silk 帛 230, p.61

With all these meanings & readings:

mián [棉] **1** cotton

A certain *tree* (well, alright, it's a plant) produces *silk*-like fibers that are good for clothes. We call this **cotton**.

637

奇

SIMP & TRAD

This character with the definition:

odd

Pinyin **jī** *and Frequency Rank* **563**

Contains **8 strokes** in the following order:

一 ナ 大 本 奇 奇 奇 奇

Contains these components:

☐ big 大 544, p.129

☐ can, may 可 60, p.23

With all these meanings & readings:

jī [奇] **1** odd (number)
qí [奇] **1** strange **2** odd **3** weird **4** wonderful

How **odd**! A *big* man is teetering across the high-wire that forms the top of the '可' element. Why is he doing this? Because he *can*!

638

寄

SIMP & TRAD

This character with the definition:

send, mail, consign

Pinyin **jì** *and Frequency Rank* **1611**

Contains **11 strokes** in the following order:

丶 冖 宀 宀 宀 宎 宎 寄 寄 寄 寄

Contains these components:

☐ roof r 宀 271, p.70

☐ odd 奇 637, p.151

With all these meanings & readings:

jì [寄] **1** to live (in a house) **2** to lodge **3** to mail **4** to send **5** to entrust **6** to depend

The postage stamps needed to **send** a letter to your friend's *house* often cost an *odd* number of cents.

639

骑

TRAD SIMPLIFIED

This character with the definition:

ride, sit astride

Pinyin **qí** *and Frequency Rank* **1398**

Contains **11 strokes** in the following order:

フ 马 马 马 马 马 骑 骑 骑 骑 骑

Contains these components:

☐ horse 马 388, p.95

☐ odd 奇 637, p.151

With all these meanings & readings:

qí [骑] **1** to ride (an animal or bike) **2** to sit astride

The young girl **rides** the *horse* in an *odd* way because the *horse* it too large for her—she would sit better on a pony.

640

This character with the definition:

chair

Pinyin **yǐ** *and Frequency Rank* **1663**

SIMP & TRAD   Contains **12 strokes** in the following order:

一 十 才 木 术 术 杧 柞 柞 椅 椅 椅

Contains these components:

■ tree 木 562, p. 133
■ odd 奇 637, p. 151

With all these meanings & readings:

yǐ [椅] **1** chair

The *tree* must think it *odd* that its wood is used to make a **chair**, an artifact for supporting a type of animal (human) in a posture that is neither lying nor standing.

641

This character with the definition:

do not, not

Pinyin **mò** *and Frequency Rank* **955**

SIMP & TRAD   Contains **10 strokes** in the following order:

一 十 艹 艹 芍 苎 苩 苩 莒 莫

Contains these components:

□ grass r 艹 87, p. 29
▬ day, sun 日 64, p. 24
■ big 大 544, p. 129

With all these meanings & readings:

mò [莫] **1** surname Mo
mò [莫] **1** do not **2** there is none who

To grow *big*, tall *grasses* need ample amounts of *sun*light, so **do not** plant them in the shade.

642

This character with the definition:

grope, touch

Pinyin **mō** *and Frequency Rank* **1367**

SIMP & TRAD   Contains **13 strokes** in the following order:

一 十 才 扩 扩 扩 扩 措 措 措 摸 摸 摸

Contains these components:

■ hand r 扌 25, p. 15
■ do not, not 莫 641, p. 152

With all these meanings & readings:

mō [摸] **1** to feel with the hand **2** to touch **3** to stroke **4** to grope **5** to feel (one's pulse)
mó [摸] **1** imitate **2** copy

Groping is putting your *hand* where it's *not* supposed to be and it's not proper.

643

This character with the definition:

stage curtain

Pinyin **mù** *and Frequency Rank* **1315**

SIMP & TRAD   Contains **13 strokes** in the following order:

一 十 艹 艹 芍 苎 苩 莒 莒 莫 莫 莫 幕 幕

Contains these components:

■ do not, not 莫 641, p. 152
□ towel 巾 118, p. 35

With all these meanings & readings:

mù [幕] **1** stage curtain **2** tent **3** by extension, act of a play

A **stage curtain** is a heavy piece of special *cloth* intended to make sure audience members *do not* see the stagehands preparing the stage set before it is complete.

644

This character with the definition:

model, imitation

Pinyin **mó** *and Frequency Rank* **689**

SIMP & TRAD   Contains **14 strokes** in the following order:

一 十 才 木 术 术 朾 朾 柑 槙 槙 槙 模 模

Contains these components:

■ tree 木 562, p. 133
■ do not, not 莫 641, p. 152

With all these meanings & readings:

mó [模] **1** imitate **2** model **3** norm **4** pattern

You *do not* need to use a whole *tree* to construct a wooden **model** of a ship.

645

漢

SIMP & TRAD

This character with the definition:

desert

Pinyin **mò** *and Frequency Rank* **1777**

Contains **13 strokes** in the following order:

丶丶氵汀汀汴洪淓淓淓漠漠

A **desert** is a place where *water* is *not* present.

Contains these components:

■ water r 氵 314, p. 80
■ do not, not 莫 641, p. 152

With all these meanings & readings:

mò [漢] **1** desert **2** unconcerned

646

墓

SIMP & TRAD

This character with the definition:

tomb

Pinyin **mù** *and Frequency Rank* **1816**

Contains **13 strokes** in the following order:

一十艹艹芦芦芦苜莫莫墓墓墓

Once you pass through a **tomb** into the *earth*, you *do not* return.

Contains these components:

■ do not, not 莫 641, p. 152
■ earth, soil 土 9, p. 11

With all these meanings & readings:

mù [墓] **1** tomb

647

弋

SIMP & TRAD

This character with the definition:

kind of arrow

Pinyin **yì** *and Frequency Rank* **4265**

Contains **3 strokes** in the following order:

一弋弋

Imagine this **kind of arrow** striking the *big* warrior in his left leg; as he begins to topple over, a *bit* of blood flies away from him (in the upper right). • You can also picture this **kind of arrow** traveling on a downward path. The arrow head is pointing down to the right and the aerodynamic feathered fins are at the top.

Contains these components:

■ big 大 (altered) 544, p. 129
□ dab r 丶 176, p. 48

With all these meanings & readings:

yì [弋] **1** to shoot

648

式

SIMP & TRAD

This character with the definition:

model, standard

Pinyin **shì** *and Frequency Rank* **303**

Contains **6 strokes** in the following order:

一二亍王式式

The boy is busy carving a **model** ship. You see, it's difficult *work* for him since he has only a sharp *kind of arrow* to use as his carving tool.

Contains these components:

■ labor, work 工 12, p. 12
■ kind of arrow 弋 647, p. 153

With all these meanings & readings:

shì [式] **1** type **2** form **3** pattern **4** style

649

试

TRAD SIMPLIFIED

This character with the definition:

test, try

Pinyin **shì** *and Frequency Rank* **643**

Contains **8 strokes** in the following order:

丶讠讠讠讠讠试试

He's **trying** to learn Mandarin Chinese, but every time he uses the *standard* language in his *speech* his Chinese friends break into laughter!

Contains these components:

■ speech r 讠 352, p. 88
■ model, standard 式 648, p. 153

With all these meanings & readings:

shì [試] **1** to test **2** to try **3** experiment **4** examination **5** test

650

SIMP & TRAD

This character with the definition:

halberd

Pinyin **gē** *and Frequency Rank* **1695**

Contains **4 strokes** in the following order:

一 弋 戈 戈

Contains these components:

■ kind of arrow 弋 647, p.153

■ scepter c ｜ (altered) 5, p.10

With all these meanings & readings:

gē [戈] **1** spear **2** surname Ge

A **halberd** is a medieval weapon formed by joining a spear with a battle-ax. Imagine the *scepter*-like diagonal as the main handle leading to the spear blade and the cross-strokes are the ax blades—complete with a drop of blood splashing in the air!

651

SIMP & TRAD

This character with the definition:

seek

Pinyin **zhǎo** *and Frequency Rank* **466**

Contains **7 strokes** in the following order:

一 十 才 扌 扌 找 找

Contains these components:

■ hand r 扌 25, p.15

■ halberd 戈 650, p.154

With all these meanings & readings:

zhǎo [找] **1** to try to find **2** to look for **3** to call on sb **4** to find **5** to seek **6** to return **7** to give change

As the pirates set out to **seek** the lost treasure, each one kept his *hand* tightly wrapped around his *halberd* as a precaution.

652

戰
TRAD

SIMPLIFIED

This character with the definition:

war

Pinyin **zhàn** *and Frequency Rank* **145**

Contains **9 strokes** in the following order:

丨 卜 𠃌 占 占 占 战 战 战

Contains these components:

■ practice divination 占 188, p.51

■ halberd 戈 650, p.154

With all these meanings & readings:

zhàn [戰] **1** to fight **2** fight **3** war **4** battle

No matter how prepared you are, **war** is as chancy as *divination* regardless of the state of your *swords* and weapons.

653

SIMP & TRAD

This character with the definition:

fifth (in a series)

Pinyin **wù** *and Frequency Rank* **3689**

Contains **5 strokes** in the following order:

一 厂 戊 戊 戊

Contains these components:

■ scepter c ｜ (altered) 5, p.10

■ halberd 戈 650, p.154

With all these meanings & readings:

wù [戊] **1** fifth of 10 heavenly stems 十天干 **2** fifth in order **3** letter "E" or roman "V" in list "A, B, C", or "I, II, III" etc **4** penta

Scepters and *halberds* are both weapons that must be grasped firmly with all **five** fingers of a hand. (Notice how this character is completed by the **fifth** stroke.)

654

鹹
咸
TRAD

SIMPLIFIED

This character with the definition:

all, everyone

Pinyin **xián** *and Frequency Rank* **2525**

Contains **9 strokes** in the following order:

一 厂 厂 斤 后 咸 咸 咸 咸

Contains these components:

■ fifth (in a series) 戊 653, p.154

■ eye 目 (altered) 75, p.26

With all these meanings & readings:

xián [咸] **1** surname Xian
xián [咸] **1** all **2** everyone
xián [鹹] **1** salted **2** salty

All the single women's *eyes* were focused on the *fifth* person who appeared in the town parade—the handsome young hero who had just returned home from war!

655

喊

SIMP & TRAD

This character with the definition:

cry out

Pinyin **hǎn** *and Frequency Rank* **1183**

Contains **12 strokes** in the following order:

丶 丆 口 口⁻ 叮 呀 呀 咸 咸 喊 喊 喊

Contains these components:

■ mouth 口 37, p.17
■ all, everyone 咸 654, p.154

With all these meanings & readings:

hǎn [喊] **1** call **2** cry **3** to shout

Babies know how to quickly capture *everyone*'s attention—by using their *mouths* to **cry out** very loud.

656

减
TRAD

减
SIMPLIFIED

This character with the definition:

lower, reduce

Pinyin **jiǎn** *and Frequency Rank* **857**

Contains **11 strokes** in the following order:

丶 冫 冫 冫 沪 浐 泜 泜 减 减 减

Contains these components:

■ ice r 冫 348, p.87
■ all, everyone 咸 654, p.154

With all these meanings & readings:

jiǎn [减] **1** to lower **2** to decrease **3** to reduce **4** to subtract **5** to diminish

Whenever *everyone* brings a piece of *ice* into the room, it **lowers** the temperature.

657

成

SIMP & TRAD

This character with the definition:

become, turn into

Pinyin **chéng** *and Frequency Rank* **59**

Contains **6 strokes** in the following order:

一 厂 厅 成 成 成

Contains these components:

■ fifth (in a series) 戊 653, p.154
■ fourth (in a series) 丁 (altered) 19, p.13

With all these meanings & readings:

chéng [成] **1** finish **2** complete **3** accomplish **4** become **5** turn into **6** win **7** succeed **8** one tenth **9** surname Cheng

After reading the *fourth* or *fifth* paragraph of a student's essay, most teachers know what its grade will **become**.

658

城

SIMP & TRAD

This character with the definition:

city wall, wall

Pinyin **chéng** *and Frequency Rank* **413**

Contains **9 strokes** in the following order:

一 十 土 圵 圵 坊 城 城 城

Contains these components:

■ earth, soil 土 9, p.11
■ become, turn into 成 657, p.155

With all these meanings & readings:

chéng [城] **1** city walls **2** city **3** town **4** m 座[zuò], 道[dào], 个[個][gè]

The ancients moved mounds of *earth* and *turned* them *into* flourishing towns surrounded by high **walls**.

659

盛

This character with the definition:

dish out, ladle

Pinyin **chéng** *and Frequency Rank* **1142**

SIMP & TRAD

Contains **11 strokes** in the following order:

一 厂 厅 成 成 成 成 戚 盛 盛 盛

Contains these components:

■ become, turn into 成 657, p.155
■ vessel, container 皿 101, p.32

With all these meanings & readings:

chéng [盛] **1** to hold **2** contain **3** to ladle **4** pick up with a utensil
shèng [盛] **1** flourishing **2** vigorous **3** magnificent **4** extensively **5** surname Sheng

When you **ladle** delicious chicken soup from the big cooking *vessel* into serving dishes, it *becomes* a nourishing meal.

Unit 29

660

TRAD 誠 · SIMPLIFIED

This character with the definition:

sincere

Pinyin **chéng** *and Frequency Rank* **1154**

Contains these components:

☐ speech r 讠 352, p.88
☐ become, turn into 成 657, p.155

With all these meanings & readings:

chéng [誠] **1** honest **2** sincere **3** true

Contains **8 strokes** in the following order:

丶 讠 讠 计 讦 诫 诚 诚

People *become* uplifted when they listen to *speeches* that are **sincere**.

661

SIMP & TRAD

This character with the definition:

I

Pinyin **wǒ** *and Frequency Rank* **9**

Contains these components:

☐ hand r 扌 (altered) 25, p.15
☐ halberd 戈 650, p.154

With all these meanings & readings:

wǒ [我] **1** I **2** me **3** my

Contains **7 strokes** in the following order:

丿 一 于 手 我 我 我

With my *halberd* in *hand*, **I** am filled with the confidence that **I** can conquer any foe.

662

SIMP & TRAD

This character with the definition:

chant softly

Pinyin **é** *and Frequency Rank* **1913**

Contains these components:

☐ mouth 口 37, p.17
☐ I 我 661, p.156

With all these meanings & readings:

é [哦] **1** to chant
ó [哦] **1** oh

Contains **10 strokes** in the following order:

丿 冂 口 口 口 吁 吁 哦 哦 哦

To calm myself, *I* will use my *mouth* to **chant softly**.

663

SIMP & TRAD

This character with the definition:

or

Pinyin **huò** *and Frequency Rank* **160**

Contains these components:

☐ dawn 旦 (altered) 70, p.25
☐ halberd 戈 650, p.154

With all these meanings & readings:

huò [或] **1** maybe **2** perhaps **3** might **4** possibly **5** or

Contains **8 strokes** in the following order:

一 丆 万 可 豇 或 或 或

Every *dawn*, my friend's biggest question is whether to stay in bed **or** to venture forth—with 'sword in hand'—into the world.

664

SIMP & TRAD

This character with the definition:

region, area

Pinyin **yù** *and Frequency Rank* **847**

Contains these components:

☐ earth, soil 土 9, p.11
☐ or 或 663, p.156

With all these meanings & readings:

yù [域] **1** field **2** region **3** area **4** domain (taxonomy)

Contains **11 strokes** in the following order:

一 十 土 土 圹 坷 垣 垣 域 域 域

In some rural **regions**, you must work the *soil or* you do not eat.

665

戔

戔 TRAD   SIMPLIFIED

This character with the definition:

tiny, fragmentary

Pinyin **jiān** *and Frequency Rank* **6653**

Contains **5 strokes** in the following order:

一 二 も も 戔

Contains these components:

■ halberd (×2, altered) 戈 650, p.154

With all these meanings & readings:

jiān [戔] **1** narrow **2** small

Two *halberds* will quickly reduce most things to **tiny** pieces.

666

浅

淺 TRAD   SIMPLIFIED

This character with the definition:

shallow, superficial

Pinyin **qiǎn** *and Frequency Rank* **1721**

Contains **8 strokes** in the following order:

丶 丶 氵 氵 泸 浅 浅 浅

Contains these components:

■ water r 氵 314, p.80

■ tiny, fragmentary 戔 665, p.157

With all these meanings & readings:

jiān [淺] **1** sound of moving water

qiǎn [淺] **1** shallow **2** light (color)

Vain and **superficial** bathing suit models never take more than a few *tiny* steps into the *water*.

667

尧

堯 TRAD   SIMPLIFIED

This character with the definition:

legendary emperor

Pinyin **yáo** *and Frequency Rank* **3264**

Contains **6 strokes** in the following order:

一 七 戈 戈 垚 尧

Contains these components:

■ tiny, fragmentary 戔 (altered) 665, p.157

■ dollar 元 (altered) 295, p.76

With all these meanings & readings:

Yáo [堯] **1** surname Yao **2** Yao or Tang Yao (c. 2200 BC), one of Five legendary Emperors 五帝, second son of Di Ku 帝喾 [~嚳]

This **legendary emperor** took the many *fragmentary monetary* systems in ancient China and merged them into one unified system of *currency*.

668

晓

曉 TRAD   SIMPLIFIED

This character with the definition:

daybreak

Pinyin **xiǎo** *and Frequency Rank* **1357**

Contains **10 strokes** in the following order:

丨 冂 日 日 日一 旪 畔 睦 睦 晓

Contains these components:

■ day, sun 日 64, p.24

■ legendary emperor 尧 667, p.157

With all these meanings & readings:

xiǎo [曉] **1** dawn **2** daybreak **3** to know **4** to let sb know **5** to make explicit

According to the story, this *legendary emperor* will rise with the *sun* to save his homeland at **daybreak**.

669

臧

SIMP & TRAD

This character with the definition:

goodness, luck

Pinyin **zāng** *and Frequency Rank* **4304**

Contains **14 strokes** in the following order:

一 厂 疒 疒 疒 疒 疒 疒 疒 疒 疧 臧 臧 臧

Contains these components:

■ slice, flake 片 (altered) 488, p.116

■ halberd 戈 650, p.154

■ subject of a ruler 臣 154, p.43

With all these meanings & readings:

zāng [臧] **1** good **2** lucky **3** surname Zang

It was the emperor's good **luck** that a *subject* armed with a *halberd* was nearby to take a *slice* of flesh from the approaching attacker.

670

SIMP & TRAD

This character with the definition:

hide, conceal

Pinyin **cáng** *and Frequency Rank* **907**

Contains these components:

☐ grass r ⺬ 87, p. 29

■ goodness, luck 臧 669, p. 157

With all these meanings & readings:

cáng [藏] **1** Tibet **2** Xizang 西藏

cáng [藏] **1** to conceal **2** to hide away **3** to harbor **4** to store **5** to collect

zàng [藏] **1** storehouse **2** depository **3** cache (computer) **4** Buddhist or Taoist scripture

Contains **17 strokes** in the following order:

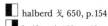

The *lucky* man found a pile of gold coins and now a pile of *grass* **hides** his treasure.

671

劃
TRAD

SIMPLIFIED

This character with the definition:

delimit

Pinyin **huà** *and Frequency Rank* **522**

Contains these components:

■ halberd 戈 650, p. 154

■ knife r 刂 169, p. 46

With all these meanings & readings:

huá [划] **1** to row **2** to paddle **3** to scratch a surface **4** profitable **5** worth (the effort) **6** it pays (to do sth)

huá [劃] **1** to scratch

huà [劃] **1** to delimit **2** to transfer **3** to assign **4** to differentiate **5** to mark off **6** to draw (a line) **7** to delete **8** stroke of a Chinese character

Contains **6 strokes** in the following order:

一 弋 戈 戈 划 划

Human history contains many examples of the use of weapons—for instance, your *knife* versus my *halberd*—to **delimit** personal boundaries.

672

SIMP & TRAD

This character with the definition:

martial, military

Pinyin **wǔ** *and Frequency Rank* **501**

Contains these components:

■ to correct, rectify 正 (altered) 193, p. 52

■ kind of arrow 弋 647, p. 153

With all these meanings & readings:

wǔ [武] **1** martial **2** military **3** surname Wu

Contains **8 strokes** in the following order:

一 二 干 亍 禾 正 武 武

After the new commander *corrected* the behavior of his troops and replaced the *kind of arrows* they used, he began to achieve overwhelming **military** success.

673

SIMP & TRAD

This character with the definition:

dog

Pinyin **quǎn** *and Frequency Rank* **2649**

Contains these components:

■ big 大 544, p. 129

■ dab r 丶 176, p. 48

With all these meanings & readings:

quǎn [犬] **1** dog

Contains **4 strokes** in the following order:

一 ナ 大 犬

A *big* **dog** needs much more to eat than a *dab* of canned food!

674

SIMP & TRAD

This character with the definition:

weep

Pinyin **kū** *and Frequency Rank* **1210**

Contains these components:

☐ mouth (×2) 口 37, p. 17

■ dog 犬 673, p. 158

With all these meanings & readings:

kū [哭] **1** to cry **2** to weep

Contains **10 strokes** in the following order:

丶 口 口 口 叩 吅 一 罗 哭 哭

Imagine this character as the face of someone who is **weeping**. The '*dog*' component is the lower half of the face and the two '*mouth*' components represent eyes from which a tear is falling.

675

This character with the definition:

implement, tool

Pinyin **qì** *and Frequency Rank* **441**

SIMP & TRAD   Contains **16 strokes** in the following order:

丶 口 口 吅 吅 吅 罒 罘 哭 哭 哭 哭 器 器 器 器

Contains these components:

■ weep 哭 674, p.158
■ mouth (×2) 口 37, p.17

With all these meanings & readings:

qì [器] **1** device **2** tool **3** utensil
4 m 台 [臺][tái]

The only time I ever saw my father *weep* and use his *mouth* to cry out in pain was after he injured himself with a power **tool**.

676

厭
TRAD   SIMPLIFIED

This character with the definition:

be sick of, disgusted with

Pinyin **yàn** *and Frequency Rank* **1633**

Contains **6 strokes** in the following order:

一 厂 厂 厌 厌 厌

Contains these components:

■ cliff r 厂 399, p.97
■ dog 犬 673, p.158

With all these meanings & readings:

yàn [厭] **1** to loathe

Towards the end of his life, the rich old man grew to **detest** the entire world. He shuttered himself in a fortress-like mansion atop a *cliff*, and kept vicious *dogs* that guarded the premises.

677

This character with the definition:

entreat

Pinyin **yāng** *and Frequency Rank* **800**

SIMP & TRAD   Contains **5 strokes** in the following order:

丨 冂 冂 央 央

Contains these components:

■ big 大 544, p.129
■ middle 中 (altered) 38, p.18

With all these meanings & readings:

yāng [央] **1** beg **2** center

The *middle* school boys ignored their female teacher's instructions even after she **entreated** them to stop misbehaving, so the principal solved the problem by hiring a *big* athletic man to be their new teacher.

678

This character with the definition:

reflect, shine

Pinyin **yìng** *and Frequency Rank* **1316**

SIMP & TRAD   Contains **9 strokes** in the following order:

丨 冂 日 日 日 旷 旷 映 映

Contains these components:

■ day, sun 日 64, p.24
■ entreat 央 677, p.159

With all these meanings & readings:

yìng [映] **1** reflect **2** shine

Ancient worshippers *entreated* the *Sun* god to **shine** his blessings down on them.

679

This character with the definition:

hero

Pinyin **yīng** *and Frequency Rank* **371**

SIMP & TRAD   Contains **8 strokes** in the following order:

一 十 艹 艹 芇 苧 英 英

Contains these components:

■ grass r 艹 87, p.29
■ entreat 央 677, p.159

With all these meanings & readings:

Yīng [英] **1** English **2** brave
3 surname Ying

The war **hero** was so highly revered that he never had to *entreat* anyone for assistance—not even when he needed someone to mow his *grass*!

680

唤

唤
TRAD SIMPLIFIED

This character with the definition:

call, call out to

Pinyin **huàn** and Frequency Rank **1835**

Contains **10 strokes** in the following order:

㇐ ㇑ �口 ㇿ 吖 吢 呜 唤 唤 唤

Contains these components:

☐ mouth 口 37, p.17

☐ man 人 (altered) 537, p.127

☐ entreat 奂 677, p.159

With all these meanings & readings:

huàn [唤] **1** to call

Why **call out** to someone? You use your *mouth* to make the call when you want to *entreat* a *man* to do something with you or for you.

681

立

SIMP & TRAD

This character with the definition:

to stand

Pinyin **lì** and Frequency Rank **197**

Contains **5 strokes** in the following order:

㇔ ㇐ ㇖ ㇉ 立

Contains these components:

☐ big 大 (altered) 544, p.129

☐ one 一 1, p.10

With all these meanings & readings:

lì [立] **1** set up **2** to stand

Even though participating in the Olympics is a *big* honor for athletes, they all want to be *one* of the select few who will wear a gold medal and **stand** on the podium as their country's anthem is played.

682

端

SIMP & TRAD

This character with the definition:

end, extremity

Pinyin **duān** and Frequency Rank **916**

Contains **14 strokes** in the following order:

㇔ ㇐ ㇖ ㇉ 立 立 立 立 立 端 端 端 端 端

Contains these components:

☐ to stand 立 681, p.160

☐ concentrate on, specialize in 耑 80, p.27

With all these meanings & readings:

duān [端] **1** end **2** extremity **3** item **4** port **5** to hold sth level with both hands **6** to carr **7** regular

I *stood* so close to the Eiffel Tower, so that I could *concentrate on* its intricate structure; however, that kept me from seeing its **end**, high above me.

683

站

SIMP & TRAD

This character with the definition:

stop, station

Pinyin **zhàn** and Frequency Rank **544**

Contains **10 strokes** in the following order:

㇔ ㇐ ㇖ ㇉ 立 立 站 站 站 站

Contains these components:

☐ to stand 立 681, p.160

☐ practice divination 占 188, p.51

With all these meanings & readings:

zhàn [站] **1** station **2** to stand **3** to halt **4** to stop

Many pilgrims *stood* on the crowded platform until the train arrived at the **station** where the famous spiritualist *practiced divination*.

684

辛

SIMP & TRAD

This character with the definition:

hardworking

Pinyin **xīn** and Frequency Rank **1463**

Contains **7 strokes** in the following order:

㇔ ㇐ ㇖ ㇉ 立 音 辛

Contains these components:

☐ to stand 立 681, p.160

☐ ten 十 7, p.11

With all these meanings & readings:

xīn [辛] **1** tired **2** eighth of 10 heavenly stems 十天干 **3** eighth in order **4** letter"H" or roman"VIII" in list"A, B, C", or"I, II, III" etc **5** octa

A worker who can *stand* for more than *ten* hours is a genuinely **hardworking** employee.

Unit 30

685
關
辟
TRAD SIMPLIFIED

辟

This character with the definition:

penal law

Pinyin **pì** *and Frequency Rank* **2140**

Contains **13 strokes** in the following order:

丶 ﹁ ﹁ ﹁ ﹁ ﹁ ﹁ ﹁ ﹁ ﹁ ﹁ 辟 辟

Contains these components:

corpse 尸 499, p.119

mouth 口 37, p.17

hardworking 辛 684, p.160

With all these meanings & readings:

bì [辟] **1** king **2** emperor **3** monarc **4** royal **5** ward off
pì [辟] **1** law
pì [闢] **1** to dispel **2** to refute **3** to repudiate **4** to open up (for development) **5** penal law

In a murder trial, a smart, *hardworking* prosecutor will find ways to use the **penal law** to enable the *mouth* of the victim's *corpse* to 'testify' from the grave.

686
壁

壁

SIMP & TRAD

This character with the definition:

like a wall

Pinyin **bì** *and Frequency Rank* **1380**

Contains **16 strokes** in the following order:

丶 ﹁ ﹁ ﹁ ﹁ ﹁ ﹁ ﹁ ﹁ ﹁ 辟 辟 辟 辟 壁 壁

Contains these components:

penal law 辟 685, p.161

earth, soil 土 9, p.11

With all these meanings & readings:

bì [壁] **1** wall **2** rampart

A people without the rule of *penal law* are as unprotected as those hiding behind a mound that looks **like a wall** but is only a pile of *earth*.

687
拉

拉

SIMP & TRAD

This character with the definition:

pull, draw, tug

Pinyin **lā** *and Frequency Rank* **324**

Contains **8 strokes** in the following order:

一 十 扌 扩 扩 扩 拉 拉

Contains these components:

hand r 扌 25, p.15

to stand 立 681, p.160

With all these meanings & readings:

lā [拉] **1** to pull **2** to play (string instruments) **3** to drag **4** to draw

Human *hands* can make a puppet *stand* and move about by **pulling** on its strings.

688
啦

啦

SIMP & TRAD

This character with the definition:

s-end: surprise

Pinyin **la** *and Frequency Rank* **1194**

Contains **11 strokes** in the following order:

丶 丨 口 口 口 叮 叮 叮 呀 啦 啦

Contains these components:

mouth 口 37, p.17

pull, draw, tug 拉 687, p.161

With all these meanings & readings:

lā [啦] **1** (onomat.) **2** (phonetic)
la [啦] **1** (sentence-final particle, contraction of "了啊") **2** (follows after each item in a list of examples)

You can **signal surprise** by making a statement about the way you *pull* your *mouth*.

689
音

音

SIMP & TRAD

This character with the definition:

sound

Pinyin **yīn** *and Frequency Rank* **540**

Contains **9 strokes** in the following order:

丶 二 亠 立 立 音 音 音 音

Contains these components:

to stand 立 681, p.160

day, sun 日 64, p.24

With all these meanings & readings:

yīn [音] **1** sound **2** noise **3** note (of musical scale) **4** tone **5** news **6** syllable **7** reading (phonetic value of a character)

As each new *day* begins, people get out of bed, *stand* up, and begin to make all kinds of **sounds**.

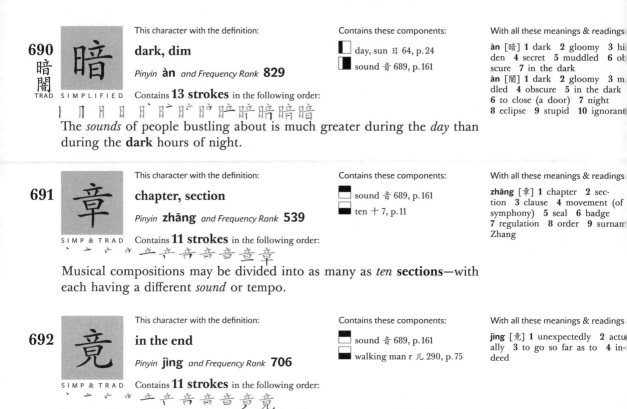

690
暗
闇
TRAD

暗
SIMPLIFIED

This character with the definition:

dark, dim

Pinyin **àn** *and Frequency Rank* **829**

Contains these components:

day, sun 日 64, p. 24

sound 音 689, p. 161

Contains **13 strokes** in the following order:

丨 冂 冂 日 日 日' 日" 日" 日产 暗 暗 暗 暗

With all these meanings & readings

àn [暗] **1** dark **2** gloomy **3** hidden **4** secret **5** muddled **6** obscure **7** in the dark
àn [闇] **1** dark **2** gloomy **3** muddled **4** obscure **5** in the dark **6** to close (a door) **7** night **8** eclipse **9** stupid **10** ignorant

The *sounds* of people bustling about is much greater during the *day* than during the **dark** hours of night.

691
章
SIMP & TRAD

This character with the definition:

chapter, section

Pinyin **zhāng** *and Frequency Rank* **539**

Contains these components:

sound 音 689, p. 161

ten 十 7, p. 11

Contains **11 strokes** in the following order:

丶 亠 亠 立 立 音 音 音 音 章 章

With all these meanings & readings

zhāng [章] **1** chapter **2** section **3** clause **4** movement (of symphony) **5** seal **6** badge **7** regulation **8** order **9** surname Zhang

Musical compositions may be divided into as many as *ten* **sections**—with each having a different *sound* or tempo.

692
竟
SIMP & TRAD

This character with the definition:

in the end

Pinyin **jìng** *and Frequency Rank* **706**

Contains these components:

sound 音 689, p. 161

walking man r 儿 290, p. 75

Contains **11 strokes** in the following order:

丶 亠 亠 立 立 音 音 音 音 竟 竟

With all these meanings & readings

jìng [竟] **1** unexpectedly **2** actually **3** to go so far as to **4** indeed

In the nineteenth-century, platoons of *walking men* entered battle to the stirring *sound* of bagpipes, hopeful that the men would return victorious **in the end**.

693
境
SIMP & TRAD

This character with the definition:

territory

Pinyin **jìng** *and Frequency Rank* **582**

Contains these components:

earth, soil 土 9, p. 11

in the end 竟 692, p. 162

Contains **14 strokes** in the following order:

一 十 土 土' 土" 圹 圹 圹 垆 培 培 培 境 境

With all these meanings & readings

jìng [境] **1** border **2** place **3** condition **4** boundary **5** circumstances **6** territory

No matter how extensive your piece of **territory** is, *in the end* if you travel far enough, you will reach *soil* that belongs to someone else.

694
童
SIMP & TRAD

This character with the definition:

child

Pinyin **tóng** *and Frequency Rank* **1229**

Contains these components:

to stand 立 681, p. 160

neighborhood 里 40, p. 18

Contains **12 strokes** in the following order:

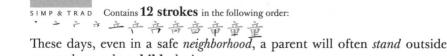

丶 亠 亠 立 立 音 音 音 音 童 童 童

With all these meanings & readings

tóng [童] **1** surname Tong **2** bare **3** child **4** children

These days, even in a safe *neighborhood*, a parent will often *stand* outside to watch over her **child** playing.

695

撞

SIMP & TRAD

This character with the definition:

run into, collide

Pinyin **zhuàng** *and Frequency Rank* **1540**

Contains **15 strokes** in the following order:

一 十 扌 扩 扩 扩 扩 扩 捧 捧 捧 撞 撞

Contains these components:

▮ hand r 扌 25, p.15

▯ child 童 694, p.162

With all these meanings & readings:

zhuàng [撞] **1** to hit **2** to strike **3** to meet by accident **4** to run into **5** to bump against **6** to bump into

The young *child* was just about to **run into** the busy street when an observant pedestrian saw and pulled him back with his *hand*.

696

帝

SIMP & TRAD

This character with the definition:

emperor*

Pinyin **dì** *and Frequency Rank* **612**

Contains **9 strokes** in the following order:

丶 二 广 亠 产 产 帝 帝 帝

Contains these components:

▯ to stand 立 (altered) 681, p.160

▮ towel 巾 118, p.35

With all these meanings & readings:

dì [帝] **1** emperor

In the presence of the **emperor**, every subject is required to wear special *clothing* and *stand* at attention until the **emperor** acknowledges him.

697

啻

SIMP & TRAD

This character with the definition:

not only

Pinyin **chì** *and Frequency Rank* **4249**

Contains **12 strokes** in the following order:

丶 二 广 亠 产 产 帝 帝 帝 帝 啻 啻

Contains these components:

▮ emperor* 帝 696, p.163

▯ mouth 口 37, p.17

With all these meanings & readings:

chì [啻] **1** only (classical, usually follows negative or question words) **2** (not) just

The *emperor* impresses his people **not only** with his physical presence, but also with the words that emerge from his *mouth*.

698

滴

SIMP & TRAD

This character with the definition:

drip

Pinyin **dī** *and Frequency Rank* **1896**

Contains **14 strokes** in the following order:

丶 丶 氵 氵 沪 沪 沪 沪 滴 滴 滴 滴 滴 滴

Contains these components:

▮ water r 氵 314, p.80

▯ not only 啻 (altered) 697, p.163

With all these meanings & readings:

dī [滴] **1** a drop **2** to drip

Not only is the *water* radical part of this character, but its form also resembles **drips** of *water* splashing out from a fountain or bird bath.

699

蒂

SIMP & TRAD

This character with the definition:

base of fruit

Pinyin **dì** *and Frequency Rank* **1429**

Contains **12 strokes** in the following order:

一 十 艹 艹 芒 芒 芦 芦 芾 蒂 蒂 蒂

Contains these components:

▯ grass r 艹 87, p.29

▮ emperor* 帝 696, p.163

With all these meanings & readings:

dì [蒂] **1** stem (of fruit)

The *emperor* ordered his villagers to plant fruit trees in the *grass*. After the fruits were harvested, they were served to the *emperor*, who refused to eat the **base of the fruit**.

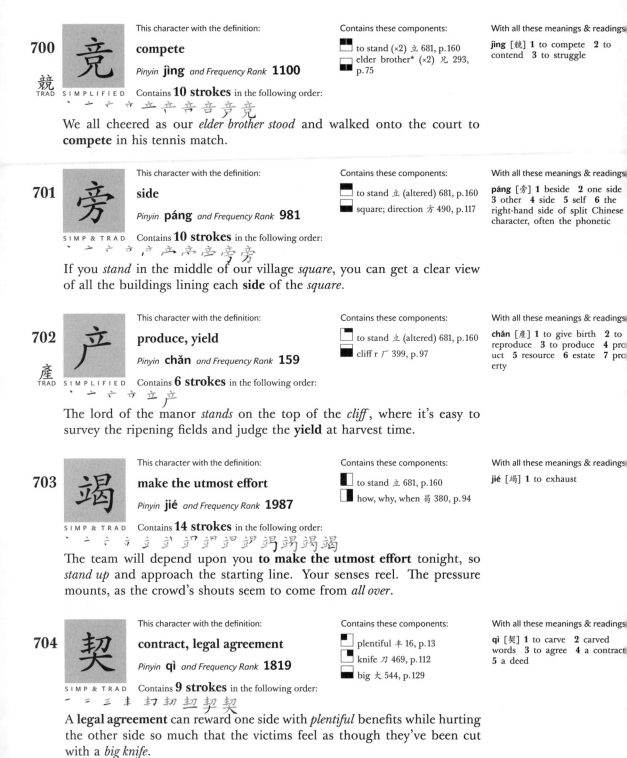

700

竞

競
TRAD   SIMPLIFIED

This character with the definition:

compete

Pinyin **jìng** *and Frequency Rank* **1100**

Contains **10 strokes** in the following order:

Contains these components:

to stand (×2) 立 681, p.160

elder brother* (×2) 兄 293, p.75

With all these meanings & readings

jìng [競] **1** to compete **2** to contend **3** to struggle

We all cheered as our *elder brother stood* and walked onto the court to **compete** in his tennis match.

701

旁

SIMP & TRAD

This character with the definition:

side

Pinyin **páng** *and Frequency Rank* **981**

Contains **10 strokes** in the following order:

Contains these components:

to stand 立 (altered) 681, p.160

square; direction 方 490, p.117

With all these meanings & readings

páng [旁] **1** beside **2** one side **3** other **4** side **5** self **6** the right-hand side of split Chinese character, often the phonetic

If you *stand* in the middle of our village *square*, you can get a clear view of all the buildings lining each **side** of the *square*.

702

产

産
TRAD   SIMPLIFIED

This character with the definition:

produce, yield

Pinyin **chǎn** *and Frequency Rank* **159**

Contains **6 strokes** in the following order:

Contains these components:

to stand 立 (altered) 681, p.160

cliff r 厂 399, p.97

With all these meanings & readings

chǎn [産] **1** to give birth **2** to reproduce **3** to produce **4** product **5** resource **6** estate **7** property

The lord of the manor *stands* on the top of the *cliff*, where it's easy to survey the ripening fields and judge the **yield** at harvest time.

703

竭

SIMP & TRAD

This character with the definition:

make the utmost effort

Pinyin **jié** *and Frequency Rank* **1987**

Contains **14 strokes** in the following order:

Contains these components:

to stand 立 681, p.160

how, why, when 曷 380, p.94

With all these meanings & readings

jié [竭] **1** to exhaust

The team will depend upon you **to make the utmost effort** tonight, so *stand up* and approach the starting line. Your senses reel. The pressure mounts, as the crowd's shouts seem to come from *all over*.

704

契

SIMP & TRAD

This character with the definition:

contract, legal agreement

Pinyin **qì** *and Frequency Rank* **1819**

Contains **9 strokes** in the following order:

Contains these components:

plentiful 丰 16, p.13

knife 刀 469, p.112

big 大 544, p.129

With all these meanings & readings

qì [契] **1** to carve **2** carved words **3** to agree **4** a contract **5** a deed

A **legal agreement** can reward one side with *plentiful* benefits while hurting the other side so much that the victims feel as though they've been cut with a *big knife*.

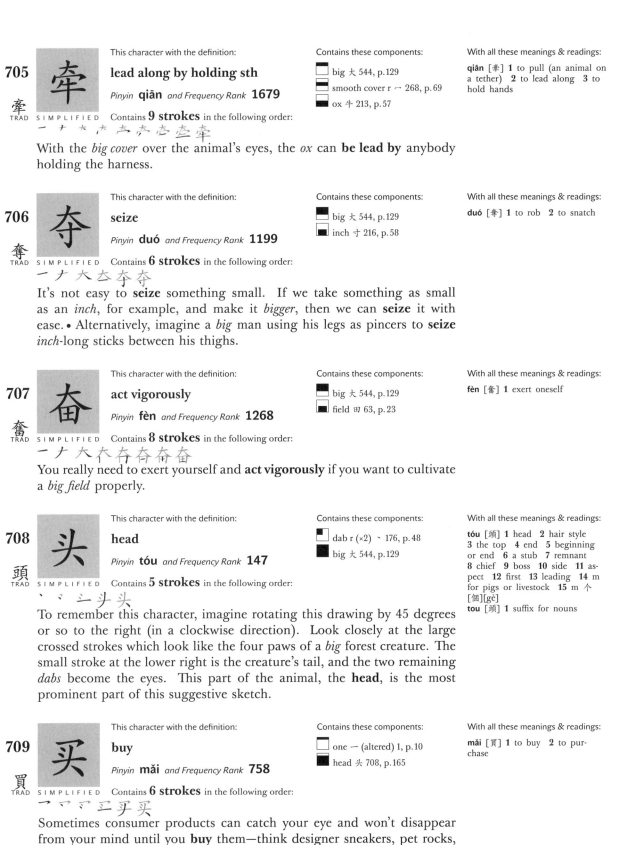

705

牵

牽 TRAD   SIMPLIFIED

This character with the definition:

lead along by holding sth

Pinyin **qiān** *and Frequency Rank* **1679**

Contains **9 strokes** in the following order:

一 十 大 大 立 牢 牢 牵 牵

Contains these components:

big 大 544, p.129

smooth cover r 冖 268, p.69

ox 牛 213, p.57

With all these meanings & readings:

qiān [牽] **1** to pull (an animal on a tether) **2** to lead along **3** to hold hands

With the *big cover* over the animal's eyes, the *ox* can **be lead by** anybody holding the harness.

706

夺

奪 TRAD   SIMPLIFIED

This character with the definition:

seize

Pinyin **duó** *and Frequency Rank* **1199**

Contains **6 strokes** in the following order:

一 ナ 大 太 夺 夺

Contains these components:

big 大 544, p.129

inch 寸 216, p.58

With all these meanings & readings:

duó [奪] **1** to rob **2** to snatch

It's not easy to **seize** something small. If we take something as small as an *inch*, for example, and make it *bigger*, then we can **seize** it with ease. • Alternatively, imagine a *big* man using his legs as pincers to **seize** *inch*-long sticks between his thighs.

707

奋

奮 TRAD   SIMPLIFIED

This character with the definition:

act vigorously

Pinyin **fèn** *and Frequency Rank* **1268**

Contains **8 strokes** in the following order:

一 ナ 大 大 存 存 奋 奋

Contains these components:

big 大 544, p.129

field 田 63, p.23

With all these meanings & readings:

fèn [奮] **1** exert oneself

You really need to exert yourself and **act vigorously** if you want to cultivate a *big field* properly.

708

头

頭 TRAD   SIMPLIFIED

This character with the definition:

head

Pinyin **tóu** *and Frequency Rank* **147**

Contains **5 strokes** in the following order:

丶 丶 二 头 头

Contains these components:

dab r (×2) 丶 176, p.48

big 大 544, p.129

With all these meanings & readings:

tóu [頭] **1** head **2** hair style **3** the top **4** end **5** beginning or end **6** a stub **7** remnant **8** chief **9** boss **10** side **11** aspect **12** first **13** leading **14** m for pigs or livestock **15** m 个 [個][gè]

tou [頭] **1** suffix for nouns

To remember this character, imagine rotating this drawing by 45 degrees or so to the right (in a clockwise direction). Look closely at the large crossed strokes which look like the four paws of a *big* forest creature. The small stroke at the lower right is the creature's tail, and the two remaining *dabs* become the eyes. This part of the animal, the **head**, is the most prominent part of this suggestive sketch.

709

买

買 TRAD   SIMPLIFIED

This character with the definition:

buy

Pinyin **mǎi** *and Frequency Rank* **758**

Contains **6 strokes** in the following order:

一 ⼀ 乛 三 买 买

Contains these components:

one 一 (altered) 1, p.10

head 头 708, p.165

With all these meanings & readings:

mǎi [買] **1** to buy **2** to purchase

Sometimes consumer products can catch your eye and won't disappear from your mind until you **buy** them—think designer sneakers, pet rocks, certain dolls, and so on. In this character, the horizontal 'one' stroke has been altered to look like a hook. It signifies how *one* single item can hook your imagination, the center of which is in your *head*, and hangs on tight until you **buy** it.

Unit 31

710

卖

TRAD SIMPLIFIED

This character with the definition:

sell

Pinyin **mài** *and Frequency Rank* **974**

Contains **8 strokes** in the following order:

一 十 土 士 吏 吏 卖 卖

Contains these components:

☐ ten 十 7, p.11

■ buy 买 709, p.165

With all these meanings & readings:

mài [賣] **1** to sell

"Buy low, sell high"—everyone who trades stocks knows this cliché. In this character, one 'sell' equals *ten buy*'s, so a 'buy' costs less than a 'sell'. Also, due to the 'ten' (十) on top of 'sell' 卖, it is indeed higher than 'buy' 买.

711

读

讀 SIMPLIFIED

This character with the definition:

attend school

Pinyin **dú** *and Frequency Rank* **752**

Contains **10 strokes** in the following order:

丶 讠 讠 讠 讠 讠 读 读 读 读

Contains these components:

■ speech r 讠 352, p.88

☐ sell 卖 710, p.167

With all these meanings & readings:

dòu [讀] **1** comma **2** phrase marked by pause
dú [讀] **1** to read **2** to study **3** reading of word (i.e. pronunciation), similar to 拼音[pin yin]

In order to **attend school**, I must earn money by working as a salesman; the persuasiveness of my *speech* determines how many products I will *sell* in a given day.

712

实

實 SIMPLIFIED

This character with the definition:

solid, substantial

Pinyin **shí** *and Frequency Rank* **100**

Contains **8 strokes** in the following order:

丶 丷 宀 宀 宔 宔 实 实

Contains these components:

☐ roof r 宀 271, p.70

■ head 头 708, p.165

With all these meanings & readings:

shí [實] **1** real **2** true **3** honest **4** really **5** solid **6** fruit **7** seed

The *roof* covering this man's *head* makes him feel that his station in life is **solid** and **substantial**.

713

奔

SIMP & TRAD

This character with the definition:

head for

Pinyin **bēn** *and Frequency Rank* **1285**

Contains **8 strokes** in the following order:

一 ノ 大 太 本 本 奔 奔

Contains these components:

☐ big 大 544, p.129

☐ decorative grasses 卉 93, p.30

With all these meanings & readings:

bēn [奔] **1** to hurry or rush **2** to run quickly **3** to elope
bèn [奔] **1** go to **2** towards

As soon as the farmer dumped that *big* pile of *decorative grasses*, the farm animals immediately began to **head for** it—mealtime!

714

庆

慶 TRAD SIMPLIFIED

This character with the definition:

celebrate

Pinyin **qìng** *and Frequency Rank* **1269**

Contains **6 strokes** in the following order:

丶 一 广 广 庆 庆

Contains these components:

☐ shelter r 广 427, p.103

■ big 大 544, p.129

With all these meanings & readings:

qìng [慶] **1** celebrate

We need a *big shelter* to hold the crowd that is coming to **celebrate** the victory. • The sole difference between 厌 'be sick of, disgusted with' (panel 676) and this character 庆 'celebrate' is the placement of the little 'dab' dot. In 'celebrate', the dot is nearer heaven, because celebration is a heavenly occasion.

715

This character with the definition:

castrate, spay

Pinyin **yān** *and Frequency Rank* **3462**

SIMP & TRAD Contains **8 strokes** in the following order:

一 ナ 大 大 夺 夵 奋 奄

Contains these components:

■ big 大 544, p. 129
■ electric current 电 149, p. 42

With all these meanings & readings

yān [奄] **1** castrate **2** to delay
yǎn [奄] **1** suddenly **2** to embrace

When you apply *electricity* to the tender regions between this *big* man's legs, you **castrate** and cauterize him all at once.

716

This character with the definition:

cover, hide

Pinyin **yǎn** *and Frequency Rank* **1514**

SIMP & TRAD Contains **11 strokes** in the following order:

一 十 扌 扌 扩 扴 扵 拚 掩 掩 掩

Contains these components:

■ hand r 扌 25, p. 15
■ castrate, spay 奄 715, p. 168

With all these meanings & readings

yǎn [掩] **1** to cover up **2** to surprise

The poor guy we met in panel 715 moves his *hand* over the *castrated* region to **cover** himself and **hide** his embarrassment.

717

This character with the definition:

fertile, rich

Pinyin **wò** *and Frequency Rank* **1808**

SIMP & TRAD Contains **7 strokes** in the following order:

丶 丶 氵 氵 沪 汙 沃

Contains these components:

■ water r 氵 314, p. 80
■ dab r 丶 176, p. 48
■ big 大 544, p. 129

With all these meanings & readings

wò [沃] **1** fertile **2** rich **3** to irrigate **4** to wash (of river)

Crops that begin as *little* seeds grow into *big* plants with the addition of *water* and sunlight, both of which enhance the natural **fertility** of soil.

718
夫
侠

This character with the definition:

man (spiffy)

Pinyin **fū** *and Frequency Rank* **377**

TRAD SIMPLIFIED Contains **4 strokes** in the following order:

一 二 夫 夫

Contains these components:

■ man 人 537, p. 127
■ two 二 2, p. 10

With all these meanings & readings

fū [侠] **1** porter
fū [夫] **1** husband **2** man

Many *men* envied the *spiffy man* because he was always seen with *two* attractive women at his side—one draped around each arm.

719

This character with the definition:

for, on behalf of

Pinyin **tì** *and Frequency Rank* **1079**

SIMP & TRAD Contains **12 strokes** in the following order:

一 二 丰 夫 夫 丰 丰 扶 扶 替 替 替

Contains these components:

■ man (spiffy) (×2) 夫 718, p. 168
■ day, sun 日 64, p. 24

With all these meanings & readings

tì [替] **1** to substitute for **2** to take the place of **3** to replace **4** for **5** on behalf of **6** to star in for

Not a *day* goes by in which one of the *spiffy men* shown here doesn't do something **on behalf of** the other *spiffy man*, his best friend.

720

潜

潜
TRAD   SIMPLIFIED

This character with the definition:

hide

Pinyin **qián** *and Frequency Rank* **1112**

Contains these components:

■ water r 氵314, p. 80
■ for, on behalf of 替 719, p. 168

With all these meanings & readings:

qián [潜] **1** hidden   **2** secret
3 latent   **4** to hide   **5** to conceal
6 to submerge   **7** to dive

Contains **15 strokes** in the following order:

丶 丶 丿 氵 氵 氵 泮 泮 泮 泮 湗 湗 潜 潜 潜

Allan Quartermain (or is it James Bond?) submerges himself beneath *four-and-one-half* (sounds like *for, on behalf of*) feet of murky river *water*. This will effectively **hide** him from Dr. No, or Goldfinger, or whoever is the villain du jour.

721

失

SIMP & TRAD

This character with the definition:

lose

Pinyin **shī** *and Frequency Rank* **375**

Contains these components:

□ dab r 丶 176, p. 48
■ man (spiffy) 夫 718, p. 168

With all these meanings & readings:

shī [失] **1** to lose   **2** to miss
3 to fail

Contains **5 strokes** in the following order:

丿 丿 二 牛 失

When the *spiffy man* noticed that he had started to **lose** a *little bit* of his hair, he suddenly felt his life slipping away.

722

秩

SIMP & TRAD

This character with the definition:

order*, sequence*

Pinyin **zhì** *and Frequency Rank* **1749**

Contains these components:

■ rice, grain (crop) 禾 593, p. 140
■ lose 失 721, p. 169

With all these meanings & readings:

zhì [秩] **1** order   **2** orderliness

Contains **10 strokes** in the following order:

丿 二 千 禾 禾 利 利 利 秩 秩

The artist's latest masterpiece consists of an **orderly sequence** of *grains* glued to a mirror. The patterns are quite intricate; you could stare at them and *lose* yourself in the work.

723

规

规
TRAD   SIMPLIFIED

This character with the definition:

rules, regulations

Pinyin **guī** *and Frequency Rank* **321**

Contains these components:

■ man (spiffy) 夫 718, p. 168
■ see 见 307, p. 78

With all these meanings & readings:

guī [规] **1** compass   **2** a rule
3 regulation   **4** to admonish
5 to plan   **6** to scheme

Contains **8 strokes** in the following order:

一 二 丰 夫 刼 刼 规 规

Even *spiffy men see* the value in adhering to certain **rules** to keep society in order.

724

庚

SIMP & TRAD

This character with the definition:

age

Pinyin **gēng** *and Frequency Rank* **3072**

Contains these components:

□ shelter r 广 427, p. 103
■ big 大 544, p. 129
■ man (spiffy) 夫 718, p. 168

With all these meanings & readings:

gēng [庚] **1** age   **2** seventh of the 10 Heavenly Stems 十天干
3 seventh in order   **4** letter "G" or roman "VII" in list "A, B, C", or "I, II, III" etc   **5** hepta

Contains **8 strokes** in the following order:

丶 二 广 广 庐 庐 庚 庚

A *spiffy man* is more interested in keeping his youth, signs of **age** at bay, and appearance than in having a *big* family or protective *shelter*.

725

This character with the definition:

Tang dynasty

Pinyin **táng** *and Frequency Rank* **973**

SIMP & TRAD   Contains **10 strokes** in the following order:

丶 一 广 广 广 庐 庐 庚 唐 唐

Contains these components:

■ age 庚 (abbrev) 724, 169

■ mouth 口 (altered) 37, p.17

With all these meanings & reading

Táng [唐] **1** Tang dynasty (618-907) **2** surname Tang

The three centuries of the great **Tang dynasty** (600-900) were a Golden *Age* of Chinese culture—so many forms of creative *speech*, such as poetry, were written and published.

726

This character with the definition:

healthy

Pinyin **kāng** *and Frequency Rank* **900**

SIMP & TRAD   Contains **11 strokes** in the following order:

丶 一 广 广 广 庐 庐 庚 唐 康 康

Contains these components:

■ age 庚 (abbrev) 724, 169

■ water 水 315, p.81

With all these meanings & reading

kāng [康] **1** healthy **2** peacefu **3** abundant **4** surname Kang **5** see also 糠

Healthy people of great *age* attribute their longevity to drinking pure *water* regularly.

727

This character with the definition:

use a hand to support

Pinyin **fú** *and Frequency Rank* **1612**

SIMP & TRAD   Contains **7 strokes** in the following order:

一 十 扌 扌 扶 扶 扶

Contains these components:

■ hand r 扌 25, p.15

■ man (spiffy) 夫 718, p.168

With all these meanings & reading

fú [扶] **1** to support with hand **2** to help sb up **3** to help

This tall *man* has had a rough night (too much drinking perhaps?) and he can hardly remain upright. A kind passerby uses his *hand* to **support** him.

728

This character with the definition:

wizard

Pinyin **wū** *and Frequency Rank* **2189**

SIMP & TRAD   Contains **7 strokes** in the following order:

一 丁 丌 丌 巫 巫 巫

Contains these components:

■ labor, work 工 12, p.12

■ man (×2) 人 537, p.127

With all these meanings & reading

wū [巫] **1** witch **2** surname W **3** Taiwan pr wú

A **wizard**'s voodoo *work* can impact two different *men* at the same time.

729

This character with the definition:

foot

Pinyin **zú** *and Frequency Rank* **527**

SIMP & TRAD   Contains **7 strokes** in the following order:

丨 口 口 口 口 足 足

Contains these components:

■ mouth 口 37, p.17

■ man 人 537, p.127

■ foretell 卜 187, p.51

With all these meanings & reading

zú [足] **1** foot **2** to be sufficie

A *man* figurativly puts 'his **foot** in his *mouth*' when he tries to *foretell* events he knows nothing about. • Some students find it helpful to see the extended 'man' component as the side view of a human **foot**.

730

SIMP & TRAD

This character with the definition:

seize, capture

Pinyin **zhuō** *and Frequency Rank* **1822**

Contains **10 strokes** in the following order:

一 十 扌 扌 护 护 护 护 捉 捉

Contains these components:

■ hand r 扌 25, p.15

▨ foot 足 729, p.170

With all these meanings & readings:

zhuō [捉] **1** to clutch **2** to grab **3** to capture

Stealthy *foot*steps and skilled *hands* are required to **capture** any wild creature successfully.

731 走

SIMP & TRAD

This character with the definition:

to walk

Pinyin **zǒu** *and Frequency Rank* **207**

Contains **7 strokes** in the following order:

一 十 土 キ キ 走 走

Contains these components:

▢ earth, soil 土 9, p.11

■ foot 足 (altered) 729, p.170

With all these meanings & readings:

zǒu [走] **1** to walk **2** to go **3** to run **4** to move (of vehicle) **5** to visit **6** to leave **7** to go away **8** to die (euph.) **9** from **10** through **11** away (in compound verbs, such as 撤走) **12** to change (shape, form, meaning)

If you want **to walk**, you must use your *feet* and move them over sections of *earth*.

732 捷

SIMP & TRAD

This character with the definition:

victorious, nimble, quick

Pinyin **jié** *and Frequency Rank* **1789**

Contains **11 strokes** in the following order:

一 十 扌 扌 护 护 护 捗 捷 捷 捷

Contains these components:

▮ hand r 扌 25, p.15

■ to walk 走 731, p.171

▬ boar's head r ⼹ 30, p.16

With all these meanings & readings:

jié [捷] **1** victory **2** triumph **3** quick **4** nimble **5** prompt **6** abbr for 捷克 Czech (Republic)

The soldiers of the **victorious** army *walked* in triumph, each one holding in his *hand* the head of an enemy soldier as if it were a *boar's head*.

733 赶

趕

TRAD SIMPLIFIED

This character with the definition:

rush

Pinyin **gǎn** *and Frequency Rank* **908**

Contains **10 strokes** in the following order:

一 十 土 キ キ 走 走 走 赶 赶

Contains these components:

■ to walk 走 731, p.171

▬ dry 干 17, p.13

With all these meanings & readings:

gǎn [趕] **1** to catch up **2** to overtake **3** to hurry **4** to rush **5** to drive away

The neurotic fellow who went out for a *walk* has an ominous feeling. It's *dry* now, but rain clouds are darkening the sky. Best for him to **rush** home.

734 越

SIMP & TRAD

This character with the definition:

exceed

Pinyin **yuè** *and Frequency Rank* **440**

Contains **12 strokes** in the following order:

一 十 土 キ キ 走 走 走 起 越 越 越

Contains these components:

■ to walk 走 731, p.171

▨ fifth (in a series) 戊 (altered) 653, p.154

With all these meanings & readings:

yuè [越] **1** generic word for peoples or states of south China or south Asia at different historical periods **2** abbr for Vietnam 越南

yuè [越] **1** to exceed **2** to climb over **3** to surpass **4** the more... the more

The doctor ordered my father to *walk* 30 minutes each day. After the *fifth* day, he **exceeded** his doctor's orders.

735 超

This character with the definition:

overtake, surpass, super-

Pinyin **chāo** *and Frequency Rank* **754**

SIMP & TRAD Contains **12 strokes** in the following order:

一 十 土 + 丰 丰 走 赴 起 起 超 超

Contains these components:

to walk 走 731, p.171

call, convene 召 484, p.115

With all these meanings & readings

chāo [超] **1** to exceed **2** overtake **3** surpass **4** transcend **5** ultra- **6** super- **7** to pass **8** to cross

As soon as I heard that our boss had *called* an important meeting, I began to *walk* very fast so that I could **overtake** my colleagues and get a front-row seat before it started.

736 起

This character with the definition:

rise

Pinyin **qǐ** *and Frequency Rank* **75**

SIMP & TRAD Contains **10 strokes** in the following order:

一 十 土 + 丰 丰 走 赴 起 起

Contains these components:

to walk 走 731, p.171

self* 己 135, p.39

With all these meanings & readings

qǐ [起] **1** to rise **2** to raise **3** to get up **4** to set out **5** to start **6** to appear **7** to launch **8** to initiate (action) **9** to draft **10** to establish **11** to get (from a depot or counter) **12** verb suffix, to start **13** (before place or time) starting from **14** m for occurrences or unpredictable events: case, instance **15** m for groups: batch, group

The most exercise I can do when I first **rise** in the morning is *to walk* my*self* to the bathroom!

737 赴

This character with the definition:

go to, attend

Pinyin **fù** *and Frequency Rank* **1843**

SIMP & TRAD Contains **9 strokes** in the following order:

一 十 土 + 丰 丰 走 赴 赴

Contains these components:

to walk 走 731, p.171

foretell 卜 187, p.51

With all these meanings & readings

fù [赴] **1** to go **2** to visit (another country) **3** to attend (a banquet)

Employees are often compelled to **attend** company dinners. As each one listlessly *walks* in, it's easy to *foretell* the events of the evening—indifferent food, boring speakers, and insincere conversation.

738 楚

This character with the definition:

clear

Pinyin **chǔ** *and Frequency Rank* **859**

SIMP & TRAD Contains **13 strokes** in the following order:

一 十 才 木 木 杧 朴 材 林 林 埜 梵 梵 楚

Contains these components:

forest 林 611, p.146

foot 足 729, p.170

With all these meanings & readings

chǔ [楚] **1** surname Chu
chǔ [楚] **1** ancient place name **2** distinct **3** clear **4** orderly **5** pain **6** suffering

I traveled through the *forest* by *foot* to the lake with water so **clear** that the trees reflected off the lake's surface, **clear**ly shown here.

739 兔

This character with the definition:

rabbit

Pinyin **tù** *and Frequency Rank* **2364**

SIMP & TRAD Contains **8 strokes** in the following order:

丿 亇 亇 午 免 免 兔 兔

Contains these components:

man 人 (altered) 537, p.127

mouth 口 (altered) 37, p.17

walking man r 儿 290, p.75

dab r 丶 176, p.48

With all these meanings & readings

tù [兔] **1** rabbit

The *man* was very upset that the **rabbit** used its *mouth* to chew on a *few* of his vegetables. Next day, the *walking man* left his house with his hunting rifle and returned that evening with a dead **rabbit** for dinner!

740

免

SIMP & TRAD

This character with the definition:

dismiss, fire, exempt

Pinyin **miǎn** *and Frequency Rank* **755**

Contains **7 strokes** in the following order:

丿 ⺈ ⺈ ⺈ 各 争 免

Contains these components:

■ rabbit 兔 (abbrev) 739, 172

With all these meanings & readings:

miǎn [免] **1** to exempt **2** to remove **3** to avoid **4** to excuse

It may help if you compare the '*rabbit*' component—altered by losing its 'tail'—with an employee who got **fired** and lost his job.

741

晚

SIMP & TRAD

This character with the definition:

evening

Pinyin **wǎn** *and Frequency Rank* **641**

Contains **11 strokes** in the following order:

丨 冂 日 日 日' 日⺈ 日⺈ 昭 昭 睁 晚

Contains these components:

■ day, sun 日 64, p.24
■ dismiss, fire, exempt 免 740, p.173

With all these meanings & readings:

wǎn [晚] **1** evening **2** night **3** late

Evening signals the time to *dismiss* workers from the *day*'s activities.

742

勉

SIMP & TRAD

This character with the definition:

strive to, do with effort

Pinyin **miǎn** *and Frequency Rank* **2078**

Contains **9 strokes** in the following order:

丿 ⺈ ⺈ 各 各 争 免 免 勉

Contains these components:

■ dismiss, fire, exempt 免 740, p.173
■ strength 力 471, p.113

With all these meanings & readings:

miǎn [勉] **1** exhort **2** to make an effort

If a boss *fires* too many employees with *strong* skills, he will keep himself in business only **with effort**.

743

挽

SIMP & TRAD

This character with the definition:

draw, pull

Pinyin **wǎn** *and Frequency Rank* **2222**

Contains **10 strokes** in the following order:

一 丨 扌 扌 扩 护 护 护 护 挽

Contains these components:

■ hand r 扌 25, p.15
■ dismiss, fire, exempt 免 740, p.173

With all these meanings & readings:

wǎn [挽] **1** to pull **2** to draw (a cart or a bow) **3** to lead (an animal) **4** an elegy (for use in funeral procession) **5** to turn (change direction) **6** to roll up (a scroll) **7** to coil

The employee refused to leave the office after being *fired*, so I used my *hand* to forcibly **pull** him out of his chair and send him out the door and on his way.

744

欠

SIMP & TRAD

This character with the definition:

owe, lack

Pinyin **qiàn** *and Frequency Rank* **1948**

Contains **4 strokes** in the following order:

丿 ⺈ 𠂉 欠

Contains these components:

□ man 人 (altered) 537, p.127
■ man 人 537, p.127

With all these meanings & readings:

qiàn [欠] **1** deficient **2** owe **3** to lack **4** yawn

Imagine this character as the '*man*' component on top being smaller because he **owes** money to the larger '*man*' component on the bottom.

745

This character with the definition:

blow, puff

Pinyin **chuī** *and Frequency Rank* **1390**

SIMP & TRAD Contains **7 strokes** in the following order:

丨 冂 口 口′ 吚 吹 吹

Contains these components:

mouth 口 37, p.17

owe, lack 欠 744, p.173

With all these meanings & readings

chuī [吹] **1** to blow **2** to play wind instrument **3** to blast **4** puff **5** to boast **6** to brag **7** end in failure **8** to fall throug

Humanity *owes* so much to the person who created music by putting his *mouth* over a hollow reed and **blowing** air into it.

746

This character with the definition:

song

Pinyin **gē** *and Frequency Rank* **1040**

SIMP & TRAD Contains **14 strokes** in the following order:

一 丆 丆 罒 可 叿 叿 哥 哥 哥 哥 哥′ 歌 歌

Contains these components:

elder brother 哥 61, p.23

owe, lack 欠 744, p.173

With all these meanings & readings

gē [歌] **1** song **2** m 支[zhī], [個][gè], 首[shǒu]

"There once was a fine *elder brother*
Who borrowed money from the other.
The guy soon wanted it back
But bro' said, "Money I *lack*
But I know I can cadge from my mother."

How's that for an impromptu **song**? Alternatively: My *elder brother* dreamed of being a pop music star. Unfortunately, he *lacked* a voice that could sing even the simplest **song** well.

747

This character with the definition:

swallow, choke

Pinyin **jì** *and Frequency Rank* **9999**

SIMP & TRAD Contains **4 strokes** in the following order:

一 匚 歺 旡

Contains these components:

one 一 1, p.10

owe, lack 欠 (altered) 744, p.173

With all these meanings & readings

jì [旡] **1** choke on something eaten

When you **choke** on food, you *lack one* breath.

748

This character with the definition:

time, occurrence

Pinyin **cì** *and Frequency Rank* **183**

SIMP & TRAD Contains **6 strokes** in the following order:

丶 冫 冫 次 次 次

Contains these components:

ice r 冫 348, p.87

owe, lack 欠 744, p.173

With all these meanings & readings

cì [次] **1** next in sequence **2** s ond **3** the second (day, time etc) **4** secondary **5** vice- **6** su **7** infra- **8** inferior quality **9** s standard **10** order **11** sequence **12** hypo- (chemistry) **13** m for enumerated events: time

Most people *lack* the ability to walk any distance on smooth *ice*, without falling at least one **time**.

749

This character with the definition:

steal, burglarize

Pinyin **dào** *and Frequency Rank* **1619**

盗 SIMPLIFIED
TRAD Contains **11 strokes** in the following order:

丶 冫 冫 冸 冹 次 次 咨 盗 盗 盗

Contains these components:

time, occurrence 次 (altered) 748, p.174

vessel, container 皿 101, p.32

With all these meanings & readings

dào [盗] **1** steal **2** rob **3** plun der **4** a thief **5** bandit **6** rob ber

The first *time* I couldn't find the antique *vessel*, I thought I misplaced it. When the second one vanished, I realized I had been **burglarized**.

750

This character with the definition:

thatch

Pinyin **cí** *and Frequency Rank* **1936**

SIMP & TRAD   Contains **9 strokes** in the following order:

一十艹艹艹茨茨茨茨

Contains these components:

☐ grass r 艹 87, p. 29

■ time, occurrence 次 748, p. 174

With all these meanings & readings:

cí [茨] **1** Caltrop (Tribulus terrestris) **2** thatched hut

Any time a mouse falls from the ceiling and lands in the soup, you know it's *time* to replace the *grass* and straw in a **thatched** roof.

751

This character with the definition:

have a rest

Pinyin **xiē** *and Frequency Rank* **1828**

SIMP & TRAD   Contains **13 strokes** in the following order:

丨冂日日尸尸号号号号号号歇歇

Contains these components:

■ how, why, when 曷 380, p. 94

☐ owe, lack 欠 744, p. 173

With all these meanings & readings:

xiē [歇] **1** to rest

I was working hard and running *all over the place* today, so now I *lack* the strength to do anything else except **have a rest**.

752

This character with the definition:

happy

Pinyin **xīn** *and Frequency Rank* **1523**

SIMP & TRAD   Contains **8 strokes** in the following order:

丿丿斤斤斤斤欣欣

Contains these components:

■ catty 斤 403, p. 98

☐ owe, lack 欠 744, p. 173

With all these meanings & readings:

xīn [欣] **1** happy

Lack of *unbalance* in your life makes you **happy**.

753 肉

This character with the definition:

meat

Pinyin **ròu** *and Frequency Rank* **1009**

SIMP & TRAD   Contains **6 strokes** in the following order:

丨冂冂内肉肉

Contains these components:

■ borders r 冂 114, p. 34

☐ man (×2) 人 537, p. 127

With all these meanings & readings:

ròu [肉] **1** meat **2** flesh **3** pulp (of a fruit)

This pictograph represents a carcass that has been cut open in preparation for a feast. The scribes were careful to use strokes that were bilaterally symmetric—that is, the right and left halves are the same, as if resembling a real life body. The *borders* element represents the animal's external corpse and its hide, with *several men* representing those who will feast on the inner **meat**. • 肉 is frequently used as an element in other glyphs, but in those cases it often takes on an altered appearance, namely '月'. Unfortunately, another common glyph—meaning 'moon' or 'month'—looks exactly the same! When 'meat' appears as '月', it often means 'body part'.

754
背
揹
TRAD SIMPLIFIED

This character with the definition:

back of the body

Pinyin **bèi** *and Frequency Rank* **787**

Contains **9 strokes** in the following order:

丨丬丬丬北背背背背

Contains these components:

☐ north 北 131, p. 38

■ meat 肉 (altered) 753, p. 175

With all these meanings & readings:

bēi [揹] **1** variant of 背[背][bēi]
bēi [背] **1** to be burdened **2** to carry on the back or shoulder
bèi [背] **1** the back of a body or object **2** to turn one's back **3** to hide something from **4** to learn by heart **5** to recite from memory

For animals that walk on four legs, the *northern*-most part of their *bodies* is their **back**.

755

This character with the definition:

belly, abdomen

Pinyin **dù** *and Frequency Rank* **1800**

SIMP & TRAD   Contains **7 strokes** in the following order:

丿 刀 月 月 肚 肚 肚

Contains these components:

◼ meat 肉 (altered) 753, p.175
◼ earth, soil 土 9, p.11

With all these meanings & readings

dǔ [肚] **1** tripe
dù [肚] **1** belly

You can only reduce the size of your **belly** by eating less *meat* from animals and more fresh food from the *earth*, such as vegetables.

756

This character with the definition:

womb, sibling

Pinyin **bāo** *and Frequency Rank* **1341**

SIMP & TRAD   Contains **9 strokes** in the following order:

丿 刀 月 月 肚 肋 朐 胞 胞

Contains these components:

◼ meat 肉 (altered) 753, p.175
◼ wrap, bag 包 385, p.95

With all these meanings & readings

bāo [胞] **1** placenta **2** womb **3** born of the same parents

A **womb** can be thought of as the *part of the body* that protectively *wraps* the fetus during its development.

757

This character with the definition:

upper arm, shoulder

Pinyin **bǎng** *and Frequency Rank* **1941**

SIMP & TRAD   Contains **14 strokes** in the following order:

丿 刀 月 月 肚 肛 肪 肪 胯 胯 胯 胯 膀 膀

Contains these components:

◼ meat 肉 (altered) 753, p.175
◼ side 旁 701, p.164

With all these meanings & readings

bǎng [膀] **1** upper arm **2** wing
bàng [膀] **1** to flirt
pāng [膀] **1** puffed (swollen)
páng [膀] **1** bladder

The *side* of a human *carcass* is comprised of the **upper arm** or **shoulder**.

758

肠
TRAD SIMPLIFIED

This character with the definition:

intestines

Pinyin **cháng** *and Frequency Rank* **1921**

Contains **7 strokes** in the following order:

丿 刀 月 月 肋 肠 肠

Contains these components:

◼ meat 肉 (altered) 753, p.175
◼ glorious, bright 昜 463, p.111

With all these meanings & readings

cháng [腸] **1** intestines

During dissections in biology lab, all the organs looked the same to me except for the **intestines**. The latter were by far the *brightest* part of the *body* that I identified, by virtue of their shiny, slimy ropiness.

759

脉
TRAD SIMPLIFIED

This character with the definition:

arteries and veins

Pinyin **mài** *and Frequency Rank* **1594**

Contains **9 strokes** in the following order:

丿 刀 月 月 肮 肮 胁 脉 脉

Contains these components:

◼ meat 肉 (altered) 753, p.175
◼ forever, always 永 319, p.81

With all these meanings & readings

mài [脈] **1** arteries and veins
2 vein (on a leaf, insect wing, etc.)
mò [脈] **1** see 脉脉 [脈脈][mò mò]

The right part looks like '*water*' (panel 315), but altered a bit. After all, the **arteries and veins** are the *parts of the body* that channel blood, the main fluid of the body.

Unit 33

760

This character with the definition:

liver

Pinyin **gān** *and Frequency Rank* **1760**

SIMP & TRAD   Contains **7 strokes** in the following order:

丿 刀 月 月 肝 肝 肝

Contains these components:

■ meat 肉 (altered) 753, p.175

□ dry 干 17, p.13

With all these meanings & readings:

gǎn [肝] **1** liver **2** m 页 [頁][yè], 个 [個][gè]

The **liver** is the *body part* that drunks need to keep '*dry*' if they don't want to succumb to cirrhosis.

761

肤
TRAD SIMPLIFIED

This character with the definition:

skin

Pinyin **fū** *and Frequency Rank* **1790**

Contains **8 strokes** in the following order:

丿 刀 月 月 肝 肝 肤 肤

Contains these components:

■ meat 肉 (altered) 753, p.175

□ man (spiffy) 夫 718, p.168

With all these meanings & readings:

fū [膚] **1** skin

The *body part* that the handsome *man* likes best is his **skin**.

---

762 膜

This character with the definition:

membrane, film, thin coating

Pinyin **mó** *and Frequency Rank* **1945**

SIMP & TRAD   Contains **14 strokes** in the following order:

丿 刀 月 月 肝 肝 肝 肝 膜 膜 膜 膜 膜 膜

Contains these components:

■ meat 肉 (altered) 753, p.175

□ do not, not 莫 641, p.152

With all these meanings & readings:

mó [膜] **1** membrane **2** film

A **membrane** is the *body part* that covers choice cuts of *meat* (steaks, chops, and so on) when an animal is freshly butchered. *Do not* eat this this part!

763

两
TRAD SIMPLIFIED

This character with the definition:

both, two

Pinyin **liǎng** *and Frequency Rank* **133**

Contains **7 strokes** in the following order:

一 丆 丙 丙 两 两 两

Contains these components:

□ one 一 1, p.10

■ borders 冂 114, p.34

■ man (×2) 人 537, p.127

With all these meanings & readings:

liǎng [兩] **1** both **2** two **3** ounce **4** some **5** a few **6** tael **7** weight equal to 50 grams

Within the *borders* of the local community, **two** *men* are carrying *one* long thing that resembles a pole or plank.

764

满
TRAD SIMPLIFIED

This character with the definition:

full, complete

Pinyin **mǎn** *and Frequency Rank* **436**

Contains **13 strokes** in the following order:

丶 丶 氵 汁 汁 洪 洪 满 满 满 满 满 满

Contains these components:

■ water r 氵 314, p.80

□ grass r 艹 87, p.29

■ both, two 两 763, p.177

With all these meanings & readings:

mǎn [滿] **1** full **2** filled **3** packed **4** fully **5** completely **6** quite **7** to reach the limit **8** to satisfy **9** satisfied **10** contented **11** to fill **12** abbr for Manchurian

In old China, access to *two* resources made a household **full** and **complete**: *water*, *grass*, and other crops. • Another meaning for this character is 'Manchu'. The 满族—Mǎnzú—were a foreign people that ruled China from the seventeenth to the twentieth centuries. One class of Manchu officials were the 满大人—mǎndàrén—which came into English as 'mandarin' and lent its name to the modern Chinese language.

765

SIMP & TRAD

This character with the definition:

three to five am

Pinyin **yín** *and Frequency Rank* **3422**

Contains **11 strokes** in the following order:

Contains these components:
- to face 向 (altered) 282, p. 72
- dry 干 17, p. 13
- man 人 537, p. 127

With all these meanings & readings

yín [寅] **1** 3rd earthly branch: 3-5 a.m., 1st solar month (4th February-5th March), year of the Tiger

Here we see a *man* unexpectedly *facing* an old and dear friend. In honor of this reunion, they go out drinking although both have been *dry* till now. They don't return home until sometime in the wee hours between **three to five am**.

766

SIMP & TRAD

This character with the definition:

perform, play, act

Pinyin **yǎn** *and Frequency Rank* **715**

Contains **14 strokes** in the following order:

Contains these components:
- water r 氵 314, p. 80
- three to five am 寅 765, p. 178

With all these meanings & readings

yǎn [演] **1** to develop **2** to evolve **3** to practice **4** to perform **5** to play **6** to act

Rain *water* leaked onto my head *very early this morning*, causing me to jump out of bed and dance around as if I were **performing** in some surreal **play**.

767
千
轠
TRAD

SIMPLIFIED

This character with the definition:

thousand

Pinyin **qiān** *and Frequency Rank* **599**

Contains **3 strokes** in the following order:

Contains these components:
- man 人 (altered) 537, p. 127
- ten 十 7, p. 11

With all these meanings & readings

qiān [千] **1** thousand
qiān [鞦] **1** a swing

We interpret these characters as they relate to periods of time. *Ten* generations of *men* live roughly a **thousand** years.

768

SIMP & TRAD

This character with the definition:

heavy

Pinyin **zhòng** *and Frequency Rank* **140**

Contains **9 strokes** in the following order:

Contains these components:
- thousand 千 767, p. 178
- neighborhood 里 40, p. 18

With all these meanings & readings

chóng [重] **1** to double **2** to repeat **3** repetition **4** iteration **5** again **6** a layer
zhòng [重] **1** heavy **2** serious

One thousand people assembled into the assembly hall of our old *neighborhood*'s school, placing a **heavy** load on the old wooden floorboards.

769

SIMP & TRAD

This character with the definition:

director

Pinyin **dǒng** *and Frequency Rank* **1629**

Contains **12 strokes** in the following order:

Contains these components:
- grass r ⺾ 87, p. 29
- heavy 重 768, p. 178

With all these meanings & readings

dǒng [董] **1** supervise **2** to direct **3** director **4** surname Dong

Nowadays, trustees, members of Boards of **Directors**, and other bigwigs wear clothes suitable for their high position in life. In ancient days, their equivalent elite status would have been signified by *grassy* laurels resting on their heads and *heavy*, overweight bodies.

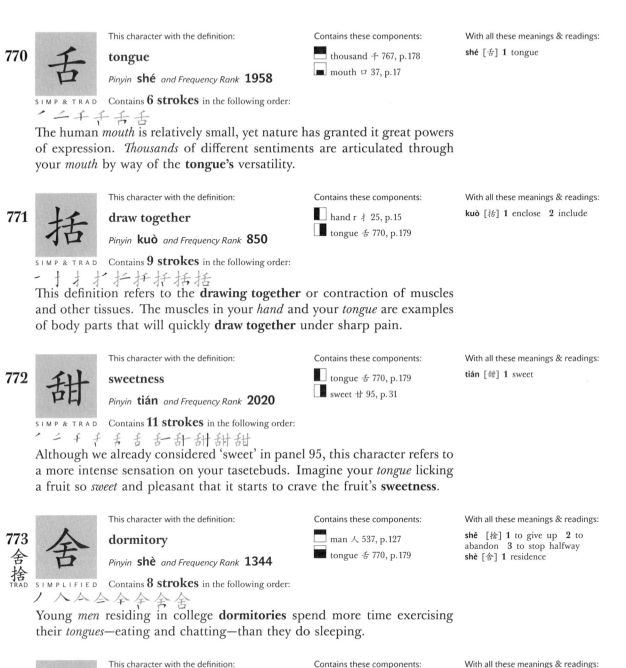

770

舌

SIMP & TRAD

This character with the definition:

tongue

Pinyin **shé** *and Frequency Rank* **1958**

Contains **6 strokes** in the following order:

Contains these components:

thousand 千 767, p.178

mouth 口 37, p.17

With all these meanings & readings:

shé [舌] **1** tongue

The human *mouth* is relatively small, yet nature has granted it great powers of expression. *Thousands* of different sentiments are articulated through your *mouth* by way of the **tongue's** versatility.

771

括

SIMP & TRAD

This character with the definition:

draw together

Pinyin **kuò** *and Frequency Rank* **850**

Contains **9 strokes** in the following order:

Contains these components:

hand r 扌 25, p.15

tongue 舌 770, p.179

With all these meanings & readings:

kuò [括] **1** enclose   **2** include

This definition refers to the **drawing together** or contraction of muscles and other tissues. The muscles in your *hand* and your *tongue* are examples of body parts that will quickly **draw together** under sharp pain.

772

甜

SIMP & TRAD

This character with the definition:

sweetness

Pinyin **tián** *and Frequency Rank* **2020**

Contains **11 strokes** in the following order:

Contains these components:

tongue 舌 770, p.179

sweet 甘 95, p.31

With all these meanings & readings:

tián [甜] **1** sweet

Although we already considered 'sweet' in panel 95, this character refers to a more intense sensation on your tastebuds. Imagine your *tongue* licking a fruit so *sweet* and pleasant that it starts to crave the fruit's **sweetness**.

773

舍
捨

TRAD   SIMPLIFIED

This character with the definition:

dormitory

Pinyin **shè** *and Frequency Rank* **1344**

Contains **8 strokes** in the following order:

Contains these components:

man 人 537, p.127

tongue 舌 770, p.179

With all these meanings & readings:

shě [捨] **1** to give up   **2** to abandon   **3** to stop halfway
shè [舍] **1** residence

Young *men* residing in college **dormitories** spend more time exercising their *tongues*—eating and chatting—than they do sleeping.

774

啥

SIMP & TRAD

This character with the definition:

what? (dialect)

Pinyin **shá** *and Frequency Rank* **2082**

Contains **11 strokes** in the following order:

Contains these components:

mouth 口 37, p.17

dormitory 舍 773, p.179

With all these meanings & readings:

shá [啥] **1** (dialect) what

Students who live in the *dormitories* come from all over China, with all kinds of accents coming out of their *mouths*. Sometimes it's hard to understand their **dialect** so I'll often have to ask: "Excuse me, **what** did you say?"

775

SIMP & TRAD

This character with the definition:

alive

Pinyin **huó** *and Frequency Rank* **219**

Contains **9 strokes** in the following order:

丶 丶 氵 氵 汗 汗 沽 活 活

Contains these components:

□ water r 氵 314, p.80

□ tongue 舌 770, p.179

With all these meanings & reading

huó [活] **1** to live **2** alive **3** I ing **4** work **5** workmanship

An ancient maxim on the essence of being **alive**: You only require *water* to keep you walking and a *tongue* to keep you talking!

776

阔

TRAD   SIMPLIFIED

This character with the definition:

wide, broad*

Pinyin **kuò** *and Frequency Rank* **1675**

Contains **12 strokes** in the following order:

丶 丨 门 门 门 门 阔 阔 阔 阔 阔 阔

Contains these components:

□ doorway 门 243, p.64

■ alive 活 775, p.180

With all these meanings & reading

kuò [闊] **1** rich **2** wide **3** bro

A young person who is fresh out of college is about to embark on her own. She looks out the *doorway*, where *life* beckons, and sees a **wide** canvas ready for her to make her mark.

777

话

TRAD   SIMPLIFIED

This character with the definition:

dialect, vernacular

Pinyin **huà** *and Frequency Rank* **170**

Contains **8 strokes** in the following order:

丶 讠 讠 讠 话 话 话 话

Contains these components:

□ speech r 讠 352, p.88

□ tongue 舌 770, p.179

With all these meanings & reading

huà [話] **1** dialect **2** language **3** spoken words **4** speech **5** t **6** words **7** conversation **8** wha sb said **9** m 种[種][zhǒng], 席[xí], 句[jù], 口[kǒu]

The kind of *speech* that I can really wrap my *tongue* around is the one in my local **dialect**.

778

辞

TRAD   SIMPLIFIED

This character with the definition:

diction

Pinyin **cí** *and Frequency Rank* **1469**

Contains **13 strokes** in the following order:

丿 二 千 千 舌 舌 舌 舌 舌 辞 辞 辞 辞

Contains these components:

□ tongue 舌 770, p.179

□ hardworking 辛 684, p.160

With all these meanings & reading

cí [辭] **1** refined language **2** w ing **3** poetic genre (so far, inte changeable with 词[詞]) **4** to take leave **5** to resign **6** to dismiss **7** to decline

While learning Chinese, your *tongue works hard* to get the **diction** right.

779

乱

TRAD   SIMPLIFIED

This character with the definition:

in disorder

Pinyin **luàn** *and Frequency Rank* **765**

Contains **7 strokes** in the following order:

丿 二 千 千 舌 舌 乱

Contains these components:

□ tongue 舌 770, p.179

□ mineshaft c ㄴ 122, p.36

With all these meanings & reading

luàn [亂] **1** in confusion **2** dis derly

Go ahead, wrap your *tongue* around a live *wire*. You'll find your thoughts and sensations temporarily jumbled up and in great **disorder**.

780

插

SIMP & TRAD

This character with the definition:

insert, put in

Pinyin **chā** *and Frequency Rank* **1495**

Contains **12 strokes** in the following order:

一 十 扌 扩 扩 杆 杆 杆 抾 插 插 插

Contains these components:

▉ hand r 扌 25, p. 15

▉ thousand 千 767, p. 178

▉ mortar 臼 373, p. 92

With all these meanings & readings:

chā [插] **1** to insert **2** stick in **3** pierce **4** to take part in **5** to interfere **6** to interpose

To build one brick wall, a *thousand hand* movements are needed just to **insert** the *mortar* in between the bricks.

781

垂

SIMP & TRAD

This character with the definition:

droop

Pinyin **chuí** *and Frequency Rank* **1592**

Contains **8 strokes** in the following order:

丿 二 千 壬 壬 垂 垂 垂

Contains these components:

▉ thousand 千 767, p. 178

▉ grass r 艹 87, p. 29

▉ knight 士 8, p. 11

With all these meanings & readings:

chuí [垂] **1** to hang (down) **2** droop **3** dangle **4** bend down **5** hand down **6** bequeath **7** nearly **8** almost **9** to approach

When you load one *thousand* pounds of *grass* onto the back of a *knight*, no matter how noble, he will inevitably start to **droop** under the weight of the *grass*.

782

睡

SIMP & TRAD

This character with the definition:

sleep

Pinyin **shuì** *and Frequency Rank* **964**

Contains **13 strokes** in the following order:

丨 冂 月 目 目 盯 盯 旴 肝 肝 睡 睡 睡

Contains these components:

▉ eye 目 75, p. 26

▉ droop 垂 781, p. 181

With all these meanings & readings:

shuì [睡] **1** to sleep

When you lie down and your *eyes* begin to *droop*, the onset of **sleep** won't be far behind.

783

定

SIMP & TRAD

This character with the definition:

decide*

Pinyin **dìng** *and Frequency Rank* **77**

Contains **8 strokes** in the following order:

丶 丶 宀 宀 宇 宇 定 定

Contains these components:

▉ roof r 宀 271, p. 70

▉ under 下 199, p. 54

▉ man 人 537, p. 127

With all these meanings & readings:

dìng [定] **1** to set **2** to fix **3** to determine **4** to decide **5** to order

Before you **decide** to buy a house, be sure to have an inspection *man* examine it from the top of its *roof* to *under*neath its foundation. • Some people prefer to think of the construction '*man*'+'*under*' as an altered form of '*to correct, rectify*' (panel 193).

784

入

SIMP & TRAD

This character with the definition:

go in, enter

Pinyin **rù** *and Frequency Rank* **210**

Contains **2 strokes** in the following order:

丿 入

Contains these components:

▉ man 人 (altered) 537, p. 127

With all these meanings & readings:

rù [入] **1** to enter **2** see also 入声 [~聲][rù shēng]

Although this looks like a *man* with his head tipped to the left, it's more useful to think of it as a fledgling plant, whose roots are just beginning to **enter** the depths of the earth.

Unit 34

785

內
TRAD ‎ SIMPLIFIED

This character with the definition:

inside*

Pinyin **nèi** *and Frequency Rank* **175**

Contains **4 strokes** in the following order:

丨 冂 内 内

Contains these components:

■ borders r 冂 114, p.34
■ go in, enter 入 (altered) 784, p.181

With all these meanings & reading

nèi [內] **1** inside **2** inner **3** internal **4** within **5** interior

You *enter* a country when you cross its *borders*; at that point, you are **inside** the country.

---

786 丙

SIMP & TRAD

This character with the definition:

third (in a series)

Pinyin **bǐng** *and Frequency Rank* **2645**

Contains **5 strokes** in the following order:

一 丆 丙 丙 丙

Contains these components:

□ one 一 1, p.10
■ inside* 内 785, p.182

With all these meanings & reading

bǐng [丙] **1** third of 10 heaven stems 十天干 **2** third in order **3** letter "C" or roman "III" in list "A, B, C", or "I, II, III" etc **4** propyl

The downward '*borders r*' element looks like a downward-pointing 'C', the **third** highest mark in school. Given how little he'd stayed *inside* to study, *one* of my friends felt fortunate to receive *one*.

787

SIMP & TRAD

This character with the definition:

become sick

Pinyin **bìng** *and Frequency Rank* **427**

Contains **10 strokes** in the following order:

丶 一 广 广 疒 疒 疒 病 病 病

Contains these components:

□ sick r 疒 434, p.104
■ third (in a series) 丙 786, p.182

With all these meanings & reading

bìng [病] **1** ailment **2** sickness **3** illness **4** disease **5** fall ill **6** sick r **7** defect **8** m 场 [場][cháng]

This man is *sick* for the *third* time this month. We fear that he has **become sick** with something serious.

---

788 商

SIMP & TRAD

This character with the definition:

business

Pinyin **shāng** *and Frequency Rank* **402**

Contains **11 strokes** in the following order:

丶 亠 产 产 产 商 商 商 商 商 商

Contains these components:

□ to stand 立 681, p.160
■ inside* 内 785, p.182
■ mouth 口 37, p.17

With all these meanings & reading

shāng [商] **1** the Shang dynasty 16th to 11th century BC
shāng [商] **1** commerce **2** to consult **3** quotient **4** 2nd not in pentatonic scale

The customer *stands* on the boulevard, looking through the window to the wonderful goods *inside*. His *mouth* hangs open, astonished by the goods for sale in this **business**.

789

SIMP & TRAD

This character with the definition:

host, multitude

Pinyin **lí** *and Frequency Rank* **1476**

Contains **15 strokes** in the following order:

丿 一 千 禾 禾 利 利 利 黎 黎 黎 黎 黎 黎 黎

Contains these components:

■ sharp 利 (altered) 604, p.142
■ go in, enter 入 784, p.181
■ water 水 315, p.81

With all these meanings & reading

lí [黎] **1** Li ethnic group of Hainan Province **2** surname Li **3** abbreviation of 黎巴嫩[lí nèn]
lí [黎] **1** black

Here are some strategies for luring a **multitude** of people to an event: (1) Use a *sharp* tool to slice a gold coin into **numerous** small pieces and promise you will hand them to patrons. (2) Use free tickets to lure a **host** of people to *go into* a theater. (3) Use a hose to spray *water* droplets into a **multitude** of drops into a crowd of people.

790

SIMP & TRAD

This character with the definition:

woman

Pinyin **nǚ** *and Frequency Rank* **224**

Contains **3 strokes** in the following order:

〈 女 女

Contains these components:

■ man 人 (altered) 537, p.127
□ one 一 1, p.10
■ action path c ⟋ 438, p.105

With all these meanings & readings:

nǚ [女] **1** female **2** woman **3** daughter

Whatever *men* can do, **women** can do better. **Women** are able to take *action* against a *man*'s achievement and turn his success on its side, thereby *leveling* the playing field.

791

SIMP & TRAD

This character with the definition:

baby

Pinyin **wá** *and Frequency Rank* **1833**

Contains **9 strokes** in the following order:

〈 女 女 女‐ 女‡ 妵 娃 娃 娃

Contains these components:

■ woman 女 790, p.183
■ jade tablet 圭 10, p.11

With all these meanings & readings:

wá [娃] **1** baby **2** doll

The *woman*'s new *jade brooch* is the most beautiful gift she's ever received; she coddles it like her **baby**.

792

SIMP & TRAD

This character with the definition:

paternal aunt

Pinyin **gū** *and Frequency Rank* **994**

Contains **8 strokes** in the following order:

〈 女 女 女‐ 女† 妵 姑 姑

Contains these components:

■ woman 女 790, p.183
■ ancient 古 53, p.21

With all these meanings & readings:

gū [姑] **1** paternal aunt

That *'ancient'* *woman* is my father's sister, my **paternal aunt**.

793

SIMP & TRAD

This character with the definition:

be like

Pinyin **rú** *and Frequency Rank* **67**

Contains **6 strokes** in the following order:

〈 女 女 如 如 如

Contains these components:

■ woman 女 790, p.183
□ enclosure r 口 36, p.17

With all these meanings & readings:

rú [如] **1** as **2** as if **3** such as

A *woman* who is wise and nurturing can **be like** a safe, emotional *'enclosure'* to those around her.

794

SIMP & TRAD

This character with the definition:

older sister

Pinyin **jiě** *and Frequency Rank* **830**

Contains **8 strokes** in the following order:

〈 女 女 如 如 如 姐 姐

Contains these components:

■ woman 女 790, p.183
■ moreover 且 84, p.28

With all these meanings & readings:

jiě [姐] **1** older sister

The *woman* who is my math professor physically resembles my **older sister**; *moreover*, they share the same bossy personality.

795

耍

SIMP & TRAD

This character with the definition:

play (a role, tricks)

Pinyin **shuǎ** *and Frequency Rank* **2260**

Contains these components:

☐ but, yet (contrast) 而 78, p. 26

☐ woman 女 790, p. 183

With all these meanings & readings:

shuǎ [耍] **1** to play with **2** to juggle

Contains **9 strokes** in the following order:

一 ㄷ ㄏ 币 而 而 耍 耍 耍

Some attractive *women* enjoy using their beauty to **play** tricks on men's hearts; *but*, after their looks fade, such *women* are often left single, lonely, and bitter.

796

妇

婦
TRAD SIMPLIFIED

This character with the definition:

married woman

Pinyin **fù** *and Frequency Rank* **932**

Contains these components:

☐ woman 女 790, p. 183

☐ boar's head r ⇒ 30, p. 16

With all these meanings & readings:

fù [婦] **1** woman

Contains **6 strokes** in the following order:

乚 ㄑ 女 如 妇 妇

Married women view themselves as *women* who are paired with men that are as heavy as *boar's heads* to carry around.

797

她

SIMP & TRAD

This character with the definition:

she

Pinyin **tā** *and Frequency Rank* **91**

Contains these components:

☐ woman 女 790, p. 183

☐ also, too* 也 132, p. 38

With all these meanings & readings:

tā [她] **1** she

Contains **6 strokes** in the following order:

乚 ㄑ 女 如 她 她

Human beings are human precisely because we each are capable of storing all our different traits in a single body. In this case, we will focus on one *woman*: **she** can be clever but *also* dumb, considerate but *also* selfish, outgoing but *also* shy.

798

姓

SIMP & TRAD

This character with the definition:

family name

Pinyin **xìng** *and Frequency Rank* **1149**

Contains these components:

☐ woman 女 790, p. 183

☐ give birth to 生 210, p. 57

With all these meanings & readings:

xìng [姓] **1** family name **2** surname **3** name **4** m 个 [個][gè]

Contains **8 strokes** in the following order:

乚 ㄑ 女 女 女 妙 姓 姓

As soon as a *woman gives birth* to a child, the newborn is given the **family name**.

799

要

SIMP & TRAD

This character with the definition:

want, wish, request

Pinyin **yào** *and Frequency Rank* **26**

Contains these components:

☐ west 西 (altered) 301, p. 77

☐ woman 女 790, p. 183

With all these meanings & readings:

yāo [要] **1** demand **2** ask **3** request **4** coerce
yào [要] **1** important **2** vital **3** to want **4** will **5** going to (a future auxiliary) **6** may **7** mus

Contains **9 strokes** in the following order:

一 ㄏ 币 而 西 西 要 要 要

'*West*' (where the sun sets) is symbolic of evening time, when the working day is over. This *woman* is enjoying the quiet evening by catering to her own **wishes**.

800

SIMP & TRAD

This character with the definition:

waist

Pinyin **yāo** *and Frequency Rank* **1458**

Contains these components:

☐ meat 肉 (altered) 753, p.175
☐ want, wish, request 要 799, p.184

With all these meanings & readings:

yāo [腰] **1** waist **2** lower back **3** pocket **4** middle **5** loins

Contains **13 strokes** in the following order:

丿 刀 月 月 肀 肀 胛 腭 腭 腰 腰 腰 腰

The *body part* that most people *want* to slender is their **waist**.

801

SIMP & TRAD

This character with the definition:

matchmaker, go-between

Pinyin **méi** *and Frequency Rank* **1506**

Contains these components:

☐ woman 女 790, p.183
☐ certain, some 某 572, p.135

With all these meanings & readings:

méi [媒] **1** medium **2** intermediary **3** matchmaker **4** go-between **5** abbr for 媒体[méi tǐ], media, especially news media

Contains **12 strokes** in the following order:

乚 夕 女 女 奸 妊 姄 姄 媒 媒 媒 媒

Traditionally, the **matchmaker** would match a young *woman* with a *certain* special appeal to an eligible bachelor.

802

SIMP & TRAD

This character with the definition:

younger sister

Pinyin **mèi** *and Frequency Rank* **1185**

Contains these components:

☐ woman 女 790, p.183
☐ have not yet 未 582, p.137

With all these meanings & readings:

mèi [妹] **1** younger sister

Contains **8 strokes** in the following order:

乚 夕 女 女 奻 奸 妷 妹

A **younger sister** is someone who *has not yet* grown into a *woman*.

803

SIMP & TRAD

This character with the definition:

listless, dejected

Pinyin **wěi** *and Frequency Rank* **457**

Contains these components:

☐ rice, grain (crop) 禾 593, p.140
☐ woman 女 790, p.183

With all these meanings & readings:

wēi [委] **1** same as 逶 in 逶迤 winding, curved
wěi [委] **1** give up **2** indeed **3** to commission

Contains **8 strokes** in the following order:

丿 二 千 禾 禾 季 委 委

The load of *grain* on this poor *woman*'s back is more than she can bear. No wonder she appears **listless** and **dejected**.

804 矮

SIMP & TRAD

This character with the definition:

short of stature

Pinyin **ǎi** *and Frequency Rank* **2027**

Contains these components:

☐ arrow 矢 552, p.130
☐ listless, dejected 委 803, p.185

With all these meanings & readings:

ǎi [矮] **1** low **2** short (in length)

Contains **13 strokes** in the following order:

丿 𠂉 𠂉 矢 矢 矢 矧 矫 矫 矮 矮 矮 矮

William Tell shot an *arrow* at the apple on his son's head, a duty imposed on him by the evil governor and a task which made Tell very nervous and *dejected*. As every schoolboy knows, the child lived because his **short stature** made the shot easier for his dad to make.

805

This character with the definition:

ill will, hard feeling

Pinyin **xián**   and Frequency Rank **1826**

Contains these components:

▪ woman 女 790, p.183
▪ double, twice 兼 600, p.142

With all these meanings & readings

xián [嫌] **1** to dislike   **2** to suspect

SIMP & TRAD   Contains **13 strokes** in the following order:

乚 乙 女 女 女 妈 妈 妈 娕 娕 婷 嫌 嫌

If *two* people in a room bear **ill will** toward each other, the best way to calm things down between them is to send in a kind-hearted *woman* to mediate a frank discussion.

806

This character with the definition:

power, might

Pinyin **wēi**   and Frequency Rank **622**

Contains these components:

▪ fifth (in a series) 戊 653, p.154
▪ one 一 1, p.10
▪ woman 女 790, p.183

With all these meanings & readings

wēi [威] **1** power   **2** might   **3** prestige

SIMP & TRAD   Contains **9 strokes** in the following order:

一 厂 厂 厃 厈 厈 威 威 威

Even though that *single woman* is *fifth* in a series of people, she stands out because she radiates a quiet **power** and **might**.

807

This character with the definition:

looks, appearance

Pinyin **zī**   and Frequency Rank **1899**

Contains these components:

▪ time, occurrence 次 748, p.174
▪ woman 女 790, p.183

With all these meanings & readings

zī [姿] **1** beauty   **2** disposition   **3** looks   **4** appearance

SIMP & TRAD   Contains **9 strokes** in the following order:

丶 冫 冫 冫 次 次 姿 姿 姿

The famous actress was such a beautiful *woman* that every *time* she made a public **appearance**, she impressed the world with her grace and poise.

808

This character with the definition:

rest content

Pinyin **ān**   and Frequency Rank **232**

Contains these components:

▪ roof r 宀 271, p.70
▪ woman 女 790, p.183

With all these meanings & readings

ān [安] **1** content   **2** calm   **3** st   **4** quiet   **5** safe   **6** secure   **7** in good health   **8** to find a place for   **9** to install   **10** to fix   **11** fit   **12** to bring (a charge again sb)   **13** to pacify   **14** security   **15** safety   **16** peace   **17** ampere   **18** surname An

SIMP & TRAD   Contains **6 strokes** in the following order:

丶 丷 宀 它 安 安

The epitome of **resting contently** is living in a home (whose *roof* is all we can see here) in which the *woman* of the house is respected and maintains order.

809

This character with the definition:

press, push down, according to

Pinyin **àn**   and Frequency Rank **573**

Contains these components:

▪ hand r 扌 25, p.15
▪ rest content 安 808, p.186

With all these meanings & readings

àn [按] **1** to press (with the hand)   **2** to push   **3** to control   **4** to restrain   **5** to check   **6** pressing down (brush movement in painting)   **7** according   **8** in the light of

SIMP & TRAD   Contains **9 strokes** in the following order:

一 十 扌 扌 扩 扩 按 按 按

A family gathering is in full swing and things are getting crazy! **In accordance with** his standing as head of family, dad motions his *hand* to make sure we all stop fighting and *rest content*.

Unit 35

810

This character with the definition:

record, law case

Pinyin **àn** *and Frequency Rank* **518**

SIMP & TRAD   Contains **10 strokes** in the following order:

丶 冖 宀 疒 疒 安 安 室 宰 案

Contains these components:

rest content 安 808, p.186

tree 木 562, p.133

With all these meanings & readings:

àn [案] **1** (legal) case **2** incident **3** record **4** file **5** table

I *rest content* when I sit at the top of the tallest *tree* around, quietly **recording** the day's events in my diary without encountering any interruptions.

811

This character with the definition:

must not, no

Pinyin **wú** *and Frequency Rank* **2876**

SIMP & TRAD   Contains **4 strokes** in the following order:

乚 凵 毋 毋

Contains these components:

woman 女 (altered) 790, p.183

place of refuge c 丁 105, p.33

one 一 1, p.10

With all these meanings & readings:

Ancient husbands strongly felt that their close female relatives **must not** be free—and here, a *woman* behind a *barred refuge* **must not** escape.

812

This character with the definition:

poison

Pinyin **dú** *and Frequency Rank* **947**

SIMP & TRAD   Contains **9 strokes** in the following order:

一 二 キ 丰 圭 青 毒 毒 毒

Contains these components:

plentiful 丰 (altered) 16, p.13

must not, no 毋 (altered) 811, p.187

With all these meanings & readings:

dú [毒] **1** poison **2** narcotics **3** evil

Poison is *plentiful* substance you *must not* eat.

813

This character with the definition:

wife

Pinyin **qī** *and Frequency Rank* **1076**

SIMP & TRAD   Contains **8 strokes** in the following order:

一 ⼀ 三 ⺕ 圭 妻 妻 妻

Contains these components:

ten 十 7, p.11

towel 巾 (altered) 118, p.35

woman 女 790, p.183

With all these meanings & readings:

qī [妻] **1** wife

qì [妻] **1** to marry off (a daughter)

The element '*woman*' combined with many garments ('*ten*' + '*towels*') shows that the ancient scribes valued a **wife** for her laundering ability.

814

This character with the definition:

chilly, sad

Pinyin **qī** *and Frequency Rank* **2352**

SIMP & TRAD   Contains **10 strokes** in the following order:

丶 冫 冫 沪 沪 沪 津 凄 凄 凄

Contains these components:

ice r 冫 348, p.87

wife 妻 813, p.187

With all these meanings & readings:

qī [凄] **1** intense cold **2** frigid **3** dismal **4** grim **5** lamentable **6** mournful

Nothing is **chillier** (or **sadder**) than a sour marriage, when the *wife* has turned *icy* towards her husband, and vice versa.

815

妡

SIMP & TRAD

This character with the definition:

concubine

Pinyin **qiè** *and Frequency Rank* **3242**

Contains **8 strokes** in the following order:

丶　丶　亠　立　立　产　产　妡

Contains these components:

to stand 立 681, p.160

woman 女 790, p.183

With all these meanings & readings

qiè [妾] **1** concubine **2** I, your servant (deprecatory self-reference for women)

A **concubine** is a *woman* who is paid to *stand* by her man.

816

接

SIMP & TRAD

This character with the definition:

come into contact with

Pinyin **jiē** *and Frequency Rank* **247**

Contains **11 strokes** in the following order:

一　十　扌　扩　扩　护　护　拉　接　接　接

Contains these components:

hand r 扌 25, p.15

concubine 妾 815, p.188

With all these meanings & readings

jiē [接] **1** to receive **2** to answer (the phone) **3** to meet or welcome sb **4** to connect **5** to catch **6** to join **7** to extend **8** to take one's turn on duty **9** take over for sb

The salacious nobleman was overcome with delight when he **came into contact with** his *concubine*'s *hand*.

817

母

SIMP & TRAD

This character with the definition:

mother

Pinyin **mǔ** *and Frequency Rank* **565**

Contains **5 strokes** in the following order:

乚　刀　毋　母　母

Contains these components:

woman 女 (altered) 790, p.183

dab r (×2) 丶 176, p.48

With all these meanings & readings

mǔ [母] **1** female **2** mother

A **mother** is a *woman* who can take little *bits* of anything and find ways to use them all to nourish and protect her family.

818

姆

SIMP & TRAD

This character with the definition:

nursemaid, mother

Pinyin **mǔ** *and Frequency Rank* **1061**

Contains **8 strokes** in the following order:

乚　女　女　奻　奻　姆　姆　姆

Contains these components:

woman 女 790, p.183

mother 母 817, p.188

With all these meanings & readings

mǔ [姆] **1** governess

A *woman* who acts like a *mother* is a **nursemaid**.

819

每

SIMP & TRAD

This character with the definition:

every

Pinyin **měi** *and Frequency Rank* **359**

Contains **7 strokes** in the following order:

丿　亠　仁　勹　每　每　每

Contains these components:

man 人 (altered) 537, p.127

mother 母 817, p.188

With all these meanings & readings

měi [每] **1** each **2** every

A *man* and his *mother* can do anything and **every**thing together, at least according to the *mother*.

820

梅

SIMP & TRAD

This character with the definition:

plum flower

Pinyin **méi** and Frequency Rank **1159**

Contains **11 strokes** in the following order:

一 十 才 木 栉 栉 梅 梅 梅 梅

Contains these components:

tree 木 562, p.133

every 每 819, p.188

With all these meanings & readings:

méi [梅] **1** plum **2** plum flower **3** Japanese apricot (Prunus mume) **4** surname Mei

The **plum flower** distinguishes that *tree* from *every* other one.

821

海

SIMP & TRAD

This character with the definition:

sea

Pinyin **hǎi** and Frequency Rank **189**

Contains **10 strokes** in the following order:

丶 丶 氵 氵 沂 汇 海 海 海 海

Contains these components:

water r 氵 314, p.80

every 每 819, p.188

With all these meanings & readings:

hǎi [海] **1** ocean **2** sea **3** m 个 [個][gè], 片[piàn]

Every channel of flowing *water*, in *every* part of the globe, empties into a **sea**.

822

舟

SIMP & TRAD

This character with the definition:

boat

Pinyin **zhōu** and Frequency Rank **2224**

Contains **6 strokes** in the following order:

丿 丿 月 舟 舟 舟

Contains these components:

dab r 丶 176, p.48

mother 母 (altered) 817, p.188

With all these meanings & readings:

zhōu [舟] **1** boat

A *mother* protects you from the evils of the world when you are *little*; **boats** protect you from the bruises and mishaps of the sea.

823

舰

艦
TRAD   SIMPLIFIED

This character with the definition:

naval vessel

Pinyin **jiàn** and Frequency Rank **851**

Contains **10 strokes** in the following order:

丿 丿 月 舟 舟 舟 舸 舰 舰 舰

Contains these components:

boat 舟 822, p.189

see 见 307, p.78

With all these meanings & readings:

jiàn [艦] **1** warship

Warships are always big and imposing. The idea is to intimidate your opponents when they *see* this frightening *boat* sailing towards them.

824

盘

盤
TRAD   SIMPLIFIED

This character with the definition:

small dish

Pinyin **pán** and Frequency Rank **1049**

Contains **11 strokes** in the following order:

丿 丿 月 舟 舟 舟 舟 舟 舟 盘 盘

Contains these components:

boat 舟 822, p.189

vessel, container 皿 101, p.32

With all these meanings & readings:

pán [盤] **1** dish **2** tray **3** to build **4** to check **5** to examine **6** to transfer **7** m for food: dish, helping **8** to coil **9** m for coils of wire **10** tectonic plate

How did we get the picky child to eat? The toy *boat* sailing in his cereal *vessel* captured his attention, and then we told him to open his mouth so the *boat* could enter! From now on, that's what I'll always think about when I envision a **dish**.

825

This character with the definition:

hinder, impede

Pinyin **fáng** *and Frequency Rank* **1873**

SIMP & TRAD Contains **7 strokes** in the following order:

丶 丿 女 女 女 妒 妒 妨

Contains these components:

woman 女 790, p.183

square; direction 方 490, p.117

With all these meanings & readings:

fáng [妨] **1** hinder **2** harm

The well-known movie star tried to walk briskly in the *direction* of the town *square*, but hordes of adoring *women* **impeded** his progress.

826

This character with the definition:

breast, milk

Pinyin **nǎi** *and Frequency Rank* **1278**

SIMP & TRAD Contains **5 strokes** in the following order:

丶 丿 女 奶 奶

Contains these components:

woman 女 790, p.183

so, therefore 乃 (altered) 520, p.124

With all these meanings & readings:

nǎi [奶] **1** breast **2** lady **3** milk

The *woman* is pregnant; *therefore*, her **breast** will naturally swell, *resulting* in **milk** being available for her newborn.

827

This character with the definition:

good, OK

Pinyin **hǎo** *and Frequency Rank* **82**

SIMP & TRAD Contains **6 strokes** in the following order:

丶 丿 女 女 奵 好

Contains these components:

woman 女 790, p.183

son, child 子 24, p.15

With all these meanings & readings:

hǎo [好] **1** good **2** well **3** prop **4** good to **5** easy to **6** very **7** so **8** (suffix indicating comple tion or readiness)
hào [好] **1** to be fond of

No scene better suggests a sense of **good**ness than that of a *woman* together with her *child*.

828

This character with the definition:

wed, marry

Pinyin **hūn** *and Frequency Rank* **942**

SIMP & TRAD Contains **11 strokes** in the following order:

丶 丿 女 女 奵 妒 妒 姄 婚 婚 婚

Contains these components:

woman 女 790, p.183

dusk 昏 416, p.101

With all these meanings & readings:

hūn [婚] **1** to marry **2** marriage **3** wedding **4** to take a wife

A hundred years ago, a *woman* could not go out after *dusk* unless she was **married**.

829

妈

媽
TRAD SIMPLIFIED

This character with the definition:

mom

Pinyin **mā** *and Frequency Rank* **750**

Contains **6 strokes** in the following order:

丶 丿 女 奵 妈 妈

Contains these components:

woman 女 790, p.183

horse 马 388, p.95

With all these meanings & readings:

mā [媽] **1** ma **2** mom **3** mother

My **mom** has won many awards as an expert *horse-woman*.

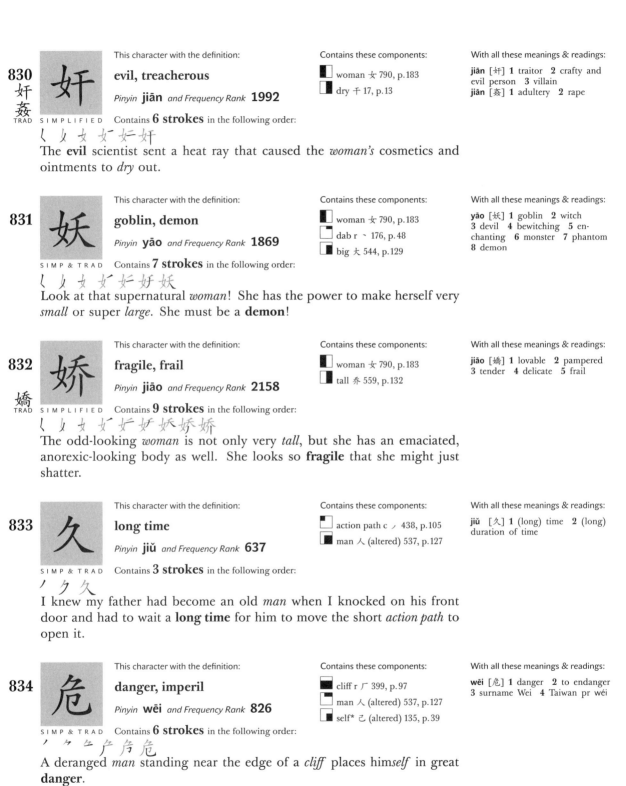

830
奸
姦
TRAD   SIMPLIFIED

This character with the definition:

evil, treacherous

Pinyin **jiān** and Frequency Rank **1992**

Contains **6 strokes** in the following order:

Contains these components:
- woman 女 790, p.183
- dry 干 17, p.13

With all these meanings & readings:

jiān [奸] **1** traitor **2** crafty and evil person **3** villain
jiān [姦] **1** adultery **2** rape

The **evil** scientist sent a heat ray that caused the *woman's* cosmetics and ointments to *dry* out.

831
SIMP & TRAD

This character with the definition:

goblin, demon

Pinyin **yāo** and Frequency Rank **1869**

Contains **7 strokes** in the following order:

Contains these components:
- woman 女 790, p.183
- dab r ⟍ 176, p.48
- big 大 544, p.129

With all these meanings & readings:

yāo [妖] **1** goblin **2** witch **3** devil **4** bewitching **5** enchanting **6** monster **7** phantom **8** demon

Look at that supernatural *woman*! She has the power to make herself very *small* or super *large*. She must be a **demon**!

832
嬌
TRAD   SIMPLIFIED

This character with the definition:

fragile, frail

Pinyin **jiāo** and Frequency Rank **2158**

Contains **9 strokes** in the following order:

Contains these components:
- woman 女 790, p.183
- tall 乔 559, p.132

With all these meanings & readings:

jiāo [嬌] **1** lovable **2** pampered **3** tender **4** delicate **5** frail

The odd-looking *woman* is not only very *tall*, but she has an emaciated, anorexic-looking body as well. She looks so **fragile** that she might just shatter.

833
SIMP & TRAD

This character with the definition:

long time

Pinyin **jiǔ** and Frequency Rank **637**

Contains **3 strokes** in the following order:

Contains these components:
- action path c ⟋ 438, p.105
- man 人 (altered) 537, p.127

With all these meanings & readings:

jiǔ [久] **1** (long) time **2** (long) duration of time

I knew my father had become an old *man* when I knocked on his front door and had to wait a **long time** for him to move the short *action path* to open it.

834
SIMP & TRAD

This character with the definition:

danger, imperil

Pinyin **wēi** and Frequency Rank **826**

Contains **6 strokes** in the following order:

Contains these components:
- cliff r 厂 399, p.97
- man 人 (altered) 537, p.127
- self* 己 (altered) 135, p.39

With all these meanings & readings:

wēi [危] **1** danger **2** to endanger **3** surname Wei **4** Taiwan pr wéi

A deranged *man* standing near the edge of a *cliff* places him*self* in great **danger**.

Unit 36

835 脆

SIMP & TRAD

This character with the definition:

fragile, brittle

Pinyin **cuì** *and Frequency Rank* **1976**

Contains **10 strokes** in the following order:

丿 刀 月 月 月 月' 朊 脃 脆 脆

Contains these components:

boat 舟 (altered) 822, p.189

danger, imperil 危 834, p.191

With all these meanings & readings:

cuì [脆] **1** brittle **2** fragile **3** crisp **4** crunchy **5** clear and loud voice **6** neat

Because the *boat* is so **fragile** and **brittle**, allowing so many of us to ride in it places all our lives in *danger*.

---

836 乞

SIMP & TRAD

This character with the definition:

beg*

Pinyin **qǐ** *and Frequency Rank* **2429**

Contains **3 strokes** in the following order:

丿 乛 乞

Contains these components:

man 人 (altered) 537, p.127

second (in a series) 乙 (altered) 146, p.41

With all these meanings & readings:

qǐ [乞] **1** beg

Times were so bad that the *man* felt fortunate to be only the *second* person standing in the long line that had gathered to **beg** for food at the charity pantry.

---

837 吃

SIMP & TRAD

This character with the definition:

eat

Pinyin **chī** *and Frequency Rank* **475**

Contains **6 strokes** in the following order:

丨 口 口 口' 吖 吃

Contains these components:

mouth 口 37, p.17

beg* 乞 836, p.192

With all these meanings & readings:

chī [吃] **1** to eat **2** to have one meal **3** to eradicate **4** to destro **5** to absorb **6** to suffer **7** to exhaust
jí [吃] **1** stammer

The homeless man was so weak that he could only *beg* for something to **eat** by pointing a finger to his open *mouth*.

---

838 气

氣 气

TRAD SIMPLIFIED

This character with the definition:

air, spirit, vital energy

Pinyin **qì** *and Frequency Rank* **217**

Contains **4 strokes** in the following order:

丿 乛 乞 气

Contains these components:

man 人 (altered) 537, p.127

one 一 1, p.10

second (in a series) 乙 146, p.41

With all these meanings & readings:

qì [氣] **1** gas **2** air **3** smell **4** weather **5** vital breath **6** to anger **7** to get angry **8** to be enraged

A person's inner **spirit** is so 'visible' that it can make *one man* appear to be bursting with **vital energy** while a *second* resembles a flat tire, with no '**air**' in him. • This character was originally designed to represent the curling shapes of heavenly clouds.

---

839 汽

SIMP & TRAD

This character with the definition:

steam, vapor

Pinyin **qì** *and Frequency Rank* **1200**

Contains **7 strokes** in the following order:

丶 氵 氵 氵 汽 汽 汽

Contains these components:

water r 氵 314, p.80

air, spirit, vital energy 气 838, p.192

With all these meanings & readings:

qì [汽] **1** steam **2** vapor

Steam is the 'moist *air*' that forms over very hot *water*, or near a mammal's nostrils during very cold temperatures.

840

色

SIMP & TRAD

This character with the definition:

color*

Pinyin **sè** *and Frequency Rank* **304**

Contains **6 strokes** in the following order:

丿 ⺈ ⺈ 各 各 色

Contains these components:

☐ man 人 (altered) 537, p.127

■ cling to, stick to 巴 137, p.39

With all these meanings & readings:

sè [色] **1** color **2** look **3** appearance **4** sex **5** m 种[種][zhǒng]

shǎi [色] **1** color **2** dice

The face of the *man* sitting next to me turned the **color** red after I pointed out the bit of shaving cream still *clinging to* his chin.

841

六

SIMP & TRAD

This character with the definition:

six

Pinyin **liù** *and Frequency Rank* **478**

Contains **4 strokes** in the following order:

丶 一 亠 六

Contains these components:

☐ cover r 亠 250, p.66

■ man 人 (altered) 537, p.127

With all these meanings & readings:

liù [六] **1** six **2** 6

We *cover* a *man* with soil when he's dead and bury him **six** feet underground.

842

亦

SIMP & TRAD

This character with the definition:

also, too

Pinyin **yì** *and Frequency Rank* **886**

Contains **6 strokes** in the following order:

丶 一 亠 亣 亦 亦

Contains these components:

■ six 六 841, p.193

■ son 儿 (altered) 312, p.80

With all these meanings & readings:

yì [亦] **1** also

Six sons are way **too** many!

843

赤

SIMP & TRAD

This character with the definition:

red, be flushed

Pinyin **chì** *and Frequency Rank* **1660**

Contains **7 strokes** in the following order:

一 十 土 亓 赤 赤 赤

Contains these components:

☐ earth, soil 土 9, p.11

■ also, too 亦 (altered) 842, p.193

With all these meanings & readings:

chì [赤] **1** red **2** scarlet **3** bare **4** naked

Ditch-digging involves carrying *soil* out of the *earth*. Sometimes, workers carry *too* much out at one time and their faces become **flushed red** from exertion.

844

赫

SIMP & TRAD

This character with the definition:

awe-inspiring

Pinyin **hè** *and Frequency Rank* **1346**

Contains **14 strokes** in the following order:

一 十 土 亓 赤 赤 赤 赤 赤 赫 赫 赫 赫 赫

Contains these components:

■ red, be flushed (×2) 赤 843, p.193

With all these meanings & readings:

hè [赫] **1** surname He **2** awe-inspiring **3** hertz

The highly unlikely odds of two women arriving at the same formal event wearing identically-styled dresses could be considered **awe-inspiring**—in reality, it will more likely result in both women *being flushed* and turning *red* with embarrassment.

845

彎
TRAD   SIMPLIFIED

This character with the definition:

bent, curved

Pinyin **wān** *and Frequency Rank* **1662**

Contains **9 strokes** in the following order:

Contains these components:

☐ also, too 亦 842, p.193

☐ bow (weapon) 弓 140, p.40

With all these meanings & readings

wān [彎] **1** bend **2** bent **3** m
道[dào]

Imagine *two* (sounds like '*too*') *bows* lying in a heap. What a tangled mess of **bent** wood!

846

灣
TRAD   SIMPLIFIED

This character with the definition:

gulf, bay

Pinyin **wān** *and Frequency Rank* **855**

Contains **12 strokes** in the following order:

Contains these components:

☐ water r 氵 314, p.80

☐ bent, curved 弯 845, p.194

With all these meanings & readings

wān [灣] **1** bay **2** gulf

A **bay** is defined by a *bent* coastline that encloses a body of *water*.

847

倉
TRAD   SIMPLIFIED

This character with the definition:

barn, storehouse

Pinyin **cāng** *and Frequency Rank* **1882**

Contains **4 strokes** in the following order:

Contains these components:

☐ man 人 537, p.127

☐ self* 己 (altered) 135, p.39

With all these meanings & readings

cāng [倉] **1** barn **2** granary
3 storehouse **4** cabin **5** hold (
ship)

The self-made *man* built a **barn** for you to **store** food and supplies for your*self* and your family.

848

搶
TRAD   SIMPLIFIED

This character with the definition:

pillage, loot

Pinyin **qiǎng** *and Frequency Rank* **1412**

Contains **7 strokes** in the following order:

Contains these components:

☐ hand r 扌 25, p.15

☐ barn, storehouse 仓 847, p.194

With all these meanings & readings

qiǎng [搶] **1** see 抢风[搶風] con
trary wind
qiǎng [搶] **1** fight over **2** to ru
3 to scramble **4** to grab **5** to
rob **6** to snatch

After the riot, the *barn* doors gaped open and the villagers used their *hands* to **pillage** and **loot** whatever they could from the *barn*.

849

蒼
TRAD   SIMPLIFIED

This character with the definition:

dark green

Pinyin **cāng** *and Frequency Rank* **1728**

Contains **7 strokes** in the following order:

Contains these components:

☐ grass r 艹 87, p.29

☐ barn, storehouse 仓 847, p.194

With all these meanings & readings

cāng [蒼] **1** dark blue **2** deep
green **3** housefly (Musca domes
tica) **4** surname Cang

This character takes its meaning from the color of the wilted *grass* that's kept in a well-stocked *barn* and peeks out of the windows. From a distance, it looks **dark green**.

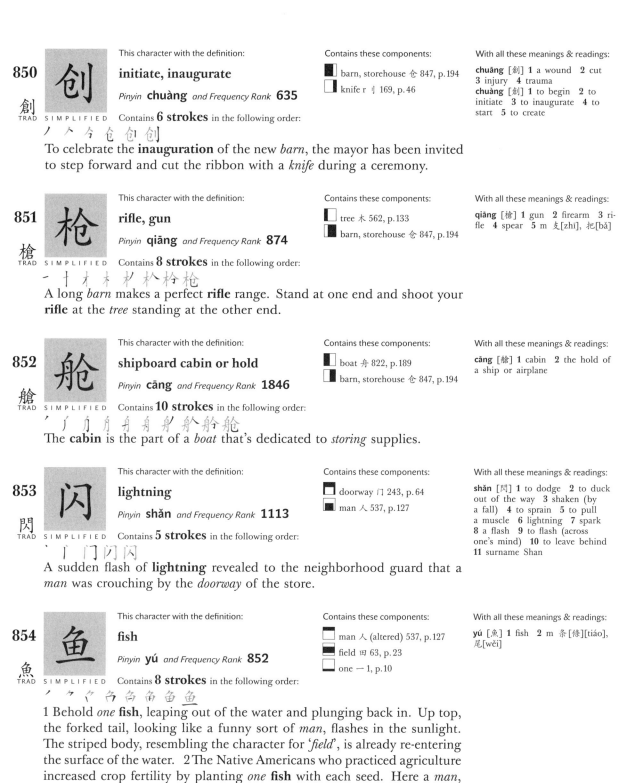

850

創

創
TRAD SIMPLIFIED

This character with the definition:

initiate, inaugurate

Pinyin **chuàng** *and Frequency Rank* **635**

Contains **6 strokes** in the following order:

ノ 人 今 仓 刍 創

Contains these components:

■ barn, storehouse 仓 847, p.194
▯ knife r 刂 169, p.46

With all these meanings & readings:

chuǎng [創] **1** a wound **2** cut **3** injury **4** trauma
chuàng [創] **1** to begin **2** to initiate **3** to inaugurate **4** to start **5** to create

To celebrate the **inauguration** of the new *barn*, the mayor has been invited to step forward and cut the ribbon with a *knife* during a ceremony.

851

枪

槍
TRAD SIMPLIFIED

This character with the definition:

rifle, gun

Pinyin **qiāng** *and Frequency Rank* **874**

Contains **8 strokes** in the following order:

一 十 才 木 朾 朳 枪 枪

Contains these components:

▯ tree 木 562, p.133
■ barn, storehouse 仓 847, p.194

With all these meanings & readings:

qiāng [槍] **1** gun **2** firearm **3** rifle **4** spear **5** m 支[zhī], 把[bǎ]

A long *barn* makes a perfect **rifle** range. Stand at one end and shoot your **rifle** at the *tree* standing at the other end.

852

舱

艙
TRAD SIMPLIFIED

This character with the definition:

shipboard cabin or hold

Pinyin **cāng** *and Frequency Rank* **1846**

Contains **10 strokes** in the following order:

′ ⺁ 丿 月 舟 舟 舟 舧 舱 舱

Contains these components:

■ boat 舟 822, p.189
■ barn, storehouse 仓 847, p.194

With all these meanings & readings:

cāng [艙] **1** cabin **2** the hold of a ship or airplane

The **cabin** is the part of a *boat* that's dedicated to *storing* supplies.

853

闪

閃
TRAD SIMPLIFIED

This character with the definition:

lightning

Pinyin **shǎn** *and Frequency Rank* **1113**

Contains **5 strokes** in the following order:

′ ⺆ 门 闪 闪

Contains these components:

▯ doorway 门 243, p.64
■ man 人 537, p.127

With all these meanings & readings:

shǎn [閃] **1** to dodge **2** to duck out of the way **3** shaken (by a fall) **4** to sprain **5** to pull a muscle **6** lightning **7** spark **8** a flash **9** to flash (across one's mind) **10** to leave behind **11** surname Shan

A sudden flash of **lightning** revealed to the neighborhood guard that a *man* was crouching by the *doorway* of the store.

854

鱼

魚
TRAD SIMPLIFIED

This character with the definition:

fish

Pinyin **yú** *and Frequency Rank* **852**

Contains **8 strokes** in the following order:

ノ 勹 ⺈ 勽 鱼 鱼 鱼 鱼

Contains these components:

▯ man 人 (altered) 537, p.127
■ field 田 63, p.23
▯ one 一 1, p.10

With all these meanings & readings:

yú [魚] **1** fish **2** m 条[條][tiáo], 尾[wěi]

1 Behold *one* **fish**, leaping out of the water and plunging back in. Up top, the forked tail, looking like a funny sort of *man*, flashes in the sunlight. The striped body, resembling the character for '*field*', is already re-entering the surface of the water.   **2** The Native Americans who practiced agriculture increased crop fertility by planting *one* **fish** with each seed. Here a *man*, the farmer, is in his *field* inserting the poor **fish** below the *horizontal surface* of the soil.

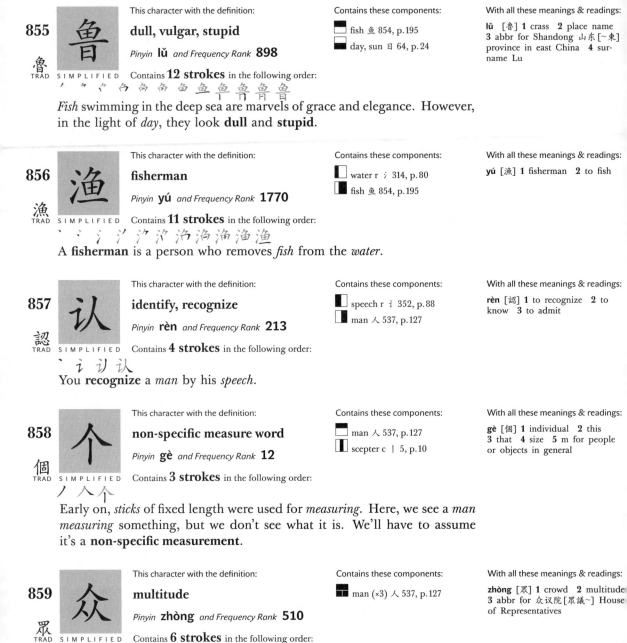

855

鲁

魯
TRAD · SIMPLIFIED

This character with the definition:

dull, vulgar, stupid

Pinyin **lǔ** *and Frequency Rank* **898**

Contains **12 strokes** in the following order:

ノ ク ケ 凸 凸 魚 鱼 鱼 魯 鲁 鲁 鲁

Contains these components:

▢ fish 鱼 854, p.195

▢ day, sun 日 64, p.24

With all these meanings & readings:

lǔ [魯] **1** crass **2** place name **3** abbr for Shandong 山东 [~东] province in east China **4** surname Lu

Fish swimming in the deep sea are marvels of grace and elegance. However, in the light of *day*, they look **dull** and **stupid**.

856

渔

漁
TRAD · SIMPLIFIED

This character with the definition:

fisherman

Pinyin **yú** *and Frequency Rank* **1770**

Contains **11 strokes** in the following order:

丶 丶 氵 氵 沕 泎 泊 泃 渔 渔 渔

Contains these components:

▢ water r 氵 314, p.80

▢ fish 鱼 854, p.195

With all these meanings & readings:

yú [漁] **1** fisherman **2** to fish

A **fisherman** is a person who removes *fish* from the *water*.

857

认

認
TRAD · SIMPLIFIED

This character with the definition:

identify, recognize

Pinyin **rèn** *and Frequency Rank* **213**

Contains **4 strokes** in the following order:

丶 讠 认 认

Contains these components:

▢ speech r 讠 352, p.88

▢ man 人 537, p.127

With all these meanings & readings:

rèn [認] **1** to recognize **2** to know **3** to admit

You **recognize** a *man* by his *speech*.

858

个

個
TRAD · SIMPLIFIED

This character with the definition:

non-specific measure word

Pinyin **gè** *and Frequency Rank* **12**

Contains **3 strokes** in the following order:

ノ 人 个

Contains these components:

▢ man 人 537, p.127

▢ scepter c 丨 5, p.10

With all these meanings & readings:

gè [個] **1** individual **2** this **3** that **4** size **5** m for people or objects in general

Early on, *sticks* of fixed length were used for *measuring*. Here, we see a *man measuring* something, but we don't see what it is. We'll have to assume it's a **non-specific measurement**.

859

众

眾
TRAD · SIMPLIFIED

This character with the definition:

multitude

Pinyin **zhòng** *and Frequency Rank* **510**

Contains **6 strokes** in the following order:

ノ 人 介 众 分 众

Contains these components:

▢ man (×3) 人 537, p.127

With all these meanings & readings:

zhòng [眾] **1** crowd **2** multitude **3** abbr for 众议院 [眾議~] House of Representatives

The components say it all—you see here a **multitude** of *men*.

Unit 37

860

從
TRAD SIMPLIFIED

This character with the definition:

from

Pinyin **cóng** *and Frequency Rank* **98**

Contains **4 strokes** in the following order:

ノ 人 从 从

Contains these components:

man (×2) 人 537, p.127

cōng [從] **1** lax **2** yielding **3** unhurried
cóng [從] **1** from **2** via **3** passing through **4** through (a gap) **5** past **6** ever (followed by negative, meaning never) **7** (formerly pr **zòng** and related to 纵 [縱]) to follow **8** to comply with **9** to obey **10** to join **11** to engage in **12** adopting some mode of action or attitude **13** follower **14** retainer **15** accessory **16** accomplice **17** related by common paternal grandfather or earlier ancestor **18** surname Cong
zòng [從] **1** second cousin

Here the components are two pictures of the same man. The left component shows the same man's original position where he came **from**, while the right picture shows him in his present location. • We sometimes use 从 for the concept of '**source**', since this character shows the progress made by somebody traveling from this source to his present position.

861

叢
TRAD SIMPLIFIED

This character with the definition:

cluster

Pinyin **cóng** *and Frequency Rank* **1678**

Contains **5 strokes** in the following order:

ノ 人 从 从 丛

Contains these components:

from 从 860, p.197

one 一 1, p.10

With all these meanings & readings:
cóng [叢] **1** cluster **2** collection **3** collection of books **4** thicket

A **cluster** is a group of *people* or other things bound together by *one* common characteristic.

862

聳
TRAD SIMPLIFIED

This character with the definition:

to tower

Pinyin **sǒng** *and Frequency Rank* **2163**

Contains **10 strokes** in the following order:

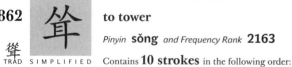

Contains these components:

from 从 860, p.197

ear 耳 76, p.26

With all these meanings & readings:
sǒng [聳] **1** to excite **2** to raise up **3** to shrug **4** high **5** lofty **6** towering

If you stand on top of the **tower** you can see *from 'ear* (sounds like 'here'—ouch!) to eternity.

863

爭
TRAD SIMPLIFIED

This character with the definition:

struggle

Pinyin **zhēng** *and Frequency Rank* **344**

Contains **6 strokes** in the following order:

Contains these components:

man 人 (altered) 537, p.127

boar's head r ヨ (altered) 30, p.16

scepter c 丨 5, p.10

With all these meanings & readings:
zhēng [爭] **1** struggle **2** fight

The **struggle** is between the *man* with a *stick* and a *wild boar*. It's not looking good for the man.

864

淨
TRAD SIMPLIFIED

This character with the definition:

clean, net (price)

Pinyin **jìng** *and Frequency Rank* **1377**

Contains **8 strokes** in the following order:

Contains these components:

ice r 冫 348, p.87

struggle 争 863, p.197

With all these meanings & readings:
jìng [淨] **1** clean **2** completely **3** only

It's hard to keep **clean** in the winter. The water turns to *ice*, and the bitter cold makes simple washing a constant *struggle*.

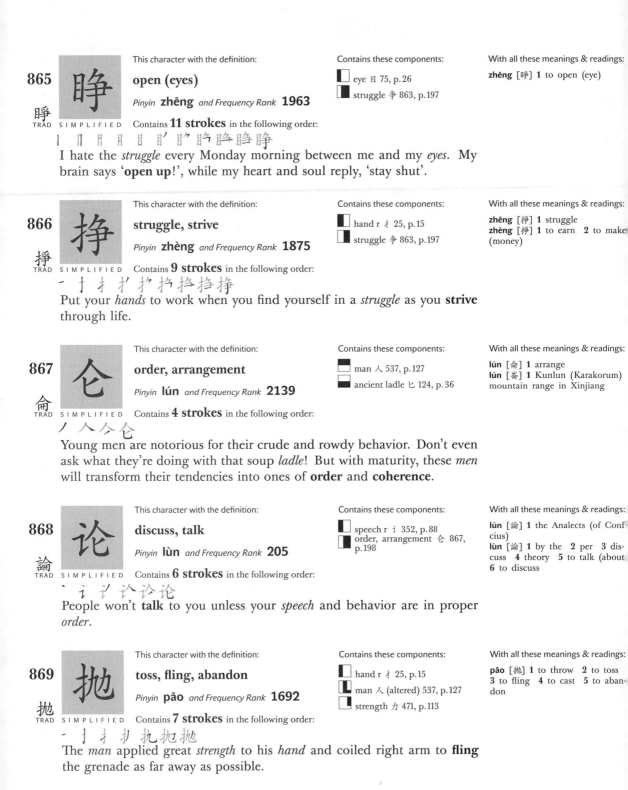

865

睁

睁
TRAD   SIMPLIFIED

This character with the definition:

open (eyes)

Pinyin **zhēng** *and Frequency Rank* **1963**

Contains **11 strokes** in the following order:

丨 冂 冂 月 目 目 目' 目'' 睁 睁 睁

Contains these components:

■ eye 目 75, p.26
■ struggle 争 863, p.197

With all these meanings & readings:

zhēng [睜] **1** to open (eye)

I hate the *struggle* every Monday morning between me and my *eyes*. My brain says 'open up!', while my heart and soul reply, 'stay shut'.

866

挣

挣
TRAD   SIMPLIFIED

This character with the definition:

struggle, strive

Pinyin **zhèng** *and Frequency Rank* **1875**

Contains **9 strokes** in the following order:

一 亅 扌 扌' 扩 护 挣 挣 挣

Contains these components:

■ hand r 扌 25, p.15
■ struggle 争 863, p.197

With all these meanings & readings:

zhēng [掙] **1** struggle
zhèng [掙] **1** to earn   **2** to make (money)

Put your *hands* to work when you find yourself in a *struggle* as you **strive** through life.

867

仑

仑
TRAD   SIMPLIFIED

This character with the definition:

order, arrangement

Pinyin **lún** *and Frequency Rank* **2139**

Contains **4 strokes** in the following order:

丿 人 仒 仑

Contains these components:

□ man 人 537, p.127
■ ancient ladle 匕 124, p.36

With all these meanings & readings:

lún [侖] **1** arrange
lún [崙] **1** Kunlun (Karakorum) mountain range in Xinjiang

Young men are notorious for their crude and rowdy behavior. Don't even ask what they're doing with that soup *ladle*! But with maturity, these *men* will transform their tendencies into ones of **order** and **coherence**.

868

论

论
TRAD   SIMPLIFIED

This character with the definition:

discuss, talk

Pinyin **lùn** *and Frequency Rank* **205**

Contains **6 strokes** in the following order:

丶 讠 讠 讼 论 论

Contains these components:

■ speech r 讠 352, p.88
■ order, arrangement 仑 867, p.198

With all these meanings & readings:

lún [論] **1** the Analects (of Confucius)
lùn [論] **1** by the **2** per **3** discuss **4** theory **5** to talk (about **6** to discuss

People won't **talk** to you unless your *speech* and behavior are in proper *order*.

869

抛

抛
TRAD   SIMPLIFIED

This character with the definition:

toss, fling, abandon

Pinyin **pāo** *and Frequency Rank* **1692**

Contains **7 strokes** in the following order:

一 亅 扌 扌 执 抛 抛

Contains these components:

■ hand r 扌 25, p.15
■ man 人 (altered) 537, p.127
□ strength 力 471, p.113

With all these meanings & readings:

pāo [抛] **1** to throw **2** to toss **3** to fling **4** to cast **5** to abandon

The *man* applied great *strength* to his *hand* and coiled right arm to **fling** the grenade as far away as possible.

870

翰

SIMP & TRAD

This character with the definition:

writing brush

Pinyin **hàn** *and Frequency Rank* **1881**

Contains **16 strokes** in the following order:

Contains these components:

☐ ten 十 7, p.11
■ morning 早 65, p.24
■ man 人 537, p.127
■ feather, wing 羽 107, p.33

With all these meanings & readings:

hàn [翰] **1** pen

一 十 十 古 古 古 直 卓 卓 龺 龺 幹 幹 翰 翰 翰 翰

Practicing Chinese calligraphy with a proper **writing brush** is demanding. The best time to do this is at *ten* in the *morning*. A *man* begins by picking up the **brush** whose hairs are as fine as *feathers*.

871

盐

鹽
TRAD   SIMPLIFIED

This character with the definition:

salt

Pinyin **yán** *and Frequency Rank* **1885**

Contains **10 strokes** in the following order:

Contains these components:

■ earth, soil 土 9, p.11
■ man 人 (altered) 537, p.127
■ vessel, container 皿 101, p.32

With all these meanings & readings:

yán [鹽] **1** salt   **2** m 粒[lì]

一 十 土 圤 圤 圤 卦 卦 盐 盐

Men can collect **salt** from the *earth*. I store some of that **salt** in a small *dish*, and set it on the table to season my meals.

872

乾

SIMP & TRAD

This character with the definition:

male principle, heaven

Pinyin **qián** *and Frequency Rank* **1999**

Contains **11 strokes** in the following order:

Contains these components:

☐ ten 十 7, p.11
■ morning 早 65, p.24
☐ man 人 (altered) 537, p.127
■ second (in a series) 乙 146, p.41

With all these meanings & readings:

qián [乾] **1** surname Qian **2** strong **3** one of the Eight Trigrams 八卦 representing sky **4** male principle

一 十 十 古 古 古 直 卓 卓 龺 乾

Every *morning*, for the last *ten* days in a row, *the man* has gotten up early to start work; he lives in fear that someone else will beat him to the office, making him *second in a series*. This is the **male principle** in action.

873

刍

芻
TRAD   SIMPLIFIED

This character with the definition:

hay for fodder

Pinyin **chú** *and Frequency Rank* **4465**

Contains **5 strokes** in the following order:

Contains these components:

■ man 人 (altered) 537, p.127
■ boar's head r ⺕ 30, p.16

With all these meanings & readings:

chú [芻] **1** cut grass **2** hay **3** straw **4** fodder **5** surname Chu

丿 ⺈ 刍 刍 刍

The *man* subdued the *wild boar* by providing **hay** for it.

874

趋

趨
TRAD   SIMPLIFIED

This character with the definition:

hasten

Pinyin **qū** *and Frequency Rank* **1486**

Contains **12 strokes** in the following order:

Contains these components:

☐ to walk 走 731, p.171
☐ hay for fodder 刍 873, p.199

With all these meanings & readings:

qū [趨] **1** to hasten **2** to hurry **3** to walk fast **4** to approach **5** to tend towards **6** to converge

一 十 土 十 丰 丰 走 走 赳 赵 趋 趋

The oxen *walk* slowly toward the *hay fodder* until they can smell it; at that point, I can barely control them as they **hasten** toward their dinner.

875

This character with the definition:

夕 **dusk***

Pinyin **xī** *and Frequency Rank* **2003**

SIMP & TRAD Contains **3 strokes** in the following order:

ノ ク 夕

Contains these components:

▪ action path c ノ 438, p.105
▪ place of refuge c ㇆ (altered) 105, p.33
▪ dab r 丶 176, p.48

With all these meanings & readings:

xī [夕] **1** evening
xì [夕] **1** dusk

At **dusk**, the dim light provides a *place of refuge* for *little* creatures in danger of attack from the aggressive *actions* of predators. • Note that the character itself is a stylized sketch of a crescent moon whose appearance in the sky announces the coming of **dusk**.

876

This character with the definition:

名 **personal name**

Pinyin **míng** *and Frequency Rank* **203**

SIMP & TRAD Contains **6 strokes** in the following order:

ノ ク 夕 夕 名 名

Contains these components:

▪ dusk* 夕 875, p.200
▪ mouth 口 37, p.17

With all these meanings & readings:

míng [名] **1** name **2** noun (part of speech) **3** place (e.g. among winners) **4** famous **5** m for people

In the *evening*, when it's hard to be identified, it's wise to use your *mouth* to clearly identify yourself by your **personal name** to people you encounter in your neighborhood.

877

This character with the definition:

外 **outside, external**

Pinyin **wài** *and Frequency Rank* **131**

SIMP & TRAD Contains **5 strokes** in the following order:

ノ ク 夕 夕卜 外

Contains these components:

▪ dusk* 夕 875, p.200
▪ foretell 卜 187, p.51

With all these meanings & readings:

wài [外] **1** outside **2** in addition **3** foreign **4** external

By *dusk*, the events of your day are nearly over and already becoming part of your past. It is impossible to *foretell* what lies **outside** of the present or past—because that is the future!

878

This character with the definition:

多 **many, much**

Pinyin **duō** *and Frequency Rank* **61**

SIMP & TRAD Contains **6 strokes** in the following order:

ノ ク 夕 夕 多 多

Contains these components:

▪ dusk* (×2) 夕 875, p.200

With all these meanings & readings:

duō [多] **1** many **2** much **3** a lot of **4** numerous **5** multi-

This character is especially useful because it can be used to describe 'large number'—such as '**many** moons', '**many** nights' (*evening* after *evening*)—as well as 'large quantity'—such as '**much** time' or '**much** food'.

879

This character with the definition:

移 **change, alter**

Pinyin **yí** *and Frequency Rank* **880**

SIMP & TRAD Contains **11 strokes** in the following order:

ノ 二 千 禾 禾 禾' 移 移 移 移 移

Contains these components:

▪ rice, grain (crop) 禾 593, p.140
▪ many, much 多 878, p.200

With all these meanings & readings:

yí [移] **1** to move **2** to shift **3** to change **4** to alter **5** to remove

Historically, *rice* and *grain* symbolized much wealth and *abundance*, which usually signaled an opportunity for drastic **change** and **alteration** in lifestyle.

880

够

夠
TRAD SIMPLIFIED

This character with the definition:

be enough

Pinyin **gòu** *and Frequency Rank* **538**

Contains **11 strokes** in the following order:

ノ 勹 勺 句 句 句 句 够 够 够 够

Contains these components:

■ many, much 多 878, p. 200
■ sentence 句 369, p. 91

With all these meanings & readings:

gòu [夠] **1** to reach **2** to be enough

Sentences should only contain as *many* words as necessary to be **enough** to get their point across.

881

歹

SIMP & TRAD

This character with the definition:

evil, vicious

Pinyin **dǎi** *and Frequency Rank* **2905**

Contains **4 strokes** in the following order:

一 丆 歹 歹

Contains these components:

□ one 一 1, p. 10
■ dusk* 夕 875, p. 200

With all these meanings & readings:

dǎi [歹] **1** bad **2** wicked **3** evil

One person with intentions to do something **evil** and **vicious** needs the cover of *dusk* to keep his identity obscure.

882

死

SIMP & TRAD

This character with the definition:

die

Pinyin **sǐ** *and Frequency Rank* **317**

Contains **6 strokes** in the following order:

一 丆 歹 歹 歹 死

Contains these components:

■ evil, vicious 歹 (altered) 881, p. 201
■ ancient ladle 匕 124, p. 36

With all these meanings & readings:

sǐ [死] **1** to die **2** impassable **3** uncrossable **4** inflexible **5** rigid **6** extremely

A great *evil* has befallen our leader, who has fallen down. See him there, upside-down, looking like a bent *spoon*. As a result, he **died**.

883

殊

SIMP & TRAD

This character with the definition:

different, special

Pinyin **shū** *and Frequency Rank* **1191**

Contains **10 strokes** in the following order:

一 丆 歹 歹 歹 歼 歼 殊 殊 殊

Contains these components:

■ evil, vicious 歹 881, p. 201
■ bright red 朱 584, p. 138

With all these meanings & readings:

shū [殊] **1** unique

Violent and *vicious* acts against others are **different** than petty crimes because the former usually produce a *bright red* color while the latter leaves the victim physically intact

---

884

残

残
TRAD SIMPLIFIED

This character with the definition:

incomplete, deficient

Pinyin **cán** *and Frequency Rank* **1150**

Contains **9 strokes** in the following order:

一 丆 歹 歹 歹 歼 残 残 残

Contains these components:

■ evil, vicious 歹 881, p. 201
□ tiny, fragmentary 戋 665, p. 157

With all these meanings & readings:

cán [殘] **1** to destroy **2** to spoil **3** to ruin **4** to injure **5** cruel **6** oppressive **7** savage **8** brutal **9** incomplete **10** disabled **11** to remain **12** to survive **13** remnant **14** surplus

The villain's plans were **incomplete** because his force of *evil* was defeated and converted into *tiny* and *fragmentary* forces of good.

Unit 38

885

列

SIMP & TRAD

This character with the definition:

arrange, line up

Pinyin **liè** *and Frequency Rank* **500**

Contains **6 strokes** in the following order:

一 ㄱ � 歹 歹刂 列

Contains these components:

■ evil, vicious 歹 881, p. 201

□ knife r 刂 169, p. 46

With all these meanings & readings:

liè [列] **1** to arrange **2** to line up **3** row **4** file **5** series **6** column

The *evil* mugger used his *knife* to force people to **line up** for easy pick-pocketing.

886

殖

SIMP & TRAD

This character with the definition:

propagate

Pinyin **zhí** *and Frequency Rank* **1438**

Contains **12 strokes** in the following order:

一 ㄱ � 歹 歹一 歹卜 歹 殖 殖 殖 殖 殖

Contains these components:

■ evil, vicious 歹 881, p. 201

□ straight, vertical 直 85, p. 29

With all these meanings & readings:

zhí [殖] **1** to grow **2** to reproduce

Winter is a necessary *evil*, killing plants but sparing their seeds by dropping them to the ground. In the spring, the seeds grow into *straight* and tall plants, thereby **propagating** the species.

887

殲

TRAD

歼

SIMPLIFIED

This character with the definition:

annihilate

Pinyin **jiān** *and Frequency Rank* **1815**

Contains **7 strokes** in the following order:

一 ㄱ � 歹 歹一 歹一 歼

Contains these components:

■ evil, vicious 歹 881, p. 201

□ thousand 千 767, p. 178

With all these meanings & readings:

jiān [殲] **1** to annihilate **2** abbr for 歼击机 [殲擊機], fighter plane **3** Jianji, PRC fighter plane based on Soviet MiG **4** usually 殲擊8歼击 [型]8型

If you magnify *evil* thoughts by a *thousand*, you have the power to **annihilate** your enemies.

888

夢

TRAD

梦

SIMPLIFIED

This character with the definition:

dream

Pinyin **mèng** *and Frequency Rank* **865**

Contains **11 strokes** in the following order:

一 十 オ 木 朳一 朴 材 林 林 梦 梦

Contains these components:

■ forest 林 611, p. 146

□ dusk* 夕 (altered) 875, p. 200

With all these meanings & readings:

mèng [夢] **1** to dream **2** m 场 [場][cháng], 个 [個][gè]

The *forest* at *evening* is scary. Things that look normal in daylight appear eerie at night. It's a nightmare **dream**scape.

889

將

TRAD

将

SIMPLIFIED

This character with the definition:

handle, deal with sth

Pinyin **jiāng** *and Frequency Rank* **132**

Contains **9 strokes** in the following order:

丶 ㇀ 丬 丬 将 将 将 将 将

Contains these components:

■ slice, flake 片 (altered) 488, p. 116

□ dusk* 夕 875, p. 200

□ inch 寸 216, p. 58

With all these meanings & readings:

jiāng [將] **1** will **2** shall **3** to use **4** to take **5** to checkmate **6** just a short while ago
jiàng [將] **1** general; commander-in-chief (military) **2** king (chess piece) **3** to command **4** to lead
qiāng [將] **1** to desire **2** to invi **3** to request

My spouse has never figured out how to barbecue meat; it always burns and takes on the taste of charcoal! I **handle the matter** tactfully by *slicing* the meat, which is dark as *night*, into small *inch*-size pieces that I force myself to swallow.

890

蔣
TRAD SIMPLIFIED

This character with the definition:

surname, Chiang Kai-Shek

Pinyin **jiǎng** *and Frequency Rank* **1172**

Contains these components:

☐ grass r 艹 87, p. 29
■ handle, deal with sth 将 889, p. 202

With all these meanings & readings:

Jiǎng [蔣] **1** surname Jiang **2** refers to Chiang Kai-shek 蔣介石 [蔣~~]

Contains **12 strokes** in the following order:

Chiang Kai-Shek achieved prominence by virtue of his leadership and capability for *handling* matters. The *grass* laurels he wears on top demonstrate the honor accorded him by the Chinese people. • Chiang Kai-Shek (Cantonese pronunciation) was the leader of the Republic of China from 1928 through 1975; his Mandarin name is Jiǎng Jièshí.

891

奖
TRAD SIMPLIFIED

This character with the definition:

award, prize, reward

Pinyin **jiǎng** *and Frequency Rank* **1233**

Contains these components:

■ handle, deal with sth 将 889, p. 202
☐ big 大 544, p. 129

With all these meanings & readings:

jiǎng [奖] **1** prize **2** award **3** encouragement **4** m 个 [個][gè]

Contains **9 strokes** in the following order:

You get a **prize** for your ability to *handle matters* effectively and expediently. The **prize** means you're *great*!

892

宛
SIMP & TRAD

This character with the definition:

winding

Pinyin **wǎn** *and Frequency Rank* **2528**

Contains these components:

☐ roof r 宀 271, p. 70
■ dusk* 夕 875, p. 200
■ self* 己 (altered) 135, p. 39

With all these meanings & readings:

wǎn [宛] **1** similar **2** winding **3** surname Wan

Contains **8 strokes** in the following order:

It's past *evening* so it's bedtime. Under your own *roof* and in your bed, it's so easy to conform your*self* to familiar **winding** postures that are the most comfortable for your body.

893

碗
SIMP & TRAD

This character with the definition:

bowl

Pinyin **wǎn** *and Frequency Rank* **1939**

Contains these components:

☐ stone, rock 石 522, p. 124
■ winding 宛 892, p. 203

With all these meanings & readings:

wǎn [碗] **1** bowl **2** cup **3** m 只 [隻][zhī], 个 [個][gè]

Contains **13 strokes** in the following order:

一 丆 丆 石 石 石 砑 砑 砑 砑 碗 碗

With practice, I can propel a small *stone* so that it hugs the inside curved wall of a **bowl** as it travels a *winding* path to the bottom.

894

罗
TRAD SIMPLIFIED

This character with the definition:

bird net

Pinyin **luó** *and Frequency Rank* **392**

Contains these components:

☐ net r 罒 100, p. 32
■ dusk* 夕 875, p. 200

With all these meanings & readings:

luō [囉] **1** fussy **2** talkative
luó [囉] **1** subordinate in a gang of bandits
luó [羅] **1** gauze **2** to collect; to gather **3** to catch **4** to sift; to sieve **5** surname Luo

Contains **8 strokes** in the following order:

丶 ㄇ 罒 罒 罒 罗 罗 罗

What's the best way **to catch birds**? It's hard no matter how, but it's easiest if you use a *net* and wait till *evening* when they are at rest, so they can't see you.

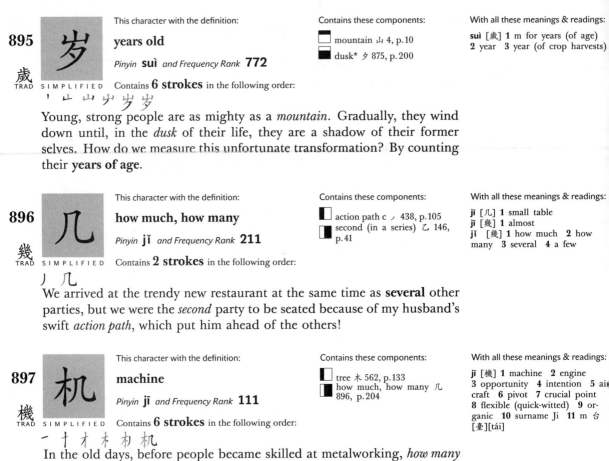

895

岁

歲
TRAD SIMPLIFIED

This character with the definition:

years old

Pinyin **suì** *and Frequency Rank* **772**

Contains **6 strokes** in the following order:

Contains these components:

☐ mountain 山 4, p.10
☐ dusk* 夕 875, p.200

With all these meanings & readings:

suì [歲] **1** m for years (of age) **2** year **3** year (of crop harvests)

Young, strong people are as mighty as a *mountain*. Gradually, they wind down until, in the *dusk* of their life, they are a shadow of their former selves. How do we measure this unfortunate transformation? By counting their **years of age**.

896

几

幾
TRAD SIMPLIFIED

This character with the definition:

how much, how many

Pinyin **jǐ** *and Frequency Rank* **211**

Contains **2 strokes** in the following order:

Contains these components:

☐ action path c ノ 438, p.105
☐ second (in a series) 乙 146, p.41

With all these meanings & readings:

jī [几] **1** small table
jī [幾] **1** almost
jǐ [幾] **1** how much **2** how many **3** several **4** a few

We arrived at the trendy new restaurant at the same time as **several** other parties, but we were the *second* party to be seated because of my husband's swift *action path*, which put him ahead of the others!

897

机

機
TRAD SIMPLIFIED

This character with the definition:

machine

Pinyin **jī** *and Frequency Rank* **111**

Contains **6 strokes** in the following order:

Contains these components:

☐ tree 木 562, p.133
☐ how much, how many 几 896, p.204

With all these meanings & readings:

jī [機] **1** machine **2** engine **3** opportunity **4** intention **5** aircraft **6** pivot **7** crucial point **8** flexible (quick-witted) **9** organic **10** surname Ji **11** m 台 [臺][tái]

In the old days, before people became skilled at metalworking, *how many trees* did it take to construct a **machine**?

898

亮

SIMP & TRAD

This character with the definition:

light, bright

Pinyin **liàng** *and Frequency Rank* **840**

Contains **9 strokes** in the following order:

Contains these components:

☐ tall 乔 (abbrev) 559, 132
☐ how much, how many 几 896, p.204

With all these meanings & readings:

liàng [亮] **1** light **2** bright

All fireworks are **bright** and colorful, but some shoot up in a straight '*tall*' line while others burst out to a sparkling ball in *several* directions.

899

沿

SIMP & TRAD

This character with the definition:

alongside

Pinyin **yán** *and Frequency Rank* **1182**

Contains **8 strokes** in the following order:

Contains these components:

☐ water r 氵 314, p.80
☐ how much, how many 几 896, p.204
☐ mouth 口 37, p.17

With all these meanings & readings:

yán [沿] **1** along **2** following (a line)
yàn [沿] **1** riverside (often with 儿[兒] erhua)

Several large stone markers, each one shaped like a big open *mouth*, were placed **alongside** the *water's* edge to alert weary travelers of the danger of high tide.

900

SIMP & TRAD

This character with the definition:

nautical vessel

Pinyin **chuán** and Frequency Rank **614**

Contains **11 strokes** in the following order:

丿 丿 丿 丹 丹 舟 舟 舟 舟 船 船

Contains these components:

■ boat 舟 822, p.189

■ how much, how many 几 896, p.204

■ mouth 口 37, p.17

With all these meanings & readings:

chuán [船] **1** a boat **2** vessel **3** ship **4** m 条[條][tiáo], 艘[sōu], 只 [隻][zhī]

An authentic **nautical vessel** is large enough to carry a small *boat* for short trips to the shore, and requires *several* crew members and a captain with a large *mouth* to shout loud orders during a storm.

901

SIMP & TRAD

This character with the definition:

commonplace

Pinyin **fán** and Frequency Rank **1013**

Contains **3 strokes** in the following order:

丿 几 凡

Contains these components:

■ how much, how many 几 896, p.204

■ dab r ﹅ 176, p.48

With all these meanings & readings:

fán [凡] **1** ordinary **2** commonplace **3** mundane **4** temporal **5** of the material world (as opposed to supernatural or immortal levels) **6** every **7** all **8** whatever **9** altogether **10** gist **11** outline **12** note of Chinese musical scale

I have *several* older sisters and my family was not wealthy so all my dresses were always 'hand-me-down's'. In order to make my prom dress look less **commonplace**, my mother sewed *dabs* of glittery sequins around the neckline.

902

訊 TRAD SIMPLIFIED

This character with the definition:

message, dispatch

Pinyin **xùn** and Frequency Rank **1238**

Contains **5 strokes** in the following order:

丶 讠 讥 讯 讯

Contains these components:

■ speech r 讠 352, p.88

■ commonplace 凡 (altered) 901, p.205

With all these meanings & readings:

xùn [訊] **1** to question **2** to ask **3** to interrogate **4** rapid **5** speedy **6** fast **7** news **8** information

The officer used **commonplace speech** in his military **dispatch** to disguise its importance from the enemy.

903

鞏 TRAD SIMPLIFIED

This character with the definition:

secure, solid

Pinyin **gǒng** and Frequency Rank **2384**

Contains **6 strokes** in the following order:

一 丆 工 刁 巩 巩

Contains these components:

■ labor, work 工 12, p.12

■ commonplace 凡 901, p.205

With all these meanings & readings:

gǒng [鞏] **1** secure **2** solid

It's hard *work* building a road. The first thing you need to do is to gather together all kinds of *commonplace* rocks and stones and lay them on the roadbed. This will create a **secure** foundation.

904

築 TRAD SIMPLIFIED

This character with the definition:

construct

Pinyin **zhù** and Frequency Rank **1130**

Contains **12 strokes** in the following order:

丿 ⺮ ⺮ ⺮ 竹 竹 竺 笁 筑 筑 筑 筑

Contains these components:

■ bamboo r ⺮ 264, p.68

■ secure, solid 巩 903, p.205

With all these meanings & readings:

zhú [筑] **1** to build **2** five-string lute **3** another word for Guiyang 贵阳[貴陽], capital of Guizhou province 贵州[貴~]
zhù [筑] **1** five-string lute or zither
zhù [築] **1** to build **2** to construct **3** to strike **4** Taiwan pr zhú

In olden times, you would **build** a house out of *bamboo* stems by anchoring and attaching them together in a *secure* manner.

905

This character with the definition:

m for flowers

Pinyin **duǒ** *and Frequency Rank* **1571**

SIMP & TRAD   Contains **6 strokes** in the following order:

Contains these components:
- how much, how many 几 896, p.204
- tree 木 562, p.133

With all these meanings & readings

duǒ [朵] **1** flower **2** earlobe **3** fig. item on both sides **4** m for flowers, clouds etc

The small child asked his mother, "*How many* flowers does that cherry blossom *tree* have?" His mother answered "*Several*." Unsatisfied, the child insisted that she tell him the exact **number of flowers** in the *tree*.

906

This character with the definition:

hide oneself

Pinyin **duǒ** *and Frequency Rank* **1644**

SIMP & TRAD   Contains **13 strokes** in the following order:

Contains these components:
- body 身 529, p.125
- m for flowers 朵 905, p.206

With all these meanings & readings

duǒ [躲] **1** to hide **2** to dodge **3** to avoid

The lush garden of my childhood home had many places for a clever child to **hide oneself**. My favorite was behind the hanging vines covered with *hundreds* of flowers—no one could see my *body* behind that 'curtain'!

907

This character with the definition:

overbearing, haughty

Pinyin **kàng** *and Frequency Rank* **3268**

SIMP & TRAD   Contains **4 strokes** in the following order:

Contains these components:
- cover r 亠 250, p.66
- how much, how many 几 896, p.204

With all these meanings & readings

kàng [亢] **1** overbearing **2** surname Kang **3** one of 28 constellations

The **overbearing** master chef lifted the *cover* of the main entree, tasted it, and smiled. *Several* of the kitchen staff sighed with relief.

908

This character with the definition:

resist, defy

Pinyin **kàng** *and Frequency Rank* **766**

SIMP & TRAD   Contains **7 strokes** in the following order:

Contains these components:
- hand r 扌 25, p.15
- overbearing, haughty 亢 907, p.206

With all these meanings & readings

kàng [抗] **1** to resist **2** to fight **3** to defy **4** anti-

The manager had become so *overbearing* that his employees organized a campaign to **defy** him and used disrespectful *hand* signals behind his back.

909

This character with the definition:

ship

Pinyin **háng** *and Frequency Rank* **773**

SIMP & TRAD   Contains **10 strokes** in the following order:

Contains these components:
- boat 舟 822, p.189
- overbearing, haughty 亢 907, p.206

With all these meanings & readings

háng [航] **1** boat **2** ship **3** cra **4** to navigate **5** to sail **6** to fl

The local fishing *boat* looked tiny as it pulled up to the luxury cruise **ship** to deliver the fresh fish that would provide the **ship**'s *haughty* passengers with gourmet meals.

Unit 39

910
虎

SIMP & TRAD

This character with the definition:

tiger

Pinyin **hǔ** *and Frequency Rank* **1083**

Contains **8 strokes** in the following order:

Contains these components:

⬜ action path c ノ 438, p.105
⬜ on 上 189, p.52
⬜ ancient ladle ヒ 124, p.36
⬜ how much, how many 几 896, p.204

With all these meanings & readings:

hǔ [虎] **1** tiger **2** m 只[隻][zhī]

In a rapid *action path*, the female **tiger** landed *on* the neck of the smallest antelope in the herd. She dragged it back to her *several* cubs; each one used its paw like an *ancient ladle* to claw 'bite-size' pieces from the antelope's flesh. • When this character is itself used as an element in other characters, the '*several; how many?*' element is often left off, so that the '**tiger**' appears in an abbreviated form (see below).

911
虛
TRAD

虚
SIMPLIFIED

This character with the definition:

empty, unoccupied

Pinyin **xū** *and Frequency Rank* **1071**

Contains **11 strokes** in the following order:

Contains these components:

⬜ tiger 虎 (abbrev) 910, 207
⬜ horned animal c (×2, altered) 卄94, p.30

With all these meanings & readings:

xū [虛] **1** devoid of content **2** void **3** false **4** empty **5** vain

Our cow was our sole source of milk and butter—until a hungry *tiger* killed it. Now our pasture is **unoccupied** by any *horned animal* and our stomachs sit **empty**.

912
殼
TRAD

壳
SIMPLIFIED

This character with the definition:

shell, housing, case

Pinyin **ké** *and Frequency Rank* **1937**

Contains **7 strokes** in the following order:

Contains these components:

⬜ knight 士 8, p.11
⬜ smooth cover r 冖 268, p.69
⬜ how much, how many 几 896, p.204

With all these meanings & readings:

ké [殼] **1** shell
qiào [殼] **1** shell **2** hard carapace **3** crust (e.g. earth's crust, etc.)

The *scholar* invented some special *coverings* for a new piece of lab equipment. *How many*? I'm not sure, but with this new tool, she can make as many **housings** herself for any of her future research needs.

913
冗

SIMP & TRAD

This character with the definition:

superfluous, redundant

Pinyin **rǒng** *and Frequency Rank* **3642**

Contains **4 strokes** in the following order:

Contains these components:

⬜ smooth cover r 冖 268, p.69
⬜ how much, how many 几 896, p.204

With all these meanings & readings:

rǒng [冗] **1** extraneous **2** redundant **3** superfluous **4** busy schedule

Instead of doing their jobs, *several* workers are gathered under the shade of the *roof*. Surely, management will make them **redundant** if they continue to stay there!

914

SIMP & TRAD

This character with the definition:

submerge, lower

Pinyin **chén** *and Frequency Rank* **747**

Contains **7 strokes** in the following order:

丶 丶 氵 氵 沪 沪 沉

Contains these components:

■ water r 氵 314, p.80
■ superfluous, redundant 冘 913, p.207

With all these meanings & readings:

chēn [沉] **1** see 黑沉沉[hēi chēn chēn]

chén [沉] **1** to submerge **2** to immerse **3** to sink **4** to keep down **5** to lower **6** to drop **7** deep **8** profound **9** heavy

When you become *redundant* to an organized crime 'family', your body is 'buried' under the *water*, where it **submerges** and becomes shark food.

915

凱
TRAD SIMPLIFIED

This character with the definition:

triumphant

Pinyin **kǎi** *and Frequency Rank* **1447**

Contains **8 strokes** in the following order:

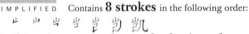
丿 屮 屮 屵 岂 岂 凯 凯

Contains these components:

■ how could it be? 岂 144, p.41
■ how much, how many 几 896, p.204

With all these meanings & readings:

kǎi [凱] **1** triumphant **2** victorious **3** chi (Greek letter Χχ)

Nothing is sweeter than a final **triumphant** victory. *How could it be* that we had to wait *several* years before our team finally won the playoffs?

916

SIMP & TRAD

This character with the definition:

flesh, muscle

Pinyin **jī** *and Frequency Rank* **1935**

Contains **6 strokes** in the following order:

丿 月 月 月 肌 肌

Contains these components:

■ meat 肉 (altered) 753, p.175
■ how much, how many 几 896, p.204

With all these meanings & readings

jī [肌] **1** flesh **2** muscle

Muscles are the kind of *meaty tissue* that enable us to perform the *several* physical tasks we do each day.

917

萬
TRAD SIMPLIFIED

This character with the definition:

ten thousand

Pinyin **wàn** *and Frequency Rank* **322**

Contains **3 strokes** in the following order:

一 丁 万

Contains these components:

□ one 一 1, p.10
■ action path c 丿 438, p.105
■ place of refuge c 𠃌 105, p.33

With all these meanings & readings

wàn [萬] **1** surname Wan **2** ten thousand **3** a great number

The enemy action was devastating. *One action* filled the *place of refuge* with **ten thousand** wounded soldiers.

918

屬
TRAD SIMPLIFIED

This character with the definition:

harsh, severe

Pinyin **lì** *and Frequency Rank* **1339**

Contains **5 strokes** in the following order:

一 厂 厂 厉 厉

Contains these components:

■ cliff r 厂 399, p.97
■ ten thousand 万 917, p.208

With all these meanings & readings

lì [厲] **1** severe **2** surname Li

The elite mountain club required every prospective member to pass a **harsh** test—to climb *ten thousand* feet to the top of a *cliff* while carrying heavy camping gear.

919

長 励
TRAD SIMPLIFIED

This character with the definition:

encourage

Pinyin **lì** *and Frequency Rank* **1468**

Contains **7 strokes** in the following order:

一 厂 尸 斤 厉 励 励

Contains these components:

■ harsh, severe 厉 918, p.208
■ strength 力 471, p.113

With all these meanings & readings:

lì [勵] **1** exhort

The best military leaders know how to **encourage** their troops to find the *strength* to survive even the most *severe* battle conditions.

920

長
TRAD SIMPLIFIED

This character with the definition:

long, length

Pinyin **cháng** *and Frequency Rank* **109**

Contains **4 strokes** in the following order:

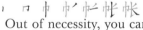

Contains these components:

▭ one 一 1, p.10
▯ scepter c ｜ (altered) 5, p.10
▭ action path c ノ 438, p.105
▭ action path c ノ (altered) 438, p.105

With all these meanings & readings:

cháng [長] **1** length **2** long **3** forever **4** always **5** constantly
zhǎng [長] **1** chief **2** head **3** elder **4** to grow **5** to develop

The vertical *scepter*, the *horizontal line*, and the two *action paths* form the right half of a compass rose (a display of the principal directions printed on a map or chart). With this device, would-be explorers are ready to travel the **length** of the earth.

921

帳
TRAD SIMPLIFIED

This character with the definition:

canopy

Pinyin **zhàng** *and Frequency Rank* **1603**

Contains **7 strokes** in the following order:

丨 冂 巾 帄 帒 帪 帐

Contains these components:

■ towel 巾 118, p.35
▯ long, length 长 920, p.209

With all these meanings & readings:

zhàng [帳] **1** covering veil **2** canopy **3** screen **4** tent **5** variant of 账 [賬][zhàng]

Out of necessity, you can make a **canopy** out of a *long towel*.

922

套
SIMP & TRAD

This character with the definition:

sheath, cover

Pinyin **tào** *and Frequency Rank* **1091**

Contains **10 strokes** in the following order:

一 ナ 大 太 本 本 查 套 套 套

Contains these components:

▭ big 大 544, p.129
■ long, length 长 (altered) 920, p.209

With all these meanings & readings:

tào [套] **1** cover **2** sheath **3** to encase **4** a case **5** to overlap **6** to interleave **7** bend (of a river or mountain range, in place names) **8** harness **9** m for sets, collections **10** tau (Greek letter Tτ)

As my grandmother used to say, every pot has a **cover**. That is, the **cover** must match the container exactly in terms of *size*, *length*, and shape.

923

張
TRAD SIMPLIFIED

This character with the definition:

expand, stretch

Pinyin **zhāng** *and Frequency Rank* **318**

Contains **7 strokes** in the following order:

フ ヲ 弓 引 弜 张 张

Contains these components:

■ bow (weapon) 弓 140, p.40
▯ long, length 长 920, p.209

With all these meanings & readings:

zhāng [張] **1** to open up **2** to spread **3** sheet of paper **4** m for flat objects, sheet **5** m for votes **6** surname Zhang

How does a *bow* manage to change its *length* without snapping? It gets **stretched** and **expanded** under the expert hands of a skillful archer.

924

涨
TRAD SIMPLIFIED

This character with the definition:

rise (water, prices)

Pinyin **zhǎng** *and Frequency Rank* **1803**

Contains these components:

■ water r 氵 314, p. 80

■ expand, stretch 张 923, p. 209

With all these meanings & readings

zhǎng [涨] **1** to rise (of prices, rivers)
zhàng [涨] **1** to swell **2** distend

Contains **10 strokes** in the following order:

` 氵 氵 汀 汀 汈 涨 涨 涨 涨

A river '*expands*' when its *water* level **rises**.

925

匆

SIMP & TRAD

This character with the definition:

hasty

Pinyin **cōng** *and Frequency Rank* **1622**

Contains these components:

■ spoon 勺 371, p. 92
■ action path c (×2) ╱ 438, p. 105

With all these meanings & readings

cōng [匆] **1** hurried **2** hasty

Contains **5 strokes** in the following order:

╱ 勹 勺 匆 匆

I was supposed to take this *spoonful* of medicine but I moved too **hastily** and the medicine streamed off the spoon's edge, in two *action paths*. • It's very tempting to mistake this character as 勿 'do not' (panel 460) which *does not* have any *dab*-like stroke. (You might even prefer this decomposition.)

926

卬

COMPONENT

This component has the meaning:

head held high c

And contains these subcomponents:

■ basket, box r ⌐ 152, p. 42
■ single ear r 卩 165, p. 46

The *box* and the *single ear* resemble a prominent pair of ears that are clearly visible when their owner **holds his head high**.

927

卯

SIMP & TRAD

This character with the definition:

early morning

Pinyin **mǎo** *and Frequency Rank* **3926**

Contains these components:

■ head held high c 卬 926, p. 210
■ action path c ╱ 438, p. 105

With all these meanings & readings

mǎo [卯] **1** mortise (slot cut into wood to receive a tenon) **2** 4th earthly branch: 5-7 a.m., 2nd solar month (6th March-4th April), year of the Rabbit

Contains **5 strokes** in the following order:

╱ ㇄ 卯 卯 卯

This character is the fourth of the so-called Earthly Branches and refers to the period between 5 and 7 AM. During that time of day, in **early morning**, *my head is held high* only by my pillow and performing any meaningful *action* is a dubious prospect.

928

留

SIMP & TRAD

This character with the definition:

retain, stay

Pinyin **liú** *and Frequency Rank* **554**

Contains these components:

■ early morning 卯 (altered) 927, p. 210
■ field 田 63, p. 23

With all these meanings & readings

liú [留] **1** leave (message) **2** to retain **3** to stay **4** to remain **5** to keep **6** to preserve

Contains **10 strokes** in the following order:

╱ ㇄ ㇆ 夗 夘 卯 留 留 留 留

To **retain** ownership of your *fields*, you must start work very *early in the morning* every day of the week for several years.

929

SIMP & TRAD

This character with the definition:

slide, glide, sneak off

Pinyin **liū** *and Frequency Rank* **1923**

Contains **13 strokes** in the following order:

Contains these components:

☐ water r 氵 314, p. 80
☐ retain, stay 留 928, p. 210

With all these meanings & readings:

liū [溜] **1** to slip away **2** to escape in stealth **3** to skate

No crops grow in the winter. Starting in January, I allow my fields to *retain* all the *water* they collect so that it can freeze and friends can **skate** and **glide** across the surface.

930

SIMP & TRAD

This character with the definition:

to chat

Pinyin **liáo** *and Frequency Rank* **1932**

Contains **11 strokes** in the following order:

Contains these components:

☐ ear 耳 76, p. 26
☐ early morning 卯 927, p. 210

With all these meanings & readings:

liáo [聊] **1** to chat **2** to have a chat **3** to kill time

You're all *ears* when you just get going in the *early morning*; that's the best time to **chat** with you.

931

SIMP & TRAD

This character with the definition:

willow

Pinyin **liǔ** *and Frequency Rank* **1557**

Contains **9 strokes** in the following order:

Contains these components:

☐ tree 木 562, p. 133
☐ early morning 卯 927, p. 210

With all these meanings & readings:

liǔ [柳] **1** willow **2** surname Liu

The **willow** was a *tree* thought to bloom in the *early morning*.

932

SIMP & TRAD

This character with the definition:

hold your head high

Pinyin **áng** *and Frequency Rank* **1952**

Contains **8 strokes** in the following order:

Contains these components:

☐ day, sun 日 64, p. 24
☐ head held high c 卬 926, p. 210

With all these meanings & readings:

áng [昂] **1** to lift **2** to raise **3** to raise one's head **4** high **5** high spirits **6** soaring **7** expensive

When you **hold your head high**, you position yourself closer to the *sun*.

933

SIMP & TRAD

This character with the definition:

restrain, restrict

Pinyin **yì** *and Frequency Rank* **1748**

Contains **7 strokes** in the following order:

Contains these components:

☐ hand r 扌 25, p. 15
☐ head held high c 卬 926, p. 210

With all these meanings & readings:

yì [抑] **1** to restrain **2** to restrict **3** to keep down **4** or

Could the *hand* in his face, forcing him to *hold his head high*, suggest that someone's trying to bully him? It looks like it—his movements are **restricted**.

934

This component has the meaning:

bone r

COMPONENT

Since brush strokes cannot produce round figures, you need to imagine these elements as roundish objects—in fact, as stacked vertebrae in a spine with the skull resting on top and a few openings in each.

Flashcards *Interlude 3*

Can you rely on narratives like ours to learn over two thousand character meanings? You can certainly 'learn' them, but you'll need the assistance of other, more traditional techniques for review and practice. Review is important to make visual recognition the automatic process it needs to be when you read Chinese in traditional settings such as language courses. To this end, we provide many review materials on our website to download for **free**. Additional interludes will describe these resources fully. Here, we discuss *flashcards*, and what technique could be more tried-and-true? There's a lot of power left in this technique when you hitch this low-tech horse (flashcard decks) to a high-tech cart (computer, cell phone, or music player).

In the past, you might have worked your way through a deck of paper flashcards, separating the cards into two piles—the facts you know from facts you don't. But now suppose that the decks are electronic in form, and managed by a computer. Suppose further that for facts you're sure of, you can specify your degree of assuredness. And perhaps the computer uses well-defined algorithms to decide when you will review the cards you're not quite sure of. Suddenly, learning with flashcards becomes a sophisticated matter little dreamed of when, in the fifth grade, you used index cards to learn state capitals!

The flashcards that you can download for free work with a shareware program called Anki, developed by Damien Elmes. Various versions of Anki work on Linux, Macintosh, and PC boxes; smartphones; flash-drives; portable music players; and, by now, who-knows-what-other devices. Moreover, there's a large user community and forum to help resolve problems and to provide assistance. You can find the Anki program at

`www.ankisrs.net`.

(If the site has changed by the time you read this, use your favorite search engine to search for 'Anki + srs'.) The program exploits the concept of *spaced repetition* to present material back to you in the best way and according to the most efficient schedule. (The 'srs' above stands for 'spaced repetition system'.)

We contend that it is not enough to recognize the meaning of a character you see—you must be able to recreate the character in your mind when given its meaning and pronunciation. (Without the pinyin pronunciation, there are many characters with such close definitions that it would otherwise be difficult to distinguish between them.) Flashcards for each character come in pairs—one which presents the character and expects you to supply the meaning and pronunciation, and one which shows the reverse. When recreating the character, you can use the stroke order diagrams in the text to 'draw' them with one finger, say, on the palm of your other hand. (That's why we provide these diagrams!) The cards in the electronic decks are prepared in the order they appear in the book, but you can ask that Anki show them to you in random order, which I recommend.

When given a card, you provide the answer to yourself, and signal that you're ready for the next card by rating your answer on ease of recall, using a sliding scale. The scale runs from 1 ('I don't know')—to 4 ('trivially easy') although the developer of Anki phrases these category names more diplomatically. Regardless of your actual response, Anki uses a sophisticated method (based on a spaced repetition method) to decide when you will be presented with this card again.

This electronic method confers several advantages to you, the learner. You can do away with untidy piles of small cards that inevitably wind up on the floor. Most important, you can do your reviewing anywhere—at home, on the bus, while waiting to pay on the supermarket checkout line, etc. In the Anki system, your cards are automatically uploaded to the master Anki server (somewhere in Japan), and all platforms accessed by you use the same 'deck' of cards. Of course, you will need internet access for your reviewing.

To get started, download and install the Anki program.

Then, proceed to www.EZChinesey.com and download the file with a name like **EZCflashcardssimp.anki** from the 'download' section. Information on the Anki website helps you install this file properly (but it's easy, at least on my Mac; simply place the Anki deck in a directory or folder that Anki knows to read).

Anki is such a powerful tool that I strongly advise taking several days (at least!) to get familiar with it.

The current author *does* use Anki—I rely on it, actually—but I tweak this procedure slightly because I like to study on a unit-by-unit basis. Suppose I am learning a new unit's-worth of characters. There is a main deck of cards, in which this unit's cards are *suspended* (Anki-speak for "ignore them all until you say otherwise"). Anki lets me create a special *cram* deck with all the cards for this current unit, which I use to practice for a few days. Go to ankisrs.net, click on the links

```
Documentation->User Manual->The Rest->Cramming For Tests
```

and follow the instructions.

When I feel comfortable with this batch, I release them back into the main deck, delete the cram deck, and move on to the next unit. (You'll want to check Anki's documentation for further details.) I can never plead lack of time or access—Anki works on my Android phone and I can review anywhere and anytime (as long as there is cell phone reception).

Your own method may be different from this, but I believe the important thing is consistency coupled with daily practice. If you come up with a new study method that is different and better, please let us know!

Although Anki is free for you to use, its developer welcomes donations to help support this work and its continuing development. We at EZChinesey have contributed, and we encourage you to do so as well.

Unit 40

935

SIMP & TRAD

This character with the definition:

bone

Pinyin **gǔ** *and Frequency Rank* **1036**

Contains these components:

☐ bone r 咼 (altered) 934, p. 212

■ meat 肉 (altered) 753, p. 175

With all these meanings & readings:

gǔ ［骨］ **1** bone **2** Taiwan pr **gū**

Contains **9 strokes** in the following order:

This character represents a bare **bone**, but also *bones* with the *meaty* muscles and tendons still attached.

936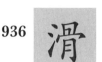

SIMP & TRAD

This character with the definition:

slippery, smooth, cunning

Pinyin **huá** *and Frequency Rank* **1480**

Contains these components:

▌ water r 氵 314, p. 80

■ bone 骨 935, p. 215

With all these meanings & readings:

gǔ ［滑］ **1** comical
huá ［滑］ **1** comical **2** cunning **3** slippery **4** smooth **5** surname Hua

Contains **12 strokes** in the following order:

A dry *bone* is very rough, but if you place it in *water*, its texture will feel **smooth** and **slippery**.

937

This component has the meaning:

wound c

COMPONENT

And contains these subcomponents:

☐ earth, soil 土 9, p. 11

▌ halberd 戈 650, p. 154

In this case, the small criss-cross of lines in the upper left of this component doesn't represent the *earth* but rather the lines of a nasty **wound** inflicted by a *halberd*-wielding soldier.

938

This component has the meaning:

surprised man c

COMPONENT

And contains these subcomponents:

☐ man (spiffy) 夫 (altered) 718, p. 168

This component differs from the character 夫, '*man (spiffy)*' with the presence of a small extra vertical stroke off the upper topknot. If the horizontals represent colorful strings by which this traditional **man** binds up his hair, then this additional stroke shows him 'letting his hair down' after an unexpected **surprise** startles him.

939

SIMP & TRAD

This character with the definition:

be short of, lack

Pinyin **quē** *and Frequency Rank* **875**

Contains these components:

▌ archaeological vessel 缶 181, p. 49

▌ surprised man c 夬 938, p. 215

With all these meanings & readings:

quē ［缺］ **1** deficiency **2** lack **3** scarce **4** vacant post **5** to run short of

Contains **10 strokes** in the following order:

The visiting scientist was a very *surprised man*; he never expected to encounter such primitive conditions at the excavation site. **Lacking** supplies, the team sat around and drank their coffee out of priceless *archaeological vessels*.

940

决
TRAD SIMPLIFIED

This character with the definition:

decide

Pinyin **jué** *and Frequency Rank* **273**

Contains **6 strokes** in the following order:

Contains these components:

■ ice r 冫 348, p. 87

▯ surprised man c 夬 938, p. 215

With all these meanings & readings:

jué [决] **1** breach (a dike) **2** to decide **3** to determine

` 冫 冫 冫 冫 决

The young *man* was always *surprised* by how hurtful his colleagues' mocking humor was. Still, he **decided** to act like he had *ice* in his veins, so as not to be bothered by it.

941

块
TRAD SIMPLIFIED

This character with the definition:

lump

Pinyin **kuài** *and Frequency Rank* **793**

Contains **7 strokes** in the following order:

Contains these components:

■ earth, soil 土 9, p. 11

▯ surprised man c 夬 938, p. 215

With all these meanings & readings:

kuài [塊] **1** lump (of earth) **2** chunk **3** piece **4** m for piece of cloth, cake, soap etc **5** colloquial word for yuan (or other unit of currency such as Hong Kong or US dollar etc), usually as 块钱[塊錢]

一 十 土 土 圵 圵 块

While taking a walk on some unexplored *soil*, a *surprised man* trips over an unexpected clod of dirt and lands on top of a **lump** of soil.

942

COMPONENT

This component has the meaning:

hills r

When you see this component to the left of a character (see below), it represents a range of **small hills**. To see the **hills**, imagine rotating this radical counter-clockwise to the left (so the vertical spine becomes horizontal) so that the soft mounds of two small **hills** are visible.

943

阻
SIMP & TRAD

This character with the definition:

block, impede

Pinyin **zǔ** *and Frequency Rank* **1175**

Contains **7 strokes** in the following order:

Contains these components:

■ hills r 阝 942, p. 216

▯ moreover 且 84, p. 28

With all these meanings & readings:

zǔ [阻] **1** to hinder **2** to block **3** to obstruct

乛 阝 阝 阝 阳 阳 阻

The surrounding *hills* **impede** travel to and from our valley. *Moreover*, they **block** out the sunlight!

944

院
SIMP & TRAD

This character with the definition:

institution

Pinyin **yuàn** *and Frequency Rank* **338**

Contains **9 strokes** in the following order:

Contains these components:

■ hills r 阝 942, p. 216

▯ to complete, finish 完 297, p. 76

With all these meanings & readings:

yuàn [院] **1** courtyard **2** institution **3** m 个[個][gè]

乛 阝 阝 阝 阝 阮 阮 院 院

I'm confined to this **institution** until my term is *complete*. In the meantime, I will continue gaze longingly through the windows at the beautiful *hills*.

945 阿

SIMP & TRAD

This character with the definition:

particle before names

Pinyin **ā** *and Frequency Rank* **471**

Contains **7 strokes** in the following order:

阝 丆 阝 阽 阿 阿 阿

Contains these components:

hills r 阝 942, p. 216

can, may 可 60, p. 23

ā [阿] **1** initial particle **2** familiar prefix to name such as 阿扁 for Chen Shui-Bian 陈水扁 [陳~~][chén shuǐ biǎn] or Dad 阿爹[ā diē] **3** used as phonetic A in transliteration **4** abbr for Afghanistan 阿富汗
à [阿] **1** (phonetic character)
a [阿] **1** (final particle expressing approval or doubt) **2** (interjection equivalent to punctuating sentence with "you see")
ē [阿] **1** flatter

Chinese speakers use this particle to indicate familiarity or to indicate some kind of relationship, often familial (阿大 'ā dà', the eldest; 阿哥 'ā gē', elder brother). • When I return home after a trip, the sight of the distant *hills* near my home *can* fill me with warm feelings of **familiarity**.

946 啊

SIMP & TRAD

This character with the definition:

phrase suffix

Pinyin **a** *and Frequency Rank* **753**

Contains **10 strokes** in the following order:

丨 冂 口 口阝 叮 呵 呀 唡 啁 啊

Contains these components:

mouth 口 37, p. 17

particle before names 阿 945, p. 217

ā [啊] **1** interjection of surprise **2** Ah! **3** Oh!
á [啊] **1** interjection expressing doubt or requiring answer **2** Eh? **3** what? **4** to show realization **5** to stress
ǎ [啊] **1** interjection of surprise or doubt **2** Eh? **3** My! **4** what's up?
à [啊] **1** interjection or grunt of agreement **2** uhm **3** Ah, OK **4** expression of recognition **5** Oh, it's you!
a [啊] **1** modal particle ending sentence, showing affirmation, approval, or consent

Chinese scribes often use the *mouth* radical to draw interjections and particles, perhaps to signify an exhalation of breath on an occasion that's slightly out of the ordinary. 啊 has many alternate pronunciations, all of which, including the main one treated here, refer to interjections (exclamations).

947 障

SIMP & TRAD

This character with the definition:

obstruct, hinder

Pinyin **zhàng** *and Frequency Rank* **1237**

Contains **13 strokes** in the following order:

阝 阝 阝 阹 阹 阹 阹 陪 陪 障 障 障 障

Contains these components:

hills r 阝 942, p. 216

chapter, section 章 691, p. 162

With all these meanings & readings:

zhàng [障] **1** to block **2** to hinder **3** to obstruct

I go to the *hills* to read a *chapter* or two of my favorite book; sometimes, I get so caught up in the story that it **hinders** my speedy return to work.

948 阳

陽 TRAD   SIMPLIFIED

This character with the definition:

sun

Pinyin **yáng** *and Frequency Rank* **650**

Contains **5 strokes** in the following order:

阝 阝 阳 阳 阳

Contains these components:

hills r 阝 942, p. 216

day, sun 日 64, p. 24

With all these meanings & readings:

yáng [陽] **1** positive (electric.) **2** sun **3** male principle (Taoism) **4** Yang, opposite: 阴 [陰][yin] ⊠

The **sun** peeks overs the *hills* at break of *day*.

949 防

SIMP & TRAD

This character with the definition:

guard, defend against

Pinyin **fáng** *and Frequency Rank* **548**

Contains **6 strokes** in the following order:

阝 阝 阝 阽 防 防

Contains these components:

hills r 阝 942, p. 216

square; direction 方 490, p. 117

With all these meanings & readings:

fáng [防] **1** to protect **2** to defend **3** to guard (against)

The *hills* located on the north side of the city provide a natural **guard** to **defend against** the city's enemies—who live in the *direction* to the north, on the far side of the protective *hills*.

950

This character with the definition:

pitfall, trap

Pinyin **xiàn** *and Frequency Rank* **1262**

SIMP & TRAD Contains **10 strokes** in the following order:

阝 阝 阝 阝⁄ 阝⁊ 阝⁊ 阝⁊ 阝⁊ 阝⁊ 陷

Contains these components:

■ hills r 阝 942, p. 216
■ man 人 (altered) 537, p. 127
■ mortar 臼 373, p. 92

With all these meanings & reading

xiàn [陷] **1** pitfall **2** trap **3** t
get stuck **4** to sink **5** to cave
6 to frame (false charge) **7** to
capture (a city in battle) **8** to
fall (to the enemy) **9** defect

After heavy rains washed away part of the popular hiking trail in the nearby *hills*, the skilled work*men* in our town filled the dangerous **pitfalls** with *mortar*.

951

隊 TRAD SIMPLIFIED

This character with the definition:

team

Pinyin **duì** *and Frequency Rank* **268**

Contains **4 strokes** in the following order:

阝 阝 阝 队

Contains these components:

■ hills r 阝 942, p. 216
■ man 人 537, p. 127

With all these meanings & reading

duì [隊] **1** squadron **2** team
3 group **4** m 个[個][gè]

The **team** is lined up for inspection. I forgot my glasses though, so when I look at the *men* on the team, their features appear indistinct and their heads look like a rolling row of *hills*.

952

薩 TRAD SIMPLIFIED

This character with the definition:

Buddha, kind-hearted person

Pinyin **sà** *and Frequency Rank* **1046**

Contains **11 strokes** in the following order:

一 十 艹 艹 萨 萨 萨 萨 萨 萨 萨

Contains these components:

■ grass r 艹 87, p. 29
■ hills r 阝 942, p. 216
■ produce, yield 产 702, p. 164

With all these meanings & reading

Sà [薩] **1** Bodhisattva **2** surna
Sa

Many ancient myths about the *birth* of **Buddha** and other divinities were created on *grass*-covered *hills*.

953

陸 TRAD SIMPLIFIED

This character with the definition:

land, continent

Pinyin **lù** *and Frequency Rank* **675**

Contains **7 strokes** in the following order:

阝 阝 阝⁻ 阝二 阡 陆 陆

Contains these components:

■ hills r 阝 942, p. 216
■ earth, soil 土 9, p. 11
■ mountain 山 4, p. 10

With all these meanings & reading

liù [陸] **1** six (banker's anti-fra
numeral)
lù [陸] **1** surname Lu **2** shore
3 land **4** continent

How might we describe a **continent**? By the presence of *hills*, *mountains*, and other types of *earth*.

954

SIMP & TRAD

This character with the definition:

pottery

Pinyin **táo** *and Frequency Rank* **1601**

Contains **10 strokes** in the following order:

阝 阝 阝⁄ 匋 匋 陶 陶 陶 陶

Contains these components:

■ hills r 阝 942, p. 216
■ wrap r 勹 364, p. 90
■ archaeological vessel 缶 181, p. 49

With all these meanings & reading

táo [陶] **1** pottery **2** pleased
3 surname Tao

Out in the *hills* beyond town, the archaeologists dug deep and found some old *wrapped pots* that appear to be some of the most ancient forms of **pottery** ever discovered.

955

This component has the meaning:

town r

COMPONENT

This component appears identical to 'hills' of panel 942 (阝), except that that element always appears on a character's left, whereas this one always appears on a character's right (see below for a few of many examples). On a character's right, this component represents the skyline of a **town**.
• How can we distinguish between these two variants? When alphabetized, 'hills' appears to the left of **town** and **town** appears to the right of 'hills'. The element on a character's left represents 'hills'; its sibling on the right depicts a **town**.

956

SIMP & TRAD

This character with the definition:

nation state

Pinyin **bāng** *and Frequency Rank* **1363**

Contains **6 strokes** in the following order:

一 二 三 丰 邦 邦

Contains these components:

■ plentiful 丰 (altered) 16, p. 13
□ town r 阝 955, p. 219

With all these meanings & readings:

bāng [邦] **1** a state **2** country or nation

Prosperous **nations** are formed from confederations of *towns* with thriving economies and *plentiful* goods for sale, all of which bode well for their future.

957

幫

TRAD SIMPLIFIED

This character with the definition:

help

Pinyin **bāng** *and Frequency Rank* **769**

Contains **9 strokes** in the following order:

一 二 三 丰 邦 邦 邦 帮 帮

Contains these components:

□ nation state 邦 956, p. 219
■ towel 巾 118, p. 35

With all these meanings & readings:

bāng [幫] **1** to help **2** to assist **3** to support **4** for sb (i.e. as a help) **5** hired (as worker) **6** side (of pail, boat etc) **7** outer layer **8** group **9** gang **10** clique **11** party **12** secret society

I lost track of time right before an important dinner party! When the doorbell rang, I was just getting out of the shower and wrapped in nothing but a *towel*. What a *state* I was in and boy, did I need **help** that night!

958

郵

TRAD SIMPLIFIED

This character with the definition:

post, mail

Pinyin **yóu** *and Frequency Rank* **1652**

Contains **7 strokes** in the following order:

丿 冂 日 由 由 由阝 邮

Contains these components:

■ reason, by means of 由 58, p. 22
□ town r 阝 955, p. 219

With all these meanings & readings:

yóu [郵] **1** post (office) **2** mail

The central **post** office is in mid-*town*. I'll stop in quickly to buy some stamps, which will *allow me* to send out some important mail.

959

SIMP & TRAD

This character with the definition:

s-end: interrogation

Pinyin **yé** *and Frequency Rank* **1174**

Contains **8 strokes** in the following order:

一 丆 丌 爪 月 耳 耵 耶

Contains these components:

■ ear 耳 76, p. 26
□ town r 阝 955, p. 219

With all these meanings & readings:

yē [耶] **1** (phonetic ye)
yé [耶] **1** interrogative particle (classical)

Things in the *town* are so noisy that I did not *hear* your question. I only caught your tone of voice, which seemed to **signal interrogation**.

Unit 41

960 This character with the definition:

evil, odd

Pinyin **xié** *and Frequency Rank* **1539**

SIMP & TRAD   Contains **6 strokes** in the following order:

一 二 千 牙 牙 邪

Contains these components:

  ☐ tooth* 牙 450, p.108
  ☐ town r ⻏ 955, p.219

With all these meanings & readings:

xié [邪] **1** demonic **2** iniquitou **3** nefarious **4** evil **5** unhealthy influences that cause disease (C nese medicine)

From afar, the jagged profiles of *towns* can resemble a mouth full of uneven and rotten *teeth*, and are frequently used as metaphors for **evil** and depravity.

---

961 This character with the definition:

all

Pinyin **dōu** *and Frequency Rank* **68**

SIMP & TRAD   Contains **10 strokes** in the following order:

一 十 土 耂 耂 者 者 者 者 都

Contains these components:

  ☐ -er 者 456, p.109
  ☐ town r ⻏ 955, p.219

With all these meanings & readings:

dōu [都] **1** all, both **2** entirely (due to) each **3** even **4** alread dū [都] **1** capital city **2** metropo lis **3** surname Du

Large *towns* and cities are known for attracting **all** kinds of talented people who are *able to do* **all** kinds of creative things.

---

962 This character with the definition:

outer city wall

Pinyin **guō** *and Frequency Rank* **1813**

SIMP & TRAD   Contains **10 strokes** in the following order:

丶 亠 亠 宁 宁 宁 亨 享 享 郭

Contains these components:

  ☐ enjoy 享 262, p.68
  ☐ town r ⻏ 955, p.219

With all these meanings & readings:

guō [郭] **1** surname Guo guō [郭] **1** outer city wall

We *enjoyed* our visit to Europe. Our favorite activity was seeing the remains of the **outer city wall** in every medieval *town* that we visited.

---

963 This component has the meaning:

private r

COMPONENT

This sloped profile resembles a rather prominent nose—and reminds people that no one likes strangers intruding into their **private** business. • This component is frequently used to represent a **snobbish person** or **busybody**, or sometimes just a **nose**. Also, it's often altered so that it appears upside-down.

---

964 This character with the definition:

selfish, personal, private

Pinyin **sī** *and Frequency Rank* **1023**

SIMP & TRAD   Contains **7 strokes** in the following order:

丿 二 千 禾 禾 私 私

Contains these components:

  ☐ rice, grain (crop) 禾 593, p.140
  ☐ private r 厶 963, p.220

With all these meanings & readings:

sī [私] **1** personal **2** private r **3** selfish

Since I'm known as a very **personal** and **private** person, it goes 'against the *grain*' whenever good friends try to stick their *noses* into my business.

965

瓜

SIMP & TRAD

This character with the definition:

melon

Pinyin **guā** *and Frequency Rank* **1827**

Contains **5 strokes** in the following order:

Contains these components:

cliff r 厂 399, p. 97
private r 厶 963, p. 220
mineshaft c 乚 122, p. 36

With all these meanings & readings:

guā [瓜] **1** melon **2** gourd **3** squash

一 厂 爪 瓜 瓜

Inside all of us, there resides a little boy who would like nothing more than to take a **melon**, retreat to some *private* place, and hurl the fruit off a *cliff* or down a *mineshaft* just for the fun of it!

966

孤

SIMP & TRAD

This character with the definition:

solitary, isolated

Pinyin **gū** *and Frequency Rank* **1334**

Contains **8 strokes** in the following order:

Contains these components:

son, child 子 24, p. 15
melon 瓜 965, p. 221

With all these meanings & readings:

gū [孤] **1** lone **2** lonely

一 了 子 孑 矛 孤 孤 孤

Because the *child* had misbehaved, his parents punished him by keeping him **isolated** on the back porch, with no one to talk to and only a *melon* to eat.

967

雲
云

TRAD SIMPLIFIED

This character with the definition:

say

Pinyin **yún** *and Frequency Rank* **692**

Contains **4 strokes** in the following order:

Contains these components:

two 二 2, p. 10
private r 厶 963, p. 220

With all these meanings & readings:

yún [云] **1** (classical) to say
yún [雲] **1** abbr for Yunnan 云南 [雲~] province in southwest China **2** surname Yun
yún [雲] **1** cloud **2** m 朵[duǒ]

一 二 云 云

The words that *two* people **say** to each other should be considered *private*.

968

層
层

TRAD SIMPLIFIED

This character with the definition:

layer, story, floor

Pinyin **céng** *and Frequency Rank* **699**

Contains **7 strokes** in the following order:

Contains these components:

corpse 尸 499, p. 119
say 云 967, p. 221

With all these meanings & readings:

céng [層] **1** layer **2** stratum **3** laminated **4** floor (of a building) **5** storey **6** m for layers **7** repeated **8** sheaf (math.)

一 コ 尸 尸 尼 层 层

When I *say* nice things about a *corpse*, the mourners seem to enjoy the **story**.

969

會
会

TRAD SIMPLIFIED

This character with the definition:

assemble, meet

Pinyin **huì** *and Frequency Rank* **29**

Contains **6 strokes** in the following order:

Contains these components:

man 人 537, p. 127
say 云 967, p. 221

With all these meanings & readings:

huì [會] **1** can **2** be possible **3** be able to **4** will **5** be likely to **6** be sure to **7** to assemble **8** to meet **9** to gather **10** to see **11** union **12** group **13** association **14** m 个[個][gè]
kuài [會] **1** to balance an account **2** accountancy **3** accounting

丿 人 人 仝 会 会

A **meeting** is an occasion for *men* to get together and *say* things to one another.

970

壇
TRAD

SIMPLIFIED

This character with the definition:

altar

Pinyin **tán** *and Frequency Rank* **1806**

Contains **7 strokes** in the following order:

一 十 土 扩 圹 坛 坛

Contains these components:

■ earth, soil 土 9, p.11

▨ say 云 967, p.221

With all these meanings & reading

tán [壇] **1** altar

An **altar** is a place on the *earth* where priests *say* special prayers and incantations.

971

動
TRAD

SIMPLIFIED

This character with the definition:

move

Pinyin **dòng** *and Frequency Rank* **73**

Contains **6 strokes** in the following order:

一 二 云 云 动 动

Contains these components:

▨ say 云 967, p.221

▨ strength 力 471, p.113

With all these meanings & reading

dòng [動] **1** to use **2** to act **3** to move **4** to change **5** abl for verb 动词 [動詞][dòng cí]

If you possess the inner *strength* to *say* things that are most important to you, your friends will find it **moving**.

972

SIMP & TRAD

This character with the definition:

go

Pinyin **qù** *and Frequency Rank* **64**

Contains **5 strokes** in the following order:

一 十 土 去 去

Contains these components:

▨ earth, soil 土 9, p.11

▨ private r 厶 963, p.220

With all these meanings & reading

qù [去] **1** to go **2** to leave **3** remove **4** see also 去声 [~聲][c shēng]

One good example of "**going**" is death—departure from this *earth*. For that's when you will end up in a *private* place within the *earth*.

973

法
SIMP & TRAD

This character with the definition:

method

Pinyin **fǎ** *and Frequency Rank* **65**

Contains **8 strokes** in the following order:

丶 丶 氵 氵 汁 注 法 法

Contains these components:

▨ water r 氵 314, p.80

▨ go 去 972, p.222

With all these meanings & reading

fǎ [法] **1** law **2** method **3** w **4** Buddhist teaching **5** Legalis **6** abbr for France

Developing **methods** for converting the motion of *water* into electrical energy that 'makes things *go*' marks a significant milestone in the history of mankind.

974

劫
SIMP & TRAD

This character with the definition:

rob, plunder

Pinyin **jié** *and Frequency Rank* **1825**

Contains **7 strokes** in the following order:

一 十 土 去 去 劫 劫

Contains these components:

▨ go 去 972, p.222

▨ strength 力 471, p.113

With all these meanings & reading

jié [劫] **1** to rob **2** to plunder **3** to seize by force **4** to coerce **5** calamity **6** abbr for kalpa 劫波 [jié bō]

When undisciplined soldiers *go* into villages, they often abuse their position and *strength* to **rob** and **plunder**.

975

丢

丢
TRAD SIMPLIFIED

This character with the definition:

lose, misplace

Pinyin **diū** *and Frequency Rank* **1639**

Contains **6 strokes** in the following order:

一 二 千 壬 丢 丢

Contains these components:

☐ dab r ﹑ 176, p.48

■ go 去 972, p.222

With all these meanings & readings:

diū [丢] **1** to lose **2** to put aside **3** to throw

We **lose** things, even *little bits* of pieces which somehow *go* astray.

976

却

卻
TRAD SIMPLIFIED

This character with the definition:

step back, retreat

Pinyin **què** *and Frequency Rank* **287**

Contains **7 strokes** in the following order:

一 十 土 去 去 却 却

Contains these components:

■ go 去 972, p.222

☐ single ear r 卩 165, p.46

With all these meanings & readings:

què [卻] **1** but **2** yet **3** however **4** while **5** to go back **6** to decline **7** to retreat **8** nevertheless **9** even though

Late at night, while I was *going* to my campsite, a strange animal bit my *single ear*. I was so startled that I immediately **stepped back**.

977

脚

腳
TRAD SIMPLIFIED

This character with the definition:

foot*

Pinyin **jiǎo** *and Frequency Rank* **790**

Contains **11 strokes** in the following order:

丿 几 月 月 肝 肚 胪 肤 脚 脚

Contains these components:

☐ meat 肉 (altered) 753, p.175

☐ step back, retreat 却 976, p.223

With all these meanings & readings:

jiǎo [脚] **1** foot **2** leg **3** base **4** kick **5** m 双[雙][shuāng], 只 [隻][zhī]

jué [脚] **1** role

The *body part* that soldiers value most during a *retreat* is the **foot**.

978

罢

罷
TRAD SIMPLIFIED

This character with the definition:

stop, cease

Pinyin **bà** *and Frequency Rank* **1305**

Contains **10 strokes** in the following order:

丿 冂 爫 罒 四 罒 罒 甲 罢 罢

Contains these components:

☐ net r 罒 100, p.32

■ go 去 972, p.222

With all these meanings & readings:

bà [罷] **1** to stop **2** cease **3** dismiss **4** suspend **5** to quit **6** to finish

ba [罷] **1** (final particle, same as 吧)

The *net* that some hooligans threw over my head as I was *going* home made me **stop** dead in my tracks.

979

摆

擺
TRAD SIMPLIFIED

This character with the definition:

place, set in order

Pinyin **bǎi** *and Frequency Rank* **1158**

Contains **13 strokes** in the following order:

一 十 扌 扌 扣 押 扟 押 押 挥 捏 摆 摆

Contains these components:

☐ hand r 扌 25, p.15

☐ stop, cease 罢 978, p.223

With all these meanings & readings:

bǎi [擺] **1** to arrange **2** to exhibit **3** to move to and fro **4** a pendulum

To complete a jigsaw puzzle, use your *hand* to **place** all the pieces where they belong; make sure the pieces are **set in** their proper **order** and *stop* only when they're all in **place**.

980

This character with the definition:

to, until

Pinyin **zhì** *and Frequency Rank* **267**

SIMP & TRAD   Contains **6 strokes** in the following order:

一 丁 工 云 至 至

Contains these components:

☐ one 一 1, p.10
☐ private r ㄙ 963, p.220
■ earth, soil 土 9, p.11

With all these meanings & reading

zhì [至] 1 arrive 2 most 3 t
4 until

One busybody tripped and fell **to** the *ground* as he hurried **to** share some '*dirt*' with his friend. • Beginners could be forgiven for confusing the character 去 (panel 972) with the current character 至. As a memory aid, focus on the bottom of the character. For 至, soil is something we till—sounds like 'until'. For 去, remember that 'private r' resembles someone's nose and use that to recall the foolish rhyme 'the nose goes'.

981

This character with the definition:

arrive

Pinyin **dào** *and Frequency Rank* **22**

SIMP & TRAD   Contains **8 strokes** in the following order:

一 工 工 云 至 至 到 到

Contains these components:

■ to, until 至 980, p.224
☐ knife r 刂 169, p.46

With all these meanings & reading

dào [到] 1 to (a place) 2 unt
(a time) 3 up to 4 to go 5
arrive

I'm really nervous about **arriving** at the office on time for a crucial job interview. My emotions will be on a *knife's* edge *until* I finally **arrive** there.

982

This character with the definition:

room*

Pinyin **shì** *and Frequency Rank* **708**

SIMP & TRAD   Contains **9 strokes** in the following order:

丶 丶 宀 宀 宕 宏 空 室 室

Contains these components:

☐ roof r 宀 271, p.70
■ to, until 至 980, p.224

With all these meanings & reading

shì [室] 1 room 2 m 个[個][g

I do not really feel at home and safe *until* I am under my own *roof* and in my own **room** .

983

This character with the definition:

house*

Pinyin **wū** *and Frequency Rank* **863**

SIMP & TRAD   Contains **9 strokes** in the following order:

一 コ 尸 尸 屋 层 屋 屋 屋

Contains these components:

☐ corpse 尸 499, p.119
■ to, until 至 980, p.224

With all these meanings & reading

wū [屋] 1 house 2 room 3 r
间[間][jiān], 个[個][gè]

Until recently, most people often lived in the same **house** their whole life—from the moment they were born *until* after they became a *corpse*.

984

This character with the definition:

hold tight (in hand)

Pinyin **wò** *and Frequency Rank* **1032**

SIMP & TRAD   Contains **12 strokes** in the following order:

一 十 才 扌 扌 护 护 护 捏 捏 握 握

Contains these components:

■ hand r 扌 25, p.15
☐ house* 屋 983, p.224

With all these meanings & reading

wò [握] 1 shake hands 2 to
hold 3 to grasp

As I left my *house* to go to work, I discovered that my front steps were coated with ice. To avoid slipping, I had used my *hand* to **hold tight** onto the railing until I made it to the bottom step.

Unit 42

985

This character with the definition:

bestow, award

Pinyin **yǔ** *and Frequency Rank* **925**

SIMP & TRAD Contains **4 strokes** in the following order:

フ マ 予 予

Contains these components:

■ private r ㄙ (altered) 963, p.220

■ fourth (in a series) 丁 19, p.13

With all these meanings & readings:

yú [予] **1** I (used by emperor) **2** me **3** variant of 余[餘], surplus

yǔ [予] **1** to give

Focus on the appearance of the entire character. The bottom '*fourth*' element resembles a gloved fist or some other blunt instrument which has rammed into a man's *nose* with such force that the scribes drew the *nose* upside-down. The attacker **bestowed** upon his victim a serious health problem.

986

This character with the definition:

open country

Pinyin **yě** *and Frequency Rank* **845**

SIMP & TRAD Contains **11 strokes** in the following order:

丶 口 日 日 甲 里 里 野 野 野 野

Contains these components:

■ neighborhood 里 40, p.18

■ bestow, award 予 985, p.225

With all these meanings & readings:

yě [野] **1** field **2** plain **3** open space **4** limit **5** boundary **6** rude **7** wild

The *neighborhood* banded together to *award* a prize to a troublesome teen: a one-way ticket to a faraway **open country**!

987

This character with the definition:

relax

Pinyin **shū** *and Frequency Rank* **1459**

SIMP & TRAD Contains **12 strokes** in the following order:

ノ 人 ト 企 全 余 舍 舍 舍 舍 舒 舒 舒

Contains these components:

■ dormitory 舍 773, p.179

■ bestow, award 予 985, p.225

With all these meanings & readings:

shū [舒] **1** to relax **2** surname Shu

I was so excited about my academic *award* that I needed to return to my *dormitory* to **relax**.

988

This character with the definition:

order, sequence

Pinyin **xù** *and Frequency Rank* **836**

SIMP & TRAD Contains **7 strokes** in the following order:

丶 二 广 广 庁 庁 序

Contains these components:

□ shelter r 广 427, p.103

■ bestow, award 予 985, p.225

With all these meanings & readings:

xù [序] **1** order **2** sequence **3** preface

The Olympic athlete built a special *shelter* to house his numerous *awards*. They are lined up in the chronological **order** in which he won them.

989

This character with the definition:

lance, pike, spear

Pinyin **máo** *and Frequency Rank* **1441**

SIMP & TRAD Contains **5 strokes** in the following order:

フ マ 予 予 矛

Contains these components:

■ bestow, award 予 985, p.225

■ action path c ノ 438, p.105

With all these meanings & readings:

máo [矛] **1** spear **2** lance **3** pike

When hunters accurately launch their **spears** on '*action paths*', they earn an '*award*'—food to eat!

990

This character with the definition:

supple, soft, gentle

Pinyin **róu** and Frequency Rank **1573**

SIMP & TRAD   Contains **9 strokes** in the following order:

フ マ マ 予 予 圣 予 矛 柔

Contains these components:

■ lance, pike, spear 矛 989, p. 225

□ tree 木 562, p. 133

With all these meanings & readings

róu [柔] **1** soft **2** flexible **3** supple **4** yielding **5** rho (Greek letter ρ)

Ancient warriors knew that the best *spear* was formed from a *tree* with very **supple** wood. Such a *spear* flexes aerodynamically as it flies toward its target.

991
台臺
颱檯
TRAD

This character with the definition:

you (literary)

Pinyin **tái** and Frequency Rank **388**

SIMPLIFIED   Contains **5 strokes** in the following order:

ㄥ ム 스 台 台

Contains these components:

■ private r ㄙ 963, p. 220

■ mouth 口 37, p. 17

With all these meanings & readings

tái [台] **1** surname Tai **2** (classical) you (in letters) **3** platform **4** Taiwan (abbr.)
tái [檯] **1** desk **2** platform
tái [臺] **1** platform **2** stage **3** terrace **4** stand **5** support **6** desk **7** station **8** broadcasting station **9** m for vehicles or machines **10** Taiwan (abbr.)
tái [颱] **1** typhoon

That cute pointy *nose* above your pert *mouth* is how I think of **you** when we're apart.

992

This character with the definition:

raise, lift

Pinyin **tái** and Frequency Rank **1386**

SIMP & TRAD   Contains **8 strokes** in the following order:

一 十 才 扌 扣 扣 抬 抬

Contains these components:

■ hand r 扌 25, p. 15

■ you (literary) 台 991, p. 226

With all these meanings & readings

tái [抬] **1** to lift **2** to raise **3** (of two or more persons) to carry

Before the Crown Prince received his official title, he had to **raise** his *hand* and swear his loyalty to the Queen. Afterwards, she said, "I appoint *you* Crown Prince."

993

This character with the definition:

govern, rule

Pinyin **zhì** and Frequency Rank **274**

SIMP & TRAD   Contains **8 strokes** in the following order:

丶 冫 氵 汁 沿 治 治 治

Contains these components:

■ water r 氵 314, p. 80

■ you (literary) 台 991, p. 226

With all these meanings & readings

zhì [治] **1** to rule **2** to govern **3** to manage **4** to control **5** to harness (a river) **6** cure **7** treatment **8** to heal

In many regions, when *you* accept responsibility to **govern** an area, you are expected to provide clean *water* to its people.

994

This character with the definition:

begin, start

Pinyin **shǐ** and Frequency Rank **381**

SIMP & TRAD   Contains **8 strokes** in the following order:

㇀ 乚 女 女 如 奶 始 始

Contains these components:

■ woman 女 790, p. 183

■ you (literary) 台 991, p. 226

With all these meanings & readings

shǐ [始] **1** begin

The beautiful *woman* **began** to cry when she heard the words: "I crown *you* Miss Universe."

995 允

SIMP & TRAD

This character with the definition:

permit, allow

Pinyin **yǔn** *and Frequency Rank* **1443**

Contains **4 strokes** in the following order:

ㄥ ㄙ ㄆ 允

Contains these components:

私 private r ㄙ 963, p.220

儿 walking man r 儿 290, p.75

With all these meanings & readings:

yǔn [允] **1** just **2** fair **3** to permit **4** to allow

On his own, the *walking man*—with just his two legs and no other body parts—is quite helpless. But with the addition of a *nose*, his abilities expand to limitless possibilities, **allowing** him to navigate his moves by sense of smell!

996 充

SIMP & TRAD

This character with the definition:

ample, sufficient

Pinyin **chōng** *and Frequency Rank* **690**

Contains **5 strokes** in the following order:

丶 亠 云 云 充

Contains these components:

cover r ⼧ 250, p.66

permit, allow 允 995, p.227

With all these meanings & readings:

chōng [充] **1** fill **2** satisfy **3** fulfill **4** to act in place of **5** substitute **6** sufficient **7** full

My husband is on a strict diet. After I serve him a **sufficient** amount of food, I *cover* the serving dish and do not *allow* him access to it.

997 矣

SIMP & TRAD

This character with the definition:

s-end: completed action

Pinyin **yǐ** *and Frequency Rank* **2069**

Contains **7 strokes** in the following order:

ㄥ ㄙ ㄆ ㄥ 丝 矣 矣

Contains these components:

私 private r ㄙ 963, p.220

arrow 矢 552, p.130

With all these meanings & readings:

yǐ [矣] **1** archaic final particle similar to modern 了

This character represents a Chinese grammatical character, that dates back to classical times. It marks the completion of an action, thus functioning like the modern 了, 'le'. • When my big *nose* stops the *arrow*'s flight, the **mark** on my face shows evidence of a **completed action**.

998 埃

SIMP & TRAD

This character with the definition:

dirt, dust

Pinyin **āi** *and Frequency Rank* **1121**

Contains **10 strokes** in the following order:

一 十 土 圵 圵 圹 垆 坯 埃 埃

Contains these components:

earth, soil 土 9, p.11

s-end: completed action 矣 997, p.227

With all these meanings & readings:

āi [埃] **1** dust **2** dirt **3** Angstrom or Ångström, unit of length equal to 1/10,000,000,000 meters **4** phonetic ai or e **5** abbr for Egypt 埃及[āi jí]

At my life's end, which marks the *completion of my activity* on this *earth*, my body will turn into **dust**.

999 幺

SIMP & TRAD

This character with the definition:

youngest

Pinyin **yāo** *and Frequency Rank* **4505**

Contains **3 strokes** in the following order:

ㄥ ㄠ 幺

Contains these components:

private r ㄙ (altered) 963, p.220

private r ㄙ 963, p.220

With all these meanings & readings:

yāo [幺] **1** youngest **2** most junior **3** tiny **4** one (unambiguous spoken form when spelling out numbers, especially on telephone or in military) **5** one or ace on dice or dominoes **6** variant of 吆, to shout

Two neighbors stick their pointy *noses* up close to see the adorable new baby—she's the **youngest** addition to the family!

1000

幻

SIMP & TRAD

This character with the definition:

fantasy

Pinyin **huàn** *and Frequency Rank* **1417**

Contains these components:

youngest 幺 999, p. 227

place of refuge c ㄱ 105, p. 33

With all these meanings & readings

huàn [幻] **1** fantasy

Contains **4 strokes** in the following order:

幺 幺 幺 幻

My *youngest* child frequently seeks *refuge* in his own **fantasy** world.

1001

幽

SIMP & TRAD

This character with the definition:

remote, secluded

Pinyin **yōu** *and Frequency Rank* **1636**

Contains these components:

mountain 山 4, p. 10

youngest (×2) 幺 999, p. 227

With all these meanings & readings

yōu [幽] **1** quiet **2** secluded **3** Hades

Contains **9 strokes** in the following order:

丨 丨 纟 幺 纱 纱 纱 幽 幽

The two '*youngest*' elements resemble large bushes disguising the *mountain* pass, keeping it **remote** and **secluded**.

1002

玄

SIMP & TRAD

This character with the definition:

incredible

Pinyin **xuán** *and Frequency Rank* **1717**

Contains these components:

cover r 亠 250, p. 66

youngest 幺 999, p. 227

With all these meanings & readings

xuán [玄] **1** black **2** mysterious

Contains **5 strokes** in the following order:

丶 亠 宀 玄 玄

Our neighbors behave strangely because there is something **incredibly** wrong with their *youngest*; they take elaborate actions to *cover* up his very existence.

1003

兹

兹
TRAD SIMPLIFIED

This character with the definition:

now, at present*

Pinyin **zī** *and Frequency Rank* **1781**

Contains these components:

incredible (×2) 玄 1002, p. 228

With all these meanings & readings

zī [兹] **1** herewith

Contains **9 strokes** in the following order:

丶 丷 兰 产 兰 兹 兹 兹 兹

There's no time like the **present**; put another way, nothing is as *incredible* as **now**.

1004

滋

SIMP & TRAD

This character with the definition:

spurt

Pinyin **zī** *and Frequency Rank* **1931**

Contains these components:

water r 氵 314, p. 80
now, at present* 兹 1003, p. 228

With all these meanings & readings

zī [滋] **1** excite **2** nourish **3** t

Contains **12 strokes** in the following order:

丶 冫 氵 汗 浐 浐 涔 滋 滋 滋 滋 滋

The three dots of the *water* component plus the two dots of the '*now, at present*' element suggest—at least visually—that there's lots of water around. At home, that might mean that water is **spurting** from a burst pipe—*now*!

005

This character with the definition:

magnetism

Pinyin **cí** *and Frequency Rank* **1771**

SIMP & TRAD   Contains **14 strokes** in the following order:

一 ナ 石 石 石 石' 矿 砼 磁 磁 磁 磁 磁

Contains these components:

stone, rock 石 522, p. 124

now, at present* 兹 1003, p. 228

With all these meanings & readings:

cí [磁] **1** magnetic **2** magnetism **3** porcelain

He used to be a real nerd, but *now* his personal **magnetism** is so great that even *stone* is attracted to him.

006

This character with the definition:

livestock

Pinyin **chù** *and Frequency Rank* **2030**

SIMP & TRAD   Contains **10 strokes** in the following order:

丶 一 亠 玄 玄 玄 畜 畜 畜 畜

Contains these components:

incredible 玄 1002, p. 228

field 田 63, p. 23

With all these meanings & readings:

chù [畜] **1** livestock **2** domesticated animal **3** domestic animal **xù** [畜] **1** to raise (animals)

The farmer's *field* is an *incredible* mess—filthy, smelly, and ugly. But that's what he gets when he chooses to keep his **livestock** there.

007

This character with the definition:

store, save up

Pinyin **xù** *and Frequency Rank* **1985**

SIMP & TRAD   Contains **13 strokes** in the following order:

一 十 艹 艹 芓 苎 苎 莕 荟 蓄 蓄 蓄 蓄

Contains these components:

grass r 艹 87, p. 29

livestock 畜 1006, p. 229

With all these meanings & readings:

xù [蓄] **1** to store

Winter is coming. If I don't **store** hay and *grass* now, the *livestock* will starve to death during those cold months.

008

This character with the definition:

young

Pinyin **yòu** *and Frequency Rank* **1577**

SIMP & TRAD   Contains **5 strokes** in the following order:

乙 幺 幺 幻 幼

Contains these components:

youngest 幺 999, p. 227

strength 力 471, p. 113

With all these meanings & readings:

yòu [幼] **1** young

All **young** creatures begin life as the *youngest* beings, but they constantly mature and develop their *strength*.

009

This character with the definition:

huh? what?

Pinyin **me** *and Frequency Rank* **63**

麼
TRAD   SIMPLIFIED   Contains **3 strokes** in the following order:

丿 乙 么

Contains these components:

action path c 丿 438, p. 105

private r 厶 963, p. 220

With all these meanings & readings:

me [麼] **1** suffix, used to form interrogative 什么 [甚麼], what?, indefinite 这么 [這麼] thus etc
ma [麼] **1** interrogative final particle

What type of *action path* is that fly tracing along my neighbor's *nose*? (I'm not close enough to see.)

Unit 43

1010

SIMP & TRAD

This character with the definition:

ghost, spirit

Pinyin **guǐ** *and Frequency Rank* **1042**

Contains **9 strokes** in the following order:

´ ⸍ ⼍ ⽩ 白 甶 鬼 鬼 鬼

Contains these components:

■☐ white 白 225, p. 60
■■ walking man r 儿 (altered) 290, p. 75
■☐ private r 厶 963, p. 220

With all these meanings & readings:

guǐ [鬼] **1** ghost **2** sly **3** cra
4 m 个 [個][gè]

In European folklore, a **ghost** is this big *white* thing that *walks around* where you least expect him. You certainly don't expect to see a *nose* appear on his leg, but it only emphasizes how distorted and scary **ghosts** can be!

1011

SIMP & TRAD

This character with the definition:

devil, monster

Pinyin **mó** *and Frequency Rank* **1180**

Contains **20 strokes** in the following order:

` ⼀ 广 广 庁 庁 庐 庐 庐 庐 麻 麻 麻 靡 靡 靡 麿 魔 魔 魔

Contains these components:

■☐ hemp 麻 (altered) 613, p. 146
■☐ ghost, spirit 鬼 1010, p. 230

With all these meanings & readings:

mó [魔] **1** devil

A *ghost* wearing Armani *hemp* clothing makes the scariest **devil** of all!

1012

SIMP & TRAD

This character with the definition:

soul, spirit

Pinyin **hún** *and Frequency Rank* **1348**

Contains **13 strokes** in the following order:

⼀ ⼆ 丐 云 云 试 动 动 䰟 䰟 魂 魂 魂

Contains these components:

■☐ say 云 967, p. 221
■☐ ghost, spirit 鬼 1010, p. 230

With all these meanings & readings:

hún [魂] **1** soul

Most Chinese *ghosts* are silent, but the ones who can *talk* are actually **souls**.

1013

SIMP & TRAD

This character with the definition:

Wei dynasty

Pinyin **wèi** *and Frequency Rank* **1648**

Contains **17 strokes** in the following order:

´ ⼆ 千 禾 禾 委 委 委 委 毵 魏 䶹 䶹 魏 魏 魏 魏

Contains these components:

■☐ listless, dejected 委 803, p. 185
■☐ ghost, spirit 鬼 1010, p. 230

With all these meanings & readings:

Wèi [魏] **1** lofty **2** surname W
3 name of vassal state of Zhou dynasty from 661 BC in Shanxi one of the Seven Hero Warring States **4** Wei state, founded by Cao Cao 曹操, one of the Thre Kingdoms from the fall of the Han **5** the Wei dynasty 221-26. **6** Wei prefecture and Wei count at different historical periods

Perhaps the **Wei** emperors chose this graph—composed of *dejected* and *ghostly* images—to show that they could rise above such matters.

1014

SIMP & TRAD

This character with the definition:

use, take

Pinyin **yǐ** *and Frequency Rank* **23**

Contains **4 strokes** in the following order:

⼁ ㇄ 以 以

Contains these components:

■☐ private r 厶 (altered) 963, p. 220
■☐ man 人 537, p. 127

With all these meanings & readings:

yǐ [以] **1** abbr for Israel 以色列 sè liè]
yǐ [以] **1** to use **2** according **3** so as to **4** by means of **5** i order to **6** by **7** with **8** because

Private medical facilities exist so that *men* can **use** special equipment and **take** their medicines away from the public eye.

1015

拟

擬
TRAD   SIMPLIFIED

This character with the definition:

plan, intend

Pinyin **nǐ** *and Frequency Rank* **1541**

Contains **7 strokes** in the following order:

一 ㄧ 扌 扌 扚 扨 拟 拟

You *use* your *hands* to carry out a bold **plan**.

Contains these components:

☐ hand r 扌 25, p.15
☐ use, take 以 1014, p.230

With all these meanings & readings:

nǐ [擬] **1** to draft (a plan) **2** to have an intention (to do sth) **3** to emulate **4** to follow (a model) **5** pseudo- **6** para-

---

1016

虫

蟲
虫
TRAD   SIMPLIFIED

This character with the definition:

insect

Pinyin **chóng** *and Frequency Rank* **1287**

Contains **6 strokes** in the following order:

丶 ㄇ 口 中 虫 虫

Insects are crawling all over the house! No matter how secure, they can get into the *middle* of the most *private* of places.

Contains these components:

☐ middle 中 38, p.18
☐ private r 厶 (altered) 963, p.220

With all these meanings & readings:

chóng [蟲] **1** an animal **2** an invertebrate **3** a worm **4** an insect **5** m 条 [條][tiáo], 只 [隻][zhī]

1017

属

屬
TRAD   SIMPLIFIED

This character with the definition:

category

Pinyin **shǔ** *and Frequency Rank* **610**

Contains **12 strokes** in the following order:

一 ㄱ ㄇ 尸 尺 尼 居 居 属 属 属 属

To a scientist, *insects* are of great interest to study because there are so many distinct opportunities to study them. You can study the entire *body*, or you can focus on the *little* component bits. The hard *insect* shells serve as distinct *borders* between one part and the next. As you can appreciate, one *insect* offers many **categories** in which to examine it.

Contains these components:

☐ corpse 尸 499, p.119
☐ dab r 丶 176, p.48
☐ insect 虫 1016, p.231
☐ borders r 冂 114, p.34

With all these meanings & readings:

shǔ [屬] **1** category **2** genus (taxonomy) **3** family members **4** dependents **5** to belong to **6** subordinate to **7** affiliated with **8** be born in the year of (one of the 12 animals) **9** to be **10** to prove to be **11** to constitute
zhǔ [屬] **1** to join together **2** to fix one's attention on **3** to concentrate on

---

1018

蛋

SIMP & TRAD

This character with the definition:

egg

Pinyin **dàn** *and Frequency Rank* **1387**

Contains **11 strokes** in the following order:

㇇ ㇆ 尸 ㇏ 足 足 蛋 蛋 蛋 蛋 蛋

Birds aren't the only creatures who lay **eggs**. While on safari a few years back, a nasty *insect* used my *foot* to deposit an **egg** that left me with a parasitic disease.

Contains these components:

☐ foot 足 (altered) 729, p.170
☐ insect 虫 1016, p.231

With all these meanings & readings:

dàn [蛋] **1** egg **2** oval shaped **3** m 个 [個][gè], 打[dá]

1019

虽

雖
TRAD   SIMPLIFIED

This character with the definition:

although, even though

Pinyin **suī** *and Frequency Rank* **504**

Contains **9 strokes** in the following order:

丶 ㄇ 口 尸 吕 吕 虽 虽 虽

Even though I opened my *mouth* only to speak, and only for a couple of seconds, an *insect* somehow flew into it.

Contains these components:

☐ mouth 口 37, p.17
☐ insect 虫 1016, p.231

With all these meanings & readings:

suī [雖] **1** although **2** even though

1020

強
TRAD   SIMPLIFIED

This character with the definition:

powerful

Pinyin **qiáng** *and Frequency Rank* **292**

Contains **12 strokes** in the following order:

乛 コ 弓 弖 弖ˊ 弖ˋ 弜 弨 弨 弨 強 強

Contains these components:

▯ bow (weapon) 弓 140, p.40
▯ although, even though 虽 1019, p.231

With all these meanings & readings:

jiàng [強] **1** stubborn **2** unyielding
qiáng [強] **1** strong **2** powerful **3** better **4** slightly more than **5** vigorous **6** violent **7** surnam Qiang
qiǎng [強] **1** to strive **2** to mak an effort

Although the chieftain carried the huge *bow* into the peace talks, we knew he didn't need it to signify his presence. As it was, he was the most **powerful** man there.

1021

蛇
SIMP & TRAD

This character with the definition:

snake, serpent

Pinyin **shé** *and Frequency Rank* **1689**

Contains **11 strokes** in the following order:

丶 丶 口 中 虫 虫 虫 虫ˊ 虴 蛇 蛇

Contains these components:

▯ insect 虫 1016, p.231
▯ it 它 277, p.71

With all these meanings & readings:

shé [蛇] **1** snake **2** serpent **3** r 条 [條][tiáo]

To many people, a **snake** is the essence of creepy-crawliness. *It* engenders primeval disgust as many *insects* do.

1022

縣
TRAD   SIMPLIFIED

This character with the definition:

county

Pinyin **xiàn** *and Frequency Rank* **877**

Contains **7 strokes** in the following order:

丨 冂 冃 日 且 县 县

Contains these components:

▯ moreover 且 84, p.28
▯ private r 厶 963, p.220

With all these meanings & readings:

xiàn [縣] **1** county, PRC administrative division below prefecture 地区 [～區][dì qù] **2** m 个 [個][gè]

A **county** is a government entity which organizes its own records in a *private* room that's filled with a long series of '*moreover*'-like bookshelves.

1023

勾
SIMP & TRAD

This character with the definition:

cross out

Pinyin **gōu** *and Frequency Rank* **2034**

Contains **4 strokes** in the following order:

丿 勹 勾 勾

Contains these components:

▯ wrap r 勹 364, p.90
▯ private r 厶 963, p.220

With all these meanings & readings:

gōu [勾] **1** to attract **2** to arous **3** to tick **4** to strike out **5** to delineate **6** to collude
gòu [勾] **1** affair **2** to reach for (with hand)

Somebody must have *wrapped* that snob's *nose*. It looks likes he's been **rubbed out**.

1024

構
TRAD   SIMPLIFIED

This character with the definition:

construct, form

Pinyin **gòu** *and Frequency Rank* **511**

Contains **8 strokes** in the following order:

一 十 才 木 木 杓 杓 构 构

Contains these components:

▯ tree 木 562, p.133
▯ cross out 勾 1023, p.232

With all these meanings & readings:

gòu [構] **1** Broussonetia papyrifera **2** to construct **3** to form **4** to make up **5** to compose

We were able to **construct** a *cross out* of *wood* (ouch!) for the neighborhood church.

1025

溝
TRAD

沟
SIMPLIFIED

This character with the definition:

trench, groove

Pinyin **gōu** *and Frequency Rank* **1610**

Contains these components:

■ water r 氵 314, p. 80
■ cross out 勾 1023, p. 232

With all these meanings & readings:

gōu [溝] **1** ditch **2** gutter **3** groove
4 gully **5** ravine **6** m 道[dào]

Contains **7 strokes** in the following order:

丶 冫 氵 沟 沟 沟

Imagine a catastrophic flood. In an effort to cancel or *cross out* these *water* paths, the authorities have dug a series of **trenches** to divert the flow.

1026

This component has the meaning:

fire r

COMPONENT

These are several blue **flames** on a gas burner. • **Fire** consumes resources and objects by burning them to ash, so we will sometimes refer to the meaning of 'consume'. Also, the flavors of a dish are intensified after being cooked over a **fire**, so sometimes this component will signify the concept of 'intense'.

1027

然
SIMP & TRAD

This character with the definition:

-ly

Pinyin **rán** *and Frequency Rank* **55**

Contains these components:

■ meat 肉 (altered) 753, p. 175
■ dog 犬 673, p. 158
■ fire r ⺗ 1026, p. 233

With all these meanings & readings:

rán [然] **1** to correct, rectify
2 right **3** so **4** thus **5** like
this **6** -ly

Contains **12 strokes** in the following order:

丿 勹 夕 夕 夕- 外 狄 狄 狄 狄 然 然

This suffix's meaning is similar to that of our English adverb suffix '-ly', but it applies chiefly to some descriptions of a change of state, as in 'suddenly', 'obviously', and 'happily'. • When you cook *meat* over an open *fire*, you **change its state**—obvious**ly**—and every *dog* in the neighborhood can smell it.

1028

烈
SIMP & TRAD

This character with the definition:

intense

Pinyin **liè** *and Frequency Rank* **802**

Contains these components:

■ arrange, line up 列 885, p. 202
■ fire r ⺗ 1026, p. 233

With all these meanings & readings:

liè [烈] **1** ardent **2** intense
3 fierce **4** stern **5** upright **6** to
give one's life for a noble cause
7 exploits **8** achievements

Contains **10 strokes** in the following order:

一 丆 歹 歹 列 列 列 列 烈 烈

When you start a *fire* in the fireplace or barbecue grill, the more strategically you *arrange* the charcoal bricks, the more **intense** will be the fire!

1029

庶
SIMP & TRAD

This character with the definition:

myriad, multitudinous

Pinyin **shù** *and Frequency Rank* **3016**

Contains these components:

■ shelter r 广 427, p. 103
■ horned animal c 廿 94, p. 30
■ fire r ⺗ 1026, p. 233

With all these meanings & readings:

shù [庶] **1** numerous **2** all
3 common people **4** nearly **5** to
hope **6** born of a concubine

Contains **11 strokes** in the following order:

丶 一 广 广 庐 庐 庶 庶 庶 庶 庶

Imagine a blizzard out west in *cattle* country. The ornery *cows* happily gather in the barn's *shelter*, where they huddle by the large *fire*. You know the weather's bad when there is a **myriad** of these cold cattle.

1030 席

SIMP & TRAD

This character with the definition:

mat

Pinyin **xí** *and Frequency Rank* **894**

Contains **10 strokes** in the following order:

丶 一 广 广 产 庐 庐 席 席 席

Contains these components:

☐ myriad, multitudinous 庶 (abbrev) 1029, 233

■ towel 巾 118, p.35

With all these meanings & readings

xí [席] **1** banquet **2** woven mat **3** seat **4** place in a democratic assembly **5** surname Xi

A large piece of *cloth* can be spread out on the ground and used as a resting **mat** for what seems like a *myriad* of people gathered around to sit and relax.

1031 照

SIMP & TRAD

This character with the definition:

shine, illuminate

Pinyin **zhào** *and Frequency Rank* **443**

Contains **13 strokes** in the following order:

丨 冂 日 日 日² 趵 趵 昭 昭 照 照 照 照

Contains these components:

■ clear, obvious 昭 486, p.116

■ fire r ⺣ 1026, p.233

With all these meanings & readings

zhào [照] **1** according to **2** in accordance with **3** to shine **4** illuminate **5** to reflect **6** photograph

The *fire* **illuminated** the study room, making all of its details *clearly* visible.

1032 熟

SIMP & TRAD

This character with the definition:

ripe, cooked

Pinyin **shú** *and Frequency Rank* **1035**

Contains **15 strokes** in the following order:

丶 一 亠 亠 古 亨 亨 享 郭 孰 孰 孰 熟 熟 熟

Contains these components:

■ who? what? which? (literary) 孰 534, p.126

■ fire r ⺣ 1026, p.233

With all these meanings & readings

shóu [熟] **1** see 熟 [熟][shú] **shú** [熟] **1** cooked (of food) **2** ripe (of fruit) **3** mature (of seeds) **4** familiar **5** skilled **6** done

Which foods are selected by the master chef to be **cooked** over an open *fire*? Only the most **ripe** and flawless fruits and vegetables.

1033 点

點 TRAD   SIMPLIFIED

This character with the definition:

dot

Pinyin **diǎn** *and Frequency Rank* **128**

Contains **9 strokes** in the following order:

丨 卜 ㆑ 占 占 占 点 点 点

Contains these components:

■ practice divination 占 188, p.51

■ fire r ⺣ 1026, p.233

With all these meanings & readings

diǎn [點] **1** point **2** dot **3** spe **4** drop **5** decimal point **6** poi of a scale **7** point in a theory or argument **8** downwards-righ convex character stroke **9** a lit **10** see also 一点 [~點][yī diǎn] **11** a jot **12** beat (of percussion instrument) **13** to draw a dot **14** to touch slightly **15** to drip **16** m for items **17** m for small indeterminate quantities **18** to nod **19** to select item from a l **20** to order (food in a restaurant) **21** to count **22** o'clock **23** one fifth of a two hour watc (old) **24** hour **25** point of tim **26** iron bell (used to mark time **27** pastry **28** dimsum **29** see also 点心 [點~][diǎn xin] **30** m 个 [個][gè]

The fortune teller failed to *foretell* the *fire* that would break out during the night, and the family's vast possessions were reduced to **dots**.

1034 杰

傑 TRAD   SIMPLIFIED

This character with the definition:

outstanding person

Pinyin **jié** *and Frequency Rank* **1129**

Contains **8 strokes** in the following order:

一 十 才 木 木 朩 杰 杰

Contains these components:

■ tree 木 562, p.133

■ fire r ⺣ 1026, p.233

With all these meanings & readings

jié [傑] **1** hero **2** heroic

A *tree* survived a raging *conflagration*? It must be as outstanding as, by analogy, an **outstanding person**.

Unit 44

1035

热

熱
TRAD SIMPLIFIED

This character with the definition:

hot, fervent

Pinyin **rè** *and Frequency Rank* **606**

Contains **10 strokes** in the following order:

一 十 扌 扌 执 执 执 热 热 热

Contains these components:

■ take charge of 执 535, p.127

■ fire r ⺍ 1026, p.233

With all these meanings & readings:

rè [热] **1** heat **2** to heat up **3** fervent **4** hot (of weather) **5** warm up

In ancient times, a special servant *took charge of* the *fire*place, making sure there was enough *fire*wood to remain **hot**. Otherwise, the winter cold would penetrate the house.

1036

燕

SIMP & TRAD

This character with the definition:

swallow bird

Pinyin **yàn** *and Frequency Rank* **1705**

Contains **16 strokes** in the following order:

一 十 艹 艹 芢 芇 芇 苗 莊 莊 莊 燕 燕 燕 燕 燕

Contains these components:

□ horned animal c 廿 94, p.30

■ north 北 (altered) 131, p.38

■ mouth 口 37, p.17

■ fire r ⺍ 1026, p.233

With all these meanings & readings:

Yàn [燕] **1** Yan, a vassal state of Zhou in modern Hebei and Liaoning **2** north Hebei **3** the four Yan kingdoms of the Sixteen Kingdoms, namely: Former Yan 前燕 (337-370), Later Yan 后燕 [後~] (384-409), Southern Yan 南燕 (398-410), Northern Yan 北燕 (409-436) **4** surname Yan

yàn [燕] **1** swallow (a type of bird)

Here's a parent **swallow** returning to feed her fledglings. Look, there they are, the four hungry dots each with a *burning* appetite. That's not an *animal* up top, but rather their distinctive tail. Compared with other birds, their wings appear short and stubby, but the bird's natural habitat is way up *north*, so it's no wonder its wings resemble the '*north*' component. We use an open *mouth* to represent the bird's compact body.

1037

This component has the meaning:

silk r

COMPONENT

This image is intended to represent **silk** threads twisted together. • The use of **silk** has traditionally been reserved for special occasions and people. Not only does this element retain its obvious interpretation as **silk** cloth, but it also often appears in characters that call attention to noteworthy occasions, situations, or people.

1038

组

組
TRAD SIMPLIFIED

This character with the definition:

organize, arrange

Pinyin **zǔ** *and Frequency Rank* **358**

Contains **8 strokes** in the following order:

乚 纟 纟 纠 纽 组 组 组

Contains these components:

■ silk r 纟 1037, p.235

■ moreover 且 84, p.28

With all these meanings & readings:

zǔ [组] **1** to form **2** compose **3** make up **4** group **5** to organize **6** cord **7** m 个 [個][gè]

Visualize the '*moreover*' element in this character as shelves that a storekeeper uses to **arrange** his fine *silk* cloths in brightly-colored displays.

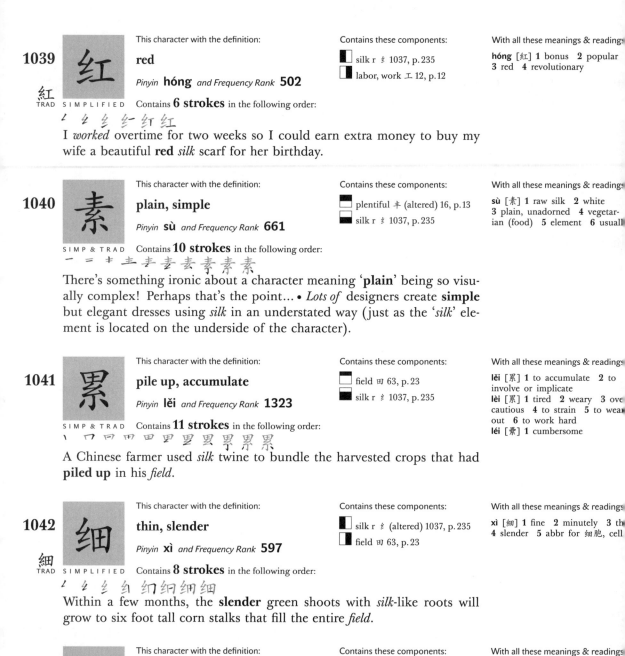

1039

红
红
TRAD SIMPLIFIED

This character with the definition:

red

Pinyin **hóng** *and Frequency Rank* **502**

Contains **6 strokes** in the following order:

Contains these components:

silk r 纟 1037, p. 235

labor, work 工 12, p. 12

With all these meanings & readings

hóng [红] **1** bonus **2** popular **3** red **4** revolutionary

I *worked* overtime for two weeks so I could earn extra money to buy my wife a beautiful **red** *silk* scarf for her birthday.

1040

素

SIMP & TRAD

This character with the definition:

plain, simple

Pinyin **sù** *and Frequency Rank* **661**

Contains **10 strokes** in the following order:

Contains these components:

plentiful 丰 (altered) 16, p. 13

silk r 纟 1037, p. 235

With all these meanings & readings

sù [素] **1** raw silk **2** white **3** plain, unadorned **4** vegetarian (food) **5** element **6** usually

There's something ironic about a character meaning '**plain**' being so visually complex! Perhaps that's the point... • *Lots of* designers create **simple** but elegant dresses using *silk* in an understated way (just as the '*silk*' element is located on the underside of the character).

1041

累

SIMP & TRAD

This character with the definition:

pile up, accumulate

Pinyin **lěi** *and Frequency Rank* **1323**

Contains **11 strokes** in the following order:

Contains these components:

field 田 63, p. 23

silk r 纟 1037, p. 235

With all these meanings & readings

lěi [累] **1** to accumulate **2** to involve or implicate
lèi [累] **1** tired **2** weary **3** over cautious **4** to strain **5** to wear out **6** to work hard
léi [累] **1** cumbersome

A Chinese farmer used *silk* twine to bundle the harvested crops that had **piled up** in his *field*.

1042

细
细
TRAD SIMPLIFIED

This character with the definition:

thin, slender

Pinyin **xì** *and Frequency Rank* **597**

Contains **8 strokes** in the following order:

Contains these components:

silk r 纟 (altered) 1037, p. 235

field 田 63, p. 23

With all these meanings & readings

xì [细] **1** fine **2** minutely **3** thin **4** slender **5** abbr for 细胞, cell

Within a few months, the **slender** green shoots with *silk*-like roots will grow to six foot tall corn stalks that fill the entire *field*.

1043

结
结
TRAD SIMPLIFIED

This character with the definition:

tie, knit, knot, weave

Pinyin **jié** *and Frequency Rank* **236**

Contains **9 strokes** in the following order:

Contains these components:

silk r 纟 (altered) 1037, p. 235

lucky 吉 47, p. 20

With all these meanings & readings

jiē [结] **1** to bear fruit **2** to produce **3** firm **4** solid
jié [结] **1** knot **2** sturdy **3** bond **4** to tie **5** to bind **6** to check out (of a hotel)

The Chinese believe that an intricately **tied**, decorative *silk* **knot** is a kind of *lucky* charm.

1044 纯 純 TRAD SIMPLIFIED

This character with the definition:

pure, unmixed

Pinyin **chún** *and Frequency Rank* **1125**

Contains **7 strokes** in the following order:

The merchant usually kept a *stockpile* of **pure** *silk*. He knew that it was often difficult to procure high-quality, **unmixed** material.

Contains these components:

- silk r 纟 1037, p. 235
- stockpile, store up 屯 (altered) 159, p. 44

With all these meanings & readings:

chún [純] **1** pure **2** simple **3** unmixed **4** genuine

1045 系 係 繫 TRAD SIMPLIFIED

This character with the definition:

academic department

Pinyin **xì** *and Frequency Rank* **216**

Contains **7 strokes** in the following order:

At many college graduation ceremonies, it is customary for professors in every **academic department** to wear long black robes trimmed with *dabs* of colored *silk* cloth.

Contains these components:

- dab r 丶 176, p. 48
- silk r 纟 1037, p. 235

With all these meanings & readings:

xì [係] **1** to connect **2** to relate to **3** to tie up **4** to bind **5** to be (literary)
xì [系] **1** system **2** department **3** faculty
jì [繫] **1** to tie **2** to fasten **3** to button up
xì [繫] **1** to connect **2** to arrest **3** to worry

1046 紫 SIMP & TRAD

This character with the definition:

purple

Pinyin **zǐ** *and Frequency Rank* **1646**

Contains **12 strokes** in the following order:

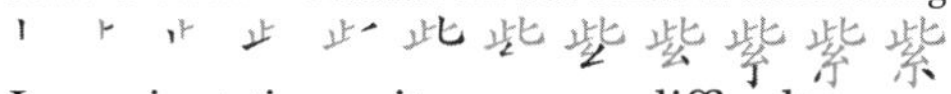

In ancient times, it was very difficult to produce deep **purple**-colored cloth, so *this* color was reserved strictly for royal garments, which were usually woven from *silk*.

Contains these components:

- this 此 196, p. 53
- silk r 纟 1037, p. 235

With all these meanings & readings:

zǐ [紫] **1** purple **2** violet **3** amethyst **4** Lithospermum erythrorhizon (flowering plant whose root provides red purple dye) **5** Japanese: murasaki

1047 索 SIMP & TRAD

This character with the definition:

scout around, look for

Pinyin **suǒ** *and Frequency Rank* **805**

Contains **10 strokes** in the following order:

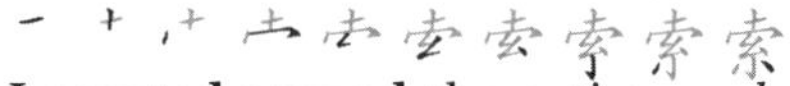

I **scouted around** the entire *market* **looking for** the best *silk* that my customers demanded.

Contains these components:

- market 市 (altered) 251, p. 66
- silk r 纟 1037, p. 235

With all these meanings & readings:

suǒ [索] **1** surname Suo
suǒ [索] **1** to search **2** to demand **3** to ask **4** to exact **5** large rope **6** isolated

1048 绕 繞 TRAD SIMPLIFIED

This character with the definition:

wind, coil

Pinyin **rào** *and Frequency Rank* **1485**

Contains **9 strokes** in the following order:

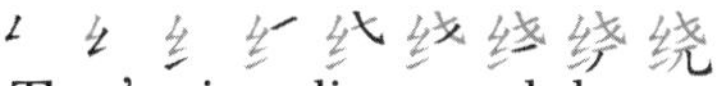

They've just discovered the mummified body of the *legendary emperor* Yao. It had been preserved by spools of *silk* thread **coiled** around the royal corpse.

Contains these components:

- silk r 纟 1037, p. 235
- legendary emperor 尧 667, p. 157

With all these meanings & readings:

rào [繞] **1** to wind **2** to coil (thread) **3** to rotate around **4** to spiral **5** to move around **6** to go round (an obstacle) **7** to by-pass **8** to make a detour **9** to confuse **10** to perplex

1049

納
TRAD　SIMPLIFIED

This character with the definition:

accept, receive

Pinyin **nà** *and Frequency Rank* **684**

Contains **7 strokes** in the following order:

乚 纟 纟 纟 纳 纳 纳

Contains these components:

■ silk r 纟 1037, p. 235
■ inside* 内 785, p. 182

With all these meanings & readings:

nà [納] **1** surname Na
nà [納] **1** to receive **2** to accept **3** to enjoy **4** to bring into **5** to pay (tax etc) **6** nano- (one billionth) **7** to reinforce sole of shoes or stockings by close sewing

After **receiving** a shipment of fine quality *silk*, I prominently displayed it *inside* my store.

1050

線
TRAD　SIMPLIFIED

This character with the definition:

thread, string, wire

Pinyin **xiàn** *and Frequency Rank* **430**

Contains **8 strokes** in the following order:

乚 纟 纟 纟 纟 线 线 线

Contains these components:

■ silk r 纟 1037, p. 235
■ tiny, fragmentary 戋 665, p. 157

With all these meanings & readings:

xiàn [線] **1** thread **2** string **3** wire **4** line **5** m 条 [條][tiáo] 股[gǔ], 根[gēn]

When you take *silk* and shred it into *fragmentary* bits, you get silk **thread**.

1051

綠
TRAD　SIMPLIFIED

This character with the definition:

green

Pinyin **lǜ** *and Frequency Rank* **1088**

Contains **11 strokes** in the following order:

乚 纟 纟 纟 纟 纟 纟 绿 绿 绿 绿

Contains these components:

■ silk r 纟 1037, p. 235
■ record, write down 录 324, p. 82

With all these meanings & readings:

lǜ [綠] **1** green

The ministers *recorded* the proclamation in gold letters on *silk* brocade. Alas, time revealed the gold was false and the characters soon turned **green**.

1052

約
TRAD　SIMPLIFIED

This character with the definition:

ask, invite

Pinyin **yuē** *and Frequency Rank* **424**

Contains **6 strokes** in the following order:

乚 纟 纟 纟 约 约

Contains these components:

■ silk r 纟 1037, p. 235
■ spoon 勺 371, p. 92

With all these meanings & readings:

yāo [約] **1** weigh
yuē [約] **1** appointment **2** agreement **3** to arrange **4** to restrict **5** approximately

My best *silk* outfits and formal *spoons* and silverware are on display whenever I **invite** guests to my home.

1053

藥
TRAD　SIMPLIFIED

This character with the definition:

medicine

Pinyin **yào** *and Frequency Rank* **662**

Contains **9 strokes** in the following order:

一 十 艹 艹 苏 艻 药 药 药

Contains these components:

□ grass r 艹 87, p. 29
■ ask, invite 约 1052, p. 238

With all these meanings & readings:

yào [藥] **1** medicine **2** drug **3** cure **4** m 种 [種][zhǒng], 服[fù]

Especially in olden times, **medicine** was created out of *grass* and other herbal components. These potions *invited* people to improve their health.

1054

统

统
TRAD SIMPLIFIED

This character with the definition:

unite, gather

Pinyin **tǒng** *and Frequency Rank* **264**

Contains **9 strokes** in the following order:

Contains these components:

silk r ⻕ 1037, p. 235

ample, sufficient 充 996, p. 227

With all these meanings & readings:

tǒng [统] **1** to gather **2** to unite **3** to unify **4** whole

If I **gather** an *ample* number of *silk* threads, I'll be ready to begin a big embroidery project.

1055

丝

絲
TRAD SIMPLIFIED

This character with the definition:

silk*

Pinyin **sī** *and Frequency Rank* **1026**

Contains **5 strokes** in the following order:

Contains these components:

silk r (×2) ⻕ 1037, p. 235

With all these meanings & readings:

sī [絲] **1** silk **2** thread **3** trace **4** m 条 [條][tiáo]

Notice how the two bottom portions of the *silk* components resemble *silk* threads twisted and tangled together to yield a superior strength of **silk** fabric.

1056

绪

緒
TRAD SIMPLIFIED

This character with the definition:

matter's beginning

Pinyin **xù** *and Frequency Rank* **1413**

Contains **11 strokes** in the following order:

Contains these components:

silk r ⻕ 1037, p. 235

-er 者 456, p. 109

With all these meanings & readings:

xù [緒] **1** beginnings **2** clues **3** mental state **4** thread

Pretend that the **beginning of an important matter** were commemorated by exchanging a small, precious token, such as a piece of worked *silk*: Delivery of the *silk* gifts would have to be entrusted exclusively to a person *capable of carrying out* the duty.

1057

绍

紹
TRAD SIMPLIFIED

This character with the definition:

connect, introduce

Pinyin **shào** *and Frequency Rank* **1234**

Contains **8 strokes** in the following order:

Contains these components:

silk r ⻕ 1037, p. 235

call, convene 召 484, p. 115

With all these meanings & readings:

shào [紹] **1** connect **2** to introduce

Silk invitations were sent out to *convene* a meeting so that the boss could *introduce* our new employees.

1058

纪

紀
TRAD SIMPLIFIED

This character with the definition:

historical record

Pinyin **jì** *and Frequency Rank* **584**

Contains **6 strokes** in the following order:

Contains these components:

silk r ⻕ 1037, p. 235

self* 己 135, p. 39

With all these meanings & readings:

jǐ [紀] **1** Ji (surname)
jì [紀] **1** discipline **2** age **3** era **4** period **5** order **6** record

The ancient town commissioned an artist to portray its impressive **historical record** by weaving a huge *silk* tapestry of its major events. The artist slyly inserted him*self* as a participant in that history.

1059

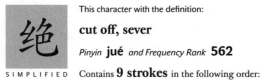

绝
绝
TRAD SIMPLIFIED

This character with the definition:

cut off, sever

Pinyin **jué** *and Frequency Rank* **562**

Contains **9 strokes** in the following order:

Contains these components:

■ silk r 纟 (altered) 1037, p. 235
□ color* 色 (altered) 840, p. 193

With all these meanings & readings:

jué [絕] **1** to cut short **2** extinct **3** to disappear **4** to vanish **5** absolutely **6** by no means

A maker of fine *silk* knows to **cut off** the roll of cloth when it is time to change the dye *color*.

Unit 45

1060

纸

纸
TRAD SIMPLIFIED

This character with the definition:

paper

Pinyin **zhǐ** *and Frequency Rank* **1020**

Contains **7 strokes** in the following order:

Contains these components:

◻ silk r 纟 (altered) 1037, p. 235
◻ surname 氏 413, p. 100

With all these meanings & readings:

zhǐ [紙] **1** paper **2** m 张 [張][zhāng], 沓[dá]

My husband insists that the banner announcing the opening of his new restaurant be made of expensive *silk* and not cheap **paper** because his family *surname* will appear on it.

1061

纵

縱
TRAD SIMPLIFIED

This character with the definition:

vertical

Pinyin **zòng** *and Frequency Rank* **1236**

Contains **7 strokes** in the following order:

Contains these components:

◻ silk r 纟 (altered) 1037, p. 235
◻ from 从 860, p. 197

With all these meanings & readings:

zòng [縱] **1** warp (the vertical threads in weaving) **2** vertical **3** longitudinal **4** north-south (lines of longitude) **5** lengthwise **6** to release **7** to indulge **8** even if

You test the quality of *silk* thread by holding it taut in a **vertical** line *from* top to bottom.

1062

续

續
TRAD SIMPLIFIED

This character with the definition:

replenish

Pinyin **xù** *and Frequency Rank* **552**

Contains **11 strokes** in the following order:

Contains these components:

◻ silk r 纟 1037, p. 235
◻ sell 卖 710, p. 167

With all these meanings & readings:

xù [續] **1** continue **2** replenish

We *sell silk* to **replenish** our bank account, which is constantly drained by our lavish lifestyle.

1063

绘

繪
TRAD SIMPLIFIED

This character with the definition:

paint, draw

Pinyin **huì** *and Frequency Rank* **1809**

Contains **9 strokes** in the following order:

Contains these components:

◻ silk r 纟 (altered) 1037, p. 235
◻ assemble, meet 会 969, p. 221

With all these meanings & readings:

huì [繪] **1** to draw **2** to paint

The artists agreed to *meet* at the loft so that they could **paint** on *silk*screens together.

1064

鄉
TRAD SIMPLIFIED

This character with the definition:

township

Pinyin **xiāng** *and Frequency Rank* **922**

Contains **3 strokes** in the following order:

Contains these components:

◼ silk r 纟 (altered) 1037, p. 235

With all these meanings & readings:

xiāng [鄉] **1** country **2** village

Silk is the kind of product you need only if you live in a **township**.

1065

纽

纽
TRAD SIMPLIFIED

This character with the definition:

button

Pinyin **niǔ** *and Frequency Rank* **1767**

Contains **7 strokes** in the following order:

Contains these components:

◼ silk r 纟 1037, p. 235
◻ clown 丑 33, p. 17

With all these meanings & readings:

niǔ [纽] **1** to turn **2** to wrench **3** button **4** nu (Greek letter ν)

In the funniest part of his act, the *clown* used pieces of *silk* to try and **button** his pants!

1066

绳

繩
TRAD SIMPLIFIED

This character with the definition:

rope

Pinyin **shéng** *and Frequency Rank* **1983**

Contains **11 strokes** in the following order:

Contains these components:

◼ silk r 纟 1037, p. 235
◻ tadpole 黾 150, p. 42

With all these meanings & readings:

shéng [繩] **1** rope **2** m 根[gēn]

Silk threads are pretty weak. But make a paste out of *tadpole* bodies and smear it on the silk, and—presto—you have a strong **rope**.

1067

This component has the meaning:

clothing r

COMPONENT

A favorite gown—a piece of **clothing** only worn on special occasions—has become crushed while hanging in the closet and waiting for the next fancy event.

1068

衣

SIMP & TRAD

This character with the definition:

clothing

Pinyin **yī** *and Frequency Rank* **725**

Contains **6 strokes** in the following order:

Contains these components:

◼ clothing r 衤 (altered) 1067, p. 242

With all these meanings & readings:

yī [衣] **1** clothes **2** m 件[jiàn]
yì [衣] **1** to dress **2** to wear **3** to put on (clothes)

Imagine your 'special event' **clothing**, in this case a **gown**, resting on a hanger just after it's come back from the cleaners. The character's lines suggest the lines of your fine garment: see the stylish collar (encircling the 'dab' head) above the flowing sleeves and the drape of the gown.

1069

哀

SIMP & TRAD

This character with the definition:

grief, sorrow

Pinyin **āi** *and Frequency Rank* **1751**

Contains **9 strokes** in the following order:

Contains these components:

◼ clothing 衣 (altered) 1068, p. 242
◻ mouth 口 37, p. 17

With all these meanings & readings:

āi [哀] **1** sorrow **2** grief **3** pity **4** to grieve for **5** to pity **6** to lament **7** to condole

People all over the world express **sorrow** by wearing a specific color on their *clothing* and letting out incomprehensible sounds from their *mouths*.

1070
表
錶
TRAD

SIMPLIFIED

This character with the definition:

outward, exterior appearance

Pinyin **biǎo** *and Frequency Rank* **177**

Contains **8 strokes** in the following order:

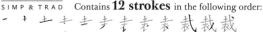

Contains these components:

☐ hair 毛 (altered) 184, p. 50
☐ clothing 衣 (altered) 1068, p. 242

With all these meanings & readings:

biǎo [表] **1** exterior surface **2** family relationship via females **3** to show (one's opinion) **4** a model **5** a table (listing information) **6** a form **7** a meter (measuring sth)
biǎo [錶] **1** a wrist watch or pocket watch

When a stray *hair* clings to an article of *clothing*, it detracts from the garment's **outward appearance**.

1071

裁

SIMP & TRAD

This character with the definition:

cut, cut cloth

Pinyin **cái** *and Frequency Rank* **1203**

Contains **12 strokes** in the following order:

Contains these components:

☐ wound c 弋 937, p. 215
☐ clothing 衣 1068, p. 242

With all these meanings & readings:

cái [裁] **1** cut out (as a dress) **2** cut **3** trim **4** reduce **5** diminish **6** decision **7** judgment

The soldier's *wound* was bleeding so profusely that the surgeon had to **cut cloth** pieces from the soldier's *clothing* for makeshift bandages.

1072

裂

SIMP & TRAD

This character with the definition:

split, divide up

Pinyin **liè** *and Frequency Rank* **1317**

Contains **12 strokes** in the following order:

Contains these components:

☐ arrange, line up 列 885, p. 202
☐ clothing 衣 1068, p. 242

With all these meanings & readings:

liè [裂] **1** to split **2** to crack **3** to break open **4** to rend

The volunteers *lined up* at the table, ready to **divide up** and distribute the used *clothing* among the worthy poor.

1073

袁

SIMP & TRAD

This character with the definition:

Yuan Shikai

Pinyin **yuán** *and Frequency Rank* **1755**

Contains **10 strokes** in the following order:

Contains these components:

☐ earth, soil 土 9, p. 11
☐ mouth 口 37, p. 17
☐ clothing 衣 (abbrev) 1068, 242

With all these meanings & readings:

Yuán [袁] **1** surname Yuan **2** often refers to Yuan Shikai 袁世凱 [~~凱]

Yuan Shikai (also written 'Yuan Shih-kai') (袁世凱, Yúan Shìkǎi), first President of the Republic of China (1912–15), declared himself Emperor in 1916. • Imagine **Yuan Shikai**'s imperial aspirations flowing out of his *robes* and being *grounded* in edicts that are issued from his *mouth* to justify the resurrection of imperialism.

1074

卒

SIMP & TRAD

This character with the definition:

foot soldier

Pinyin **zú** *and Frequency Rank* **2584**

Contains **8 strokes** in the following order:

Contains these components:

☐ clothing 衣 (altered) 1068, p. 242
☐ ten 十 7, p. 11

With all these meanings & readings:

cù [卒] **1** abruptly **2** hurriedly
zú [卒] **1** die **2** soldier

The **foot soldier**'s uniform looked completely different from his street *clothing*. Notice his pants, whose knife-edge creases makes them look like a Chinese 'ten'.

1075

SIMP & TRAD

This character with the definition:

drunk

Pinyin **zuì** *and Frequency Rank* **1783**

Contains these components:

■ five to seven pm 酉 302, p. 77
■ foot soldier 卒 1074, p. 243

With all these meanings & readings:

zuì [醉] **1** intoxicated

Contains **15 strokes** in the following order:

一 厂 厂 兀 酉 酉 酉 酉 酉 酉 醉 醉 醉 醉 醉

If you pour large amounts of *wine* into one *foot soldier*, you get a **drunk** soldier.

1076

SIMP & TRAD

This character with the definition:

to smash, break

Pinyin **suì** *and Frequency Rank* **1420**

Contains these components:

■ stone, rock 石 522, p. 124
■ foot soldier 卒 1074, p. 243

With all these meanings & readings:

suì [碎] **1** to break down **2** to break into pieces **3** fragmentary

Contains **13 strokes** in the following order:

一 ノ 丆 石 石 石 砕 砕 砕 砕 碎 碎 碎

The force of the bomb explosion sent a *stone* toward the *soldier* that then **smashed** his helmet.

1077 农

農
TRAD SIMPLIFIED

This character with the definition:

agriculture

Pinyin **nóng** *and Frequency Rank* **465**

Contains these components:

■ clothing 衣 (altered) 1068, p. 242

With all these meanings & readings:

nóng [農] **1** agriculture

Contains **6 strokes** in the following order:

丶 一 ニ 少 农 农

Scholars speculate that **agriculture** was the first accomplishment of civilization. By altering parts of the fruits and vegetables that early farmers cultivated, people made it possible to create warm and durable *clothing*.

1078 浓

濃
TRAD SIMPLIFIED

This character with the definition:

dense, thick

Pinyin **nóng** *and Frequency Rank* **1585**

Contains these components:

■ water r 氵 314, p. 80
■ agriculture 农 1077, p. 244

With all these meanings & readings:

nóng [濃] **1** concentrated **2** dens[e]

Contains **9 strokes** in the following order:

丶 丶 氵 氵 汀 沙 波 浓 浓

Every type of *agriculture* requires a steady supply of *water* in order to produce a **thick** harvest.

1079

SIMP & TRAD

This character with the definition:

decline, wane, feeble

Pinyin **shuāi** *and Frequency Rank* **1702**

Contains these components:

■ clothing 衣 (altered) 1068, p. 242
■ day, sun 日 (altered) 64, p. 24

With all these meanings & readings:

cuī [衰] **1** mourning garments
shuāi [衰] **1** weak **2** feeble **3** decline **4** wane

Contains **10 strokes** in the following order:

丶 一 亠 产 卉 亩 声 表 衰 衰

Look how gaudy this guy's *clothes* are—so much so that the *sun* seems to radiate out of it. As men's clothing becomes more outrageous, so does civilization **decline**.

1080

This character with the definition:

at first

Pinyin **chū** *and Frequency Rank* **667**

SIMP & TRAD   Contains **7 strokes** in the following order:

Contains these components:

■ clothing r 衤 1067, p. 242
■ knife 刀 469, p. 112

With all these meanings & readings:

chū [初] **1** at first **2** (at the) beginning **3** first **4** junior **5** basic

` ﾗ ﾈ ﾈ ﾈ 初 初

The jewelry store owner was fooled **at first** by the customer's expensive-looking *clothing*, and eagerly brought out his most valuable items. He realized his mistake when he turned around and the 'customer' suddenly pointed a *knife* at him.

1081

補
TRAD

This character with the definition:

mend, patch

Pinyin **bǔ** *and Frequency Rank* **944**

SIMPLIFIED   Contains **7 strokes** in the following order:

Contains these components:

■ clothing r 衤 1067, p. 242
■ foretell 卜 187, p. 51

With all these meanings & readings:

bǔ [補] **1** to repair **2** to patch **3** to mend **4** to make up for **5** to fill (a vacancy) **6** to supplement

` ﾗ ﾈ ﾈ ﾈ 礼 补

Because I'm a man, I don't have a clue how to **mend** torn *clothes*. As far as I'm concerned, somebody takes a *magic wand* and waves it over the tear to make it disappear.

1082

This character with the definition:

sleeve

Pinyin **xiù** *and Frequency Rank* **1686**

SIMP & TRAD   Contains **10 strokes** in the following order:

Contains these components:

■ clothing r 衤 1067, p. 242
■ reason, by means of 由 58, p. 22

With all these meanings & readings:

xiù [袖] **1** sleeve

` ﾗ ﾈ ﾈ ﾈ 衤 初 初 袖 袖

Imagine that *clothes* originally took the form of table cloth-like garments draped over a person's head. It was hard to maneuver in them until some fashion genius created **sleeves by means of** which people could do whatever they wanted.

1083

This character with the definition:

robe, gown

Pinyin **páo** *and Frequency Rank* **2324**

SIMP & TRAD   Contains **10 strokes** in the following order:

Contains these components:

■ clothing r 衤 1067, p. 242
■ wrap, bag 包 385, p. 95

With all these meanings & readings:

páo [袍] **1** gown (lined)

` ﾗ ﾈ ﾈ ﾈ 衤 初 袍 袍 袍

A **robe** is an article of *clothing* that *wraps* you from head to toe.

1084

This component has the meaning:

dog r

COMPONENT

Imagine, viewed from above, a stylized form of a family **dog** curled up in front of the fireplace. The main curve represents its spine in repose, with its tail tucked in at the bottom. The top stroke represents its front pair of legs opposite from its ears while the bottom stroke represents its hind legs.

Unit 46

1085

狂

SIMP & TRAD

This character with the definition:

mad, crazy

Pinyin **kuáng** *and Frequency Rank* **1147**

Contains **7 strokes** in the following order:

丿 丬 犭 犭 犴 狂 狂

Contains these components:

▮ dog r 犭 1084, p. 245
▮ king 王 15, p. 12

With all these meanings & readings:

kuáng [狂] **1** mad **2** wild **3** violent

The *king*'s subjects were well aware of the *king*'s 'mad as a hatter' disposition; so they were not surprised to learn that the *king*'s *dog* was just as **crazy** as its owner.

1086

猫

TRAD

SIMPLIFIED

This character with the definition:

cat

Pinyin **māo** *and Frequency Rank* **1673**

Contains **11 strokes** in the following order:

丿 丬 犭 犭 犴 犵 犳 猎 猫 猫 猫

Contains these components:

▮ dog r 犭 (altered) 1084, p. 245
▮ seedling 苗 91, p. 30

With all these meanings & readings:

māo [猫] **1** cat **2** m 只 [隻][zhi]

The Chinese regard **cats** as *dog*-like animals, and allow their **cats** to roam around the *seedlings* in the fields to kill mice and farm pests.

1087

犯

SIMP & TRAD

This character with the definition:

break law, commit crime

Pinyin **fàn** *and Frequency Rank* **767**

Contains **5 strokes** in the following order:

丿 丬 犭 犭 犯

Contains these components:

▮ dog r 犭 1084, p. 245
▮ single ear r 卩 (altered) 165, p. 46

With all these meanings & readings:

fàn [犯] **1** to violate **2** to offend **3** to assault **4** criminal **5** crime **6** to make a mistake **7** recurrence (of mistake or sth bad)

The *dog* with *one ear* looked so threatening I could easily imagine him **committing** a doggy **crime**.

1088

貌

SIMP & TRAD

This character with the definition:

appearance*

Pinyin **mào** *and Frequency Rank* **1595**

Contains **14 strokes** in the following order:

丿 丆 爫 夕 豸 豸 豸 豸 豹 豹 貃 貌 貌

Contains these components:

▮ dog r 犭 (altered) 1084, p. 245
▮ white 白 225, p. 60
▮ walking man r 儿 290, p. 75

With all these meanings & readings:

mào [貌] **1** appearance

You can see that the *dog* is vicious by how the scribes placed emphasis on its teeth. Upon confronting it, the *walking man* froze and his **appearance** turned *white* with fright.

1089

獄

TRAD

SIMPLIFIED

This character with the definition:

prison, jail

Pinyin **yù** *and Frequency Rank* **1597**

Contains **9 strokes** in the following order:

丿 丬 犭 犭 狂 犾 犾 狱 狱

Contains these components:

▮ dog r 犭 1084, p. 245
▮ speech r 讠 352, p. 88
▮ dog 犬 673, p. 158

With all these meanings & readings:

yù [獄] **1** prison

The two *dogs* flank the man and listen to his *speech* for commands. Because they are big, fierce, and yet well-disciplined, both are used as **prison** guards.

1090

SIMP & TRAD

This character with the definition:

dog*

Pinyin **gǒu** *and Frequency Rank* **1281**

Contains these components:

■ dog r 犭 1084, p. 245
■ sentence 句 369, p. 91

With all these meanings & readings:

gǒu [狗] **1** dog **2** m 只 [隻][zhī], 条 [條][tiáo]

Contains **8 strokes** in the following order:

ノ ノ 犭 犭 犭 狗 狗 狗

A **dog** is known as Man's Best Friend partly because only *dogs* seem able to understand—and eager to obey—a simple command *sentence* from its master.

1091

SIMP & TRAD

This character with the definition:

valiant

Pinyin **měng** *and Frequency Rank* **1157**

Contains these components:

■ dog r 犭 1084, p. 245
■ eldest brother 孟 102, p. 32

With all these meanings & readings:

měng [猛] **1** ferocious **2** suddenly **3** fierce **4** violent **5** abrupt

Contains **11 strokes** in the following order:

ノ ノ 犭 犭 犭 狆 狆 猛 猛 猛 猛

A home intruder tried to attack my *eldest brother*, that is, until the loyal and **valiant** response of his *dog* sent the intruder fleeing.

1092

猪
TRAD SIMPLIFIED

This character with the definition:

hog, pig

Pinyin **zhū** *and Frequency Rank* **1762**

Contains these components:

■ dog r 犭 1084, p. 245
■ -er 者 456, p. 109

With all these meanings & readings:

zhū [豬] **1** hog **2** pig **3** swine **4** m 口 [kǒu], 头 [頭][tóu]

Contains **11 strokes** in the following order:

ノ ノ 犭 犭 犭 狆 狆 猪 猪 猪 猪

Believe it or not, a **pig** shares many similar *abilities* with a *dog*. It's loyal, smart, trainable, long-lived—and you can eat it, too.

1093

犹
TRAD SIMPLIFIED

This character with the definition:

just as, just like

Pinyin **yóu** *and Frequency Rank* **1230**

Contains these components:

■ dog r 犭 1084, p. 245
■ dog 犬 (altered) 673, p. 158

With all these meanings & readings:

yóu [猶] **1** also **2** as if **3** still **4** to scheme **5** a Jew

Contains **7 strokes** in the following order:

ノ ノ 犭 犭 犭 犹 犹

(We'll use this term to mean **similarity** or **the same as**.) If you look at wildly distinct breeds of *dogs* (such as Irish wolfhounds and Boston terriers), it's hard to believe they belong to the **same** species.

1094

获
TRAD SIMPLIFIED

This character with the definition:

capture, catch

Pinyin **huò** *and Frequency Rank* **688**

Contains these components:

□ grass r 艹 87, p. 29
■ just as, just like 犹 (altered) 1093, p. 247

With all these meanings & readings:

huò [獲] **1** to catch **2** to obtain **3** to capture
huò [穫] **1** to reap **2** to harvest

Contains **10 strokes** in the following order:

一 十 艹 艹 艻 艻 芥 芥 获 获

I have *two dogs* that **capture** prey in the *grassy* fields and meadows.

1095

獨
TRAD SIMPLIFIED

This character with the definition:

on one's own

Pinyin **dú** *and Frequency Rank* **627**

Contains these components:

■ dog r 犭 1084, p. 245
■ insect 虫 1016, p. 231

With all these meanings & readings:

dú [獨] **1** alone **2** independent **3** single **4** sole **5** only

Contains **9 strokes** in the following order:

ノ 丿 犭 犭 犯 狆 独 独 独

The pathetic individual smells like a *dog* and is covered with *insects*. Gross! No wonder he is **on his own**!

1096

This component has the meaning:

heart (fat) r

COMPONENT

This is the first of two forms for 'heart'; this form occurs when the component appears on the bottom of characters. As in Western prose and poetry, the **heart** element will correspond with an emotion or emotional event.

1097

SIMP & TRAD

This character with the definition:

heart

Pinyin **xīn** *and Frequency Rank* **90**

Contains these components:

■ heart (fat) r 心 (altered) 1096, p. 248

With all these meanings & readings:

xīn [心] **1** heart **2** mind **3** m [顆][kē], 个[個][gè], 颗[顆][kē]

Contains **4 strokes** in the following order:

ノ 心 心 心

The central curve suggests the physical **heart** is partitioned into its four chambers.

1098

悶
TRAD SIMPLIFIED

This character with the definition:

stuffy, muggy

Pinyin **mēn** *and Frequency Rank* **1830**

Contains these components:

□ doorway 门 243, p. 64
■ heart 心 1097, p. 248

With all these meanings & readings:

mēn [悶] **1** stuffy **2** shut indoo **3** to smother **4** to cover tightly
mèn [悶] **1** bored **2** depressed **3** melancholy **4** sealed **5** airtig **6** tightly closed

Contains **7 strokes** in the following order:

丶 冂 门 门 闷 闷 闷

Imagine the dabs in the *'heart'* component as invisible drops of water hanging in the air inside the *doorway* of a room on a **muggy** day.

1099

SIMP & TRAD

This character with the definition:

must

Pinyin **bì** *and Frequency Rank* **248**

Contains these components:

■ heart 心 1097, p. 248
■ action path c 丿 438, p. 105

With all these meanings & readings:

bì [必] **1** certainly **2** must **3** will **4** necessarily

Contains **5 strokes** in the following order:

ノ 心 心 必 必

Your *heart* **must** be constantly in *action*—otherwise you die.

1100

SIMP & TRAD

This character with the definition:

宓

tranquil

Pinyin **mì** *and Frequency Rank* **4271**

Contains **8 strokes** in the following order:

`丶丷宀宀宓宓宓宓`

Contains these components:

☐ roof r 宀 271, p. 70
■ must 必 1099, p. 248

With all these meanings & readings:

mì [宓] **1** still **2** silent **3** surname Mi

My grandparents' house was **tranquil** because, while under their *roof*, we were told that we *must* not make noise.

1101

SIMP & TRAD

This character with the definition:

密

thick, dense, intimate

Pinyin **mì** *and Frequency Rank* **591**

Contains **11 strokes** in the following order:

`丶丷宀宀宓宓宓宓密密密`

Contains these components:

☐ tranquil 宓 1100, p. 249
■ mountain 山 4, p. 10

With all these meanings & readings:

mì [密] **1** secret **2** confidential **3** close **4** thick **5** dense

The **thick, dense** vegetation that shrouds the *mountain* keeps it *tranquil*.

1102
秘
祕
TRAD SIMPLIFIED

This character with the definition:

秘

secret

Pinyin **mì** *and Frequency Rank* **896**

Contains **10 strokes** in the following order:

`丿二千千禾禾禾秋秘秘秘`

Contains these components:

☐ rice, grain (crop) 禾 593, p. 140
☐ must 必 1099, p. 248

With all these meanings & readings:

bì [秘] **1** see 秘鲁 [~鲁] [bì lǔ]
mì [秘] **1** secret **2** secretary

The *grains* for the troops *must* be delivered in **secret** to prevent the enemy from disrupting our plans or gaining knowledge of our strength.

1103

SIMP & TRAD

This character with the definition:

瑟

rustling sound

Pinyin **sè** *and Frequency Rank* **1694**

Contains **13 strokes** in the following order:

`一二千王王王王王珏珏瑟瑟瑟`

Contains these components:

☐ king (×2) 王 15, p. 12
☐ must 必 1099, p. 248

With all these meanings & readings:

sè [瑟] **1** a type of standing harp, smaller than konghou 箜篌, with 5–25 strings

It's a solemn moment when a *pair of kings* from neighboring states gather to sign a treaty that *must* be signed! No one dares make noise to interrupt the proceedings—only the **rustling sounds** of the rulers' robes can be heard.

1104

SIMP & TRAD

This character with the definition:

悲

sad, sorrow

Pinyin **bēi** *and Frequency Rank* **1166**

Contains **12 strokes** in the following order:

`丿丿丬丬刲非非非非悲悲悲`

Contains these components:

☐ not 非 6, p. 11
■ heart (fat) r 心 1096, p. 248

With all these meanings & readings:

bēi [悲] **1** sad **2** sadness **3** sorrow **4** grief

Sadness and **sorrow** are prime examples of *negative emotions*.

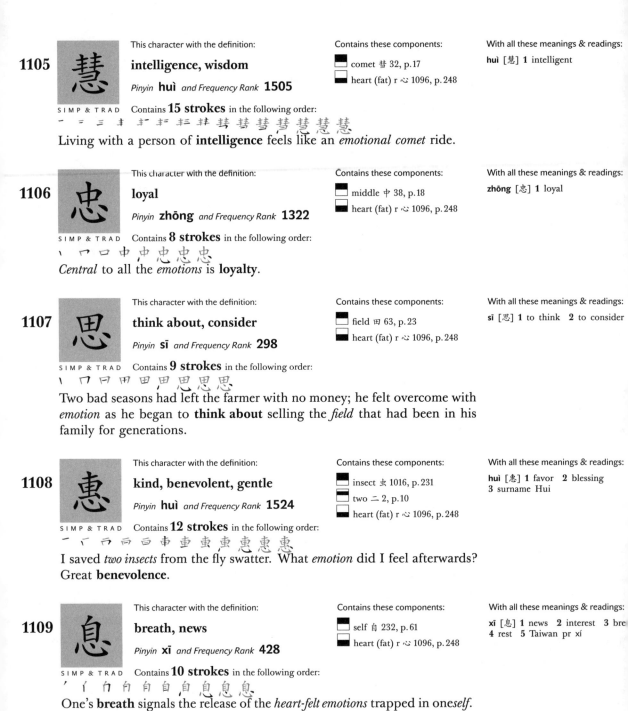

1105

慧

SIMP & TRAD

This character with the definition:

intelligence, wisdom

Pinyin **huì** *and Frequency Rank* **1505**

Contains **15 strokes** in the following order:

Contains these components:

☐ comet 彗 32, p.17
☐ heart (fat) r 心 1096, p.248

With all these meanings & readings:

huì [慧] **1** intelligent

Living with a person of **intelligence** feels like an *emotional comet* ride.

1106

忠

SIMP & TRAD

This character with the definition:

loyal

Pinyin **zhōng** *and Frequency Rank* **1322**

Contains **8 strokes** in the following order:

Contains these components:

☐ middle 中 38, p.18
☐ heart (fat) r 心 1096, p.248

With all these meanings & readings:

zhōng [忠] **1** loyal

Central to all the *emotions* is **loyalty**.

1107

思

SIMP & TRAD

This character with the definition:

think about, consider

Pinyin **sī** *and Frequency Rank* **298**

Contains **9 strokes** in the following order:

Contains these components:

☐ field 田 63, p.23
☐ heart (fat) r 心 1096, p.248

With all these meanings & readings:

sī [思] **1** to think **2** to consider

Two bad seasons had left the farmer with no money; he felt overcome with *emotion* as he began to **think about** selling the *field* that had been in his family for generations.

1108

惠

SIMP & TRAD

This character with the definition:

kind, benevolent, gentle

Pinyin **huì** *and Frequency Rank* **1524**

Contains **12 strokes** in the following order:

Contains these components:

☐ insect 虫 1016, p.231
☐ two 二 2, p.10
☐ heart (fat) r 心 1096, p.248

With all these meanings & readings:

huì [惠] **1** favor **2** blessing **3** surname Hui

I saved *two insects* from the fly swatter. What *emotion* did I feel afterwards? Great **benevolence**.

1109

息

SIMP & TRAD

This character with the definition:

breath, news

Pinyin **xī** *and Frequency Rank* **428**

Contains **10 strokes** in the following order:

Contains these components:

☐ self 自 232, p.61
☐ heart (fat) r 心 1096, p.248

With all these meanings & readings:

xī [息] **1** news **2** interest **3** bre **4** rest **5** Taiwan pr xí

One's **breath** signals the release of the *heart-felt emotions* trapped in one*self*.

Unit 47

1110

This character with the definition:

daughter-in-law

Pinyin **xí** *and Frequency Rank* **2393**

SIMP & TRAD Contains **13 strokes** in the following order:

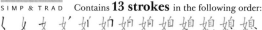

Contains these components:

woman 女 790, p. 183

breath, news 息 1109, p. 250

With all these meanings & readings:

xí [媳] **1** daughter in law

Family relations are emotion-laden connections. When a son introduces as a prospective **daughter-in-law** a *woman*, he hopes that she will serve as a *breath* of fresh air into the family.

1111

This character with the definition:

forget

Pinyin **wàng** *and Frequency Rank* **1056**

SIMP & TRAD Contains **7 strokes** in the following order:

Contains these components:

perish 亡 259, p. 67

heart (fat) r 心 1096, p. 248

With all these meanings & readings:

wàng [忘] **1** to forget **2** to overlook **3** to neglect

In this character, the 'perish' element seems like a heavy anvil hammering down on the heart beneath it—in the same way that **forgetting** a rival can sometimes resemble the *perishing* of negative *emotion*.

1112

This character with the definition:

be puzzled, bewildered

Pinyin **huò** *and Frequency Rank* **1600**

SIMP & TRAD Contains **12 strokes** in the following order:

Contains these components:

or 或 663, p. 156

heart (fat) r 心 1096, p. 248

With all these meanings & readings:

huò [惑] **1** confuse

The young man was **puzzled** over which path to follow—his *heart* by marrying his true love *or* his head by going away to college.

1113

This character with the definition:

think, believe

Pinyin **xiǎng** *and Frequency Rank* **99**

SIMP & TRAD Contains **13 strokes** in the following order:

Contains these components:

appearance 相 587, p. 139

heart (fat) r 心 1096, p. 248

With all these meanings & readings:

xiǎng [想] **1** to think **2** to believe **3** to suppose **4** to wish **5** to want **6** to miss

It's amazing how often the Chinese embed charming metaphors into their characters. For example, here we see the *appearance* of an *emotion* as if to say a **thought** or **belief** originates in the *heart*.

1114

This character with the definition:

feel, sense

Pinyin **gǎn** *and Frequency Rank* **243**

SIMP & TRAD Contains **13 strokes** in the following order:

Contains these components:

all, everyone 咸 654, p. 154

heart (fat) r 心 1096, p. 248

With all these meanings & readings:

gǎn [感] **1** to feel **2** to move **3** to touch **4** to affect

To **feel** and to **sense** show empathic awareness from *everyone's heart*.

1115

This character with the definition:

compassionate, kind

Pinyin **cí** *and Frequency Rank* **1487**

SIMP & TRAD   Contains **13 strokes** in the following order:

Contains these components:

■ now, at present* 兹 1003, p. 228

■ heart (fat) r 心 1096, p. 248

With all these meanings & readings:

cí [慈] **1** compassionate **2** gentle **3** merciful **4** kind **5** humane

Major religions teach people to live in the *present* moment and to have a *heart* that is **compassionate, kind,** and loving.

1116

This character with the definition:

feel attached to

Pinyin **liàn** *and Frequency Rank* **1464**

戀 TRAD   SIMPLIFIED   Contains **10 strokes** in the following order:

Contains these components:

■ also, too 亦 842, p. 193

■ heart (fat) r 心 1096, p. 248

With all these meanings & readings:

liàn [戀] **1** to feel attached to **2** long for **3** love

Two (sounds like *too*) *hearts* are joined together because their owners **feel attached to one another**.

1117

This character with the definition:

envy, be jealous

Pinyin **jì** *and Frequency Rank* **1922**

SIMP & TRAD   Contains **7 strokes** in the following order:

Contains these components:

■ self* 己 135, p. 39

■ heart (fat) r 心 1096, p. 248

With all these meanings & readings:

jì [忌] **1** avoid as taboo **2** jealous

A *heart* that is concerned only with the *self* is prone to **be jealous** of others, since there is no room in it to allow the in the feeling of generosity.

1118

This character with the definition:

blame, reproach, reprove

Pinyin **yuàn** *and Frequency Rank* **1637**

SIMP & TRAD   Contains **9 strokes** in the following order:

Contains these components:

■ dusk* 夕 875, p. 200

■ self* 己 (altered) 135, p. 39

■ heart (fat) r 心 1096, p. 248

With all these meanings & readings:

yuàn [怨] **1** to blame **2** to complain

Lying awake in bed at *night* is the worst—you're prey to all sorts of thoughts and *emotions* that lead you to **blame** *yourself* for everything that's wrong in your life.

1119

This character with the definition:

aspiration

Pinyin **zhì** *and Frequency Rank* **542**

志誌 TRAD   SIMPLIFIED   Contains **7 strokes** in the following order:

Contains these components:

■ knight 士 8, p. 11

■ heart (fat) r 心 1096, p. 248

With all these meanings & readings:

zhì [志] **1** aspiration **2** ambition **3** the will

zhì [誌] **1** sign **2** mark **3** to record **4** write a footnote

The *emotions* of a true *knight* are aligned with his noble **aspirations**: to do good and protect his sovereign.

1120 恩

This character with the definition:

kindness, favor

Pinyin **ēn** *and Frequency Rank* **888**

SIMP & TRAD   Contains **10 strokes** in the following order:

丨 冂 冂 因 因 因 因 恩 恩 恩

Contains these components:

因 because 困 545, p.129

心 heart (fat) r 心 1096, p.248

With all these meanings & readings:

ēn [恩] **1** favor **2** grace **3** kindness

Gestures of **kindness** *cause* the *heart* to feel *emotions*.

1121 嗯

This character with the definition:

how come? why?

Pinyin **ňg** *and Frequency Rank* **2042**

SIMP & TRAD   Contains **13 strokes** in the following order:

丨 口 口 叮 叮 叮 叮 叩 咽 咽 嗯 嗯 嗯

Contains these components:

口 mouth 口 37, p.17

恩 kindness, favor 恩 1120, p.253

With all these meanings & readings:

ēn [嗯] **1** (a groaning sound)
èn [嗯] **1** (nonverbal grunt as interjection) **2** OK, yeah **3** what?
ēn [嗯] **1** interjection indicating approval, appreciation or agreement

His open *mouth* revealed his **surprise** at being the recipient of unexpected *kindness*.

1122 意

This character with the definition:

idea, meaning

Pinyin **yì** *and Frequency Rank* **104**

SIMP & TRAD   Contains **13 strokes** in the following order:

丶 亠 亠 立 立 音 音 音 音 意 意 意

Contains these components:

音 sound 音 689, p.161

心 heart (fat) r 心 1096, p.248

With all these meanings & readings:

yì [意] **1** idea **2** meaning **3** though **4** to think **5** wish **6** desire **7** intention **8** to expect **9** to anticipate **10** abbr for Italy 意大利

This character symbolically depicts an **idea** as the '*sound*' of an *emotion*.

1123 怎

This character with the definition:

how, why

Pinyin **zěn** *and Frequency Rank* **382**

SIMP & TRAD   Contains **9 strokes** in the following order:

丿 乍 乍 乍 乍 怎 怎 怎 怎

Contains these components:

乍 abruptly 乍 447, p.107

心 heart (fat) r 心 1096, p.248

With all these meanings & readings:

zěn [怎] **1** how

How is the human *heart* connected to the brain? The brain transmits signals of intense *emotion* to different parts of the body, including the *heart*, which is **why** one's *heart abruptly* beats faster sometimes.

1124 忽

This character with the definition:

suddenly

Pinyin **hū** *and Frequency Rank* **912**

SIMP & TRAD   Contains **8 strokes** in the following order:

丿 勹 勿 勿 勿 忽 忽 忽

Contains these components:

勿 do not 勿 460, p.111

心 heart (fat) r 心 1096, p.248

With all these meanings & readings:

hū [忽] **1** suddenly

Do not scare me like that again. My *heart* is still beating wildly from the **sudden** (and unwanted!) kiss you planted on me.

1125 忍

SIMP & TRAD

This character with the definition:

bear, endure, forbear

Pinyin **rěn** *and Frequency Rank* **1127**

Contains these components:

▭ blade edge 刃 487, p.116

▬ heart (fat) r 心 1096, p. 248

With all these meanings & readings:

rěn [忍] **1** to beat **2** to endure **3** to tolerate

Contains **7 strokes** in the following order:

フ刀刃刃忍忍忍

This character focuses on the *emotional* balancing that is required during times of **forbearance** and **endurance**—when it feels like you're living on the *edge of a blade*.

1126 急

SIMP & TRAD

This character with the definition:

impatient, anxious

Pinyin **jí** *and Frequency Rank* **657**

Contains these components:

▬ hay for fodder 刍 873, p.199

▭ heart (fat) r 心 1096, p. 248

With all these meanings & readings:

jí [急] **1** urgent **2** pressing **3** rapid **4** hurried **5** worried

Contains **9 strokes** in the following order:

ノ 勹 刍 刍 刍 刍 急 急 急

The **impatient** guests were anxious to try the chef's latest avant-garde masterpiece: *hay* and *heart* hotpot.

1127 稳

穩
TRAD

SIMPLIFIED

This character with the definition:

steady, steadfast

Pinyin **wěn** *and Frequency Rank* **1055**

Contains these components:

▯ rice, grain (crop) 禾 593, p.140

▮ impatient, anxious 急 1126, p. 254

With all these meanings & readings:

wěn [穩] **1** settled **2** steady **3** stable

Contains **14 strokes** in the following order:

′ ニ 千 禾 禾 禾' 禾" 秒 秒 稳 稳 稳 稳 稳

Careful—the cup of *rice* is filled to the brim. If you are *anxious* or *impatient* while carrying the cup, it won't hold **steady** and the *rice* will spill all over the floor.

1128 隐

隱
TRAD

SIMPLIFIED

This character with the definition:

conceal, hide, latent

Pinyin **yǐn** *and Frequency Rank* **1034**

Contains these components:

▯ hills r ⻖ 942, p. 216

▮ impatient, anxious 急 1126, p. 254

With all these meanings & readings:

yǐn [隱] **1** secret **2** hidden **3** concealed **4** Greek stem: crypto-

yìn [隱] **1** to lean upon

Contains **11 strokes** in the following order:

⻖ ⻏ ⻏' ⻏" 阶 阵 隐 隐 隐 隐 隐

Blackbeard the Pirate is *anxious* to get back to the *hills*, for that's where his buried treasure lies **hidden**.

1129 愿

願
TRAD

SIMPLIFIED

This character with the definition:

be willing

Pinyin **yuàn** *and Frequency Rank* **598**

Contains these components:

▬ original, unprocessed 原 400, p.97

▬ heart (fat) r 心 1096, p. 248

With all these meanings & readings:

yuàn [願] **1** to hope **2** to wish **3** to desire **4** hoped-for **5** reac **6** willing **7** sincere

Contains **14 strokes** in the following order:

一 厂 厂 厂 厉 厉 盾 原 原 原 原 愿 愿 愿

What *emotion* do you feel when you visit a mountain spring in its *original* environment? Whatever it is, it's sure to be **honest** and **sincere**.

1130 态

态 TRAD

态 SIMPLIFIED

This character with the definition:

attitude

Pinyin **tài** *and Frequency Rank* **528**

Contains **8 strokes** in the following order:

一 ナ 大 太 太 态 态 态

Contains these components:

☐ too (much) 太 547, p.129

■ heart (fat) r 心 1096, p.248

With all these meanings & readings:

tài [態] **1** attitude

That guy's got a real **attitude**. It's as if there's *too much emotion* leaking out of his *heart*.

1131 恐

SIMP & TRAD

This character with the definition:

afraid, frightened

Pinyin **kǒng** *and Frequency Rank* **891**

Contains **10 strokes** in the following order:

一 丆 工 丮 巩 巩 巩 恐 恐 恐

Contains these components:

☐ labor, work 工 12, p.12

☐ commonplace 凡 901, p.205

■ heart (fat) r 心 1096, p.248

With all these meanings & readings:

kǒng [恐] **1** afraid **2** frightened **3** to fear

It is almost *commonplace* for coal miners' families to live feeling constantly **afraid** and *emotional* about the safety of their loved ones while they *work* deep underground.

1132 虑

虑 TRAD

虑 SIMPLIFIED

This character with the definition:

anxiety

Pinyin **lǜ** *and Frequency Rank* **901**

Contains **10 strokes** in the following order:

丨 丆 匕 广 卢 虍 虎 虑 虑 虑

Contains these components:

☐ tiger 虎 (abbrev) 910, 207

■ heart (fat) r 心 1096, p.248

With all these meanings & readings:

lǜ [慮] **1** to think over **2** to consider **3** anxiety

Standing in the presence of a charging *tiger* will cause your *heart* to beat wildly because of severe **anxiety**.

1133 患

SIMP & TRAD

This character with the definition:

trouble, disaster

Pinyin **huàn** *and Frequency Rank* **1249**

Contains **11 strokes** in the following order:

丶 宀 口 吕 吕 吕 串 串 患 患 患

Contains these components:

☐ strung together 串 51, p.21

■ heart (fat) r 心 1096, p.248

With all these meanings & readings:

huàn [患] **1** to suffer (from illness) **2** to contract (a disease) **3** misfortune **4** trouble **5** danger **6** worry

It may be a sign of **trouble** when several *emotions* are *strung together*. **Disaster** brings with it many emotions. It may help to view the 'strung together' component as a couple of weights attached to a sharp spear. An enemy is attacking your *heart*, and only **trouble** or **disaster** will follow.

1134 悬

悬 TRAD

悬 SIMPLIFIED

This character with the definition:

suspend, hang*

Pinyin **xuán** *and Frequency Rank* **1879**

Contains **11 strokes** in the following order:

丨 冂 冂 日 且 且 县 县 悬 悬 悬

Contains these components:

☐ county 县 1022, p.232

■ heart (fat) r 心 1096, p.248

With all these meanings & readings:

xuán [懸] **1** hang **2** suspend **3** unresolved

The *county* bigwig keeps his private clothes rack in his office. He is so forthright and outgoing that it's as if he **hangs** his *heart* there each day.

Unit 48

1135

This component has the meaning:

heart (skinny) r

COMPONENT

This is the second of the 'heart' components, which scribes use whenever a 'heart' element appears on the left. Imagine the bottom curve of panel 1096 stretched taut and combining with one of the drops of blood. The remaining two drops suggest the importance of a healthy **heart** for keeping the blood flowing.

1136

This character with the definition:

realize

Pinyin **wù** *and Frequency Rank* **1668**

SIMP & TRAD Contains **10 strokes** in the following order:

丶丶忄忄忄忔忤悟悟悟悟

It took me a long time to **realize** that the *heart* inside *me* is the source for the real *me*.

Contains these components:

■ heart (skinny) r 忄 1135, p. 256
■ me 吾 46, p. 20

With all these meanings & readings:

wù [悟] 1 comprehend

1137

This character with the definition:

understand, know

Pinyin **dǒng** *and Frequency Rank* **1211**

SIMP & TRAD Contains **15 strokes** in the following order:

丶丶忄忄忄忄忄忄忄忄悼悼懂懂懂

You know that you fully **understand** a situation when you can turn your *heart* to *direct* your behavior.

Contains these components:

■ heart (skinny) r 忄 1135, p. 256
■ director 董 769, p. 178

With all these meanings & readings:

dǒng [懂] 1 to understand 2 to know

1138

This character with the definition:

fear, be afraid

Pinyin **pà** *and Frequency Rank* **631**

SIMP & TRAD Contains **8 strokes** in the following order:

丶丶忄忄忄怕怕怕

When a person **is afraid**, the *heart* beats faster and blood drains from their body's extremities, including the face—which is the reason for the phrase '*white* with fear'.

Contains these components:

■ heart (skinny) r 忄 1135, p. 256
■ white 白 225, p. 60

With all these meanings & readings:

pà [怕] 1 to be afraid 2 to fear

1139

This character with the definition:

nature, character, sex

Pinyin **xìng** *and Frequency Rank* **122**

SIMP & TRAD Contains **8 strokes** in the following order:

丶丶忄忄忄忓性性

The *heart gives birth to* the true **nature** and **character** of a person.

Contains these components:

■ heart (skinny) r 忄 1135, p. 256
■ give birth to 生 210, p. 57

With all these meanings & readings:

xìng [性] 1 nature 2 character 3 property 4 quality 5 attribute 6 sexuality 7 sex 8 gender 9 surname 10 suffix forming adjective from verb 11 suffix forming noun from adjective, corresponding to -ness or -ity 12 essence 13 m 个 [個][gè]

1140 busy

Pinyin **máng** *and Frequency Rank* **827**

SIMP & TRAD   Contains **6 strokes** in the following order:

Contains these components:
- heart (skinny) r 忄 1135, p. 256
- perish 亡 259, p. 67

With all these meanings & readings:
máng [忙] **1** busy **2** hurriedly

When you're truly **busy**, your *heart* is working so hard that you can be in danger of *perishing*. For instance, truly **busy** people sometimes forget to eat and become as skinny as the '*heart*' component. • It's easy to confuse 忙 with 忘 'forget' (panel 1111) since both characters use the same phonetic element (亡). To remember which different radical variant for 'heart' is used, recall that 'forget' uses the 'fat' heart component (both words begin with the same letter).

1141 快 fast

Pinyin **kuài** *and Frequency Rank* **366**

SIMP & TRAD   Contains **7 strokes** in the following order:

Contains these components:
- heart (skinny) r 忄 1135, p. 256
- surprised man c 夬 938, p. 215

With all these meanings & readings:
kuài [快] **1** rapid **2** quick **3** speed **4** rate **5** soon **6** shortly **7** quick-witted **8** clever **9** sharp (of knives or wits) **10** forthright **11** plain-spoken **12** gratified **13** pleased **14** pleasant **15** police runner (in former times, official to arrest criminals)

An extremely *surprised man* finds his *heart* beating wildly and very **fast**. It takes a couple of minutes for him to regain control of his heart rate.

1142 悔 regret, repent

Pinyin **huǐ** *and Frequency Rank* **1853**

SIMP & TRAD   Contains **10 strokes** in the following order:

Contains these components:
- heart (skinny) r 忄 1135, p. 256
- every 每 819, p. 188

With all these meanings & readings:
huǐ [悔] **1** regret

Shoulda, woulda, coulda. **Regret** is an *emotion* that *every*body feels at one point or another.

1143 恒 permanent

恆
TRAD

Pinyin **héng** *and Frequency Rank* **1764**

SIMPLIFIED   Contains **9 strokes** in the following order:

Contains these components:
- heart (skinny) r 忄 1135, p. 256
- speak 曰 67, p. 24
- two 二 2, p. 10

With all these meanings & readings:
héng [恒] **1** permanent **2** constant

That *speech* of love was so sincere that it carved not one but *two marks* on my *heart*. I know that you weren't toying with my emotions—our love is of a **permanent** form.

1144 state of mind

懷
TRAD

Pinyin **huái** *and Frequency Rank* **762**

SIMPLIFIED   Contains **7 strokes** in the following order:

Contains these components:
- heart (skinny) r 忄 1135, p. 256
- no! 不 493, p. 117

With all these meanings & readings:
huái [懷] **1** to think of **2** to cherish **3** mind **4** heart **5** bosom **6** surname Huai

This character implores to *not* pay attention to our *emotions*, relying instead on our **state of mind**.

1145

忆

憶 TRAD   SIMPLIFIED

This character with the definition:

recall, remember

Pinyin **yì** *and Frequency Rank* **1333**

Contains **4 strokes** in the following order:

丶 丶 忄 忆

Contains these components:

■ heart (skinny) r 忄 1135, p. 256
■ second (in a series) 乙 146, p. 41

With all these meanings & readings

yì [憶] **1** remember

"Fool me once, shame on you. Fool me twice, shame on me." The *second* exposure to an *emotional* experience ensures that we will **remember** it.

1146

怔

SIMP & TRAD

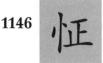

This character with the definition:

panic-stricken

Pinyin **zhēng** *and Frequency Rank* **2191**

Contains **8 strokes** in the following order:

丶 丶 忄 忄 怔 怔 怔 怔

Contains these components:

■ heart (skinny) r 忄 1135, p. 256
■ to correct, rectify 正 193, p. 52

With all these meanings & readings

zhēng [怔] **1** to stare blankly **2** startled
zhèng [怔] **1** stumped for words **2** to stare blankly

After a **panic attack**, the *heart* will *correct* its rhythms.

1147

慌

SIMP & TRAD

This character with the definition:

panic, nervous

Pinyin **huāng** *and Frequency Rank* **1650**

Contains **12 strokes** in the following order:

丶 丶 忄 忄 忄 忄 忄 忄 忄 慌 慌 慌

Contains these components:

■ heart (skinny) r 忄 1135, p. 256
■ barren, desolate 荒 445, p. 107

With all these meanings & readings

huāng [慌] **1** to get panicky **2** lose one's head

My *heart* palpitates madly in the presence of great *desolation*. I become **nervous** to the point of **panic** when I think of what will happen of us?

1148

足

This component has the meaning:

foot r

COMPONENT

And contains these subcomponents:

■ mouth 口 37, p. 17
■ stop! 止 190, p. 52

It has been said that there are some people so dumb that they cannot walk and talk at the same time. This component depicts as much: using their *mouths*, they come to a complete *stop*, and are now standing still on their **feet**. (Many people regard this component as a distorted and squished version of the character 足 'foot'.)

1149

距

SIMP & TRAD

This character with the definition:

be apart or away from

Pinyin **jù** *and Frequency Rank* **1202**

Contains **11 strokes** in the following order:

丶 口 口 𧾷 𧾷 𧾷 距 距 距 距 距

Contains these components:

■ foot r 𧾷 1148, p. 258
■ huge 巨 153, p. 42

With all these meanings & readings

jù [距] **1** at a distance of **2** distance **3** to be apart

With one step of his *foot*, the *huge* man from panel 153 can quickly move himself **away from** trouble.

150 跳

jump

Pinyin **tiào** *and Frequency Rank* **999**

SIMP & TRAD   Contains **13 strokes** in the following order:

丶 ㇇ 口 口 ⻊ ⻊ ⻊ 趴 趴 跳 跳 跳 跳

This character with the definition:

Contains these components:

foot r ⻊ 1148, p. 258
omen 兆 236, p. 63

With all these meanings & readings:

tiào [跳] **1** jump **2** hop **3** skip (a grade) **4** to leap **5** to bounce **6** to beat

My superstitious sister lifted her *foot* to **jump** over the cracked pavement. She believes that stepping on any crack is a bad *omen*.

151 跌

fall, tumble

Pinyin **diē** *and Frequency Rank* **1590**

SIMP & TRAD   Contains **12 strokes** in the following order:

丶 ㇇ 口 口 ⻊ ⻊ ⻊ 趴 趺 趺 跌 跌

This character with the definition:

Contains these components:

foot r ⻊ 1148, p. 258
lose 失 721, p. 169

With all these meanings & readings:

diē [跌] **1** to drop **2** to fall **3** to tumble **4** Taiwan pr diê

You **fall** or **tumble** when you *lose* your *footing*.

152 踏

step on, tread, stamp

Pinyin **tà** *and Frequency Rank* **1753**

SIMP & TRAD   Contains **15 strokes** in the following order:

丶 ㇇ 口 口 ⻊ ⻊ ⻊ 趴 趴 趴 跆 跆 踏 踏 踏

This character with the definition:

Contains these components:

foot r ⻊ 1148, p. 258
repeat sth numerous times 沓 316, p. 81

With all these meanings & readings:

tà [踏] **1** to tread **2** to stamp **3** to step on **4** to press a pedal **5** to investigate on the spot

What does a *foot* do *repeatedly*? It **steps on** things and **stamps** itself in place during times of frustration, that's what.

153 跑

run

Pinyin **pǎo** *and Frequency Rank* **864**

SIMP & TRAD   Contains **12 strokes** in the following order:

丶 ㇇ 口 口 ⻊ ⻊ ⻊ 趴 趵 跑 跑 跑

This character with the definition:

Contains these components:

foot r ⻊ 1148, p. 258
wrap, bag 包 385, p. 95

With all these meanings & readings:

pǎo [跑] **1** to run **2** to escape **3** race

I *wrap* my *feet* in special shoes to **run** as fast as the wind.

154 跃

leap, jump

Pinyin **yuè** *and Frequency Rank* **1516**

躍
TRAD   SIMPLIFIED   Contains **11 strokes** in the following order:

丶 ㇇ 口 口 ⻊ ⻊ ⻊ 趴 趺 趺 跃

This character with the definition:

Contains these components:

foot r ⻊ 1148, p. 258
dab r 丶 176, p. 48
big 大 544, p. 129

With all these meanings & readings:

yuè [躍] **1** to jump **2** to leap

Whenever you **jump**, your *feet* leave the ground for a *small bit* of time. Now try to **jump** as *high* as you can.

155 践

trample, tread upon

Pinyin **jiàn** *and Frequency Rank* **1578**

踐
TRAD   SIMPLIFIED   Contains **12 strokes** in the following order:

丶 ㇇ 口 口 ⻊ ⻊ ⻊ 趴 趺 践 践 践

This character with the definition:

Contains these components:

foot r ⻊ 1148, p. 258
tiny, fragmentary 戋 665, p. 157

With all these meanings & readings:

jiàn [踐] **1** fulfill (a promise) **2** tread **3** walk

The teenage neighbors **trampled** all over my garden with their huge, Doc Martens-shod *feet* and destroyed my *tiny* sprouts.

1156

This component has the meaning:

man r

COMPONENT

And contains these subcomponents:

■ man 人 (altered) 537, p.127

Here's the squished form of 人 (panel 537). In this form, it fits into the character square while leaving room for other elements.

1157

This character with the definition:

benevolence

Pinyin **rén** and Frequency Rank **1360**

SIMP & TRAD   Contains **4 strokes** in the following order:

ノ 亻 仁 仁

Contains these components:

■ man r 亻 1156, p.260
■ two 二 2, p.10

With all these meanings & readings:

rén [仁] **1** humane **2** kernel

One of the most noble feelings that can be shared between *two men* is **benevolence**.

1158

This character with the definition:

immortal

Pinyin **xiān** and Frequency Rank **1255**

SIMP & TRAD   Contains **5 strokes** in the following order:

ノ 亻 亻 仙 仙

Contains these components:

■ man r 亻 1156, p.260
■ mountain 山 4, p.10

With all these meanings & readings:

xiān [仙] **1** immortal

If you visualize this character as the '*man*' component standing at the base of the '*mountain*' element, you can remember the image as *man* standing in awe facing **immortal** Mother Nature.

1159

This character with the definition:

what

Pinyin **shén** and Frequency Rank **156**

SIMP & TRAD   Contains **4 strokes** in the following order:

ノ 亻 仁 什

Contains these components:

■ man r 亻 1156, p.260
■ ten 十 7, p.11

With all these meanings & readings:

shí [什] **1** tenth (used in fractions)
shén [甚] **1** what

An abstract word such as 'what' is sometimes combined with well-known concrete phrases, such as '**What** the hell!?' Here we associate that phrase to visualize 什. For me, the definition of 'hell' is spending eternity with the *ten men* closest to me in life.

Unit 49

1160 伍 SIMP & TRAD

This character with the definition: **five-man squad**

Pinyin **wǔ** *and Frequency Rank* **1472**

Contains **6 strokes** in the following order:

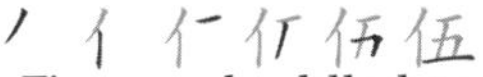

Contains these components:
- man r 亻 1156, p. 260
- five 五 13, p. 12

With all these meanings & readings:
wǔ [伍] **1** squad of five soldiers **2** to associate with **3** five (banker's anti-fraud numeral) **4** surname Wu

Five men huddled together in a special group makes a **squad**: it doesn't get any more obvious than that!

1161 佳 SIMP & TRAD

This character with the definition: **lovely, beautiful**

Pinyin **jiā** *and Frequency Rank* **1583**

Contains **8 strokes** in the following order:

Contains these components:
- man r 亻 1156, p. 260
- jade tablet 圭 10, p. 11

With all these meanings & readings:
jiā [佳] **1** excellent

The *man* contemplates buying the *jade tablet* because it is so extraordinarily **fine** and **beautiful**.

1162 值 SIMP & TRAD

This character with the definition: **be worth**

Pinyin **zhí** *and Frequency Rank* **600**

Contains **10 strokes** in the following order:

Contains these components:
- man r 亻 1156, p. 260
- straight, vertical 直 85, p. 29

With all these meanings & readings:
zhí [值] **1** value **2** (to be) worth **3** to happen

Here's a silly image. If you want to buy a person, go to a *person* store, where all the available people are hung neatly, *straight* and *vertical*, on the walls. There will even be labels fixed on each piece of merchandise telling you exactly how much each *person* **is worth**!

1163 估 SIMP & TRAD

This character with the definition: **estimate**

Pinyin **gū** *and Frequency Rank* **1326**

Contains **7 strokes** in the following order:

Contains these components:
- man r 亻 1156, p. 260
- ancient 古 53, p. 21

With all these meanings & readings:
gū [估] **1** estimate
gù [估] **1** old **2** second-hand (clothes)

Even in *ancient* times, a *man* knew how to **estimate** the value of goods.

1164 仲 SIMP & TRAD

This character with the definition: **second in seniority**

Pinyin **zhòng** *and Frequency Rank* **1706**

Contains **6 strokes** in the following order:

Contains these components:
- man r 亻 1156, p. 260
- middle 中 38, p. 18

With all these meanings & readings:
zhòng [仲] **1** surname Zhong
zhòng [仲] **1** second month of the season **2** middle **3** intermediate **4** 2nd in seniority

In smaller groups, the **second in seniority** is often the proverbial *man* in the *middle*.

1165

This character with the definition:

stretch, extend

Pinyin **shēn** *and Frequency Rank* **1161**

SIMP & TRAD   Contains **7 strokes** in the following order:

ノ 亻 亻 亻⼁ 伸 伸 伸

Contains these components:

man r 亻 1156, p. 260

express 申 57, p. 22

With all these meanings & readings

shēn [伸] **1** to stretch **2** to extend

It takes a *man* who is not afraid to *express* his opinion to **extend** his influence beyond that of the average *man*.

1166

This character with the definition:

but

Pinyin **dàn** *and Frequency Rank* **95**

SIMP & TRAD   Contains **7 strokes** in the following order:

ノ 亻 亻 亻⼁ 但 但 但

Contains these components:

man r 亻 1156, p. 260

dawn 旦 70, p. 25

With all these meanings & readings

dàn [但] **1** but **2** yet **3** however **4** only **5** merely **6** still

This *man* is still lingering over his morning breakfast, **but** he should be well on his way to work—it's well past *dawn*, **but** he's not out (sounds like 'down, but not out')!

1167

This character with the definition:

invade

Pinyin **qīn** *and Frequency Rank* **1086**

SIMP & TRAD   Contains **9 strokes** in the following order:

ノ 亻 亻⼁ 亻⼁ 伊 伊 侵 侵 侵

Contains these components:

man r 亻 1156, p. 260

broom 帚 (altered) 121, p. 36

With all these meanings & readings

qīn [侵] **1** to invade **2** to encroach **3** to infringe **4** to approach

Visualize an army of *men* armed with *brooms*! The 'towel' element of *broom* has been altered to a form showing lines that cross. The *men* are crossing the boundary to **invade** their neighboring country.

1168

This character with the definition:

he

Pinyin **tā** *and Frequency Rank* **10**

SIMP & TRAD   Contains **5 strokes** in the following order:

ノ 亻 亻⼁ 他 他

Contains these components:

man r 亻 1156, p. 260

also, too* 也 132, p. 38

With all these meanings & readings

tā [他] **1** he **2** him

Human beings are human precisely because we all store our different traits in a single body. If we focus on this one *man*, we can see **he** can be clever but *also* dumb, considerate but *also* selfish, outgoing but *also* shy.

1169

This character with the definition:

look up

Pinyin **yǎng** *and Frequency Rank* **1368**

SIMP & TRAD   Contains **6 strokes** in the following order:

ノ 亻 亻⼁ 化 仰 仰

Contains these components:

man r 亻 1156, p. 260

head held high c 卬 926, p. 210

With all these meanings & readings

yǎng [仰] **1** to look up **2** surname Yang

Even with his *head held high*, the *man* still **looked up** at the sky when he heard the loud burst of thunder.

1170

This character with the definition:

m for items, things, etc

Pinyin **jiàn** *and Frequency Rank* **250**

SIMP & TRAD   Contains **6 strokes** in the following order:

ノ 亻 亻 亻 仁 件

Contains these components:

■ man r 亻 1156, p. 260
■ ox 牛 213, p. 57

With all these meanings & readings:

jiàn [件] **1** item **2** component **3** m for events, things, clothes etc

In the old days, the only '**things**' that mattered were *cattle* and their handlers, the former being the source of a *man*'s wealth. So it makes sense to put a *man* and his '*oxen*' (cattle) together to **count** the number of *cattle* he owns.

1171

This character with the definition:

father's elder brother

Pinyin **bó** *and Frequency Rank* **821**

SIMP & TRAD   Contains **7 strokes** in the following order:

ノ 亻 亻 亻 伯 伯 伯

Contains these components:

■ man r 亻 1156, p. 260
■ white 白 225, p. 60

With all these meanings & readings:

bó [伯] **1** father's elder brother **2** senior **3** paternal elder uncle **4** eldest of brothers **5** respectful form of address **6** Count, third of five orders of nobility 五等爵位[wǔ děng jué wèi]

My **father's elder brother** was so cruel to him as a child that even now my father, a grown *man*, turns *white* with fear at the mention of his brother's name.

1172

This character with the definition:

live, dwell (in a place)

Pinyin **zhù** *and Frequency Rank* **309**

SIMP & TRAD   Contains **7 strokes** in the following order:

ノ 亻 亻 亻 住 住 住

Contains these components:

■ man r 亻 1156, p. 260
■ master 主 179, p. 49

With all these meanings & readings:

zhù [住] **1** to live **2** to dwell **3** to stay **4** to reside **5** to stop

The *man* once felt he was the *master* of his home and all that fell within it; ironically, after his divorce, he was not allowed **to live** there anymore.

1173

This character with the definition:

assume a post

Pinyin **rèn** *and Frequency Rank* **186**

SIMP & TRAD   Contains **6 strokes** in the following order:

ノ 亻 亻 仁 任 任

Contains these components:

■ man r 亻 1156, p. 260
■ knight 士 8, p. 11
□ dab r 丶 176, p. 48

With all these meanings & readings:

rèn [任] **1** to assign **2** to appoint **3** to take up a post **4** office **5** responsibility **6** to let **7** to allow **8** to give free rein to **9** no matter (how, what etc) **10** surname Ren

The right element of 任 is not the 'king' of panel 15! Look closely—the middle horizontal stroke is longer than those above or below it. • As he **assumes a new post**, the administration views this *man* as a *small knight*. He gained stature with his cavalier behavior!

1174 凭

憑
TRAD   SIMPLIFIED

This character with the definition:

lean on, rely on

Pinyin **píng** *and Frequency Rank* **1410**

Contains **8 strokes** in the following order:

ノ 亻 亻 仁 任 任 凭 凭

Contains these components:

□ assume a post 任 1173, p. 263
□ how much, how many 几 896, p. 204

With all these meanings & readings:

píng [憑] **1** to lean against **2** to rely on **3** on the basis of **4** no matter (how, what etc) **5** proof

Management knows they can **rely on** you so they allowed you to *assume a post* with *many* responsibilities.

1175

This character with the definition:

letter

Pinyin **xìn** *and Frequency Rank* **176**

SIMP & TRAD   Contains **9 strokes** in the following order:

丿 亻 亻 信 信 信 信 信 信

Contains these components:

man r 亻 1156, p. 260

speech 言 256, p. 67

With all these meanings & readings:

xìn [信] **1** letter **2** m 封[fēng] **3** true **4** to believe **5** sign **6** evidence

In the old days, a written **letter** was the best way to permanently record a *person's speech.*

1176

This character with the definition:

seem, appear

Pinyin **sì** *and Frequency Rank* **431**

SIMP & TRAD   Contains **6 strokes** in the following order:

丿 亻 亻 似 似 似

Contains these components:

man r 亻 1156, p. 260

use, take 以 1014, p. 230

With all these meanings & readings:

sì [似] **1** to seem **2** to appear **3** to resemble **4** similar **5** -like **6** pseudo-

During Mardi Gras, *men use* unusual costumes to **appear** to be something they are not.

1177

This character with the definition:

promote, urge

Pinyin **cù** *and Frequency Rank* **1102**

SIMP & TRAD   Contains **9 strokes** in the following order:

丿 亻 亻 亻 伲 伲 伲 促 促

Contains these components:

man r 亻 1156, p. 260

foot 足 729, p. 170

With all these meanings & readings:

cù [促] **1** to hurry **2** to rush **3** to hasten **4** near **5** to promote

If a *man* wants to **promote** silence in the home, he may start by tapping his *foot* impatiently whenever his wife opens her mouth to speak.

1178

This character with the definition:

rest

Pinyin **xiū** *and Frequency Rank* **1082**

SIMP & TRAD   Contains **6 strokes** in the following order:

丿 亻 亻 什 休 休

Contains these components:

man r 亻 1156, p. 260

tree 木 562, p. 133

With all these meanings & readings:

xiū [休] **1** to rest

A *person* leans against a *tree* for a **rest.**

1179

This character with the definition:

safeguard, protect

Pinyin **bǎo** *and Frequency Rank* **266**

SIMP & TRAD   Contains **9 strokes** in the following order:

丿 亻 亻 伊 伊 伊 俣 保 保

Contains these components:

man r 亻 1156, p. 260

dull-witted 呆 566, p. 134

With all these meanings & readings:

bǎo [保] **1** to defend **2** to protect **3** to insure or guarantee **4** to maintain **5** hold or keep **6** to guard **7** abbr for Bulgaria

To **protect** and **safeguard** the health and dignity of his *dull-witted* younger brother are the duties of every responsible *man.*

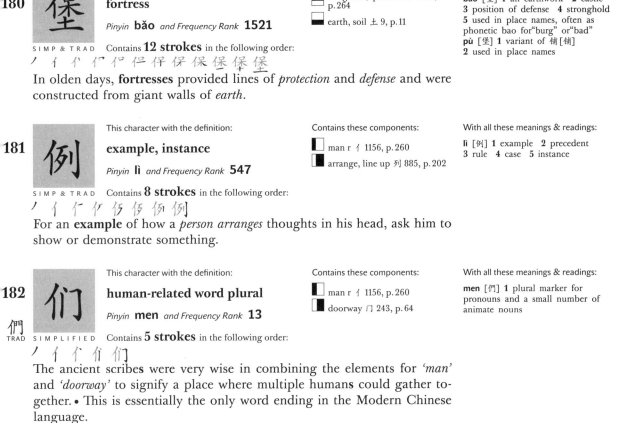

180

堡

fortress

Pinyin **bǎo** *and Frequency Rank* **1521**

SIMP & TRAD   Contains **12 strokes** in the following order:

ノ 亻 亻 亻 伊 伊 伊 伊 保 保 保 堡

This character with the definition:

Contains these components:

safeguard, protect 保 1179, p. 264

earth, soil 土 9, p. 11

With all these meanings & readings:

bǎo [堡] **1** an earthwork **2** castle **3** position of defense **4** stronghold **5** used in place names, often as phonetic bao for"burg" or"bad" **pù** [堡] **1** variant of 铺[铺] **2** used in place names

In olden days, **fortresses** provided lines of *protection* and *defense* and were constructed from giant walls of *earth*.

181

例

example, instance

Pinyin **lì** *and Frequency Rank* **547**

SIMP & TRAD   Contains **8 strokes** in the following order:

ノ 亻 亻 亻 佅 佅 例 例

This character with the definition:

Contains these components:

man r 亻 1156, p. 260

arrange, line up 列 885, p. 202

With all these meanings & readings:

lì [例] **1** example **2** precedent **3** rule **4** case **5** instance

For an **example** of how a *person arranges* thoughts in his head, ask him to show or demonstrate something.

182

们

human-related word plural

Pinyin **men** *and Frequency Rank* **13**

TRAD SIMPLIFIED   Contains **5 strokes** in the following order:

ノ 亻 亻 们 们

This character with the definition:

Contains these components:

man r 亻 1156, p. 260

doorway 门 243, p. 64

With all these meanings & readings:

men [们] **1** plural marker for pronouns and a small number of animate nouns

The ancient scribes were very wise in combining the elements for '*man*' and '*doorway*' to signify a place where multiple humans could gather together. • This is essentially the only word ending in the Modern Chinese language.

183

倒

topple, fall over

Pinyin **dǎo** *and Frequency Rank* **608**

SIMP & TRAD   Contains **10 strokes** in the following order:

ノ 亻 亻 伒 伭 佫 倒 倒 倒 倒

This character with the definition:

Contains these components:

man r 亻 1156, p. 260

arrive 到 981, p. 224

With all these meanings & readings:

dǎo [倒] **1** to fall **2** to collapse **3** to topple **4** to fail **5** to go bankrupt **6** to change (trains or buses) **7** to move around **8** to sell **9** to speculate (buying and selling, also 捣[捣]) **10** profiteer **dào** [倒] **1** upset **2** turn over **3** to tip **4** to pour **5** to go home **6** to the contrary **7** inverted

The *man arrived* in such haste that he **toppled** over when he stopped.

184

依

count on, depend on

Pinyin **yī** *and Frequency Rank* **568**

SIMP & TRAD   Contains **8 strokes** in the following order:

ノ 亻 亻 广 伝 佐 依 依

This character with the definition:

Contains these components:

man r 亻 1156, p. 260

clothing 衣 1068, p. 242

With all these meanings & readings:

yī [依] **1** according to **2** depend on **3** near to

The sales *man* knew that he could persuade strangers to **depend on** him if he wore expensive *clothing*.

Unit 50

1185

This character with the definition:

why, how

Pinyin **hé** *and Frequency Rank* **229**

SIMP & TRAD Contains **7 strokes** in the following order:

丿 亻 仁 仃 何 何 何

Contains these components:

■ man r 亻 1156, p. 260

□ can, may 可 60, p. 23

With all these meanings & reading

hé [何] 1 surname He
hé [何] 1 what 2 how 3 why
4 which 5 carry

Men are the ones born with the *ability* to achieve anything—at least that was the perceived wisdom for centuries. Modern science has since turned that statement on its head. **How** could you still say that today, and *why* would you even want to?

1186

This character with the definition:

lotus

Pinyin **hé** *and Frequency Rank* **1427**

SIMP & TRAD Contains **10 strokes** in the following order:

一 十 艹 艹 花 芢 荇 荷 荷 荷

Contains these components:

□ grass r 艹 87, p. 29

■ why, how 何 1185, p. 266

With all these meanings & reading

hé [荷] 1 lotus 2 abbr for the Netherlands or Holland 荷兰 [~蘭]
hè [荷] 1 peppermint 2 to ca burden

The **lotus** is a *flower* used by many Eastern cultures because it is believed to have the power to *answer universal questions* of existence.

1187

This character with the definition:

change, transform

Pinyin **huà** *and Frequency Rank* **178**

SIMP & TRAD Contains **4 strokes** in the following order:

丿 亻 化 化

Contains these components:

■ man r 亻 1156, p. 260

□ ancient ladle 匕 124, p. 36

With all these meanings & reading

huā [化] 1 variant of 花
huà [化] 1 to make into 2 to change into 3 -ization 4 to . -ize 5 to transform 6 abbrevi tion of 化学 [~學][huà xué]

The *man* stirs the pot with an *ancient ladle*. Soon, the bland mixture of vegetables, spices, and other ingredients **changes** into a tasty soup.

1188

This character with the definition:

blossom, flower

Pinyin **huā** *and Frequency Rank* **410**

SIMP & TRAD Contains **7 strokes** in the following order:

一 十 艹 艹 花 花 花

Contains these components:

□ grass r 艹 87, p. 29
■ change, transform 化 1187, p. 266

With all these meanings & reading

huā [花] 1 flower 2 blossom
3 fancy pattern 4 m 朵[duǒ], 支[zhī], 束[shù], 把[bǎ], 盆[pé 簇[cù] 5 to spend (money, tin
6 surname Hua

An amazing *transformation* occurs in nature when a *green plant* becomes covered with beautiful, fragrant **blossoms**.

1189

This character with the definition:

glory, splendor

Pinyin **huá** *and Frequency Rank* **412**

華 SIMPLIFIED
TRAD Contains **6 strokes** in the following order:

丿 亻 亻 化 华 华

Contains these components:

□ change, transform 化 1187, p. 266
■ ten 十 7, p. 11

With all these meanings & reading

huá [華] 1 Mt Hua 华山[华~] Shaanxi 2 surname Hua
huá [華] 1 abbr for China
2 magnificent 3 splendid 4 f ery

The court magician is not very powerful. It took him *ten* sets of *transformations* to create a jewel that radiated with **splendor**.

190

SIMP & TRAD

This character with the definition:

hundred (fraud proof)

Pinyin **bǎi** *and Frequency Rank* **5437**

Contains **8 strokes** in the following order:

ノ 亻 亻 仁 佰 佰 佰 佰

Contains these components:

man r 亻 1156, p. 260

hundred 百 226, p. 60

With all these meanings & readings:

bǎi [佰] **1** hundred (banker's anti-fraud numeral)

Gather a *hundred men* and group them together. They will keep each other accountable and ensure that each person stays honest. The '**fraud proof**' test depends on the honesty among this group of a **hundred** men.

191

SIMP & TRAD

This character with the definition:

stay overnight

Pinyin **sù** *and Frequency Rank* **1752**

Contains **11 strokes** in the following order:

丶 丶 宀 宀 宀 宿 宿 宿 宿 宿 宿

Contains these components:

roof r 宀 271, p. 70

hundred (fraud proof) 佰 1190, p. 267

With all these meanings & readings:

sù [宿] **1** lodge for the night **2** old **3** former **4** surname Su
xiǔ [宿] **1** night **2** m for nights
xiù [宿] **1** constellation

I can sleep anywhere. All I need is a *roof* over my head to get *one hundred* winks of blissful sleep. Since I'm always calm in these situations, you might call me *frightproof* (sounds like '*fraud proof*'). I prefer to **stay overnight** so as to better enjoy the company of others.

192

缩
TRAD   SIMPLIFIED

This character with the definition:

contract, shrink

Pinyin **suō** *and Frequency Rank* **1304**

Contains **14 strokes** in the following order:

乙 乡 纟 纟 纩 纩 纩 纩 绽 绽 缩 缩 缩 缩

Contains these components:

silk r 纟 1037, p. 235

stay overnight 宿 1191, p. 267

With all these meanings & readings:

suō [缩] **1** to withdraw **2** to pull back **3** to contract **4** to shrink **5** to reduce **6** abbreviation

Whenever I let my *silk* underwear *stay overnight* in the washtub, they **shrink**! Now they're too tight for my own comfort.

193

SIMP & TRAD

This character with the definition:

short-tailed bird

Pinyin **zhuī** *and Frequency Rank* **5837**

Contains **8 strokes** in the following order:

ノ 亻 亻 仁 仆 佯 佯 隹

Contains these components:

man r 亻 1156, p. 260

master 主 (altered) 179, p. 49

With all these meanings & readings:

zhuī [隹] **1** short-tailed bird

It's easy to confuse the right part with 主, 'master' (panel 179). But note carefully: '*master*' has only three horizontals, while '**bird**' has four. **Birds** fly over *masters* and over other ordinary *men*, so they deserve a 'higher' rank, and the additional horizontal stroke emphasizes this. (**Short-tailed birds** include pigeons, crows, chickens, and the like.)

194

堆

This character with the definition:

heap up

Pinyin **duī** *and Frequency Rank* **1370**

SIMP & TRAD

Contains **11 strokes** in the following order:

一 十 土 圵 圵 圵 坫 堆 堆 堆 堆

Contains these components:

earth, soil 土 9, p. 11

short-tailed bird 隹 1193, p. 267

With all these meanings & readings:

duī [堆] **1** a pile **2** a mass **3** heap **4** stack

No matter how high you **heap up** a pile of *earth*, no *short-tailed bird* will ever build a nest at the top. Their instinct 'tells them' that their four-legged enemies can still climb up a tall pile of **heaped up** *earth*.

1195

This character with the definition:

push

Pinyin **tuī** *and Frequency Rank* **505**

Contains these components:

■ hand r 扌 25, p.15
■ short-tailed bird 隹 1193, p.267

With all these meanings & reading

tuī [推] **1** to push **2** to cut **3** to refuse **4** to reject **5** to decline **6** to shirk (responsibil **7** to put off **8** to delay **9** to push forward **10** to nominate **11** to elect

SIMP & TRAD   Contains **11 strokes** in the following order:

一 亅 扌 扌 扩 扩 拃 拃 拃 推 推

Of all the *short-tailed birds*, bluejays are the most aggressive. Sometimes I want to use my *hand* to **push** them away from the bird-feeder so the other *short-tailed birds* can have a chance to get some food.

1196

This character with the definition:

alone, only

Pinyin **wéi** *and Frequency Rank* **1094**

Contains these components:

■ mouth 口 37, p.17
■ short-tailed bird 隹 1193, p.267

With all these meanings & reading

wéi [唯] **1** -ism **2** only **3** alor
wěi [唯] **1** yes

SIMP & TRAD   Contains **11 strokes** in the following order:

丶 口 口 叨 叩 吖 咔 咔 唯 唯

In rural areas, just before dawn, the early riser might feel all **alone** until he hears the cheerful songs and chirps from the *mouths* of many *short-tailed birds* as they greet the new day.

1197

This character with the definition:

sell*

Pinyin **shòu** *and Frequency Rank* **1114**

Contains these components:

■ short-tailed bird 隹 1193, p.267
□ mouth 口 37, p.17

With all these meanings & reading

shòu [售] **1** to sell

SIMP & TRAD   Contains **11 strokes** in the following order:

丿 亻 亻 仁 仁 仨 伟 隹 隹 隹 售

The child's *mouth* dropped open in shock when he heard about his parents plans to **sell** his *short-tailed bird* and its beautiful gilt cage.

1198

This character with the definition:

gather, collect

Pinyin **jí** *and Frequency Rank* **406**

Contains these components:

■ short-tailed bird 隹 1193, p.267
■ tree 木 562, p.133

With all these meanings & reading

jí [集] **1** to gather **2** to collect **3** collected works **4** m for sections of a TV series etc: episo

SIMP & TRAD   Contains **12 strokes** in the following order:

丿 亻 亻 仁 仁 仨 伟 隹 隹 隼 集 集

Often, different species of *short-tailed birds* will **gather** together around sunset in a particularly large *tree*.

1199

This character with the definition:

who

Pinyin **shuí** *and Frequency Rank* **648**

Contains these components:

■ speech r 讠 352, p.88
■ short-tailed bird 隹 1193, p.267

With all these meanings & reading

shéi [谁] **1** who **2** also pronounced shui2

TRAD SIMPLIFIED   Contains **10 strokes** in the following order:

丶 讠 讠 讠 讠 诈 诈 谁 谁 谁

An owl is a *short-tailed bird* whose cry sounds eerily close to human *speech*— "Hoo, hoo—**who, who**."

200

维

维
TRAD   SIMPLIFIED

This character with the definition:

hold together

Pinyin **wéi** *and Frequency Rank* **520**

Contains **11 strokes** in the following order:

Contains these components:

silk r 纟 1037, p. 235

short-tailed bird 隹 1193, p. 267

With all these meanings & readings:

wéi [维] **1** to preserve **2** to maintain **3** to hold together **4** dimension **5** abbr for Uighur 维吾尔 [维~爾]

Silk fibers are so delicate that they can be used to **hold together** the damaged wings of *short-tailed birds*.

201

翟

SIMP & TRAD

This character with the definition:

long-tailed pheasant

Pinyin **dí** *and Frequency Rank* **3919**

Contains **14 strokes** in the following order:

Contains these components:

feather, wing 羽 107, p. 33

short-tailed bird 隹 1193, p. 267

With all these meanings & readings:

dí [翟] **1** surname Zhai
dí [翟] **1** long-tail pheasant

It would appear that the scribes simply added the element for *'feather'* to the one for *'short-tailed bird'* to construct this character meaning **long-tailed pheasant**.

202

准

準
准
TRAD   SIMPLIFIED

This character with the definition:

standard, criterion

Pinyin **zhǔn** *and Frequency Rank* **379**

Contains **10 strokes** in the following order:

Contains these components:

ice r 冫 348, p. 87

short-tailed bird 隹 1193, p. 267

With all these meanings & readings:

zhǔn [准] **1** to allow **2** to grant **3** in accordance with **4** in the light of
zhǔn [準] **1** (old) horizontal **2** accurate **3** standard **4** definetely **5** certainly

A **criterion** for cooking *short-tailed birds* is that they be kept on *ice* and defrosted only just before they are to be cooked.

203

焦

SIMP & TRAD

This character with the definition:

burnt, scorched

Pinyin **jiāo** *and Frequency Rank* **1554**

Contains **12 strokes** in the following order:

Contains these components:

short-tailed bird 隹 1193, p. 267

fire r ⺍ 1026, p. 233

With all these meanings & readings:

jiāo [焦] **1** burnt **2** scorched **3** worried **4** anxious **5** surname Jiao

The best example of something being **burnt** intentionally for good flavor is a large *short-tailed bird* that is slow roasted over a *fire*.

204

瞧

SIMP & TRAD

This character with the definition:

look at

Pinyin **qiáo** *and Frequency Rank* **1551**

Contains **17 strokes** in the following order:

Contains these components:

eye 目 75, p. 26

burnt, scorched 焦 1203, p. 269

With all these meanings & readings:

qiáo [瞧] **1** look at

On a winter evening, your *eyes* can become mesmerized by the *burning* logs in a fireplace—the *burnt* embers accumulate under the bright, dancing flames to produce a warm glow that you can't help but continue to **look at**.

1205

This character with the definition:

wild goose

Pinyin **yàn** *and Frequency Rank* **2553**

SIMP & TRAD   Contains **12 strokes** in the following order:

一 厂 厂 厂 厂 厂 厂 厂 雁 雁 雁 雁

Contains these components:

- cliff r 厂 399, p. 97
- man r 亻 1156, p. 260
- short-tailed bird 隹 1193, p. 267

With all these meanings & reading

yàn [雁] **1** wild goose

How do flocks of birds fly in China? Not in a V-formation, for they don't have this letter! In China, they say that migrating birds fly in a 人-shape (panel 537; but here we use the more compact radical form, 亻, panel 1156). The Chinese, therefore, see **wild geese** as a flock of *short-tailed birds* that fly by the *cliff* in 人-formation.

1206

鷹
TRAD   SIMPLIFIED

This character with the definition:

eagle

Pinyin **yīng** *and Frequency Rank* **1927**

Contains **18 strokes** in the following order:

` 一 广 广 广 庐 庐 庐 庐 庐 庐 雁 雁 膺 膺 鹰 鹰

Contains these components:

- wild goose 雁 (altered) 1205, p. 270
- bird 鸟 394, p. 96

With all these meanings & reading

yīng [鷹] **1** eagle **2** falcon **3** hawk

Scribes emphasize the nobility and grandeur of the **eagle** by making the *bird*-ness of the *wild goose* more complex.

1207

This character with the definition:

elegant

Pinyin **yǎ** *and Frequency Rank* **1139**

SIMP & TRAD   Contains **12 strokes** in the following order:

一 匚 牙 牙 邪 邪 邪 邪 雅 雅 雅 雅

Contains these components:

- tooth* 牙 450, p. 108
- short-tailed bird 隹 1193, p. 267

With all these meanings & reading

yǎ [雅] **1** elegant

Imagine wearing an **elegant** necklace made from the *teeth* of *birds*.

1208

This character with the definition:

lofty

Pinyin **cuī** *and Frequency Rank* **2552**

SIMP & TRAD   Contains **11 strokes** in the following order:

丿 屮 山 屵 屵 岽 岸 崖 崖 崔 崔

Contains these components:

- mountain 山 4, p. 10
- short-tailed bird 隹 1193, p. 267

With all these meanings & reading

cuī [崔] **1** high mountain **2** precipitous **3** surname Cui

When the *short-tailed bird* flies to the top of the *mountain*, it takes a **lofty** flight path.

1209 催

This character with the definition:

to urge*

Pinyin **cuī** *and Frequency Rank* **2064**

SIMP & TRAD   Contains **13 strokes** in the following order:

丿 亻 亻 伫 仳 佟 催 催 催 催 催 催 催

Contains these components:

- man r 亻 1156, p. 260
- lofty 崔 1208, p. 270

With all these meanings & reading

cuī [催] **1** to urge **2** to press **3** to prompt **4** to rush sb **5** hasten sth **6** to expedite

We **urged** our *friend* to cut down on her *lofty* behavior before things got too out of hand at the party.

Unit 51

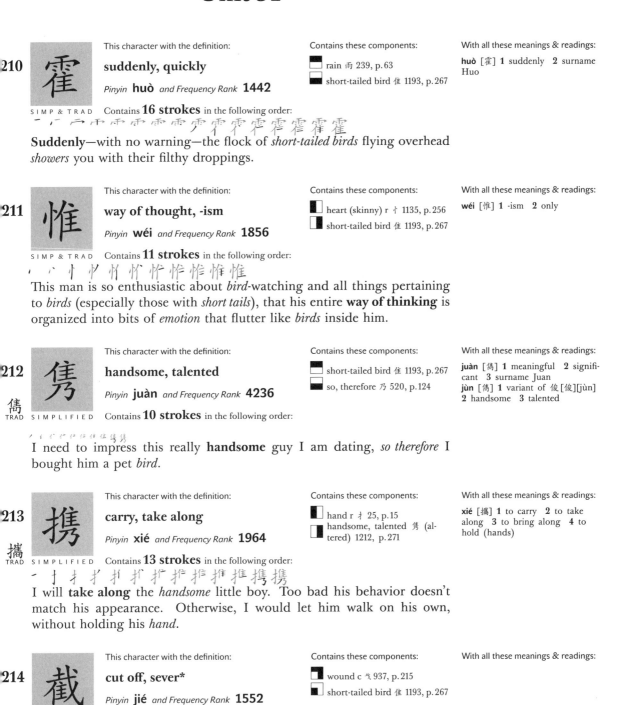

210 霍
SIMP & TRAD

This character with the definition:

suddenly, quickly

Pinyin **huò** *and Frequency Rank* **1442**

Contains **16 strokes** in the following order:

Contains these components:
- rain 雨 239, p. 63
- short-tailed bird 隹 1193, p. 267

With all these meanings & readings:

huò [霍] **1** suddenly **2** surname Huo

Suddenly—with no warning—the flock of *short-tailed birds* flying overhead *showers* you with their filthy droppings.

---

211 惟
SIMP & TRAD

This character with the definition:

way of thought, -ism

Pinyin **wéi** *and Frequency Rank* **1856**

Contains **11 strokes** in the following order:

Contains these components:
- heart (skinny) r 忄 1135, p. 256
- short-tailed bird 隹 1193, p. 267

With all these meanings & readings:

wéi [惟] **1** -ism **2** only

This man is so enthusiastic about *bird*-watching and all things pertaining to *birds* (especially those with *short tails*), that his entire **way of thinking** is organized into bits of *emotion* that flutter like *birds* inside him.

---

212 隽
TRAD 儁 SIMPLIFIED

This character with the definition:

handsome, talented

Pinyin **juàn** *and Frequency Rank* **4236**

Contains **10 strokes** in the following order:

Contains these components:
- short-tailed bird 隹 1193, p. 267
- so, therefore 乃 520, p. 124

With all these meanings & readings:

juàn [儁] **1** meaningful **2** significant **3** surname Juan
jùn [儁] **1** variant of 俊 [俊][jùn] **2** handsome **3** talented

I need to impress this really **handsome** guy I am dating, *so therefore* I bought him a pet *bird*.

---

213 携
TRAD 攜 SIMPLIFIED

This character with the definition:

carry, take along

Pinyin **xié** *and Frequency Rank* **1964**

Contains **13 strokes** in the following order:

Contains these components:
- hand r 扌 25, p. 15
- handsome, talented 隽 (altered) 1212, p. 271

With all these meanings & readings:

xié [攜] **1** to carry **2** to take along **3** to bring along **4** to hold (hands)

I will **take along** the *handsome* little boy. Too bad his behavior doesn't match his appearance. Otherwise, I would let him walk on his own, without holding his *hand*.

---

214 截
SIMP & TRAD

This character with the definition:

cut off, sever*

Pinyin **jié** *and Frequency Rank* **1552**

Contains **14 strokes** in the following order:

Contains these components:
- wound c 戈 937, p. 215
- short-tailed bird 隹 1193, p. 267

With all these meanings & readings:

The samurai knight was able to *wound* the *short-tailed bird*; thereafter it was easy to capture and **cut off** its head.

1215

This character with the definition:

pay

Pinyin **fù** *and Frequency Rank* **820**

SIMP & TRAD   Contains **5 strokes** in the following order:

ノ 亻 亻 付 付

Contains these components:

■ man r 亻 1156, p. 260
■ inch 寸 216, p. 58

With all these meanings & reading

fù [付] **1** to pay **2** to hand o
to **3** surname Fu

We are witnessing a commercial transaction. The *man* wants to **pay** for some merchandise with *inch*-sized coins.

1216

This character with the definition:

symbol, mark, sign

Pinyin **fú** *and Frequency Rank* **1205**

SIMP & TRAD   Contains **11 strokes** in the following order:

ノ 𠂉 ⺮ ⺮ ⺮ ⺮ 符 符 符 符 符

Contains these components:

□ bamboo r ⺮ 264, p. 68
■ pay 付 1215, p. 272

With all these meanings & reading

fú [符] **1** mark **2** sign **3** talis
man **4** to seal **5** to correspo
to **6** tally **7** symbol **8** writte
charm **9** to coincide **10** surname Fu

In ancient days, a simple **sign** made from *bamboo* and inscribed with the word '*pay*' directed customers to the cashier.

1217

This character with the definition:

mansion

Pinyin **fǔ** *and Frequency Rank* **417**

SIMP & TRAD   Contains **8 strokes** in the following order:

丶 亠 广 广 庁 庁 府 府

Contains these components:

□ shelter r 广 427, p. 103
■ pay 付 1215, p. 272

With all these meanings & reading

fǔ [府] **1** seat of government
2 government repository (archi
3 official residence **4** mansion
5 presidential palace **6** (hon-
orific) Your home **7** prefectur
(from Tang to Qing times)

If you buy a **mansion**, you will *pay* and *pay* for this luxurious *shelter*.

1218

This character with the definition:

rotten, putrid, stale

Pinyin **fǔ** *and Frequency Rank* **1576**

SIMP & TRAD   Contains **14 strokes** in the following order:

丶 亠 广 广 庁 庁 府 府 府 腐 腐 腐 腐 腐

Contains these components:

■ mansion 府 (altered) 1217, p. 272
□ meat 肉 753, p. 175

With all these meanings & reading

fǔ [腐] **1** decay **2** rotten

One of the workmen left a *meat* sandwich in one of the rooms in the *mansion* that they had worked in. They realized it only days later when the stench of **rotting** *meat* filled the house.

1219 附

This character with the definition:

add on, attach

Pinyin **fù** *and Frequency Rank* **923**

SIMP & TRAD   Contains **7 strokes** in the following order:

𠃌 阝 阝 阝 阶 附 附

Contains these components:

■ hills r 阝 942, p. 216
■ pay 付 1215, p. 272

With all these meanings & reading

fù [附] **1** to add **2** to attach
3 to be close to **4** to be attached

We are so **attached** to the picturesque *hills* outside of our town that we are glad to *pay* extra taxes and fees to keep them pristine and beautiful for us and future generations to use.

1220

This character with the definition:

to instruct, exhort

Pinyin **fù** *and Frequency Rank* **2093**

SIMP & TRAD   Contains **8 strokes** in the following order:

丶 丆 口 叮 叮 叮 咐 咐

Contains these components:

☐ mouth 口 37, p. 17
☐ pay 付 1215, p. 272

With all these meanings & readings:

fù [咐] **1** to order

I *pay* a tutor to **instruct** me on Chinese. The '*mouth*' part shows him delivering his lecture as loudly as possible. I must *pay* attention so that I learn how to pronounce these characters with my *mouth*.

1221

This character with the definition:

take the place of

Pinyin **dài** *and Frequency Rank* **174**

SIMP & TRAD   Contains **5 strokes** in the following order:

丿 亻 仁 代 代

Contains these components:

☐ man r 亻 1156, p. 260
☐ kind of arrow 弋 647, p. 153

With all these meanings & readings:

dài [代] **1** to substitute **2** to act on behalf of others **3** to replace **4** generation **5** dynasty **6** age **7** period **8** (historical) era **9** (geological) eon

After waiting hours in line, I see this *man* who is holding a sharp *kind of arrow* in a very threatening manner approaching me. Sure enough, he's determined **to take my place** in line.

1222

This character with the definition:

pouch, bag, pocket

Pinyin **dài** *and Frequency Rank* **1310**

SIMP & TRAD   Contains **11 strokes** in the following order:

丿 亻 仁 代 代 代 袋 袋 袋 袋 袋

Contains these components:

☐ take the place of 代 1221, p. 273
☐ clothing 衣 1068, p. 242

With all these meanings & readings:

dài [袋] **1** a pouch **2** bag **3** sack **4** pocket

Pouches and **bags** *take the place of* bulky **pockets** sewn into *clothing*.

1223

This character with the definition:

marquis

Pinyin **hóu** *and Frequency Rank* **1756**

SIMP & TRAD   Contains **9 strokes** in the following order:

丿 亻 仁 仃 仅 伫 侯 侯 侯

Contains these components:

☐ man r 亻 1156, p. 260
☐ cover r 冖 (altered) 250, p. 66
☐ arrow 矢 552, p. 130

With all these meanings & readings:

hóu [侯] **1** Marquis, second of five orders of nobility 五等爵位[wǔ děng jué wèi] **2** nobleman **3** surname Hou **4** used erroneously for 候[hòu]

A **marquis** is a type of nobleman. He's noble by virtue of the special hat which *covers* his head and by the fact that he's practicing his *arrow* shooting skills as an archer, a leisure activity available only to noblemen at the **marquis** rank.

1224

This character with the definition:

time, season

Pinyin **hòu** *and Frequency Rank* **341**

SIMP & TRAD   Contains **10 strokes** in the following order:

丿 亻 仁 仃 仁 仃 侍 侯 候 候

Contains these components:

☐ marquis 侯 1223, p. 273
☐ scepter c 丨 5, p. 10

With all these meanings & readings:

hòu [候] **1** wait

The *scepter* is an appropriate symbol of authority to combine with one representing the *marquis*, a kind of nobleperson. However, the **time** when noblemen played a leading role in society has long passed, so that's why the *scepter* is so short.

1225

This character with the definition:

m for persons (polite)

Pinyin **wèi** *and Frequency Rank* **182**

SIMP & TRAD   Contains **7 strokes** in the following order:

ノ 亻 亻 亻 仁 位 位

Contains these components:

man r 亻 1156, p. 260

to stand 立 681, p. 160

With all these meanings & readings

wèi [位] **1** position **2** location **3** m for people **4** place **5** seat **6** m for binary bits (e.g. 十六位 16-bit or 2 bytes)

Formal occasions generally demand that *people stand straighter* than they usually do. So '*people stand*' represents this **formal counting word**.

1226

億
TRAD   SIMPLIFIED

This character with the definition:

hundred million

Pinyin **yì** *and Frequency Rank* **1057**

Contains **3 strokes** in the following order:

ノ 亻 亿

Contains these components:

man r 亻 1156, p. 260

second (in a series) 乙 146, p. 41

With all these meanings & readings

yì [億] **1** a hundred million **2** calculate

If you stick a knife into a *man*, the first thing you encounter is his skin. But the *second in a series* of human tissue is his blood. There are approximately one **hundred million** blood cells in an adult man's body.

1227

This character with the definition:

make, write, compose

Pinyin **zuò** *and Frequency Rank* **49**

SIMP & TRAD   Contains **7 strokes** in the following order:

ノ 亻 亻 亻 乍 作 作

Contains these components:

man r 亻 1156, p. 260

abruptly 乍 447, p. 107

With all these meanings & readings

zuò [作] **1** to do **2** to make **3** to regard as **4** to take sb for

Even though we *men* are notorious couch potatoes, when a creative idea *abruptly* strikes us, we immediately start to figure out how to **make** this new invention.

1228 伤

傷
TRAD   SIMPLIFIED

This character with the definition:

injure, wound

Pinyin **shāng** *and Frequency Rank* **660**

Contains **6 strokes** in the following order:

ノ 亻 亻 亻 伤 伤

Contains these components:

man r 亻 1156, p. 260

man 人 (altered) 537, p. 127

strength 力 471, p. 113

With all these meanings & readings

shāng [傷] **1** injure **2** injury **3** wound

Two men are doing something that involves great *strength*; it must be a fight. One *man* is trying his best to **injure** the other *man*.

1229 仍

This character with the definition:

remain, continue as before

Pinyin **réng** *and Frequency Rank* **601**

SIMP & TRAD   Contains **4 strokes** in the following order:

ノ 亻 乃 仍

Contains these components:

man r 亻 1156, p. 260

so, therefore 乃 520, p. 124

With all these meanings & readings

réng [仍] **1** still **2** yet **3** to remain

The *man's* wife told him he had ignored her requests to stop his gambling addiction. *Therefore* she could no longer **remain** married to him. He promised her he would stop if she gave him one more chance. This time, he kept his promise to her, with the *result* being that he also kept his wife.

1230

佛
佛
佛

TRAD   SIMPLIFIED

This character with the definition:

Buddha

Pinyin **fó** *and Frequency Rank* **771**

Contains **7 strokes** in the following order:

ノ 亻 亻 伫 佀 佛 佛

Contains these components:

▪ man r 亻 1156, p. 260
▪ not (literary works) 弗 142, p. 40

With all these meanings & readings:

fó [佛] **1** Buddha **2** Buddhism
fú [彿] **1** seemingly

The ancient book described a *man* striving to become like the great **Buddha**—that is, learning to think and behave like a god, and *not* a *man*.

1231

低

SIMP & TRAD

This character with the definition:

low, below average

Pinyin **dī** *and Frequency Rank* **592**

Contains **7 strokes** in the following order:

ノ 亻 亻 低 仾 低 低

Contains these components:

▪ man r 亻 1156, p. 260
▪ basic 氐 414, p. 100

With all these meanings & readings:

dī [低] **1** low **2** beneath **3** to lower (one's head) **4** to let droop **5** to hang down **6** to incline

A *man* with **below average** intelligence does not possess the *basic* skills to survive on his own.

1232

仔

SIMP & TRAD

This character with the definition:

animal young

Pinyin **zǐ** *and Frequency Rank* **1572**

Contains **5 strokes** in the following order:

ノ 亻 亻 仔 仔

Contains these components:

▪ man r 亻 1156, p. 260
▪ son, child 子 24, p. 15

With all these meanings & readings:

zǐ [仔] **1** duty **2** responsibility
zǐ [仔] **1** minutely **2** young

A *man* takes his *son* to the zoo, where their favorite exhibits are those that feature **animal young**.

1233

仇

SIMP & TRAD

This character with the definition:

hatred

Pinyin **chóu** *and Frequency Rank* **1536**

Contains **4 strokes** in the following order:

ノ 亻 仇 仇

Contains these components:

▪ man r 亻 1156, p. 260
▪ nine 九 532, p. 126

With all these meanings & readings:

chóu [仇] **1** hatred **2** animosity **3** enmity **4** a rival **5** an enemy **6** feud
qiú [仇] **1** match **2** mate **3** surname Qiu

Some believe that every *man* and woman on earth is born with the same *nine* vices, with **hatred** being one of them.

1234

体
體

TRAD   SIMPLIFIED

This character with the definition:

body*

Pinyin **tǐ** *and Frequency Rank* **149**

Contains **7 strokes** in the following order:

ノ 亻 亻 什 休 体 体

Contains these components:

▪ man r 亻 1156, p. 260
▪ root or stem of plant 本 586, p. 139

With all these meanings & readings:

tǐ [體] **1** body **2** form **3** style **4** system

The **body** is the *root* of a *man* or *woman*'s physical essence.

Unit 52

1235

伦

倫
TRAD SIMPLIFIED

This character with the definition:

human relationship

Pinyin **lún** *and Frequency Rank* **970**

Contains **6 strokes** in the following order:

ノ 亻 伙 伙 伶 伦

Contains these components:

man r 亻 1156, p. 260

order, arrangement 仑 867, p. 198

With all these meanings & readings

lún [倫] 1 human relationship **2** order **3** coherence

In a healthy **human relationship**, one *person* brings *order* to the life of the other and vice versa.

1236

伟

偉
TRAD SIMPLIFIED

This character with the definition:

great, imposing

Pinyin **wěi** *and Frequency Rank* **1107**

Contains **6 strokes** in the following order:

ノ 亻 仁 伫 伟 伟

Contains these components:

man r 亻 1156, p. 260

leather 韦 109, p. 33

With all these meanings & readings

wěi [偉] 1 big **2** large **3** great

My shy brother looks very **imposing** whenever he dresses in black *leather* to ride his motorcycle. Perhaps the clothes really do 'make the *man*'!

1237

佩

珮
TRAD SIMPLIFIED

This character with the definition:

girdle

Pinyin **pèi** *and Frequency Rank* **1507**

Contains **8 strokes** in the following order:

ノ 亻 刂 佩 佩 佩 佩 佩

Contains these components:

man r 亻 1156, p. 260

commonplace 凡 901, p. 205

towel 巾 118, p. 35

With all these meanings & readings

pèi [佩] 1 to respect **2** to wear (belt etc)
pèi [珮] 1 girdle ornaments

On tropical islands, it is *commonplace* for a *man* **to girdle** his waist with only a *towel*-like cloth.

1238

侍

SIMP & TRAD

This character with the definition:

serve, wait upon

Pinyin **shì** *and Frequency Rank* **1871**

Contains **8 strokes** in the following order:

ノ 亻 仁 仕 仕 侍 侍 侍

Contains these components:

man r 亻 1156, p. 260

Buddhist temple 寺 220, p. 59

With all these meanings & readings

shì [侍] 1 attend on

Men who work in religious *Buddhist temples* do so to **serve** God.

1239

仆

僕
仆
TRAD SIMPLIFIED

This character with the definition:

fall forward

Pinyin **pū** *and Frequency Rank* **1812**

Contains **4 strokes** in the following order:

ノ 亻 仆 仆

Contains these components:

man r 亻 1156, p. 260

foretell 卜 187, p. 51

With all these meanings & readings

pū [仆] 1 to fall forward **2** to fall prostrate
pú [僕] 1 servant

The clumsy magician has a tendency to **fall forward**, especially after he drinks too much, but here's magic to the rescue! He uses his powers to *foretell* the situation and rights himself.

240

俩

TRAD SIMPLIFIED

This character with the definition:

two (colloquial)

Pinyin **liǎ** *and Frequency Rank* **1574**

Contains **9 strokes** in the following order:

丿 亻 亻 仃 仃 俩 俩 俩 俩

Contains these components:

man r 亻 1156, p. 260

both, two 两 763, p. 177

With all these meanings & readings:

liǎ [俩] **1** two (equivalent to 两个) **2** both (of us) **3** some **liǎng** [俩] **1** craft **2** cunning

This means almost the same thing as **both** or *two*, but it tends to be spoken whenever there are *two people* involved.

241

伐

SIMP & TRAD

This character with the definition:

cut down

Pinyin **fá** *and Frequency Rank* **1810**

Contains **6 strokes** in the following order:

丿 亻 亻 代 伐 伐

Contains these components:

man r 亻 1156, p. 260

halberd 戈 650, p. 154

With all these meanings & readings:

fá [伐] **1** to cut down **2** to fell **3** to dispatch an expedition against **4** to attack **5** to boast

In times of peace, *men* use their *swords* to **cut down** trees and crops.

242

俄

SIMP & TRAD

This character with the definition:

Russian

Pinyin **é** *and Frequency Rank* **975**

Contains **9 strokes** in the following order:

丿 亻 亻 仁 仁 仨 俄 俄 俄

Contains these components:

man r 亻 1156, p. 260

I 我 661, p. 156

With all these meanings & readings:

é [俄] **1** suddenly **2** very soon **3** Russian

Russian men are very *egotistical*.

243

伏

SIMP & TRAD

This character with the definition:

bend over

Pinyin **fú** *and Frequency Rank* **1389**

Contains **6 strokes** in the following order:

丿 亻 亻 伙 伏 伏

Contains these components:

man r 亻 1156, p. 260

dog 犬 673, p. 158

With all these meanings & readings:

fú [伏] **1** to lean over **2** to fall (go down) **3** to hide (in ambush) **4** to conceal oneself **5** to lie low **6** hottest days of summer **7** to submit **8** to concede defeat **9** to overcome **10** to subdue **11** volt **12** surname Fu

The only way the *man* can pet the cute small *dog* is if he **bends over** to reach it.

244

仿

仿 倣

TRAD SIMPLIFIED

This character with the definition:

imitate, copy, resemble

Pinyin **fǎng** *and Frequency Rank* **1259**

Contains **6 strokes** in the following order:

丿 亻 亻 仁 仿 仿

Contains these components:

man r 亻 1156, p. 260

square; direction 方 490, p. 117

With all these meanings & readings:

fǎng [仿] **1** to imitate **2** to copy

fǎng [倣] **1** variant of 仿[仿][fǎng]

fǎng [彷] **1** seemingly

The *man* followed my cooking *directions*, and his mousse was a perfect **imitation**.

245

储

储 儲

TRAD SIMPLIFIED

This character with the definition:

store up, save

Pinyin **chǔ** *and Frequency Rank* **1526**

Contains **12 strokes** in the following order:

丿 亻 亻 亻 伫 仁 仁 伫 伫 储 储 储

Contains these components:

man r 亻 1156, p. 260

speech r 讠 352, p. 88

-er 者 456, p. 109

With all these meanings & readings:

chǔ [储] **1** savings **2** to save **3** to deposit **4** to store **5** surname Chu **6** Taiwan pr chú

Whoever **saves up** his lifetime experiences shouldn't hesitate to draw upon them to make a point during a debate. Such a *man* makes a fine *speak-er*.

1246

This character with the definition:

false, fake, bogus

Pinyin **wěi** *and Frequency Rank* **1556**

Contains these components:

☐ man r 亻 1156, p. 260

☐ do, accomplish 为 481, p. 115

With all these meanings & readings:

wěi [偽] **1** false **2** fake **3** forg
4 bogus **5** Taiwan pr **wèi**

SIMPLIFIED   Contains **6 strokes** in the following order:

丿 亻 亻 仂 伪 伪

Men who claim they've *done* something when they haven't are **bogus**!

1247

This component has the meaning:

left step r

COMPONENT

And contains these subcomponents:

☐ action path c 丿 438, p. 105

☐ man r 亻 1156, p. 260

Imagine a person in front of you facing left. Although the heel of the foot is missing, this component clearly shows the **left foot**. The *action path* suggests the presence of the right foot, just visible next to it, as the **left** foot takes a **step**.

1248

This character with the definition:

direction toward

Pinyin **wǎng** *and Frequency Rank* **369**

Contains these components:

☐ left step r 亻 1247, p. 278

☐ master 主 179, p. 49

With all these meanings & readings:

wǎng [往] **1** to go (in a direction) **2** to **3** towards **4** (of a train) bound for **5** past **6** pre
ous

SIMP & TRAD   Contains **8 strokes** in the following order:

丿 亻 亻 彳 彳 往 往 往

The *master* takes a *step* confidently in the **direction toward** his goal.

1249

This character with the definition:

firm, business

Pinyin **háng** *and Frequency Rank* **53**

Contains these components:

☐ left step r 亻 1247, p. 278

☐ one 一, p. 10

☐ fourth (in a series) 丁 19, p. 13

With all these meanings & readings:

háng [行] **1** a row **2** series
3 age order (of brothers) **4** pre
fession **5** professional **6** relatin
to company
xíng [行] **1** to walk **2** to go
3 to travel **4** a visit **5** tempo-
rary **6** makeshift **7** current **8** circulation **9** to do **10** to perform **11** capable **12** competen
13 effective **14** all right **15** O
16 will do
xìng [行] **1** behavior **2** conduc

SIMP & TRAD   Contains **6 strokes** in the following order:

丿 亻 亻 彳 行 行

The right hand '*one fourth*' pair of elements is a reverse image of '*left step*'; think of it perhaps as '*right step*'. Step by step, we build a sound **busi-ness**.

1250 街

This character with the definition:

street

Pinyin **jiē** *and Frequency Rank* **1101**

Contains these components:

☐ firm, business 行 (altered) 1249, p. 278

☐ jade tablet 圭 10, p. 11

With all these meanings & readings:

jiē [街] **1** street **2** m 条 [條][tiá

SIMP & TRAD   Contains **12 strokes** in the following order:

丿 亻 亻 彳 彳 彴 往 往 街 街 街 街

Streets are more durable when their surfaces are laid as *firm* as a *jade tablet*.

1251

This character with the definition:

law, rule

Pinyin **lǜ**   *and Frequency Rank* **526**

SIMP & TRAD   Contains **9 strokes** in the following order:

丿 彡 彳 彳 彳 律 律 律 律

Contains these components:

■ left step r 彳 1247, p. 278
■ writing instrument, pen 聿 31, p. 16

With all these meanings & readings:
lǜ [律] **1** law

Step by *step*, the actions of *writing instruments* create **laws** that **rule** us all.

1252

This character with the definition:

go on a journey

Pinyin **zhēng**   *and Frequency Rank* **739**

SIMP & TRAD   Contains **8 strokes** in the following order:

丿 彡 彳 彳 彳 征 征 征

Contains these components:

■ left step r 彳 1247, p. 278
■ to correct, rectify 正 193, p. 52

With all these meanings & readings:
zhēng [征] **1** journey **2** trip **3** expedition **4** to go on long campaign **5** to attack
zhēng [徵] **1** to request **2** to impose (taxes) **3** to levy (troops) **4** to draft (for military service) **5** phenomenon **6** symptom **7** characteristic sign (used as proof) **8** evidence

To **go on a journey**, one must start by taking one *left step* forward properly. The trip will be easy on your feet if you *rectify* improper walking habits.

1253

懲
TRAD   SIMPLIFIED

This character with the definition:

punish, discipline

Pinyin **chéng**   *and Frequency Rank* **1821**

Contains **12 strokes** in the following order:

丿 彡 彳 彳 彳 征 征 征 征 惩 惩 惩

Contains these components:

□ go on a journey 征 1252, p. 279
■ heart (fat) r 心 1096, p. 248

With all these meanings & readings:
chéng [懲] **1** punish **2** discipline

Proper **discipline** is a *journey* filled with *emotion*. For example, you will experience frustration and (im)patience as you raise your children to follow the proper path.

1254

This character with the definition:

stay

Pinyin **dāi**   *and Frequency Rank* **673**

SIMP & TRAD   Contains **9 strokes** in the following order:

丿 彡 彳 彳 彳 待 待 待 待

Contains these components:

■ left step r 彳 1247, p. 278
■ Buddhist temple 寺 220, p. 59

With all these meanings & readings:
dāi [待] **1** stay **2** delay
dài [待] **1** to wait **2** to treat **3** to deal with **4** to need **5** going to (do sth) **6** about to **7** intending to

A *Buddhist temple* is a place to enter and seek refuge. This character depicts how a practitioner *steps* into the *temple*, and prepares to **stay** for some time.

1255

This character with the definition:

verbal particle

Pinyin **de**   *and Frequency Rank* **39**

SIMP & TRAD   Contains **11 strokes** in the following order:

丿 彡 彳 彳 彳 得 得 得 得 得 得

Contains these components:

■ left step r 彳 1247, p. 278
□ dawn 旦 70, p. 25
□ inch 寸 216, p. 58

With all these meanings & readings:
dé [得] **1** to obtain **2** to get **3** to gain **4** to catch (a disease) **5** proper **6** suitable **7** proud **8** contented **9** to allow **10** to permit **11** ready **12** finished
de [得] **1** structural particle: used after a verb (or adjective as main verb), linking it to following phrase indicating effect, degree, possibility etc
děi [得] **1** to have to **2** must **3** ought to **4** to need to

Careful where you take a *left step* as the plain is a hiker's minefield. As you can see at *dawn*'s light, the ground is littered with these *inch*-long **particles**. Stepping on these sharp objects the wrong way can unleash a barrage of **verbal particles**.

1256

SIMP & TRAD

This character with the definition:

disciple, pupil, follower

Pinyin **tú** *and Frequency Rank* **1060**

Contains **10 strokes** in the following order:

ノ ㇇ 彳 彳 彳 彳 彳 徉 徒 徒

Contains these components:

◧ left step r 彳 1247, p. 278
◨ to walk 走 731, p. 171

With all these meanings & readings

tú [徒] **1** apprentice **2** disciple **3** prison sentence

The **disciple** always takes *steps* behind his master, who *walks* ahead and exudes confidence.

1257

SIMP & TRAD

This character with the definition:

morality

Pinyin **dé** *and Frequency Rank* **256**

Contains **15 strokes** in the following order:

ノ ㇇ 彳 彳 彳 彳 德 德 德 德 德 德 德 德 德

Contains these components:

◧ left step r 彳 1247, p. 278
◨ straight, vertical 直 (altered) 85, p. 29
◨ heart (fat) r 心 1096, p. 248

With all these meanings & readings

dé [德] **1** Germany **2** virtue **3** goodness **4** morality **5** ethic **6** kindness **7** favor **8** character **9** kind

When your spiritual and *emotional* life is just like that of a virtuous man, then taking *left step* after step on a *straight* path will ensure your life exhibits a level of **morality**. • The alteration to the '*straight, vertical*' element is unusual, for it involves turning the 'net' sub-element on its side.

1258

徹
TRAD

SIMPLIFIED

This character with the definition:

thorough, complete

Pinyin **chè** *and Frequency Rank* **1240**

Contains **7 strokes** in the following order:

ノ ㇇ 彳 彳 彳 彻 彻

Contains these components:

◧ left step r 彳 1247, p. 278
◨ ancient ladle 匕 124, p. 36
◨ knife 刀 469, p. 112

With all these meanings & readings

chè [徹] **1** thorough **2** penetrating **3** to pervade **4** to pass through

To get the maximum **penetrating** power of floor stain, you need to *stomp* on it, mash it with a *spoon*, and cut it with a *knife*.

1259

禦
御
TRAD

SIMPLIFIED

This character with the definition:

control, manage

Pinyin **yù** *and Frequency Rank* **1381**

Contains **12 strokes** in the following order:

ノ ㇇ 彳 彳 彳 彳 彳 徉 徉 御 御 御

Contains these components:

◧ left step r 彳 1247, p. 278
◨ unload, take sth off 卸 198, p. 53

With all these meanings & readings

yù [御] **1** defend **2** imperial **3** to drive
yù [禦] **1** defend **2** resist

Effective bosses **manage** their work *step* by *step* and make sure to *offload* each task properly as they are completed.

Study Tips *Interlude 4*

Below are a few suggestions to help you use the material in this book most effectively.

Your 'learning' session must always involve two activities—the first is adding new characters to memory, and the second is reviewing those you have already learned. Reviewing characters that you have already learned is essential to the "learning and remembering" process, and **must** be done every day! We strongly suggest you use flashcards to do this review. We suggest even more strongly that you should download our free electronic card decks together with the Anki flashcard program (see *Flashcards*, Interlude 3, for more details).

Use whatever techniques work best in learning new material. For example, perhaps setting a daily quota for yourself is most advantageous for you. If you decide on a plan of five new characters per day, you will complete one unit a week **and** have your weekends off (although even then, you should still spend some time reviewing earlier material!). Or, you may prefer to study an entire unit all at once, and then review parts of it separately for several days before you incorporate it into a master review deck.

Finally, here are three tips to help you get the most out of the **EZChinesey** method:

■ First, every day you must review earlier material.

■ Second, as you read each new memory story, get into the habit of mentally visualizing the appearance of each component used in the story in your mind. "Seeing" the Chinese forms in your mind will help you learn more quickly and remember better. And in your daily review, when you forget a character, re-learn it then and there by "seeing" the components.

■ Third, if you feel that *our* memory story does not work for you, make up your own. We all respond differently to different types of cues. Some memory books suggest making the stories as absurd, and therefore as memorable, as possible. Others recommend using very intimate or graphic images—but you're on your own if you travel that route!

In fact, we encourage you to try constructing your own stories for characters now and then. Why? Because once you begin to read Chinese on your own, sooner or later you will come across a character not included in this guide. If you have taught yourself to create your own memory story, you will quickly be able to learn and remember that new character and its meaning!

Unit 53

1260 This component has the meaning:

eight r
COMPONENT

Hands tented together in prayer form a powerful attraction to photographers of all kinds. Here, an amateur attempts a shot by aiming the camera in front of his model's hands. However, his camera slips at the last moment and he catches only the two thumbs in a relaxed position. Nevertheless, this 'thumbnail' photo reminds us of the **eight** fingers out of the frame, and, by extension, of the number **eight**. • We often ascribe this component with a meaning of **abundance** and **plenty**; see below for further discussion.

1261 This character with the definition:

eight

Pinyin **bā** *and Frequency Rank* **451**

SIMP & TRAD   Contains **2 strokes** in the following order:

ノ 八

Contains these components:

■ eight r ˇ (altered) 1260, p. 282

With all these meanings & readings

bā [八] **1** eight **2** 8

The same photographer from the panel '*eight r*' (panel 1260) attempts again to capture prayerful hands on film but his own hands slip yet again. This time he catches only the upper portions of the hands, **eight** fingers in profile set against each other. • Chinese scribes liked to associate '**eight**' with the concept of **abundance**, because in Cantonese, the pronunciation of 八 sounds similar to the word meaning 'rich' or 'abundant'. As '**eight**' acquired a 'lucky' connotation, the Chinese regarded the number with special significance, which has since spread to Mandarin-speaking regions as well.

1262 This character with the definition:

small

Pinyin **xiǎo** *and Frequency Rank* **83**

SIMP & TRAD   Contains **3 strokes** in the following order:

亅 小 小

Contains these components:

■ eight 八 1261, p. 282
▯ hooked stick c 亅 18, p. 13

With all these meanings & readings

xiǎo [小] **1** small **2** tiny **3** few **4** young

The '*eight*' stands for abundance, the fortune I earned by my own efforts, and that someone with a *stick-like* weapon is trying to rob from me. As a result, my previous *abundance* shrunk to a **small** amount.

1263 This character with the definition:

point, tip

Pinyin **jiān** *and Frequency Rank* **1321**

SIMP & TRAD   Contains **6 strokes** in the following order:

丨 小 小 尐 尖 尖

Contains these components:

□ small 小 (altered) 1262, p. 282
■ big 大 544, p. 129

With all these meanings & readings

jiān [尖] **1** point (of needle) **2** sharp **3** shrewd **4** pointed

The **point** or **tip** can be defined as the place where a *small* space begins to grow *bigger* and *bigger* as one moves away from it.

1264 慕

This character with the definition:

admire*

Pinyin **mù** *and Frequency Rank* **1990**

SIMP & TRAD   Contains **14 strokes** in the following order:

一　十　艹　艹　艹　苩　苩　苩　莫　莫　慕　慕　慕　慕

Not a *small* number of people **admire** him.

Contains these components:

do not, not 莫 641, p. 152

small 小 (altered) 1262, p. 282

With all these meanings & readings:

mù [慕] **1** admire

1265 示

This character with the definition:

show, indicate

Pinyin **shì** *and Frequency Rank* **425**

SIMP & TRAD   Contains **5 strokes** in the following order:

一　二　于　亓　示

That young mother has *two small* children who she's always **showing** off to others.

Contains these components:

two 二 2, p. 10

small 小 1262, p. 282

With all these meanings & readings:

shì [示] **1** to show **2** reveal

1266 奈

This character with the definition:

how can one help?

Pinyin **nài** *and Frequency Rank* **1624**

SIMP & TRAD   Contains **8 strokes** in the following order:

一　ナ　大　太　杰　夲　夲　奈

After TV reports *showed* the devastation of the *big* flood, volunteers arrived and asked '**How can we help?**'.

Contains these components:

big 大 (altered) 544, p. 129

show, indicate 示 1265, p. 283

With all these meanings & readings:

nài [奈] **1** how can one help

1267 禁

This character with the definition:

prohibit

Pinyin **jìn** *and Frequency Rank* **986**

SIMP & TRAD   Contains **13 strokes** in the following order:

一　十　オ　木　朷　村　材　林　林　林　梦　埜　禁

Even though the *forest shows* you its wonderful offerings, a barrier **prohibits** you from entering it.

Contains these components:

forest 林 611, p. 146

show, indicate 示 1265, p. 283

With all these meanings & readings:

jīn [禁] **1** to endure
jìn [禁] **1** to prohibit **2** to forbid

1268 款

This character with the definition:

clause in contract

Pinyin **kuǎn** *and Frequency Rank* **807**

SIMP & TRAD   Contains **12 strokes** in the following order:

一　十　士　圭　圭　青　青　素　款　款　款　款

In China, *knights* were employed to enforce contracts; they convincingly *showed* each party what they *owed* in each **clause in the contract**.

Contains these components:

knight 士 8, p. 11

show, indicate 示 1265, p. 283

owe, lack 欠 744, p. 173

With all these meanings & readings:

kuǎn [款] **1** section **2** paragraph **3** funds **4** m 笔 [筆][bǐ], 个 [個][gè] **5** m for versions or models (e.g. a version of a device, software, etc.)

1269

SIMP & TRAD

This character with the definition:

clan, sect, faction

Pinyin **zōng** *and Frequency Rank* **727**

Contains **8 strokes** in the following order:

丶 丷 宀 宀 宀 宇 宗 宗

Contains these components:

▢ roof r 宀 271, p. 70

▧ show, indicate 示 1265, p. 283

With all these meanings & readings

zōng [宗] **1** school **2** sect **3** ppose **4** model **5** ancestor **6** family **7** m for batches, itemcases (medical or legal), reservo **8** surname Zong

People of like mind or tradition usually belong to the same **sect** and often *show* their common bond by gathering together in the same place, under the same *roof*.

1270

SIMP & TRAD

This character with the definition:

sublime

Pinyin **chóng** *and Frequency Rank* **1482**

Contains **11 strokes** in the following order:

丨 屵 山 中 屵 屵 崇 崇 崇 崇 崇

Contains these components:

▢ mountain 山 4, p. 10

▧ clan, sect, faction 宗 1269, p. 284

With all these meanings & readings

chóng [崇] **1** high **2** dignified **3** lofty **4** to honor

One *mountain* so dominated those around it with its permanently snow-capped peak majestic view, that the tribal *clan* regarded this **sublime** *mountain* as the gods' dwelling-place.

1271

综

TRAD   SIMPLIFIED

This character with the definition:

sum up, add together

Pinyin **zōng** *and Frequency Rank* **1425**

Contains **11 strokes** in the following order:

乚 纟 纟 纟 纩 纩 综 综 综 综 综

Contains these components:

▮ silk r 纟 (altered) 1037, p. 235

▯ clan, sect, faction 宗 1269, p. 284

With all these meanings & readings

zōng [综] **1** to sum up **2** to ptogether **3** heddle (device to form warp in weaving textiles) **4** Taiwan pr zòng

The political *faction* realized that it would acquire significantly more power if it could convince all the *silk* merchants in the district to **add** their voting power **together** and support the *faction*'s interests in the upcoming election.

1272

蹤

TRAD   SIMPLIFIED

This character with the definition:

footprint, trace, tracks

Pinyin **zōng** *and Frequency Rank* **1532**

Contains **15 strokes** in the following order:

丶 丷 口 口 甲 甲 呈 足 足 趵 趵 趵 踉 踪 踪

Contains these components:

▮ foot r 足 1148, p. 258

▯ clan, sect, faction 宗 1269, p. 284

With all these meanings & readings

zōng [蹤] **1** footprint **2** trace **3** tracks

When you march on *foot* along with the rest of your *clan*, you leave plenty of **footprints** on the path.

1273

SIMP & TRAD

This character with the definition:

ticket

Pinyin **piào** *and Frequency Rank* **910**

Contains **11 strokes** in the following order:

一 一 一 两 两 西 西 覀 票 票 票

Contains these components:

▢ west 西 (altered) 301, p. 77

▧ show, indicate 示 1265, p. 283

With all these meanings & readings

piào [票] **1** bank note **2** ticket **3** a vote **4** m 张 [張][zhāng]

I boarded the *train* headed *west*, but not before I was asked to *show* my **ticket**.

1274

SIMP & TRAD

This character with the definition:

drift, float

Pinyin **piāo** *and Frequency Rank* **1568**

Contains these components:

■ water r 氵 314, p. 80
■ ticket 票 1273, p. 284

With all these meanings & readings:

piāo [漂] **1** to float **2** to drift
piǎo [漂] **1** to bleach
piào [漂] **1** elegant **2** polished

Contains **14 strokes** in the following order:

丶 丶 氵 汀 汀 沪 沪 洏 洏 漂 漂 漂 漂 漂

As soon as the ferry left shore, my superstitious brother dropped his *ticket* into the *water* to see how far it would **drift** away. The longer it stayed **a**float, the luckier he felt.

1275

标

標
TRAD   SIMPLIFIED

This character with the definition:

mark, label

Pinyin **biāo** *and Frequency Rank* **473**

Contains these components:

■ tree 木 562, p. 133
■ show, indicate 示 1265, p. 283

With all these meanings & readings:

biāo [標] **1** the topmost branches of a tree **2** surface **3** sign **4** to mark **5** (outward) sign **6** indication **7** prize **8** award **9** bid

Contains **9 strokes** in the following order:

一 十 十 木 杧 杧 杬 标 标

In those ancient days, we would have used *wooden* sticks to **mark** our belongings to *show* others what belongs to us.

1276

SIMP & TRAD

This character with the definition:

surplus, spare

Pinyin **yú** *and Frequency Rank* **729**

Contains these components:

■ man 人 537, p. 127
■ show, indicate 示 (altered) 1265, p. 283

With all these meanings & readings:

yú [余] **1** I (used by emperor) **2** variant of 余[餘], surplus
yú [餘] **1** extra **2** surplus **3** remaining **4** remainder after division **5** (following numerical value) or more **6** in excess of (some number) **7** residue (math.) **8** after **9** I **10** me **11** surname Yu

Contains **7 strokes** in the following order:

丿 人 𠆢 合 仐 余 余

When *men* get interested in *showing off* their possessions, it is a sign that they have a **surplus** of resources beyond the basics needed for survival. To emphasize this fact, the ancient scribes inserted a **surplus** vertical stroke near the top of the '*show*' element.

1277

茶

SIMP & TRAD

This character with the definition:

tea

Pinyin **chá** *and Frequency Rank* **1272**

Contains these components:

■ grass r 艹 87, p. 29
■ surplus, spare 余 (altered) 1276, p. 285

With all these meanings & readings:

chá [茶] **1** tea **2** tea plant **3** m 杯[bēi], 壶[壺][hú]

Contains **9 strokes** in the following order:

一 十 艹 艻 艻 苃 苳 茶 茶

Tea is brewed from a kind of dried *grass* and is so enjoyable that there is hardly ever any *surplus*!

1278

SIMP & TRAD

This character with the definition:

remove, eliminate

Pinyin **chú** *and Frequency Rank* **464**

Contains these components:

■ hills r 阝 942, p. 216
■ surplus, spare 余 1276, p. 285

With all these meanings & readings:

chú [除] **1** to get rid of **2** to remove **3** to exclude **4** to eliminate **5** to wipe out **6** to divide **7** except **8** not including

Contains **9 strokes** in the following order:

了 阝 阝 阹 阹 阼 除 除 除

My parents had to **eliminate** all their *surplus* possessions before they could move into their retirement home in the *hills*.

1279

This character with the definition:

slowly, gently

Pinyin **xú** and Frequency Rank **1313**

SIMP & TRAD   Contains **10 strokes** in the following order:

ノ ク 彳 彳 彴 仒 佘 佘 徐 徐

Contains these components:

■ left step r 彳 1247, p. 278

■ surplus, spare 余 1276, p. 285

With all these meanings & readings:

xú [徐] **1** slow **2** gentle **3** surname Xu

After surgery, my movements were so limited that no *spare* gestures were possible. I needed physical therapy so that I could **slowly** re-learn how to take one *left step* without falling over.

1280
塗
涂
TRAD   SIMPLIFIED

This character with the definition:

smear, apply

Pinyin **tú** and Frequency Rank **1735**

Contains **10 strokes** in the following order:

丶 丶 氵 氵 汄 汄 泠 涂 涂 涂

Contains these components:

■ water r 氵 314, p. 80

■ surplus, spare 余 1276, p. 285

With all these meanings & readings:

tú [塗] **1** to apply (paint etc) **2** to smear **3** to daub **4** to blo[t] out **5** to scribble **6** to scrawl **7** mud (literary)
tú [涂] **1** to smear **2** daub **3** [to] apply (paint) **4** to spread **5** sur[name Tu]

A *surplus* of rainfall this year allowed the farmers to expand their irrigation systems and **apply** the accumulated rain*water* to new crops.

1281

This character with the definition:

oblique, slanting

Pinyin **xié** and Frequency Rank **1786**

SIMP & TRAD   Contains **11 strokes** in the following order:

ノ 人 乀 仒 仒 仒 佘 佘 佘 佘 斜

Contains these components:

■ surplus, spare 余 1276, p. 285

■ cup-shaped 斗 185, p. 51

With all these meanings & readings:

xié [斜] **1** slanting

Tea spills out when I hold my *cup-shaped* bowl. At first, I thought there was a *too much* tea in the cup, but then I realized it was me being clumsy—I was holding the cup in a **slanted** manner.

1282
親
TRAD   SIMPLIFIED

This character with the definition:

relatives

Pinyin **qīn** and Frequency Rank **362**

Contains **9 strokes** in the following order:

丶 二 亠 立 立 辛 辛 亲 亲

Contains these components:

■ to stand 立 681, p. 160

■ show, indicate 示 (altered) 1265, p. 283

With all these meanings & readings:

qīn [親] **1** parent **2** one's own (flesh and blood) **3** relative **4** related **5** marriage **6** bride **7** close **8** intimate **9** in person **10** first-hand **11** in favor o[f] **12** pro- **13** to kiss
qìng [親] **1** parents-in-law of one[']s offspring

The combination of elements in this character may indicate that the ancient scribes intended to depict that we *stand* more erect at formal events—such as weddings and funerals—in order to *show* respect to our **relatives**.

1283

This character with the definition:

new

Pinyin **xīn** and Frequency Rank **161**

SIMP & TRAD   Contains **13 strokes** in the following order:

丶 二 亠 立 立 辛 辛 亲 亲 新 新 新 新

Contains these components:

■ relatives 亲 1282, p. 286

■ catty 斤 403, p. 98

With all these meanings & readings:

xīn [新] **1** new **2** newly **3** abb[r] for 新疆[xin jiāng] **4** meso- (chemistry)

The acquisition of **new** *relatives*—say by marriage—may lead to a state of *unbalance* as traditional pecking orders are fought and re-affirmed.

1284

SIMP & TRAD

This character with the definition:

military official

Pinyin **wèi** *and Frequency Rank* **2126**

Contains **11 strokes** in the following order:

一 コ 尸 尸 尸 尽 层 层 层- 尉 尉

Contains these components:

⬚ corpse 尸 499, p. 119

⬚ show, indicate 示 1265, p. 283

⬛ inch 寸 216, p. 58

With all these meanings & readings:

wèi [尉] **1** military officer **2** to quiet **3** surname Wei

After the intense battle ended, the **military official** surveyed the casualties and was greatly distressed to find the *corpse* of his best lieutenant, which *showed* an *inch*-long fatal wound to the heart.

Unit 54

1285 慰

SIMP & TRAD

This character with the definition:

console, comfort

Pinyin **wèi** *and Frequency Rank* **1632**

Contains **15 strokes** in the following order:

一 コ 尸 尸 尸 屋 屋 屋 尉 尉 尉 尉 慰 慰

Contains these components:

■ military official 尉 1284, p. 287

■ heart (fat) r 心 1096, p. 248

With all these meanings & readings:

wèi [慰] **1** to comfort **2** to console **3** to reassure

After experiencing the awfulness of war first hand, the *military official* knew that his next challenge would be to provide *compassion* and **comfort** while attempting to **console** many grieving widows and orphans.

1286 杂

雜
TRAD

SIMPLIFIED

This character with the definition:

mixed, composite

Pinyin **zá** *and Frequency Rank* **853**

Contains **6 strokes** in the following order:

丿 九 九 杂 杂 杂

Contains these components:

■ nine 九 532, p. 126

□ show, indicate 示 (abbrev) 1265, 283

With all these meanings & readings:

zá [雜] **1** mixed **2** miscellaneou **3** various **4** to mix

A curious **mixture** of things always accumulates in desk and dresser drawers. In mine, I can *show* you at least *nine* objects that bear no relation to one another.

1287 际

際
TRAD SIMPLIFIED

This character with the definition:

border, boundary

Pinyin **jì** *and Frequency Rank* **423**

Contains **7 strokes** in the following order:

Contains these components:

■ hills r ⻖ 942, p. 216

■ show, indicate 示 1265, p. 283

With all these meanings & readings:

jì [際] **1** border **2** edge **3** bou ary **4** between **5** among **6** in terval **7** while

The distant *hills show* the country's **borders**.

1288 东

東
TRAD SIMPLIFIED

This character with the definition:

east

Pinyin **dōng** *and Frequency Rank* **194**

Contains **5 strokes** in the following order:

一 七 车 东 东

Contains these components:

■ show, indicate 示 (altered) 1265, p. 283

■ action path c 丿 438, p. 105

With all these meanings & readings:

dōng [東] **1** east **2** host (i.e. sitting on east side of guest) **3** landlord **4** surname Dong

As the sun ascends in the **east**, its rays *indicate* the *action path* that it will trace in the sky throughout the day.

1289 陈

陳
TRAD SIMPLIFIED

This character with the definition:

put on display

Pinyin **chén** *and Frequency Rank* **525**

Contains **7 strokes** in the following order:

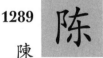

Contains these components:

■ hills r ⻖ 942, p. 216

■ east 东 1288, p. 288

With all these meanings & readings:

chén [陳] **1** surname Chen **2** C of the Southern dynasties (557-589)

chén [陳] **1** to lay out **2** to exhibit **3** to display **4** to narrate **5** to state **6** to explain **7** to te **8** old **9** stale

When the sun rises over the *hills* in the *east*, it vividly lights up the special landscaping that we've **put on display**.

1290

練
TRAD   SIMPLIFIED

This character with the definition:

practice, train, drill

Pinyin **liàn** *and Frequency Rank* **1005**

Contains **8 strokes** in the following order:

丿 乙 纟 纟 纩 纩 练 练

Contains these components:

silk r 纟 1037, p. 235

east 东 1288, p. 288

With all these meanings & readings:

liàn [練] **1** to practice **2** to train **3** to drill **4** to perfect (one's skill) **5** exercise

While still wearing my *silk* pajamas, I get out of bed and face *east* to **practice** Chinese martial arts every morning.

1291

車
TRAD   SIMPLIFIED

This character with the definition:

car

Pinyin **chē** *and Frequency Rank* **361**

Contains **4 strokes** in the following order:

一 t 车 车

Contains these components:

east 东 (altered) 1288, p. 288

ten 十 7, p. 11

With all these meanings & readings:

chē [車] **1** surname Che
chē [車] **1** car **2** vehicle **3** m 辆[輛][liàng] **4** machine **5** to shape with a lathe
jū [車] **1** war chariot (archaic) **2** rook (in Chinese chess) **3** rook (in chess)

In the old days, how would you have travelled from California to New York? You would have climbed in your **car**, and driven *east*. After *ten* days, more or less, you would find yourself bucking crowds in Times Square. • Also: 车 shows the outline of the front of your new, fire-engine red Lexus, seen from above. The car's hood is on the left. The horizontals represent the wheels on the right and left. The front right door is open, and if you look inside, you'll see the front row of bucket seats (that's the vertical line) neatly bisected in two.

1292

輩
TRAD   SIMPLIFIED

This character with the definition:

lifetime

Pinyin **bèi** *and Frequency Rank* **1477**

Contains **12 strokes** in the following order:

丨 丬 刌 非 非 非 非 非 韭 辈 辈 辈

Contains these components:

not 非 6, p. 11

car 车 1291, p. 289

With all these meanings & readings:

bèi [輩] **1** contemporaries **2** generation **3** lifetime

I still remember those horrible years 'BDL'—before driver's license. *Not* having access to a *car* made completing every day errands seem a **lifetime**!

1293

輯
TRAD   SIMPLIFIED

This character with the definition:

compile, edit

Pinyin **jí** *and Frequency Rank* **1362**

Contains **13 strokes** in the following order:

一 t 车 车 车 车' 车¹ 轺 辑 辑 辑 辑 辑

Contains these components:

car 车 1291, p. 289

mouth 口 37, p. 17

ear 耳 76, p. 26

With all these meanings & readings:

jí [輯] **1** gather up **2** collect **3** edit **4** compile

To be an effective **editor**, you need a working *car*, a glib *mouth*, and a sympathetic *ear*.

1294

軍
TRAD   SIMPLIFIED

This character with the definition:

military

Pinyin **jūn** *and Frequency Rank* **102**

Contains **6 strokes** in the following order:

丿 冖 冖 军 军 军

Contains these components:

smooth cover r 冖 268, p. 69

car 车 1291, p. 289

With all these meanings & readings:

jūn [軍] **1** army **2** military **3** arms **4** m 个[個][gè]

By installing a strong and protective yet *smooth cover* onto a normal *car*, you can convert it to a weapon-resistant vehicle suitable for **military** use.

1295

挥

挥
TRAD   SIMPLIFIED

This character with the definition:

brandish

Pinyin **huī** *and Frequency Rank* **742**

Contains **9 strokes** in the following order:

一 丨 扌 扩 护 护 挥 挥 挥

Contains these components:

hand r 扌 25, p.15

military 军 1294, p.289

With all these meanings & readings

huī [挥] **1** to wave **2** to brandi
3 to wipe away **4** to command
5 to conduct **6** to scatter **7** to
disperse

A great *military* leader knows the importance of making a symbolic gesture, such as raising his *hand* high to **brandish** his sword for all to see, before leading his troops into battle.

1296

浑

浑
TRAD   SIMPLIFIED

This character with the definition:

muddy

Pinyin **hún** *and Frequency Rank* **1991**

Contains **9 strokes** in the following order:

丶 丶 氵 氵 汇 沪 浑 浑 浑

Contains these components:

water r 氵 314, p.80

military 军 1294, p.289

With all these meanings & readings

hún [浑] **1** muddy

Military vehicles are big and heavy. After a rainstorm, this heaviness churns up a lot of earth, which mixes with rain *water* to create dismal, **muddy** conditions.

1297

斩

斩
TRAD   SIMPLIFIED

This character with the definition:

behead

Pinyin **zhǎn** *and Frequency Rank* **2463**

Contains **8 strokes** in the following order:

一 七 车 车 车 斩 斩 斩

Contains these components:

car 车 1291, p.289

catty 斤 403, p.98

With all these meanings & readings

zhǎn [斩] **1** to behead (as form of capital punishment) **2** to chop

In a terrible accident, one of the *car's* wheels came flying off; the car became *unbalanced* and the driver was **beheaded**.

1298

暂

暂
TRAD   SIMPLIFIED

This character with the definition:

temporarily

Pinyin **zàn** *and Frequency Rank* **1325**

Contains **12 strokes** in the following order:

一 七 车 车 车 斩 斩 斩 斩 暂 暂 暂

Contains these components:

behead 斩 1297, p.290

speak 日 67, p.24

With all these meanings & readings

zàn [暂] **1** temporary **2** Taiwan
pr zhàn

If you *behead* a chicken, it will continue to *speak* **temporarily**.

1299

渐

渐
TRAD   SIMPLIFIED

This character with the definition:

gradually

Pinyin **jiàn** *and Frequency Rank* **870**

Contains **11 strokes** in the following order:

丶 丶 氵 氵 汁 汢 沌 浐 渐 渐 渐

Contains these components:

water r 氵 314, p.80

behead 斩 1297, p.290

With all these meanings & readings

jiān [渐] **1** imbue
jiàn [渐] **1** gradual **2** gradually

The dead rat had floated in the *water* for several days with only its head exposed above water. A sort of natural *beheading* process, or decomposition, **gradually** separated of the head from the body.

1300

库

庫 TRAD SIMPLIFIED

This character with the definition:

warehouse, storehouse

Pinyin **kù** *and Frequency Rank* **1097**

Contains **7 strokes** in the following order:

丶 亠 广 广 庄 庄 库

Contains these components:

▢ shelter r 广 427, p.103
▣ car 车 1291, p.289

With all these meanings & readings:

kù [库] **1** warehouse **2** store-house

A **warehouse** used to function as a *shelter* for surplus goods. Now, we shop at 'warehouse stores' that are so large that store managers require a small *car* to inspect it all.

1301

软

軟 TRAD SIMPLIFIED

This character with the definition:

soft, pliant

Pinyin **ruǎn** *and Frequency Rank* **1043**

Contains **8 strokes** in the following order:

一 七 车 车 车 车 轩 软

Contains these components:

▣ car 车 1291, p.289
▣ owe, lack 欠 744, p.173

With all these meanings & readings:

ruǎn [软] **1** soft **2** flexible

A luxury *car* without **soft** leather seats will surely *lack* buyers!

1302

辆

輛 TRAD SIMPLIFIED

This character with the definition:

m for vehicles

Pinyin **liàng** *and Frequency Rank* **1375**

Contains **11 strokes** in the following order:

一 七 车 车 车 车 轩 轩 辆 辆 辆

Contains these components:

▣ car 车 1291, p.289
▣ both, two 两 763, p.177

With all these meanings & readings:

liàng [辆] **1** m for vehicles

This picture of *both cars* helps us remember that this character is the **measure word for vehicles** such as cars. • There is no English-word equivalent so a useful analogy is the measurement units used in cooking, for example: one cup of sugar, a pinch of salt.

1303

载

載 TRAD SIMPLIFIED

This character with the definition:

carry, convey

Pinyin **zǎi** *and Frequency Rank* **977**

Contains **10 strokes** in the following order:

一 十 土 吉 去 幸 幸 载 载 载

Contains these components:

▢ wound c 弋 937, p.215
▢ car 车 1291, p.289

With all these meanings & readings:

zǎi [载] **1** year **2** to record in writing
zài [载] **1** to carry **2** to convey **3** to load **4** to hold **5** to fill up **6** and **7** also **8** as well as **9** simultaneously

Quick—we need to **convey** the *wounded* soldier to a hospital with our *car*.

1304

阵

陣 TRAD SIMPLIFIED

This character with the definition:

battle formation

Pinyin **zhèn** *and Frequency Rank* **788**

Contains **6 strokes** in the following order:

丨 阝 阝 阵 阵 阵

Contains these components:

▣ hills r 阝 942, p.216
▣ car 车 1291, p.289

With all these meanings & readings:

zhèn [阵] **1** disposition of troops **2** wave **3** spate **4** burst **5** spell **6** short period of time **7** m for events or states of short duration

Since the troops' **battle formation** extended far into the foot*hills*, the army commander was driven around the area in an open-topped *car* to inspect the troops.

1305

轮

輪 TRAD SIMPLIFIED

This character with the definition:

wheel, wheel-like

Pinyin **lún** *and Frequency Rank* **1096**

Contains **8 strokes** in the following order:

一 ㄟ 车 车 车 轮 轮 轮

Contains these components:

■ car 车 1291, p. 289
■ order, arrangement 仑 867, p. 198

With all these meanings & readings:

lún [輪] **1** wheel **2** disk **3** ring **4** steamship **5** to take turns **6** to rotate **7** by turn **8** m for big round objects: disk, or recurring events: round, turn

The **wheels** bring *order* to a *car* and a car provides the freedom to make convenient *arrangements* in your life.

1306

辖

轄 TRAD SIMPLIFIED

This character with the definition:

have jurisdiction over

Pinyin **xiá** *and Frequency Rank* **1643**

Contains **14 strokes** in the following order:

一 ㄟ 车 车 车 车 轩 轩 轩 轩 辖 辖 辖 辖

Contains these components:

■ car 车 1291, p. 289
■ harm, injure 害 280, p. 72

With all these meanings & readings:

xiá [轄] **1** to govern **2** to control **3** having jurisdiction over **4** linchpin of a wheel (archaic) **5** noise of a barrow

That *car* ran into yours and *injured* you. You can't do anything for yourself now so let the courts **have jurisdiction over** the matter.

1307

轨

軌 TRAD SIMPLIFIED

This character with the definition:

course, path

Pinyin **guǐ** *and Frequency Rank* **1883**

Contains **6 strokes** in the following order:

一 ㄟ 车 车 轨 轨

Contains these components:

■ car 车 1291, p. 289
■ nine 九 532, p. 126

With all these meanings & readings:

guǐ [軌] **1** course **2** path **3** track **4** rail

Why are there *nine cars* driving so fast and close to each other? It must be a race and their **path** is determined by the race **course**.

1308

乐

樂 TRAD SIMPLIFIED

This character with the definition:

glad to, enjoy

Pinyin **lè** *and Frequency Rank* **619**

Contains **5 strokes** in the following order:

一 ㇠ 乐 乐 乐

Contains these components:

■ show, indicate 示 (altered) 1265, p. 283

With all these meanings & readings:

lè [樂] **1** happy **2** laugh **3** cheerful **4** surname Le
yuè [樂] **1** surname Yue **2** music

When people **enjoy** life, they can't help but *show* this emotion on their faces and, indeed, in every action they make. On the left, the extra curvy stroke connecting the horizontals represents the crinkle line that forms around the eyes of genuinely **happy** people when they smile.

1309

肖

SIMP & TRAD

This character with the definition:

like, similar to

Pinyin **xiào** *and Frequency Rank* **2019**

Contains **7 strokes** in the following order:

丨 丶 丷 丬 肖 肖 肖

Contains these components:

■ small 小 (altered) 1262, p. 282
■ meat 肉 (altered) 753, p. 175

With all these meanings & readings:

xiào [肖] **1** similar **2** resembling **3** to resemble **4** to be like

The young child looked at his portion of *meat*, which was *small* compared to his older brother's, and cried out: 'I want *meat* **like** his!'

Unit 55

1310

稍

SIMP & TRAD

This character with the definition:

slightly, somewhat

Pinyin **shāo** *and Frequency Rank* **1373**

Contains **12 strokes** in the following order:

一 二 千 禾 禾 利 利 秒 秒 稍 稍 稍

Contains these components:

■ rice, grain (crop) 禾 593, p. 140
■ like, similar to 肖 1309, p. 292

With all these meanings & readings:

shāo [稍] **1** somewhat   **2** a little

Grains will look *similar to* one another if their genetic makeups are **somewhat** alike.

1311

消

SIMP & TRAD

This character with the definition:

disappear, vanish

Pinyin **xiāo** *and Frequency Rank* **439**

Contains **10 strokes** in the following order:

丶 丶 氵 汀 汀 泸 消 消 消

Contains these components:

■ water r 氵 314, p. 80
■ like, similar to 肖 1309, p. 292

With all these meanings & readings:

xiāo [消] **1** consume   **2** news   **3** subside   **4** to disappear   **5** to vanish   **6** have to   **7** need

Sometimes, water can work *like* magic and make stains **vanish** from clothes!

1312

削

SIMP & TRAD

This character with the definition:

pare, peel with knife

Pinyin **xiāo** *and Frequency Rank* **1794**

Contains **9 strokes** in the following order:

丨 丬 少 肖 肖 肖 削 削

Contains these components:

■ like, similar to 肖 1309, p. 292
■ knife r 刂 169, p. 46

With all these meanings & readings:

xiāo [削] **1** to scrape
xuē [削] **1** to reduce   **2** to pare (away)   **3** to cut (down)

With a deftly wielded *knife*, you can make a piece of shapeless wood *look like* something else by means of skillfully **peeling away** parts of the wood.

1313

悄

SIMP & TRAD

This character with the definition:

quiet, silent

Pinyin **qiǎo** *and Frequency Rank* **1434**

Contains **10 strokes** in the following order:

丶 丶 忄 忄 忄 忄 忙 悄 悄 悄

Contains these components:

■ heart (skinny) r 忄 1135, p. 256
■ like, similar to 肖 1309, p. 292

With all these meanings & readings:

qiǎo [悄] **1** quiet   **2** sad

Silence is a lot *like* a subdued *emotion*.

1314

京

SIMP & TRAD

This character with the definition:

capital city

Pinyin **jīng** *and Frequency Rank* **566**

Contains **8 strokes** in the following order:

丶 一 亠 宁 古 亨 京 京

Contains these components:

■ cover r 冖 250, p. 66
■ mouth 口 37, p. 17
■ small 小 1262, p. 282

With all these meanings & readings:

jīng [京] **1** capital   **2** Beijing (abbr.)

As a country bumpkin visiting the **capital** for the first time, you will *cover* your *mouth* in astonishment at the sight of the monumental buildings because they will make you feel so *small*.

1315 景

SIMP & TRAD

This character with the definition:

view, scene

Pinyin **jǐng** *and Frequency Rank* **814**

Contains **12 strokes** in the following order:

丶 冂 冂 日 旦 旱 昌 昌 景 景 景 景

Contains these components:

☐ day, sun 日 64, p. 24
■ capital city 京 1314, p. 293

With all these meanings & readings:

jǐng [景] **1** bright **2** circumstance **3** scenery **4** surname Jing

In the *light of day*, nothing surpasses the spectacular **view** of any *capital city*.

1316 凉
凉
TRAD   SIMPLIFIED

This character with the definition:

cool

Pinyin **liáng** *and Frequency Rank* **1581**

Contains **10 strokes** in the following order:

丶 冫 冫 广 亠 泞 泞 涼 涼 涼

Contains these components:

☐ ice r 冫 348, p. 87
■ capital city 京 1314, p. 293

With all these meanings & readings:

liáng [凉] **1** cool **2** cold **3** the five Liang of the Sixteen Kingdoms, namely: Former Liang 前凉 [~涼] (314-376), Later Liang 後凉 [~涼] (386-403), Northern Liang 北凉 [~涼] (398-439), Southern Liang 南凉 [~涼] (397-414), Western Liang 西凉 [~涼] (400-421)

Have you ever been to *capital city* in mid-winter? It's perceptibly warmer than the surrounding countryside. When it's *icy* in the 'burbs, it's merely **cool** in the *capital*.

1317 惊
驚
TRAD   SIMPLIFIED

This character with the definition:

alarmed

Pinyin **jīng** *and Frequency Rank* **659**

Contains **11 strokes** in the following order:

丶 丶 忄 忄 忙 忙 怕 怕 惊 惊 惊

Contains these components:

☐ heart (skinny) r 忄 1135, p. 256
■ capital city 京 1314, p. 293

With all these meanings & readings:

jīng [驚] **1** to start **2** to be frightened **3** to be scared **4** ala

My cousin from the countryside feels very ill at ease in his country's *capital*. His *emotions* are getting a fierce workout as a succession of unexpected sights continually **alarms** him.

1318 琼
瓊
TRAD   SIMPLIFIED

This character with the definition:

fine jade

Pinyin **qióng** *and Frequency Rank* **2205**

Contains **12 strokes** in the following order:

一 二 王 王 王 扩 玗 玙 琤 琼 琼 琼

Contains these components:

☐ king 王 15, p. 12
■ capital city 京 1314, p. 293

With all these meanings & readings:

qióng [瓊] **1** jasper **2** fine jade **3** beautiful **4** exquisite (e.g. wine, food) **5** abbreviation for Hainan province

We've established in panel 177 that there is a connection between 'jade' and the monarchy. The *capital* was the best part of the *king's* domain, which he regarded as a piece of **fine jade**.

1319 掠

SIMP & TRAD

This character with the definition:

plunder

Pinyin **lüè** *and Frequency Rank* **1868**

Contains **11 strokes** in the following order:

一 十 扌 扩 扩 扩 拘 拘 掠 掠 掠

Contains these components:

☐ hand r 扌 25, p. 15
■ capital city 京 1314, p. 293

With all these meanings & readings:

lüè [掠] **1** to take over by force **2** to rob **3** to plunder

The government officials who infest a country's *capital* always seem to have their *hands* stretched out to collect fees, bribes, or worse. It's legal **plunder**!

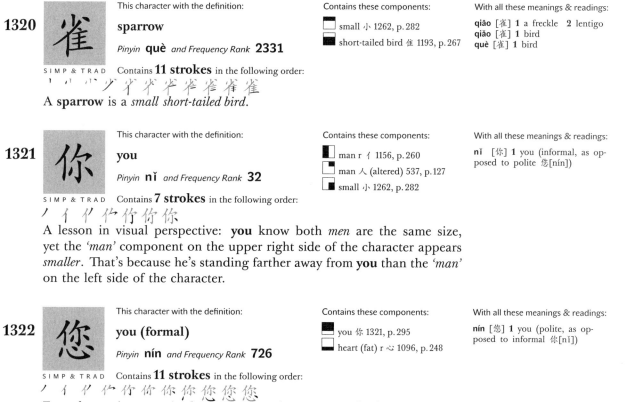

1320

雀

SIMP & TRAD

que

This character with the definition:

sparrow

Pinyin **què** *and Frequency Rank* **2331**

Contains **11 strokes** in the following order:

一 丨 小 少 少 犭 犭 犭 雀 雀 雀

Contains these components:

small 小 1262, p. 282

short-tailed bird 隹 1193, p. 267

With all these meanings & readings:

qiǎo [雀] **1** a freckle **2** lentigo
qiǎo [雀] **1** bird
què [雀] **1** bird

A **sparrow** is a *small short-tailed bird*.

1321

你

SIMP & TRAD

This character with the definition:

you

Pinyin **nǐ** *and Frequency Rank* **32**

Contains **7 strokes** in the following order:

ノ 亻 亻 仁 佗 你 你

Contains these components:

man r 亻 1156, p. 260

man 人 (altered) 537, p. 127

small 小 1262, p. 282

With all these meanings & readings:

nǐ [你] **1** you (informal, as opposed to polite 您[nín])

A lesson in visual perspective: **you** know both *men* are the same size, yet the *'man'* component on the upper right side of the character appears *smaller*. That's because he's standing farther away from **you** than the *'man'* on the left side of the character.

1322

您

SIMP & TRAD

This character with the definition:

you (formal)

Pinyin **nín** *and Frequency Rank* **726**

Contains **11 strokes** in the following order:

ノ 亻 亻 仁 佗 你 你 你 您 您 您

Contains these components:

you 你 1321, p. 295

heart (fat) r 心 1096, p. 248

With all these meanings & readings:

nín [您] **1** you (polite, as opposed to informal 你[nǐ])

Formal occasions require less *emotion* and more control when I speak to *you*, certainly less so than when I speak to **you** normally.

1323

少

SIMP & TRAD

This character with the definition:

few, little

Pinyin **shǎo** *and Frequency Rank* **233**

Contains **4 strokes** in the following order:

丨 丿 小 少

Contains these components:

small 小 1262, p. 282

action path c 丿 438, p. 105

With all these meanings & readings:

shǎo [少] **1** few **2** little **3** lack
shào [少] **1** young

The character 小 (panel 1262) refers to the relative size of things, while this character refers to the relative number of things. To distinguish them, remember that only a **few** *small* tools are required to perform an *activity*— and you make sure to keep count of those **few** tools so you won't lose them.

1324

省

SIMP & TRAD

This character with the definition:

economize, be frugal

Pinyin **shěng** *and Frequency Rank* **666**

Contains **9 strokes** in the following order:

丨 丿 小 少 少 省 省 省 省

Contains these components:

few, little 少 1323, p. 295

eye 目 75, p. 26

With all these meanings & readings:

shěng [省] **1** to save **2** to economize **3** to do without **4** to omit
5 to leave out **6** province **7** m
个[個][gè]
xǐng [省] **1** introspection **2** to
examine oneself critically **3** awareness **4** to visit (an elderly relative)

If you plan to **economize**, you will need to learn to **be frugal** and to keep one *eye* alert for bargains that allow you to save a *few* dollars on purchases.

1325

This character with the definition:

quarrel, make noise

Pinyin **chǎo** *and Frequency Rank* **2040**

SIMP & TRAD　Contains **7 strokes** in the following order:

Contains these components:

☐ mouth 口 37, p. 17
■ few, little 少 1323, p. 295

With all these meanings & readings:

chǎo [吵] **1** to quarrel **2** to make a noise **3** noisy **4** to disturb by making a noise

You use your *mouth* to **quarrel**. If you become too good at **quarreling**, you will end up with *few* close friends.

1326

This character with the definition:

wonderful

Pinyin **miào** *and Frequency Rank* **1250**

SIMP & TRAD　Contains **7 strokes** in the following order:

Contains these components:

■ woman 女 790, p. 183
■ few, little 少 1323, p. 295

With all these meanings & readings:

miào [妙] **1** clever **2** wonderful

In contrast to ancient thinking, modern day thinking says that *women* have *few* natural disadvantages; in fact, *women* are actually quite **wonderful**!

1327

This character with the definition:

sand

Pinyin **shā** *and Frequency Rank* **848**

SIMP & TRAD　Contains **7 strokes** in the following order:

Contains these components:

■ water r 氵 314, p. 80
■ few, little 少 1323, p. 295

With all these meanings & readings:

shā [沙] **1** granule **2** hoarse **3** raspy **4** sand **5** powder **6** abbr for Tsar or Tsarist Russia **7** surname Sha **8** m 粒[lì]

We usually associate **sand** with *water* and the *little* grains of **sand** at the seashore. In the northern part of China, **sand** implies lack of *water* and is the source of terrible **sand**-storms; sometimes *little* particles of **sand** travel as far as Beijing.

1328

This character with the definition:

katydid

Pinyin **shā** *and Frequency Rank* **2125**

SIMP & TRAD　Contains **10 strokes** in the following order:

Contains these components:

☐ grass r 艹 87, p. 29
■ sand 沙 1327, p. 296

With all these meanings & readings:

shā [莎] **1** phonetic "sha" used in transliterations
suō [莎] **1** see 莎草[suō cǎo] **2** see 摩莎[mó suō]

In North America, many species of **katydid** are very small in size—analogous to grains of living *sand* in a sea of *grass*.

1329

This character with the definition:

step

Pinyin **bù** *and Frequency Rank* **349**

SIMP & TRAD　Contains **7 strokes** in the following order:

Contains these components:

■ stop! 止 190, p. 52
☐ few, little 少 (altered) 1323, p. 295

With all these meanings & readings:

bù [步] **1** a step **2** a pace **3** walk **4** march **5** stages in a process

My dog had taken only a *few* **steps** toward the open gate when I issued one command *'Stop!'* The well-trained dog immediately obeyed and remained where he was.

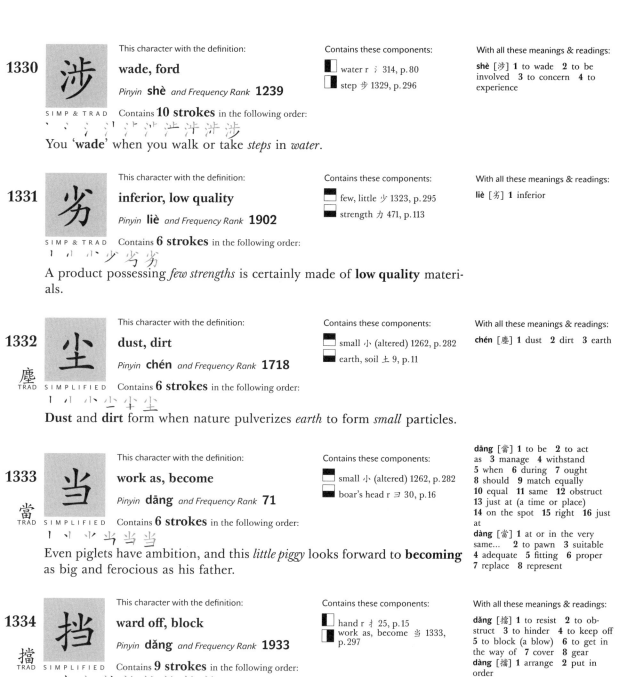

1330 涉

This character with the definition:

wade, ford

Pinyin **shè** *and Frequency Rank* **1239**

SIMP & TRAD   Contains **10 strokes** in the following order:

Contains these components:

□ water r 氵 314, p. 80
□ step 步 1329, p. 296

With all these meanings & readings:

shè [涉] **1** to wade **2** to be involved **3** to concern **4** to experience

You '**wade**' when you walk or take *steps* in *water*.

1331 劣

This character with the definition:

inferior, low quality

Pinyin **liè** *and Frequency Rank* **1902**

SIMP & TRAD   Contains **6 strokes** in the following order:

Contains these components:

□ few, little 少 1323, p. 295
□ strength 力 471, p. 113

With all these meanings & readings:

liè [劣] **1** inferior

A product possessing *few strengths* is certainly made of **low quality** materials.

1332 尘

塵 TRAD   SIMPLIFIED

This character with the definition:

dust, dirt

Pinyin **chén** *and Frequency Rank* **1718**

Contains **6 strokes** in the following order:

Contains these components:

□ small 小 (altered) 1262, p. 282
□ earth, soil 土 9, p. 11

With all these meanings & readings:

chén [塵] **1** dust **2** dirt **3** earth

Dust and **dirt** form when nature pulverizes *earth* to form *small* particles.

1333 当

當 TRAD   SIMPLIFIED

This character with the definition:

work as, become

Pinyin **dāng** *and Frequency Rank* **71**

Contains **6 strokes** in the following order:

Contains these components:

□ small 小 (altered) 1262, p. 282
□ boar's head r ⼹ 30, p. 16

With all these meanings & readings:

dāng [當] **1** to be **2** to act as **3** manage **4** withstand **5** when **6** during **7** ought **8** should **9** match equally **10** equal **11** same **12** obstruct **13** just at (a time or place) **14** on the spot **15** right **16** just at
dàng [當] **1** at or in the very same... **2** to pawn **3** suitable **4** adequate **5** fitting **6** proper **7** replace **8** represent

Even piglets have ambition, and this *little piggy* looks forward to **becoming** as big and ferocious as his father.

1334 挡

擋 TRAD   SIMPLIFIED

This character with the definition:

ward off, block

Pinyin **dǎng** *and Frequency Rank* **1933**

Contains **9 strokes** in the following order:

Contains these components:

□ hand r 扌 25, p. 15
□ work as, become 当 1333, p. 297

With all these meanings & readings:

dǎng [擋] **1** to resist **2** to obstruct **3** to hinder **4** to keep off **5** to block (a blow) **6** to get in the way of **7** cover **8** gear
dàng [擋] **1** arrange **2** put in order

Many parents believe that if their children *become* '*hand*-laborers' (manual laborers), they will be **blocked** from earning lots of money and prestige.

Unit 56

1335 档
檔
TRAD SIMPLIFIED

This character with the definition:

file, archive

Pinyin **dàng** *and Frequency Rank* **1787**

Contains **10 strokes** in the following order:

一 十 才 木 札 杧 杧 料 档 档

Contains these components:

■ tree 木 562, p.133
■ work as, become 当 1333, p.297

With all these meanings & readings:

dàng [檔] **1** official records **2** grade (of goods) **3** file **4** rec **5** shelves **6** cross-piece **7** (classifier for cross-pieces)

My son achieved his dream of *becoming* a forest ranger; now he has a mental **file** of every *tree* under his watch.

1336 尔
爾
TRAD SIMPLIFIED

This character with the definition:

you, thou

Pinyin **ěr** *and Frequency Rank* **220**

Contains **5 strokes** in the following order:

丿 ㇇ 尓 尔 尔

Contains these components:

■ man 人 (altered) 537, p.127
■ small 小 1262, p.282

With all these meanings & readings:

ěr [爾] **1** thus **2** so **3** like that **4** you **5** thou

Suppose I am speaking to you from a great distance. **You** appear to be a *small man* because **you** are standing far away from me.

1337 弥
彌
TRAD SIMPLIFIED

This character with the definition:

full, overflowing

Pinyin **mí** *and Frequency Rank* **1785**

Contains **8 strokes** in the following order:

㇇ ㇆ 弓 弘 弥 弥 弥 弥

Contains these components:

■ bow (weapon) 弓 140, p.40
■ you, thou 尔 1336, p.298

With all these meanings & readings:

mí [彌] **1** full **2** to fill **3** completely **4** to fix up
mí [瀰] **1** overflowing

When *you* stand in the doorway with your giant *bow* and arrow aimed directly at me, I **overflow** with fear.

1338 称
稱
TRAD SIMPLIFIED

This character with the definition:

to nickname

Pinyin **chēng** *and Frequency Rank* **449**

Contains **10 strokes** in the following order:

丿 二 千 禾 禾 利 秆 称 称 称

Contains these components:

■ rice, grain (crop) 禾 593, p.140
■ you, thou 尔 1336, p.298

With all these meanings & readings:

chèn [稱] **1** to fit **2** balanced **3** suitable
chēng [稱] **1** to weigh **2** to stat **3** to name **4** name **5** appellation **6** to praise
chèng [稱] **1** variant of 秤 [秤][c] **2** steelyard

I called out to *you* like a *thous*and times, and even threw some *rice* your way to get your attention. But it was no use! You deserve the **nickname** 'No Use' because you are so self-absorbed.

1339 添
SIMP & TRAD

This character with the definition:

increase

Pinyin **tiān** *and Frequency Rank* **1859**

Contains **11 strokes** in the following order:

丶 丶 氵 沃 沃 沃 添 添 添 添

Contains these components:

■ water r 氵 314, p.80
■ heaven 天 548, p.129
■ small 小 (altered) 1262, p.282
■ dab r 丶 176, p.48

With all these meanings & readings:

tiān [添] **1** to add **2** to increase **3** to replenish

It looked like a *little something* fell from *heaven*, but it was a coconut from the tall palm tree by the pool. The little boy had *watered* the tree faithfully and watched as it sprouted and rapidly **increased** in height.

1340

孫
TRAD

孙
SIMPLIFIED

This character with the definition:

grandson

Pinyin **sūn** *and Frequency Rank* **995**

Contains **6 strokes** in the following order:

丁 了 孑 孑 孙 孙

Contains these components:

■ son, child 子 24, p.15
■ small 小 1262, p.282

With all these meanings & readings:

sūn [孙] **1** grandson **2** descendant **3** surname Sun

A **grandson** is like a *son*, but the filial relationship has been diluted—made *small*—by the intervening generation.

1341

其
SIMP & TRAD

This character with the definition:

his, hers, its, theirs

Pinyin **qí** *and Frequency Rank* **85**

Contains **8 strokes** in the following order:

一 十 甘 甘 甘 其 其 其

Contains these components:

■ eye 目 (altered) 75, p.26
■ eight 八 1261, p.282

With all these meanings & readings:

qí [其] **1** his **2** her **3** its **4** theirs **5** that **6** such **7** it (refers to sth preceding it)

One *eye* times *eight* equals the *eyes* in **his**, **her**, **its**, and **their** head.

1342

基
SIMP & TRAD

This character with the definition:

base, foundation

Pinyin **jī** *and Frequency Rank* **280**

Contains **11 strokes** in the following order:

一 十 甘 甘 甘 其 其 其 基 基 基

Contains these components:

■ his, hers, its, theirs 其 1341, p.299
■ earth, soil 土 9, p.11

With all these meanings & readings:

jī [基] **1** base **2** foundation **3** basic **4** radical (chemistry)

The ruthless Emperor was notorious for conquering other nations by destroying their towns, and then using the rubble in the *soil* to lay the **foundation** for *his* own buildings.

1343

斯
SIMP & TRAD

This character with the definition:

this (literary)

Pinyin **sī** *and Frequency Rank* **168**

Contains **12 strokes** in the following order:

一 十 甘 甘 甘 其 其 其 其´ 斯 斯 斯

Contains these components:

■ his, hers, its, theirs 其 1341, p.299
■ catty 斤 403, p.98

With all these meanings & readings:

sī [斯] **1** (phonetic) **2** this

The alternate meaning for the element '*catty*' is illustrated in **this** character by *its* two '*unbalanced*' elements.

1344

欺
SIMP & TRAD

This character with the definition:

deceive, cheat*

Pinyin **qī** *and Frequency Rank* **1699**

Contains **12 strokes** in the following order:

一 十 甘 甘 甘 其 其 其 其´ 欺 欺 欺

Contains these components:

■ his, hers, its, theirs 其 1341, p.299
■ owe, lack 欠 744, p.173

With all these meanings & readings:

qī [欺] **1** take unfair advantage of **2** to deceive **3** to cheat

Any man who constantly **deceives** others *lacks* honesty in *his* character.

1345

This character with the definition:

extremely

Pinyin **shèn** *and Frequency Rank* **626**

SIMP & TRAD Contains **9 strokes** in the following order:

一 十 卄 井 甘 其 其 其 甚

Contains these components:

his, hers, its, theirs 其 1341, p. 299

mineshaft c ㄴ 122, p. 36

With all these meanings & readings:

shèn [甚] **1** what **2** very **3** extremely **4** any

My husband is still **extremely** upset about losing *his* brother in the *mineshaft* accident last week.

1346

This character with the definition:

be capable of

Pinyin **kān** *and Frequency Rank* **1811**

SIMP & TRAD Contains **12 strokes** in the following order:

一 十 土 址 圤 坩 坩 坩 堪 堪 堪 堪

Contains these components:

earth, soil 土 9, p. 11

extremely 甚 1345, p. 300

With all these meanings & readings:

kān [堪] **1** to endure **2** may **3** can

Some ancient civilizations flourished in certain regions because their leaders decided, "Our people **are capable of** thriving in this location with its fresh water source and *extremely* fertile *soil.*"

1347

This character with the definition:

cave, den

Pinyin **xué** *and Frequency Rank* **1940**

SIMP & TRAD Contains **5 strokes** in the following order:

丶 丷 宀 宀 穴

Contains these components:

roof r 宀 271, p. 70

eight 八 1261, p. 282

With all these meanings & readings:

xué [穴] **1** cave **2** cavity **3** hol **4** acupuncture point **5** Taiwan xuè

The topmost *roof* emphasizes the shelter provided by a **cave**, and the strokes of the '*eight*' depict its sloping walls which severely limit its interior space. • When this character appears as an element of another, it often appears without the topmost dab, as in 探 and 深.

1348

窝
TRAD SIMPLIFIED

This character with the definition:

nest, lair

Pinyin **wō** *and Frequency Rank* **1962**

Contains **12 strokes** in the following order:

丶 丷 宀 宀 穴 宋 宋 宏 宏 窝 窝 窝

Contains these components:

cave, den 穴 1347, p. 300

mouth 口 37, p. 17

inside* 内 785, p. 182

With all these meanings & readings:

wō [窝] **1** nest

What's a **nest** anyway but a horizontal *cave* or lair *inside* of which gape the many open *mouths* of the fledgelings?

1349 突

This character with the definition:

dash forward

Pinyin **tū** *and Frequency Rank* **484**

SIMP & TRAD Contains **9 strokes** in the following order:

丶 丷 宀 宀 穴 宊 突 突 突

Contains these components:

cave, den 穴 1347, p. 300

dog 犬 673, p. 158

With all these meanings & readings:

tū [突] **1** to dash **2** to move forward quickly **3** to bulge **4** to protrude **5** to break through **6** to rush out **7** sudden **8** Taiwan pr tú

The thieves tried to rob the banker's house, but they failed to detect the *dog* lying in the *den*. He **dashed forward** and grabbed one of the robbers by the seat of his pants.

1350 探

This character with the definition:

look for, explore

Pinyin **tàn** *and Frequency Rank* **917**

SIMP & TRAD   Contains **11 strokes** in the following order:

一 十 扌 扌 扩 扩 扩 护 护 探 探

Contains these components:

■ hand r 扌 25, p.15
□■ cave, den 穴 (altered) 1347, p.300
■ tree 木 562, p.133

With all these meanings & readings:

tàn [探] **1** to explore **2** to search out **3** to scout **4** to visit **5** to stretch forward

My friend used his *hand* to point out the cypress *tree* that marked the entrance to the *cave* that we planned to **explore**.

1351 深

This character with the definition:

deep

Pinyin **shēn** *and Frequency Rank* **401**

SIMP & TRAD   Contains **11 strokes** in the following order:

丶 丶 氵 氵 氵 氵 氵 氵 深 深 深

Contains these components:

■ water r 氵 314, p.80
□■ cave, den 穴 (altered) 1347, p.300
■ tree 木 562, p.133

With all these meanings & readings:

shēn [深] **1** close **2** deep **3** late **4** profound **5** dark (of color, water, etc.)

Imagine a body of *water* so **deep** that it fills the depths of *caves* and reaches the highest of *trees*.

1352 空

This character with the definition:

empty

Pinyin **kōng** *and Frequency Rank* **272**

SIMP & TRAD   Contains **8 strokes** in the following order:

丶 丷 宀 宀 穴 空 空 空

Contains these components:

□ cave, den 穴 1347, p.300
■ labor, work 工 12, p.12

With all these meanings & readings:

kōng [空] **1** air **2** sky **3** empty **4** free time **5** in vain
kòng [空] **1** emptied **2** leisure

After hours of hard *labor* digging at the spot in the *cave* where the ancient map showed the pirate's gold was buried, we finally uncovered a chest—but it was **empty**!

1353 控

This character with the definition:

accuse, charge

Pinyin **kòng** *and Frequency Rank* **780**

SIMP & TRAD   Contains **11 strokes** in the following order:

一 十 扌 扌 扩 扩 护 护 控 控 控

Contains these components:

■ hand r 扌 25, p.15
□ empty 空 1352, p.301

With all these meanings & readings:

kòng [控] **1** to accuse **2** to charge **3** to control **4** to sue

After the border guard **accused** me of smuggling drugs, I had to raise my *hands* so that he could check that my pockets and all other areas of my body were completely *empty*.

1354 腔

This character with the definition:

body cavity

Pinyin **qiāng** *and Frequency Rank* **1914**

SIMP & TRAD   Contains **12 strokes** in the following order:

丿 月 月 月 月 肜 腔 腔 腔 腔 腔 腔

Contains these components:

■ meat 肉 (altered) 753, p.175
□ empty 空 1352, p.301

With all these meanings & readings:

qiāng [腔] **1** cavity of body **2** barrel (e.g. engine cylinder) **3** compartment **4** tune **5** accent of speech

The *empty* part of a *body* is a **body cavity**.

1355   穿

SIMP & TRAD

This character with the definition:

penetrate, pierce

Pinyin **chuān** *and Frequency Rank* **785**

Contains **9 strokes** in the following order:

丶 丶 宀 宀 空 空 空 穿 穿

Contains these components:

☐ cave, den 穴 1347, p. 300

▨ tooth* 牙 450, p. 108

With all these meanings & readings:

chuān [穿] **1** to bore through **2** pierce **3** perforate **4** penetra **5** pass through **6** to dress **7** to wear **8** to put on **9** to thread

My dentist told me that the *hole* on the inside of my *tooth* was so big that it threatened to **penetrate** down to the root of my *tooth*.

1356   奂

奂
TRAD   SIMPLIFIED

This character with the definition:

excellent

Pinyin **huàn** *and Frequency Rank* **3774**

Contains **9 strokes** in the following order:

丿 夕 夕 鱼 鱼 奂 奂

Contains these components:

☐ man 人 (altered) 537, p. 127

▨ cave, den 穴 (altered) 1347, p. 300

▨ big 大 544, p. 129

With all these meanings & readings:

huàn [奂] **1** excellent **2** surnam Huan

The *man*, an aspiring Olympian athlete, leaped across a *big hole* and gave an **excellent** performance.

1357   换

换
TRAD   SIMPLIFIED

This character with the definition:

barter

Pinyin **huàn** *and Frequency Rank* **824**

Contains **10 strokes** in the following order:

一 十 扌 扌 扩 扩 抻 拹 换 换

Contains these components:

▨ hand r 扌 25, p. 15

▨ excellent 奂 1356, p. 302

With all these meanings & readings:

huàn [换] **1** change **2** exchang

A **barter** system is based on the belief that your trading partner will *hand* you goods of *excellent* quality.

1358   穷

穷
TRAD   SIMPLIFIED

This character with the definition:

impoverished, exhausted

Pinyin **qióng** *and Frequency Rank* **1343**

Contains **7 strokes** in the following order:

丶 丶 宀 宀 穴 穷 穷

Contains these components:

▨ cave, den 穴 1347, p. 300

▨ strength 力 471, p. 113

With all these meanings & readings:

qióng [穷] **1** exhausted **2** poor

The hike was so **exhausting** that we had to use our last reserves of *strength* to crawl into the *cave*.

1359   挖

SIMP & TRAD

This character with the definition:

dig, excavate

Pinyin **wā** *and Frequency Rank* **1860**

Contains **9 strokes** in the following order:

一 十 扌 扌 扩 扩 护 挖 挖

Contains these components:

▨ hand r 扌 25, p. 15

☐ cave, den 穴 1347, p. 300

☐ second (in a series) 乙 146, p. 41

With all these meanings & readings:

wā [挖] **1** to dig **2** to excavate **3** to scoop out

To **excavate** the ancient buried tomb, the archaeologists first planned to **dig** a series of *holes* in the desert sand using only their *hands*. They were delighted to find the remains of a royal coffin by the *second hole*!

Unit 57

1360

This character with the definition:

study carefully

Pinyin **jiū** *and Frequency Rank* **429**

SIMP & TRAD   Contains **7 strokes** in the following order:

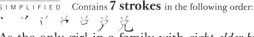

Contains these components:

☐ cave, den 穴 1347, p. 300
■ nine 九 532, p. 126

With all these meanings & readings:

jiū [究] **1** after all **2** to investigate **3** to study carefully **4** Taiwan pr jiù

All *nine* members of our diving team plan to **study carefully** the safety manual before we go explore the underwater *cave*.

1361

This character with the definition:

exchange, convert

Pinyin **duì** *and Frequency Rank* **2424**

兑
TRAD   SIMPLIFIED   Contains **7 strokes** in the following order:

Contains these components:

☐ eight 八 1261, p. 282
■ elder brother* 兄 293, p. 75

With all these meanings & readings:

duì [兑] **1** to cash

As the only girl in a family with *eight elder brothers* it was easy to **convert** me into a tom-boy.

1362

This character with the definition:

shed, take off

Pinyin **tuō** *and Frequency Rank* **943**

脱
TRAD   SIMPLIFIED   Contains **11 strokes** in the following order:

Contains these components:

■ meat 肉 (altered) 753, p. 175
☐ exchange, convert 兑 1361, p. 303

With all these meanings & readings:

tuō [脱] **1** to shed **2** to take off **3** to escape **4** to get away from

Whenever I want to **shed** weight, I simply eat more *meat* and protein, and exercise more to *convert* that fat into muscle!

1363 税

This character with the definition:

tax, duty

Pinyin **shuì** *and Frequency Rank* **781**

税
TRAD   SIMPLIFIED   Contains **12 strokes** in the following order:

Contains these components:

■ rice, grain (crop) 禾 593, p. 140
☐ exchange, convert 兑 1361, p. 303

With all these meanings & readings:

shuì [税] **1** taxes **2** duties

Every government imposes a **tax** on its people. Today it is a portion of your earnings; in ancient times it was a portion of your *rice crop*. In *exchange*, the government agrees to provide its people with services.

1364

This character with the definition:

speak*

Pinyin **shuō** *and Frequency Rank* **24**

說
TRAD   SIMPLIFIED   Contains **9 strokes** in the following order:

Contains these components:

■ speech r 讠 352, p. 88
☐ exchange, convert 兑 1361, p. 303

With all these meanings & readings:

shuì [說] **1** to canvass **2** to persuade **3** see 游说 [遊說][yóu shuì], to canvass and 说客 [說~][shuì kè], persuasive speaker
shuō [說] **1** to speak **2** to say **3** a theory (usually in compounds such as 日心说 heliocentric theory)

When you **speak** with someone on the telephone, there is an electronic *exchange* of *speech* between the two of you.

1365

閲
TRAD SIMPLIFIED

阅

This character with the definition:

read, review

Pinyin **yuè** and *Frequency Rank* **1489**

Contains **10 strokes** in the following order:

丶 亠 门 门 门 阅 阅 阅 阅 阅

Contains these components:

▢ doorway 门 243, p. 64
▢ exchange, convert 兑 1361, p. 303

With all these meanings & readings:

yuè [閲] 1 peruse 2 review 3 read

The tourist was in a foreign country and needed to *exchange* some currency. So he passed through the *doorway* of the nearest bank and began to **read** the instructions on the Currency Exchange form.

1366

悦
TRAD SIMPLIFIED

悦

This character with the definition:

pleased, happy, delighted

Pinyin **yuè** and *Frequency Rank* **1995**

Contains **10 strokes** in the following order:

丶 丶 忄 忄 忄 忄 悦 悦 悦 悦

Contains these components:

▢ heart (skinny) r 忄 1135, p. 256
▢ exchange, convert 兑 1361, p. 303

With all these meanings & readings:

yuè [悦] 1 pleased

A person would need to have a *heart* of stone to not be **happy** for a wedding couple at the moment they *exchange* their vows.

1367

谷
谷穀
TRAD SIMPLIFIED

谷

This character with the definition:

valley

Pinyin **gǔ** and *Frequency Rank* **1095**

Contains **7 strokes** in the following order:

丿 八 夕 夂 谷 谷 谷

Contains these components:

▢ eight 八 1261, p. 282
▢ man 人 537, p. 127
▢ enclosure r 口 36, p. 17

With all these meanings & readings:

gǔ [穀] 1 grain 2 corn
gǔ [谷] 1 surname Yu
gǔ [谷] 1 valley

Many (symbolized by '*eight*') *people* live within a natural *enclosure* such as a **valley**.

1368

容
SIMP & TRAD

容

This character with the definition:

tolerate, excuse

Pinyin **róng** and *Frequency Rank* **442**

Contains **10 strokes** in the following order:

丶 丶 宀 宀 穴 穴 突 容 容 容

Contains these components:

▢ roof r 宀 271, p. 70
▢ valley 谷 (altered) 1367, p. 304

With all these meanings & readings:

róng [容] 1 to hold 2 to conta 3 to allow 4 appearance 5 loc 6 countenance

Our river *valley* is very humid, with warm, moist air hanging over it like an invisible *roof* in the summertime. People who cannot **tolerate** such conditions temporarily move into the surrounding mountains for cool, fresh air.

1369

裕
SIMP & TRAD

裕

This character with the definition:

abundant

Pinyin **yù** and *Frequency Rank* **2023**

Contains **12 strokes** in the following order:

丶 丿 礻 礻 礻 礻 礻 袷 袷 裕 裕 裕

Contains these components:

▢ clothing r 礻 1067, p. 242
▢ valley 谷 1367, p. 304

With all these meanings & readings:

yù [裕] 1 abundant

Since the surrounding high mountains prevent sunlight from warming the base of the *valley*, we are used to wearing **abundant** layers of *clothing* for warmth.

1370 俗

SIMP & TRAD

This character with the definition:

vulgar

Pinyin **sú** *and Frequency Rank* **1354**

Contains these components:

☐ man r 亻 1156, p. 260
☐ valley 谷 1367, p. 304

With all these meanings & readings:

sú [俗] **1** custom **2** convention **3** popular **4** common **5** coarse **6** vulgar **7** secular

Contains **9 strokes** in the following order:

丿 亻 亻 亻 俗 俗 俗 俗 俗

Only **vulgar** *people* live in the *valley*; it's too unpleasant for the upper classes!

1371 欲

SIMP & TRAD

This character with the definition:

wish, desire, want

Pinyin **yù** *and Frequency Rank* **1045**

Contains these components:

☐ valley 谷 1367, p. 304
☐ owe, lack 欠 744, p. 173

With all these meanings & readings:

yù [欲] **1** desire **2** longing **3** appetite **4** wish

Contains **11 strokes** in the following order:

丿 丷 夕 夕 谷 谷 谷 谷 谷 欲 欲

This *valley* is dark, damp, gloomy, and *lacks* any redeeming value. I **wish** we lived somewhere else!

1372 公

SIMP & TRAD

This character with the definition:

public affairs

Pinyin **gōng** *and Frequency Rank* **115**

Contains these components:

☐ eight 八 1261, p. 282
☐ private r 厶 963, p. 220

With all these meanings & readings:

gōng [公] **1** public **2** collectively owned **3** common **4** international (e.g. high seas, metric system, calendar) **5** make public **6** fair **7** just **8** Duke, highest of five orders of nobility 五等爵位[wǔ děng jué wèi] **9** honorable (gentlemen) **10** father-in-law **11** male (animal)

Contains **4 strokes** in the following order:

丿 八 公 公

Eight private events happening all at one time can't possibly be kept *private* for long. Before you know it, everything has become a **public affair**.

1373 松

松
鬆
TRAD SIMPLIFIED

This character with the definition:

pine tree

Pinyin **sōng** *and Frequency Rank* **895**

Contains these components:

☐ tree 木 562, p. 133
☐ public affairs 公 1372, p. 305

With all these meanings & readings:

sōng [松] **1** surname Song
sōng [松] **1** pine **2** m 棵[kē]
sōng [鬆] **1** loose **2** to loosen **3** to relax

Contains **8 strokes** in the following order:

一 十 才 木 朳 松 松 松

Since people who work in *public affairs* are supposed to stand as upright as **pine trees**, the **pine tree** character symbolically combines '*tree*' with '*public affairs*'.

1374 袞

袞
TRAD SIMPLIFIED

This character with the definition:

imperial robes

Pinyin **gǔn** *and Frequency Rank* **4843**

Contains these components:

☐ clothing 衣 (altered) 1068, p. 242
☐ public affairs 公 1372, p. 305

With all these meanings & readings:

gǔn [袞] **1** imperial robe

Contains **10 strokes** in the following order:

丶 一 亠 六 夺 玄 夺 穵 窏 袞

Imperial robes were special *clothes* designed to create dramatic impressions at *public affairs*.

1375

滚
TRAD   SIMPLIFIED

This character with the definition:

roll, tumble

Pinyin **gǔn**   *and Frequency Rank* **1542**

Contains **13 strokes** in the following order:

丶 丶 氵 氵 泸 泸 泸 滚 滚 滚 滚 滚 滚

Contains these components:

water r 氵 314, p. 80

imperial robes 衮 1374, p. 305

With all these meanings & readings

gǔn [滚] **1** to boil **2** to roll **3** get lost (imperative) **4** take a hike

As the Emperor was being lifted into the royal boat, his long *imperial robes* became caught on the edge of the dock. Everyone froze in shock as they watched him **tumble** and splash into the *water*!

1376

訟
TRAD   SIMPLIFIED

This character with the definition:

litigation

Pinyin **sòng**   *and Frequency Rank* **1862**

Contains **6 strokes** in the following order:

丶 讠 讠 讠 讼 讼

Contains these components:

speech r 讠 352, p. 88

public affairs 公 1372, p. 305

With all these meanings & readings

sòng [訟] **1** litigation

In ancient times, personal *speech* was subject to **litigation** even in the context of *public affairs*.

1377

SIMP & TRAD

This character with the definition:

tool, utensil

Pinyin **jù**   *and Frequency Rank* **391**

Contains **8 strokes** in the following order:

丨 冂 冂 月 目 且 具 具

Contains these components:

eye 目 (altered) 75, p. 26

eight 八 1261, p. 282

With all these meanings & readings

jù [具] **1** tool **2** device **3** utensil **4** equipment **5** instrument **6** talent **7** ability **8** to possess **9** to have **10** to provide **11** to furnish **12** to state **13** m for devices, coffins, dead bodies

I (sounds like '*eye*') can become *abundantly* productive when *I* have the *eight* proper **tools** within reach.

1378

SIMP & TRAD

This character with the definition:

entirely

Pinyin **jù**   *and Frequency Rank* **1909**

Contains **10 strokes** in the following order:

丿 亻 亻 仴 俔 俱 俱 俱 俱 俱

Contains these components:

man r 亻 1156, p. 260

tool, utensil 具 1377, p. 306

With all these meanings & readings

jù [俱] **1** entirely **2** without exception

With the right *tool*, a *man* can be **entirely** self-sufficient.

1379

SIMP & TRAD

This character with the definition:

real

Pinyin **zhēn**   *and Frequency Rank* **204**

Contains **10 strokes** in the following order:

一 十 十 古 古 吉 直 直 真 真

Contains these components:

ten 十 7, p. 11

tool, utensil 具 1377, p. 306

With all these meanings & readings

zhēn [真] **1** really **2** truly **3** indeed **4** real **5** true **6** genuine

Since I'm a very amateur handyman, I like to adopt the look of a **real** contractor on my weekend projects. I sport a professional-looking leather belt and have at least *ten tools* hanging off it.

1380

This character with the definition:

fill out (form)

Pinyin **tián** *and Frequency Rank* **1970**

SIMP & TRAD   Contains **13 strokes** in the following order:

一 十 土 土 圹 圹 圹 圹 圹 垍 埴 埴 填 填

Contains these components:

earth, soil 土 9, p. 11

real 真 1379, p. 306

With all these meanings & readings:

tián [填] **1** to fill in

Whenever you purchase a parcel of *land*, you need to **fill out** and sign formal documents so that the you will be legally recognized as the '*real*' owner.

1381

懼
TRAD   SIMPLIFIED

This character with the definition:

fear, dread

Pinyin **jù** *and Frequency Rank* **1616**

Contains **11 strokes** in the following order:

丿 丶 忄 忄 忉 忉 怕 怕 惧 惧 惧

Contains these components:

heart (skinny) r 忄 1135, p. 256

tool, utensil 具 1377, p. 306

With all these meanings & readings:

jù [懼] **1** to fear

The evil overseer walks around with a heavy *tool* in his hand, threatening the slaves who exhibit the slightest infraction. He created an *emotional* climate of **fear and dread**.

1382

This character with the definition:

cautious, careful

Pinyin **shèn** *and Frequency Rank* **1765**

SIMP & TRAD   Contains **13 strokes** in the following order:

丿 丶 忄 忄 忄 忄 忏 怕 怕 愼 愼 愼 慎

Contains these components:

fear, dread 惧 (altered) 1381, p. 307

ten 十 7, p. 11

With all these meanings & readings:

shèn [慎] **1** cautious

When you've been *frightened* by the same thing *ten* times in a row, you develop a degree of **caution**.

1383 州

This character with the definition:

state, province

Pinyin **zhōu** *and Frequency Rank* **721**

SIMP & TRAD   Contains **6 strokes** in the following order:

丶 丿 小 州 州 州

Contains these components:

river 川 444, p. 107

eight 八 1261, p. 282

dab r 丶 176, p. 48

With all these meanings & readings:

zhōu [州] **1** province   **2** subprefecture   **3** state (e.g. of US)

Imagine the large '*river*' element as a region so vast that it forms an entire **state**. It is so large that some areas have an *abundance* of resources (represented by the '*eight*' element 'embedded' on the left side), while other areas have *very few* (the '*dab*' 'embedded' on the right side of the character).

1384 洲

This character with the definition:

continent

Pinyin **zhōu** *and Frequency Rank* **701**

SIMP & TRAD   Contains **9 strokes** in the following order:

丶 丶 氵 氵 沪 沙 洲 洲 洲

Contains these components:

water r 氵 314, p. 80

state, province 州 1383, p. 307

With all these meanings & readings:

zhōu [洲] **1** continent   **2** island

A **continent** is defined as a land mass of *states* surrounded by *water*.

Unit 58

1385

This character with the definition:

divide, separate

Pinyin **fēn** *and Frequency Rank* **79**

SIMP & TRAD   Contains **4 strokes** in the following order:

ノ 八 分 分

An orange is wonderful because you do not need a *knife* to peel and **separate** it into *eight* pieces to share with your friends.

Contains these components:

◻ eight 八 1261, p. 282
◼ knife 刀 469, p. 112

With all these meanings & readings:

fēn [分] **1** to divide **2** to separate **3** to allocate **4** to distinguish (good and bad) **5** part or subdivision **6** fraction **7** one tenth (of certain units) **8** unit of length equivalent to 0.33 cm **9** minute **10** a point (in sports or games) **11** 0.01 yuan (unit of money)
fèn [分] **1** part **2** ingredient **3** component

1386 芬

This character with the definition:

sweet smell, fragrance

Pinyin **fēn** *and Frequency Rank* **1890**

SIMP & TRAD   Contains **7 strokes** in the following order:

一 十 廾 芍 芬 芬 芬

Freshly-mowed lawns release a specially **sweet smell**—one of the great **fragrances**—as the lawnmower slices and *divides* the blades of *grass*.

Contains these components:

◻ grass r ⺾ 87, p. 29
◼ divide, separate 分 1385, p. 308

With all these meanings & readings:

fēn [芬] **1** perfume **2** fragrance

1387

This character with the definition:

diverse

Pinyin **fēn** *and Frequency Rank* **1181**

 TRAD   SIMPLIFIED   Contains **7 strokes** in the following order:

乚 乡 纟 纟 纠 纷 纷

I forgot to hem the *silk* handkerchief and the cloth quickly *separated* into **diverse** threads.

Contains these components:

◼ silk r 纟 1037, p. 235
◻ divide, separate 分 1385, p. 308

With all these meanings & readings:

fēn [纷] **1** numerous **2** confused **3** disorderly

1388

This character with the definition:

share, portion

Pinyin **fèn** *and Frequency Rank* **784**

SIMP & TRAD   Contains **6 strokes** in the following order:

ノ 亻 仁 仏 份 份

If we take that *man's* money, we can *divide* it so that we each can pocket an equal **share**.

Contains these components:

◼ man r 亻 1156, p. 260
◻ divide, separate 分 1385, p. 308

With all these meanings & readings:

fèn [份] **1** part **2** share **3** portion **4** copy **5** m for gifts, newspaper, magazine, papers, reports, contracts etc

---

1389

This character with the definition:

dress up as, disguise as

Pinyin **bàn** *and Frequency Rank* **1974**

SIMP & TRAD   Contains **7 strokes** in the following order:

一 十 扌 扩 扮 扮 扮

The best **disguises** are those created out of everyday materials. To prepare for the Halloween party, we used our *hands* to *separate* articles of clothing for the ultimate costume.

Contains these components:

◼ hand r 扌 25, p. 15
◻ divide, separate 分 1385, p. 308

With all these meanings & readings:

bàn [扮] **1** to disguise oneself **2** to dress up **3** adorn

390

This character with the definition:

introduce

Pinyin **jiè** *and Frequency Rank* **831**

SIMP & TRAD   Contains **4 strokes** in the following order:

ノ 入 介 介

Contains these components:

☐ man 人 537, p.127
■ eight 八 (altered) 1261, p.282

With all these meanings & readings:

jiè [介] **1** introduce **2** lie between **3** between

Confusion reigns when there are *eight men* in a room! Things calm down as soon as everyone is **introduced** to each other.

391 界

This character with the definition:

boundary, scope

Pinyin **jiè** *and Frequency Rank* **288**

SIMP & TRAD   Contains **9 strokes** in the following order:

丶 冂 日 田 田 尸 甼 界 界

Contains these components:

☐ field 田 63, p.23
■ introduce 介 1390, p.309

With all these meanings & readings:

jiè [界] **1** boundary **2** scope **3** extent **4** circles **5** group **6** kingdom (taxonomy)

The '*introduce*' element of this character resembles an oversized arrow pointing to the **boundary** of the *field*.

392 价

TRAD 價   SIMPLIFIED

This character with the definition:

price

Pinyin **jià** *and Frequency Rank* **409**

Contains **6 strokes** in the following order:

ノ 亻 亻 亻 价 价

Contains these components:

■ man r 亻 1156, p.260
☐ introduce 介 1390, p.309

With all these meanings & readings:

jià [價] **1** price **2** value **3** valence (on an atom)
jie [價] **1** great **2** good **3** middleman **4** servant

The matchmaker is the *man* who *introduces* the partners to a future marriage. In return, he stipulates a **price** for this service that the parties must pay.

393

TRAD 階   SIMPLIFIED

This character with the definition:

stairs, rank or step

Pinyin **jiē** *and Frequency Rank* **745**

Contains **6 strokes** in the following order:

阝 阝 阝 阶 阶 阶

Contains these components:

■ hills r 阝 942, p.216
☐ introduce 介 1390, p.309

With all these meanings & readings:

jiē [階] **1** rank or step **2** stairs

He'll (sounds like '*hill*') *introduce* me to the boss who will permit me to ride in the executive elevator so that I don't have to take the **stairs** to my office all the time.

394

TRAD 貝   SIMPLIFIED

This character with the definition:

cowrie

Pinyin **bèi** *and Frequency Rank* **1133**

Contains **4 strokes** in the following order:

丨 冂 贝 贝

Contains these components:

☐ eye 目 (abbrev) 75, 26
■ eight 八 (altered) 1261, p.282

With all these meanings & readings:

bèi [貝] **1** cowries **2** shell **3** valuables **4** shellfish **5** surname Bei

1 *I* (sounds like '*eye*') love *plenty* of **money**! **2** Mollusks are shellfish that make **shells** yet leave them behind for human enjoyment after (their) death. They all have a common structure—a fleshy foot that sticks out of its enclosing shell, and this glyph displays this structure. • The **cowrie** shell was an early form of currency. When used as a component, it takes on a meaning related to money, like 'valuable', 'wealth', or 'money'!

1395

贡

贡
TRAD SIMPLIFIED

This character with the definition:

tribute, gifts

Pinyin **gòng** *and Frequency Rank* **1548**

Contains **7 strokes** in the following order:

一 丁 工 丌 吉 贡 贡

Contains these components:

labor, work 工 12, p.12

cowrie 贝 1394, p.309

With all these meanings & reading

gòng [貢] **1** tribute **2** gifts

Part of the *money* we receive in wages for our *work* is exacted from us as tax, a **tribute** to our government to fund the public services.

1396

贵

贵
TRAD SIMPLIFIED

This character with the definition:

expensive

Pinyin **guì** *and Frequency Rank* **873**

Contains **9 strokes** in the following order:

丶 一 口 中 虫 虫 贵 贵 贵

Contains these components:

middle 中 38, p.18

one 一 1, p.10

cowrie 贝 1394, p.309

With all these meanings & reading

guì [貴] **1** expensive **2** noble **3** your (name) **4** precious

They say that it is wiser to spend your *money* on one **expensive** high-quality item than on several cheaper items of *middle* or lower quality.

1397

溃

溃
TRAD SIMPLIFIED

This character with the definition:

burst, break through

Pinyin **kuì** *and Frequency Rank* **1916**

Contains **12 strokes** in the following order:

丶 丶 氵 氵 汭 汭 沖 浀 浀 溃 溃 溃

Contains these components:

water r 氵 314, p.80

expensive 贵 1396, p.310

With all these meanings & reading

kuì [潰] **1** be dispersed **2** break down

The raging *water* will attack the *expensive* seawall with gusto and **break through**. It will destroy the expensive beachfront properties, not caring how much money was involved to build them.

1398

质

质
TRAD SIMPLIFIED

This character with the definition:

quality

Pinyin **zhì** *and Frequency Rank* **404**

Contains **8 strokes** in the following order:

一 厂 斤 斤 斤 质 质 质

Contains these components:

catty 斤 (altered) 403, p.98

cowrie 贝 1394, p.309

With all these meanings & reading

zhì [質] **1** hostage **2** substance **3** nature **4** quality **5** Taiwan zhí

An avid *shell* collector assesses and double checks the **quality** of *shells* by inspecting how *unbalanced* they are.

1399

则

则
TRAD SIMPLIFIED

This character with the definition:

standard, norm

Pinyin **zé** *and Frequency Rank* **284**

Contains **6 strokes** in the following order:

丨 冂 冂 贝 则 则

Contains these components:

cowrie 贝 1394, p.309

knife r 刂 169, p.46

With all these meanings & reading

zé [則] **1** conjunction used to express contrast with a previous sentence or clause **2** standard **3** norm **4** rule **5** to imitate **6** to follow **7** then **8** principle **9** m for written items (such as official statement)

You can imagine this character as representing the Federal mint. You use a *knife* to cut large amounts of *money* into **standard** units, such as dollars into quarters, dimes, nickels, etc.

400 测
测
TRAD SIMPLIFIED

This character with the definition:

to survey, measure

Pinyin **cè** *and Frequency Rank* **861**

Contains **9 strokes** in the following order:

丶 丶 氵 沪 沪 沏 浉 浉 测

Contains these components:

■ water r 氵 314, p. 80

■ standard, norm 则 1399, p. 310

With all these meanings & readings:

cè [测] **1** side **2** to lean **3** to survey **4** to measure **5** conjecture

Ancient records show that **measuring** the flood plains of rivers such as the Nile in Egypt and the Yangtze in China were *standard* procedures **to survey** every year. The records of the high-low *water norms* were of vital importance to farmers and the welfare of the entire country.

401 侧
侧
TRAD SIMPLIFIED

This character with the definition:

inclined to

Pinyin **cè** *and Frequency Rank* **1220**

Contains **8 strokes** in the following order:

丿 亻 亻 仴 伵 侧 侧 侧

Contains these components:

■ man r 亻 1156, p. 260

■ standard, norm 则 1399, p. 310

With all these meanings & readings:

cè [侧] **1** the side **2** to incline towards **3** to lean **4** inclined **5** lateral **6** side
zhāi [侧] **1** lean on one side

People who do *normal* things routinely are **inclined** to keep doing them that way.

402 贴
贴
TRAD SIMPLIFIED

This character with the definition:

paste, stick to

Pinyin **tiē** *and Frequency Rank* **1454**

Contains **9 strokes** in the following order:

丨 冂 贝 贝 贝 贴 贴 贴 贴

Contains these components:

■ cowrie 贝 1394, p. 309

■ practice divination 占 188, p. 51

With all these meanings & readings:

tiē [贴] **1** to stick **2** to paste **3** to keep close to **4** to fit snugly **5** to subsidize **6** allowance (e.g. money for food or housing) **7** sticker **8** m for sticking plaster: strip

The only way to **paste** or **stick** the heavy *shell* to the wall was to apply a bit of *magic* on it beforehand.

403 责
责
TRAD SIMPLIFIED

This character with the definition:

responsibility

Pinyin **zé** *and Frequency Rank* **535**

Contains **8 strokes** in the following order:

一 二 丰 主 青 青 责 责

Contains these components:

■ master 主 (altered) 179, p. 49

■ cowrie 贝 1394, p. 309

With all these meanings & readings:

zé [责] **1** duty **2** responsibility **3** to reproach **4** to blame

When someone entrusts a *master* with a *valuable object*, he immediately incurs a **responsibility**, if only to care for the *valuable object*.

404 绩
绩
TRAD SIMPLIFIED

This character with the definition:

merit, accomplishment

Pinyin **jì** *and Frequency Rank* **1547**

Contains **11 strokes** in the following order:

乙 乡 乡 乡 纟一 纟三 纟丰 结 绩 绩 绩

Contains these components:

■ silk r 纟 1037, p. 235

■ responsibility 责 1403, p. 311

With all these meanings & readings:

jì [绩] **1** merit **2** accomplishment **3** grade **4** Taiwan pr jī

The *silk* worker felt a genuine sense of **accomplishment**. By quickly moving it away from the area where a sudden roof leak had developed, he had fulfilled his *responsibility* to protect the valuable *silk* fabric.

1405

债

债
TRAD   SIMPLIFIED

This character with the definition:

debt

Pinyin **zhài** *and Frequency Rank* **1223**

Contains **10 strokes** in the following order:

ノ 亻 亻⁻ 亻⁼ 伫 佳 佳 佳 债 债

Paying off **debt** is a *man*'s primary *responsibility*.

Contains these components:

■ man r 亻 1156, p.260

■ responsibility 责 1403, p.311

With all these meanings & reading

zhài [债] **1** debt   **2** m 笔 [筆] [b

1406

贾

贾
TRAD   SIMPLIFIED

This character with the definition:

merchant

Pinyin **gǔ** *and Frequency Rank* **2051**

Contains **10 strokes** in the following order:

一 亠 帀 帀 西 西 覀 覀 贾 贾

This Chinese **merchant** is so good at his job of selling worthless *shells* to companies in the *West*.

Contains these components:

■ west 西 (altered) 301, p.77

■ cowrie 贝 1394, p.309

With all these meanings & reading

gǔ [賈] **1** surname Jia
gǔ [賈] **1** merchant   **2** to buy

1407

赞

赞
TRAD   SIMPLIFIED

This character with the definition:

commend

Pinyin **zàn** *and Frequency Rank* **1179**

Contains **16 strokes** in the following order:

ノ 一 十 土 未 先 牛 牛 牛 牛 牜 牜 牜 赞 赞 赞

Many art experts **commend** my friend on his talent—he has received lots of prize *money* and *first*-place rankings at art shows.

Contains these components:

■ first (×2) 先 291, p.75

■ cowrie 贝 1394, p.309

With all these meanings & reading

zàn [讚] **1** to praise
zàn [贊] **1** to patronize   **2** to support   **3** to praise

---

1408

页

頁
TRAD   SIMPLIFIED

This character with the definition:

page, leaf

Pinyin **yè** *and Frequency Rank* **1128**

Contains **6 strokes** in the following order:

一 丁 丆 页 页 页

The pattern on *one bit of a shell* sometimes reminds me of patterns on a small **leaf**. • This character must surely have looked to ancient scribes like the unfinished stick figure of a man. The simplified head is connected by a short neck to a broad-shouldered body on top of two legs. Therefore, we often interpret this character as being a sketch of a '**man**' which the scribes will then complete by adding another element.

Contains these components:

■ one 一 1, p.10

■ dab r 丶 176, p.48

■ cowrie 贝 1394, p.309

With all these meanings & reading

yè [頁] **1** page   **2** leaf

1409

项

項
TRAD   SIMPLIFIED

This character with the definition:

nape of neck

Pinyin **xiàng** *and Frequency Rank* **571**

Contains **9 strokes** in the following order:

一 丅 工 工 巧 巧 项 项 项

I sweated so much while performing yard *work* that *leaves* stuck to the **nape of my neck**.

Contains these components:

■ labor, work 工 12, p.12

■ page, leaf 页 1408, p.312

With all these meanings & reading

xiàng [項] **1** surname Xiang
xiàng [項] **1** back of neck   **2** it **3** thing   **4** term (in a mathema ical formula)   **5** sum (of money **6** m for principles, items, claus tasks, research projects etc

Unit 59

1410

顶
TRAD SIMPLIFIED

This character with the definition:

carry on your head

Pinyin **dǐng** *and Frequency Rank* **1000**

Contains **8 strokes** in the following order:

一 丁 丁 丁 丌 丌 顶 顶 顶

Contains these components:

fourth (in a series) 丁 19, p. 13

page, leaf 页 1408, p. 312

With all these meanings & readings:

dǐng [顶] **1** apex **2** crown of the head **3** top **4** roof r **5** to carry on the head **6** to push to the top **7** to go against **8** most **9** to replace **10** to substitute **11** m for headwear, hats, veils etc **12** to agree or support (internet slang, similar to digg)

On the *fourth page* of his instruction manual, the novice hiker learned that to cross a stream successfully, he would need to pack all his gear in a way that it could all be **carried on his head**.

1411

项
TRAD SIMPLIFIED

This character with the definition:

in an instant

Pinyin **qǐng** *and Frequency Rank* **2724**

Contains **8 strokes** in the following order:

一 匕 上 上 巨 巧 顷 顷

Contains these components:

ancient ladle 匕 124, p. 36

page, leaf 页 1408, p. 312

With all these meanings & readings:

qǐng [顷] **1** unit of area equal to 100 亩 [畝][mǔ] or 6.67 hectares **2** a short while **3** a little while ago **4** circa. (for approximate dates) **5** Taiwan pr qīng

Even a huge *ancient ladle* would not be adequate to clear the autumn *leaves* from your lawn; the slightest breeze causes more to fall **in an instant**.

1412

倾
TRAD SIMPLIFIED

This character with the definition:

incline, lean

Pinyin **qīng** *and Frequency Rank* **1260**

Contains **10 strokes** in the following order:

丿 亻 亻 化 亿 你 你 倾 倾 倾

Contains these components:

man r 亻 1156, p. 260

in an instant 顷 1411, p. 313

With all these meanings & readings:

qīng [倾] **1** to overturn **2** to collapse **3** to lean **4** to tend **5** to incline **6** to pour out

During the span of his life, a *man* is vigorous and strong in his youth; yet needs to **lean** forward just to walk in his old age.

1413

顿
TRAD SIMPLIFIED

This character with the definition:

m for meals

Pinyin **dùn** *and Frequency Rank* **794**

Contains **10 strokes** in the following order:

一 匚 屯 屯 屯 盯 盱 顿 顿 顿

Contains these components:

stockpile, store up 屯 159, p. 44

page, leaf 页 1408, p. 312

With all these meanings & readings:

dùn [顿] **1** stop **2** pause **3** to arrange **4** to lay out **5** to kowtow **6** to stamp **7** at once **8** m for meals, beating, tellings off etc: time, bout, spell, meal

I used a blank *page* to make a grocery list of goods to *stockpile* in preparation for the hurricane. I'm planning to *store up* enough food for a **week's worth of meals**.

1414

题
TRAD SIMPLIFIED

This character with the definition:

topic, subject, title

Pinyin **tí** *and Frequency Rank* **218**

Contains **15 strokes** in the following order:

丨 冂 日 日 旦 早 旱 昂 是 是 是 题 题 题 题

Contains these components:

is 是 194, p. 53

page, leaf 页 1408, p. 312

With all these meanings & readings:

tí [题] **1** topic **2** problem for discussion **3** exam question **4** subject **5** to inscribe **6** to mention **7** surname Ti **8** m 个 [個][gè], 道[dào]

The **topic** of the main article *is* usually found on the front *page* of a newspaper.

1415

頑
TRAD   SIMPLIFIED

This character with the definition:

stupid, stubborn

Pinyin **wán** *and Frequency Rank* **2024**

Contains **10 strokes** in the following order:

一 二 テ 元 元 玩 玩 顽 顽 顽

Contains these components:

☐ dollar 元 295, p.76

☐ page, leaf 页 1408, p.312

With all these meanings & reading

wán [頑] **1** mischievous **2** obstinate **3** to play **4** stupid **5** stubborn **6** naughty

Only a **stupid** person would sell an original *page* from a rare book for a *dollar*.

1416

顆
TRAD   SIMPLIFIED

This character with the definition:

m for small, roundish things

Pinyin **kē** *and Frequency Rank* **1448**

Contains **14 strokes** in the following order:

丨 冂 曰 日 旦 甲 罗 果 果 颗 颗 颗 颗 颗

Contains these components:

☐ fruit 果 567, p.134

☐ page, leaf 页 1408, p.312

With all these meanings & reading

kē [顆] **1** m for small spheres, pearls, corn grains, teeth, heart satellites etc

The humongous *fruit* trees' *leaves* did not deter us from gathering a **basket of apples** and a large **bowl of peaches**.

1417

預
TRAD   SIMPLIFIED

This character with the definition:

in advance

Pinyin **yù** *and Frequency Rank* **647**

Contains **10 strokes** in the following order:

フ マ 子 予 予 矛 矛 预 预 预

Contains these components:

☐ bestow, award 予 985, p.225

☐ page, leaf 页 1408, p.312

With all these meanings & reading

yù [預] **1** to advance **2** in advance **3** beforehand **4** to prepare

In advance of the book's release to the general public, I *bestowed* some *pages* of my new novel upon the influential critic.

1418

顧
TRAD   SIMPLIFIED

This character with the definition:

attend to, look after

Pinyin **gù** *and Frequency Rank* **815**

Contains **10 strokes** in the following order:

一 厂 厅 厄 后 后 顾 顾 顾 顾

Contains these components:

☐ trapped in a difficult situation 厄 426, p.103

☐ page, leaf 页 1408, p.312

With all these meanings & reading

gù [顧] **1** to look after **2** to t into consideration **3** to attend **4** surname Gu

I was *trapped in a difficult situation* after I tripped over the *pages* of an open book. After I regained my balance, I was able to **attend to** the troublesome situation and fix it.

1419

順
TRAD   SIMPLIFIED

This character with the definition:

in the direction of

Pinyin **shùn** *and Frequency Rank* **938**

Contains **9 strokes** in the following order:

丿 刂 川 川 𠂤 𠂤 顺 顺 顺

Contains these components:

☐ river 川 444, p.107

☐ page, leaf 页 1408, p.312

With all these meanings & reading

shùn [順] **1** to obey **2** to follow **3** to arrange **4** to make reasonable **5** along **6** favorab

A floating *leaf* will always move **in the direction of** a *river's* current.

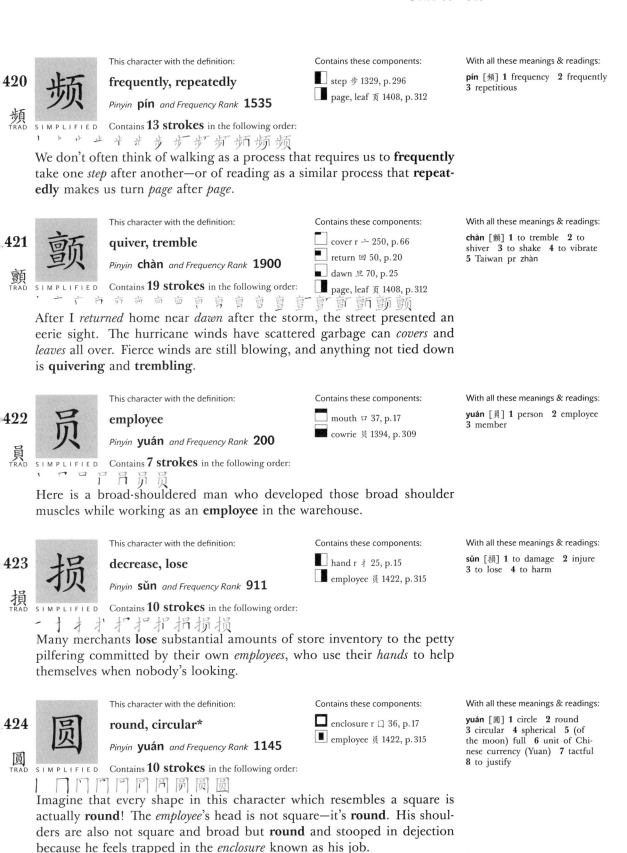

420
频
频
TRAD SIMPLIFIED

This character with the definition:

frequently, repeatedly

Pinyin **pín** *and Frequency Rank* **1535**

Contains **13 strokes** in the following order:

Contains these components:
step 步 1329, p. 296
page, leaf 页 1408, p. 312

With all these meanings & readings:
pín [频] **1** frequency **2** frequently **3** repetitious

We don't often think of walking as a process that requires us to **frequently** take one *step* after another—or of reading as a similar process that **repeatedly** makes us turn *page* after *page*.

421
颤
颤
TRAD SIMPLIFIED

This character with the definition:

quiver, tremble

Pinyin **chàn** *and Frequency Rank* **1900**

Contains **19 strokes** in the following order:

Contains these components:
cover r 宀 250, p. 66
return 回 50, p. 20
dawn 旦 70, p. 25
page, leaf 页 1408, p. 312

With all these meanings & readings:
chàn [顫] **1** to tremble **2** to shiver **3** to shake **4** to vibrate **5** Taiwan pr zhàn

After I *returned* home near *dawn* after the storm, the street presented an eerie sight. The hurricane winds have scattered garbage can *covers* and *leaves* all over. Fierce winds are still blowing, and anything not tied down is **quivering** and **trembling**.

422
员
員
TRAD SIMPLIFIED

This character with the definition:

employee

Pinyin **yuán** *and Frequency Rank* **200**

Contains **7 strokes** in the following order:

Contains these components:
mouth 口 37, p. 17
cowrie 贝 1394, p. 309

With all these meanings & readings:
yuán [員] **1** person **2** employee **3** member

Here is a broad-shouldered man who developed those broad shoulder muscles while working as an **employee** in the warehouse.

423
损
損
TRAD SIMPLIFIED

This character with the definition:

decrease, lose

Pinyin **sǔn** *and Frequency Rank* **911**

Contains **10 strokes** in the following order:

Contains these components:
hand r 扌 25, p. 15
employee 员 1422, p. 315

With all these meanings & readings:
sǔn [損] **1** to damage **2** injure **3** to lose **4** to harm

Many merchants **lose** substantial amounts of store inventory to the petty pilfering committed by their own *employees*, who use their *hands* to help themselves when nobody's looking.

424
圆
圓
TRAD SIMPLIFIED

This character with the definition:

round, circular*

Pinyin **yuán** *and Frequency Rank* **1145**

Contains **10 strokes** in the following order:

Contains these components:
enclosure r 囗 36, p. 17
employee 员 1422, p. 315

With all these meanings & readings:
yuán [圓] **1** circle **2** round **3** circular **4** spherical **5** (of the moon) full **6** unit of Chinese currency (Yuan) **7** tactful **8** to justify

Imagine that every shape in this character which resembles a square is actually **round**! The *employee's* head is not square—it's **round**. His shoulders are also not square and broad but **round** and stooped in dejection because he feels trapped in the *enclosure* known as his job.

1425

赢

赢
TRAD SIMPLIFIED

This character with the definition:

gain, win

Pinyin **yíng** *and Frequency Rank* **1836**

Contains **17 strokes** in the following order:

丶 亠 亡 宀 宀 言 言 言 亯 亯 贏 贏 贏 贏 贏 贏 贏

- perish 亡 259, p. 67
- meat 肉 (altered) 753, p. 175
- employee 员 1422, p. 315
- commonplace 凡 (altered) 901, p. 205

With all these meanings & reading

yíng [赢] **1** to beat **2** to win **3** to profit

For food bank *employees*, local restaurants and grocery stores are *commonplace* sources of surplus food that can *perish* quickly. This practice reduces waste and allows the food bank to **gain** free vegetables, fruit, and *meat* for those who cannot afford to buy such items.

1426

贯

贯
TRAD SIMPLIFIED

This character with the definition:

link up

Pinyin **guàn** *and Frequency Rank* **1478**

Contains **8 strokes** in the following order:

乚 口 田 毌 毌 毌 贯 贯

Contains these components:

- field 田 (altered) 63, p. 23
- cowrie 贝 1394, p. 309

With all these meanings & reading

guàn [贯] **1** to pierce through **2** to string together **3** string of 1000 cash

The farmer used the *money* he inherited to purchase his neighbor's *field* so that he could **link up** the two adjacent *fields*—and create his own huge '*Field* of Dreams'.

1427

惯

惯
TRAD SIMPLIFIED

This character with the definition:

accustomed, used to

Pinyin **guàn** *and Frequency Rank* **1226**

Contains **11 strokes** in the following order:

丶 丶 忄 忄 忄 忭 忭 惯 惯 惯 惯

Contains these components:

- heart (skinny) r 忄 1135, p. 256
- link up 贯 1426, p. 316

With all these meanings & reading

guàn [惯] **1** accustomed to **2** used to **3** indulge; spoil (someone, usually a child)

While recovering from his *heart* attack, my father learned to mentally *link up* exercise with his very survival. As a result, he has become so **used to** exercising that it is now part of his daily routine.

1428

资

资
TRAD SIMPLIFIED

This character with the definition:

money, expenses

Pinyin **zī** *and Frequency Rank* **257**

Contains **10 strokes** in the following order:

丶 冫 冫 次 次 次 次 咨 资 资

Contains these components:

- time, occurrence 次 748, p. 174
- cowrie 贝 1394, p. 309

With all these meanings & reading

zī [资] **1** resources **2** capital **3** to provide **4** to supply **5** to support **6** money **7** expense

Any *time* I earn *money*, I use it to pay off my **expenses**.

1429

贞

贞
TRAD SIMPLIFIED

This character with the definition:

chaste

Pinyin **zhēn** *and Frequency Rank* **2366**

Contains **9 strokes** in the following order:

丨 卜 ㇆ 卢 贞 贞

Contains these components:

- foretell 卜 187, p. 51
- cowrie 贝 1394, p. 309

With all these meanings & reading

zhēn [贞] **1** chaste

The beautiful girl is famous for her *shell*-like ears, and she's constantly being **chased** (sounds like '**chaste**') by aggressive men. Who can *foretell* the outcome?

430

侦

侦
TRAD SIMPLIFIED

This character with the definition:

investigate, detect

Pinyin **zhēn** *and Frequency Rank* **1479**

Contains **8 strokes** in the following order:

ノ イ イ´ イ宀 イ占 侦 侦 侦

Contains these components:

man r 亻 1156, p. 260

chaste 贞 1429, p. 316

With all these meanings & readings:

zhēn [侦] **1** to scout **2** to spy
3 to detect

In certain cultures, it is acceptable for certain *men* to **investigate** their daughters' activities to make sure they remain *chaste* until marriage.

431

货

货
TRAD SIMPLIFIED

This character with the definition:

goods

Pinyin **huò** *and Frequency Rank* **818**

Contains **8 strokes** in the following order:

ノ イ 亻 化 化 货 货 货

Contains these components:

change, transform 化 1187, p. 266

cowrie 贝 1394, p. 309

With all these meanings & readings:

huò [货] **1** goods **2** money
3 commodity **4** m 个 [個][gè]

This character encompasses half of a freshman economics course. *Wealth* supports the *transformation* of resources into **goods** and commodities that you can then sell to create even more *wealth*!

432

财

财
TRAD SIMPLIFIED

This character with the definition:

wealth, riches

Pinyin **cái** *and Frequency Rank* **680**

Contains **7 strokes** in the following order:

丨 冂 冂 贝 贝 一 财 财

Contains these components:

cowrie 贝 1394, p. 309
sth just happened 才 449, p. 108

With all these meanings & readings:

cái [财] **1** money **2** wealth
3 riches **4** property **5** valuables

My friend *just found* an ancient rare *shell* that will surely bring him **wealth** if he sells it.

433

赌

赌
TRAD SIMPLIFIED

This character with the definition:

bet, gamble

Pinyin **dǔ** *and Frequency Rank* **2037**

Contains **12 strokes** in the following order:

丨 冂 冂 贝 贝 丿 财丿 财丬 财少 财耂 赌 赌 赌

Contains these components:

cowrie 贝 1394, p. 309

-er 者 456, p. 109

With all these meanings & readings:

dǔ [赌] **1** to bet **2** to gamble

A scribe once thought that *wealth* fostered one major *activity*—**gambling**.

434

贺

贺
TRAD SIMPLIFIED

This character with the definition:

congratulate

Pinyin **hè** *and Frequency Rank* **1690**

Contains **9 strokes** in the following order:

フ 力 加 加 加 加 智 贺 贺

Contains these components:

cowrie 贝 1394, p. 309

add, increase 加 476, p. 114

With all these meanings & readings:

hè [贺] **1** surname He
hè [贺] **1** to congratulate

From a Chinese point of view, a sudden *increase* in *wealth* calls for **congratulations**.

Unit 60

1435

费

费 TRAD SIMPLIFIED

This character with the definition:

cost, spend, expend

Pinyin **fèi** *and Frequency Rank* **486**

Contains these components:

▫ not (literary works) 弗 142, p.40

▪ cowrie 贝 1394, p.309

With all these meanings & reading

fèi [费] **1** to cost **2** to spend **3** fee **4** wasteful **5** expenses **6** surname Fei

Contains **9 strokes** in the following order:

Many sad stories have been written about the '**cost**' of gambling away one's *money*: *not* having enough left to **spend** on basic needs such as food and shelter.

1436

负

負 TRAD SIMPLIFIED

This character with the definition:

carry on shoulders, bear

Pinyin **fù** *and Frequency Rank* **691**

Contains these components:

▫ man 人 (altered) 537, p.127

▪ cowrie 贝 1394, p.309

With all these meanings & reading

fù [負] **1** lose **2** negative (ma etc) **3** to bear **4** to carry (or one's back)

Contains **6 strokes** in the following order:

This *man* is making *money* because he is now old enough to **bear** more responsibilities and earn rewards for his actions.

1437

赖

賴 TRAD SIMPLIFIED

This character with the definition:

rely, depend on

Pinyin **lài** *and Frequency Rank* **1365**

Contains these components:

▪ bundle, bunch 束 590, p.140
▫ carry on shoulders, bear 负 1436, p.318

With all these meanings & reading

lài [賴] **1** surname Lai
lài [賴] **1** to depend on **2** reliance **3** to renege (on promis **4** to disclaim **5** to rat (on det **6** to blame sb else

Contains **13 strokes** in the following order:

Since I'm too old to do the job, I **rely** on my son to *carry* the heavy *bundles on his shoulders*.

1438

赋

賦 TRAD SIMPLIFIED

This character with the definition:

endow, bestow

Pinyin **fù** *and Frequency Rank* **1747**

Contains these components:

▪ cowrie 贝 1394, p.309
▪ martial, military 武 672, p.158

With all these meanings & reading

fù [賦] **1** poetic essay **2** taxati **3** bestow on **4** endow with

Contains **12 strokes** in the following order:

The rebel *army* confiscates *money* from villagers for their warlord, who is the source of their monetary **endowments**.

1439

购

購 TRAD SIMPLIFIED

This character with the definition:

buy*

Pinyin **gòu** *and Frequency Rank* **1078**

Contains these components:

▪ cowrie 贝 1394, p.309
▪ cross out 勾 1023, p.232

With all these meanings & reading

gòu [購] **1** to buy **2** to purchase

Contains **8 strokes** in the following order:

丨 冂 刀 贝 贝' 购 购 购

I have my shopping list in one hand and my *money* in the other. Each time I **buy** something on the list, I *cross out* the item.

440

贲
贲
TRAD SIMPLIFIED

This character with the definition:

run quickly, dash

Pinyin **bēn** *and Frequency Rank* **4733**

Contains **9 strokes** in the following order:

一 十 士 击 赤 贲 贲 贲 贲

Contains these components:

☐ decorative grasses 卉 93, p. 30
■ cowrie 贝 1394, p. 309

With all these meanings & readings:

bēn [贲] **1** energetic **2** surname Ben
bì [贲] **1** bright

On village holidays, we hold a children's game by burying a bag of *money* deep within a big pile of *decorative grasses*; the children then **hasten** to dig through it to be the first one to find the *money*.

441

喷
喷
TRAD SIMPLIFIED

This character with the definition:

spout, gush

Pinyin **pēn** *and Frequency Rank* **1729**

Contains **12 strokes** in the following order:

丨 冂 口 口丨 口十 吐 吐 呣 哧 喷 喷 喷

Contains these components:

☐ mouth 口 37, p. 17
■ run quickly, dash 贲 1440, p. 319

With all these meanings & readings:

pēn [喷] **1** to puff **2** to spout **3** to spray **4** to spurt
pèn [喷] **1** fragrant

The small boy had to *run quickly* around the fountain and position his *mouth* to catch the water as it **spouted** from the fountain. (It may be helpful to visualize the *'run quickly, dash'* element as an ornate water fountain, with an open *mouth* poised beside it.)

442

愤
愤
TRAD SIMPLIFIED

This character with the definition:

anger

Pinyin **fèn** *and Frequency Rank* **1508**

Contains **12 strokes** in the following order:

丶 丷 忄 忄 忭 忭 忭 忭 愤 愤 愤 愤

Contains these components:

■ heart (skinny) r 忄 1135, p. 256
☐ run quickly, dash 贲 1440, p. 319

With all these meanings & readings:

fèn [愤] **1** indignant **2** anger **3** resentment

Anger is often the result of an *emotion* that develops with too much *haste*. If we force ourselves to stay calm in a stressful situation, we can more easily control angry feelings which threaten to arise.

443

贷
贷
TRAD SIMPLIFIED

This character with the definition:

loan, borrow

Pinyin **dài** *and Frequency Rank* **1605**

Contains **9 strokes** in the following order:

丿 亻 仁 代 代 代 贷 贷 贷

Contains these components:

☐ take the place of 代 1221, p. 273
■ cowrie 贝 1394, p. 309

With all these meanings & readings:

dài [贷] **1** to lend on interest **2** to borrow **3** a loan **4** leniency **5** to make excuses **6** to pardon **7** to forgive

A **loan** *takes the place of* your own *money* when you don't have any.

444

赔
赔
TRAD SIMPLIFIED

This character with the definition:

pay for, compensate

Pinyin **péi** *and Frequency Rank* **1734**

Contains **12 strokes** in the following order:

丨 冂 贝 贝 贝 贮 贮 贮 赔 赔 赔 赔

Contains these components:

■ cowrie 贝 1394, p. 309
■ to stand 立 681, p. 160
☐ mouth 口 37, p. 17

With all these meanings & readings:

péi [赔] **1** lose in trade **2** pay damage

When you damage your neighbor's lawnmower, you *stand up* like a man, open your *mouth*, and give him *money* to **compensate** for the damage.

1445

贸

贸
TRAD   SIMPLIFIED

This character with the definition:

commerce, trade

Pinyin **mào** *and Frequency Rank* **1092**

Contains **9 strokes** in the following order:

丿 𠂉 𠂆 𠂏 卯 卯 留 贸 贸

Contains these components:

◼ early morning 卯 (altered) 927, p. 210

◼ cowrie 贝 1394, p. 309

With all these meanings & readings

mào [貿] **1** commerce   **2** trade

"The *early morning* bird catches the worm." As such, stock brokers rise *very early* to **trade** *money*.

1446

贫

貧
TRAD   SIMPLIFIED

This character with the definition:

poor

Pinyin **pín** *and Frequency Rank* **1359**

Contains **8 strokes** in the following order:

丿 八 分 分 分 谷 贫 贫

Contains these components:

◻ divide, separate 分 1385, p. 308

◼ cowrie 贝 1394, p. 309

With all these meanings & readings

pín [貧] **1** poor   **2** inadequate   **3** deficient   **4** garrulous

When *money* is *divided* among many people, nobody gets enough, nobody is happy, and everyone stays **poor**.

1447

只

只
TRAD   SIMPLIFIED

This character with the definition:

only

Pinyin **zhǐ** *and Frequency Rank* **97**

Contains **5 strokes** in the following order:

丶 口 口 尸 只

Contains these components:

◻ mouth 口 37, p. 17

◼ eight 八 1261, p. 282

With all these meanings & readings

zhǐ [只] **1** only   **2** merely   **3** just   **4** but
zhǐ [祇] **1** but   **2** only
zhī [隻] **1** m for birds and certain animals, one of a pair, some utensils, vessels etc

My *mouth* watered as the dish heaped with *eight* cups of fried rice was placed before me. I soon learned that one person can **only** eat so much, and that pile of fried rice was too much for me to finish by myself. • Because of this interpretation this character will sometimes take on the meaning '**restricted amount**' when it appears as an element.

1448

职

職
TRAD   SIMPLIFIED

This character with the definition:

duty, job

Pinyin **zhí** *and Frequency Rank* **616**

Contains **11 strokes** in the following order:

一 厂 丌 币 月 月 耳 耴 职 职 职

Contains these components:

◼ ear 耳 76, p. 26

◼ only 只 1447, p. 320

With all these meanings & readings

zhí [職] **1** office   **2** duty

A guy with big *ears* shaped like jugs has a strange **job**—he *only* has to scoop up leaves with them.

1449

识

識
TRAD   SIMPLIFIED

This character with the definition:

recognize

Pinyin **shí** *and Frequency Rank* **340**

Contains **7 strokes** in the following order:

丶 讠 讠 识 识 识 识

Contains these components:

◼ speech r 讠 352, p. 88

◼ only 只 1447, p. 320

With all these meanings & readings

shí [識] **1** to know   **2** knowledge   **3** Taiwan pr shì
zhì [識] **1** to record   **2** write a footnote

How can you **recognize** a friend in the dark? It is *only* when they *speak* that you can identify him.

1450

织

織
TRAD   SIMPLIFIED

This character with the definition:

weave

Pinyin **zhī** *and Frequency Rank* **578**

Contains **8 strokes** in the following order:

乙 乡 乡 纟 纟 织 织 织 织

Contains these components:

■ silk r ⽷ 1037, p. 235
□ only 只 1447, p. 320

With all these meanings & readings:

zhī [織] **1** to weave **2** to knit

Historically, seamstresses were *only* allowed to use *silk* thread with which to **weave**.

1451

积

積
TRAD   SIMPLIFIED

This character with the definition:

amass, accumulate

Pinyin **jī** *and Frequency Rank* **728**

Contains **10 strokes** in the following order:

⼃ ⼆ 千 禾 禾 和 和 和 积 积

Contains these components:

■ rice, grain (crop) 禾 593, p. 140
□ only 只 1447, p. 320

With all these meanings & readings:

jī [積] **1** to amass **2** to accumulate **3** to store **4** measured quantity (such as area of volume) **5** product (the result of multiplication) **6** to integrate (math.) **7** to solve (or integrate) an ordinary differential equation (math.) **8** old **9** long-standing

Picture a small pile of *grain*. The pile contains a *restricted amount*. However, if we acquire lots of piles, we will have **amassed** valuable property.

1452

函

SIMP & TRAD

This character with the definition:

case, casket

Pinyin **hán** *and Frequency Rank* **1950**

Contains **8 strokes** in the following order:

⼅ 了 了 矛 承 承 函 函

Contains these components:

■ s-end le 了 23, p. 15
■ eight (×2, altered) ⼋1261, p. 282
□ receptacle r ⼐ 157, p. 43

With all these meanings & readings:

hán [函] **1** envelope **2** case **3** letter

A *casket* is a *receptacle* for a body which has undergone the *transformation* of death. Visualize the main character as a corpse viewed from above in an open **casket**, which is depicted by the 'receptacle' element; the 'le' element is the corpse (with the head at the top); and the two 'eight' elements represent the arm and leg on each side of the corpse.

1453

豕

SIMP & TRAD

This character with the definition:

pig, boar

Pinyin **shǐ** *and Frequency Rank* **4953**

Contains **7 strokes** in the following order:

⼀ ⼇ 了 了 豸 豸 豕

Contains these components:

□ one 一 1, p. 10
■ do not 勿 (altered) 460, p. 111
□ eight ⼋ (altered) 1261, p. 282

With all these meanings & readings:

shǐ [豕] **1** hog **2** swine

A **boar** is *one* animal that you *do not* want to take for granted. It has a foul temper, and can be vicious, with temperaments that can turn on a dime. But if you can capture and butcher one, you will have an *abundant* supply of meat.

1454

豪

SIMP & TRAD

This character with the definition:

super-talented person

Pinyin **háo** *and Frequency Rank* **1513**

Contains **14 strokes** in the following order:

⼂ ⼀ ⼗ 亠 古 亩 高 亭 亭 亭 亭 豪 豪 豪

Contains these components:

□ high 高 (abbrev) 253, 66
■ pig, boar 豕 1453, p. 321

With all these meanings & readings:

háo [豪] **1** grand **2** heroic

A *pig* is part of the character representing a **super-talented person**! *Pigs* are fat, prosperous, and happy in Chinese tradition. Someone with *high* levels of *pig*ness might be a **super-talented person**.

1455
蒙
曚
TRAD   SIMPLIFIED

This character with the definition:

cheat, hoodwink

Pinyin **mēng**   and Frequency Rank **1039**

Contains **13 strokes** in the following order:

一 艹 艹 艹 艹 艹 芦 苎 莒 芦 夢 蒙 蒙 蒙

Contains these components:

- grass r 艹 87, p. 29
- smooth cover r ⌐ (altered) 268, p. 69
- one 一 1, p. 10
- pig, boar 豕 (altered) 1453, p. 321

With all these meanings & readings:

Méng [矇] **1** surname Meng
mēng [矇] **1** (knocked) unconscious **2** to deceive **3** to cheat **4** to hoodwink
méng [矇] **1** dim sighted **2** ignorant **3** drizzle **4** receive a favor (敬词 polite)
měng [蒙] **1** Mongolia **2** cover

Feral *pigs* are smart and strong. We have to **hoodwink** them to catch them. Here is *one* that's already been trapped, and the extra horizontal stroke represents the effectiveness of the *cover*. It is in a deep pit, covered by a reinforcing *cover*; that extra *horizontal* stroke provides further reinforcement. A layer of *grass* fooled the *pig* into walking over the trap.

1456

彖

SIMP & TRAD

This character with the definition:

determine, make a judgment

Pinyin **tuàn**   and Frequency Rank **6434**

Contains **9 strokes** in the following order:

彑 彑 彑 彖 彖 彖 彖 彖 彖

Contains these components:

- mutual 互 (altered) 14, p. 12
- pig, boar 豕 1453, p. 321

With all these meanings & readings:

tuàn [彖] **1** to foretell the future using the trigrams of the Book Changes 易经 [~經]

My neighbor and I got together to buy a *pig*. But when we sold it, we couldn't *mutually* agree on our individual shares of the profit, so we went to court for a **judgment**.

1457

缘
缘
TRAD   SIMPLIFIED

This character with the definition:

reason, cause

Pinyin **yuán**   and Frequency Rank **1274**

Contains **12 strokes** in the following order:

纟 纟 纟 纟 纩 纩 纩 绔 绔 缘 缘 缘

Contains these components:

- silk r 纟 1037, p. 235
- determine, make a judgment 彖 1456, p. 322

With all these meanings & readings:

yuán [緣] **1** cause **2** reason **3** karma **4** fate **5** predestined affinity **6** margin **7** hem **8** edge **9** along

The **reason** that judges wear *silk robes* is judges they appear more impressive in robes when they *make a judgment*.

1458

家

SIMP & TRAD

This character with the definition:

home

Pinyin **jiā**   and Frequency Rank **56**

Contains **10 strokes** in the following order:

丶 宀 宀 宀 宀 宁 穷 家 家 家

Contains these components:

- roof r 宀 271, p. 70
- pig, boar 豕 1453, p. 321

With all these meanings & readings:

jiā [家] **1** home **2** family **3** m for families or businesses **4** ref to the philosophical schools of pre-Han China **5** noun suffix for specialists in some activity such as musician or revolutionar corresponds to English -ist, -er, -ary or -ian **6** surname Jia **7** m 个 [個][gè]

The people who live in my **home**, under my *roof*, are *pigs*!

1459

象

SIMP & TRAD

This character with the definition:

elephant

Pinyin **xiàng**   and Frequency Rank **300**

Contains **11 strokes** in the following order:

丿 丿 匃 匄 匄 务 务 象 象 象 象

Contains these components:

- man r 亻 (altered) 1156, p. 260
- eye 目 (altered) 75, p. 26
- pig, boar 豕 (altered) 1453, p. 321

With all these meanings & readings:

xiàng [象] **1** elephant **2** shape **3** form **4** appearance **5** of that shape **6** comparable to **7** such as... **8** image under a map (math.) **9** m 只 [隻][zhī]

What an animal! Vaguely *pig*-like in form, **elephants** have huge *eyes* positioned at a funny angle and that fixate on you with almost *human* expressiveness. An **elephant** is so big that a *man* can ride on top.

Unit 61

460

This character with the definition:

resemble

Pinyin **xiàng** *and Frequency Rank* **294**

SIMP & TRAD   Contains **13 strokes** in the following order:

丿 亻 亻 仹 伃 伃 伃 伃 伊 傍 像 像 像

Contains these components:

■ man r 亻 1156, p. 260

■ elephant 象 1459, p. 322

With all these meanings & readings:

xiàng [像] **1** (look) like **2** similar (to) **3** appearance **4** to appear **5** to seem **6** image **7** portrait **8** resemble **9** seem

Some readers may be old enough to remember *elephant* jokes. Why does a *man* **resemble** an *elephant*? They both walk on two legs—except for the *elephant*. (This joke would have garnered huge laughs in 1963.)

461

This character with the definition:

pleased, content

Pinyin **yù** *and Frequency Rank* **1956**

SIMP & TRAD   Contains **15 strokes** in the following order:

フ マ 予 予 予 予 预 预 预 豫 豫 豫 豫 豫 豫

Contains these components:

■ bestow, award 予 985, p. 225

■ elephant 象 1459, p. 322

With all these meanings & readings:

Yù [豫] **1** abbr for Henan province 河南 in central China **2** variant of 预 [預] **3** beforehand **4** to prepare

That's me—the guy on the back of the *elephant*—and the *elephant* is *bestowing* on me the ride of my life. I am **pleased** with the novelty of this experience.

462

This character with the definition:

rate, proportion

Pinyin **lǜ** *and Frequency Rank* **625**

SIMP & TRAD   Contains **11 strokes** in the following order:

丶 一 亠 玄 玄 玄 浐 浐 浐 率 率

Contains these components:

■ incredible 玄 1002, p. 228

■■ eight (×2, altered) 八 1261, p. 282

□ ten 十 7, p. 11

With all these meanings & readings:

shuài [率] **1** rate **2** frequency
shuài [率] **1** to lead **2** to command **3** rash **4** hasty **5** frank **6** straightforward **7** generally **8** usually

The **rate** of increase is *incredible*—at over eighty percent. How can we tell? Not only is there one *eight* on the left side of this character, but a second *eight* on the right as well. Two *eight*'s over the same *ten* (8/10=80%) emphasizes this *incredible* result.

463

This character with the definition:

manage

Pinyin **bàn** *and Frequency Rank* **367**

辦
TRAD   SIMPLIFIED   Contains **4 strokes** in the following order:

フ 力 办 办

Contains these components:

■ strength 力 471, p. 113

□ eight 八 (altered) 1261, p. 282

With all these meanings & readings:

bàn [辦] **1** to do **2** to manage **3** to handle **4** to go about **5** to run **6** to set up **7** to deal with

The '*eight*' that should have been at the top represents something that's indivisible, yet the task at hand is to split the item in two. By applying great *strength*, we **manage** this.

1464

脅
TRAD

胁
SIMPLIFIED

This character with the definition:

coerce, force

Pinyin **xié** *and Frequency Rank* **1494**

Contains **8 strokes** in the following order:

丿 刀 月 月 肕 肋 肋 胁

Contains these components:

◻ meat 肉 (altered) 753, p.175
◻ manage 办 1463, p.323

With all these meanings & readings

xié [脅] **1** side of body **2** thre

I use a rotting, stinking piece of *meat* to torture people, which is how I *manage* to get my way. This enables me to **force** you to do what I want you to do.

1465

協
TRAD

协
SIMPLIFIED

This character with the definition:

harmonize, cooperate

Pinyin **xié** *and Frequency Rank* **735**

Contains **6 strokes** in the following order:

一 十 オ 协 协 协

Contains these components:

◻ ten 十 7, p.11
◻ manage 办 1463, p.323

With all these meanings & readings

xié [協] **1** cooperate **2** harmon
3 to help **4** to assist **5** to join

Only with **cooperation** and inter-personal **harmony** can *ten* people *manage* to finish the job.

1466

蘇
TRAD

苏
SIMPLIFIED

This character with the definition:

revive*

Pinyin **sū** *and Frequency Rank* **590**

Contains **7 strokes** in the following order:

一 十 艹 艻 艻 苏 苏

Contains these components:

◻ grass r ⺿ 87, p.29
◻ manage 办 1463, p.323

With all these meanings & readings

sū [甦] **1** revive
sū [蘇] **1** Perilla frutescens (Chi
nese basil or wild red basil)
2 place name **3** to revive **4** u
as phonetic in transliteration
5 abbr for Soviet Union 苏维埃
[蘇維~] or 苏联[蘇聯], Jiangsu
province 江苏[~蘇] and Suzhou
city 苏州[蘇~] **6** surname Su

The old fool *managed* to run into a lamp post and knock himself out cold. A wandering healer threw some aromatic *grass* over him and **managed** to **revive** him.

1467

飛
TRAD

飞
SIMPLIFIED

This character with the definition:

to fly

Pinyin **fēi** *and Frequency Rank* **347**

Contains **3 strokes** in the following order:

乁 飞 飞

Contains these components:

◻ second (in a series) 乙 146, p.41
◻ eight 八 (altered) 1261, p.282

With all these meanings & readings

fēi [飛] **1** to fly

Tickets to London are scarce on short notice. The only way I could **fly** was by agreeing to stand-by status. I was number *eight* originally, but rapidly moved up to be *second in the series* of would-be travelers.

1468

肅
TRAD

肃
SIMPLIFIED

This character with the definition:

esteem, respect

Pinyin **sù** *and Frequency Rank* **1518**

Contains **8 strokes** in the following order:

フ ㄱ ヨ 肀 肀 肃 肃 肃

Contains these components:

◻ boar's head r ヨ 30, p.16
◻ scepter c ｜ 5, p.10
◻ eight 八 1261, p.282
◻ eight 八 (altered) 1261, p.282

With all these meanings & readings

sù [肅] **1** Gansu **2** respectful

The village hero killed so many wild pigs (see the pile of *super-abundant boar's heads*?) that he was awarded a royal *scepter*, which symbolized the king's **esteem** and **repect** towards him

469

萧

萧
TRAD SIMPLIFIED

This character with the definition:

desolate, bleak

Pinyin **xiāo** *and Frequency Rank* **1898**

Contains **11 strokes** in the following order:

一 十 艹 艻 芏 莑 茟 萧 萧 萧 萧

Contains these components:

☐ grass r 艹 87, p. 29

◼ esteem, respect 肃 1468, p. 324

With all these meanings & readings:

xiāo [萧] **1** mournful **2** desolate **3** surname Xiao

Our new neighbors began to treat us with *respect* only after we planted lush green *grass* on our **bleak**-looking property.

470

啸

啸
TRAD SIMPLIFIED

This character with the definition:

to whistle

Pinyin **xiào** *and Frequency Rank* **2301**

Contains **11 strokes** in the following order:

丨 冂 口 口┐ 口⁼ 吐 吀 啸 啸 啸 啸

Contains these components:

◼ mouth 口 37, p. 17

◧ esteem, respect 肃 1468, p. 324

With all these meanings & readings:

xiào [啸] **1** to hiss **2** to whistle

Finally, you caught your breath after witnessing the beauty of this presentation (panel 1468). Now make a sound to show your appreciation and *esteem*, and use your *mouth* to **whistle**!

471

兰

蘭
TRAD SIMPLIFIED

This character with the definition:

orchid

Pinyin **lán** *and Frequency Rank* **642**

Contains **5 strokes** in the following order:

丶 ⺌ 丷 兰 兰

Contains these components:

☐ eight r ⺌ 1260, p. 282

◼ three 三 3, p. 10

With all these meanings & readings:

lán [蘭] **1** orchid (兰花 [蘭~] Cymbidium goeringii) **2** fragrant thoroughwort (兰草 [蘭~] Eupatorium fortunei) **3** lily magnolia (木兰 [~蘭]) **4** surname Lan

The **orchid** is a flower with an *abundance* of positive attributes which is what makes it such a special flower. Fragrance, brilliant color, and longevity are its *three* most important qualities.

472

拦

攔
TRAD SIMPLIFIED

This character with the definition:

to bar or block

Pinyin **lán** *and Frequency Rank* **1996**

Contains **8 strokes** in the following order:

一 十 扌 扌 扗 拦 拦 拦

Contains these components:

◧ hand r 扌 25, p. 15

◼ orchid 兰 1471, p. 325

With all these meanings & readings:

lán [攔] **1** cut off **2** hinder

Here we see someone's *hand* intent on cutting off and stealing a rare *orchid* specimen. At the last moment, the *orchid*'s beauty captivates him and **bars** him from committing this destructive deed.

473

南

SIMP & TRAD

This character with the definition:

south

Pinyin **nán** *and Frequency Rank* **307**

Contains **9 strokes** in the following order:

一 十 十 冇 南 南 南 南 南

Contains these components:

☐ ten 十 7, p. 11

◼ borders r 冂 114, p. 34

▭ eight r ⺌ 1260, p. 282

◼ dry 干 17, p. 13

With all these meanings & readings:

nán [南] **1** south

As you travel **south** from anywhere in the Northern Hemisphere, the temperature increases about *ten* degrees soon after you cross the *borders* of each territory. Eventually you will approach the Equator, where the tropical heat is so *abundant* that conditions become oppressively hot and *dry*.

1474

献

獻
TRAD   SIMPLIFIED

This character with the definition:

offer, donate

Pinyin **xiàn** *and Frequency Rank* **1192**

Contains **13 strokes** in the following order:

一 十 ナ 古 古 古 南 南 南 南 献 献 献

Contains these components:

south 南 1473, p. 325

dog 犬 673, p. 158

With all these meanings & readings

xiàn [献] **1** to offer

America's *south* is hot and *south* plus *dog* equals 'hot dog'. I'm famous for my hot dogs so the next time we have a barbecue, come on over—I'd like to **offer** you one.

1475

喃

SIMP & TRAD

This character with the definition:

mumbling

Pinyin **nán** *and Frequency Rank* **2233**

Contains **12 strokes** in the following order:

丨 口 口 口一 叶 叶 呐 呐 喃 喃 喃

Contains these components:

mouth 口 37, p. 17

south 南 1473, p. 325

With all these meanings & readings

nán [喃] **1** mumble in repetition

Northern people are full of their own special prejudices, often regarding people from southern tropical regions as doing things slowly, perhaps in response to the stifling heat they live in. Language is the worst. The sounds that these *southerners* make with their *mouths* sound like **mumbling** to unaccustomed Northern ears.

1476

酋

SIMP & TRAD

This character with the definition:

tribal chief

Pinyin **qiú** *and Frequency Rank* **3403**

Contains **9 strokes** in the following order:

丶 丷 丬 丬 丬 丙 酉 酉 酋

Contains these components:

eight r ㇔ 1260, p. 282

five to seven pm 酉 302, p. 77

With all these meanings & readings

qiú [酋] **1** tribal chief

It's easy to select the new **tribal chief**. The person who eats and drinks the most *abundant* amount during supper, which is served between *five and seven o'clock in the evening*, is the one chosen.

1477

尊

SIMP & TRAD

This character with the definition:

honor, venerate

Pinyin **zūn** *and Frequency Rank* **1134**

Contains **12 strokes** in the following order:

丶 丷 丬 丬 丬 丙 酉 酉 酋 尊 尊 尊

Contains these components:

tribal chief 酋 1476, p. 326

inch 寸 216, p. 58

With all these meanings & readings

zūn [尊] **1** to honor   **2** to respe
3 (classifier for cannons and statues)   **4** ancient wine vessel

You know the elder is **honored** when even the *tribal chief* behaves as if he's only one *inch* tall in the elder's presence.

1478

拳

SIMP & TRAD

This character with the definition:

fist

Pinyin **quán** *and Frequency Rank* **1784**

Contains **10 strokes** in the following order:

丶 丷 丷 一 丷 半 关 养 养 养 拳

Contains these components:

eight r ㇔ 1260, p. 282

man (spiffy) 夫 718, p. 168

hand 手 21, p. 14

With all these meanings & readings

quán [拳] **1** fist

This sketch depicts part of a *man's hand* knocking down another *man*, and in the process shaking loose a *couple of drops* of blood or sweat. Only a **fist** is capable of unleashing that power.

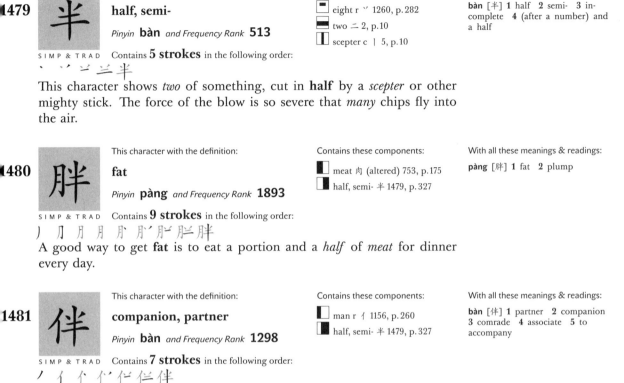

1479 半 **half, semi-**

Pinyin **bàn** *and Frequency Rank* **513**

SIMP & TRAD   Contains **5 strokes** in the following order:

Contains these components:

eight r `ˇ` 1260, p. 282

two 二 2, p. 10

scepter c 丨 5, p. 10

With all these meanings & readings:

bàn [半] **1** half **2** semi- **3** incomplete **4** (after a number) and a half

This character shows *two* of something, cut in **half** by a *scepter* or other mighty stick. The force of the blow is so severe that *many* chips fly into the air.

1480 胖 **fat**

Pinyin **pàng** *and Frequency Rank* **1893**

SIMP & TRAD   Contains **9 strokes** in the following order:

Contains these components:

meat 肉 (altered) 753, p. 175

half, semi- 半 1479, p. 327

With all these meanings & readings:

pàng [胖] **1** fat **2** plump

A good way to get **fat** is to eat a portion and a *half* of *meat* for dinner every day.

1481 伴 **companion, partner**

Pinyin **bàn** *and Frequency Rank* **1298**

SIMP & TRAD   Contains **7 strokes** in the following order:

Contains these components:

man r 亻 1156, p. 260

half, semi- 半 1479, p. 327

With all these meanings & readings:

bàn [伴] **1** partner **2** companion **3** comrade **4** associate **5** to accompany

A *person* is only *half* a soul without his life **partner** by his side.

1482 判 **judge, decide**

Pinyin **pàn** *and Frequency Rank* **719**

SIMP & TRAD   Contains **7 strokes** in the following order:

Contains these components:

half, semi- 半 (altered) 1479, p. 327

knife r 刂 (altered) 169, p. 46

With all these meanings & readings:

pàn [判] **1** to judge **2** to sentence **3** to discriminate **4** to discern

The **judgment** of the court: split the items with a *knife* so each party receives *half*.

1483 鬲 **cooking cauldron**

Pinyin **lì** *and Frequency Rank* **6855**

SIMP & TRAD   Contains **10 strokes** in the following order:

Contains these components:

high 高 (abbrev) 253, 66

half, semi- 半 (altered) 1479, p. 327

With all these meanings & readings:

gé [鬲] **1** surname Ge **2** earthen pot **3** iron cauldron
lì [鬲] **1** ancient ceramic three-legged vessel used for cooking with cord markings on the outside and hollow legs

This ancient **cooking cauldron**, often found in archaeological sites, is poorly designed. It's so *high* off the ground that the meat is only *half-*cooked in the time that it would take to roast over a fire.

1484

This character with the definition:

melt, thaw

Pinyin **róng** *and Frequency Rank* **1225**

SIMP & TRAD Contains **16 strokes** in the following order:

Contains these components:

▮ cooking cauldron 鬲 1483, p. 327

▮ insect 虫 1016, p. 231

With all these meanings & readings:

róng [融] **1** harmonious **2** melt **3** mild

一 一 一 一 一 冂 冂 冃 冐 鬲 鬲 鬲 鬲 融 融 融

After the freezing soldiers had finished packing ice into their *cooking cauldron* to **melt** for drinking water, they were shocked to discover that the water contained dozens of *insects*.

Unit 62

◀485

隔

SIMP & TRAD

This character with the definition:

separate, impede

Pinyin **gé** *and Frequency Rank* **1319**

Contains **12 strokes** in the following order:

亻 阝 阝 阿 阿 阿 阿 隔 隔 隔 隔 隔

Contains these components:

hills r 阝 942, p. 216

cooking cauldron 鬲 1483, p. 327

With all these meanings & readings:

gé [隔] **1** to separate **2** to partition **3** to stand or lie between **4** at a distance from **5** after or at an interval of

The *hill* tribesmen not only threatened to **impede** our progress but also to **separate** our bodies from our limbs and toss the pieces into their huge *cooking cauldrons*. After that, we ran for our lives!

◀486

羊

SIMP & TRAD

This character with the definition:

sheep

Pinyin **yáng** *and Frequency Rank* **1337**

Contains **6 strokes** in the following order:

丶 丷 兰 兰 兰 羊

Contains these components:

eight r 丷 1260, p. 282

three 三 3, p. 10

scepter c 丨 5, p. 10

With all these meanings & readings:

yáng [羊] **1** surname Yang
yáng [羊] **1** sheep **2** m 头 [頭][tóu], 只 [隻][zhī]

Imagine looking at a fat, plump **sheep** from top to bottom: we would see its two ears at the top, next a face, then its four legs, and finally a tail at the bottom.

◀487

善

SIMP & TRAD

This character with the definition:

kind, good

Pinyin **shàn** *and Frequency Rank* **749**

Contains **12 strokes** in the following order:

丶 丷 兰 兰 兰 羊 羊 羊 善 善 善 善

Contains these components:

sheep 羊 (altered) 1486, p. 329

speech 言 (altered) 256, p. 67

With all these meanings & readings:

shàn [善] **1** good (virtuous) **2** benevolent **3** well-disposed **4** good at sth **5** to improve or perfect

Sheep are well-known to be gentle animals. A person whose *speech* resembles that of a *sheep* is sure to be **good** and **kind**.

◀488

鮮

鮮
TRAD   SIMPLIFIED

This character with the definition:

fresh, new

Pinyin **xiān** *and Frequency Rank* **958**

Contains **14 strokes** in the following order:

ノ ク 夕 各 各 毎 鱼 鱼 鱼 鱼' 鲜 鲜 鲜 鲜

Contains these components:

fish 鱼 854, p. 195

sheep 羊 1486, p. 329

With all these meanings & readings:

xiān [鮮] **1** fresh
xiǎn [鮮] **1** few **2** rare

Fish and *sheep* both need to keep moving in order to locate **new** sources of food.

◀489

美

SIMP & TRAD

This character with the definition:

beautiful

Pinyin **měi** *and Frequency Rank* **151**

Contains **9 strokes** in the following order:

丶 丷 兰 兰 羊 羊 差 美 美

Contains these components:

sheep 羊 (altered) 1486, p. 329

big 大 544, p. 129

With all these meanings & readings:

měi [美] **1** America **2** beautiful

For a shepherd, there's no sight more **beautiful** than one of a *big*, plump *sheep*.

1490

SIMP & TRAD

This character with the definition:

ocean

Pinyin **yáng** *and Frequency Rank* **803**

Contains **9 strokes** in the following order:

丶 丶 氵 氵 泬 泮 泮 洋 洋

Contains these components:

☐ water r 氵 314, p. 80
☐ sheep 羊 1486, p. 329

With all these meanings & readings

yáng [洋] **1** foreign **2** ocean

Growing up on my father's large *sheep* farm was similar to living in Paradise—there was a bubbling stream of fresh *water* flowing through its pastures and the vast blue **ocean** was visible from its hills.

1491

様
TRAD

SIMPLIFIED

This character with the definition:

shape, pattern

Pinyin **yàng** *and Frequency Rank* **88**

Contains **10 strokes** in the following order:

一 十 才 木 杉 杉 栏 栏 样 样

Contains these components:

☐ tree 木 562, p. 133
☐ sheep 羊 1486, p. 329

With all these meanings & readings

yàng [様] **1** manner **2** pattern **3** way **4** appearance **5** shape **6** m 个 [個][gè]

In agrarian settings, what counted most towards a landowner's peace of mind was the proper **appearance** of wealth—agriculture, symbolized by a *tree*, and livestock, represented by a *sheep*.

1492

詳
TRAD   SIMPLIFIED

This character with the definition:

detailed

Pinyin **xiáng** *and Frequency Rank* **1439**

Contains **8 strokes** in the following order:

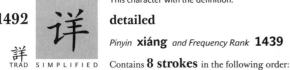

Sheep are not very smart animals so they could never learn to do a simple 'trick', even after many *speeches*, with **detailed** instructions given by the best animal trainers in the world.

Contains these components:

☐ speech r 讠 352, p. 88
☐ sheep 羊 1486, p. 329

With all these meanings & readings

xiáng [詳] **1** detailed **2** comprehensive

1493

幸
倖
TRAD   SIMPLIFIED

This character with the definition:

luck, good fortune

Pinyin **xìng** *and Frequency Rank* **902**

Contains **8 strokes** in the following order:

一 十 士 击 击 击 査 幸

Contains these components:

☐ earth, soil 土 9, p. 11
☐ sheep 羊 (altered) 1486, p. 329

With all these meanings & readings

xìng [倖] **1** lucky
xìng [幸] **1** fortunate **2** lucky **3** surname Xing

In virtually every civilization, from mankind's earliest days to the present, a person's **good fortune** often begins by acquiring a few domesticated animals such as *sheep* or cattle, and enough fertile *soil* for them to graze on.

1494

弟

SIMP & TRAD

This character with the definition:

younger brother

Pinyin **dì** *and Frequency Rank* **816**

Contains **7 strokes** in the following order:

丶 丷 兰 兰 芇 弟 弟

Contains these components:

☐ sheep 羊 1486, p. 329
☐ bow (weapon) 弓 140, p. 40
☐ action path c 丿 438, p. 105

With all these meanings & readings

dì [弟] **1** younger brother **2** junior male **3** I (modest word in letter)
tì [弟] **1** variant of 悌 [悌][tì]

In hunter societies, a **younger brother** proves himself by completing a successful *action*, such as using his *bow* to kill a *sheep* for dinner.

1495

第

SIMP & TRAD

This character with the definition:

prefix for number in series

Pinyin **dì** *and Frequency Rank* **114**

Contains **11 strokes** in the following order:

ノ ト ⺮ ⺮ ⺮ ⺮ 竺 笃 第 第 第

Contains these components:

☐ bamboo r ⺮ 264, p. 68
☐ younger brother 弟 (altered) 1494, p. 330

With all these meanings & readings:

dì [第] **1** (prefix indicating ordinal number, e.g. first, number two etc)

Chinese scribes often include the *bamboo radical* in contexts involving calculation or record-keeping, probably symbolic of the use of *bamboo* in the abacus, the traditional Chinese calculator. The '*younger brother*' element makes a fine companion to it, not only because its pronunciation matches that of the whole character, but also because keeping track of a boy's **position in the sequence** of sons in a family was so important to Chinese fathers.

1496

梯

SIMP & TRAD

This character with the definition:

ladder

Pinyin **tī** *and Frequency Rank* **1672**

Contains **11 strokes** in the following order:

一 十 才 木 术 术 杧 杧 棉 梯 梯

Contains these components:

☐ tree 木 562, p. 133
☐ younger brother 弟 1494, p. 330

With all these meanings & readings:

tī [梯] **1** ladder

Ladders are made from *trees*, and the horizontal strokes of the '*younger brother*' element resemble those of a **ladder**'s rungs.

1497

差

SIMP & TRAD

This character with the definition:

lack, be short of

Pinyin **chà** *and Frequency Rank* **732**

Contains **9 strokes** in the following order:

丶 丷 丷 ⺍ 兰 羊 羊 差 差

Contains these components:

☐ sheep 羊 1486, p. 329
☐ labor, work 工 12, p. 12

With all these meanings & readings:

chā [差] **1** difference **2** discrepancy **3** to differ **4** error **5** to err **6** to make a mistake
chà [差] **1** differ from **2** short of **3** to lack **4** poor
chāi [差] **1** to send **2** to commission **3** messenger **4** mission
cī [差] **1** uneven

The *sheep* are running wild! We're **short on** time so we will need to *work* hard to retrieve them.

1498

羞

SIMP & TRAD

This character with the definition:

shame, embarrass

Pinyin **xiū** *and Frequency Rank* **2048**

Contains **10 strokes** in the following order:

丶 丷 丷 ⺍ 兰 羊 羔 着 羞 羞

Contains these components:

☐ sheep 羊 (altered) 1486, p. 329
☐ clown 丑 33, p. 17

With all these meanings & readings:

xiū [羞] **1** shy **2** ashamed **3** shame **4** bashful **5** used for 馐 [饈][xiū], delicacies

A professional *clown* is trained to perform **embarrassing** acts that will cause the crowd to laugh *sheep*ishly.

499

养

养
TRAD   SIMPLIFIED

This character with the definition:

provide for

Pinyin **yǎng** *and Frequency Rank* **760**

Contains **9 strokes** in the following order:

丶 丷 丷 ⺍ 兰 羊 美 养 养

Contains these components:

☐ sheep 羊 (altered) 1486, p. 329
☐ introduce 介 1390, p. 309

With all these meanings & readings:

yǎng [養] **1** to raise (animals) **2** to bring up (children) **3** to keep (pets) **4** to support **5** to give birth

It's easy for a shepherd to **provide for** his family. The prosperity due to his *sheep* allows him to *introduce* his family to some finer things.

1500

SIMP & TRAD

This character with the definition:

oxygen

Pinyin **yǎng** *and Frequency Rank* **1863**

Contains these components:

air, spirit, vital energy 气 838, p. 192

sheep 羊 1486, p. 329

With all these meanings & readings:

yǎng [氧] **1** oxygen (chemistry)

Contains **10 strokes** in the following order:

丿 一 七 气 气 气 氕 氧 氧 氧

Be careful when you buy carpet made of *wool*. If you want to find out whether it's real *wool*, burn a bit in the presence of **oxygen**. If the carpet is authentic, the *'vital spirit'* of *sheep* will yield a horrendous stink. Otherwise, if there is no smell, the fiber is synthetic and you've been cheated.

1501

著
TRAD

SIMPLIFIED

This character with the definition:

action in progress

Pinyin **zhe** *and Frequency Rank* **41**

Contains these components:

sheep 羊 (altered) 1486, p. 329

eye 目 75, p. 26

With all these meanings & readings:

zhāo [著] **1** catch **2** receive **3** suffer
zháo [著] **1** to touch **2** to come in contact with **3** to feel **4** to be affected by **5** to catch fire **6** to fall asleep **7** to burn
zhe [著] **1** particle attached after verb to indicate action in progress, like -ing ending
zhuó [著] **1** to wear (clothes) **2** to contact **3** to use **4** to apply

Contains **11 strokes** in the following order:

丶 丷 丷 䒑 兰 羊 羊 着 着 着 着

Little *sheep* never keep still so the shepherd must use his *eye* to keep track of their **continuing progress**.

1502

SIMP & TRAD

This character with the definition:

level, flat, even

Pinyin **píng** *and Frequency Rank* **215**

Contains these components:

eight r ㇀ 1260, p. 282

dry 干 17, p. 13

With all these meanings & readings:

píng [平] **1** surname Ping
píng [平] **1** flat **2** level **3** equal **4** to tie (make the same score) **5** to draw (score) **6** calm **7** peaceful **8** see also 平声 [~聲][píng shēng]

Contains **5 strokes** in the following order:

一 丷 丆 亚 平

When *dry* and arid conditions are especially *abundant*, it's easy for the wind and weather to wear down all the high peaks and fill in the earth's natural depressions, making the landscape becomes **level**, **flat**, and **even**.

1503

評
TRAD

SIMPLIFIED

This character with the definition:

comment on, criticize

Pinyin **píng** *and Frequency Rank* **809**

Contains these components:

speech r 讠 352, p. 88

level, flat, even 平 1502, p. 332

With all these meanings & readings:

píng [評] **1** to discuss **2** to comment **3** to criticize **4** to judge **5** to choose (by public appraisal)

Contains **7 strokes** in the following order:

丶 讠 订 评 评 评 评

If you are going to **criticize** someone, you should first plan your *speech* beforehand and then deliver it in a calm, *even* tone of voice.

1504

蘋
苹
TRAD   SIMPLIFIED

This character with the definition:

apple

Pinyin **píng** *and Frequency Rank* **2478**

Contains these components:

grass r 艹 87, p. 29

level, flat, even 平 1502, p. 332

With all these meanings & readings:

píng [苹] **1** (artemisia) **2** duckweed
pín [蘋] **1** marsiliaceae **2** clover fern
píng [蘋] **1** apple

Contains **8 strokes** in the following order:

一 十 艹 艹 芍 苆 苈 苹

Legend has it that William Tell shot an **apple** off his son's head with an arrow. Good thing the boy's head was sufficiently *flat* and *level* enough to keep the apple from rolling off his head and onto the *grass* before his dad shot it!

1505

This character with the definition:

duckweed

Pinyin **píng** *and Frequency Rank* **2180**

SIMP & TRAD   Contains **8 strokes** in the following order:

一十艹艹艹艹艹艹蓱萍

Contains these components:

■ water r 氵 314, p. 80
■ apple 苹 (altered) 1504, p. 332

With all these meanings & readings:

píng [萍] **1** duckweed

Although the components here have been subtly altered from the previous panel, nevertheless they somehow suggest that an *apple* is growing in *water*. Although **duckweed** primarily provides nutrition for ducks, like an *apple*, it can also be gathered and eaten by people.

1506

This character with the definition:

s-end: conjecture

Pinyin **hū** *and Frequency Rank* **458**

SIMP & TRAD   Contains **5 strokes** in the following order:

丿㇋几乎乎

Contains these components:

■ eight r ㇑ 1260, p. 282
■ in, at, to 于 20, p. 13

With all these meanings & readings:

hū [乎] **1** (final particle in classical Chinese, expressing question or doubt, similar to 吗 [嗎])

The character 于, an old friend from panel 20, carries an *abundance* of *prepositional meanings*, and makes a reasonable element for this character. So, I hope I can determine your meaning, but you need to **signal** which **conjecture** is correct.

1507

This character with the definition:

exhale

Pinyin **hū** *and Frequency Rank* **843**

SIMP & TRAD   Contains **8 strokes** in the following order:

丨口口口㇆㇆呼呼

Contains these components:

■ mouth 口 37, p. 17
■ s-end: conjecture 乎 1506, p. 333

With all these meanings & readings:

hū [呼] **1** to call **2** to cry **3** to shout **4** to breath out **5** to exhale

We **exhale** puffs of air from our *mouth* as expressions of *surprise* or *doubt*.

1508

This character with the definition:

once, formerly

Pinyin **céng** *and Frequency Rank* **463**

SIMP & TRAD   Contains **12 strokes** in the following order:

丶丷丷丷㕫㕫曽曽曽曾曾

Contains these components:

■ eight r (×2) ㇑ 1260, p. 282
■ day, sun 日 (altered) 64, p. 24
■ day, sun 日 64, p. 24

With all these meanings & readings:

céng [曾] **1** once **2** already **3** former **4** previously **5** (past tense marker used before verb or clause)
zēng [曾] **1** surname Zeng **2** great-grand (father)

In Chinese culture, time is seen as a scroll, with the most recent events appearing on the bottom. In this character, things are currently full of *sun*shine, but up top, in the old days, it was not only *sunny*, but super-*abundantly sunny* (although the *sun* has been turned on its side for artistic purposes). **Formerly** things were much better than they are now.

1509

This character with the definition:

increase, add

Pinyin **zēng** *and Frequency Rank* **446**

SIMP & TRAD   Contains **15 strokes** in the following order:

一十土圹圹圹圹垍增增增增增增增

Contains these components:

■ earth, soil 土 9, p. 11
■ once, formerly 曾 1508, p. 333

With all these meanings & readings:

zēng [增] **1** to increase **2** to expand **3** to add

Formerly, when everyone farmed, people depended solely on the *earth*'s natural fertility to **increase** the yield on their fields.

Unit 63

1510

SIMP & TRAD

This character with the definition:

monk

Pinyin **sēng** *and Frequency Rank* **2013**

Contains **14 strokes** in the following order:

ノ イ イ゙ イ゙ イ゙ 伫 伫 伫 俏 俏 俏 僧 僧 僧

Contains these components:

◼ man r 亻 1156, p. 260
◼ once, formerly 曾 1508, p. 333

With all these meanings & readings:

sēng [僧] **1** monk **2** Sangha, the Buddhist monastic order

Many religions postulate that a soul has multiple lifetimes. This character suggests that a *man's former* life was **as a monk**.

1511

SIMP & TRAD

This character with the definition:

fire

Pinyin **huǒ** *and Frequency Rank* **433**

Contains **4 strokes** in the following order:

丶 丷 少 火

Contains these components:

◼ man 人 537, p. 127
◼ eight r 丷 1260, p. 282

With all these meanings & readings:

huǒ [火] **1** fire **2** m 把[bǎ]

Observe here the visceral reaction of a *man* observing a roaring **fire**—fixed still in surprise, arms raised in awe.

1512

烧
TRAD   SIMPLIFIED

This character with the definition:

burn, cook, run a fever

Pinyin **shāo** *and Frequency Rank* **1201**

Contains **10 strokes** in the following order:

丶 丷 少 火 火 灶 灶 烂 烆 烧

Contains these components:

◼ fire 火 1511, p. 334
◼ legendary emperor 尧 667, p. 157

With all these meanings & readings:

shāo [烧] **1** to burn **2** to cook **3** to stew **4** to bake **5** to roast **6** fever

When the *legendary emperor* died of a dreadful disease, his courtiers used a huge pyre of *fire* to **burn** his body in order to prevent the disease from spreading throughout the court and the country.

1513

煙
TRAD   SIMPLIFIED

This character with the definition:

smoke

Pinyin **yān** *and Frequency Rank* **967**

Contains **10 strokes** in the following order:

丶 丷 少 火 灯 灯 炯 炯 烟 烟

Contains these components:

◼ fire 火 1511, p. 334
◼ because 因 545, p. 129

With all these meanings & readings:

yān [煙] **1** cigarette **2** tobacco **3** smoke **4** m 缕[縷][lǚ], 根[gēn]

There's always **smoke** *because* of *fire*.

1514 灭

滅
TRAD   SIMPLIFIED

This character with the definition:

extinguish

Pinyin **miè** *and Frequency Rank* **953**

Contains **5 strokes** in the following order:

一 ⼀ 二 灭 灭

Contains these components:

◻ one 一 1, p. 10
◼ fire 火 1511, p. 334

With all these meanings & readings:

miè [滅] **1** to extinguish **2** to overthrow (a former regime)

If you put *one* lid on a *fire*, you will **extinguish** it.

1515 **燃** burn, ignite

Pinyin **rán** *and Frequency Rank* **1553**

SIMP & TRAD   Contains **16 strokes** in the following order:

Contains these components:

◻ fire 火 1511, p. 334
◼ -ly 然 1027, p. 233

With all these meanings & readings:

rán [燃] **1** to burn **2** to ignite **3** to light **4** fig. to spark off (hopes) **5** to start (debate) **6** to raise (hopes)

丶 丶 丬 丬 火 灶 灶 灼 燃 燃 燃 燃 燃 燃 燃 燃

When a *fire* flares up sudden*ly* and violent*ly*, it can **ignite** and **burn** everything in sight.

1516 **伙** partner, mate

Pinyin **huǒ** *and Frequency Rank* **1047**

SIMP & TRAD   Contains **6 strokes** in the following order:

Contains these components:

◻ man r 亻 1156, p. 260
◼ fire 火 1511, p. 334

With all these meanings & readings:

huǒ [伙] **1** assistant **2** furniture **3** partner **4** m for a group of people

丿 亻 仃 仃 伙 伙

When a *man* finds his love **partner**, his heart feels as if it is on *fire* with desire.

1517 **光** ray (of light)

Pinyin **guāng** *and Frequency Rank* **290**

SIMP & TRAD   Contains **6 strokes** in the following order:

Contains these components:

◻ fire 火 (altered) 1511, p. 334
◼ walking man r 儿 290, p. 75

With all these meanings & readings:

guāng [光] **1** light **2** ray **3** bright **4** only **5** merely **6** to use up **7** m 道[dào]

丨 丬 ⺌ ⺌ 光 光

This character shows an aspect of *fire* which *travels* (like a *walking man*)— the **rays of light** it emits. Another interpretation: The central horizontal line represents the horizon of the sea, which cuts off part of the setting or rising sun. The curved lines on the bottom show the reflection of the sun's **rays** on the water, and the strokes above are the **rays** of light from the sun itself.

1518 **耀** dazzling

Pinyin **yào** *and Frequency Rank* **1804**

SIMP & TRAD   Contains **20 strokes** in the following order:

Contains these components:

◻ ray (of light) 光 1517, p. 335
◼ long-tailed pheasant 翟 1201, p. 269

With all these meanings & readings:

yào [耀] **1** brilliant **2** glorious

丨 丬 ⺌ ⺌ 光 光 耂 耂 耖 耖 耖 耖 耀 耀 耀 耀 耀 耀 耀 耀

Driving along the country road at night, we came to a sudden stop when we saw the beautiful *long-tailed pheasant* standing in the middle of the road, illuminated by our **dazzling** head*lights*.

1519 **晃** to dazzle

Pinyin **huǎng** *and Frequency Rank* **1796**

SIMP & TRAD   Contains **10 strokes** in the following order:

Contains these components:

◻ day, sun 日 64, p. 24
◼ ray (of light) 光 1517, p. 335

With all these meanings & readings:

huǎng [晃] **1** dazzle
huàng [晃] **1** sway **2** to shade

 丨 冂 冂 日 旦 旱 昇 晃 晃 晃

The *rays* from the *sun* can easily **dazzle** an onlooker.

1520

辉
TRAD SIMPLIFIED

This character with the definition:

brightness, splendor

Pinyin **huī** *and Frequency Rank* **1623**

Contains **12 strokes** in the following order:

丿 亅 ⺌ ⺌ 半 半 米 米 扩 扩 粍 辉 辉

Contains these components:

■ ray (of light) 光 1517, p. 335
■ military 军 1294, p. 289

With all these meanings & readings:

huī [輝] **1** bright **2** glorious

In the old days, people believed *military* victories created a special *light* that brought **splendor** to the reigning monarch.

1521

秋
鞦
TRAD SIMPLIFIED

This character with the definition:

autumn

Pinyin **qiū** *and Frequency Rank* **1151**

Contains **9 strokes** in the following order:

丿 二 千 千 禾 禾 禾 秋 秋

Contains these components:

■ rice, grain (crop) 禾 593, p. 140
■ fire 火 1511, p. 334

With all these meanings & readings:

qiū [秋] **1** autumn **2** fall **3** harvest time **4** a swing **5** surname Qiu
qiū [鞦] **1** a swing

In **autumn**, the leaves, plants, *rice*, and *grain* take on the colors of *fire*.

1522
愁
SIMP & TRAD

This character with the definition:

worry about

Pinyin **chóu** *and Frequency Rank* **2113**

Contains **13 strokes** in the following order:

丿 二 千 千 禾 禾 禾 秋 秋 秋 愁 愁 愁

Contains these components:

■ autumn 秋 1521, p. 336
■ heart (fat) r 心 1096, p. 248

With all these meanings & readings:

chóu [愁] **1** worry about

When I was a child, the arrival of *autumn* meant the start of a new school year, and I would be filled with *emotions* of **worry about** the new term.

1523
炎
SIMP & TRAD

This character with the definition:

scorching hot

Pinyin **yán** *and Frequency Rank* **1324**

Contains **8 strokes** in the following order:

丶 丷 丷 火 火 炎 炎 炎

Contains these components:

■ fire (×2) 火 1511, p. 334

With all these meanings & readings:

yán [炎] **1** flame **2** inflammation **3** -itis

Two fires yield **scorching hot** temperatures.

1524

淡
SIMP & TRAD

This character with the definition:

bland, weak

Pinyin **dàn** *and Frequency Rank* **1293**

Contains **11 strokes** in the following order:

丶 丶 氵 氵 氵 沙 浃 浃 淡 淡 淡

Contains these components:

■ water r 氵 314, p. 80
■ scorching hot 炎 1523, p. 336

With all these meanings & readings:

dàn [淡] **1** insipid **2** diluted **3** weak **4** mild **5** light in color **6** tasteless **7** fresh **8** indifferent **9** nitrogen

If you add too much *scorching hot water* to the teapot, you will brew a cup of **weak** tea.

1525

谈
談
TRAD SIMPLIFIED

This character with the definition:

chat, talk

Pinyin **tán** *and Frequency Rank* **474**

Contains **10 strokes** in the following order:

丶 讠 讠 讠 讣 谈 谈 谈 谈 谈

Contains these components:

■ speech r 讠 352, p. 88
■ scorching hot 炎 1523, p. 336

With all these meanings & readings:

tán [談] **1** to speak **2** to talk **3** to converse **4** to chat **5** to discuss **6** surname Tan

Adolescent girls can **chat** for hours, with long *speeches* filled with *scorching hot* gossip about boys.

1526 烂

爛 TRAD   SIMPLIFIED

This character with the definition:

rot, fester

Pinyin **làn** *and Frequency Rank* **1754**

Contains **9 strokes** in the following order:

丶 丷 丬 火 火 火 灯 烂 烂

Contains these components:

■ fire 火 1511, p. 334

□ orchid 兰 1471, p. 325

With all these meanings & readings:

làn [爛] **1** soft **2** mushy **3** well-cooked and soft **4** to rot **5** to decompose **6** rotten **7** worn out **8** chaotic **9** messy **10** utterly **11** thoroughly

Why would anyone want to cook an *orchid*? Nevertheless, you can imagine that improperly applying *heat* to an *orchid* or other fine flower will accelerate its rate of decay and cause it to **rot**.

1527 灾

災 TRAD   SIMPLIFIED

This character with the definition:

disaster, calamity

Pinyin **zāi** *and Frequency Rank* **1349**

Contains **7 strokes** in the following order:

丶 丷 宀 宀 灾 灾 灾

Contains these components:

□ roof r 宀 271, p. 70

■ fire 火 1511, p. 334

With all these meanings & readings:

zāi [災] **1** disaster **2** calamity

The *roof* is on *fire*! Help us put it out and avoid a **disaster**!

1528 炸

SIMP & TRAD

This character with the definition:

blow up, explode

Pinyin **zhà** *and Frequency Rank* **976**

Contains **9 strokes** in the following order:

丶 丷 丬 火 火 灯 灯 炸 炸

Contains these components:

■ fire 火 1511, p. 334

□ abruptly 乍 447, p. 107

With all these meanings & readings:

zhá [炸] **1** to deep fry
zhà [炸] **1** to explode

Whenever you play with *fire*, something dangerous can occur *abruptly*—including an **explosion**.

1529 烦

煩 TRAD   SIMPLIFIED

This character with the definition:

vexed, annoyed

Pinyin **fán** *and Frequency Rank* **1253**

Contains **10 strokes** in the following order:

丶 丷 丬 火 火 灯 灯 炻 烦 烦

Contains these components:

■ fire 火 1511, p. 334

□ page, leaf 页 1408, p. 312

With all these meanings & readings:

fán [煩] **1** to feel vexed **2** to bother **3** to trouble **4** superfluous and confusing **5** edgy

The homeowner set his *leaves* on *fire*, which created ashes that blew around and greatly **annoyed** his neighbors.

1530 灯

燈 TRAD   SIMPLIFIED

This character with the definition:

lamp, light

Pinyin **dēng** *and Frequency Rank* **1115**

Contains **6 strokes** in the following order:

丶 丷 丬 火 火 灯

Contains these components:

■ fire 火 1511, p. 334

□ fourth (in a series) 丁 19, p. 13

With all these meanings & readings:

dēng [燈] **1** lamp **2** light **3** lantern **4** m 盏 [盞][zhǎn]

It's hard to light a **lamp** in the face of a fierce wind. It took *four* tries to light the *fire*.

1531

SIMP & TRAD

This character with the definition:

coal

Pinyin **méi** *and Frequency Rank* **1740**

Contains **13 strokes** in the following order:

丶 丷 ナ 火 灯 灯 炓 炓 炓 炑 煤 煤 煤

Contains these components:

▮ fire 火 1511, p. 334
▮ certain, some 某 572, p. 135

With all these meanings & readings

méi [煤] **1** coal **2** m 块 [塊][ku...

In the old days, we needed a *certain* something to keep the *fires* well stoked during the winter. That something was **coal**.

1532

砲
TRAD SIMPLIFIED

This character with the definition:

gun, cannon

Pinyin **pào** *and Frequency Rank* **914**

Contains **9 strokes** in the following order:

丶 丷 ナ 火 灯 灼 炲 炮 炮

Contains these components:

▮ fire 火 1511, p. 334
▮ wrap, bag 包 385, p. 95

With all these meanings & readings

pào [炮] **1** gun **2** cannon **3** fir... cracker **4** m 座 [zuò]

Cannon *fire* generates tremendous noise, and the bursting shells *wrap* you in smoke.

1533

靈
TRAD SIMPLIFIED

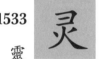

This character with the definition:

clever, sharp

Pinyin **líng** *and Frequency Rank* **734**

Contains **7 strokes** in the following order:

フ ユ ヨ ヨ ヨ 尹 灵

Contains these components:

▯ boar's head r ⼹ 30, p. 16
▮ fire 火 1511, p. 334

With all these meanings & readings

líng [靈] **1** quick **2** alert **3** efficacious **4** effective **5** spirit **6** departed soul **7** coffin

Imagine a scene from your worst nightmare—in front of you is an enraged wild *boar* that is charging directly at you. Behind you rages an out-of-control forest *fire*. What do you do? You'll need every dose of **cleverness** and **sharpness** to escape this pickle.

1534

煉
TRAD SIMPLIFIED

This character with the definition:

smelt, refine

Pinyin **liàn** *and Frequency Rank* **1763**

Contains **9 strokes** in the following order:

丶 丷 ナ 火 灯 灶 烆 烆 炼

Contains these components:

▮ fire 火 1511, p. 334
▮ east 东 (altered) 1288, p. 288

With all these meanings & readings

liàn [煉] **1** refine **2** smelt

The blowing wind forces the *fire* to travel *east*. What a disaster! The *fire* is so hot that it **smelts** the metal in all the houses as it destroys everything in its path.

Unit 64

1535

SIMP & TRAD

This character with the definition:

rice (food)

Pinyin **mǐ** *and Frequency Rank* **575**

Contains **6 strokes** in the following order:

丶 丷 二 半 米 米

Contains these components:

☐ tree 木 562, p.133
☐ eight r ⸜ 1260, p.282

With all these meanings & readings:

mǐ [米] **1** meter (classifier)
2 rice (food) **3** surname Mi
4 m 粒[lì]

The presence of *eight* different strokes in all different directions is supposed to suggest **rice** grains shaken loose from the *stalk* and scattered all over the floor.

1536

粗

SIMP & TRAD

This character with the definition:

coarse

Pinyin **cū** *and Frequency Rank* **1414**

Contains **11 strokes** in the following order:

丶 丷 二 半 米 米 籼 籼 籼 粗 粗

Contains these components:

☐ rice (food) 米 1535, p.339
☐ moreover 且 84, p.28

With all these meanings & readings:

cū [粗] **1** coarse **2** rough **3** thick
4 unfinished **5** vulgar **6** rude
7 crude

A bowl of *rice* is usually served hot. *Moreover*, hot water is required to cook the **coarse** grains. • It is easy to mistake this character 粗 'coarse' with 租 'rent' (panel 594), especially since the left elements of both refer to rice. But 禾 (panel 593) refers to rice crops, portions of which could be remitted as rent. The character 米 (panel 1535) refers to cooked rice, which is definitely not suitable for rent.

1537
糟
蹧
TRAD

糟

SIMPLIFIED

This character with the definition:

a mess

Pinyin **zāo** *and Frequency Rank* **1918**

Contains **17 strokes** in the following order:

丶 丷 二 半 米 米 籿 籼 籼 糟 糟 糟 糟 糟 糟 糟 糟

Contains these components:

☐ rice (food) 米 1535, p.339
☐ medium-sized group of people 曹 97, p.31

With all these meanings & readings:

zāo [糟] **1** dregs **2** to waste
3 spoil
zāo [蹧] **1** to waste **2** spoil

After the wedding, the *medium-sized group* of family and guests threw handfuls of *rice* at the bride and groom as they departed. The festive send off created quite **a mess** in front of the church!

1538

料

SIMP & TRAD

This character with the definition:

stuff

Pinyin **liào** *and Frequency Rank* **557**

Contains **10 strokes** in the following order:

丶 丷 二 半 米 米 米 料 料 料

Contains these components:

☐ rice (food) 米 1535, p.339
☐ cup-shaped 斗 185, p.51

With all these meanings & readings:

liào [料] **1** material **2** stuff
3 grain **4** feed **5** to expect
6 to anticipate **7** to guess

She picked up her **stuff** for dinner, which consisted of a *cup-shaped* portion of *rice for food*.

1539

This character with the definition:

powder

Pinyin **fěn** *and Frequency Rank* **1498**

SIMP & TRAD   Contains **10 strokes** in the following order:

丶 丷 二 斗 斗 米 米 籵 籵 粉 粉

Contains these components:

■ rice (food) 米 1535, p. 339
■ divide, separate 分 1385, p. 308

With all these meanings & readings:

fěn [粉] **1** powder **2** cosmetic face powder **3** food prepared from starch **4** noodles or pasta made from any kind of flour **5** whitewash **6** white **7** pink

If you start with cooked *rice for food* and keep *dividing* it into ever smaller particles, you will eventually end up with mushy **powder**.

1540

類
TRAD   SIMPLIFIED

This character with the definition:

kind, type, class

Pinyin **lèi** *and Frequency Rank* **311**

Contains **9 strokes** in the following order:

丶 丷 二 斗 斗 米 米 类 类

Contains these components:

□ rice (food) 米 1535, p. 339
■ dog 犬 (altered) 673, p. 158

With all these meanings & readings:

lèi [類] **1** kind **2** type **3** class **4** category **5** similar **6** like **7** to resemble

Here are two prototypical **types** of organisms in the vegetable and animal kingdoms: *rice* and blind *dogs* (which is why there are no eyes!).

1541

This character with the definition:

grain, granule, pellet

Pinyin **lì** *and Frequency Rank* **1714**

SIMP & TRAD   Contains **11 strokes** in the following order:

丶 丷 二 斗 斗 米 米 籵 粒 粒 粒

Contains these components:

□ rice (food) 米 1535, p. 339
□ to stand 立 681, p. 160

With all these meanings & readings:

lì [粒] **1** a grain **2** a granule **3** m for small round things (peas, bullets, peanuts, pills, grains, etc.)

Someone threw *rice* on the floor where I was *standing* in my bare feet. I could feel each and every **grain** with my soles.

1542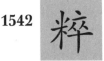

This character with the definition:

pure*, unmixed*

Pinyin **cuì** *and Frequency Rank* **1736**

SIMP & TRAD   Contains **14 strokes** in the following order:

丶 丷 二 斗 斗 米 米 籵 籵 粹 粹 粹 粹 粹

Contains these components:

■ rice (food) 米 1535, p. 339
■ foot soldier 卒 1074, p. 243

With all these meanings & readings:

cuì [粹] **1** pure **2** unmixed **3** essence

The prince (disguised as a *soldier*) went to the wedding. The guests threw *rice* at him, but the grains simply rolled off him because he was so **pure**.

1543

This character with the definition:

sugar, sweets, carbs

Pinyin **táng** *and Frequency Rank* **1746**

SIMP & TRAD   Contains **16 strokes** in the following order:

丶 丷 二 斗 斗 米 米 籵 籵 糖 糖 糖 糖 糖 糖 糖

Contains these components:

■ rice (food) 米 1535, p. 339
■ Tang dynasty 唐 725, p. 170

With all these meanings & readings:

táng [糖] **1** sugar **2** sweets **3** candy **4** m 颗 [顆][kē], 块 [塊][kuài]

In the collective Chinese memory, nothing was **sweeter** than life during the *Tang dynasty*. Back then, Chinese **candy** would be separated into pieces and sprinkled with *rice* flour to keep them from sticking together.

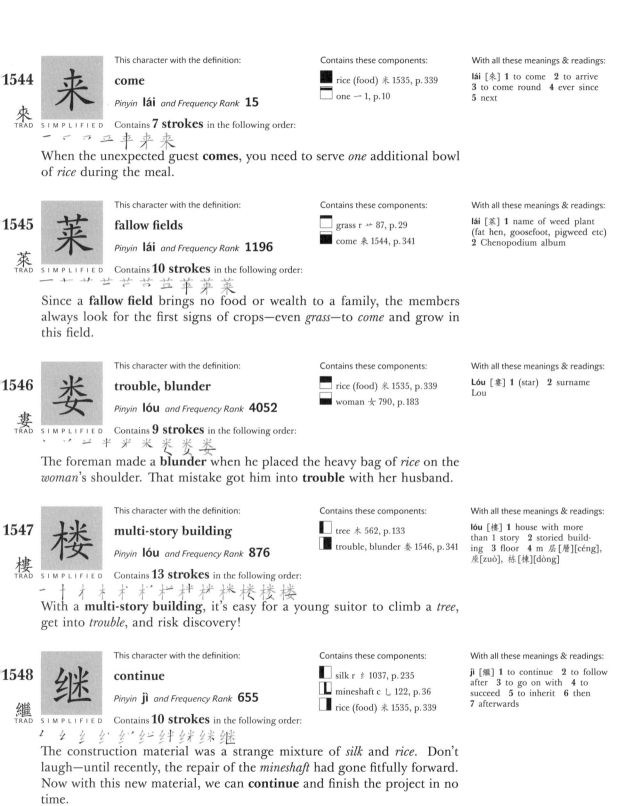

1544 来 来 TRAD SIMPLIFIED

This character with the definition:

come

Pinyin **lái** *and Frequency Rank* **15**

Contains **7 strokes** in the following order:

一 丷 冂 卫 半 来 来

Contains these components:

rice (food) 米 1535, p. 339

one 一 1, p. 10

With all these meanings & readings:

lái [來] **1** to come **2** to arrive **3** to come round **4** ever since **5** next

When the unexpected guest **comes**, you need to serve *one* additional bowl of *rice* during the meal.

1545 莱 莱 TRAD SIMPLIFIED

This character with the definition:

fallow fields

Pinyin **lái** *and Frequency Rank* **1196**

Contains **10 strokes** in the following order:

一 十 艹 芊 芐 苧 苧 苙 莁 莱 莱

Contains these components:

grass r 艹 87, p. 29

come 来 1544, p. 341

With all these meanings & readings:

lái [萊] **1** name of weed plant (fat hen, goosefoot, pigweed etc) **2** Chenopodium album

Since a **fallow field** brings no food or wealth to a family, the members always look for the first signs of crops—even *grass*—to *come* and grow in this field.

1546 娄 婁 TRAD SIMPLIFIED

This character with the definition:

trouble, blunder

Pinyin **lóu** *and Frequency Rank* **4052**

Contains **9 strokes** in the following order:

丶 丷 一 半 半 米 娄 娄 娄

Contains these components:

rice (food) 米 1535, p. 339

woman 女 790, p. 183

With all these meanings & readings:

Lóu [婁] **1** (star) **2** surname Lou

The foreman made a **blunder** when he placed the heavy bag of *rice* on the *woman*'s shoulder. That mistake got him into **trouble** with her husband.

1547 楼 樓 TRAD SIMPLIFIED

This character with the definition:

multi-story building

Pinyin **lóu** *and Frequency Rank* **876**

Contains **13 strokes** in the following order:

一 十 才 木 术 栌 杧 桦 桦 楼 楼 楼 楼

Contains these components:

tree 木 562, p. 133

trouble, blunder 娄 1546, p. 341

With all these meanings & readings:

lóu [樓] **1** house with more than 1 story **2** storied building **3** floor **4** m 层 [層][céng], 座 [zuò], 栋 [棟][dòng]

With a **multi-story building**, it's easy for a young suitor to climb a *tree*, get into *trouble*, and risk discovery!

1548 继 繼 TRAD SIMPLIFIED

This character with the definition:

continue

Pinyin **jì** *and Frequency Rank* **655**

Contains **10 strokes** in the following order:

乙 纟 纟 纟 纩 纩 纤 绀 继 继

Contains these components:

silk r 纟 1037, p. 235

mineshaft c ⼅ 122, p. 36

rice (food) 米 1535, p. 339

With all these meanings & readings:

jì [繼] **1** to continue **2** to follow after **3** to go on with **4** to succeed **5** to inherit **6** then **7** afterwards

The construction material was a strange mixture of *silk* and *rice*. Don't laugh—until recently, the repair of the *mineshaft* had gone fitfully forward. Now with this new material, we can **continue** and finish the project in no time.

1549

断
斷
TRAD   SIMPLIFIED

This character with the definition:

break, snap, cut

Pinyin **duàn** *and Frequency Rank* **434**

Contains **11 strokes** in the following order:

、 ⺍ ⺊ 爿 米 米 斷 斷 断 断 断

Contains these components:

☐ mineshaft c ㄴ (altered) 122, p. 36

☐ rice (food) 米 1535, p. 339

☐ catty 斤 403, p. 98

With all these meanings & readings:

duàn [断] **1** to break **2** to break off **3** to decide **4** to judge **5** (in negative sentences) absolutely **6** definitely **7** decidedly

An axle **snapped** just as the vehicle approached the mine. This caused the whole load of *rice* to fall off the *unbalanced* car and down the *mineshaft*.

1550

金

SIMP & TRAD

This character with the definition:

gold

Pinyin **jīn** *and Frequency Rank* **260**

Contains **8 strokes** in the following order:

丿 入 亼 合 仐 余 余 金

Contains these components:

■ entire 全 540, p. 128

■■ eight r ˅ 1260, p. 282

With all these meanings & readings:

jīn [金] **1** gold **2** metal **3** money **4** the Jurchen Jin dynasty (1115-1234) **5** surname Jin or Kim

In a time of war, you want to transform all your wealth into a form which makes it easy to transport. You choose the solution that worked centuries ago and still works now: convert your *entire* fortune, all of your *abundance*, into **gold**.

1551

针
針
TRAD   SIMPLIFIED

This character with the definition:

needle, pin

Pinyin **zhēn** *and Frequency Rank* **1116**

Contains **7 strokes** in the following order:

丿 卜 ヒ 乍 全 钅 针 针

Contains these components:

■ gold 金 1550, p. 342

■ ten 十 7, p. 11

With all these meanings & readings:

zhēn [针] **1** injection **2** needle **3** pin **4** m 根[gēn], 支[zhī]

In the old days, you needed one *gold* coin to buy *ten* **needles**.

1552

锦
錦
TRAD   SIMPLIFIED

This character with the definition:

brocade

Pinyin **jǐn** *and Frequency Rank* **1947**

Contains **13 strokes** in the following order:

丿 卜 ヒ 乍 全 钅 针 钉 钌 铝 锠 锦 锦

Contains these components:

■ gold 金 1550, p. 342

■ silk 帛 230, p. 61

With all these meanings & readings:

jǐn [锦] **1** brocade **2** embroidered work **3** bright

Brocade is a luxurious fabric made of *silk* shot with *gold* and other shiny metallic threads.

1553

钱
錢
TRAD   SIMPLIFIED

This character with the definition:

money, coins

Pinyin **qián** *and Frequency Rank* **603**

Contains **10 strokes** in the following order:

丿 卜 ヒ 乍 全 钅 钆 钱 钱 钱

Contains these components:

■ gold 金 1550, p. 342

■ tiny, fragmentary 戋 665, p. 157

With all these meanings & readings:

qián [钱] **1** coin **2** money **3** surname Qian **4** m 笔[bǐ][bǐ]

Solid *gold* can be used as **money** when you chop it up into *tiny* **coin**-like pieces.

1554

銳

锐

TRAD   SIMPLIFIED

This character with the definition:

sharp, acute

Pinyin **ruì** *and Frequency Rank* **1851**

Contains these components:

■ gold 金 1550, p. 342

■ exchange, convert 兑 1361, p. 303

With all these meanings & readings:

ruì [銳] **1** acute

Contains **12 strokes** in the following order:

丿 ㇊ ㅌ ㅌ 钅 金 金 钊 钊 钊 锐 锐 锐

A **sharp** businessman is one who can *convert* goods into *golden* profits.

1555

鎮

镇

TRAD   SIMPLIFIED

This character with the definition:

garrison

Pinyin **zhèn** *and Frequency Rank* **1002**

Contains these components:

■ gold 金 1550, p. 342

■ real 真 1379, p. 306

With all these meanings & readings:

zhèn [鎮] **1** composed   **2** small town   **3** to suppress   **4** to press down   **5** to post

Contains **15 strokes** in the following order:

丿 ㇊ ㅌ ㅌ 钅 金 金 钊 钟 钟 锁 镇 镇 镇 镇

Gold only becomes *real* currency at the **garrison** because that's the only place where it can be exchanged for practical goods.

1556

銷

销

TRAD   SIMPLIFIED

This character with the definition:

melt metal

Pinyin **xiāo** *and Frequency Rank* **904**

Contains these components:

■ gold 金 1550, p. 342

■ like, similar to 肖 1309, p. 292

With all these meanings & readings:

xiāo [銷] **1** to melt   **2** to do away with   **3** to sell

Contains **12 strokes** in the following order:

丿 ㇊ ㅌ ㅌ 钅 钊 钊 钊 钊 销 销 销

A kiln will **melt metal** so that distinct pieces of *gold* will emerge looking *like* a single lump of *gold*.

1557

鏡

镜

TRAD   SIMPLIFIED

This character with the definition:

mirror

Pinyin **jìng** *and Frequency Rank* **1251**

Contains these components:

■ gold 金 1550, p. 342

■ in the end 竟 692, p. 162

With all these meanings & readings:

jìng [鏡] **1** mirror

Contains **16 strokes** in the following order:

丿 ㇊ ㅌ ㅌ 钅 金 钊 钊 钊 镗 镗 镜 镜 镜 镜 镜

Even with the help of a **mirror**, it is very difficult for most people to see themselves as who they really are *in the end*—and not to cling to a false image of themselves. The ability to be aware of your true strengths and weaknesses is as valuable as *gold*.

1558

鎖

锁

TRAD   SIMPLIFIED

This character with the definition:

lock up, lock

Pinyin **suǒ** *and Frequency Rank* **1558**

Contains these components:

■ gold 金 1550, p. 342

□ small 小 1262, p. 282

■ cowrie 贝 1394, p. 309

With all these meanings & readings:

suǒ [鎖] **1** to lock up   **2** to lock   **3** m 把[bǎ]

Contains **12 strokes** in the following order:

丿 ㇊ ㅌ ㅌ 钅 钊 钊 钊 钊 锁 锁 锁

The wealthy man **locked up** his *small* collection of rare *shells* in the same safe that contained his *gold*.

1559

鑒
TRAD　SIMPLIFIED

This character with the definition:

reflect, mirror

Pinyin **jiàn** *and Frequency Rank* **1655**

Contains **13 strokes** in the following order:

丨　刂　刂ノ　刂⻌　刂⻌丶　⺊⻌　⺊⻌丶　⺊⻌丶　竖　鉴　鉴　鉴　鉴

Contains these components:

⬛ inspect, supervise 监 (altered) 207, p. 55

⬛ gold 金 1550, p. 342

With all these meanings & readings:

jiàn [鑒] **1** example **2** mirror **3** to view **4** reflection **5** to reflect **6** to inspect **7** to warn **8** (ancient bronze mirror)

Note that in the '*inspect*' portion at the top of this character, the bloody vessel has been abbreviated to a single bloody dot. • If we *inspect* a sheet of *gold*, our image will **reflect** off its surface.

Unit 65

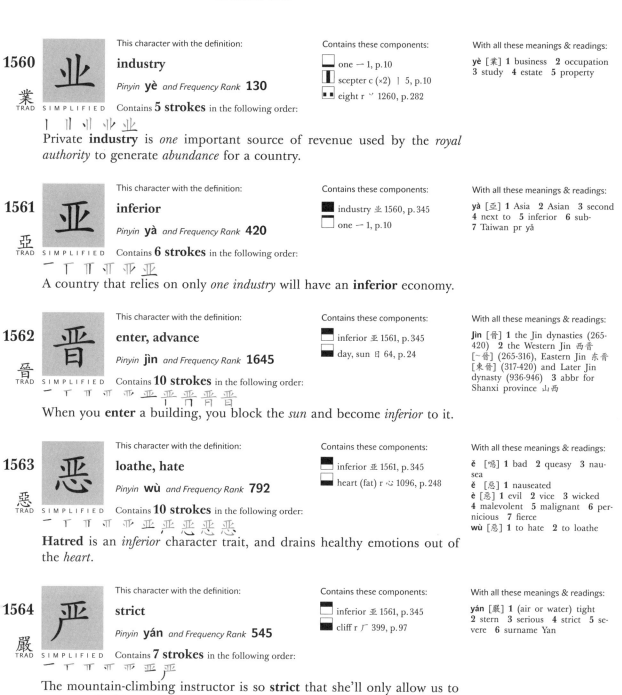

1560
业
業 TRAD SIMPLIFIED

This character with the definition:

industry

Pinyin **yè** *and Frequency Rank* **130**

Contains **5 strokes** in the following order:

丨 丨丨 业业 业

Contains these components:

one 一 1, p.10

scepter c (×2) 丨 5, p.10

eight r ˅ 1260, p.282

With all these meanings & readings:

yè [業] **1** business **2** occupation **3** study **4** estate **5** property

Private **industry** is *one* important source of revenue used by the *royal authority* to generate *abundance* for a country.

1561
亚
亞 TRAD SIMPLIFIED

This character with the definition:

inferior

Pinyin **yà** *and Frequency Rank* **420**

Contains **6 strokes** in the following order:

一 丁 亓 亓 亚 亚

Contains these components:

industry 业 1560, p.345

one 一 1, p.10

With all these meanings & readings:

yà [亞] **1** Asia **2** Asian **3** second **4** next to **5** inferior **6** sub- **7** Taiwan pr yǎ

A country that relies on only *one industry* will have an **inferior** economy.

1562
晋
晉 TRAD SIMPLIFIED

This character with the definition:

enter, advance

Pinyin **jìn** *and Frequency Rank* **1645**

Contains **10 strokes** in the following order:

一 丁 亓 亓 亚 亚 亚 亚 亚 晋
丨 冂 日 晋

Contains these components:

inferior 亚 1561, p.345

day, sun 日 64, p.24

With all these meanings & readings:

Jìn [晉] **1** the Jin dynasties (265-420) **2** the Western Jin 西晋 [～晉] (265-316), Eastern Jin 东晋 [東晉] (317-420) and Later Jin dynasty (936-946) **3** abbr for Shanxi province 山西

When you **enter** a building, you block the *sun* and become *inferior* to it.

1563
恶
惡 TRAD SIMPLIFIED

This character with the definition:

loathe, hate

Pinyin **wù** *and Frequency Rank* **792**

Contains **10 strokes** in the following order:

一 丁 亓 亓 亚 亚 亚 恶 恶 恶

Contains these components:

inferior 亚 1561, p.345

heart (fat) r 心 1096, p.248

With all these meanings & readings:

ě [噁] **1** bad **2** queasy **3** nausea

ě [惡] **1** nauseated

è [惡] **1** evil **2** vice **3** wicked **4** malevolent **5** malignant **6** pernicious **7** fierce

wù [惡] **1** to hate **2** to loathe

Hatred is an *inferior* character trait, and drains healthy emotions out of the *heart*.

1564
严
嚴 TRAD SIMPLIFIED

This character with the definition:

strict

Pinyin **yán** *and Frequency Rank* **545**

Contains **7 strokes** in the following order:

一 丁 亓 亓 亚 亚 严

Contains these components:

inferior 亚 1561, p.345

cliff r 厂 399, p.97

With all these meanings & readings:

yán [嚴] **1** (air or water) tight **2** stern **3** serious **4** strict **5** severe **6** surname Yan

The mountain-climbing instructor is so **strict** that she'll only allow us to attempt climbing *inferior cliffs*.

1565

顯
TRAD SIMPLIFIED

This character with the definition:

be obvious

Pinyin **xiǎn** *and Frequency Rank* **469**

Contains these components:

□ day, sun 日 64, p.24
□ industry 业 1560, p.345

With all these meanings & readings:

xiǎn [顯] **1** prominent **2** conspic uous **3** Greek stem: phanero-

Contains **9 strokes** in the following order:

丶 丨 冂 曰 日 昌 昌 显 显

Most technological advances work by taking an existing technique and expanding upon it. Every so often, someone creates something truly innovative. It's as if someone shines a bright light, bright as the *sun*, on an existing *industry* to discover an unresolved problem which, in hindsight, **appears obvious.** • It's easy to forget whether the 日 component goes above or below in 1565 (显) and 1562 (晋). With 显, the 'sun' goes up top, as befits a guiding light which makes things **obvious**. In 晋, 'enter, advance', it's better to think about how the '日' is a light beckoning us through the doorway through which we enter, and so belongs on the bottom.

1566

濕
TRAD SIMPLIFIED

This character with the definition:

wet, damp

Pinyin **shī** *and Frequency Rank* **1743**

Contains these components:

□ water r 氵 314, p.80
□ be obvious 显 1565, p.346

With all these meanings & readings:

shī [濕] **1** moist **2** wet

Contains **12 strokes** in the following order:

丶 丶 氵 氵 沪 沪 泪 浭 湿 湿 湿 湿

When a silk dress gets **wet**, the spot where the *water* dropped is *obvious*.

1567

SIMP & TRAD

This character with the definition:

to esteem

Pinyin **shàng** *and Frequency Rank* **878**

Contains these components:

□ eight r ⸯ 1260, p.282
□ to face 向 (altered) 282, p.72

With all these meanings & readings:

shàng [尚] **1** still **2** yet **3** to value **4** to esteem **5** surname Shang

Contains **8 strokes** in the following order:

丨 丷 屵 屵 尚 尚 尚 尚

The student holds his professor in such high **esteem** that he seeks *to face* his professor an *abundance* of times.

1568

SIMP & TRAD

This character with the definition:

special room

Pinyin **táng** *and Frequency Rank* **980**

Contains these components:

□ to esteem 尚 1567, p.346
□ earth, soil 土 9, p.11

With all these meanings & readings:

táng [堂] **1** (main) hall **2** large room for a specific purpose **3** r lationship between cousins etc on the paternal side of a family **4** of the same clan **5** m for sets (or suites) of furniture, classes e **6** m 间 [間][jiān]

Contains **11 strokes** in the following order:

丨 丷 屵 屵 尚 尚 尚 堂 堂 堂 堂

A **special room** that you *esteem* is apt to be treated as a special place on *earth*.

1569

掌
SIMP & TRAD

This character with the definition:

palm (of hand)

Pinyin **zhǎng** *and Frequency Rank* **890**

Contains these components:

□ to esteem 尚 1567, p.346
□ hand 手 21, p.14

With all these meanings & readings:

zhǎng [掌] **1** in charge of **2** pal of hand

Contains **12 strokes** in the following order:

丨 丷 屵 屵 尚 尚 尚 堂 堂 堂 掌

Applause is the special noise made by clapping the **palms** of your *hands* together, which demonstrates your level of *esteem*.

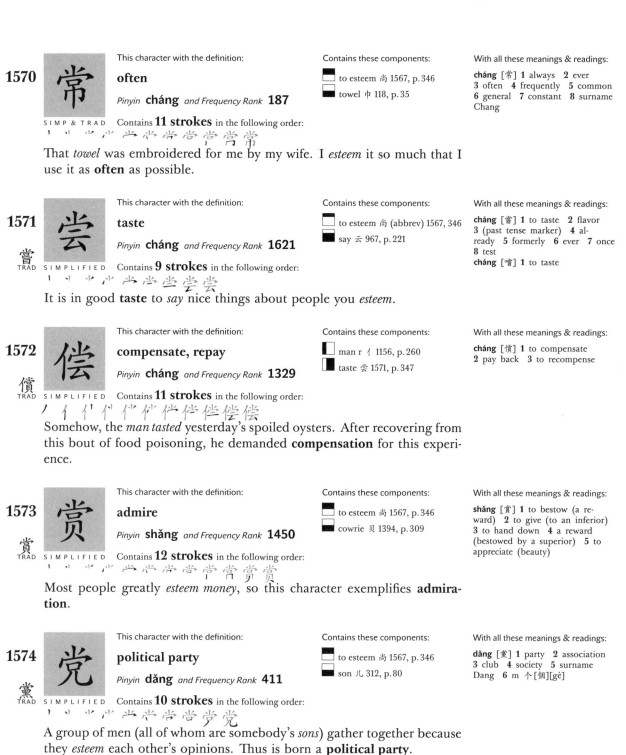

1570

常

SIMP & TRAD

This character with the definition:

often

Pinyin **cháng** *and Frequency Rank* **187**

Contains **11 strokes** in the following order:

丨丷丷丷丷当当常常常常

Contains these components:

☐ to esteem 尚 1567, p. 346
☐ towel 巾 118, p. 35

With all these meanings & readings:

cháng [常] **1** always **2** ever **3** often **4** frequently **5** common **6** general **7** constant **8** surname Chang

That *towel* was embroidered for me by my wife. I *esteem* it so much that I use it as **often** as possible.

1571

尝

嘗
TRAD   SIMPLIFIED

This character with the definition:

taste

Pinyin **cháng** *and Frequency Rank* **1621**

Contains **9 strokes** in the following order:

丨丷丷丷当当尝尝尝

Contains these components:

☐ to esteem 尚 (abbrev) 1567, 346
☐ say 云 967, p. 221

With all these meanings & readings:

cháng [嘗] **1** to taste **2** flavor **3** (past tense marker) **4** already **5** formerly **6** ever **7** once **8** test
cháng [嚐] **1** to taste

It is in good **taste** to *say* nice things about people you *esteem*.

1572

偿

償
TRAD   SIMPLIFIED

This character with the definition:

compensate, repay

Pinyin **cháng** *and Frequency Rank* **1329**

Contains **11 strokes** in the following order:

丿亻亻亻伫伫伫偿偿偿偿

Contains these components:

☐ man r 亻 1156, p. 260
☐ taste 尝 1571, p. 347

With all these meanings & readings:

cháng [償] **1** to compensate **2** pay back **3** to recompense

Somehow, the *man tasted* yesterday's spoiled oysters. After recovering from this bout of food poisoning, he demanded **compensation** for this experience.

1573

赏

賞
TRAD   SIMPLIFIED

This character with the definition:

admire

Pinyin **shǎng** *and Frequency Rank* **1450**

Contains **12 strokes** in the following order:

丨丷丷丷当当常常常赏赏赏

Contains these components:

☐ to esteem 尚 1567, p. 346
☐ cowrie 贝 1394, p. 309

With all these meanings & readings:

shǎng [賞] **1** to bestow (a reward) **2** to give (to an inferior) **3** to hand down **4** a reward (bestowed by a superior) **5** to appreciate (beauty)

Most people greatly *esteem money*, so this character exemplifies **admiration**.

1574

党

黨
TRAD   SIMPLIFIED

This character with the definition:

political party

Pinyin **dǎng** *and Frequency Rank* **411**

Contains **10 strokes** in the following order:

丨丷丷丷当当常常党党

Contains these components:

☐ to esteem 尚 1567, p. 346
☐ son 儿 312, p. 80

With all these meanings & readings:

dǎng [黨] **1** party **2** association **3** club **4** society **5** surname Dang **6** m 个[個][gè]

A group of men (all of whom are somebody's *sons*) gather together because they *esteem* each other's opinions. Thus is born a **political party**.

1575

This character with the definition:

lie down

Pinyin **tǎng** *and Frequency Rank* **1608**

SIMP & TRAD — Contains **15 strokes** in the following order:

Contains these components:

body 身 529, p.125
to esteem 尚 1567, p.346

With all these meanings & readings:

tǎng [躺] **1** to recline **2** to lie down

The athlete *esteems* his *body*, so he makes sure to **lie down** and get rest after each of his workouts.

1576

This character with the definition:

if, in case

Pinyin **tǎng** *and Frequency Rank* **2118**

SIMP & TRAD — Contains **10 strokes** in the following order:

Contains these components:

man r 亻 1156, p.260
to esteem 尚 1567, p.346

With all these meanings & readings:

tǎng [倘] **1** if **2** supposing **3** in case

The *man* on the left is short-hand for all things human—affairs, events, possessions, and so on. The '*still, yet*' component implies division. For human affairs, the division is between reality and imagination or between what has happened and not (yet) happened—in other words, the same relation as determined by **if** or **in case of**.

1577

This character with the definition:

black

Pinyin **hēi** *and Frequency Rank* **519**

SIMP & TRAD — Contains **12 strokes** in the following order:

Contains these components:

neighborhood 里 (altered) 40, p.18
eight r ⌄ 1260, p.282
fire r 灬 1026, p.233

With all these meanings & readings:

hēi [黑] **1** black **2** dark **3** abbr for Heilongjiang 黑龙江 [~龍~] province in northeast China

Fire has utterly ravaged the *neighborhood* and the evidence of devastation is *abundant*. Everything has either been burned **black** or is covered in **black** ash.

1578

This character with the definition:

ink, ink stick

Pinyin **mò** *and Frequency Rank* **1493**

SIMP & TRAD — Contains **15 strokes** in the following order:

Contains these components:

black 黑 1577, p.348
earth, soil 土 9, p.11

With all these meanings & readings:

mò [墨] **1** ink stick **2** China ink **3** corporal punishment consisting of carving and inking characters on the victim's forehead **4** abbr for 墨西哥 Mexico **5** m 块 [塊][kuài]

Scribes ground *black* material from the *earth* to make their **ink**.

1579

This character with the definition:

silent, keep silent

Pinyin **mò** *and Frequency Rank* **1031**

SIMP & TRAD — Contains **16 strokes** in the following order:

Contains these components:

black 黑 1577, p.348
dog 犬 673, p.158

With all these meanings & readings:

mò [默] **1** silent **2** write from memory

Since our *black dog* remained **silent** during last night's burglary, we suspect that he must have known the culprit.

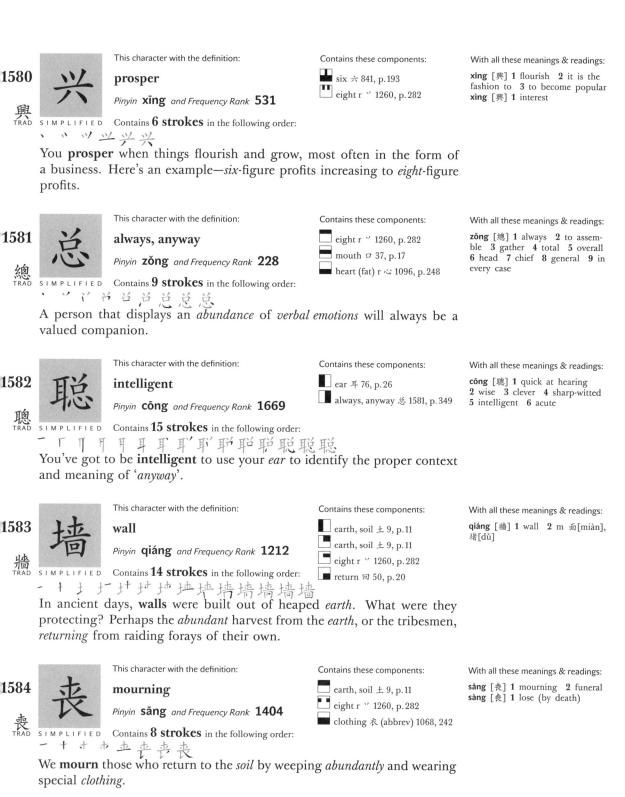

1580 兴

興 TRAD   SIMPLIFIED

This character with the definition:

prosper

Pinyin **xīng** *and Frequency Rank* **531**

Contains **6 strokes** in the following order:

丶 ⺍ ⺍ ⺍ 兴 兴

Contains these components:

六 six 六 841, p. 193

⼋ eight r ⺍ 1260, p. 282

With all these meanings & readings:

xīng [興] **1** flourish **2** it is the fashion to **3** to become popular
xìng [興] **1** interest

You **prosper** when things flourish and grow, most often in the form of a business. Here's an example—*six*-figure profits increasing to *eight*-figure profits.

1581 总

總 TRAD   SIMPLIFIED

This character with the definition:

always, anyway

Pinyin **zǒng** *and Frequency Rank* **228**

Contains **9 strokes** in the following order:

丶 ⺍ ⼇ 台 台 台 总 总 总

Contains these components:

⼋ eight r ⺍ 1260, p. 282

口 mouth 口 37, p. 17

心 heart (fat) r 心 1096, p. 248

With all these meanings & readings:

zǒng [總] **1** always **2** to assemble **3** gather **4** total **5** overall **6** head **7** chief **8** general **9** in every case

A person that displays an *abundance* of *verbal emotions* will always be a valued companion.

1582 聪

聰 TRAD   SIMPLIFIED

This character with the definition:

intelligent

Pinyin **cōng** *and Frequency Rank* **1669**

Contains **15 strokes** in the following order:

一 丆 冂 冂 月 耳 耳 耳' 耶' 耶 聡 聡 聪 聪 聪

Contains these components:

耳 ear 耳 76, p. 26

总 always, anyway 总 1581, p. 349

With all these meanings & readings:

cōng [聰] **1** quick at hearing **2** wise **3** clever **4** sharp-witted **5** intelligent **6** acute

You've got to be **intelligent** to use your *ear* to identify the proper context and meaning of '*anyway*'.

1583 墙

牆 TRAD   SIMPLIFIED

This character with the definition:

wall

Pinyin **qiáng** *and Frequency Rank* **1212**

Contains **14 strokes** in the following order:

一 十 土 土' 圤 圤 圤 垆 墙 墙 墙 墙 墙 墙

Contains these components:

土 earth, soil 土 9, p. 11

土 earth, soil 土 9, p. 11

⼋ eight r ⺍ 1260, p. 282

回 return 回 50, p. 20

With all these meanings & readings:

qiáng [牆] **1** wall **2** m 面[miàn], 堵[dǔ]

In ancient days, **walls** were built out of heaped *earth*. What were they protecting? Perhaps the *abundant* harvest from the *earth*, or the tribesmen, *returning* from raiding forays of their own.

1584 丧

喪 TRAD   SIMPLIFIED

This character with the definition:

mourning

Pinyin **sāng** *and Frequency Rank* **1404**

Contains **8 strokes** in the following order:

一 十 十 ⼟ 圭 尭 尭 丧

Contains these components:

土 earth, soil 土 9, p. 11

⼋ eight r ⺍ 1260, p. 282

衣 clothing 衣 (abbrev) 1068, 242

With all these meanings & readings:

sāng [喪] **1** mourning **2** funeral
sàng [喪] **1** lose (by death)

We **mourn** those who return to the *soil* by weeping *abundantly* and wearing special *clothing*.

Additional Resources *Interlude 5*

This interlude describes resources that we've gathered at the time this book was prepared. We're always adding fresh material so we urge you to check back often to see what's new.

If you're not a flashcard person, or if flashcards are impractical for you (let's face it, they require a substantial outlay of resources: either a smart phone and computer for e-files, or the time and expense to prepare print versions), you might prefer to review words on a unit-by-unit basis. You can view this material (and use it) on your computer, or easily and affordably print out bits on an as-needed basis.

The file **EZCsimpshuffles.pdf** contains several types of listings, each in two columns. Some of the pages are labeled '**Characters to Definitions**' because the unit's characters (on the left) are paired to their definition and pinyin pronunciation (on the right). You can print or preview each of these files and use them to reinforce character meanings.

Other pages, headed '**Definitions to Characters**', ask you to supply the forms of the characters when you read the definition/pinyin pair on the left.

But after you have done this a couple of times, how can you truly be sure that you're practicing the characters properly? You might only have been memorizing the order in which the characters appear on the page.

For that reason, we present several "shuffle" lists. For each shuffle list, the order of character presentation in one shuffle is completely different from that of any other shuffle. It's harder to remember the order in which characters are presented in successive shuffles, so you are more likely to see results in the effectiveness of this review method if you use all the different shuffles when you practice.

It's easy to work with these lists because there are a variety of ways to preview them. And if you feel like printing them, you can do so using any printer and any kind of paper. Please note, however, that all this reviewing is done on a unit-by-unit basis only; there's no effective way to review across unit groups with this material as there is with the Anki smart flashcard decks. This end-of-unit review material, used in conjunction with the graded reading practice file (see below), may be as good as using electronic flashcards.

If you regularly review earlier characters along with those in your current unit, here's how to really ensure that you will achieve great progress: You'll find the graded reading file, **EZCsimprdr.pdf**, on our website. It uses Chinese phrases and words formed from your current crop of glyphs along with their predecessors. While you *can* print this large file (equivalent to more than 900 printed pages), it will almost surely be more convenient to view it onscreen with a viewer such as Adobe Acrobat, or another comparable program. (On my Mac, for instance, I use two programs, **Skim** and **TEXShop**, but there are many others so you can use whichever works on your computer platform.)

Entries in this *graded reading file* are keyed to the panels of this book. The entries consist of valid words, phrases, idioms, fixed expressions, and transliterations that use only the current character together with other characters that have already appeared in earlier panels. One can't readily

Unit Review Material

Unit 28: Shuffle 1 (Characters to Definitions)

弋   **kind of arrow** (yì) (Page 156 Panel 647)
模   **model, imitation** (mó) (Page 155 Panel 644)
试   **test, try** (shì) (Page 156 Panel 649)
摸   **grope, touch** (mō) (Page 155 Panel 642)
战   **war** (zhàn) (Page 157 Panel 652)
减   **lower, reduce** (jiǎn) (Page 158 Panel 656)
椅   **chair** (yǐ) (Page 155 Panel 640)
戈   **halberd** (gē) (Page 157 Panel 650)
漢   **desert** (mò) (Page 156 Panel 645)
骑   **ride, sit astride** (qí) (Page 154 Panel 639)
戊   **fifth (in a series)** (wù) (Page 157 Panel 653)
幕   **stage curtain** (mù) (Page 155 Panel 643)
棉   **cotton** (mián) (Page 154 Panel 636)
莫   **do not, not** (mò) (Page 155 Panel 641)
寄   **send, mail, consign** (jì) (Page 154 Panel 638)
找   **seek** (zhǎo) (Page 157 Panel 651)
喊   **cry out** (hǎn) (Page 158 Panel 655)
柯   **ax handle** (kē) (Page 154 Panel 635)
咸   **all, everyone** (xián) (Page 157 Panel 654)
式   **model, standard** (shì) (Page 156 Panel 648)
城   **city wall, wall** (chéng) (Page 158 Panel 658)
奇   **odd** (jī) (Page 154 Panel 637)
墓   **tomb** (mù) (Page 156 Panel 646)

Graded Reading Practice for Hoenig's 'Traditional Chinese Characters'

230 雨 **[yǔ]** 1. rain 2. CL:陣 [zhèn], 場 [cháng]
雨山 **[yǔ shān]** Yushan district of Ma'anshan city 马鞍山市 [mǎ ān shān shì], Anhui
雨量 **[yǔ liàng]** rainfall
冒雨 **[mào yǔ]** to brave the rain
雨山區 **[yǔ shān qū]** Yushan district of Ma'anshan city 马鞍山市 [mǎ ān shān shì], Anhui
血雨 **[xuè yǔ]** 1. rain of blood 2. heavy rain colored by loess sandstorm
毛毛雨 **[máo máo yǔ]** 1. drizzle 2. light rain
下雨 **[xià yǔ]** rainy

231 雪 **[xuě]** 1. snow 2. CL:場 [cháng]
申雪 **[shēn xuě]** 1. to right a wrong 2. to redress an injustice
瑞雪 **[ruì xuě]** timely snow
雪鞋 **[xuě xié]** 1. snowshoes 2. CL:雙 [shuāng]
下雪 **[xià xuě]** to snow
白雪 **[bái xuě]** white snow
雪白 **[xuě bái]** snow white

232 需 **[xū]** 1. to require 2. to need 3. to want 4. necessity 5. need
特需 **[tè xū]** 1. special need 2. particular requirement

233 霝 **[líng]** 1. drops of rain 2. to fall in drops

234 雷 **[léi]** surname Lei
雷 **[léi]** 1. thunder 2. (internet slang) terrifying 3. terrific
雷山 **[léi shān]** Leishan county in Qiandongnan Miao and Dong autonomous prefecture 黔东南州 [qián dōng nán zhōu], Guizhou
手雷 **[shǒu léi]** grenade
排雷 **[pái léi]** mine clearance
打雷 **[dǎ léi]** thunder
雷轟 **[léi hōng]** sound of thunder
掃雷 **[sǎo léi]** minesweeper (computer game)
地雷 **[dì léi]** landmine
弗雷 **[fú léi]** Freyr (god in Norse mythology)
雷雨 **[léi yǔ]** thunderstorm

235 電 **[diàn]** 1. electric 2. electricity 3. electrical
電工 **[diàn gōng]** electrician
手電 **[shǒu diàn]** 1. flashlight 2. torch
電子 **[diàn zǐ]** 1. electronic 2. electron
電打 **[dian4 da3]** electric typewriter (as opposed to hand typewriter), abbr. for 電打字機
回電 **[huí diàn]** 1. to reply to a telegram 2. to wire back
日電 **[Rì diàn4]** 1. NEC (Nippon Electronic Company) 2. abbr. for 日電電子
電車 **[diàn chē]** 1. trolleybus 2. CL:輛 [liàng]

(Top) Part of a typical page from the file EZCsimpshuffles.pdf. **(Bottom)** A portion of EZCsimprdr.pdf.

predict which predecessors will appear with a particular character, so you get to practice characters from earlier units. This material was compiled with the excellent dictionary word file CC-CEDICT, available for free online.

Can you think of other learning materials that you'd like to have access to? Feel free to drop us a line with any suggestions and any other comments that you may have as you work through our materials. (There is no guarantee that we'll provide it, but we promise to review all the feedback we receive.)

I'd like to conclude this interlude with a word about other materials that are available on the Web for learning Chinese, much of them free, too. There has been an explosive proliferation of these resources, and I encourage you to explore this cornucopia for yourself. Of particular interest are resources that lend themselves to EZChinesey materials, so please take note. There are several series of Chinese lessons produced by Chinese Central TV (english.cntv.cn). Many of these programs include the scripts that you can follow for additional reading practice, and they use the simplified character set that we present in this volume. Additional material, not as extensive, has been made available by the National Taiwan Normal University, but these materials use traditional characters. For further information, you can visit www.coolchinese.com. You can also enter 'ntnu + online + chinese' into your favorite search engine for even more resources.

Unit 66

1585

券

SIMP & TRAD

This character with the definition:

ticket, certificate

Pinyin **quàn** *and Frequency Rank* **1481**

Contains **8 strokes** in the following order:

丶 丷 二 兰 半 关 券 券

Contains these components:

eight r 丷 1260, p. 282

man (spiffy) 夫 718, p. 168

knife 刀 469, p. 112

With all these meanings & readings:

quàn [券] **1** deed **2** bond **3** contract **4** ticket

Tickets to the rock concert are all sold out so some thug has approached a *man* for his **tickets**; watch as the *drops* of sweat fly off his face. The mugger uses a *knife* to rob the *man* of his **tickets**.

1586

单

單
TRAD

SIMPLIFIED

This character with the definition:

single, sole

Pinyin **dān** *and Frequency Rank* **389**

Contains **8 strokes** in the following order:

丶 丷 丷 丷 严 肖 苗 单

Contains these components:

eight r 丷 1260, p. 282

first (in a series) 甲 39, p. 18

one 一 1, p. 10

With all these meanings & readings:

dān [單] **1** see 单于 [單~][chán yú]
dān [單] **1** bill **2** list **3** form **4** single **5** only **6** sole **7** odd number **8** m 个 [個][gè]
shàn [單] **1** surname Shan

Up until I was four years old, I was my parents' **sole** child and was treated like a princess. Then a second child was born, followed by a third *one* a year later. I had to accept that I was only the *first in a series* of a *great many* children.

1587

弹

彈
TRAD

SIMPLIFIED

This character with the definition:

pluck, play (an instrument)

Pinyin **tán** *and Frequency Rank* **632**

Contains **11 strokes** in the following order:

乛 ㄱ 弓 弘 弘 弹 弹 弹 弹 弹 弹

Contains these components:

bow (weapon) 弓 140, p. 40

single, sole 单 1586, p. 353

With all these meanings & readings:

dàn [彈] **1** crossball **2** bullet **3** shot **4** shell **5** ball
tán [彈] **1** impeach **2** to pluck a string **3** to play (a stringed musical instrument with fingers) **4** to snap

A tight string is the *single* item that's shared between a warrior's *bow* and musician's guitar; note, however, that one is pulled while the other is **plucked**.

1588

兽

獸
TRAD

SIMPLIFIED

This character with the definition:

wild beast

Pinyin **shòu** *and Frequency Rank* **1602**

Contains **11 strokes** in the following order:

丶 丷 丷 丷 肖 肖 鲁 单 单 兽 兽

Contains these components:

eight r 丷 1260, p. 282

field 田 63, p. 23

one 一 1, p. 10

mouth 口 37, p. 17

With all these meanings & readings:

shòu [獸] **1** beast **2** quadruped

There's an *abundance* of **wild beasts** in the *field*. *One* of them spotted me and immediately threatened me with its open *mouth*.

1589

夾
TRAD   SIMPLIFIED

This character with the definition:

place between

Pinyin **jiā**   and Frequency Rank **1758**

Contains **6 strokes** in the following order:

一 ニ ゴ 夹 夹 夹

Contains these components:

🔲 man (spiffy) 夫 718, p. 168

🔲 eight r (×2) ˅ 1260, p. 282

With all these meanings & readings

jiā [夾] **1** to press from either side **2** to place in between **3** sandwich **4** to carry sth under armpit **5** wedged between **6** b tween **7** to intersperse **8** to m **9** to mingle **10** clip **11** folder
jiá [夾] **1** hold between **2** lined 3 narrow lane

This character illustrates itself in two ways: (1) 夫 is between the two dabs of '*eight r*', and (2) these dabs are **between** the two horizontals of 夫. Metaphorically, *people* create *abundance*, and *abundance* creates *people*.

1590

俠
TRAD   SIMPLIFIED

This character with the definition:

heroic

Pinyin **xiá**   and Frequency Rank **1216**

Contains **8 strokes** in the following order:

ノ 亻 仁 仃 仃 侊 侠 侠

Contains these components:

🔲 man r 亻 1156, p. 260

🔲 place between 夹 1589, p. 354

With all these meanings & readings

xiá [俠] **1** knight-errant **2** brave and chivalrous **3** hero **4** heroi

Men placed in between two life threatening events often behave **heroically**.

1591

峽
TRAD   SIMPLIFIED

This character with the definition:

gorge, canyon

Pinyin **xiá**   and Frequency Rank **1727**

Contains **9 strokes** in the following order:

丨 山 山 山一 山一 山竹 山一 峡 峡

Contains these components:

🔲 mountain 山 4, p. 10

🔲 place between 夹 1589, p. 354

With all these meanings & readings

xiá [峽] **1** gorge

To early explorers, **gorges** and **canyons** were picturesque valleys nestled *between mountains*.

1592

蓋
TRAD   SIMPLIFIED

This character with the definition:

cover

Pinyin **gài**   and Frequency Rank **1052**

Contains **11 strokes** in the following order:

丶 ⋎ ⊻ 兰 羊 羊 羊 盖 盖 盖 盖

Contains these components:

🔲 eight r ˅ 1260, p. 282

🔲 king 王 15, p. 12

🔲 vessel, container 皿 101, p. 32

With all these meanings & readings

gài [蓋] **1** lid **2** top **3** cover **4** canopy **5** to build
gě [蓋] **1** surname Ge

The silversmith created a **cover** for the costly *vessel* that featured *several kings* cavorting in strange costumes.

1593

關
TRAD   SIMPLIFIED

This character with the definition:

shut, close

Pinyin **guān**   and Frequency Rank **127**

Contains **6 strokes** in the following order:

丶 ⋎ ⊻ 兰 关 关

Contains these components:

🔲 eight r ˅ 1260, p. 282

🔲 heaven 天 548, p. 129

With all these meanings & readings

guān [關] **1** mountain pass **2** t close **3** to shut **4** to turn off **5** to concern **6** to involve **7** surname Guan

Dealing with the public in a busy store is stressful. By the time the day ends, you've had it. Once you lock up and **close** the store, the tranquility feels *a lot* like *heaven*.

1594

聯
TRAD SIMPLIFIED

This character with the definition:

allied (forces), joint (effort)

Pinyin **lián** and Frequency Rank **356**

Contains **12 strokes** in the following order:

一 厂 厂 丌 月 耳 耳 耴 耴' 耴¯ 联 联

Contains these components:

■ ear 耳 76, p. 26
□ shut, close 关 1593, p. 354

With all these meanings & readings:

lián [聯] **1** to ally **2** to unite **3** to join

Nobody's perfect, so when you **ally** yourself with someone, you *shut* your *ears* to their negative qualities.

1595

鄭
TRAD SIMPLIFIED

This character with the definition:

serious, earnest

Pinyin **zhèng** and Frequency Rank **1132**

Contains **8 strokes** in the following order:

丶 ⺍ 丷 ⺀ 关 关 郑

Contains these components:

■ shut, close 关 1593, p. 354
□ town r 阝955, p. 219

With all these meanings & readings:

Zhèng [鄭] **1** surname Zheng

On New Year's Eve, the whole *town* was *closed* for some **serious** partying.

1596

兰

This component has the meaning:

tributaries c

COMPONENT

And contains these subcomponents:

■ eight r ⸍ 1260, p. 282
□ one 一 1, p. 10

The converging lines suggest an *abundance* of water flowing into *one* main river. These represent **tributaries**.

1597

豆
荳
TRAD SIMPLIFIED

This character with the definition:

bean

Pinyin **dòu** and Frequency Rank **1793**

Contains **7 strokes** in the following order:

一 丆 戸 吉 豆 豆 豆

Contains these components:

□ one 一 1, p. 10
■ mouth 口 37, p. 17
■ tributaries c 兰 1596, p. 355

With all these meanings & readings:

dòu [荳] **1** bean **2** peas **3** m 棵[kē], 粒[lì]
dòu [豆] **1** bean **2** sacrificial vessel

This slightly surreal image is intended to represent a bowl of steaming **beans**, with the bottom '*tributaries*' representing the table top and the profile of the bowl. A more realistic perspective would have the *mouth* of the bowl slanted more elliptically. The small horizontal that is at the top of the character suggests the abundance of beans in the bowl or perhaps rising steam.

1598

短
SIMP & TRAD

This character with the definition:

short, brief

Pinyin **duǎn** and Frequency Rank **889**

Contains **12 strokes** in the following order:

丿 ㇉ 匸 チ 矢 矢¯ 知¯ 知 短 短 短 短

Contains these components:

■ arrow 矢 552, p. 130
□ bean 豆 1597, p. 355

With all these meanings & readings:

duǎn [短] **1** lack **2** short

The expert archer honed his accuracy by aiming his **short** arrows at the dead center of his target, which is the size of a *bean*.

1599 首

SIMP & TRAD

This character with the definition:

head, leader

Pinyin **shǒu** and Frequency Rank **481**

Contains these components:

tributaries c ⺌ 1596, p. 355

self 自 232, p. 61

With all these meanings & readings

shǒu [首] **1** head **2** chief **3** fir (occasion, thing etc) **4** m for poems, songs etc

Contains **9 strokes** in the following order:

丶 丷 丷 ﾄ 产 产 首 首 首

The lines of the '*tributaries*' element reminds me of the hair on my **head**, which stands up in all directions when I look at my*self* in the mirror each morning.

1600 前

SIMP & TRAD

This character with the definition:

before, in front of

Pinyin **qián** and Frequency Rank **93**

Contains these components:

tributaries c ⺌ 1596, p. 355

boat 舟 (altered) 822, p. 189

knife r 刂 169, p. 46

With all these meanings & readings

qián [前] **1** before **2** in front **3** ago **4** former **5** previous **6** earlier **7** front **8** prefixed word denoting respect (polite 美称); foremost; premier

Contains **9 strokes** in the following order:

丶 丷 丷 产 产 前 前 前 前

The prow of the sailing *boat* in the *tributary* is as sharp as a *knife*. The thing about sailboats is they only travel one way—in the direction **in front of** the bow.

1601 箭

SIMP & TRAD

This character with the definition:

arrow*

Pinyin **jiàn** and Frequency Rank **1496**

Contains these components:

bamboo r ⺮ 264, p. 68

before, in front of 前 1600, p. 356

With all these meanings & readings

jiàn [箭] **1** arrow **2** m 支[zhī]

Contains **15 strokes** in the following order:

丿 ⺮ ⺮ ⺮ 竹 竹 竹 竹 箁 箁 箁 箁 箁 箭 箭

The *bamboo* **arrows** of the master archer flew swiftly *in front of* the advancing army.

1602 壴

This component has the meaning:

drumroll c

COMPONENT

And contains these subcomponents:

ten 十 7, p. 11

bean 豆 1597, p. 355

Ten beans artfully and forcefully thrown down against the skin of a drum creates sounds similar to a **drumroll**.

1603 喜

SIMP & TRAD

This character with the definition:

like, happy

Pinyin **xǐ** and Frequency Rank **668**

Contains these components:

drumroll c 壴 1602, p. 356

mouth 口 37, p. 17

With all these meanings & readings

xǐ [喜] **1** to be fond of **2** to like **3** to enjoy **4** to be happy **5** to feel pleased **6** happiness **7** delight **8** glad

Contains **12 strokes** in the following order:

一 十 士 圭 吉 吉 吉 吉 壴 壴 喜 喜

It's easy to tell when a child is **happy**. The constant chatter from his or her *mouth* sounds like an ever present *drumroll*!

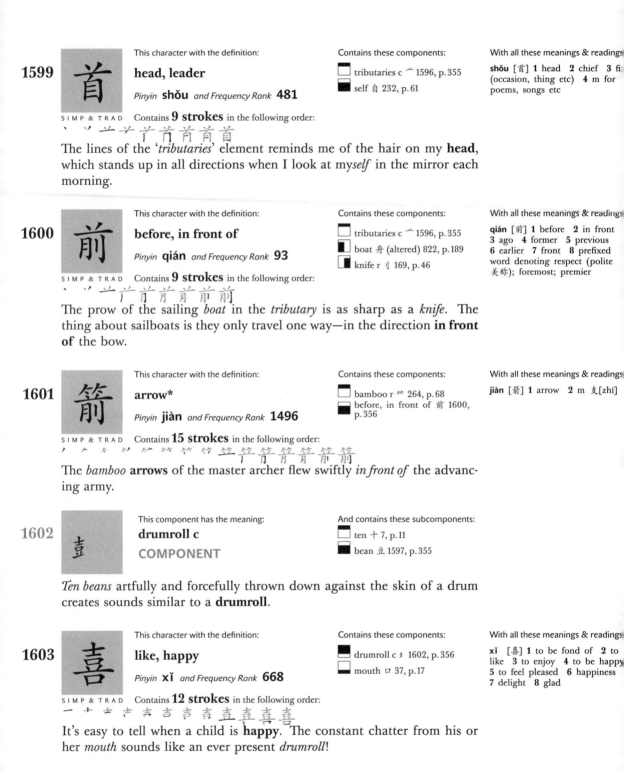

604 嘻

SIMP & TRAD

This character with the definition:

giggle

Pinyin **xī** *and Frequency Rank* **2432**

Contains **15 strokes** in the following order:

Contains these components:

mouth 口 37, p.17

like, happy 喜 1603, p.356

With all these meanings & readings:

xī [嘻] **1** laugh   **2** giggle

丨 口 口 口⁻ 口ᵗ 咕 咕 咕 咕 嘻 嘻 嘻 嘻 嘻 嘻

When you are *happy*, a contented **giggle** might slip out of your *mouth*.

605 嘉

SIMP & TRAD

This character with the definition:

commend, praise

Pinyin **jiā** *and Frequency Rank* **1845**

Contains **14 strokes** in the following order:

Contains these components:

drumroll c 壴 1602, p.356

add, increase 加 476, p.114

With all these meanings & readings:

jiā [嘉] **1** excellent

一 十 士 吉 吉 吉 吉 吉 壴 壴 嘉 嘉 嘉 嘉

I was so excited to be **commended** for my improved grades that it seemed as if a *drumroll* was announcing the *increase* in my academic performance.

606 音

COMPONENT

This component has the meaning:

contempt c

And contains these subcomponents:

to stand 立 681, p.160

mouth 口 37, p.17

When a person decides to take a *stand* and use his *mouth* to express an unpopular opinion, he may not only be ignored but also treated with **contempt**.

607 部

SIMP & TRAD

This character with the definition:

part, section

Pinyin **bù** *and Frequency Rank* **84**

Contains **10 strokes** in the following order:

Contains these components:

contempt c 音 1606, p.357

town r 阝 955, p.219

With all these meanings & readings:

bù [部] **1** ministry   **2** department   **3** section   **4** part   **5** division   **6** troops   **7** board   **8** (classifier for works of literature, films, machines etc)   **9** m 个 [個][gè]

丶 亠 立 立 立 音 音 音 咅 部 部

Even though their economy relies heavily on tourism, the *towns*people have *contempt* for the tourists who visit their **section** of the city.

608 倍

SIMP & TRAD

This character with the definition:

-fold

Pinyin **bèi** *and Frequency Rank* **1392**

Contains **10 strokes** in the following order:

Contains these components:

man r 亻 1156, p.260

contempt c 音 1606, p.357

With all these meanings & readings:

bèi [倍] **1** (two, three etc) -fold   **2** times (multiplier)   **3** double   **4** to increase or multiply

丿 亻 亻 亻 亻 佇 佇 佇 倍 倍

A *man* who holds others in *contempt* magnifies others' negative traits ten-**fold**.

609 培

SIMP & TRAD

This character with the definition:

bank up with earth

Pinyin **péi** *and Frequency Rank* **1152**

Contains **11 strokes** in the following order:

Contains these components:

earth, soil 土 9, p.11

contempt c 音 1606, p.357

With all these meanings & readings:

péi [培] **1** to cultivate   **2** to earth up

一 十 土 圵 圵 圬 坮 垃 垃 培 培

Because of my *contempt* for my neighbors, I built a fence around my property, and **banked it up with earth** to ensure that they never set foot on my *soil.*

Unit 67

610

陪

SIMP & TRAD

This character with the definition:

accompany

Pinyin **péi** *and Frequency Rank* **1664**

Contains **10 strokes** in the following order:

亻 阝 阝' 阝 阝 阡 陪 陪 陪

Contains these components:

◼ hills r 阝 942, p. 216
◼ contempt c 咅 1606, p. 357

With all these meanings & readings:

péi [陪] **1** to accompany **2** to keep sb company

Sometimes the owner of a 'showcase' property in the *hills* with beautiful views on all sides is **accompanied** by feelings of *contempt* from those envious of the owner's wealth.

611

This component has the meaning:

feathers r

COMPONENT

This component visually resembles bird **feathers** that are swept up by the wind; '**feathers**' can also suggest other elements of growth on creatures, such as hair and bristles.

612

须

須
TRAD   SIMPLIFIED

This character with the definition:

must*

Pinyin **xū** *and Frequency Rank* **444**

Contains **9 strokes** in the following order:

丿 彡 彡 彡 彡 彡 须 须 须

Contains these components:

◼ feathers r 彡 1611, p. 359
◼ page, leaf 页 1408, p. 312

With all these meanings & readings:

xū [须] **1** beard **2** necessary **3** must
xū [鬚] **1** beard **2** mustache

In the fall, when individual *leaves* flutter slowly toward the ground as *feathers* do, you know that there **must** not be even the slightest breeze blowing.

613

彭

SIMP & TRAD

This character with the definition:

surname, Peng

Pinyin **péng** *and Frequency Rank* **1501**

Contains **12 strokes** in the following order:

一 十 士 吉 吉 吉 吉 青 壴 壴 彭 彭

Contains these components:

◼ drumroll c 壴 1602, p. 356
◼ feathers r 彡 1611, p. 359

With all these meanings & readings:

Péng [彭] **1** surname Peng

This character represents the **Peng family name**, and apparently has no other meaning. How can we fix it in our minds forever? In a local theater, the performance begins with a loud *drumroll* accompanying dancing girls covered with bright *feathers*. The acronym **P E N G** hangs over the stage—'**p**lease **e**njoy our **n**ightly **g**ig'!

1614

This character with the definition:

shadow, reflection

Pinyin **yǐng** *and Frequency Rank* **390**

SIMP & TRAD   Contains **15 strokes** in the following order:

丶 冂 日 日 旦 旦 昌 昌 景 景 景 景' 影 影

Contains these components:

■ view, scene 景 1315, p. 294
■ feathers r 彡 1611, p. 359

With all these meanings & readings:

yǐng [影] **1** picture **2** image **3** film **4** movie **5** photograph **6** reflection **7** shadow **8** trace

Imagine an ocean *view* at sunset—notice how the sun's **reflection** makes the water look like it's covered with *feathers*.

1615

This character with the definition:

take advantage of

Pinyin **chèn** *and Frequency Rank* **2109**

SIMP & TRAD   Contains **12 strokes** in the following order:

一 十 土 丰 丰 走 走 赵 赵 趁 趁 趁

Contains these components:

■ to walk 走 731, p. 171
■ man 人 537, p. 127
■ feathers r 彡 1611, p. 359

With all these meanings & readings:

chèn [趁] **1** to avail oneself of **2** to take advantage of

Here's a *man walking around* and in danger of tripping over his long, luxuriant, *feathery* hair. The Royal Tonsorial Parlor is on his route—he'd better **take advantage** of this opportunity to get a haircut.

1616

This character with the definition:

respectful, dignified

Pinyin **mù** *and Frequency Rank* **1683**

SIMP & TRAD   Contains **16 strokes** in the following order:

丿 二 千 禾 禾 禾 利 和 种 秞 秞 穆 穆 穆 穆 穆

Contains these components:

■ rice, grain (crop) 禾 593, p. 140
■ silk 帛 (altered) 230, p. 61
■ feathers r 彡 1611, p. 359

With all these meanings & readings:

mù [穆] **1** surname Mu **2** sole

Here's our special suit for this **respectful** and **dignified** occasion. Of course, it is made of *silk*, tastefully accoutered with some *feathers* for decoration. The harvest provided us with much prosperity so we cram our pockets full of *grain*, which we will throw in a celebratory manner at the end of the ceremony.

1617

诊
TRAD   SIMPLIFIED

This character with the definition:

diagnose

Pinyin **zhěn** *and Frequency Rank* **1401**

Contains **7 strokes** in the following order:

丶 讠 讠 论 诊 诊 诊

Contains these components:

■ speech r 讠 352, p. 88
■ man 人 537, p. 127
■ feathers r 彡 1611, p. 359

With all these meanings & readings:

zhěn [诊] **1** examine or treat medically

My ideal doctor is a *man* whose hands feel like *feathers* on my body. He *speaks* his **diagnosis** calmly and in measured tones, no matter how serious the condition.

1618

This component has the meaning:

protective cover c

COMPONENT

And contains these subcomponents:

■ man 人 537, p. 127
■ feathers r 彡 1611, p. 359

Imagine that the 'man' element is a roof that serves as a **protective cover** for the valuable shipment of *feathers* beneath it.

619 珍

SIMP & TRAD

This character with the definition:

precious thing

Pinyin **zhēn** and Frequency Rank **1314**

Contains these components:

◼ jade 玉 (altered) 177, p. 48
◻ protective cover c 参 1618, p. 360

With all these meanings & readings:

zhēn [珍] **1** precious thing **2** treasure

Contains **9 strokes** in the following order:

一 二 ‡ 王 玛 玜 珍 珍 珍

Jade is a **precious thing** that should have a *protective cover* to conceal it from theft.

620 参

参
TRAD   SIMPLIFIED

This character with the definition:

take part in, participate

Pinyin **cān** and Frequency Rank **507**

Contains these components:

◻ private r (×3) 厶 963, p. 220
◼ protective cover c 参 1618, p. 360

With all these meanings & readings:

cān [参] **1** take part in **2** participate **3** join **4** attend **5** to join **6** unequal **7** varied **8** irregular **9** to counsel **10** uneven **11** not uniform **12** abbr for 参议院 [参議~] Senate, Upper House **shēn** [参] **1** ginseng

Contains **8 strokes** in the following order:

ㄥ ㄙ 仏 扩 夹 参 参 参

With a sufficient *protective cover* that blocks outsiders from view, people **take part in** all kinds of *private* affairs.

621 惨

惨
TRAD   SIMPLIFIED

This character with the definition:

miserable, wretched

Pinyin **cǎn** and Frequency Rank **1530**

Contains these components:

◼ heart (skinny) r 忄 1135, p. 256
◻ take part in, participate 参 1620, p. 361

With all these meanings & readings:

cǎn [惨] **1** miserable **2** wretched **3** cruel **4** inhuman **5** seriously **6** badly **7** tragic

Contains **11 strokes** in the following order:

丶 丷 忄 忙 忙 忙 忙 怏 恢 惨 惨

It's an *emotional* burden to have to *participate* in so many office parties: I'm **miserable** celebrating others' promotions but never my own.

622 丗

COMPONENT

This component has the meaning:

contented cows c

And contains these subcomponents:

◼ horned animal c 廿 94, p. 30
◻ one 一 1, p. 10

Contented cows are almost unique among all *horned animals* in that they generally are seen as behaving in only *one* way—as **contented cows**.

623 昔

SIMP & TRAD

This character with the definition:

former times, past

Pinyin **xī** and Frequency Rank **2388**

Contains these components:

◼ contented cows c 丗 1622, p. 361
◻ day, sun 日 64, p. 24

With all these meanings & readings:

xī [昔] **1** past **2** former

Contains **8 strokes** in the following order:

一 十 卄 世 苗 昔 昔 昔

An aging bull ruminates on his **past** life and how his sole job was to keep the *cows contented* all *day* long.

624 措

SIMP & TRAD

This character with the definition:

arrange

Pinyin **cuò** and Frequency Rank **1148**

Contains these components:

◼ hand r 扌 25, p. 15
◻ former times, past 昔 1623, p. 361

With all these meanings & readings:

cuò [措] **1** to handle **2** to manage **3** to put in order **4** to arrange **5** to administer **6** to execute **7** to take action on **8** to plan

Contains **11 strokes** in the following order:

一 亅 扌 扌 扗 扗 拱 拮 措 措 措

In *former times*, when it had been privately owned, the valuable rare book collection was meticulously cared for by a dedicated librarian. However, after its owner donated it to the university library in his will, these literary works became carelessly re-**arranged** by many anonymous *hands*.

1625

SIMP & TRAD

This character with the definition:

books, records

Pinyin **jí** *and Frequency Rank* **1579**

Contains **20 strokes** in the following order:

丿 ㇒ ㇏ ㇉ 竹 竹 竹 竿 竿 笋 笋 笋 笋 籍 籍 籍 籍 籍 籍

Contains these components:

☐ bamboo r ⺮ 264, p.68
■ two 二 2, p.10
■ tree 木 562, p.133
◨ former times, past 昔 1623, p.361

With all these meanings & reading

jí [籍] **1** register **2** native plac **3** record of person's identity, including surname, place of bir and ancestral shrine **4** surnam Ji

In the *past*, **books** from China were made from *bamboo* strips that were cut from *two plants* and then sewn together.

1626

SIMP & TRAD

This character with the definition:

cherish, value highly

Pinyin **xī** *and Frequency Rank* **1512**

Contains **11 strokes** in the following order:

丶 丶 忄 忄 忄 忄 惜 惜 惜 惜 惜

Contains these components:

■ heart (skinny) r 忄 1135, p.256
◨ former times, past 昔 1623, p.361

With all these meanings & reading

xī [惜] **1** pity **2** regret **3** to r **4** to begrudge **5** Taiwan pr xí

People **cherish** what has long been with them because an *emotion* is tied to the memories of *former times*.

1627

SIMP & TRAD

This character with the definition:

borrow or lend

Pinyin **jiè** *and Frequency Rank* **984**

Contains **10 strokes** in the following order:

丿 亻 仁 仁 什 供 供 借 借 借

Contains these components:

■ man r 亻 1156, p.260
◨ former times, past 昔 1623, p.361

With all these meanings & reading

jiè [借] **1** to lend **2** to borrow **3** excuse **4** pretext **5** by mea of **6** to seize (an opportunity) **7** to take (an opportunity)

You can **borrow or lend** money from *men* who know you and your credit worthiness from *former times*.

1628

错
TRAD

SIMPLIFIED

This character with the definition:

wrong, mistaken

Pinyin **cuò** *and Frequency Rank* **638**

Contains **13 strokes** in the following order:

丿 ㇒ ㇏ 乍 全 全 针 针 针 错 错 错 错

Contains these components:

■ gold 金 1550, p.342
◨ former times, past 昔 1623, p.361

With all these meanings & reading

cuò [錯] **1** mistake **2** error **3** blunder **4** fault **5** cross **6** uneven **7** wrong **8** m 个 [個][gè]

In *former times* our country's currency included *gold* pieces. Now, however, one would be **mistaken** to consider today's money any more than a devalued version of the *past*.

1629
臘
腊
TRAD

SIMPLIFIED

This character with the definition:

sausage

Pinyin **là** *and Frequency Rank* **1497**

Contains **12 strokes** in the following order:

丿 ㇉ 月 月 肝 肝 肝 脐 脐 腊 腊 腊

Contains these components:

■ meat 肉 (altered) 753, p.175
◨ former times, past 昔 1623, p.361

With all these meanings & reading

là [腊] **1** preserved (meat)
là [臘] **1** December **2** preserve (meat)

Remember the boar we butchered *some time ago*? We took the *meat* and made delicious **sausages** with it.

630

猎

獵 TRAD   SIMPLIFIED

This character with the definition:

hunt, chase

Pinyin **liè** *and Frequency Rank* **1687**

Contains **11 strokes** in the following order:

ノ 犭 犭 犭¯ 犭¹ 犭⺀ 猎 猎 猎 猎 猎

Contains these components:

■ dog r 犭 1084, p. 245

◨ former times, past 昔 1623, p. 361

With all these meanings & readings:

liè ［獵］ **1** hunting

In *times past*, there was great reliance on *dogs* to make a **hunt** successful.

631

共

SIMP & TRAD

This character with the definition:

together

Pinyin **gòng** *and Frequency Rank* **330**

Contains **6 strokes** in the following order:

一 十 卄 共 共 共

Contains these components:

◨ contented cows c 共 1622, p. 361

▤ eight 八 1261, p. 282

With all these meanings & readings:

gòng ［共］ **1** common **2** general **3** to share **4** together **5** total **6** altogether **7** abbr for 共产党 ［~産黨］[gòng chǎn dǎng], Communist party

There are *eight contented cows* huddled **together** in the shade of the large old tree.

632

翼

SIMP & TRAD

This character with the definition:

wing*

Pinyin **yì** *and Frequency Rank* **1294**

Contains **17 strokes** in the following order:

⁊ ⁊⁷ ⁊⁷⁷ ⁊⁷⁷ ⁊⁷⁷ 羽 羽 習 習 翌 翌 單 單 置 置 翼 翼

Contains these components:

▭ feather, wing 羽 107, p. 33

▬ field 田 63, p. 23

▬ together 共 1631, p. 363

With all these meanings & readings:

yì ［翼］ **1** wing

When I let my dog off the leash to run in the open *field*, the dozens of geese that had been gathered *together* there took off at once. The sound of thousands of *feathers* on nearly a hundred large **wings**, all beating the air at once, was indescribable. Even my dog look startled by the strange noise as all those geese took flight.

633

典

SIMP & TRAD

This character with the definition:

canon, dictionary

Pinyin **diǎn** *and Frequency Rank* **1044**

Contains **8 strokes** in the following order:

丨 冂 冂 曲 曲 典 典 典

Contains these components:

■ together 共 1631, p. 363

▬ borders r 冂 114, p. 34

With all these meanings & readings:

diǎn ［典］ **1** canon **2** dictionary

A **dictionary** has within its '*borders*' bound *together* the definitions of many words,

---

634

塞

SIMP & TRAD

This character with the definition:

stuff, squeeze in

Pinyin **sāi** *and Frequency Rank* **1080**

Contains **13 strokes** in the following order:

丶 丷 宀 宀 宀 宇 审 宲 実 実 寒 寒 塞

Contains these components:

▭ roof r 宀 271, p. 70

▬ together 共 (altered) 1631, p. 363

▬ earth, soil 土 9, p. 11

With all these meanings & readings:

sāi ［塞］ **1** stop up **2** to squeeze in **3** to stuff **4** Serb (abbr.) **5** Serbian
sài ［塞］ **1** strategic pass
sè ［塞］ **1** piston **2** unenlightened

If you use a *roof* to hold *together* poles or walls around a parcel of *earth*, you can **squeeze in** your things under it!

Unit 68

1635

赛

赛
TRAD　SIMPLIFIED

This character with the definition:

game, competition

Pinyin **sài** *and Frequency Rank* **1064**

Contains **14 strokes** in the following order:

、丶宀宀宀宔宔宲宲宲寒寒赛赛

Contains these components:

□ roof r 宀 271, p.70

▬ together 共 (altered) 1631, p.363

□ cowrie 贝 1394, p.309

With all these meanings & reading

sài [赛] **1** to compete **2** competition **3** match **4** to surpas **5** better than **6** superior to **7** excel

Competitions such as the Olympic **Games** are meant to transcend political differences by gathering athletic teams *together* under one *roof* to **compete** for the prize of national pride. The medals could just as well be something symbolic, such as a *seashell*.

1636

洪
SIMP & TRAD

This character with the definition:

vast, grand (water)

Pinyin **hóng** *and Frequency Rank* **1350**

Contains **9 strokes** in the following order:

、丶氵氵汁汁洪洪洪

Contains these components:

■ water r 氵 314, p.80

□ together 共 1631, p.363

With all these meanings & reading

hóng [洪] **1** flood **2** big **3** gr **4** surname Hong

When several great rivers or other flowing bodies of *water* come *together*, the result is a **vast** intersection that resembles a flood.

1637

寒
SIMP & TRAD

This character with the definition:

cold, glacial

Pinyin **hán** *and Frequency Rank* **1297**

Contains **12 strokes** in the following order:

、丶宀宀宀宔宔宲宲宲寒寒

Contains these components:

□ roof r 宀 271, p.70

▬ together 共 (altered) 1631, p.363

□ ice r 冫 (altered) 348, p.87

With all these meanings & reading

hán [寒] **1** cold **2** poor **3** to tremble

It's so **cold** outside that even though we are huddling *together* under the *roof*, *ice* has managed to form all around us.

1638

SIMP & TRAD

This character with the definition:

supply, feed

Pinyin **gōng** *and Frequency Rank* **550**

Contains **8 strokes** in the following order:

丿亻亻仕什供供供

Contains these components:

▮ man r 亻 1156, p.260

□ together 共 1631, p.363

With all these meanings & reading

gōng [供] **1** offer (information etc) **2** supply
gòng [供] **1** offer **2** sacrificial offering **3** trial statement **4** confession

An army gains strength through its stomach, so detailed plans are necessary to **feed** the large groups of *men* stationed *together*.

1639

SIMP & TRAD

This character with the definition:

respectful

Pinyin **gōng** *and Frequency Rank* **1742**

Contains **10 strokes** in the following order:

一十卅卅芈芈恭恭恭恭

Contains these components:

■ together 共 1631, p.363

▫ small 小 (altered) 1262, p.282

With all these meanings & reading

gōng [恭] **1** respectful

A *small* group of soldiers stands *together* at attention, **respectful** of their commander.

640

巷

SIMP & TRAD

This character with the definition:

lane, alley

Pinyin **xiàng** *and Frequency Rank* **2399**

Contains **9 strokes** in the following order:

一 十 艹 艹 芦 共 共 巷 巷

Contains these components:

■ together 共 1631, p. 363

■ single ear r 卩 165, p. 46

With all these meanings & readings:

xiàng [巷] **1** lane **2** alley

This old-fashioned **alley** is so narrow that we can't pass through it *together* or else a *single ear* will get scraped off by the **alley**'s walls.

641

港

SIMP & TRAD

This character with the definition:

harbor, port

Pinyin **gǎng** *and Frequency Rank* **927**

Contains **12 strokes** in the following order:

丶 丶 氵 氵 汁 沣 洪 洪 洪 港 港 港

Contains these components:

■ water r 氵 314, p. 80

■ lane, alley 巷 1640, p. 365

With all these meanings & readings:

gǎng [港] **1** harbor **2** Hong Kong (abbr for 香港) **3** m 个 [個][gè]

A backlogged **port** can be the *water* equivalent of a market square for the ships sitting at anchor there—sometimes even a makeshift *water lane* will develop to transport goods faster between the 'idle' ships!

642

暴

SIMP & TRAD

This character with the definition:

sudden and violent, savage

Pinyin **bào** *and Frequency Rank* **1028**

Contains **15 strokes** in the following order:

丶 冖 冂 日 旦 旦 旦 早 昦 暴 暴 暴 暴 暴

Contains these components:

■ day, sun 日 64, p. 24

■ together 共 1631, p. 363

■ water 水 315, p. 81

With all these meanings & readings:

bào [暴] **1** sudden **2** violent **3** cruel **4** to show or expose **5** to injure **6** surname Bao

Sometimes drops of *water* will fall on a *sunny day*. Sailors know that such drops of *water* may signal a **sudden and violent** change in weather.

643

爆

SIMP & TRAD

This character with the definition:

explode, burst

Pinyin **bào** *and Frequency Rank* **1243**

Contains **19 strokes** in the following order:

丶 丷 丬 火 火 炉 炉 炉 焊 焊 焊 煟 煁 爆 爆 爆 爆 爆

Contains these components:

■ fire 火 1511, p. 334

■ sudden and violent, savage 暴 1642, p. 365

With all these meanings & readings:

bào [爆] **1** to crack **2** to explode or burst

Fire and *sudden violence* are signs of an impending **explosion**.

644

展

SIMP & TRAD

This character with the definition:

open up, spread out

Pinyin **zhǎn** *and Frequency Rank* **275**

Contains **10 strokes** in the following order:

フ コ 尸 尸 屈 屈 屈 屈 展 展

Contains these components:

■ corpse 尸 499, p. 119

■ contented cows c 丷 1622, p. 361

■ clothing 衣 (abbrev) 1068, 242

With all these meanings & readings:

zhǎn [展] **1** to use **2** to spread out **3** to postpone **4** to unfold

Twice a year the farmer sends a few of his *contented cows* to the slaughterhouse. After their meat is sold, the hide is removed from their *corpses* and **spread out** so that it can later be made into leather *clothing*.

1645

黄

黃
TRAD   SIMPLIFIED

This character with the definition:

yellow

Pinyin **huáng**   *and Frequency Rank* **561**

Contains **11 strokes** in the following order:

一 十 卄 世 艹 芑 苂 苗 苗 黄 黄

Contains these components:

contented cows c 半 1622, p. 361

field 田 (altered) 63, p. 23

eight 八 1261, p. 282

With all these meanings & readings:

huáng [黄] **1** yellow **2** sulfur **3** surname Huang or Hwang

It's harvest time, and the farmer surveys his pasture. The *cows are contented*, the *fields* have produced an *abundance* of crops, and all is right with the world. While green is the prominent color in the spring and summer, **yellows** and browns hold sway in the fall.

1646

横

橫
TRAD   SIMPLIFIED

This character with the definition:

horizontal stroke

Pinyin **héng**   *and Frequency Rank* **1330**

Contains **15 strokes** in the following order:

一 十 才 木 木 杧 杧 柑 梺 梺 梺 横 横 横 横

Contains these components:

tree 木 562, p. 133

yellow 黄 1645, p. 366

With all these meanings & readings:

héng [横] **1** horizontal **2** across **3** (horizontal character stroke)
hèng [横] **1** harsh and unreasonable **2** see also 蛮横 [蠻横][mán hèng] **3** unexpected **4** see also 横祸 [横禍][hèng huò]

After a woodsman uses **horizontal strokes** to cut down a *tree*, the tree's bright *yellow* sap becomes visible.

1647

堇

SIMP & TRAD

This character with the definition:

clay, yellow loam

Pinyin **jǐn**   *and Frequency Rank* **5758**

Contains **11 strokes** in the following order:

一 十 卄 艹 芢 芢 苢 苜 莣 菫 堇

Contains these components:

yellow 黄 (altered) 1645, p. 366

earth, soil 土 9, p. 11

With all these meanings & readings:

jǐn [堇] **1** yellow loam **2** clay **3** season **4** few

Many types of **clay** resemble *yellow earth.*

1648

勤

SIMP & TRAD

This character with the definition:

diligent, hardworking

Pinyin **qín**   *and Frequency Rank* **1565**

Contains **13 strokes** in the following order:

一 十 卄 艹 芢 芢 苢 莣 莣 菫 堇 勤 勤

Contains these components:

clay, yellow loam 堇 1647, p. 366

strength 力 471, p. 113

With all these meanings & readings:

qín [勤] **1** diligent **2** industrious **3** hardworking **4** frequent **5** regular **6** constant

Clay is very dense. Even a potter must apply physical *strength* to mold the *clay* and must be very **hardworking** in order to produce delicate glazed pottery from a large lump of *clay.*

1649

采

COMPONENT

This component has the meaning:

distinguish, differentiate r

And contains these subcomponents:

action path c ノ 438, p. 105

rice (food) 米 1535, p. 339

Immediately after the *rice* harvest, the best cooks take *action* to sort and **differentiate** the best grains of *rice* from the inferior ones.

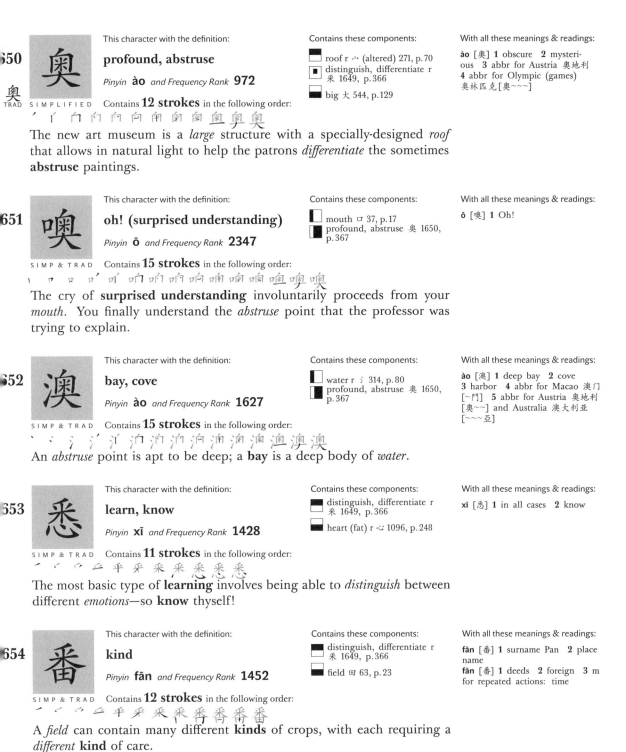

650

奥
TRAD SIMPLIFIED

This character with the definition:

profound, abstruse

Pinyin **ào** *and Frequency Rank* **972**

Contains **12 strokes** in the following order:

Contains these components:

☐ roof r 宀 (altered) 271, p.70
☐ distinguish, differentiate r 釆 1649, p.366
☐ big 大 544, p.129

With all these meanings & readings:

ào [奥] **1** obscure **2** mysterious **3** abbr for Austria 奥地利 **4** abbr for Olympic (games) 奥林匹克[奥~~~]

The new art museum is a *large* structure with a specially-designed *roof* that allows in natural light to help the patrons *differentiate* the sometimes **abstruse** paintings.

651

噢
SIMP & TRAD

This character with the definition:

oh! (surprised understanding)

Pinyin **ō** *and Frequency Rank* **2347**

Contains **15 strokes** in the following order:

Contains these components:

☐ mouth 口 37, p.17
☐ profound, abstruse 奥 1650, p.367

With all these meanings & readings:

ō [噢] **1** Oh!

The cry of **surprised understanding** involuntarily proceeds from your *mouth*. You finally understand the *abstruse* point that the professor was trying to explain.

652

澳
SIMP & TRAD

This character with the definition:

bay, cove

Pinyin **ào** *and Frequency Rank* **1627**

Contains **15 strokes** in the following order:

Contains these components:

☐ water r 氵 314, p.80
☐ profound, abstruse 奥 1650, p.367

With all these meanings & readings:

ào [澳] **1** deep bay **2** cove **3** harbor **4** abbr for Macao 澳门 [~门] **5** abbr for Austria 奥地利 [奥~~] and Australia 澳大利亚 [~~~亚]

An *abstruse* point is apt to be deep; a **bay** is a deep body of *water*.

653

悉
SIMP & TRAD

This character with the definition:

learn, know

Pinyin **xī** *and Frequency Rank* **1428**

Contains **11 strokes** in the following order:

Contains these components:

☐ distinguish, differentiate r 釆 1649, p.366
☐ heart (fat) r 心 1096, p.248

With all these meanings & readings:

xī [悉] **1** in all cases **2** know

The most basic type of **learning** involves being able to *distinguish* between different *emotions*—so **know** thyself!

654

番
SIMP & TRAD

This character with the definition:

kind

Pinyin **fān** *and Frequency Rank* **1452**

Contains **12 strokes** in the following order:

Contains these components:

☐ distinguish, differentiate r 釆 1649, p.366
☐ field 田 63, p.23

With all these meanings & readings:

fān [番] **1** surname Pan **2** place name
fān [番] **1** deeds **2** foreign **3** m for repeated actions: time

A *field* can contain many different **kinds** of crops, with each requiring a *different* **kind** of care.

1655

This character with the definition:

sow, broadcast

Pinyin **bō** *and Frequency Rank* **1275**

Contains these components:
- hand r 扌 25, p. 15
- kind 番 1654, p. 367

With all these meanings & reading
bō [播] **1** sow **2** scatter **3** sp
4 broadcast **5** Taiwan pr bò

SIMP & TRAD   Contains **15 strokes** in the following order:

一 十 扌 扩 扩 扩 护 挦 挦 採 採 播 播 播 播

A farmer uses his *hand* to **sow** different *kinds* of seeds in his field.

1656

This character with the definition:

turn over

Pinyin **fān** *and Frequency Rank* **1027**

Contains these components:
- kind 番 1654, p. 367
- feather, wing 羽 107, p. 33

With all these meanings & reading
fān [翻] **1** to turn over **2** to
flip over **3** to overturn **4** to
translate **5** to decode

SIMP & TRAD   Contains **18 strokes** in the following order:

丿 𠂆 亠 𠂉 平 乎 釆 釆 番 番 番 番 翻 翻 翻 翻 翻 翻

A bird can maneuver so quickly and gracefully during flight because each *feather* is a different *kind* and is so flexible that it can almost **turn over** in the bird's *wing*! • This character can be expanded to other meanings involving the word 'turn'—for example, '**turn upside down**' and '**turn inside out**'.

1657

This component has the meaning:

hands raised high c

COMPONENT

The three lower strokes suggest three individual **upraised** hands, and the long upper curve suggests a background filled with many **hands raised high**. • In most references and texts, this element is taken to be a radical based on the character 爪, 'claw'.

1658

This character with the definition:

proper

Pinyin **tuǒ** *and Frequency Rank* **1840**

Contains these components:
- hands raised high c ⌒ 1657, p. 368
- woman 女 790, p. 183

With all these meanings & reading
tuǒ [妥] **1** secure **2** sound

SIMP & TRAD   Contains **7 strokes** in the following order:

丿 𠂉 爫 爫 受 妥 妥

The young *woman* did not feel it was **proper** for her to join the angry protestors who were marching with their *hands raised high*.

1659
採
采

TRAD   SIMPLIFIED

This character with the definition:

pick, gather

Pinyin **cǎi** *and Frequency Rank* **585**

Contains these components:
- hands raised high c ⌒ 1657, p. 368
- tree 木 562, p. 133

With all these meanings & reading
cǎi [採] **1** to pick **2** to pluck **3** to collect **4** to select **5** to choose **6** to gather
cǎi [采] **1** affairs **2** gather
cài [采] **1** allotment to a feuda noble

Contains **8 strokes** in the following order:

丿 𠂉 爫 爫 𤔾 采 采 采

Since the best fruit sits high on the *tree*, you need to keep your *hands raised high* to be able to **pick** those succulent plums.

Unit 69

660

菜

SIMP & TRAD

This character with the definition:

course (meal)

Pinyin **cài** *and Frequency Rank* **1266**

Contains **11 strokes** in the following order:

一十艹艹苎苎苹苹苹菜菜

Contains these components:

☐ grass r ⧾ 87, p. 29

■ pick, gather 采 1659, p. 368

With all these meanings & readings:

cài [菜] **1** dish (type of food) **2** vegetables **3** vegetable **4** cuisine **5** m 盘[盤][pán], 道[dào]

This morning I went out to my garden to *gather* vegetables for the special **course** of the **meal** I'm planning for dinner; while I was in the garden, I spent time *picking* out stray growths of *grass* and weeds.

661

彩

SIMP & TRAD

This character with the definition:

colorful

Pinyin **cǎi** *and Frequency Rank* **1177**

Contains **11 strokes** in the following order:

丿丷丷丷三平平平采采彩彩彩

Contains these components:

■ pick, gather 采 1659, p. 368

☐ feathers r 彡 1611, p. 359

With all these meanings & readings:

cǎi [彩] **1** (bright) color **2** variety **3** applause **4** applaud **5** (lottery) prize

We *gather feathers* because they are so **colorful**.

662

浮

SIMP & TRAD

This character with the definition:

float

Pinyin **fú** *and Frequency Rank* **1462**

Contains **10 strokes** in the following order:

丶丶氵氵氵汒浮浮浮浮

Contains these components:

☐ water r 氵 314, p. 80

■ hands raised high c ⧾ 1657, p. 368

■ son, child 子 24, p. 15

With all these meanings & readings:

fú [浮] **1** to float **2** superficial **3** floating **4** unstable **5** movable **6** provisional **7** temporary **8** transient **9** impetuous **10** hollow **11** inflated **12** to exceed **13** superfluous **14** excessive **15** surplus

A small *child* fell into the *water* and kept his *hands raised high* in panic; fortunately, his natural buoyancy allowed him to **float** long enough to be rescued.

663

俘

SIMP & TRAD

This character with the definition:

capture, take prisoner

Pinyin **fú** *and Frequency Rank* **2057**

Contains **9 strokes** in the following order:

丿亻亻仁仵仵俘俘俘

Contains these components:

■ man r 亻 1156, p. 260

☐ hands raised high c ⧾ 1657, p. 368

■ son, child 子 24, p. 15

With all these meanings & readings:

fú [俘] **1** prisoner of war

Young soldiers—so young that they seem like *children*—have *raised their hands* to surrender to the *man* that **captured** them.

664

乳

SIMP & TRAD

This character with the definition:

breast, milk*

Pinyin **rǔ** *and Frequency Rank* **1831**

Contains **8 strokes** in the following order:

丿丷丷㓁爫孚孚乳

Contains these components:

■ hands raised high c ⧾ 1657, p. 368

■ son, child 子 24, p. 15

☐ mineshaft c ㄥ 122, p. 36

With all these meanings & readings:

rǔ [乳] **1** breast **2** milk

Young mothers owe their babies several things: protection from dangers (like a *mineshaft*) and food, which you see as she *raises her son high* to let him nurse at her **breast**.

1665

摇
搖
TRAD   SIMPLIFIED

This character with the definition:

to wave, to wag

Pinyin **yáo** *and Frequency Rank* **940**

Contains these components:
- ▮ hand r 扌 25, p.15
- ▪ hands raised high c ⺧ 1657, p.368
- ▪ archaeological vessel 缶 181, p.49

With all these meanings & readings

yáo [搖] **1** shake **2** to rock

Contains **13 strokes** in the following order:

一 十 扌 扩 扩 护 护 押 押 捏 捏 摇 摇

Some of the stranded travelers are trying to attract would-be rescuers by **waving** their *hands* vigorously. So far, no luck. Next, they will *raise their hands high*. If that still doesn't work, they will brandish a large *archaeological vessel*.

1666

应
應
TRAD   SIMPLIFIED

This character with the definition:

should, ought to

Pinyin **yīng** *and Frequency Rank* **144**

Contains these components:
- ▮ extensive 广 430, p.104
- ▪ hands raised high c ⺧ (altered) 1657, p.368

With all these meanings & readings

yīng [應] **1** ought
yìng [應] **1** surname Ying **2** to answer **3** to respond

Contains **7 strokes** in the following order:

丶 亠 广 广 应 应 应

The members *raise their hands* to affirm an *extensive* list of motions, a list of all the things we **ought** to do.

1667

This component has the meaning:

mighty tree c

COMPONENT

You know this is a **mighty tree** because of its towering profile with three levels of branches sticking out.

1668

奏
SIMP & TRAD

This character with the definition:

memorialize the emperor

Pinyin **zòu** *and Frequency Rank* **1543**

Contains these components:
- ▯ mighty tree c 夫 1667, p.370
- ▪ heaven 天 548, p.129

With all these meanings & readings

zòu [奏] **1** present a memorial **2** to play (music)

Contains **9 strokes** in the following order:

一 二 三 声 夫 表 表 奏 奏

After the emperor was buried, a *mighty tree* was planted at the site as an earthly symbol from nature to **memorialize the emperor** as the Son of *Heaven*.

1669

凑
湊
TRAD   SIMPLIFIED

This character with the definition:

assemble

Pinyin **còu** *and Frequency Rank* **2193**

Contains these components:
- ▮ ice r 冫 348, p.87
- ▪ memorialize the emperor 奏 1668, p.370

With all these meanings & readings

còu [湊] **1** assemble **2** put together **3** press near **4** come together

Contains **11 strokes** in the following order:

丶 冫 冫 冱 沣 沣 浃 湊 湊 凑 凑

Everyone **assembled** at the temple, even on this *icy* day, to *memorialize the emperor*.

670

This character with the definition:

Qin (dynasty)

Pinyin **qín** *and Frequency Rank* **1394**

SIMP & TRAD   Contains **10 strokes** in the following order:

一 二 三 丰 夫 夫 表 表 奉 秦

Contains these components:

■ mighty tree c 夫 1667, p. 370

▣ rice, grain (crop) 禾 593, p. 140

With all these meanings & readings:

Qín [秦] **1** surname Qin **2** Qin dynasty (221-207 BC) of the first emperor 秦始皇[qín shǐ huáng] **3** abbreviation of 陕西[shǎn xī]

It is thought that the word 'China' is derived from the **Qin** dynasty. More than two thousand years ago, the **Qin** introduced a centralized government, with extensive programs of public works (symbolized by the *'mighty tree'* element), and guaranteed supplies of food and *grain* to all its citizens.

671 泰

This character with the definition:

peace, quiet

Pinyin **tài** *and Frequency Rank* **1318**

SIMP & TRAD   Contains **10 strokes** in the following order:

一 二 三 丰 夫 表 表 泰 泰 泰

Contains these components:

▢ mighty tree c 夫 1667, p. 370

▬ water 水 315, p. 81

With all these meanings & readings:

tài [泰] **1** safe **2** peaceful **3** most **4** Mt Thai 泰山 in Shandong **5** abbr for Thailand **6** grand

Wind softly blowing through *mighty trees* and *water* gurgling in a nearby brook are two of the **peaceful** sounds created by nature.

672 春

This character with the definition:

spring (season)

Pinyin **chūn** *and Frequency Rank* **921**

SIMP & TRAD   Contains **9 strokes** in the following order:

一 二 三 丰 夫 表 春 春 春

Contains these components:

■ mighty tree c 夫 1667, p. 370

▬ day, sun 日 64, p. 24

With all these meanings & readings:

chūn [春] **1** spring (time) **2** gay **3** joyful **4** youthful **5** love **6** lust **7** life

The *'sun'* element at the base of the *'mighty tree'* represents a *sun* sitting low in the sky and signifies the end of winter's cold and the beginning of the balmy *days* of **spring**.

673

卷
捲
TRAD

This character with the definition:

exam paper

Pinyin **juàn** *and Frequency Rank* **1016**

SIMPLIFIED   Contains **8 strokes** in the following order:

丶 丷 一 二 丰 关 券 卷

Contains these components:

■ spring (season) 春 (altered) 1672, p. 371

▢ single ear r 卩 (altered) 165, p. 46

With all these meanings & readings:

juàn [卷] **1** chapter **2** examination paper
juǎn [捲] **1** to roll (up) **2** to sweep up **3** coil **4** to carry on **5** (classifier for small rolled things: wad of paper money, scroll, movie tape etc)

I did terribly on the *spring* mid-term **exam** because I didn't bother to listen, with even a *single ear*, to the instructions the teacher gave at the start.

674 圈

This character with the definition:

enclose

Pinyin **juàn** *and Frequency Rank* **1366**

SIMP & TRAD   Contains **11 strokes** in the following order:

丨 冂 冂 冂 冂 冃 冄 冈 圂 圈 圈

Contains these components:

▢ enclosure r 囗 36, p. 17

■ exam paper 卷 1673, p. 371

With all these meanings & readings:

juàn [圈] **1** to confine **2** enclose
juàn [圈] **1** pen (pig) **2** a fold
quān [圈] **1** circle **2** ring **3** loop **4** m for loops, orbits, laps of race etc **5** m 个[個][gè]

The pigs are quietly waiting in their *enclosure* for their favorite dinner—used *exam papers* which will soon be **enclosed** in their stomachs.

1675

SIMP & TRAD

This character with the definition:

give, present

Pinyin **fèng** and Frequency Rank **1382**

Contains **8 strokes** in the following order:

一 二 三 丰 夫 表 丢 奉

Contains these components:

▪ mighty tree c 夫 1667, p. 370

▫ plentiful 丰 (altered) 16, p. 13

With all these meanings & readings:

fèng [奉] **1** to offer (tribute) **2** to present respectfully (to superior, ancestor, deity etc) **3** to esteem **4** to revere **5** to believe in (a religion) **6** to wait upon **7** to accept orders (from superior)

The *mighty tree* is a symbol of the *plentiful* yield **presented** to us by Mother Nature.

1676

壽
TRAD

SIMPLIFIED

This character with the definition:

longevity

Pinyin **shòu** and Frequency Rank **1615**

Contains **7 strokes** in the following order:

一 二 三 丰 丰 寿 寿

Contains these components:

▪ mighty tree c 夫 (altered) 1667, p. 370

▫ inch 寸 216, p. 58

With all these meanings & readings:

shòu [寿] **1** (long) life

The *mighty tree* is in danger of toppling over. Wise forest rangers need to insert a one *inch* slab of wood to preserve its natural supports and safeguard the **longevity** of the tree.

1677

籌
TRAD

SIMPLIFIED

This character with the definition:

tally, counter

Pinyin **chóu** and Frequency Rank **1677**

Contains **13 strokes** in the following order:

丿 ㇒ ㇏ ㇏ 竹 竹 竹 竺 竺 笃 笃 筹 筹

Contains these components:

▫ bamboo r ⺮ 264, p. 68

▪ longevity 寿 1676, p. 372

With all these meanings & readings:

chóu [筹] **1** chip (in gambling) **2** token (for counting) **3** ticket **4** to prepare **5** to plan **6** to raise (funds) **7** resource **8** mea-

Bamboo plants have such *longevity* that they are used to **tally** and mark the passage of time. A natural **counter**, *bamboo* records historical events, such as the arrival of new dynasties, eclipses, floods, and earthquakes.

1678

COMPONENT

This component has the meaning:

many c

And contains these subcomponents:

▪ man 人 537, p. 127

▫ one 一 1, p. 10

This *man* stands tall on the *horizontal* platform as he's being honored for **many** achievements. • This component sometimes appears in the variant form 亼.

1679

SIMP & TRAD

This character with the definition:

join, combine

Pinyin **hé** and Frequency Rank **171**

Contains **6 strokes** in the following order:

丿 人 亼 今 合 合

Contains these components:

▫ many c 亼 1678, p. 372

▪ mouth 口 37, p. 17

With all these meanings & readings:

gě [合] **1** 100 ml **2** one-tenth a peck **3** measure for dry grain equal to one-tenth of sheng 升 liter, or one-hundredth dou 斗 **hé** [合] **1** Chinese musical note **2** fit **3** to join **4** counter for matches, battles etc

Many mouths—people—**join** together to accomplish great things.

680
拿
SIMP & TRAD

This character with the definition:

take

Pinyin **ná** *and Frequency Rank* **645**

Contains **10 strokes** in the following order:

ノ 人 人 ⼈ 合 合 合 合 合 拿

Contains these components:

join, combine 合 1679, p. 372

hand 手 21, p. 14

With all these meanings & readings:

ná [拿] **1** to hold **2** to seize **3** to catch **4** to apprehend **5** to take

A pickpocket uses his *hand* to *join* other people's belongings to his own and **takes** their things without their knowledge.

681
拾
SIMP & TRAD

This character with the definition:

pick up (from the ground)

Pinyin **shí** *and Frequency Rank* **1961**

Contains **9 strokes** in the following order:

一 十 扌 扒 扒 拾 拾 拾 拾

Contains these components:

hand r 扌 25, p. 15

join, combine 合 1679, p. 372

With all these meanings & readings:

shí [拾] **1** to pick up **2** ten (banker's anti-fraud numeral)

The ground is littered with garbage! In **picking up** this mess, I am using my *hand* to *join* this mess with the debris that other volunteers have already **picked up**.

682
哈
SIMP & TRAD

This character with the definition:

aha!

Pinyin **hā** *and Frequency Rank* **713**

Contains **9 strokes** in the following order:

丨 冖 口 叮 叭 哈 哈 哈 哈

Contains these components:

mouth 口 37, p. 17

join, combine 合 1679, p. 372

With all these meanings & readings:

hā [哈] **1** laughter **2** yawn **3** abbr for Kazakhstan
hǎ [哈] **1** a Pekinese **2** a pug

When good things happen to me, I let out an **'aha!'** sound that is released out of my open *mouth*. My lips do not *join* together when I produce this sigh of contentment.

683
答
SIMP & TRAD

This character with the definition:

answer

Pinyin **dá** *and Frequency Rank* **559**

Contains **12 strokes** in the following order:

ノ ⺊ ⺮ 竹 竹 竹 笁 笞 笞 筌 答 答

Contains these components:

bamboo r ⺮ 264, p. 68

join, combine 合 1679, p. 372

With all these meanings & readings:

dā [答] **1** to answer **2** agree
dá [答] **1** reply **2** answer **3** return **4** respond **5** echo

In ancient days, priests threw small pieces of *bamboo* on the table. The way they *joined* together provided **answers**, supposedly, to questions posed by worshipers.

684
塔
SIMP & TRAD

This character with the definition:

pagoda

Pinyin **tǎ** *and Frequency Rank* **1030**

Contains **12 strokes** in the following order:

一 十 土 圹 圹 圹 垯 垯 垯 塔 塔 塔

Contains these components:

earth, soil 土 9, p. 11

answer 答 (altered) 1683, p. 373

With all these meanings & readings:

tǎ [塔] **1** pagoda **2** tower **3** minaret **4** m 座[zuò]

The new **pagoda** was built on a parcel of meticulously cultivated *earth*; it's literally an *answer* to our prayers!

Unit 70

1685
停

This character with the definition:

stop, pause

Pinyin **tíng** *and Frequency Rank* **693**

SIMP & TRAD Contains **11 strokes** in the following order:

丿 亻 亻 亾 亾 仴 停 停 停 停 停

Contains these components:

man r 亻 1156, p. 260

pagoda 塔 1684, p. 373

With all these meanings & readings

tíng [停] **1** to stop **2** to halt **3** to park (a car)

When the *man*, a typical tourist, first encountered the beautiful *pagoda*, its beauty and grace forced him to **stop** in his tracks and admire it.

1686
搭

This character with the definition:

build

Pinyin **dā** *and Frequency Rank* **1842**

SIMP & TRAD Contains **12 strokes** in the following order:

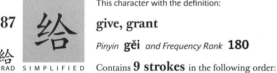

Contains these components:

hand r 扌 25, p. 15

answer 答 (altered) 1683, p. 373

With all these meanings & readings

dā [搭] **1** to put up **2** to build (scaffolding) **3** to hang (clothes on a pole) **4** to connect **5** to join **6** to arrange in pairs **7** to match **8** to add **9** to throw in (resources) **10** to take (boat, train)

The man's *hand* plucks an *answer* from the oracle and learns that his destiny is to **build**.

1687
给

給
TRAD   SIMPLIFIED

This character with the definition:

give, grant

Pinyin **gěi** *and Frequency Rank* **180**

Contains **9 strokes** in the following order:

乚 纟 纟 纟 纩 纷 纷 给 给

Contains these components:

silk r 纟 1037, p. 235

join, combine 合 1679, p. 372

With all these meanings & readings

gěi [给] **1** to **2** for **3** for the benefit of **4** to give **5** to allow **6** to do sth (for sb) **7** (passive particle)
jǐ [给] **1** to supply **2** provide

Seamstresses *join* strands of *silk* together to **give** the resulting fabric greater strength.

1688
恰

This character with the definition:

exactly, properly

Pinyin **qià** *and Frequency Rank* **1308**

SIMP & TRAD Contains **9 strokes** in the following order:

丶 丷 忄 忄 忭 恰 恰 恰 恰

Contains these components:

heart (skinny) r 忄 1135, p. 256

join, combine 合 1679, p. 372

With all these meanings & readings

qià [恰] **1** exactly **2** just

The artist has an *emotional* disposition, but somehow her *emotions join* and *combine* in a **proper** manner that allows her to produce beautiful work.

1689
俞

This character with the definition:

consent

Pinyin **yú** *and Frequency Rank* **3251**

SIMP & TRAD Contains **9 strokes** in the following order:

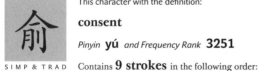

Contains these components:

join, combine 合 (altered) 1679, p. 372

meat 肉 (altered) 753, p. 175

knife r 刂 169, p. 46

With all these meanings & readings

yú [俞] **1** surname Yu
yú [俞] **1** yes (used by Emperor or ruler) **2** OK **3** to accede **4** to assent

The medical student *joins* the *knife* to the body to practice surgery—with his professor's **consent**, of course.

690

輸
TRAD
SIMPLIFIED

This character with the definition:

transport, convey

Pinyin **shū** and Frequency Rank **939**

Contains these components:
- car 车 1291, p. 289
- consent 俞 1689, p. 374

With all these meanings & readings:

shū [輸] **1** to lose **2** to transport **3** to donate **4** to enter (a password)

Contains **13 strokes** in the following order:

一 ㄥ 车 车 车 斩 轮 轮 轮 轮 输 输 输

My parents *consented* for me to use their *car* to **transport** all my friends to the dance.

691

愈
愈
癒
TRAD
SIMPLIFIED

This character with the definition:

the more—the more

Pinyin **yù** and Frequency Rank **1301**

Contains these components:
- consent 俞 1689, p. 374
- heart (fat) r 心 1096, p. 248

With all these meanings & readings:

yù [愈] **1** heal **2** the more...the more **3** to recover **4** better
yù [癒] **1** heal

Contains **13 strokes** in the following order:

ノ 人 ㄥ 介 介 合 合 俞 俞 俞 愈 愈 愈

The **more** I *consent* to go out with her, **the more** I feel a growing *emotional* attachment. How will this end?

692

愉
SIMP & TRAD

This character with the definition:

delighted, joyful

Pinyin **yú** and Frequency Rank **1982**

Contains these components:
- heart (skinny) r 忄 1135, p. 256
- consent 俞 1689, p. 374

With all these meanings & readings:

yú [愉] **1** pleased

Contains **12 strokes** in the following order:

丶 丶 忄 忄 忙 愉 愉 愉 愉 愉 愉 愉

I am **delighted** at my Master's *consent* to pour my *heart* into my poetry. I am overflowing with **joyfulness**.

693

偷
SIMP & TRAD

This character with the definition:

pilfer

Pinyin **tōu** and Frequency Rank **1284**

Contains these components:
- man r 亻 1156, p. 260
- consent 俞 1689, p. 374

With all these meanings & readings:

tōu [偷] **1** to steal **2** to pilfer

Contains **11 strokes** in the following order:

ノ 亻 亻 件 价 价 偷 偷 偷 偷 偷

A *man* **pilfers** when he take things of little value without the owner's *consent*.

694

僉
僉
TRAD
SIMPLIFIED

This character with the definition:

together, unanimous

Pinyin **qiān** and Frequency Rank **5613**

Contains these components:
- join, combine 合 (altered) 1679, p. 372
- hands raised high c ⺍ 1657, p. 368

With all these meanings & readings:

qiān [僉] **1** all

Contains **7 strokes** in the following order:

ノ 人 ㄥ 合 合 合 佥

A group of people that *raises their hands high* and *joins* **together** over the same opinions signifies **unanimous** agreement. • Although this is a low frequency character in its standalone incarnation, you'll see it frequently as a component in other characters.

1695

剑

剑
TRAD SIMPLIFIED

This character with the definition:

sword, saber

Pinyin **jiàn** *and Frequency Rank* **869**

Contains these components:

■ together, unanimous 佥 1694, p. 375

▢ knife r 刂 169, p. 46

With all these meanings & readings

jiàn [劍] **1** (double-edged) sword **2** m 口[kǒu], 把[bǎ]

Contains **9 strokes** in the following order:

ノ 𠆢 𠆢 𠆢 仑 佥 佥 剑 剑

Even though a **sword, saber,** and *knife* are similar in design and purpose, they are rarely used *together*—an attacker usually selects only one of them as his weapon of choice.

1696

签

签
TRAD SIMPLIFIED

This character with the definition:

sign one's name

Pinyin **qiān** *and Frequency Rank* **1254**

Contains these components:

▢ bamboo r 竹 264, p. 68
■ together, unanimous 佥 1694, p. 375

With all these meanings & readings

qiān [簽] **1** sign one's name
qiān [籤] **1** inscribed bamboo stick (used in divination, gambling, drawing lots etc) **2** small wood sliver **3** a label **4** a tag

Contains **13 strokes** in the following order:

ノ 𠂉 𠂉 𠂉 𥫗 𥫗 𥫗 䇛 筌 签 签 签 签

In ancient times, *bamboo* pens were used to **sign one's name**—often on a special document signifying *unanimous* agreement among the parties.

1697

险

险
TRAD SIMPLIFIED

This character with the definition:

dangerous

Pinyin **xiǎn** *and Frequency Rank* **672**

Contains these components:

▢ hills r 阝 942, p. 216
■ together, unanimous 佥 1694, p. 375

With all these meanings & readings

xiǎn [險] **1** danger **2** dangerous **3** rugged

Contains **9 strokes** in the following order:

𠃌 阝 阝′ 阶 阶 险 险 险 险

We formed a search party to travel *together* into the *hills* because it was too **dangerous** to go it alone.

1698

验

验
TRAD SIMPLIFIED

This character with the definition:

inspect, check

Pinyin **yàn** *and Frequency Rank* **534**

Contains these components:

▢ horse 马 388, p. 95
■ together, unanimous 佥 1694, p. 375

With all these meanings & readings

yàn [驗] **1** to examine **2** to test **3** to check

Contains **10 strokes** in the following order:

𠃌 马 马 马′ 驵 验 验 验 验 验

Buying a *horse* is a tricky business. Lacking any experience, you need to work *together* with an old hand to help you **inspect** which *horse* is best for you to buy.

1699

检

检
TRAD SIMPLIFIED

This character with the definition:

examine, review

Pinyin **jiǎn** *and Frequency Rank* **731**

Contains these components:

▢ tree 木 562, p. 133
■ together, unanimous 佥 1694, p. 375

With all these meanings & readings

jiǎn [檢] **1** to check **2** to examine **3** to inspect

Contains **11 strokes** in the following order:

一 十 才 木 𣏕 𣏕 松 枪 检 检 检

Whenever a large number of identical *tree* species grow closely *together,* *tree* experts **examine** them more frequently, because so many identical *trees* growing *together* are more vulnerable to insect infestation and disease.

1700

This character with the definition:

small box

Pinyin **hé** *and Frequency Rank* **2067**

SIMP & TRAD   Contains **11 strokes** in the following order:

Contains these components:

☐ join, combine 合 1679, p. 372
■ vessel, container 皿 101, p. 32

With all these meanings & readings:

hé [盒] **1** small box **2** case

I *combined* into one *vessel* the contents of several **small boxes**.

1701

This character with the definition:

today, current

Pinyin **jīn** *and Frequency Rank* **336**

SIMP & TRAD   Contains **4 strokes** in the following order:

ノ 人 𠆢 今

Contains these components:

☐ many c 厶 (altered) 1678, p. 372
☐ second (in a series) 乙 (altered) 146, p. 41

With all these meanings & readings:

jīn [今] **1** today **2** modern **3** present **4** current **5** this **6** now

The to-do list for **today** contains too *many* items for the lazy worker. His boss will be lucky if the worker gets to the *second in the series*.

1702

This character with the definition:

zither-like instrument

Pinyin **qín** *and Frequency Rank* **1701**

SIMP & TRAD   Contains **12 strokes** in the following order:

一 二 ㆌ 王 王' 玨 玨 玨 珡 琴 琴 琴

Contains these components:

☐ king (×2) 王 15, p. 12
■ today, current 今 1701, p. 377

With all these meanings & readings:

qín [琴] **1** guqin or zither, cf 古琴 **2** musical instrument in general

Imagine that the two '*king*' elements at the top of the character symbolize that one *king* has chosen *today* as the time to teach the other how to play a **zither-like instrument**.

1703

This character with the definition:

chant, recite

Pinyin **yín** *and Frequency Rank* **2015**

SIMP & TRAD   Contains **7 strokes** in the following order:

丨 𠮛 口 叻 𠮩 吟 吟

Contains these components:

■ mouth 口 37, p. 17
■ today, current 今 1701, p. 377

With all these meanings & readings:

yín [吟] **1** moan **2** to hum

The teacher told her young students, "*Today* you will use your mind and your *mouth* to **recite** the alphabet to me."

1704 含

This character with the definition:

hold (in mouth)

Pinyin **hán** *and Frequency Rank* **937**

SIMP & TRAD   Contains **7 strokes** in the following order:

ノ 人 𠆢 今 今 含 含

Contains these components:

☐ today, current 今 1701, p. 377
■ mouth 口 37, p. 17

With all these meanings & readings:

hán [含] **1** to keep **2** to contain **3** to suck (keep in your mouth without chewing)

When I go to my dentist later *today*, I know that he will ask me to **hold** tubes and other things in my *mouth* while he works on my teeth.

1705

貪

貪
TRAD   SIMPLIFIED

This character with the definition:

corrupt

Pinyin **tān** *and Frequency Rank* **1874**

Contains **8 strokes** in the following order:

丿 人 𠆢 今 今 含 貪 貪

Contains these components:

today, current 今 1701, p. 377

cowrie 貝 1394, p. 309

With all these meanings & readings

tān [貪] **1** greedy

Young people *today* believe that a person cannot earn a lot of *money* without being **corrupt**.

1706

令

SIMP & TRAD

This character with the definition:

order, decree

Pinyin **lìng** *and Frequency Rank* **378**

Contains **5 strokes** in the following order:

丿 人 𠆢 今 令

Contains these components:

today, current 今 1701, p. 377

dab r 、 176, p. 48

With all these meanings & readings

líng [令] **1** see 脊令[jǐ líng]
lǐng [令] **1** m for a ream of paper
lìng [令] **1** make or cause to be **2** order **3** command **4** decree **5** honorable

Today is a *bit* like every other day at work. I will just be following my boss's **orders**.

1707

玲

SIMP & TRAD

This character with the definition:

exquisitely made

Pinyin **líng** *and Frequency Rank* **1855**

Contains **9 strokes** in the following order:

一 二 干 王 玗 玲 玲 玲 玲

Contains these components:

king 王 15, p. 12

order, decree 令 1706, p. 378

With all these meanings & readings

líng [玲] **1** onomat. ting-a-ling (in compounds such as 玎玲 or 玲珑[~瓏]) **2** tinkling of gem-pendants

By the *order* of the *king*, any goods bestowed to the royal household had to be **exquisitely made**.

1708

零

SIMP & TRAD

This character with the definition:

zero

Pinyin **líng** *and Frequency Rank* **1342**

Contains **13 strokes** in the following order:

一 厂 厂 厂 雨 雨 雨 雪 雯 雯 零 零 零

Contains these components:

rain 雨 239, p. 63

order, decree 令 1706, p. 378

With all these meanings & readings

líng [零] **1** remnant **2** zero

There is **zero** possibility that *rain*fall will ever be produced 'By the *Order*' of any human, no matter how powerful.

1709

齡

齡
TRAD   SIMPLIFIED

This character with the definition:

duration (time)

Pinyin **líng** *and Frequency Rank* **1510**

Contains **13 strokes** in the following order:

丨 卜 𠤎 止 齿 齿 齿 齿 齿 齢 齡 齡 齡

Contains these components:

tooth 齿 543, p. 128

order, decree 令 1706, p. 378

With all these meanings & readings

líng [齡] **1** age

In ancient days, dental hygiene was primitive at best: the greater the **duration of time** since your last visit to the dentist, the more likely that the condition of your *teeth* would *decree* the quality of your epicurean life.

Unit 71

1710

This character with the definition:

cold

Pinyin **lěng** *and Frequency Rank* **700**

SIMP & TRAD   Contains **7 strokes** in the following order:

丶冫冫冷冷冷冷

Contains these components:

ice r 冫 348, p. 87

order, decree 令 1706, p. 378

With all these meanings & readings:

lěng [冷] **1** cold

The mayor issued a special *decree* that it was not safe to skate on the town's lake during the winter because the temperatures had not been **cold** enough to form solid, thick *ice*.

1711

铃
TRAD SIMPLIFIED

This character with the definition:

bell

Pinyin **líng** *and Frequency Rank* **1969**

Contains **10 strokes** in the following order:

丿𠂉𠂉车车钅钤钤铃铃

Contains these components:

gold 金 1550, p. 342

order, decree 令 1706, p. 378

With all these meanings & readings:

líng [铃] **1** (small) bell **2** m 只 [隻][zhī]

The queen rang a *gold*-plated **bell** to *order* her attendants to her private chamber.

1712

领
TRAD SIMPLIFIED

This character with the definition:

collar

Pinyin **lǐng** *and Frequency Rank* **329**

Contains **11 strokes** in the following order:

丿𠂉𠂉今令令令𠆤领领领

Contains these components:

order, decree 令 1706, p. 378

page, leaf 页 1408, p. 312

With all these meanings & readings:

lǐng [领] **1** neck **2** collar **3** to lead **4** to receive **5** m for clothes, mats, screens etc

My husband nervously loosened his **collar** as he watched the Food Inspector write a five *page order* listing the code violations in his restaurant.

1713

SIMP & TRAD

This character with the definition:

life, fate

Pinyin **mìng** *and Frequency Rank* **258**

Contains **8 strokes** in the following order:

丿人人今合合合命

Contains these components:

mouth 口 37, p. 17

order, decree 令 (altered) 1706, p. 378

With all these meanings & readings:

mìng [命] **1** life **2** fate **3** order

If you're a pessimist, then **life** is just a succession of *orders* issued to you from the *mouths* of others.

1714

邻
TRAD SIMPLIFIED

This character with the definition:

neighbor

Pinyin **lín** *and Frequency Rank* **1659**

Contains **7 strokes** in the following order:

丿𠂉𠂉今令令阝邻

Contains these components:

order, decree 令 1706, p. 378

town r 阝 955, p. 219

With all these meanings & readings:

lín [邻] **1** neighbor **2** adjacent **3** close to

A constant stream of *orders* and *decrees* were a feature of ancient *towns*. Then, you could rely on good **neighbors** to share their burdens with you.

1715

TRAD SIMPLIFIED

This character with the definition:

sympathy, pity

Pinyin **lián** *and Frequency Rank* **1599**

Contains **8 strokes** in the following order:

丶 丶 忄 忄 忄 忄 忄 忄

Contains these components:

■ heart (skinny) r 忄 1135, p. 256
■ order, decree 令 1706, p. 378

With all these meanings & readings:

lián [憐] **1** to pity

Harsh *decrees* generate so much *emotion* that you must rely on friends and loved ones for **sympathy** and **pity**.

1716

SIMP & TRAD

This character with the definition:

long for

Pinyin **niàn** *and Frequency Rank* **477**

Contains **8 strokes** in the following order:

丿 人 仝 今 念 念 念 念

Contains these components:

■ today, current 今 1701, p. 377
■ heart (fat) r 心 1096, p. 248

With all these meanings & readings:

niàn [念] **1** to read **2** to study (a degree course) **3** to read aloud **4** to miss (sb) **5** idea **6** remembrance **7** twenty (bank anti-fraud numeral corresponding to 廿, 20)

Impulsive people will desperately **long for** something *today* and then have no *feeling* for it a week or even a day later.

1717

COMPONENT

This component has the meaning:

river course c

And contains these subcomponents:

■ man 人 537, p. 127
■ labor, work 工 12, p. 12

The **course of a river** attracts many *men* who plan to harness the river's power to do useful *work*.

1718

TRAD SIMPLIFIED

This character with the definition:

light (weight)

Pinyin **qīng** *and Frequency Rank* **460**

Contains **9 strokes** in the following order:

一 七 车 车 车 轻 轻 轻 轻

Contains these components:

■ car 车 1291, p. 289
■ river course c 仝 1717, p. 380

With all these meanings & readings:

qīng [輕] **1** light **2** easy **3** gentle **4** soft **5** reckless **6** unimportant **7** frivolous **8** small in number **9** unstressed **10** neutral

The flood waters in the *river course* were so strong and violent that they carried everything—even *cars* and trucks—downstream as if they were **light** as toys.

1719

TRAD SIMPLIFIED

This character with the definition:

warp (fabric)

Pinyin **jīng** *and Frequency Rank* **62**

Contains **8 strokes** in the following order:

乙 纟 纟 纤 纤 经 经 经

Contains these components:

■ silk r 纟 1037, p. 235
■ river course c 仝 1717, p. 380

With all these meanings & readings:

jīng [經] **1** classics **2** sacred book **3** scripture **4** to pass through **5** to undergo **6** warp **7** longitude **8** abbr for economics 经济 [經濟] **9** surname Jing

Silk is made when a single layer of parallel threads, which is known as the **warp** and resembles a long *river course*, is fed through a loom which inter-weaves the **warp** with perpendicular threads to produce a fine fabric.

1720

徑
TRAD

SIMPLIFIED

This character with the definition:

path, track

Pinyin **jìng** *and Frequency Rank* **1307**

Contains **8 strokes** in the following order:

Contains these components:
- ◩ left step r ⼻ 1247, p. 278
- ◩ river course c 巠 1717, p. 380

With all these meanings & readings:
jìng [徑] **1** path **2** diameter

A **path** is like a winding *river coursing* over the forest floor, formed by imprints from the *steps* of hundreds of people and animals traveling through.

1721

劲
TRAD

勁
SIMPLIFIED

This character with the definition:

vigor, energy

Pinyin **jìn** *and Frequency Rank* **1358**

Contains **7 strokes** in the following order:

Contains these components:
- ◩ river course c 巠 1717, p. 380
- ◩ strength 力 471, p. 113

With all these meanings & readings:
jìn [勁] **1** strength **2** energy **3** enthusiasm **4** m 把[bǎ]
jìng [勁] **1** stalwart **2** sturdy **3** strong **4** powerful

The *strength* and intensity of the spring sun melts the high mountain snow into streams that cascade down into the valley below with such **vigor** that sometimes they will change the *river's course*.

1722

This component has the meaning:

wrangling c

COMPONENT

And contains these subcomponents:
- ◩ hardworking (×2) 辛 684, p. 160

Men who have to *work hard* all day are apt to be a little cranky by evening. It's no surprise to hear them **wrangle** verbally with each other.

1723

SIMP & TRAD

This character with the definition:

distinguish between

Pinyin **biàn** *and Frequency Rank* **1910**

Contains **16 strokes** in the following order:

Contains these components:
- ◪ wrangling c 辡 1722, p. 381
- ◪ knife r ⼑ 169, p. 46

With all these meanings & readings:
biàn [辨] **1** to distinguish **2** to recognize

Two men are *wrangling* and their tempers rising. One of them has a *knife*, which may help us **distinguish between** the winner and the loser.

1724

辩
TRAD

辯
SIMPLIFIED

This character with the definition:

argue, debate

Pinyin **biàn** *and Frequency Rank* **1355**

Contains **16 strokes** in the following order:

Contains these components:
- ◪ wrangling c 辡 1722, p. 381
- ◪ speech r ⻈ 352, p. 88

With all these meanings & readings:
biàn [辯] **1** dispute **2** debate **3** argue **4** discuss

The two men are *wrangling* with the "weapons" of *speech* in a heated **debate**.

1725 This component has the meaning:

moving hand c

COMPONENT

And contains these subcomponents:

☐ one 一 1, p.10

◼ action path c ⁄ 438, p.105

A magician succeeds by focusing your attention on *one* **moving hand** while his other is following an *action path* that will pull the rabbit out of the hat.

1726 This character with the definition:

to sink

Pinyin **chén** *and Frequency Rank* **1681**

SIMP & TRAD Contains **7 strokes** in the following order:

Contains these components:

◻ water r 氵 314, p.80

◼ moving hand c ⁄ (altered) 1725, p.382

◼ mineshaft c ㄴ 122, p.36

With all these meanings & readings:

chén [沈] **1** surname Shen **2** pl name

chén [沈] **1** variant of 沉 [沉][ch

丶 丶 氵 氵 氿 沙 沈

The long-abandoned *mineshaft* was a favorite dumping place because, years ago, it had filled with *water* and many a furtively *moving hand* enjoyed dropping 'unwanted' things over the *mineshaft's* edge while eyes happily watched objects **sink** and disappear forever.

1727 This character with the definition:

upper arm

Pinyin **gōng** *and Frequency Rank* **4921**

SIMP & TRAD Contains **8 strokes** in the following order:

Contains these components:

◼ meat 肉 (altered) 753, p.175

◼ moving hand c ⁄ 1725, p.382

◻ private r 厶 963, p.220

With all these meanings & readings:

gōng [肱] **1** brachium **2** humer•

丿 刀 月 月 肝 肚 肱 肱

The **upper arm** does not contain your funny bone but it is the *body part* that allows your *moving hand* to touch your *nose*.

1728 雄 This character with the definition:

male, mighty

Pinyin **xióng** *and Frequency Rank* **1054**

SIMP & TRAD Contains **12 strokes** in the following order:

Contains these components:

◼ upper arm 肱 (altered) 1727, p.382

◻ short-tailed bird 隹 1193, p.267

With all these meanings & readings:

xióng [雄] **1** heroic **2** male

一 ナ 左 左 厷 厷 厷 厷 雄 雄 雄 雄

The **males** felt strong and **mighty** after they frightened away the small group of *short-tailed birds* by simply waving their *upper arms*.

1729 宏 This character with the definition:

great, grand

Pinyin **hóng** *and Frequency Rank* **1798**

SIMP & TRAD Contains **7 strokes** in the following order:

Contains these components:

◻ roof r 宀 271, p.70

◼ upper arm 肱 (altered) 1727, p.382

With all these meanings & readings:

hóng [宏] **1** great **2** magnificent **3** macro (comp.) **4** macro-

丶 丷 宀 宀 宁 宏 宏

As the workers removed the *roof* of the buried royal tomb, they found an item of **great** interest to the experts—the thousand-year-old *upper arm* bone of a child.

1730 左

This character with the definition:

left

Pinyin **zuǒ** *and Frequency Rank* **782**

SIMP & TRAD   Contains **5 strokes** in the following order:

一 ナ 左 左 左

Contains these components:

■ moving hand c ナ 1725, p.382

□ labor, work 工 12, p.12

With all these meanings & readings:

zuǒ [左] **1** left   **2** surname Zuo

The factory employees spent the entire day seated by an assembly line that constantly moved from right to **left**, with their *moving hands* busily at *work* inserting various pieces and parts into the continuous stream of products.

1731 佐

This character with the definition:

assist

Pinyin **zuǒ** *and Frequency Rank* **2081**

SIMP & TRAD   Contains **7 strokes** in the following order:

ノ 亻 仁 仕 佐 佐 佐

Contains these components:

■ man r 亻 1156, p.260

■ left 左 1730, p.383

With all these meanings & readings:

zuǒ [佐] **1** assist

Left-handed people are so clumsy that they need a *man* to **assist** them whenever they want to do meaningful work. (The current author is a lefty.)

1732 右

This character with the definition:

right (side)

Pinyin **yòu** *and Frequency Rank* **783**

SIMP & TRAD   Contains **5 strokes** in the following order:

一 ナ 右 右 右

Contains these components:

■ moving hand c ナ 1725, p.382

■ mouth 口 37, p.17

With all these meanings & readings:

yòu [右] **1** right (-hand)

A dentist's *moving hand* usually approaches your *mouth* from the **right** because most dentists are right-handed.

1733 若

This character with the definition:

seem, like, as if

Pinyin **ruò** *and Frequency Rank* **651**

SIMP & TRAD   Contains **8 strokes** in the following order:

一 十 艹 艹 艹 若 若 若

Contains these components:

□ grass r 艹 87, p.29

■ right (side) 右 1732, p.383

With all these meanings & readings:

ruò [若] **1** to seem   **2** like   **3** as   **4** if

As I compare my house to my neighbor's on the *right*, I feel **as if** his *grass* looks greener than mine!

1734

諾

TRAD   SIMPLIFIED

This character with the definition:

promise

Pinyin **nuò** *and Frequency Rank* **969**

Contains **9 strokes** in the following order:

ﾑ 讠 讠 讧 诺 诺 诺 诺 诺

Contains these components:

■ speech r 讠 352, p.88

■ seem, like, as if 若 1733, p.383

With all these meanings & readings:

nuò [诺] **1** promise   **2** consent

His political *speech seemed* to **promise** all kinds of social improvements, but he was deceitful, just *like* all his colleagues.

Unit 72

1735 惹
SIMP & TRAD

This character with the definition:

provoke, exasperate

Pinyin **rě** *and Frequency Rank* **2272**

Contains **12 strokes** in the following order:

一 十 艹 兰 芢 芋 若 若 若 惹 惹 惹

Contains these components:

■ seem, like, as if 若 1733, p. 383
■ heart (fat) r 心 1096, p. 248

With all these meanings & readings:

rě [惹] **1** to provoke **2** to irritate **3** to vex **4** to stir up **5** anger **6** to attract (troubles) **7** to cause (problems)

When a child tries to **provoke** his or her parents, the last thing the parents should do is to act *like* the child has affected their *emotions*.

1736
布
佈
TRAD SIMPLIFIED

This character with the definition:

cloth

Pinyin **bù** *and Frequency Rank* **380**

Contains **5 strokes** in the following order:

一 ナ ナ 右 布

Contains these components:

■ moving hand c 丿 1725, p. 382
■ towel 巾 118, p. 35

With all these meanings & readings:

bù [佈] **1** to declare **2** to announce **3** to spread **4** to make known **5** spread **6** (cotton) cloth
bù [布] **1** to declare **2** to announce **3** to spread **4** to make known **5** spread **6** (cotton) cloth

Consider this *moving hand* an expert at transforming a rough *towel* into finished **cloth**.

1737 怖
SIMP & TRAD

This character with the definition:

be afraid of

Pinyin **bù** *and Frequency Rank* **1776**

Contains **8 strokes** in the following order:

丶 丷 忄 忄 忙 忭 怖 怖

Contains these components:

■ heart (skinny) r 忄 1135, p. 256
■ cloth 布 1736, p. 384

With all these meanings & readings:

bù [怖] **1** terror **2** terrified **3** afraid **4** frightened

I **am afraid of** spiders. If I see one, I become paralyzed with fear and feel as if a strip of *cloth* is wrapped tightly around my *heart*.

1738 尤
SIMP & TRAD

This character with the definition:

particularly, especially

Pinyin **yóu** *and Frequency Rank* **1099**

Contains **4 strokes** in the following order:

一 ナ 尢 尤

Contains these components:

■ moving hand c 丿 1725, p. 382
■ dab r 丶 176, p. 48
■ mineshaft c ㄥ 122, p. 36

With all these meanings & readings:

yóu [尤] **1** outstanding **2** particularly, especially **3** a fault **4** to express discontentment against **5** surname You

The criminal's shirt had an incriminating *dab* of his victim's blood on it. The *mineshaft* was the perfect place to make it 'disappear'—**especially** since it had been abandoned for years. In no time at all, his quick *moving hand* dropped the shirt down the *mineshaft* before anyone could witness this act.

1739 就
SIMP & TRAD

This character with the definition:

then

Pinyin **jiù** *and Frequency Rank* **27**

Contains **12 strokes** in the following order:

丶 一 十 亠 古 京 京 京 京 訧 就 就

Contains these components:

■ capital city 京 1314, p. 293
■ particularly, especially 尤 1738, p. 384

With all these meanings & readings:

jiù [就] **1** at once **2** right away **3** only **4** just (emphasis) **5** early as **6** already **7** as soon as **8** then **9** in that case **10** as many as **11** even if **12** to approach **13** to move towards **14** to undertake **15** to engage in **16** to suffer **17** subjected to **18** to accomplish **19** to take advantage of **20** to go with (of foods) **21** with regard to **22** concerning

It is a common pattern for young adults to move into the *capital city* for career opportunities and *especially* for a larger social life. **Then**, after marriage and the arrival of their first child, they flee the *capital city* and head to the suburbs.

1740

憂
TRAD   SIMPLIFIED

This character with the definition:

忧

worry, anxiety

Pinyin **yōu** *and Frequency Rank* **1461**

Contains **7 strokes** in the following order:

Contains these components:

■ heart (skinny) r 忄 1135, p. 256

□ particularly, especially 尤 1738, p. 384

With all these meanings & readings:

yōu [憂] **1** to worry **2** to concern oneself with **3** worried **4** anxiety **5** sorrow **6** a parent's funeral **7** inconvenienced by being orphaned

Emotions that are *especially* troublesome include **worry** and **anxiety**.

1741

擾
TRAD   SIMPLIFIED

This character with the definition:

扰

bother

Pinyin **rǎo** *and Frequency Rank* **1483**

Contains **7 strokes** in the following order:

Contains these components:

■ hand r 扌 25, p. 15

□ worry, anxiety 忧 1740, p. 385

With all these meanings & readings:

rǎo [擾] **1** disturb

My brother has an *anxiety* disorder that causes any physical contact, even the slightest touch from a friend's *hand*, to **bother** him.

1742

优
優
TRAD   SIMPLIFIED

This character with the definition:

优

excellent, superior

Pinyin **yōu** *and Frequency Rank* **774**

Contains **6 strokes** in the following order:

Contains these components:

■ man r 亻 1156, p. 260

□ worry, anxiety 忧 1740, p. 385

With all these meanings & readings:

yōu [優] **1** excellent **2** superior

ノ 亻 仁 伢 优 优

That *man* is good—**excellent**, really—at reducing other people's *anxiety*.

1743

龙
龍
TRAD   SIMPLIFIED

This character with the definition:

龙

dragon

Pinyin **lóng** *and Frequency Rank* **696**

Contains **5 strokes** in the following order:

Contains these components:

■ particularly, especially 尤 1738, p. 384

□ action path c ノ 438, p. 105

With all these meanings & readings:

lóng [龍] **1** dragon **2** imperial **3** surname Long **4** m 条 [條][tiáo]

一 ナ 尤 龙 龙

Look at this character as a pictograph. You see a man with an injured right leg (the *action path*) with a massive bandage or cast on it. The patient is trying to walk, but it's such an effort that a drop of his sweat flies in the air. And he's not really walking, either—he's just **draggin'** (sounds like **dragon**!) himself along.

1744

龐
TRAD   SIMPLIFIED

This character with the definition:

庞

very large

Pinyin **páng** *and Frequency Rank* **1849**

Contains **8 strokes** in the following order:

Contains these components:

■ shelter r 广 427, p. 103

□ dragon 龙 1743, p. 385

With all these meanings & readings:

páng [龐] **1** huge **2** enormous **3** tremendous **4** surname Pang

丶 一 广 广 庁 庞 庞 庞

Look at how the *dragon* sticks out from its *shelter*—it's so **very large**!

1745

TRAD 襲

This character with the definition:

raid, make a surprise attack

Pinyin **xí** *and Frequency Rank* **1213**

SIMPLIFIED   Contains **11 strokes** in the following order:

一 ナ 九 尤 龙 龙 龙 芯 袭 袭 袭

Contains these components:

■ dragon 龙 1743, p. 385
■ clothing 衣 1068, p. 242

With all these meanings & readings:

xí [襲] **1** to attack **2** to inherit **3** m for suits (especially of funeral robes)

Who would suspect a herd of *dragons* that wears tutus, Speedo swim trunks, and other outrageous articles of *clothing* would be preparing a **surprise attack** on the settlers?

1746

TRAD 籠

This character with the definition:

cage, coop, basket

Pinyin **lóng** *and Frequency Rank* **1928**

SIMPLIFIED   Contains **11 strokes** in the following order:

丿 ト ゲ ゲ 竹 竹 竺 笭 筶 笼 笼

Contains these components:

■ bamboo r ⺮ 264, p. 68
■ dragon 龙 1743, p. 385

With all these meanings & readings:

lóng [籠] **1** basket **2** cage **3** fl bamboo basket used to serve dimsum 点心 [點~] such as jiǎoz 饺子 [餃~], bāozi 包子 etc

How do you build a **cage** for a *dragon*? Very carefully. It turns out *bamboo* is the best material, for it flexes without breaking.

1747

This character with the definition:

gray

Pinyin **huī** *and Frequency Rank* **1311**

SIMP & TRAD   Contains **6 strokes** in the following order:

一 ナ 大 犬 灰 灰

Contains these components:

■ moving hand c ナ 1725, p. 382
■ fire 火 1511, p. 334

With all these meanings & readings:

huī [灰] **1** ash **2** dust **3** lime **4** gray **5** discouraged **6** dejected

The safest way to put out a camp*fire* is to extinguish the flames with water and then to scatter all the embers with your *moving hands* until only cold **gray** ashes remain.

1748

This character with the definition:

extensive, vast

Pinyin **huī** *and Frequency Rank* **1364**

SIMP & TRAD   Contains **9 strokes** in the following order:

丶 丷 忄 忄 忙 快 恢 恢 恢

Contains these components:

■ heart (skinny) r 忄 1135, p. 256
■ gray 灰 1747, p. 386

With all these meanings & readings:

huī [恢] **1** to restore **2** to recover **3** great

Youth is the time to embark on **extensive** trips all over the world so that your *heart* will be full of many happy memories when you are old and *gray*.

1749

TRAD 無

This character with the definition:

un-, -less

Pinyin **wú** *and Frequency Rank* **105**

SIMPLIFIED   Contains **4 strokes** in the following order:

一 二 于 无

Contains these components:

■ moving hand c ナ 1725, p. 382
□ one 一 1, p. 10
■ mineshaft c ∟ 122, p. 36

With all these meanings & readings:

wú [無] **1** -less **2** not to have **3** no **4** none **5** not **6** to lack **7** un-

Un-less I can dodge the enemy's *one moving hand*, it will push me down the *mineshaft*.

1750

抚
撫
TRAD   SIMPLIFIED

This character with the definition:

comfort, console

Pinyin **fǔ** *and Frequency Rank* **1720**

Contains **7 strokes** in the following order:

一 十 扌 扌 扩 抚 抚

Contains these components:

▪ hand r 扌 25, p.15
▪ un-, -less 无 1749, p.386

With all these meanings & readings:

fǔ [撫] **1** to comfort **2** to console **3** to stroke **4** to caress **5** an old term for province or provincial governor

The **consoling** touch of a human *hand* benefits a mourner by helping him feel *less* pain.

1751

丰

This component has the meaning:

action scaffolding c

COMPONENT

And contains these subcomponents:

▪ one 一 1, p.10
▪ action path c ノ 438, p.105
▪ scepter c ∣ 5, p.10

Visualize the curved vertical stroke on the left as the upward movement of a load of construction material, hoisted alongside the **action scaffolding** until it reaches its place on the horizontal bar at the top.

1752

丌
SIMP & TRAD

This character with the definition:

his, hers, theirs (archaic)

Pinyin **jī** *and Frequency Rank* **9999**

Contains **3 strokes** in the following order:

一 丁 丌

Contains these components:

▪ action scaffolding c 丰 (altered) 1751, p.387

With all these meanings & readings:

jī [丌] **1** surname Ji
jì [丌] **1** "pedestal" component in Chinese characters
qí [丌] **1** archaic variant of 其 [其][qí]

Imagine the '*action scaffolding c*' component as the profile of a table with **its** leg bent and **its** surface slightly tilted.

1753

畀
SIMP & TRAD

This character with the definition:

bestow, confer

Pinyin **bì** *and Frequency Rank* **5859**

Contains **8 strokes** in the following order:

丿 冂 冃 田 田 畀 畀 畀

Contains these components:

▪ field 田 63, p.23
▪ his, hers, theirs (archaic) 丌 1752, p.387

With all these meanings & readings:

bì [畀] **1** confer on **2** give to

After the father's death, his will revealed that he **bestowed** his *field* on his children, making parts of it *his, hers, and theirs*.

1754

鼻
SIMP & TRAD

This character with the definition:

nose

Pinyin **bí** *and Frequency Rank* **1335**

Contains **14 strokes** in the following order:

丿 丬 冂 白 白 自 自 鼻 鼻 鼻 鼻 畠 鼻 鼻

Contains these components:

▪ self 自 232, p.61
▪ bestow, confer 畀 1753, p.387

With all these meanings & readings:

bí [鼻] **1** nose

It is said that one's **nose** *bestows* a unique sense of *self* to one's personality.

1755

异
異
TRAD   SIMPLIFIED

This character with the definition:

different, strange, unusual

Pinyin **yì** *and Frequency Rank* **709**

Contains **6 strokes** in the following order:

ㄱ ㄱ 巳 巳 异 异

Contains these components:

▪ self* 己 (altered) 135, p.39
▪ action scaffolding c 丰 1751, p.387

With all these meanings & readings:

yì [異] **1** different **2** other **3** hetero- **4** unusual **5** strange **6** surprising **7** to distinguish **8** to separate **9** to discriminate

Our manager, a fat and bald man, can be quite a character. Here he is him*self*, climbing up the *scaffolding* to hang a 'Happy New Year' sign that is written in Chinese. Everyone thought this was **strange** and **unusual** considering that the Lunar New Year was six months away.

1756

This character with the definition:

wear, put on (clothes)

Pinyin **dài** *and Frequency Rank* **1228**

SIMP & TRAD   Contains **17 strokes** in the following order:

一 十 土 吉 吉 高 奇 奇 奇 专 童 壹 童 竞 责 戴 戴 戴

Contains these components:

■ wound c ㇇ 937, p. 215
■ different, strange, unusual 异 1755, p. 387

With all these meanings & readings:

dài [戴] **1** to put on **2** to respect **3** to bear **4** to support **5** wear (glasses, hat, gloves) **6** surname Dai

His *wound* was rather odd and located in an *unusual* part of his body. Displaying it rather embarrassed him, so he was careful to **put on clothes** that would cover it up completely.

1757

This character with the definition:

manage, handle

Pinyin **nòng** *and Frequency Rank* **1053**

SIMP & TRAD   Contains **7 strokes** in the following order:

一 二 干 王 王 手 弄

Contains these components:

■ king 王 15, p. 12
■ action scaffolding c 廾 1751, p. 387

With all these meanings & readings:

lòng [弄] **1** lane **2** alley
nòng [弄] **1** to do **2** to manage **3** to handle **4** to play with **5** t fool with **6** to mess with **7** to fix **8** to toy with

The *king* stands on top of the *scaffolding* in order to oversee his subjects and **manage** all their affairs.

1758

This character with the definition:

well

Pinyin **jǐng** *and Frequency Rank* **1431**

SIMP & TRAD   Contains **4 strokes** in the following order:

一 二 井 井

Contains these components:

■ action scaffolding c 廾 1751, p. 387
▭ one 一 1, p. 10

With all these meanings & readings:

jǐng [井] **1** warn **2** well **3** surname Jing **4** m 口 [kǒu]

The horizontals and verticals represent the division of land into neighboring fields. They can flourish despite their proximity to each other because they share the central **well**, which provides plenty of water for every *one* of the farmers. Also, the criss-cross pattern of lines can represent a protective grid across the top of the **well**. You can drop your bucket down to collect water, but children and other large objects can't fall through. Sometimes, we'll use this character to represent stick-like things.

1759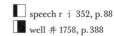

This character with the definition:

talk, speak, speaking of

Pinyin **jiǎng** *and Frequency Rank* **555**

講
TRAD SIMPLIFIED   Contains **6 strokes** in the following order:

Contains these components:

▮ speech r 讠 352, p. 88
■ well 井 1758, p. 388

With all these meanings & readings:

jiǎng [講] **1** to speak **2** to explain **3** a speech **4** a lecture

丶 讠 讠 讧 讲 讲

The genie's *speech* rose mysteriously from the *well* and asked us to **speak** our wishes more clearly to him.

Unit 73

1760

SIMP & TRAD

This character with the definition:

plow, till

Pinyin **gēng** *and Frequency Rank* **1850**

Contains **10 strokes** in the following order:

一 = 三 丰 耒 耒 耒 耕 耕 耕

Contains these components:

tree 木 562, p. 133
two 二 (altered) 2, p. 10
well 井 1758, p. 388

With all these meanings & readings:

gēng [耕] **1** to plow **2** to till

In ancient times, people made **plows** out of *two trees*: one tree was for the handle and one was for the 'blade'. The lengths of the strokes in 'two' are altered to emphasize that the length of the handle was longer than the blade, the part that digs into the soil. The four strokes of the *'well'* map out the pattern of furrows in the soil.

1761

升
昇陞
TRAD

SIMPLIFIED

This character with the definition:

move upward

Pinyin **shēng** *and Frequency Rank* **837**

Contains **4 strokes** in the following order:

丿 一 千 升

Contains these components:

dab r 丶 176, p. 48
action scaffolding c 廾 1751, p. 387

With all these meanings & readings:

shēng [升] **1** to raise **2** to hoist **3** to promote **4** metric liter (also written 公升) **5** measure for dry grain equal to one-tenth dou 斗
shēng [昇] **1** ascend **2** peaceful
shēng [陞] **1** promoted

In constructing a tall building, workers **move upward** in *small* increments by building *action scaffolding* as they progress.

1762

SIMP & TRAD

This character with the definition:

warn, guard against

Pinyin **jiè** *and Frequency Rank* **1566**

Contains **7 strokes** in the following order:

一 二 于 开 戒 戒 戒

Contains these components:

halberd 戈 650, p. 154
action scaffolding c 廾 1751, p. 387

With all these meanings & readings:

jiè [戒] **1** swear off **2** warn against

The king decided to **guard against** his enemies by placing his most trusted warrior at the top of the *action scaffolding*. The warrior's threatening *halberd* was poised for action and ready to **warn** the king of any intruders.

1763

械

SIMP & TRAD

This character with the definition:

weapons, implements

Pinyin **xiè** *and Frequency Rank* **1657**

Contains **11 strokes** in the following order:

一 十 オ 木 木 杧 杧 枞 械 械 械

Contains these components:

tree 木 562, p. 133
warn, guard against 戒 1762, p. 389

With all these meanings & readings:

xiè [械] **1** tools

It takes some ingenuity to transform a *tree* into suitable **weapons** that will effectively *guard against* danger.

1764

SIMP & TRAD

This character with the definition:

calculate, compute

Pinyin **suàn** *and Frequency Rank* **403**

Contains **14 strokes** in the following order:

Contains these components:
- bamboo r ⺮ 264, p.68
- eye 目 75, p.26
- action scaffolding c 廾 1751, p.387

With all these meanings & readings:

suàn [算] **1** regard as **2** to figur **3** to calculate **4** to compute

Even today in China, an occasional shopkeeper can be seen **calculating** his accounts at a dizzying speed on an abacus, with its *eye*-shaped beads held together by a mini-*scaffold* locked into a *bamboo* frame.

1765

This component has the meaning:

pinned bug c

COMPONENT

And contains these subcomponents:
- action path c ノ 438, p.105
- boar's head r ⺕ (altered) 30, p.16

Think of the '*action path*' element as the flight path of an unfortunate insect straight into a *wild boar's* mouth! It is trapped and becomes the ultimate **pinned bug**!

1766

SIMP & TRAD

This character with the definition:

he, she

Pinyin **yī** *and Frequency Rank* **761**

Contains **6 strokes** in the following order:

Contains these components:
- man r 亻 1156, p.260
- pinned bug c 尹 1765, p.390

With all these meanings & readings:

yī [伊] **1** he **2** she **3** surname Yi **4** abbr for Iraq or Iran

Since **he** felt as trapped as a *pinned bug* in his gender role as a *man*, '**he**' decided to become a '**she**'!

1767

SIMP & TRAD

This character with the definition:

monarch, lord

Pinyin **jūn** *and Frequency Rank* **985**

Contains **7 strokes** in the following order:

Contains these components:
- pinned bug c 尹 1765, p.390
- mouth 口 37, p.17

With all these meanings & readings:

jūn [君] **1** monarch **2** lord **3** gentleman **4** ruler (length)

In modern times, the influences of a European **monarch** is analogous to that of a *pinned bug*: a figurehead with a *mouth* for making speeches but with no real power to move.

1768 群

SIMP & TRAD

This character with the definition:

flock, herd, crowd

Pinyin **qún** *and Frequency Rank* **570**

Contains **13 strokes** in the following order:

Contains these components:
- monarch, lord 君 1767, p.390
- sheep 羊 1486, p.329

With all these meanings & readings:

qún [群] **1** group **2** crowd **3** flock, herd, pack, etc.

The shepherd was like the *lord* of his *sheep*. The **flock** blindly followed his every move—behaving precisely as sheep do!

1769

This component has the meaning:

safe place c

COMPONENT

In a dangerous situation, most people's natural response is to take quick *action* in finding a *place of refuge*, a protective **safe place**.

1770

This character with the definition:

red, cinnabar

Pinyin **dān** *and Frequency Rank* **1280**

SIMP & TRAD   Contains **4 strokes** in the following order:

丿 刀 刀 丹

Contains these components:

■ safe place c 冂 1769, p. 391
⊐ cover r 冖 250, p. 66

With all these meanings & readings:

dān [丹] **1** red **2** pellet **3** powder **4** cinnabar

Cinnabar is a **red**-colored ore that was frequently used as a pigment in traditional Chinese art. No doubt every artist kept his supply of **cinnabar** in a *safe place* and with a secure *cover* over it.

1771

This character with the definition:

moon, month

Pinyin **yuè** *and Frequency Rank* **169**

SIMP & TRAD   Contains **4 strokes** in the following order:

丿 刀 月 月

Contains these components:

■ safe place c 冂 1769, p. 391
⊐ two 二 2, p. 10

With all these meanings & readings:

yuè [月] **1** moon **2** month **3** m 个 [個][gè], 轮 [輪][lún]

Personal privacy is very difficult to find in a country as populous as China; yet, these *two* lovers find a very private, *safe place* where they could meet once a **month**, under the light of the **moon**, for some 'quality time' together. • This character often represents an altered form of 'meat' (normally 肉, panel 753), and will represent a **body part** in this variation.

1772

This character with the definition:

overlord

Pinyin **bà** *and Frequency Rank* **1838**

SIMP & TRAD   Contains **21 strokes** in the following order:

一 厂 厂 币 币 币 而 雨 雪 雪 雪 雪 雪 雪 雪 霄 霸 霸 霸

Contains these components:

☐ rain 雨 239, p. 63
■ animal hide 革 98, p. 31
■ moon, month 月 1771, p. 391

With all these meanings & readings:

bà [霸] **1** hegemon **2** tyrant **3** lord **4** feudal chief **5** to rule by force **6** to usurp **7** (in modern advertising) master

During every full *moon*, even when it *rains*, our **overlord** conducts a fertility ritual while wearing only an *animal hide*.

1773

This character with the definition:

be willing, ready to

Pinyin **kěn** *and Frequency Rank* **860**

SIMP & TRAD   Contains **8 strokes** in the following order:

丨 卜 止 止 肯 肯 肯 肯

Contains these components:

☐ stop! 止 190, p. 52
■ moon, month 月 1771, p. 391

With all these meanings & readings:

kěn [肯] **1** to agree **2** to consent **3** to be ready (to do sth) **4** willing

Since my friend and his wife had been planning their camping trip for more than a *month*, my friend was shocked when his wife ran up to him while he was packing the car. She cried "*Stop!* I'm not **willing to** go on this trip if I have to sleep outside!"

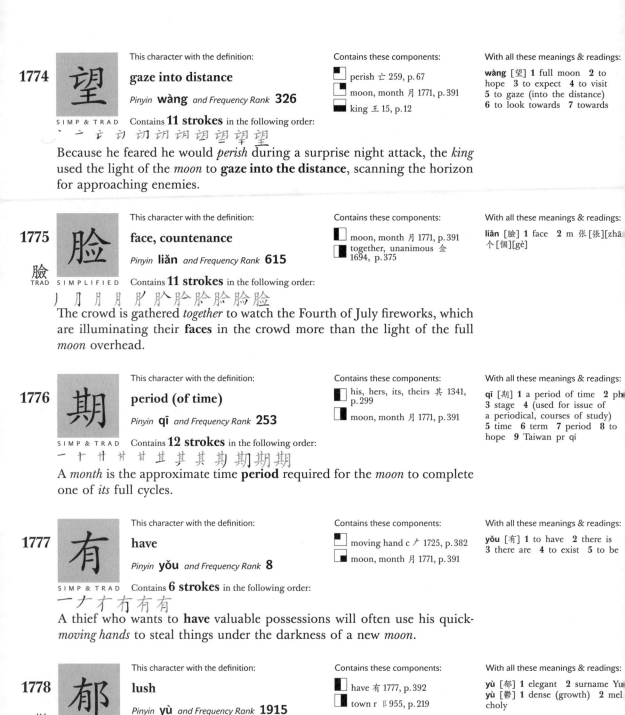

1774　望

SIMP & TRAD

This character with the definition:

gaze into distance

Pinyin **wàng**   and Frequency Rank **326**

Contains these components:

■ perish 亡 259, p. 67
■ moon, month 月 1771, p. 391
■ king 王 15, p. 12

With all these meanings & readings:

wàng [望] **1** full moon **2** to hope **3** to expect **4** to visit **5** to gaze (into the distance) **6** to look towards **7** towards

Contains **11 strokes** in the following order:

Because he feared he would *perish* during a surprise night attack, the *king* used the light of the *moon* to **gaze into the distance**, scanning the horizon for approaching enemies.

1775　脸

脸
TRAD   SIMPLIFIED

This character with the definition:

face, countenance

Pinyin **liǎn**   and Frequency Rank **615**

Contains these components:

■ moon, month 月 1771, p. 391
■ together, unanimous 佥 1694, p. 375

With all these meanings & readings:

liǎn [脸] **1** face **2** m 张 [張][zhā 个 [個][gè]

Contains **11 strokes** in the following order:

The crowd is gathered *together* to watch the Fourth of July fireworks, which are illuminating their **faces** in the crowd more than the light of the full *moon* overhead.

1776　期

SIMP & TRAD

This character with the definition:

period (of time)

Pinyin **qī**   and Frequency Rank **253**

Contains these components:

■ his, hers, its, theirs 其 1341, p. 299
■ moon, month 月 1771, p. 391

With all these meanings & readings:

qī [期] **1** a period of time **2** ph **3** stage **4** (used for issue of a periodical, courses of study) **5** time **6** term **7** period **8** to hope **9** Taiwan pr qí

Contains **12 strokes** in the following order:

A *month* is the approximate time **period** required for the *moon* to complete one of *its* full cycles.

1777　有

SIMP & TRAD

This character with the definition:

have

Pinyin **yǒu**   and Frequency Rank **8**

Contains these components:

■ moving hand c ナ 1725, p. 382
■ moon, month 月 1771, p. 391

With all these meanings & readings:

yǒu [有] **1** to have **2** there is **3** there are **4** to exist **5** to be

Contains **6 strokes** in the following order:

A thief who wants to **have** valuable possessions will often use his quick-*moving hands* to steal things under the darkness of a new *moon*.

1778　郁

鬱
TRAD   SIMPLIFIED

This character with the definition:

lush

Pinyin **yù**   and Frequency Rank **1915**

Contains these components:

■ have 有 1777, p. 392
■ town r 阝 955, p. 219

With all these meanings & readings:

yù [郁] **1** elegant **2** surname Yu **yù** [鬱] **1** dense (growth) **2** mel choly

Contains **8 strokes** in the following order:

You only *have towns* in locations where there is sufficient **lush** vegetation to support their rapid growth.

1779

SIMP & TRAD

This character with the definition:

nature's color, unripe

Pinyin **qīng** *and Frequency Rank* **497**

Contains **8 strokes** in the following order:

一　二　主　主　丰　青　青　青

Contains these components:

▭ plentiful 丰 (altered) 16, p.13

▭ moon, month 月 1771, p.391

With all these meanings & readings:

qīng [青] **1** nature's color **2** green or blue **3** greenish black **4** youth **5** young (of people) **6** abbr for Qinghai province 青海

The most visible of **nature's colors** are blue and green—they are the ones that predominate on land and sea in temperate climates. Moreover, it was once thought that intense exposure to the sun was harmful to plant growth and that *plentiful moonlight* was responsible for lush harvests. • Similarly, the Chinese associate 'green' with 'unripe', as do we English speakers.

1780

SIMP & TRAD

This character with the definition:

clear, fine (of weather)

Pinyin **qíng** *and Frequency Rank* **1968**

Contains **12 strokes** in the following order:

丨　冂　日　日　日⁻　日⁼　日⁺　昨　晴　晴　晴　晴

Contains these components:

▭ day, sun 日 64, p.24

▭ nature's color, unripe 青 1779, p.393

With all these meanings & readings:

qíng [晴] **1** clear **2** fine (weather)

Under the **clear** skies of a **fine** *day*, many shades of *green* are on brilliant display in the forest.

1781

SIMP & TRAD

This character with the definition:

eyeball

Pinyin **jīng** *and Frequency Rank* **934**

Contains **13 strokes** in the following order:

丨　冂　月　月　目　日⁻　日⁼　日⁺　睛　睛　睛　睛　睛

Contains these components:

▭ eye 目 75, p.26

▭ nature's color, unripe 青 1779, p.393

With all these meanings & readings:

jīng [睛] **1** eye

The *natural color* of a person's *eye* is not visible when it is examined as an **eyeball** by an optometrist.

1782

SIMP & TRAD

This character with the definition:

clear, clear up

Pinyin **qīng** *and Frequency Rank* **335**

Contains **11 strokes** in the following order:

丶　丶　氵　汀　汢　沣　清　清　清　清　清

Contains these components:

▭ water r 氵 314, p.80

▭ nature's color, unripe 青 1779, p.393

With all these meanings & readings:

qīng [清] **1** clear **2** distinct **3** complete **4** pure **5** the Ch'ing or Qing dynasty (1644-1911)

Even though the clean *water* in the lake was 'crystal **clear**' and colorless, its surface mirrored the color of the sky above it—*nature's color*.

1783

請
TRAD   SIMPLIFIED

This character with the definition:

polite request, ask

Pinyin **qǐng** *and Frequency Rank* **421**

Contains **10 strokes** in the following order:

丶　讠　讠⁻　讠⁼　计　请　请　请　请　请

Contains these components:

▭ speech r 讠 352, p.88

▭ nature's color, unripe 青 1779, p.393

With all these meanings & readings:

qǐng [请] **1** to ask **2** to invite **3** please (do sth) **4** to treat (to a meal etc) **5** to request

The famous naturalist's *speech* about 'experiencing' the spectacular beauty of *nature's color* prompted my wife to **politely request** that we spend time together in a good place—totally surrounded by nature.

1784

This character with the definition:

guess

Pinyin **cāi** *and Frequency Rank* **1598**

SIMP & TRAD   Contains **11 strokes** in the following order:

Contains these components:

■ dog r 犭 1084, p. 245
▯ nature's color, unripe 青 1779, p. 393

With all these meanings & readings:

cāi [猜] **1** to guess

丿 犭 犭 犭 犭 犭 狰 猜 猜 猜 猜

Most people would never **guess** that *dogs* love the 'crunch' of *unripe* vegetables.

Unit 74

1785

情

SIMP & TRAD

This character with the definition:

sentiment, sensibility

Pinyin **qíng** *and Frequency Rank* **120**

Contains **11 strokes** in the following order:

丶 丶 忄 忄 忄 忄 忄 情 情 情 情

Contains these components:

☐ heart (skinny) r 忄 1135, p. 256
☐ nature's color, unripe 青 1779, p. 393

With all these meanings & readings:

qíng [情] **1** feeling **2** emotion
3 passion **4** situation

The brilliant display of *nature's colors* in gardens can produce an *emotional* **sentiment** that lingers in one's memory.

1786

精

SIMP & TRAD

This character with the definition:

perfect, excellent

Pinyin **jīng** *and Frequency Rank* **435**

Contains **14 strokes** in the following order:

丶 丷 二 半 米 米 米 米 米 精 精 精 精 精

Contains these components:

☐ rice (food) 米 1535, p. 339
☐ nature's color, unripe 青 1779, p. 393

With all these meanings & readings:

jīng [精] **1** essence **2** extract
3 vitality **4** energy **5** semen
6 sperm **7** mythical goblin
spirit **8** highly perfected **9** elite
10 the pick of sth. **11** proficient
(refined ability) **12** extremely
(fine) **13** selected rice (archaic)

Since 'brown' is thought to be '*nature's color*' for rice, brown *rice* is considered an **excellent** health food.

1787

静

静
TRAD   SIMPLIFIED

This character with the definition:

still, quiet, calm

Pinyin **jìng** *and Frequency Rank* **722**

Contains **14 strokes** in the following order:

一 二 キ 主 丰 青 青 青 青 青 静 静 静 静

Contains these components:

☐ nature's color, unripe 青 1779, p. 393
☐ struggle 争 863, p. 197

With all these meanings & readings:

jìng [静] **1** still **2** calm **3** quiet
4 not moving

In a rural setting, surrounded by the **quiet calm** of *nature's colors*, it is easy to overlook the daily *struggle* for survival experienced by the wild animals who live there.

1788

明

SIMP & TRAD

This character with the definition:

bright, clear

Pinyin **míng** *and Frequency Rank* **121**

Contains **8 strokes** in the following order:

丨 冂 日 日 日丿 明 明 明

Contains these components:

☐ day, sun 日 64, p. 24
☐ moon, month 月 1771, p. 391

With all these meanings & readings:

míng [明] **1** clear **2** bright **3** to
understand **4** next **5** the Ming
dynasty (1368-1644) **6** surname
Ming

The **bright** lights of the *sun* and *moon* are most visible when the skies are **clear**.

1789

盟

SIMP & TRAD

This character with the definition:

alliance, pact

Pinyin **méng** *and Frequency Rank* **1163**

Contains **13 strokes** in the following order:

丨 冂 日 日 日丿 明 明 明 明 明 盟 盟 盟

Contains these components:

☐ bright, clear 明 1788, p. 395
☐ vessel, container 皿 101, p. 32

With all these meanings & readings:

méng [盟] **1** oath **2** pledge
3 union **4** to ally **5** league,
a subdivision corresponding to
prefecture in Inner Mongolia

After each member of the crime syndicate signed the secret **pact** in *bright* red blood, it was locked in a steel *container*.

1790

This character with the definition:

dynasty

Pinyin **cháo** *and Frequency Rank* **593**

SIMP & TRAD   Contains **12 strokes** in the following order:

一 十 十 古 占 直 直 卓 車 朝 朝 朝

Contains these components:

■ ten 十 7, p.11
■ morning 早 65, p.24
■ moon, month 月 1771, p.391

With all these meanings & readings:

cháo [朝] **1** to face **2** towards **3** facing **4** direct **5** dynasty **6** imperial court **7** abbr for 朝鲜 [~鲜][cháo xiǎn] Korea, especially Joseon dynasty or North Korea
zhāo [朝] **1** morning

The ruling **dynasty** had been in power for nearly *ten* centuries. The ancient Chinese consider that a time span comparable to the amount of time that passes between the first light of *morning* and the rising of the *moon*.

1791

This character with the definition:

tide, current

Pinyin **cháo** *and Frequency Rank* **1302**

SIMP & TRAD   Contains **15 strokes** in the following order:

丶 冫 氵 氵 汁 汁 沽 沽 淖 涓 潮 潮 潮

Contains these components:

■ water r 氵 314, p.80
■ dynasty 朝 1790, p.396

With all these meanings & readings:

cháo [潮] **1** tide **2** current **3** damp **4** moist **5** humid

The pre-determined and unstoppable ebb and flow of the **tide** rules every body of *water* on the earth, resembling the force of a strong *dynasty*.

1792

This character with the definition:

that

Pinyin **nà** *and Frequency Rank* **38**

SIMP & TRAD   Contains **6 strokes** in the following order:

丁 彐 彐 月 那 那

Contains these components:

■ moon, month 月 (altered) 1771, p.391
■ town r 阝 955, p.219

With all these meanings & readings:

nǎ [那] **1** variant of 哪[哪][nǎ]
nà [那] **1** that **2** those **3** commonly pr [nèi] before a classifier, especially in Beijing

It was a century-old tradition **that** on the first Saturday of every *month* the *town* hold an open-market.

1793

This character with the definition:

which? what?

Pinyin **něi** *and Frequency Rank* **652**

SIMP & TRAD   Contains **9 strokes** in the following order:

丿 丨 口 叮 叮 叮 呷 哪 哪

Contains these components:

■ mouth 口 37, p.17
■ that 那 1792, p.396

With all these meanings & readings:

nǎ [哪] **1** how **2** which
na [哪] **1** (particle equivalent to 啊 after noun ending in -n)
něi [哪] **1** which? (interrogative, followed by classifier or numeral classifier)

The combination of a small '*mouth*' element on the left with the larger '*that*' on the right may help you remember this character as the phrase 'Is *that* **what** he was talking about?'

1794

This character with the definition:

lithe, graceful

Pinyin **núo** *and Frequency Rank* **1584**

SIMP & TRAD   Contains **9 strokes** in the following order:

乀 女 女 如 妇 妇 娜 娜 娜

Contains these components:

■ woman 女 790, p.183
■ that 那 1792, p.396

With all these meanings & readings:

nà [娜] **1** (phonetic na) **2** used especially in girl's names such as Anna 安娜 or Diana 黛安娜
núo [娜] **1** elegant **2** graceful

This *particular woman* is distinguished by her **graceful** athletic abilities.

1795

This character with the definition:

be able to, can

Pinyin **néng** *and Frequency Rank* **35**

SIMP & TRAD   Contains **10 strokes** in the following order:

乙 厶 牟 台 台 肖 肖 能 能 能

Contains these components:
- private r 厶 963, p. 220
- moon, month 月 1771, p. 391
- compared with 比 (altered) 127, p. 37

With all these meanings & readings:

néng [能] **1** can **2** may **3** capable **4** energy **5** able **6** surname Neng

The new mother of triplets has resolved to take *private* time once a *month*, so that she **can** 'recharge' herself and **be able to** remain a loving mother, and not be *compared with* a tense robot.

1796

This character with the definition:

bear (animal)

Pinyin **xióng** *and Frequency Rank* **1741**

SIMP & TRAD   Contains **14 strokes** in the following order:

乙 厶 牟 台 台 肖 肖 能 能 能 熊 熊 熊 熊

Contains these components:
- be able to, can 能 1795, p. 397
- fire r ⺣ 1026, p. 233

With all these meanings & readings:

xióng [熊] **1** bear **2** to scold **3** to rebuke **4** brilliant light **5** to shine brightly **6** surname Xiong

A mother **bear** who feels her cubs are threatened *is able to* assume a protective role and *fire* vicious and deadly attacks upon usually unsuspecting human intruders.

1797

This character with the definition:

we (emperor)

Pinyin **zhèn** *and Frequency Rank* **3054**

SIMP & TRAD   Contains **10 strokes** in the following order:

丿 刀 月 月 月' 肌 肸 朕 朕 朕

Contains these components:
- moon, month 月 1771, p. 391
- eight r ⸠ 1260, p. 282
- heaven 天 548, p. 129

With all these meanings & readings:

zhèn [朕] **1** I **2** we (imperial use) **3** subtle

On a beautiful *moon*-lit night, the 'Emperor of *Heaven*' declared: "**We** would be most pleased to see *eight* maidens perform a dance in the courtyard." His attendants hastened to comply with the royal command.

1798

騰
TRAD SIMPLIFIED

This character with the definition:

gallop, prance

Pinyin **téng** *and Frequency Rank* **1635**

Contains **13 strokes** in the following order:

丿 刀 月 月 月' 肌 肸 朕 朕 腾 腾 腾

Contains these components:
- we (emperor) 朕 (altered) 1797, p. 397
- horse 马 388, p. 95

With all these meanings & readings:

téng [騰] **1** to soar **2** to gallop **3** to rise **4** to prance **5** to hover **6** to move out

If you were a *horse* that received the honor to carry the *royal 'we'*, would you do anything other than **prance** and **gallop** in the expected manner?

1799

胜

勝
TRAD SIMPLIFIED

This character with the definition:

win victory, succeed, excel

Pinyin **shèng** *and Frequency Rank* **743**

Contains **9 strokes** in the following order:

丿 刀 月 月 月' 肚 肚 胜 胜

Contains these components:
- moon, month 月 1771, p. 391
- give birth to 生 210, p. 57

With all these meanings & readings:

shèng [勝] **1** victory **2** success **3** to beat **4** to defeat **5** to surpass **6** victorious **7** superior to **8** to get the better of **9** better than **10** surpassing **11** superb (of vista) **12** beautiful (scenery) **13** wonderful (view) **14** (arch. pronunciation shēng) able to bear **15** equal to (a task)

By the light of the full *moon*, the ancient princess *gave birth to* a mighty prince, who later would **win** great **victories** for the Chinese people.

1800

This character with the definition:

friend

Pinyin **péng** *and Frequency Rank* **882**

SIMP & TRAD Contains **8 strokes** in the following order:

丿 刀 月 月 朋) 朋) 朋 朋

Contains these components:

■ moon, month (×2) 月 1771, p. 391

With all these meanings & readings:

péng [朋] **1** friend

Only a true **friend** will stay with you through your ups and downs, *month* after *month*.

1801

鵬
TRAD SIMPLIFIED

This character with the definition:

roc

Pinyin **péng** *and Frequency Rank* **1926**

Contains **13 strokes** in the following order:

丿 刀 月 月 月 朋 朋 朋 朋ʼ 朋ʼ 朋ʼ 鹏 鹏

Contains these components:

■ friend 朋 1800, p. 398
■ bird 鸟 394, p. 96

With all these meanings & readings:

péng [鹏] **1** large fabulous bird

Despite the ferocity of this large fabulous *bird*, sailors considered the **roc** to be a *friendly bird*. How so? If they managed to subdue it, they were able to feast off its flesh for a long, long time.

1802

This character with the definition:

to use

Pinyin **yòng** *and Frequency Rank* **51**

SIMP & TRAD Contains **5 strokes** in the following order:

丿 冂 月 月 用

Contains these components:

■ moon, month 月 1771, p. 391
□ scepter c ∣ 5, p. 10

With all these meanings & readings:

yòng [用] **1** to use

In rural areas with no outdoor electric lighting, under a new *moon* the only natural light comes from the stars and planets. So the wise farmer learns **to use** a *scepter*-like stick for support whenever he ventures outside after dark.

1803

This character with the definition:

just now, only

Pinyin **fǔ** *and Frequency Rank* **2152**

SIMP & TRAD Contains **7 strokes** in the following order:

一 丁 冂 冃 冃 甫 甫

Contains these components:

■ to use 用 (altered) 1802, p. 398
□ one 一 1, p. 10
□ dab r ⟍ 176, p. 48

With all these meanings & readings:

fǔ [甫] **1** just **2** just now

Imagine this character as a building for people *to use* as their *one* special meeting place. Think of the 'dab' element at the top right as a flag signaling its completion **just now** so it is ready *to use*! • When this character appears as an element in other characters, it may mean **monument** or **statue**.

1804

捕

This character with the definition:

catch, seize

Pinyin **bǔ** *and Frequency Rank* **1312**

SIMP & TRAD Contains **10 strokes** in the following order:

一 十 扌 扩 扩 拍 捅 捅 捕 捕

Contains these components:

■ hand r 扌 25, p. 15
■ just now, only 甫 1803, p. 398

With all these meanings & readings:

bǔ [捕] **1** to catch **2** to seize **3** to capture

It is one of nature's marvels to observe a bear **catch** a migrating salmon with *only* a quick swipe of its clawed '*hand*'.

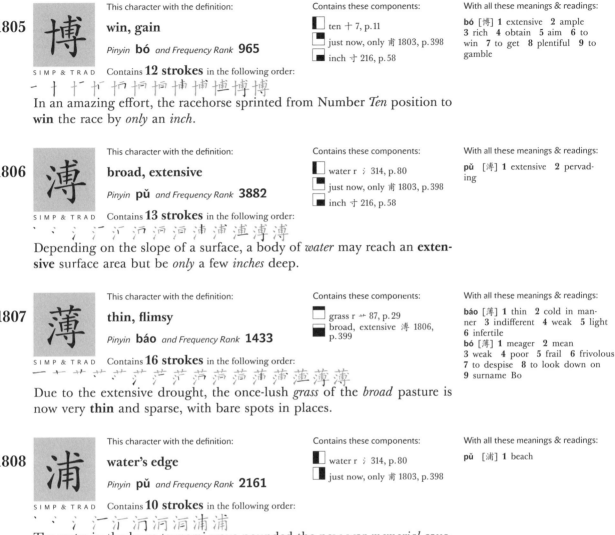

1805 博

This character with the definition:

win, gain

Pinyin **bó** *and Frequency Rank* **965**

SIMP & TRAD   Contains **12 strokes** in the following order:

一 十 十 一 十 一 一 博 博 博 博 博

In an amazing effort, the racehorse sprinted from Number *Ten* position to **win** the race by *only* an *inch*.

Contains these components:

ten 十 7, p.11

just now, only 甫 1803, p.398

inch 寸 216, p.58

With all these meanings & readings:

bó [博] **1** extensive **2** ample **3** rich **4** obtain **5** aim **6** to win **7** to get **8** plentiful **9** to gamble

---

1806 溥

This character with the definition:

broad, extensive

Pinyin **pǔ** *and Frequency Rank* **3882**

SIMP & TRAD   Contains **13 strokes** in the following order:

丶 丶 氵 汀 汀 沔 沔 沔 浦 浦 溥 溥 溥

Depending on the slope of a surface, a body of *water* may reach an **extensive** surface area but be *only* a few *inches* deep.

Contains these components:

water r 氵 314, p.80

just now, only 甫 1803, p.398

inch 寸 216, p.58

With all these meanings & readings:

pǔ [溥] **1** extensive **2** pervading

1807 薄

This character with the definition:

thin, flimsy

Pinyin **báo** *and Frequency Rank* **1433**

SIMP & TRAD   Contains **16 strokes** in the following order:

一 十 艹 艹 艹 艹 艹 茬 蒲 薄 蒲 蒲 蓮 薄 薄

Due to the extensive drought, the once-lush *grass* of the *broad* pasture is now very **thin** and sparse, with bare spots in places.

Contains these components:

grass r 艹 87, p.29

broad, extensive 溥 1806, p.399

With all these meanings & readings:

báo [薄] **1** thin **2** cold in manner **3** indifferent **4** weak **5** light **6** infertile

bó [薄] **1** meager **2** mean **3** weak **4** poor **5** frail **6** frivolous **7** to despise **8** to look down on **9** surname Bo

---

1808 浦

This character with the definition:

water's edge

Pinyin **pǔ** *and Frequency Rank* **2161**

SIMP & TRAD   Contains **10 strokes** in the following order:

丶 丶 氵 汀 汀 沔 沔 沔 浦 浦

The *water* in the huge tsunami wave pounded the new war *memorial* causing it to topple. It was so heavy that it caused all the land around it to sink. The memorial is now resting at the **water's edge**.

Contains these components:

water r 氵 314, p.80

just now, only 甫 1803, p.398

With all these meanings & readings:

pǔ [浦] **1** beach

1809 蒲

This character with the definition:

cattail

Pinyin **pú** *and Frequency Rank* **2344**

SIMP & TRAD   Contains **13 strokes** in the following order:

一 十 艹 艹 艹 艹 艹 茳 蒲 蒲 蒲 蒲 蒲

The fuzzy **cattail** is a beloved and decorative *grass* you can find at the *water's edge*.

Contains these components:

grass r 艹 87, p.29

water's edge 浦 1808, p.399

With all these meanings & readings:

pú [蒲] **1** refers to various monocotyledonous flowering plants including Acorus calamus and Typha orientalis **2** common cattail **3** bullrush **4** surname Pu **5** old place name **6** phonetic po or pu

Unit 75

1810

This character with the definition:

teacher, instructor

Pinyin **fù** *and Frequency Rank* **1887**

SIMP & TRAD Contains **12 strokes** in the following order:

ノ 亻 亻 亻 俨 佴 佴 俌 傅 傅 傅 傅

Contains these components:

☐ man r 亻 1156, p. 260
☐ just now, only 甫 1803, p. 398
☐ inch 寸 216, p. 58

With all these meanings & readings

Fù [傅] **1** tutor **2** surname Fu

That *man* is a terrific **teacher**! *Just now*, he taught me how long an *inch* is.

1811

This character with the definition:

corridor, passageway

Pinyin **yǒng** *and Frequency Rank* **4038**

SIMP & TRAD Contains **7 strokes** in the following order:

乛 ⼇ マ 7 甬 甬 甬 甬

Contains these components:

☐ son, child 子 (altered) 24, p. 15
☐ to use 用 1802, p. 398

With all these meanings & readings

tǒng [甬] **1** variant of 桶 bucket **2** (classifier) cubic dry measure pecks 五斗, approx half-liter)
yǒng [甬] **1** the Yongjiang river 甬江 through Ningbo 宁波 **2** abbr for Ningpo

Children can be especially creative in designing ways *to use* a long **corridor**!

1812

This character with the definition:

painful

Pinyin **tòng** *and Frequency Rank* **730**

SIMP & TRAD Contains **12 strokes** in the following order:

丶 亠 广 广 疒 疒 疒 疒 病 病 痈 痛

Contains these components:

☐ sick r 疒 434, p. 104
☐ corridor, passageway 甬 1811, p. 400

With all these meanings & readings

tòng [痛] **1** ache **2** pain **3** sorrow

My sister's illness required her to remain in total isolation, which kept her away from contact with people in the hospital *corridors*. The arrangement felt more **painful** for her than being *sick*.

1813

This character with the definition:

courageous

Pinyin **yǒng** *and Frequency Rank* **1206**

SIMP & TRAD Contains **9 strokes** in the following order:

乛 マ マ 丏 甬 甬 甬 勇 勇

Contains these components:

☐ corridor, passageway 甬 1811, p. 400
☐ strength 力 471, p. 113

With all these meanings & readings

yǒng [勇] **1** brave

Our **courageous** soldiers used their great *strength* to cut a long *passageway* through the dense forest so that they could make a surprise attack on the enemy camp.

1814

This character with the definition:

gush, well up

Pinyin **yǒng** *and Frequency Rank* **1642**

SIMP & TRAD Contains **10 strokes** in the following order:

丶 丶 氵 汀 沪 沪 涌 涌 涌 涌

Contains these components:

☐ water r 氵 314, p. 80
☐ corridor, passageway 甬 1811, p. 400

With all these meanings & readings

yǒng [涌] **1** to bubble up **2** to rush forth

The terrorists have blown up the dam! *Water* is flowing through the innermost *corridors* of all the houses and **gushing up** everywhere.

1815

角

SIMP & TRAD

This character with the definition:

horn, corner, angle

Pinyin **jiǎo** *and Frequency Rank* **736**

Contains **7 strokes** in the following order:

ノ ⺈ ⺈ 冎 角 角 角

Contains these components:

■ knife 刀 (altered) 469, p.112

■ to use 用 1802, p.398

With all these meanings & readings:

jiǎo [角] **1** surname Jue
jiǎo [角] **1** angle **2** horn **3** horn-shaped **4** unit of money equal to 0.1 yuan **5** m 个[個][gè]
jué [角] **1** role (theater) **2** to compete **3** ancient three legged wine vessel **4** third note of pentatonic scale

Great skill is required *to use* a *knife* to create artistic objects from large animal bones and **horns**.

1816

嘴

SIMP & TRAD

This character with the definition:

mouth, snout, bill

Pinyin **zuǐ** *and Frequency Rank* **1010**

Contains **15 strokes** in the following order:

丨 ⼝ ⼝ ⼝ ⼞ 吡 吡 吡 吡 嘴 嘴 嘴 嘴 嘴 嘴

Contains these components:

■ mouth 口 37, p.17

■ this 此 196, p.53

■ horn, corner, angle 角 1815, p.401

With all these meanings & readings:

zuǐ [嘴] **1** mouth **2** beak **3** spout (of teapot etc) **4** m 张[張][zhāng], 个[個][gè]

For her birthday *this* year my daughter preferred to pet a cat's soft *mouth* instead of a dog's *angled* **snout**.

1817

触

觸
TRAD

SIMPLIFIED

This character with the definition:

touch, contact

Pinyin **chù** *and Frequency Rank* **1207**

Contains **13 strokes** in the following order:

ノ ⺈ ⺈ 冎 角 角 角 触 触 触 触 触 触

Contains these components:

■ horn, corner, angle 角 1815, p.401

■ insect 虫 1016, p.231

With all these meanings & readings:

chù [觸] **1** to knock against **2** to touch **3** to feel

The hive of angry stinging *insects* chased me into a *corner*. I am very allergic to their stings so I was deeply fearful of **contact** with them.

1818

衡

SIMP & TRAD

This character with the definition:

weigh, measure

Pinyin **héng** *and Frequency Rank* **1340**

Contains **16 strokes** in the following order:

ノ ⼆ ⼻ ⼻ 行 衍 衍 衍 衍 衍 衡 衡 衡 衡 衡 衡

Contains these components:

■ firm, business 行 1249, p.278
■ horn, corner, angle 角 (altered) 1815, p.401
■ big 大 544, p.129

With all these meanings & readings:

héng [衡] **1** to weigh **2** weight **3** measure

My friend built a very profitable *business* out of using special equipment to **weigh** very *big* objects and to **measure** the dimensions of objects with sharp *angles* instead of 'normal' *corners*.

1819

解

SIMP & TRAD

This character with the definition:

untie, undo, take off

Pinyin **jiě** *and Frequency Rank* **201**

Contains **13 strokes** in the following order:

ノ ⺈ ⺈ 冎 角 角 角 角 解 解 解 解 解

Contains these components:

■ horn, corner, angle 角 1815, p.401

■ knife 刀 469, p.112

■ ox 牛 213, p.57

With all these meanings & readings:

jiě [解] **1** surname Xie
jiě [解] **1** to divide **2** to break up **3** to split **4** to separate **5** to dissolve **6** to solve **7** to melt **8** to remove **9** to untie **10** to loosen **11** to open **12** to emancipate **13** to explain **14** to understand **15** to know **16** a solution **17** a dissection
jiè [解] **1** transport under guard

The farmer's too-aggressive *ox* was also too valuable to be killed. So after it gored him, the farmer used a sharp *knife* to **take off** the pointed parts, its *horns*, and rendered the *ox* less dangerous to everyone who encountered it.

1820

确

碻
TRAD SIMPLIFIED

This character with the definition:

true, authentic

Pinyin **què** *and Frequency Rank* **331**

Contains **12 strokes** in the following order:

一 厂 ア 石 石 石′ 矸 矿 矿 硞 确 确

The carved image of the *horn* on the *stone* seal **authenticates** the oath.

Contains these components:

- stone, rock 石 522, p.124
- horn, corner, angle 角 1815, p.401

With all these meanings & readings

què [确] 1 authenticated   2 soli
3 firm
què [確] 1 authenticated   2 soli
3 firm   4 real   5 true

1821

拥

擁
TRAD SIMPLIFIED

This character with the definition:

embrace, hold

Pinyin **yōng** *and Frequency Rank* **1059**

Contains **8 strokes** in the following order:

一 十 扌 扩 扣 拥 拥 拥

Hands have a central *use* in a passionate **embrace**.

Contains these components:

- hand r 扌 25, p.15
- to use 用 1802, p.398

With all these meanings & readings

yōng [擁] 1 to hold   2 to embrace   3 to wrap around   4 to
gather around (sb)   5 to throng
6 to swarm   7 to support

1822

胃

SIMP & TRAD

This character with the definition:

stomach

Pinyin **wèi** *and Frequency Rank* **1957**

Contains **9 strokes** in the following order:

丨 冂 冃 冃 田 甲 胃 胃 胃

A farmer was fortunate during the growing season, because twice a *month*
his *field* of crops provided enough food to fill the **stomachs** of his human
and animal families!

Contains these components:

- field 田 63, p.23
- moon, month 月 (altered) 1771, p.391

With all these meanings & readings

wèi [胃] 1 stomach   2 m 个
[個][gè]

1823

谓

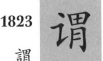

謂
TRAD SIMPLIFIED

This character with the definition:

say*

Pinyin **wèi** *and Frequency Rank* **945**

Contains **11 strokes** in the following order:

丶 讠 讠 讥 讵 谓 谓 谓 谓 谓 谓

Perhaps a hungry Chinese scribe developed this character after he heard
the grumbling *speech* of his *stomach* **say**, "Feed me!"

Contains these components:

- speech r 讠 352, p.88
- stomach 胃 1822, p.402

With all these meanings & readings

wèi [謂] 1 speak of

1824

胡
胡
鬍
TRAD SIMPLIFIED

This character with the definition:

beard, mustache

Pinyin **hú** *and Frequency Rank* **806**

Contains **9 strokes** in the following order:

一 十 廾 古 古 刮 胡 胡 胡

Even though the man's **beard** looked *ancient*, it was neatly trimmed by his
barber every *month*.

Contains these components:

- ancient 古 53, p.21
- moon, month 月 1771, p.391

With all these meanings & readings

hú [胡] 1 non-Han people, especially from central Asia   2 reckless   3 outrageous   4 what?
5 why?   6 surname Hu   7 to
complete a winning hand at
mahjong (also written 和 [和][hú

hú [鬍] 1 beard   2 mustache
3 whiskers

825 湖

This character with the definition:

lake

Pinyin **hú** *and Frequency Rank* **918**

SIMP & TRAD   Contains **12 strokes** in the following order:

丶 丶 氵 汁 汁 汁 沽 沽 沽 湖 湖 湖

Contains these components:

⬛ water r 氵 314, p. 80
◨ beard, mustache 胡 1824, p. 402

With all these meanings & readings:

hú [湖] **1** lake   **2** m 个[個][gè], 片[piàn]

The reflection of the mountains on the *water* resembled a *mustache* along the edge of the **lake**.

---

826 糊

This character with the definition:

paste, plaster

Pinyin **hú** *and Frequency Rank* **1393**

SIMP & TRAD   Contains **15 strokes** in the following order:

丶 丷 二 半 米 米 米 料 料 料 粘 糊] 糊 糊 糊

Contains these components:

⬛ rice (food) 米 1535, p. 339
◨ beard, mustache 胡 1824, p. 402

With all these meanings & readings:

hú [糊] **1** muddled   **2** paste **3** scorched
hù [糊] **1** paste   **2** cream

By the end of the day, splatters of **plaster** that looked like grains of *rice* had sprinkled into the workman's *beard*.

---

827 胎

This character with the definition:

fetus, baby

Pinyin **tāi** *and Frequency Rank* **1984**

SIMP & TRAD   Contains **9 strokes** in the following order:

丿 刀 月 月 肜 胎 胎 胎 胎

Contains these components:

◧ moon, month 月 1771, p. 391
⬛ you (literary) 台 991, p. 226

With all these meanings & readings:

tāi [胎] **1** fetus   **2** litter   **3** tire (of a wheel); abbr of 轮胎[輪~]

The royal obstetrician told the young Queen, "*You* have a double dose of good fortune. Your **baby** is a boy, and he was born during a full *moon*."

---

828 肥

This character with the definition:

fertile, rich (soil)

Pinyin **féi** *and Frequency Rank* **1620**

SIMP & TRAD   Contains **8 strokes** in the following order:

丿 刀 月 月 月⁷ 月⁷ 肥 肥

Contains these components:

◧ moon, month 月 (altered) 1771, p. 391
⬛ cling to, stick to 巴 137, p. 39

With all these meanings & readings:

féi [肥] **1** loose-fitting   **2** fat **3** fertile

My husband *clings to* our ranch's land because the pastures are so **fertile** with thick grass. His cattle always have more *meat* on them than any others.

---

829 臂

This character with the definition:

arm, upper arm

Pinyin **bì** *and Frequency Rank* **1688**

SIMP & TRAD   Contains **17 strokes** in the following order:

⁻ ⁻ 尸 尸 尸 尸 启 启 启 启 辟 辟 辟 辟 臂 臂 臂

Contains these components:

◨ penal law 辟 685, p. 161
◧ moon, month 月 1771, p. 391

With all these meanings & readings:

bì [臂] **1** arm

The upraised **arm** of a policeman getting ready to seize the crook and uphold the *penal law* resembles the shape of the crescent *moon*.

1830
腫
TRAD SIMPLIFIED

肿

This character with the definition:

to swell

Pinyin **zhǒng** *and Frequency Rank* **1792**

Contains **8 strokes** in the following order:

丿 刀 月 月 肝 肝 肝 肿

Contains these components:

moon, month 月 1771, p. 391

middle 中 38, p. 18

With all these meanings & readings

zhǒng [腫] **1** to swell **2** swelling **3** swollen

In the *middle* of the *month*, when the *moon* aligns with the earth in a certain way, extra high tides make the seas **swell** up.

1831
膽
TRAD SIMPLIFIED

胆

This character with the definition:

bravery, audacity

Pinyin **dǎn** *and Frequency Rank* **1352**

Contains **9 strokes** in the following order:

丿 刀 月 月 肝 肝 肝 胆 胆

Contains these components:

moon, month 月 1771, p. 391

dawn 旦 70, p. 25

With all these meanings & readings

dǎn [膽] **1** the gall **2** the nerve **3** courage **4** guts **5** gall bladder

The prince demonstrates his **bravery** yet again. He'll be in the Enchanted Forest until *dawn* and his only companion is the light from the full *moon*.

1832
陰
TRAD SIMPLIFIED

阴

This character with the definition:

cloudy

Pinyin **yīn** *and Frequency Rank* **987**

Contains **6 strokes** in the following order:

阝 阝 阝 阴 阴 阴

Contains these components:

hills r 阝 942, p. 216

moon, month 月 1771, p. 391

With all these meanings & readings

yīn [陰] **1** surname Yin
yīn [陰] **1** overcast (weather) **2** cloudy **3** shady **4** Yin (the negative principle of Yin and Yang) **5** negative (electric.) **6** feminine **7** moon **8** implicit **9** hidden **10** pudenda

By the light of the *moon* the **cloudy** sky appeared covered by *hills*.

1833
髒
TRAD SIMPLIFIED

脏

This character with the definition:

filthy

Pinyin **zāng** *and Frequency Rank* **1634**

Contains **10 strokes** in the following order:

丿 刀 月 月 月` 肝 肝 肝 脏 脏

Contains these components:

moon, month 月 1771, p. 391

village 庄 432, p. 104

With all these meanings & readings

zàng [臟] **1** viscera **2** (anatomy) organ
zāng [髒] **1** dirty **2** filthy

As if by the light of the *moon*, the *village* takes a bath to rid itself of the **filth** tourists bring in. What a sight—all the quaint old buildings daintily stepping into the river and washing themselves all over!

1834
週
周
TRAD SIMPLIFIED

周

This character with the definition:

week

Pinyin **zhōu** *and Frequency Rank* **490**

Contains **8 strokes** in the following order:

丿 冂 冂 冂 周 周 周 周

Contains these components:

safe place c 冂 1769, p. 391

earth, soil 土 9, p. 11

mouth 口 37, p. 17

With all these meanings & readings

zhōu [周] **1** complete **2** encircle **3** circuit **4** lap **5** week **6** cycle **7** all **8** every **9** attentive **10** thoughtful **11** the Zhou dynasty from 1027 BC **12** surname Zhou
zhōu [賙] **1** bestow alms
zhōu [週] **1** cycle **2** week

Whether your **week** involves using your *mouth* to teach others or your hands to work in the *soil*, you need a *safe place* to return to at the end of the day.

Unit 76

835
调
TRAD SIMPLIFIED

This character with the definition:

tune

Pinyin **diào** *and Frequency Rank* **400**

Contains **10 strokes** in the following order:

Contains these components:

■ speech r 讠 352, p. 88
■ week 周 1834, p. 404

With all these meanings & readings:

diào [调] **1** to transfer **2** to move (troops or cadres) **3** to investigate **4** to enquire into **5** accent **6** view **7** argument **8** key (in music) **9** mode (music) **10** tune **11** tone **12** melody
tiáo [调] **1** harmonize **2** reconcile **3** blend **4** suit well **5** provoke **6** incite

During your first *week* on a new job, you should always use polite *speech* with others and avoid humming a **tune** to yourself as you work.

836
雕
鸟彫
RAD SIMPLIFIED

This character with the definition:

carve, engrave

Pinyin **diāo** *and Frequency Rank* **1829**

Contains **16 strokes** in the following order:

Contains these components:

■ week 周 1834, p. 404
■ short-tailed bird 隹 1193, p. 267

With all these meanings & readings:

diāo [彫] **1** engrave
diāo [雕] **1** engrave **2** shrewd
diāo [鵰] **1** golden eagle

The eagle, a famous *short-tailed bird*, is attacking the sheep! But it's so *weak* (sounds like 'week') that it can't tear the sheep to pieces. It can only **carve** bloody gashes into the sheep's body.

837
乂

This component has the meaning:

harmonious crossing c

COMPONENT

When well-drawn, this character evokes peaceful feelings from the **harmonious crossing** of its graceful strokes.

838
丈
SIMP & TRAD

This character with the definition:

elder male relative

Pinyin **zhàng** *and Frequency Rank* **1242**

Contains **3 strokes** in the following order:

Contains these components:

□ ten 十 (altered) 7, p. 11
□ harmonious crossing c 乂 (altered) 1837, p. 405

With all these meanings & readings:

zhàng [丈] **1** ten feet

It is Chinese tradition to respect and maintain *harmonious* relations with an **elder male relative**—especially one who has reached the age of *ten* decades!

839
仗
SIMP & TRAD

This character with the definition:

battle

Pinyin **zhàng** *and Frequency Rank* **1712**

Contains **5 strokes** in the following order:

Contains these components:

■ man r 亻 1156, p. 260
□ elder male relative 丈 1838, p. 405

With all these meanings & readings:

zhàng [仗] **1** weaponry **2** to hold (a weapon) **3** to wield **4** to rely on **5** to depend on **6** war **7** battle

Two men are all that would fit in this character. They symbolize a larger group of men that are standing together, egging each other on and anticipating victory, as they prepare for **battle**.

1840

This character with the definition:

end, stop

Pinyin **ài** *and Frequency Rank* **1291**

SIMP & TRAD   Contains **5 strokes** in the following order:

一 十 艹 艻 艾

Contains these components:

▪ grass r ⺿ 87, p. 29
▫ harmonious crossing c 乂 1837, p. 405

With all these meanings & reading:

ài [艾] **1** surname Ai
ài [艾] **1** Chinese mugwort (Artemisia vulgaris) **2** phonetic "ai" or "i" **3** abbreviation of 艾滋病 [ài zī bìng]

Imagine this character as crossed 'pipes' with water *harmoniously* flowing through them until the overgrown '*grass*' at the top causes the flowing **to stop**.

1841

This character with the definition:

hey!*

Pinyin **āi** *and Frequency Rank* **2294**

SIMP & TRAD   Contains **8 strokes** in the following order:

丨 冂 口 口一 吖 吖 哎 哎

Contains these components:

▪ mouth 口 37, p. 17
▪ end, stop 艾 1840, p. 406

With all these meanings & reading:

āi [哎] **1** interjection of surprise or disapprobation hey! **2** why **3** look out! **4** How dare you

When I realized we were experiencing an earthquake, my *mouth* shouted "**Hey!**" and my heart felt as if it would not *stop* racing.

1842

This character with the definition:

hope

Pinyin **xī** *and Frequency Rank* **508**

SIMP & TRAD   Contains **7 strokes** in the following order:

丿 乂 ㄨ 产 关 希 希

Contains these components:

▫ harmonious crossing c 乂 1837, p. 405
▪ cloth 布 1736, p. 384

With all these meanings & reading:

xī [希] **1** rare **2** infrequent

The spiritual leader entered the Shrine of **Hope** with his arms *harmoniously crossed* under a gold-embroidered *cloth* around his shoulders.

1843

This character with the definition:

sparse

Pinyin **xī** *and Frequency Rank* **1788**

SIMP & TRAD   Contains **12 strokes** in the following order:

丿 二 千 千 禾 禾 利 利 秎 秎 稀 稀

Contains these components:

▪ rice, grain (crop) 禾 593, p. 140
▪ hope 希 1842, p. 406

With all these meanings & reading:

xī [稀] **1** diluted **2** sparse

Having too much *hope* for next year's output at the conclusion of this *grain* harvest means that the harvest was too **sparse** for everyone's well-being.

1844

This character with the definition:

simultaneous action

Pinyin **yòu** *and Frequency Rank* **126**

SIMP & TRAD   Contains **2 strokes** in the following order:

フ 又

Contains these components:

▫ one 一 1, p. 10
▪ harmonious crossing c 乂 1837, p. 405

With all these meanings & reading:

yòu [又] **1** (once) again **2** also **3** both... and... **4** again

Sometimes the choir sang with *one* voice; other times they *harmonized* in a **simultaneous blending** of alto and soprano voices. • This character frequently appears as a radical component with the meaning '**hand**'—can you visualize the horizontal stroke of the 'index finger' pinching the top left of the diagonal 'thumb'?

845

堅
TRAD SIMPLIFIED

坚

This character with the definition:

hard, firm

Pinyin **jiān** *and Frequency Rank* **748**

Contains **7 strokes** in the following order:

丨 刂 刂フ 刂又 刂又 刂又 坚

Contains these components:

■□ subject of a ruler 臣 (altered) 154, p. 43
■ simultaneous action 又 1844, p. 406
■ earth, soil 土 9, p. 11

With all these meanings & readings:

jiān [堅] **1** strong **2** solid **3** firm **4** unyielding **5** resolute

As he bows down the loyal *subject* lowers himself with both hands in a *simultaneous action* on the *earth*, knowing that the surface will be **hard** and too **firm** for comfort. ('*Subject*' 臣 is greatly altered so it will fit into the small space allotted to it.)

846

賢
TRAD SIMPLIFIED

贤

This character with the definition:

talented person

Pinyin **xián** *and Frequency Rank* **1943**

Contains **8 strokes** in the following order:

丨 刂 刂フ 刂又 刂又 刂又 贤 贤

Contains these components:

■□ subject of a ruler 臣 (altered) 154, p. 43
■ simultaneous action 又 1844, p. 406
■ cowrie 贝 1394, p. 309

With all these meanings & readings:

xián [賢] **1** worthy (person)

It takes a very **talented person** to be, in a *simultaneous action*, both a loyal *subject of the king* and capable of acquiring lots of *money* for himself. ('*Subject*' 臣 is greatly altered so it will fit into the small space allotted to it.)

847

緊
TRAD SIMPLIFIED

紧

This character with the definition:

tight, taut

Pinyin **jǐn** *and Frequency Rank* **560**

Contains **10 strokes** in the following order:

丨 刂 刂フ 刂又 刂又 坚 紧 紧 紧 紧

Contains these components:

■□ subject of a ruler 臣 (altered) 154, p. 43
■ simultaneous action 又 1844, p. 406
■ silk 帛 (altered) 230, p. 61

With all these meanings & readings:

jǐn [緊] **1** tight **2** strict **3** close at hand; near **4** urgent; tense **5** hard up; short of money **6** to tighten

Subjects are kept under **tight** control in *the same way* that *silk* threads are kept **taut** under constant tension.

848

怪
SIMP & TRAD

This character with the definition:

surprising, strange

Pinyin **guài** *and Frequency Rank* **775**

Contains **8 strokes** in the following order:

丶 丶 忄 忄フ 怏 怪 怪 怪

Contains these components:

■ heart (skinny) r 忄 1135, p. 256
■ simultaneous action 又 1844, p. 406
■ earth, soil 土 9, p. 11

With all these meanings & readings:

guài [怪] **1** bewildering **2** odd **3** queer **4** strange **5** uncanny **6** devil **7** monster **8** wonder at **9** to blame **10** quite **11** rather

It is not **surprising** that when one's *hands* work in the *soil* of a place, one's *heart* gets 'planted' into the same place.

849

雙
TRAD SIMPLIFIED

双

This character with the definition:

pair, both, dual

Pinyin **shuāng** *and Frequency Rank* **581**

Contains **4 strokes** in the following order:

フ 又 叉刀 双

Contains these components:

■■ simultaneous action (×2) 又 1844, p. 406

With all these meanings & readings:

shuāng [雙] **1** two **2** double **3** pair **4** both **5** surname Shuang

To do most things well, use **both** hands in *simultaneous actions*.

1850

轰

轟
TRAD   SIMPLIFIED

This character with the definition:

rumble

Pinyin **hōng** *and Frequency Rank* **1264**

Contains **8 strokes** in the following order:

一 亡 车 车 轰 轰 轰 轰

Contains these components:

car 车 1291, p. 289

pair, both, dual 双 1849, p. 407

With all these meanings & readings

hōng [轟] **1** explosion **2** bang **3** boom **4** rumble **5** strike (by thunder or a bomb)

A *pair* of *cars* colliding into one another makes an awful racket, a racket that resembles a loud **rumbling** sound.

1851

聂

聶
TRAD   SIMPLIFIED

This character with the definition:

whisper

Pinyin **niè** *and Frequency Rank* **2797**

Contains **10 strokes** in the following order:

一 厂 丌 丌 耳 耳 聂 聂 聂 聂

Contains these components:

ear 耳 76, p. 26

pair, both, dual 双 1849, p. 407

With all these meanings & readings

niè [聶] **1** surname Nie **2** whisper

When people insist on **whispering**, I need to use *both ears* to hear.

1852

摄

攝
TRAD   SIMPLIFIED

This character with the definition:

absorb, take in

Pinyin **shè** *and Frequency Rank* **1403**

Contains **13 strokes** in the following order:

一 十 扌 扌 扫 扫 扫 拒 捤 摄 摄 摄 摄

Contains these components:

hand r 扌 25, p. 15

whisper 聂 1851, p. 408

With all these meanings & readings

shè [攝] **1** to take in **2** to absorb **3** to assimilate **4** to act for **5** to take a photo **6** photo shoot **7** photo **8** to conserve (one's health)

Professors use different techniques to get their students to **absorb** lectures. Some *whisper* instead of yell, hoping their students will pay greater attention. Others believe a whack on the *hand* is the best way to ensure their students' undivided attention.

1853

报

報
TRAD   SIMPLIFIED

This character with the definition:

newspaper

Pinyin **bào** *and Frequency Rank* **234**

Contains **7 strokes** in the following order:

一 十 扌 扌 扫' 报 报

Contains these components:

hand r 扌 25, p. 15

single ear r 卩 165, p. 46

simultaneous action 又 1844, p. 406

With all these meanings & readings

bào [報] **1** to announce **2** to inform **3** report **4** newspaper **5** recompense **6** revenge **7** m 份[fèn], 张[張][zhāng]

Good reporters produce good **newspapers** by using their **hands** and *ears* in a *simultaneous action* to capture the news.

1854

祭

SIMP & TRAD

This character with the definition:

offer sacrifice

Pinyin **jì** *and Frequency Rank* **1782**

Contains **11 strokes** in the following order:

Contains these components:

moon, month 月 (altered) 1771, p. 391

simultaneous action 又 (altered) 1844, p. 406

show, indicate 示 1265, p. 283

With all these meanings & readings

jì [祭] **1** surname Zhai
jì [祭] **1** offer sacrifice

Ancient tribes **offered sacrifice** to the gods on nights when clear skies were *simultaneous with* a full *moon*, believing that this combination *indicated* the gods were 'open' to receiving the tribe's burnt sacrifice.

855 察

This character with the definition:

scrutinize, inspect

Pinyin **chá** *and Frequency Rank* **564**

SIMP & TRAD Contains **14 strokes** in the following order:

`丶 丶 宀 宀 宁 宁 宁 宁 宛 宛 察 察 察 察`

Contains these components:

roof r 宀 271, p.70

offer sacrifice 祭 1854, p.408

With all these meanings & readings:

chá [察] **1** to examine **2** to inquire **3** to observe **4** to inspect **5** to look into **6** obvious **7** clearly evident

To help the gods better **scrutinize** their thanksgiving ritual, the people asked the priest to *offer sacrifice* outside of the temple's *roof*.

---

856 擦

This character with the definition:

rub, scrape

Pinyin **cā** *and Frequency Rank* **1761**

SIMP & TRAD Contains **17 strokes** in the following order:

`一 亅 扌 扌 扩 扩 扩 护 护 护 挨 挨 擦 擦 擦 擦`

Contains these components:

hand r 扌 25, p.15

scrutinize, inspect 察 1855, p.409

With all these meanings & readings:

cā [擦] **1** to wipe **2** to erase **3** rubbing (brush stroke in painting) **4** to clean **5** to polish

The priest used his *hand* to gently **scrape** off the surface of the burnt offering so that he could *scrutinize* it for any special message from the gods.

---

857 友

This character with the definition:

friend*

Pinyin **yǒu** *and Frequency Rank* **594**

SIMP & TRAD Contains **4 strokes** in the following order:

`一 ナ 方 友`

Contains these components:

moving hand c ナ 1725, p.382

simultaneous action 又 1844, p.406

With all these meanings & readings:

yǒu [友] **1** friend

Just as I began to slip on the ice, my **friend's** quick *moving hand* grasped my arm and prevented me from falling.

---

858 爱

爱 TRAD SIMPLIFIED

This character with the definition:

love

Pinyin **ài** *and Frequency Rank* **394**

Contains **10 strokes** in the following order:

`爫 爫 爫 爫 爫 严 严 受 爱 爱`

Contains these components:

hands raised high c 爫 1657, p.368

smooth cover r 冖 268, p.69

friend* 友 1857, p.409

With all these meanings & readings:

ài [爱] **1** to love **2** affection **3** to be fond of **4** to like

The relationship between good *friends* is a *smooth cover* that blankets them in happiness. When the relationship blossoms into something more, such as **love**, *hands are raised high*.

---

859 发

發 TRAD SIMPLIFIED

This character with the definition:

send out, issue

Pinyin **fā** *and Frequency Rank* **47**

Contains **5 strokes** in the following order:

`一 ナ 发 发 发`

Contains these components:

friend* 友 1857, p.409

eight 八 1261, p.282

With all these meanings & readings:

fā [發] **1** to send out **2** to show (one's feeling) **3** to issue **4** to develop **5** (classifier for gunshots, "rounds")
fà [髮] **1** hair **2** Taiwan pr fǎ

You need to **issue** your message to the world, so ask *eight friends* to volunteer to be your emissaries.

Unit 77

1860

撥
TRAD   SIMPLIFIED

This character with the definition:

poke, stir

Pinyin **bō** *and Frequency Rank* **1807**

Contains **8 strokes** in the following order:

一 亅 扌 扩 扑 扨 拔 拨

Contains these components:

hand r 扌 25, p.15

send out, issue 发 1859, p.409

With all these meanings & readings

bō [撥] **1** to push aside **2** to appropriate (money) **3** to move **4** to set aside **5** to poke **6** to stir **7** group (of people) **8** ba **9** to dial

One way to let someone know you want to *send out* a message is to **poke** him or her with your *hand*. But do not be surprised if you **stir** up trouble with this person by doing this!

1861

廢
TRAD   SIMPLIFIED

This character with the definition:

useless, superfluous

Pinyin **fèi** *and Frequency Rank* **1376**

Contains **8 strokes** in the following order:

丶 亠 广 广 庐 庐 废 废

Contains these components:

shelter r 广 427, p.103

send out, issue 发 1859, p.409

With all these meanings & readings

fèi [廢] **1** abolish **2** crippled **3** abandoned **4** waste

Our local government *issued* an order that declared pets were '**superfluous**' compared to humans and that none would be allowed into any of the hurricane *shelters*.

1862

SIMP & TRAD

This character with the definition:

attire, garment

Pinyin **fú** *and Frequency Rank* **365**

Contains **8 strokes** in the following order:

丿 刀 月 月 肌 肌 服 服

Contains these components:

meat 肉 (altered) 753, p.175

single ear r 卩 165, p.46

simultaneous action 又 1844, p.406

With all these meanings & readings

fú [服] **1** clothes **2** dress **3** garment **4** to serve **5** to obey **6** to convince **7** to acclimatize **8** to take (medicine) **9** mourning clothes **10** to wear mourning clothes

fù [服] **1** dose (measure word for medicine)

Tonight was my first date in a *month*! I was so nervous that, *even as* I got dressed in my best **attire**, I managed to forget my second earring, leaving me with a *single ear* 'undressed'!

1863

SIMP & TRAD

This character with the definition:

mulberry tree

Pinyin **sāng** *and Frequency Rank* **1528**

Contains **10 strokes** in the following order:

フ マ ヌ ヌ 叒 叒 叕 桑 桑 桑

Contains these components:

simultaneous action (×3) 又 1844, p.406

tree 木 562, p.133

With all these meanings & readings

sāng [桑] **1** mulberry tree

The **mulberry tree** is known as a '*messy tree*' because it drops berries that stain sidewalks and require many *hands* to clean up.

1864

SIMP & TRAD

This character with the definition:

prop up, support

Pinyin **zhī** *and Frequency Rank* **437**

Contains **4 strokes** in the following order:

一 十 步 支

Contains these components:

ten 十 7, p.11

simultaneous action 又 1844, p.406

With all these meanings & readings

zhī [支] **1** to support **2** to sustain **3** to erect **4** to raise **5** branch **6** division **7** to draw money **8** surname Zhi **9** m for rods such as pens and guns, for army divisions and for songs or compositions **10** watt, classifier for power of light bulbs

The waiter **supports** a tray of *ten* glasses with one hand, while he *simultaneously* uses his other hand to write down a take-out order.

865

技

SIMP & TRAD

This character with the definition:

skill, ability

Pinyin **jì** *and Frequency Rank* **422**

Contains **7 strokes** in the following order:

一 十 扌 扩 拉 扗 技

Contains these components:

■ hand r 扌 25, p. 15
■ prop up, support 支 1864, p. 410

With all these meanings & readings:

jì [技] **1** skill

To do a one-armed pushup, you must *support* your body weight on only one *hand*, a **skill** that requires great strength.

866

枝

SIMP & TRAD

This character with the definition:

branch (of tree)

Pinyin **zhī** *and Frequency Rank* **1491**

Contains **8 strokes** in the following order:

一 十 才 木 朾 朾 枝 枝

Contains these components:

■ tree 木 562, p. 133
■ prop up, support 支 1864, p. 410

With all these meanings & readings:

zhī [枝] **1** branch **2** m for sticks, rods, pencils etc

The trunk of a *tree supports* (and feeds) its **branches**.

867

鼓

SIMP & TRAD

This character with the definition:

drum, rouse

Pinyin **gǔ** *and Frequency Rank* **1123**

Contains **13 strokes** in the following order:

一 十 土 士 吉 吉 吉 吉 壴 壴 壴 鼓 鼓

Contains these components:

■ drumroll c 壴 1602, p. 356
■ prop up, support 支 1864, p. 410

With all these meanings & readings:

gǔ [鼓] **1** convex **2** drum **3** to rouse **4** to beat **5** m 通[tòng], 面[miàn]

My first day in boot camp began with the sound of a bugle at dawn to **rouse** us and was followed by a *drumroll* at the door of our barracks. Even so, I still had to *support* my sleeping body against the wall of the shower.

868

皮

SIMP & TRAD

This character with the definition:

skin, leather

Pinyin **pí** *and Frequency Rank* **741**

Contains **5 strokes** in the following order:

一 厂 广 皮 皮

Contains these components:

■ action path c 丿 438, p. 105
■ prop up, support 支 1864, p. 410

With all these meanings & readings:

pí [皮] **1** leather **2** skin **3** fur **4** surname Pi **5** pico- (one trillionth) **6** m 张 [張][zhāng]

Our **skin** *supports* our muscles and skeleton so we can perform the *actions* of life.

869

坡

SIMP & TRAD

This character with the definition:

slope, plain

Pinyin **pō** *and Frequency Rank* **1550**

Contains **8 strokes** in the following order:

一 十 土 扩 圹 坍 坡 坡

Contains these components:

■ earth, soil 土 9, p. 11
■ skin, leather 皮 1868, p. 411

With all these meanings & readings:

pō [坡] **1** slope **2** m 个 [個][gè]

The farmer had spent so many years tilling the *soil* of the sun-baked **plain** that his *skin* looked like *leather*.

1870

颇

颇
TRAD　SIMPLIFIED

This character with the definition:

slanting, tilting

Pinyin **pō** *and Frequency Rank* **1560**

Contains these components:

■ skin, leather 皮 1868, p. 411

■ page, leaf 页 1408, p. 312

With all these meanings & reading

pō [颇] **1** rather **2** quite **3** c siderably (Taiwan pr pǒ) **4** o **5** inclined **6** slanting

Contains **11 strokes** in the following order:

丆 厂 广 皮 皮 皮 皮 颇 颇 颇 颇

The archaeologist could barely breathe as he gently held the fragile *page*-like *leather* sheet with **slanting** rows of pre-historic writing on it.

1871

This character with the definition:

passive signifier, by

Pinyin **bèi** *and Frequency Rank* **154**

Contains these components:

■ clothing r 衤 1067, p. 242

■ skin, leather 皮 1868, p. 411

With all these meanings & reading

bèi [被] **1** by (indicates passive voice sentences or clauses) **2** **3** to cover (literary)

SIMP & TRAD　Contains **11 strokes** in the following order:

丶 𠃌 才 礻 礻 衤 衤 衤 衤 被 被

'Man bites dog' is a standard sentence. Speakers use the passive voice to transform the sentence's object into its topic: the dog was bitten by the man. English grammar relies on special verb endings plus the preposition '**by**' to signal the passive voice. Chinese grammar uses this character 被 as the **passive signifier**. • Over the long history of human kind, the use of *leather* for *clothing* was gradually replaced **by** woven fabrics.

1872

This character with the definition:

other party, those

Pinyin **bǐ** *and Frequency Rank* **1256**

Contains these components:

■ left step r 彳 1247, p. 278

■ skin, leather 皮 1868, p. 411

With all these meanings & reading

bǐ [彼] **1** that **2** those **3** (o another)

SIMP & TRAD　Contains **8 strokes** in the following order:

丿 彳 彳 彳 𠂆 犳 彼 彼

My friend hates to dance; he claims that whenever he makes a *left step*, his foot lands on the *leather* shoe of the **other party** that's dancing with him.

1873

This character with the definition:

broken, damaged

Pinyin **pò** *and Frequency Rank* **604**

Contains these components:

■ stone, rock 石 522, p. 124

■ skin, leather 皮 1868, p. 411

With all these meanings & reading

pò [破] **1** to break **2** to split **3** broken **4** damaged **5** worn out

SIMP & TRAD　Contains **10 strokes** in the following order:

一 丆 厂 石 石 石 砂 砂 破 破

Only the hiker's sturdy *leather* boot prevented his ankle from being badly **damaged** when he tripped on a *stone* and twisted it.

1874

This character with the definition:

wave, ripple of water

Pinyin **bō** *and Frequency Rank* **664**

Contains these components:

■ water r 氵 314, p. 80

■ skin, leather 皮 1868, p. 411

With all these meanings & reading

bō [波] **1** wave **2** ripple **3** su **4** surge **5** abbr for 波兰 [~蘭] Poland

SIMP & TRAD　Contains **8 strokes** in the following order:

丶 冫 氵 氵 氵 沪 波 波

One of the pleasures of body-surfing is to feel the tumbling *water* on your *skin* as the **wave** carries your body to shore.

875 婆

SIMP & TRAD

This character with the definition:

old woman, mother-in-law

Pinyin **pó** *and Frequency Rank* **1347**

Contains these components:
- wave, ripple of water 波 1874, p.412
- woman 女 790, p.183

With all these meanings & readings:

pó [婆] **1** grandmother **2** matron **3** mother-in-law

Contains **11 strokes** in the following order:

丶 丶 氵 汀 汀 沪 波 波 波 婆 婆

My **mother-in-law** is a *woman* who enjoys creating *waves* of disharmony among my family members when she visits my house.

---

876 皱

TRAD SIMPLIFIED

This character with the definition:

wrinkle

Pinyin **zhòu** *and Frequency Rank* **1954**

Contains these components:
- hay for fodder 刍 873, p.199
- skin, leather 皮 1868, p.411

With all these meanings & readings:

zhòu [皱] **1** to wrinkle **2** wrinkled **3** to crease

Contains **10 strokes** in the following order:

丿 勹 乌 刍 刍 刍 刍 皱 皱 皱

The older you get, the more **wrinkles** you develop, and the more you are apt to attempt crackpot diets. My 'favorite' so far is the *hay* diet that claims to give you smoother *skin*.

---

877 玻

SIMP & TRAD

This character with the definition:

glass

Pinyin **bō** *and Frequency Rank* **1769**

Contains these components:
- jade 玉 (abbrev) 177, 48
- skin, leather 皮 1868, p.411

With all these meanings & readings:

bō [玻] **1** glass

Contains **9 strokes** in the following order:

一 二 千 王 玎 玎 玑 玻 玻

In olden days, peasants made windows out of *animal skins*. **Glass**, the costly alternative material used by the monied classes, was so expensive that its value was compared to *jade*.

---

878 疲

SIMP & TRAD

This character with the definition:

tired, weary*

Pinyin **pí** *and Frequency Rank* **1778**

Contains these components:
- sick r 疒 434, p.104
- skin, leather 皮 1868, p.411

With all these meanings & readings:

pí [疲] **1** weary

Contains **10 strokes** in the following order:

丶 一 广 广 疒 疒 疒 疒 疲 疲

The old doctor has had it with patients! He is so **weary** of treating *sick* and *leathery* people who never stop complaining and are slow to pay their bills.

---

879 敲

SIMP & TRAD

This character with the definition:

to strike, beat

Pinyin **qiāo** *and Frequency Rank* **1732**

Contains these components:
- high 高 253, p.66
- prop up, support 支 (abbrev) 1864, 410

With all these meanings & readings:

qiāo [敲] **1** extort **2** knock **3** to strike **4** to knock (at a door) **5** to hit

Contains **14 strokes** in the following order:

丶 亠 亠 亠 高 高 高 高 高 高 剞 剞 敲 敲

The small child did a great job using toy blocks to build a tower. It was so *high* that he needed to *prop up* several parts of it with buttresses. When the tower tumbled down, as was inevitable, it **struck** him with great force.

1880

This character with the definition:

old gentleman

Pinyin **sǒu** *and Frequency Rank* **3804**

SIMP & TRAD

Contains these components:

■ prop up, support 支 (abbrev) 1864, 410

□ speak 日 (altered) 67, p. 24

With all these meanings & reading

sǒu [叟] **1** old gentleman **2** c man

Contains **9 strokes** in the following order:

丶 丨 丨 臼 臼 臼 臼 申 申 叟 叟

It was sad to see how dependent the **old gentleman** was on physical *support* before he could *speak* even a single word.

1881

This character with the definition:

search, collect

Pinyin **sōu** *and Frequency Rank* **1564**

SIMP & TRAD

Contains these components:

■ hand r 扌 25, p. 15

□ old gentleman 叟 1880, p. 414

With all these meanings & reading

sōu [搜] **1** to search

Contains **12 strokes** in the following order:

一 十 扌 扌 扌 扌 扌 扌 扣 押 搜 搜

The *old gentlemen* uses his *hand* to **search** for things since his eyesight is no longer reliable.

1882

This character with the definition:

thin, lean

Pinyin **shòu** *and Frequency Rank* **1841**

SIMP & TRAD

Contains these components:

■ sick r 疒 434, p. 104

□ old gentleman 叟 1880, p. 414

With all these meanings & reading

shòu [瘦] **1** tight **2** thin **3** le

Contains **14 strokes** in the following order:

丶 亠 广 广 疒 疒 疒 疒 疒 疒 瘦 瘦 瘦 瘦

The *old gentlemen* became *ill* from working too hard. We noticed that he steadily lost weight, becoming **thinner** and **leaner**.

1883

This character with the definition:

m for ships and vessels

Pinyin **sōu** *and Frequency Rank* **1470**

SIMP & TRAD

Contains these components:

■ boat 舟 (altered) 822, p. 189

□ old gentleman 叟 1880, p. 414

With all these meanings & reading

sōu [艘] **1** m for ships **2** Taiw pr são

Contains **15 strokes** in the following order:

丿 丿 刀 月 舟 舟 舟 舟 舟 舟 舟 舟 艘 艘 艘

It's scary to see the *old gentleman* moving around on the *boat* by himself. He **counts** his steps on the **boat** since his vision has become so poor.

1884

This character with the definition:

take, get, obtain

Pinyin **qǔ** *and Frequency Rank* **323**

SIMP & TRAD

Contains these components:

■ ear 耳 76, p. 26

□ simultaneous action 又 1844, p. 406

With all these meanings & reading

qǔ [取] **1** to take **2** to get **3** to choose **4** to fetch

Contains **8 strokes** in the following order:

一 厂 冂 冃 月 耳 取 取

A century ago, a spy would use his own *ear* as his listening device, and press it against an interior wall, to **get** confidential information *as it was* being discussed in the next room.

Unit 78

385 最

SIMP & TRAD

This character with the definition:

most, -est

Pinyin **zuì** and Frequency Rank **139**

Contains **12 strokes** in the following order:

㇒ 冂 冃 日 旦 早 昇 昇 昇 最 最 最

Contains these components:

☐ day, sun 日 64, p. 24
☐ take, get, obtain 取 (altered) 1884, p. 414

With all these meanings & readings:

zuì [最] **1** most **2** the most **3** -est

People who want the **most** from life see every *day* as an opportunity to *obtain* it.

---

386 趣

SIMP & TRAD

This character with the definition:

interesting

Pinyin **qù** and Frequency Rank **1065**

Contains **15 strokes** in the following order:

一 十 十 土 丰 丰 走 走 走 赴 赳 趄 趄 趣 趣

Contains these components:

☐ to walk 走 731, p. 171
☐ take, get, obtain 取 1884, p. 414

With all these meanings & readings:

qù [趣] **1** interesting **2** to interest

I decided *to walk* to the store to *get* my groceries so that I could experience the **interesting** sights and sounds along the way.

---

887 聚

SIMP & TRAD

This character with the definition:

assemble, gather together

Pinyin **jù** and Frequency Rank **1306**

Contains **14 strokes** in the following order:

一 厂 冂 斤 耳 耵 取 取 取 聚 聚 聚 聚 聚

Contains these components:

☐ take, get, obtain 取 1884, p. 414
☐ water 水 (altered) 315, p. 81

With all these meanings & readings:

jù [聚] **1** to congregate **2** to assemble **3** to mass **4** to gather together **5** to amass **6** to polymerize

When people **gather together** for a celebration, each person will usually *take* a glass of *water* (or stronger beverage) and raise it during a toast of good cheer.

---

888 娶

SIMP & TRAD

This character with the definition:

take a wife

Pinyin **qǔ** and Frequency Rank **2494**

Contains **11 strokes** in the following order:

一 厂 冂 斤 耳 耵 取 取 取 娶 娶

Contains these components:

☐ take, get, obtain 取 1884, p. 414
☐ woman 女 790, p. 183

With all these meanings & readings:

qǔ [娶] **1** take a wife **2** to marry (a woman)

In the very unlamented old days, a man **takes a wife** by, uh, literally *taking* a *woman*.

---

889 曼

SIMP & TRAD

This character with the definition:

gracefully

Pinyin **màn** and Frequency Rank **1224**

Contains **11 strokes** in the following order:

㇒ 冂 冃 日 旦 昌 冒 冒 昌 曼 曼

Contains these components:

☐ brave 冒 (altered) 77, p. 26
☐ simultaneous action 又 1844, p. 406

With all these meanings & readings:

màn [曼] **1** handsome **2** large **3** long

The hunter was so skillful and *brave* that he could **gracefully** hurl his spear and kill a wild boar *just as* it began to charge at him.

1890

This character with the definition:

brim over, overflow

Pinyin **màn** *and Frequency Rank* **1455**

SIMP & TRAD   Contains **14 strokes** in the following order:

Contains these components:

☐ water r 氵 314, p.80
☐ gracefully 曼 1889, p.415

With all these meanings & readings

màn [漫] **1** free **2** unrestrained **3** inundate

The Olympic diver entered the *water* so *gracefully* that not even a ripple caused water to **overflow** out of the edge of the pool.

1891

This character with the definition:

slow

Pinyin **màn** *and Frequency Rank* **822**

SIMP & TRAD   Contains **14 strokes** in the following order:

Contains these components:

☐ heart (skinny) r 忄 1135, p.256
☐ gracefully 曼 1889, p.415

With all these meanings & readings

màn [慢] **1** slow

During the horse-jumping competition, my *heart* felt weak as I watched my horse **slow** to a painful stop while the other horses *gracefully* jumped the fence and raced ahead.

1892

This character with the definition:

slave, enslave

Pinyin **nú** *and Frequency Rank* **1402**

SIMP & TRAD   Contains **5 strokes** in the following order:

Contains these components:

☐ woman 女 790, p.183
☐ simultaneous action 又 1844, p.406

With all these meanings & readings

nú [奴] **1** slave

A modern *woman* can be **enslaved** by cultural expectations *even as* she is considered liberated by the greater society.

1893

This character with the definition:

become angry, indignant

Pinyin **nù** *and Frequency Rank* **1143**

SIMP & TRAD   Contains **9 strokes** in the following order:

Contains these components:

☐ slave, enslave 奴 1892, p.416
☐ heart (fat) r 心 1096, p.248

With all these meanings & readings

nù [怒] **1** indignant

Slaves took great risks when they **became angry** or revealed their *emotion*.

1894

This character with the definition:

exert, strive

Pinyin **nǔ** *and Frequency Rank* **1081**

SIMP & TRAD   Contains **7 strokes** in the following order:

Contains these components:

☐ slave, enslave 奴 1892, p.416
☐ strength 力 471, p.113

With all these meanings & readings

nǔ [努] **1** to exert **2** to strive

A *slave* could expect to be ordered to **exert** himself to the maximum limits of his physical *strength*.

895

This character with the definition:

anti-, oppose

Pinyin **fǎn** *and Frequency Rank* **237**

SIMP & TRAD   Contains **4 strokes** in the following order:

一 厂 反 反

Contains these components:

■ cliff r 厂 399, p.97
■ simultaneous action 又 1844, p.406

With all these meanings & readings:

fǎn [反] **1** contrary **2** in reverse **3** inside-out or upside-down **4** to reverse **5** to return **6** to oppose **7** opposite **8** against **9** anti- **10** to rebel **11** to use analogy **12** instead **13** abbr for 反切 phonetic system

Climbing a *cliff* is so difficult because the forces of gravity *simultaneously* **oppose** each step upward you take.

896

板
闆
TRAD   SIMPLIFIED

This character with the definition:

board, plank

Pinyin **bǎn** *and Frequency Rank* **930**

Contains **8 strokes** in the following order:

一 十 才 木 木 杤 板 板

Contains these components:

■ tree 木 562, p.133
■ anti-, oppose 反 1895, p.417

With all these meanings & readings:

bǎn [板] **1** board **2** plank **3** plate **4** slab **5** stiff **6** unnatural **7** pedal **8** m 块[塊][kuài]
bǎn [闆] **1** see 老板[~闆], boss

My wife vehemently *opposes* my plan to cut down our immense black walnut *tree* and convert its rare wood into **planks** to sell.

897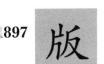

SIMP & TRAD

This character with the definition:

edition, newspaper page

Pinyin **bǎn** *and Frequency Rank* **810**

Contains **8 strokes** in the following order:

丿 丿 尸 片 片 肵 版 版

Contains these components:

■ slice, flake 片 488, p.116
■ anti-, oppose 反 1895, p.417

With all these meanings & readings:

bǎn [版] **1** a register **2** a block of printing **3** an edition **4** version **5** page

The town newspaper published a mere *slice* of the full story about the *anti-government* rally. It did not even take up a full column on one **newspaper page**.

898

SIMP & TRAD

This character with the definition:

betray, rebel, revolt

Pinyin **pàn** *and Frequency Rank* **1779**

Contains **9 strokes** in the following order:

丶 丷 ソ ゝ 半 半 扪 叛 叛

Contains these components:

■ sheep 羊 (altered) 1486, p.329
■ anti-, oppose 反 1895, p.417

With all these meanings & readings:

pàn [叛] **1** to betray **2** to rebel **3** to revolt

The slaughterers have trained a man wearing a *sheep* costume to lead the herd to the slaughterhouse (that's why there are missing legs). I *oppose* such tactics, which uses a fake sheep to **betray** her genuine comrades.

899

SIMP & TRAD

This character with the definition:

degree, other small unit

Pinyin **dù** *and Frequency Rank* **184**

Contains **9 strokes** in the following order:

丶 亠 广 广 产 庐 庐 庹 度

Contains these components:

■ shelter r 广 427, p.103
■ horned animal c 廿 94, p.30
■ simultaneous action 又 1844, p.406

With all these meanings & readings:

dù [度] **1** to pass **2** to spend (time) **3** measure **4** limit **5** extent **6** degree of intensity **7** (classifier for angles and temperature) degree **8** (classifier for events and occurrences) **9** (classifier for electricity) kilowatt-hour
duó [度] **1** estimate

Our new *bull* stubbornly refused to enter his *shelter* until the cold of winter; then, *simultaneous with* each lower **degree** in temperature, he moved a foot closer to the entrance. At thirty **degrees**, he trotted into the warm *shelter*.

1900

渡

SIMP & TRAD

This character with the definition:

ferry across

Pinyin **dù** *and Frequency Rank* **1406**

Contains **12 strokes** in the following order:

丶 氵 氵 氵 沪 沪 沪 泸 泸 渡 渡

Contains these components:

☐ water r 氵 314, p.80
☐ degree, other small unit 度 1899, p.417

With all these meanings & readings

dù [渡] **1** to cross **2** to pass through **3** to ferry

The *water* temperature was below forty *degrees* and too cold to swim in so I had to **ferry across** to get to the island.

1901

叔

SIMP & TRAD

This character with the definition:

uncle

Pinyin **shū** *and Frequency Rank* **1422**

Contains **8 strokes** in the following order:

丨 卜 上 十 丗 未 叔 叔

Contains these components:

☐ on 上 189, p.52
☐ small 小 1262, p.282
☐ simultaneous action 又 1844, p.406

With all these meanings & readings

shū [叔] **1** uncle **2** father's younger brother **3** husband's younger brother **4** Taiwan pr shú

When I was a *small* boy, my **uncle** would read me adventure stories *while* I sat *on* his lap.

1902

督

SIMP & TRAD

This character with the definition:

supervise

Pinyin **dū** *and Frequency Rank* **946**

Contains **13 strokes** in the following order:

丨 卜 上 十 丗 未 叔 叔 叔 督 督 督 督

Contains these components:

☐ uncle 叔 1901, p.418
☐ eye 目 75, p.26

With all these meanings & readings

dū [督] **1** to supervise

My *uncle* joined the family business to **supervise** the sales force, especially to keep his sharp *eye* on their expense accounts.

1903

寂

SIMP & TRAD

This character with the definition:

lonely, quiet

Pinyin **jì** *and Frequency Rank* **1739**

Contains **11 strokes** in the following order:

丶 丷 宀 宀 宀 空 宇 宋 宋 寂 寂

Contains these components:

☐ roof r 宀 271, p.70
☐ uncle 叔 1901, p.418

With all these meanings & readings

jì [寂] **1** lonesome

My shy *uncle* spent a **quiet** life under the same *roof*. He never married but was always full of good humor.

1904

SIMP & TRAD

This character with the definition:

receive

Pinyin **shòu** *and Frequency Rank* **238**

Contains **8 strokes** in the following order:

爫 爫 爫 爫 爫 受 受 受

Contains these components:

☐ hands raised high c 爫 1657, p.368
☐ smooth cover r 冖 268, p.69
☐ simultaneous action 又 1844, p.406

With all these meanings & readings

shòu [受] **1** to receive **2** to accept **3** to suffer **4** subjected to **5** to bear **6** to stand **7** pleasa **8** (passive marker)

At the same moment that the student **received** his diploma with its *smooth cover*, his family stood up with their *hands raised high* and cheered.

905

授

SIMP & TRAD

This character with the definition:

instruct, teach

Pinyin **shòu** *and Frequency Rank* **968**

Contains **11 strokes** in the following order:

一 十 扌 扌 扩 扩 护 护 护 拶 授

Contains these components:

hand r 扌 25, p. 15

receive 受 1904, p. 418

With all these meanings & readings:

shòu [授] **1** to teach **2** to instruct **3** to award **4** to give

Professors only *receive* positive feedback on how well they **teach** when their students *hand* in well-written exams.

906

爰

SIMP & TRAD

This character with the definition:

leads to, therefore

Pinyin **yuán** *and Frequency Rank* **4896**

Contains **9 strokes** in the following order:

一 ⺊ ⺊ ⺊ 呥 罒 罒 爰 爰

Contains these components:

receive 受 (altered) 1904, p. 418

moving hand c 丆 1725, p. 382

With all these meanings & readings:

yuán [爰] **1** therefore **2** consequently **3** thus **4** hence **5** thereupon **6** it follows that **7** where? **8** to change (into) **9** ancient unit of weight and money **10** surname Yuan

In many sports, the *moving hand* of a referee signals some type of rule violation; **therefore**, it is expected that someone will *receive* a penalty call.

907

缓

缓
TRAD   SIMPLIFIED

This character with the definition:

unhurried, slow, sluggish

Pinyin **huǎn** *and Frequency Rank* **1111**

Contains **12 strokes** in the following order:

乚 纟 纟 纟 纟 纩 纩 纩 綷 綷 缓 缓

Contains these components:

silk r 纟 1037, p. 235

leads to, therefore 爰 1906, p. 419

With all these meanings & readings:

huǎn [缓] **1** slow **2** unhurried **3** sluggish **4** gradual **5** not tense **6** relaxed **7** to postpone **8** to defer **9** to stall **10** to stave off **11** to revive **12** to recuperate

The **slow**, meticulous process of weaving *silk leads to* a final product of very fine fabrics.

908

援

SIMP & TRAD

This character with the definition:

help, aid, assist

Pinyin **yuán** *and Frequency Rank* **1197**

Contains **12 strokes** in the following order:

一 十 扌 扌 扩 扩 护 护 拦 拶 援 援

Contains these components:

hand r 扌 25, p. 15

leads to, therefore 爰 1906, p. 419

With all these meanings & readings:

yuán [援] **1** to help **2** to assist **3** to aid

Extending a generous *hand* to **help** someone in need can *lead to* positive outcomes for both the giver and receiver.

909

暖

SIMP & TRAD

This character with the definition:

warm, genial

Pinyin **nuǎn** *and Frequency Rank* **1745**

Contains **13 strokes** in the following order:

丨 冂 日 日 日 日⺊ 旷 旷 旷 � 暚 暖 暖

Contains these components:

day, sun 日 64, p. 24

leads to, therefore 爰 1906, p. 419

With all these meanings & readings:

nuǎn [暖] **1** warm **2** to heat **3** genial

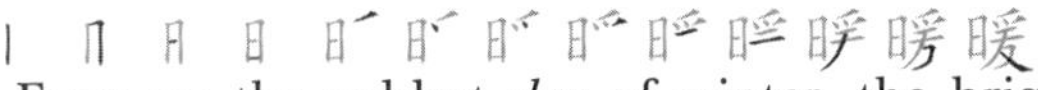

Even on the coldest *day* of winter, the bright *sun* usually generates an uplifting effect which *leads to* **warm** feelings of good cheer throughout the day.

Unit 79

1910

SIMP & TRAD

This character with the definition:

uproot

Pinyin **bá** *and Frequency Rank* **1502**

Contains **8 strokes** in the following order:

Contains these components:
- hand r 扌 25, p.15
- dog 犬 (altered) 673, p.158
- simultaneous action 又 1844, p.406

With all these meanings & reading

bá [拔] **1** to pull up **2** to pull out **3** to draw out by suction **4** to select **5** to pick **6** to sta out (above level) **7** to surpass **8** to seize

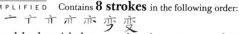

To **uproot** the old tree trunk, I needed to use my own *hands together with my dog*'s ability to pull. (Note how the lower right stroke of '*dog*' simultaneously occupies the same space as the '*simultaneous action*' element.)

1911

變 TRAD · SIMPLIFIED

This character with the definition:

change into

Pinyin **biàn** *and Frequency Rank* **225**

Contains **8 strokes** in the following order:

Contains these components:
- also, too 亦 842, p.193
- simultaneous action 又 1844, p.406

With all these meanings & reading

biàn [變] **1** to change **2** to become different **3** to transform **4** to vary **5** rebellion

One blacksmith hammering is not enough to **change** iron **into** steel. If several others *also* participate *at the same time*, however, their combined efforts will do the trick.

1912

戲 TRAD · SIMPLIFIED

This character with the definition:

play, show

Pinyin **xì** *and Frequency Rank* **1033**

Contains **6 strokes** in the following order:

Contains these components:
- simultaneous action 又 1844, p.406
- halberd 戈 650, p.154

With all these meanings & readings

xì [戲] **1** trick **2** drama **3** pla **4** show **5** m 出[chū], 场[場][c 台[臺][tái]

The renegade samurai warrior is stealing the **show**. He has *halberds* in both hands, and is twirling them in a *simultaneous action*. His skill captures the audience's attention.

1913

SIMP & TRAD

This character with the definition:

ancient bamboo spear

Pinyin **shū** *and Frequency Rank* **6005**

Contains **4 strokes** in the following order:

Contains these components:
- how much, how many 几 896, p.204
- simultaneous action 又 1844, p.406

With all these meanings & readings

shū [殳] **1** surname Shu **2** spe

The archaeologists discovered *several* weapons *at the same time* that they were exploring the royal tomb. They were amazed to find the **ancient bamboo spear** in perfect condition after being buried for four thousand years.

914

This character with the definition:

throw, fling

Pinyin **tóu** *and Frequency Rank* **516**

SIMP & TRAD Contains **7 strokes** in the following order:

一 十 才 扌 扩 投 投

Contains these components:

■ hand r 扌 25, p.15
■ ancient bamboo spear 殳 1913, p.420

With all these meanings & readings:

tóu [投] **1** to throw **2** to send **3** to invest

In order to **throw** his *ancient bamboo spear* effectively enough to wound his enemy, a warrior needed a strong arm, steady *hand*, and excellent vision.

915

This character with the definition:

section, part

Pinyin **duàn** *and Frequency Rank* **567**

SIMP & TRAD Contains **9 strokes** in the following order:

丿 亻 亻 乍 乍 身 扩 奶 段

Contains these components:

■ ear 耳 (abbrev) 76, 26
■ ancient bamboo spear 殳 1913, p.420

With all these meanings & readings:

duàn [段] **1** surname Duan **2** paragraph **3** section **4** segment **5** stage (of a process) **6** m for stories, periods of time, lengths of thread etc

The warrior heard the *ancient bamboo spear* as it whizzed past his head, but he did not realize that it had shcared off **part** of his *ear*.

916

This character with the definition:

thigh

Pinyin **gǔ** *and Frequency Rank* **644**

SIMP & TRAD Contains **8 strokes** in the following order:

丿 刀 月 月 月' 肟 股 股

Contains these components:

■ meat 肉 (altered) 753, p.175
■ ancient bamboo spear 殳 1913, p.420

With all these meanings & readings:

gǔ [股] **1** share **2** portion **3** section **4** part **5** thigh **6** (classifier for smells, electric currents, spirals etc) **7** whiff

When the *ancient bamboo spear* struck the soldier's **thigh**, it created such a large wound that his exposed flesh resembled raw *meat*.

917

This character with the definition:

set up, found, establish

Pinyin **shè** *and Frequency Rank* **302**

設
TRAD   SIMPLIFIED   Contains **6 strokes** in the following order:

丶 讠 讠' 讱 设 设

Contains these components:

■ speech r 讠 352, p.88
■ ancient bamboo spear 殳 1913, p.420

With all these meanings & readings:

shè [設] **1** to set up **2** to arrange **3** to establish **4** to found **5** to display

The soldier was skilled in both throwing an *ancient bamboo spear* more accurately than anyone else and motivating others with his *speech*. He was soon promoted to sergeant and allowed to **establish** his own battalion.

918

This character with the definition:

military service

Pinyin **yì** *and Frequency Rank* **1245**

SIMP & TRAD Contains **7 strokes** in the following order:

丿 彳 彳 彳' 狅 役 役

Contains these components:

■ left step r 彳 1247, p.278
■ ancient bamboo spear 殳 1913, p.420

With all these meanings & readings:

yì [役] **1** forced labor **2** corvée **3** obligatory task **4** military service **5** to use as servant **6** to enserf **7** a servant (in former times) **8** a war **9** a campaign **10** a battle

Basic training for **military service** in the Emperor's Army prepared soldiers to march with a raised *left step* and to throw an *ancient bamboo spear* with superior force and accuracy.

1919　毅　SIMP & TRAD

This character with the definition:

perseverance

Pinyin **yì** *and Frequency Rank* **1946**

Contains these components:

- to stand 立 681, p.160
- pig, boar 系 1453, p.321　ancient bamboo spear 殳 1913, p.420

With all these meanings & readings

yì [毅] **1** perseverance

Contains **15 strokes** in the following order:

丶　亠　六　宁　立　产　产　亨　亨　豖　豖　豙　豙　毅　毅

Learning how to throw an *ancient bamboo spear* accurately requires great **perseverance**. You must *stand* for hours and practice throwing it at a target shaped like a large *boar* with a red circle drawn around the area of its heart.

1920　般　SIMP & TRAD

This character with the definition:

sort, kind

Pinyin **bān** *and Frequency Rank* **629**

Contains these components:

- boat 舟 822, p.189
- ancient bamboo spear 殳 1913, p.420

With all these meanings & readings

bān [般] **1** sort **2** kind **3** clas **4** way **5** manner

Contains **10 strokes** in the following order:

丿　丿　冂　月　月　舟　舟　舣　船　般

The Vikings used *boats* designed with a special **kind** of bow. It had a point so sharp that the bow resembled an *ancient bamboo spear*.

1921　搬　SIMP & TRAD

This character with the definition:

take away, remove

Pinyin **bān** *and Frequency Rank* **1766**

Contains these components:

- hand r 扌 25, p.15
- sort, kind 般 1920, p.422

With all these meanings & readings

bān [搬] **1** to move **2** to shift **3** to remove **4** to transport **5** apply indiscriminately **6** to cop mechanically

Contains **13 strokes** in the following order:

一　十　扌　扩　扚　扲　捛　捐　搁　搁　搬　搬

While vacuum cleaners and electronic gadgets are convenient, only the heavy scrubbing of your own *hands* will **remove** certain *kinds* of stains.

1922　毁　TRAD　毁 SIMPLIFIED

This character with the definition:

destroy, ruin

Pinyin **huǐ** *and Frequency Rank* **1160**

Contains these components:

- mortar 臼 373, p.92
- labor, work 工 12, p.12　ancient bamboo spear 殳 1913, p.420

With all these meanings & readings

huǐ [毁] **1** to destroy **2** to damage **3** to ruin
huǐ [燬] **1** blaze **2** destroy by fire
huǐ [譭] **1** defame **2** to slander

Contains **13 strokes** in the following order:

丶　亻　仨　臼　臼　白　臼　臾　皇　皇　皂　毁　毁

The conquerors, well-equipped with their *ancient bamboo spears*, have laid waste to our lands. Bombs have created *ragged holes* in our fields and all public *works* have been thoroughly **destroyed**.

1923　殿　SIMP & TRAD

This character with the definition:

hall, palace, temple

Pinyin **diàn** *and Frequency Rank* **1555**

Contains these components:

- corpse 尸 499, p.119
- together 共 1631, p.363　ancient bamboo spear 殳 1913, p.420

With all these meanings & readings

diàn [殿] **1** palace hall

Contains **13 strokes** in the following order:

一　コ　尸　尸　尼　尼　屈　屏　屏　屏　屈　殿　殿

Only the king knows where the *dead bodies* are buried. The rebels who were *speared* to death are buried *together* deep in the bowels of the **palace**.

1924

疫

SIMP & TRAD

This character with the definition:

epidemic, plague

Pinyin **yì** *and Frequency Rank* **1791**

Contains **9 strokes** in the following order:

丶 亠 广 广 疒 疒 疒 疫 疫

Contains these components:

■ sick r 疒 434, p.104
■ ancient bamboo spear 殳 1913, p.420

With all these meanings & readings:

yì [疫] **1** epidemic **2** plague

Epidemics are *sicknesses* that move rapidly through a town. It is as if the *sick*nesses travel on swift but *ancient bamboo spears*.

1925

没

沒 TRAD SIMPLIFIED

This character with the definition:

have not

Pinyin **méi** *and Frequency Rank* **72**

Contains **7 strokes** in the following order:

丶 丶 氵 氵 沪 没 没

Contains these components:

■ water r 氵 314, p.80
■ ancient bamboo spear 殳 1913, p.420

With all these meanings & readings:

méi [沒] **1** (negative prefix for verbs) **2** have not **3** not
mò [沒] **1** drowned **2** to end **3** to die **4** to inundate

Applying *water* on a *bamboo spear* **has no** benefit. It dulls the edge and warps the fibers. What we thought would create smooth bamboo does **not**—it **has** created a knot instead!

1926

叙

敍 TRAD SIMPLIFIED

This character with the definition:

talk, chat, narrate

Pinyin **xù** *and Frequency Rank* **1607**

Contains **9 strokes** in the following order:

丿 亽 乍 佘 乎 余 余 钅 叙

Contains these components:

■ surplus, spare 余 1276, p.285
□ simultaneous action 又 1844, p.406

With all these meanings & readings:

xù [敍] **1** to narrate **2** to chat **3** abbr for Syria 叙利亚 [敍~亞]

Normally, we're so busy we have to multitask and do *several things at once*. Now that the work is finished, and we have *surplus* time to relax, we can **chat** a bit and bring ourselves up to date.

1927

邓

鄧 TRAD SIMPLIFIED

This character with the definition:

surname of Deng Xiaoping

Pinyin **dèng** *and Frequency Rank* **1614**

Contains **4 strokes** in the following order:

フ 又 邓 邓

Contains these components:

□ simultaneous action 又 1844, p.406
□ town r 阝 955, p.219

With all these meanings & readings:

Dèng [鄧] **1** surname Deng

Deng Xiaoping is a famous 20th-century Chinese leader, through whose influence and abilities caused *town* economies to thrive. The entire country became more active in various economic activities, which is what 'simultaneous action' symbolizes.

1928

圣

聖 TRAD SIMPLIFIED

This character with the definition:

sage

Pinyin **shèng** *and Frequency Rank* **960**

Contains **5 strokes** in the following order:

フ 又 圣 圣 圣

Contains these components:

□ simultaneous action 又 1844, p.406
■ earth, soil 土 9, p.11

With all these meanings & readings:

shèng [聖] **1** holy **2** sacred **3** saint **4** sage

Sages evaluated several *simultaneous conditions* in the *soil* and thus assisted primitive farmers who wanted to increase their yield.

1929

嘆
TRAD · SIMPLIFIED

This character with the definition:

sigh, exclaim

Pinyin **tàn** *and Frequency Rank* **1299**

Contains **5 strokes** in the following order:

丨 口 口 叹 叹

Contains these components:

mouth 口 37, p.17
simultaneous action 又 1844, p.406

With all these meanings & readings:

tàn [嘆] **1** sigh **2** gasp **3** exclaim
tàn [歎] **1** sigh **2** gasp **3** exclaim

When you *simultaneously* exercise your *mouth* and think of a lost opportunity, you will produce a **sigh**.

1930

漢
TRAD · SIMPLIFIED

This character with the definition:

ethnic Chinese

Pinyin **hàn** *and Frequency Rank* **711**

Contains **5 strokes** in the following order:

丶 丶 氵 汈 汉

Contains these components:

water r 氵 314, p.80
simultaneous action 又 1844, p.406

With all these meanings & readings:

Hàn [漢] **1** Chinese **2** the Han dynasty (206 BC-220 AD)

Historians are now confident that extensive systems of *water* power operating in *simultaneous conditions* were key to the development of any civilization, especially that of the **ethnic Chinese**.

1931

難
TRAD · SIMPLIFIED

This character with the definition:

difficult, hard

Pinyin **nán** *and Frequency Rank* **295**

Contains **10 strokes** in the following order:

丁 又 叉 刈 𬺭 𬺬 难 难 难 难

Contains these components:

simultaneous action 又 1844, p.406
short-tailed bird 隹 1193, p.267

With all these meanings & readings:

nán [難] **1** difficult (to...) **2** problem **3** difficulty **4** difficult **5** not good
nàn [難] **1** disaster **2** distress **3** to scold

Have you ever tried to use your *hand* to catch a *bird*? Don't bother—it's very **hard** to do.

1932

歡
TRAD · SIMPLIFIED

This character with the definition:

pleased

Pinyin **huān** *and Frequency Rank* **685**

Contains **6 strokes** in the following order:

丁 又 叉 𬺰 𬺲 欢

Contains these components:

simultaneous action 又 1844, p.406
owe, lack 欠 744, p.173

With all these meanings & readings:

huān [歡] **1** joyous **2** happy **3** pleased

When I pay off a loan I *owe*, I *simultaneously* manage to **please** two people—the person who gets his money back, and myself, because this debt becomes one less thing to worry about.

1933

權
TRAD · SIMPLIFIED

This character with the definition:

authority, power

Pinyin **quán** *and Frequency Rank* **297**

Contains **6 strokes** in the following order:

一 十 才 木 权 权

Contains these components:

tree 木 562, p.133
simultaneous action 又 1844, p.406

With all these meanings & readings:

quán [權] **1** authority **2** power **3** right **4** temporary

I know this *tree* is on your land but I am allowed to approach and put my *hand* on it because I have special **authority**.

934

劝

勧
TRAD   SIMPLIFIED

This character with the definition:

urge, persuade

Pinyin **quàn** *and Frequency Rank* **1562**

Contains **4 strokes** in the following order:

フ　又　劝　劝

Contains these components:

◨ simultaneous action 又 1844, p. 406

◨ strength 力 471, p. 113

With all these meanings & readings:

quàn [勧] **1** to advise **2** to urge
3 to try to persuade **4** exhort

The salesman's urgent *hand* movements, coupled with his great *strength* of character, **persuaded** you to buy the new product.

Unit 80

1935

觀
TRAD

SIMPLIFIED

This character with the definition:

observe

Pinyin **guān** and Frequency Rank **334**

Contains **6 strokes** in the following order:

丿 又 刄 刄 观 观

Contains these components:

■ simultaneous action 又 1844, p. 406
■ see 见 307, p. 78

With all these meanings & readings:

guān [觀] **1** to look at **2** to watch **3** to observe **4** to behold **5** concept **6** point of view
guàn [觀] **1** Taoist monastery

There is a distinction between **observing** and *seeing*. When you *simultaneously see* and evaluate what you're *seeing*, that is when you are **observing**.

1936

僅
TRAD

SIMPLIFIED

This character with the definition:

barely, merely

Pinyin **jǐn** and Frequency Rank **494**

Contains **4 strokes** in the following order:

丿 亻 仅 仅

Contains these components:

■ man r 亻 1156, p. 260
■ simultaneous action 又 1844, p. 406

With all these meanings & readings:

jǐn [僅] **1** barely **2** only **3** me

In ancient days, *men* performed many tasks *simultaneously*, which resulted in their **barely** surviving.

1937

擇
TRAD

SIMPLIFIED

This character with the definition:

choose, select*

Pinyin **zé** and Frequency Rank **961**

Contains **8 strokes** in the following order:

一 十 扌 扩 扨 择 择 择

Contains these components:

■ hand r 扌 25, p. 15
■ simultaneous action 又 1844, p. 406
■ earth, soil 土 (altered) 9, p. 11

With all these meanings & readings:

zé [擇] **1** to select **2** to choose **3** to pick **4** to differentiate
zhái [擇] **1** to choose **2** to pick over **3** to pick out **4** to take out **5** to eliminate

All kinds of treasures appear on the *soil* near houses on garbage pick-up day. I *simultaneously* use both *hands* to **selectively** pick up the best and most usable trash.

1938

澤
TRAD

SIMPLIFIED

This character with the definition:

marsh

Pinyin **zé** and Frequency Rank **951**

Contains **8 strokes** in the following order:

丶 丶 氵 沢 汊 泽 泽 泽

Contains these components:

■ water r 氵 314, p. 80
■ simultaneous action 又 1844, p. 406
■ earth, soil 土 (altered) 9, p. 11

With all these meanings & readings:

zé [澤] **1** beneficence **2** marsh

This bleak **marsh** is a slimy mixture that's somehow both scary and beautiful *at the same time*. Its main characteristic is the everpresent mixture of *water* and *soil*.

1939

譯
TRAD

SIMPLIFIED

This character with the definition:

translate

Pinyin **yì** and Frequency Rank **1198**

Contains **7 strokes** in the following order:

丶 讠 讱 讱 译 译 译

Contains these components:

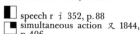

■ speech r 讠 352, p. 88
■ simultaneous action 又 1844, p. 406
■ earth, soil 土 (altered) 9, p. 11

With all these meanings & readings:

yì [譯] **1** to translate **2** to interpret

Strangers are not welcome in this town. Old timers *simultaneously* throw harsh *speech* and chunks of *earth* at newcomers. You don't need an **interpreter** to figure their intentions.

940

對
TRAD   SIMPLIFIED

This character with the definition:

correct, right

Pinyin **duì** *and Frequency Rank* **33**

Contains **5 strokes** in the following order:

Contains these components:

■ simultaneous action 又 1844, p.406

□ inch 寸 216, p.58

With all these meanings & readings:

duì [對] **1** couple **2** pair **3** to be opposite **4** to oppose **5** to face **6** versus **7** for **8** to **9** correct (answer) **10** to answer **11** to reply **12** to direct (towards sth) **13** right

It's often hard to install large objects **correctly**. For example, trying to place a huge roof beam properly requires several men to *simultaneously* make controlled movements of an *inch* to the spot where the beam should rest. They need to remain balanced and in position.

1941

樹
TRAD   SIMPLIFIED

This character with the definition:

tree*

Pinyin **shù** *and Frequency Rank* **697**

Contains **9 strokes** in the following order:

Contains these components:

■ tree 木 562, p.133

□ correct, right 对 1940, p.427

With all these meanings & readings:

shù [樹] **1** tree **2** m 棵[kē]

It's *correct* to think of a *tree* as a **tree**.

1942

釋
TRAD   SIMPLIFIED

This character with the definition:

explain

Pinyin **shì** *and Frequency Rank* **813**

Contains **12 strokes** in the following order:

Contains these components:

■ distinguish, differentiate r 采 1649, p.366

□ simultaneous action 又 1844, p.406

□ earth, soil 土 (altered) 9, p.11

With all these meanings & readings:

shì [釋] **1** explain **2** to release

My class wanted me to **explain** the concept of 'quick sand'. To do so required that I *distinguish* between types of water sources and how their *simultaneous action* interacts with elements in the *earth*.

1943

雞
TRAD   SIMPLIFIED

This character with the definition:

chicken

Pinyin **jī** *and Frequency Rank* **1391**

Contains **7 strokes** in the following order:

Contains these components:

■ simultaneous action 又 1844, p.406

□ bird 鸟 394, p.96

With all these meanings & readings:

jī [雞] **1** fowl **2** chicken **3** m 只[隻][zhī]

Chickens seem like such busy *birds*. They appear to do *many things at once*.

1944

史
SIMP & TRAD

This character with the definition:

history

Pinyin **shǐ** *and Frequency Rank* **456**

Contains **5 strokes** in the following order:

Contains these components:

■ harmonious crossing c 乂 (altered) 1837, p.405

□ middle 中 (altered) 38, p.18

With all these meanings & readings:

shǐ [史] **1** history **2** surname Shi

History books praise the *Middle* Kingdom of China for bringing *harmony* to the Far East.

1945

馶
TRAD   SIMPLIFIED

This character with the definition:

move, go quickly (vehicle)

Pinyin **shǐ** *and Frequency Rank* **1520**

Contains **8 strokes** in the following order:

フ 马 马 马 驴 驴 驶 驶

Contains these components:

■ horse 马 388, p.95
□ history 史 1944, p.427

With all these meanings & readings

shǐ   [驶] **1** hasten **2** proceed t
3 sail a vessel

Throughout most of *history*, using a *horse* was the only way to make a carriage **move quickly**.

1946

SIMP & TRAD

This character with the definition:

minor official

Pinyin **lì** *and Frequency Rank* **2311**

Contains **6 strokes** in the following order:

一 亠 一 一 亖 吏

Contains these components:

■ history 史 1944, p.427
□ one 一 1, p.10

With all these meanings & readings

lì   [吏] **1** minor official

The life story of *one* **minor official** reflected the *history* of the entire Kingdom.

1947

SIMP & TRAD

This character with the definition:

cause, make, enable

Pinyin **shǐ** *and Frequency Rank* **119**

Contains **8 strokes** in the following order:

ノ 亻 亻 亻 佢 佢 使 使

Contains these components:

■ man r 亻 1156, p.260
■ minor official 吏 1946, p.428

With all these meanings & readings

shǐ   [使] **1** to make **2** to cause
3 to enable **4** to use **5** to employ **6** messenger

Even though my uncle was a shy *man*, his position as a *minor official* in the province **enabled** him to give orders that other *men* would carry out.

1948

SIMP & TRAD

This character with the definition:

even more

Pinyin **gèng** *and Frequency Rank* **221**

Contains **7 strokes** in the following order:

一 亠 一 一 百 吏 更

Contains these components:

■ history 史 1944, p.427
□ two 二 2, p.10

With all these meanings & readings

gēng [更] **1** to change
gèng [更] **1** more **2** even more
3 further **4** still **5** still more

The *history* of a place is **even more** interesting if it involves *two* or more ethnic groups.

1949

SIMP & TRAD

This character with the definition:

cheap

Pinyin **pián** *and Frequency Rank* **271**

Contains **9 strokes** in the following order:

ノ 亻 亻 亻 佢 佢 佢 便 便

Contains these components:

■ man r 亻 1156, p.260
■ even more 更 1948, p.428

With all these meanings & readings

biàn [便] **1** ordinary **2** plain
3 convenient **4** as convenient
5 when the chance arises **6** ha
7 easy **8** informal **9** simple
10 so **11** thus **12** to relieve on
self **13** to urinate **14** to defeca
15 equivalent to 就: then **16** ir
that case **17** even if **18** soon
afterwards
pián [便] **1** advantageous **2** che

A *man* (or woman) tends to buy *even more* of an item if the price is **cheap**.

1950 鞭

SIMP & TRAD

This character with the definition:

a whip

Pinyin **biān** *and Frequency Rank* **2250**

Contains **18 strokes** in the following order:

Contains these components:

- animal hide 革 98, p. 31
- cheap 便 1949, p. 428

With all these meanings & readings:

biān [鞭] **1** a whip or lash **2** to flog **3** to whip

A **whip** only requires a thin strip of *animal hide*, so it's *cheap* to make.

1951 硬

SIMP & TRAD

This character with the definition:

hard, stiff

Pinyin **yìng** *and Frequency Rank* **1170**

Contains **12 strokes** in the following order:

Contains these components:

- stone, rock 石 522, p. 124
- even more 更 1948, p. 428

With all these meanings & readings:

yìng [硬] **1** hard **2** stiff **3** strong **4** firm

You may think the average *rock* as a **hard** object, but a diamond is *even more* so.

1952 艮

SIMP & TRAD

This character with the definition:

tough, chewy

Pinyin **gěn** *and Frequency Rank* **4564**

Contains **6 strokes** in the following order:

Contains these components:

- eye 目 (altered) 75, p. 26
- harmonious crossing c 乂 (altered) 1837, p. 405

With all these meanings & readings:

gěn [艮] **1** blunt **2** tough **3** chewy

gèn [艮] **1** one of the eight trigrams

My *eye* savored the juicy steak in front of me until I took my very first bite, and discovered how **tough** it was—way beyond '**chewy**'! My feelings of *harmony* instantly disappeared.

1953 眼

SIMP & TRAD

This character with the definition:

eye*

Pinyin **yǎn** *and Frequency Rank* **281**

Contains **11 strokes** in the following order:

Contains these components:

- eye 目 75, p. 26
- tough, chewy 艮 1952, p. 429

With all these meanings & readings:

yǎn [眼] **1** eye **2** (classifier for big hollow things:well, stove, pot etc) **3** m 双[雙][shuāng]

A piece of grit in your *eye* can be so painful that it makes you squint, making it difficult for your **eye** to see properly.

1954 根

SIMP & TRAD

This character with the definition:

plant roots

Pinyin **gēn** *and Frequency Rank* **352**

Contains **10 strokes** in the following order:

Contains these components:

- tree 木 562, p. 133
- tough, chewy 艮 1952, p. 429

With all these meanings & readings:

gēn [根] **1** root **2** basis **3** m for long slender objects, e.g. cigarettes, guitar strings **4** m 条[條][tiáo] **5** radical (chemistry)

The survival guide described those **plant roots**—some from *trees*—that maintained a *chewy* texture and contained medicinal properties in an emergency.

1955

This character with the definition:

mark, trace

Pinyin **hén** *and Frequency Rank* **1938**

SIMP & TRAD Contains **11 strokes** in the following order:

Contains these components:

☐ sick r 疒 434, p.104
◨ tough, chewy 艮 1952, p.429

With all these meanings & readings:

hén [痕] **1** scar **2** traces

The only **trace** left from my being *sick* for two weeks was the weight that I lost. Most food was too *tough* for me to eat.

1956

This character with the definition:

set a limit, restrict

Pinyin **xiàn** *and Frequency Rank* **613**

SIMP & TRAD Contains **8 strokes** in the following order:

Contains these components:

☐ hills r 阝 942, p.216
◨ tough, chewy 艮 1952, p.429

With all these meanings & readings:

xiàn [限] **1** limit **2** bound

If you **restrict** your cattle from wandering into the *hills* to graze, you are guarding against their muscles not becoming too *tough*, which will reduce the value of their meat on the market.

1957

This character with the definition:

ruthless, relentless

Pinyin **hěn** *and Frequency Rank* **1654**

SIMP & TRAD Contains **9 strokes** in the following order:

Contains these components:

☐ dog r 犭 1084, p.245
◨ tough, chewy 艮 1952, p.429

With all these meanings & readings:

hěn [狠] **1** fierce **2** very

No matter how *tough* a piece of meat, the *dog* will be **relentless** in devouring it.

1958

This character with the definition:

hate

Pinyin **hèn** *and Frequency Rank* **1295**

SIMP & TRAD Contains **9 strokes** in the following order:

Contains these components:

☐ heart (skinny) r 忄 1135, p.256
◨ tough, chewy 艮 1952, p.429

With all these meanings & readings:

hèn [恨] **1** to hate

A *heart* full of **hate** is a *tough heart* indeed.

1959

This character with the definition:

with, follow

Pinyin **gēn** *and Frequency Rank* **541**

SIMP & TRAD Contains **13 strokes** in the following order:

Contains these components:

☐ foot r 𧾷 1148, p.258
◨ tough, chewy 艮 1952, p.429

With all these meanings & readings:

gēn [跟] **1** heel **2** to follow closely **3** to go with **4** to marry sb (of woman) **5** with **6** towards **7** as (compared to) **8** from (different from) **9** and (in addition to)

The plants along the path through the tropical forest were so overgrown that they made it difficult for us to **follow** the path. The terrain was also very *tough* on our *feet*.

Unit 81

1960 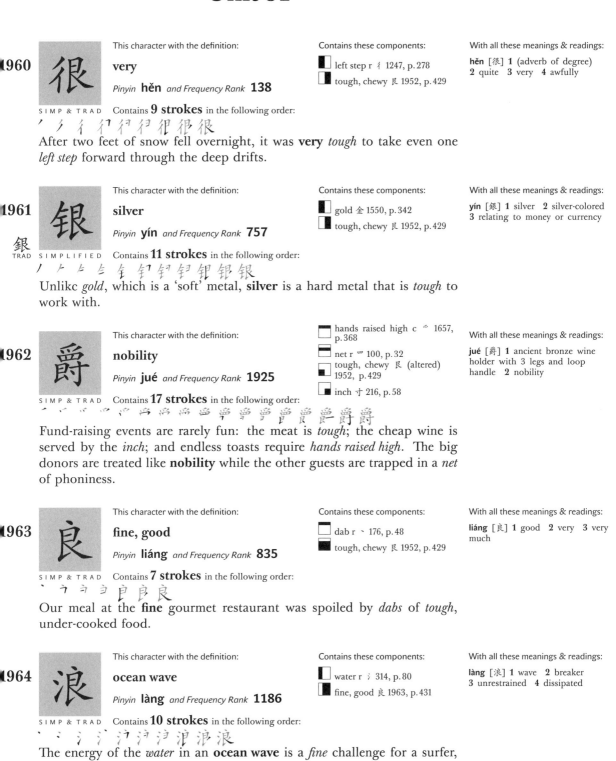 很

This character with the definition:

very

Pinyin **hěn** *and Frequency Rank* **138**

SIMP & TRAD Contains **9 strokes** in the following order:

Contains these components:

■ left step r 彳 1247, p. 278

■ tough, chewy 艮 1952, p. 429

With all these meanings & readings:

hěn [很] **1** (adverb of degree) **2** quite **3** very **4** awfully

After two feet of snow fell overnight, it was **very** *tough* to take even one *left step* forward through the deep drifts.

1961 银

This character with the definition:

silver

Pinyin **yín** *and Frequency Rank* **757**

TRAD SIMPLIFIED Contains **11 strokes** in the following order:

Contains these components:

■ gold 金 1550, p. 342

■ tough, chewy 艮 1952, p. 429

With all these meanings & readings:

yín [銀] **1** silver **2** silver-colored **3** relating to money or currency

Unlike *gold*, which is a 'soft' metal, **silver** is a hard metal that is *tough* to work with.

1962 爵

This character with the definition:

nobility

Pinyin **jué** *and Frequency Rank* **1925**

SIMP & TRAD Contains **17 strokes** in the following order:

Contains these components:

☐ hands raised high c ⌒ 1657, p. 368

▬ net r ⚏ 100, p. 32

☐ tough, chewy 艮 (altered) 1952, p. 429

☐ inch 寸 216, p. 58

With all these meanings & readings:

jué [爵] **1** ancient bronze wine holder with 3 legs and loop handle **2** nobility

Fund-raising events are rarely fun: the meat is *tough*; the cheap wine is served by the *inch*; and endless toasts require *hands raised high*. The big donors are treated like **nobility** while the other guests are trapped in a *net* of phoniness.

1963 良

This character with the definition:

fine, good

Pinyin **liáng** *and Frequency Rank* **835**

SIMP & TRAD Contains **7 strokes** in the following order:

Contains these components:

☐ dab r 、 176, p. 48

■ tough, chewy 艮 1952, p. 429

With all these meanings & readings:

liáng [良] **1** good **2** very **3** very much

Our meal at the **fine** gourmet restaurant was spoiled by *dabs* of *tough*, under-cooked food.

1964 浪

This character with the definition:

ocean wave

Pinyin **làng** *and Frequency Rank* **1186**

SIMP & TRAD Contains **10 strokes** in the following order:

Contains these components:

■ water r 氵 314, p. 80

■ fine, good 良 1963, p. 431

With all these meanings & readings:

làng [浪] **1** wave **2** breaker **3** unrestrained **4** dissipated

The energy of the *water* in an **ocean wave** is a *fine* challenge for a surfer, but not so *good* for the owner of a beach-front property.

1965
娘
孃
TRAD   SIMPLIFIED

This character with the definition:

mum, mother

Pinyin **niáng** *and Frequency Rank* **881**

Contains **10 strokes** in the following order:

Contains these components:
- woman 女 790, p. 183
- fine, good 良 1963, p. 431

With all these meanings & readings:
niáng [娘] **1** mother **2** young lady
niáng [孃] **1** mother

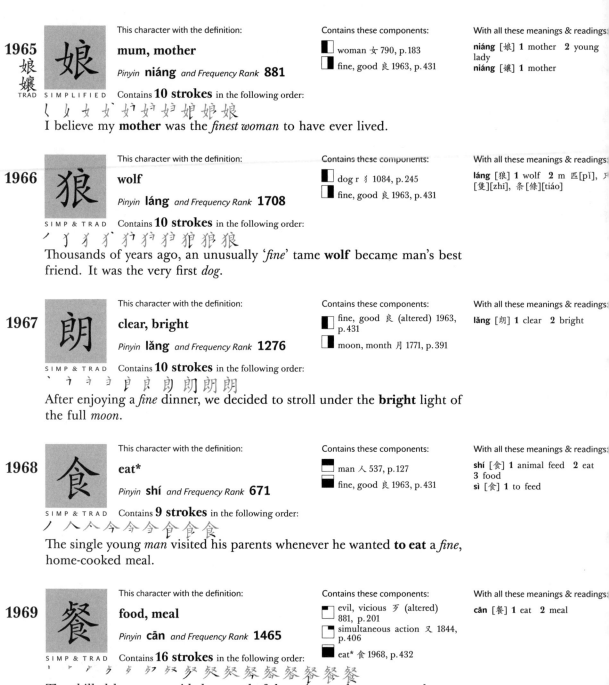

I believe my **mother** was the *finest woman* to have ever lived.

1966
狼

SIMP & TRAD

This character with the definition:

wolf

Pinyin **láng** *and Frequency Rank* **1708**

Contains **10 strokes** in the following order:

Contains these components:
- dog r 犭 1084, p. 245
- fine, good 良 1963, p. 431

With all these meanings & readings:
láng [狼] **1** wolf **2** m 匹[pǐ], 只[隻][zhī], 条[條][tiáo]

Thousands of years ago, an unusually '*fine*' tame **wolf** became man's best friend. It was the very first *dog*.

1967
朗

SIMP & TRAD

This character with the definition:

clear, bright

Pinyin **lǎng** *and Frequency Rank* **1276**

Contains **10 strokes** in the following order:

Contains these components:
- fine, good 良 (altered) 1963, p. 431
- moon, month 月 1771, p. 391

With all these meanings & readings:
lǎng [朗] **1** clear **2** bright

After enjoying a *fine* dinner, we decided to stroll under the **bright** light of the full *moon*.

1968
食

SIMP & TRAD

This character with the definition:

eat*

Pinyin **shí** *and Frequency Rank* **671**

Contains **9 strokes** in the following order:

Contains these components:
- man 人 537, p. 127
- fine, good 良 1963, p. 431

With all these meanings & readings:
shí [食] **1** animal feed **2** eat **3** food
sì [食] **1** to feed

The single young *man* visited his parents whenever he wanted **to eat** a *fine*, home-cooked meal.

1969
餐

SIMP & TRAD

This character with the definition:

food, meal

Pinyin **cān** *and Frequency Rank* **1465**

Contains **16 strokes** in the following order:

Contains these components:
- evil, vicious 歹 (altered) 881, p. 201
- simultaneous action 又 1844, p. 406
- eat* 食 1968, p. 432

With all these meanings & readings:
cān [餐] **1** eat **2** meal

The skilled hunter provided a wonderful service to the town: *at the same time* that he thought to kill the *vicious* wild animal in self-defense, he provided fresh **food**—the animal's meat—for the people to *eat*.

1970

SIMP & TRAD

This character with the definition:

郎
young man

Pinyin **láng** *and Frequency Rank* **1457**

Contains **8 strokes** in the following order:

丶 亠 亠 亖 自 良 郎 郎

Contains these components:

■ fine, good 良 (altered) 1963, p. 431

□ town r 阝 955, p. 219

With all these meanings & readings:

láng [郎] **1** (arch.) minister **2** official **3** noun prefix denoting function or status **4** a youth **5** surname Lang

The single **young man** was eager to move out of his parents' country house and into a *fine* apartment in *town* so that he could better enjoy its entertainment and social activities.

1971

糧
TRAD SIMPLIFIED

This character with the definition:

粮
grain, food, provisions

Pinyin **liáng** *and Frequency Rank* **1303**

Contains **13 strokes** in the following order:

丶 丷 一 半 米 米 米 籵 籵 粈 粮 粮 粮

Contains these components:

■ rice (food) 米 1535, p. 339

■ fine, good 良 1963, p. 431

With all these meanings & readings:

liáng [糧] **1** grain **2** food **3** provisions **4** agricultural tax paid in grain

Rice makes for mighty *fine* **provisions**.

1972

SIMP & TRAD

This character with the definition:

辰
time, day, occasion

Pinyin **chén** *and Frequency Rank* **2317**

Contains **7 strokes** in the following order:

一 厂 厂 厈 辰 辰 辰

Contains these components:

□ cliff r 厂 399, p. 97

■ tough, chewy 長 (altered) 1952, p. 429

With all these meanings & readings:

chén [辰] **1** 5th earthly branch: 7–9 a.m., 3rd solar month (5th April–4th May), year of the Dragon

It took so much **time** to hike up the *cliff* that we had to rest and eat our *chewy* protein food.

1973

SIMP & TRAD

This character with the definition:

振
rouse, shake, vibrate

Pinyin **zhèn** *and Frequency Rank* **1140**

Contains **10 strokes** in the following order:

一 十 扌 扩 扩 护 护 振 振 振

Contains these components:

■ hand r 扌 25, p. 15

■ time, day, occasion 辰 1972, p. 433

With all these meanings & readings:

zhèn [振] **1** to shake **2** to flap **3** to vibrate **4** to resonate **5** to rise up with spirit **6** to rouse oneself

On the first *day* of school, a parent's *hand* is usually needed to **rouse** sleepy children and get them ready in *time* to catch the school bus.

1974

震
SIMP & TRAD

This character with the definition:

震
shake, quake

Pinyin **zhèn** *and Frequency Rank* **1104**

Contains **15 strokes** in the following order:

一 厂 戸 乕 乕 雨 雨 雨 霎 霎 霍 震 震 震 震

Contains these components:

■ rain 雨 239, p. 63

■ time, day, occasion 辰 1972, p. 433

With all these meanings & readings:

zhèn [震] **1** to shake **2** to vibrate **3** to jolt **4** to quake **5** excited **6** shocked **7** one of the eight trigrams, symbolizing thunder

A hurricane is a dangerous *time*. Powerful winds can cause your house to **shake** and the *rain* to fall sideways.

1975

SIMP & TRAD

This character with the definition:

disgrace, dishonor

Pinyin **rǔ** *and Frequency Rank* **1907**

Contains **10 strokes** in the following order:

一 厂 厂 厂 辰 辰 辰 辰 辱 辱

Contains these components:

◻ time, day, occasion 辰 1972, p. 433

◼ inch 寸 216, p. 58

With all these meanings & readings:

rǔ [辱] **1** disgrace **2** insult **3** t⟨ humiliate **4** Taiwan pr rù **5** pr⟨ fixed word denoting respect (po- lite 谦辞)

In the Emperor's court in ancient China, an official's prestige was mea- sured by the amount of seating room he was given during each special *occasion*. The difference of only one *inch* could signal **disgrace**.

1976

SIMP & TRAD

This character with the definition:

morning*

Pinyin **chén** *and Frequency Rank* **1388**

Contains **11 strokes** in the following order:

丶 亠 冂 日 旦 尸 尸 层 昂 晨 晨

Contains these components:

◻ day, sun 日 64, p. 24

◼ time, day, occasion 辰 1972, p. 433

With all these meanings & readings:

chén [晨] **1** morning **2** dawn **3** daybreak

Morning is the *time* of *day* when the *sun* first rises above the horizon.

1977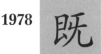

SIMP & TRAD

This character with the definition:

lip

Pinyin **chún** *and Frequency Rank* **1880**

Contains **10 strokes** in the following order:

一 厂 厂 厂 辰 辰 辰 辰 唇 唇

Contains these components:

◼ time, day, occasion 辰 (al- tered) 1972, p. 433

◻ mouth 口 37, p. 17

With all these meanings & readings:

chún [唇] **1** lip

Her **lips** were trembling on that special *occasion* when I proposed marriage. Her *mouth* opened in surprised pleasure—or was it amused contempt— when I bent down on one knee? It was hard to tell!

1978

SIMP & TRAD

This character with the definition:

already, then

Pinyin **jì** *and Frequency Rank* **724**

Contains **9 strokes** in the following order:

丿 ㇇ ㇕ 艮 艮 既 既 既 既

Contains these components:

◼ tough, chewy 艮 (altered) 1952, p. 429

◻ swallow, choke 旡 747, p. 174

With all these meanings & readings:

jì [既] **1** already **2** since **3** bot⟨ (and...)

The meat was so *tough* that I could not chew it and instead *swallowed* a large piece; **then** I began to *choke* on it.

1979 概

SIMP & TRAD

This character with the definition:

approximate, general

Pinyin **gài** *and Frequency Rank* **791**

Contains **13 strokes** in the following order:

一 十 才 木 木 术 杆 柑 根 根 栖 概 概

Contains these components:

◻ tree 木 562, p. 133

◻ already, then 既 1978, p. 434

With all these meanings & readings:

gài [概] **1** general **2** approxi- mate

An expert measured the trunk of the huge sycamore *tree* near my house, and *then* estimated that its **approximate** age was 350 years—older than the age of the United States.

1980

This character with the definition:

promptly, immediately

Pinyin **jí** *and Frequency Rank* **293**

SIMP & TRAD   Contains **7 strokes** in the following order:

フ ㄱ ㅋ 尸 尸 即 即

Contains these components:

▪ tough, chewy 艮 (altered) 1952, p. 429

▪ single ear r 卩 165, p. 46

With all these meanings & readings:

jí [即] **1** namely **2** that is **3** i.e. **4** prompt **5** at once **6** at present **7** even if **8** prompted (by the occasion) **9** to approach **10** to come into contact **11** to assume (office) **12** to draw near

My toothache was so bad that pains would **immediately** shoot up to my *ear* whenever I tried to eat anything *chewy*.

1981

艱
TRAD   SIMPLIFIED

This character with the definition:

difficult, arduous

Pinyin **jiān** *and Frequency Rank* **1647**

Contains **8 strokes** in the following order:

フ 又 ㄨ フ 又 フ 又 ㄱ 艰 艰 艰

Contains these components:

▪ simultaneous action 又 1844, p. 406

▪ tough, chewy 艮 1952, p. 429

With all these meanings & readings:

jiān [艱] **1** difficult **2** hard **3** hardship

For some unfortunate people, it is a **difficult** to perform more than one task *at the same time*, such as walking and *chewing* gum.

1982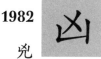

兇
TRAD   SIMPLIFIED

This character with the definition:

fiendish, ferocious

Pinyin **xiōng** *and Frequency Rank* **1378**

Contains **4 strokes** in the following order:

ノ ㄨ 凶 凶

Contains these components:

▢ receptacle r 凵 157, p. 43

▪ harmonious crossing c 乂 1837, p. 405

With all these meanings & readings:

xiōng [兇] **1** variant of 凶 [兇][xiōng]

xiōng [凶] **1** vicious **2** fierce **3** terrible **4** fearful **5** violence **6** murder **7** criminal **8** murderer **9** ominous **10** inauspicious **11** famine **12** crop failure

Like Pandora's box, this *receptacle* is open to the sky, and we see how all the buoyant forces of *harmony* are rising and escaping. What's left? In the absence of harmony, **fiendishness** and **ferocity** thrive. • Here are three characters whose meanings may blend together in a student's mind. How can we distinguish between 冈, 区, and 凶 ('mountain ridge', 'administrative division', and 'fiendish')? All three contain a harmonious cross within an open square. The open part of the square suggests a means of escape which can aid in the memorization of the character's meaning. Mountain ridges are so heavy, they fall out of the bottom. Ferocity is a boiling hot emotion and the steam from it rises out the top. To flee from a fiendish administrator, you flee to another district.

1983

SIMP & TRAD

This character with the definition:

chest, bosom

Pinyin **xiōng** *and Frequency Rank* **1356**

Contains **10 strokes** in the following order:

丿 ㄇ 月 月 月' 朐 朐 胸 胸 胸

Contains these components:

▪ moon, month 月 (altered) 1771, p. 391

▪ wrap r 勹 364, p. 90

▪ fiendish, ferocious 凶 1982, p. 435

With all these meanings & readings:

xiōng [胸] **1** chest **2** bosom **3** heart **4** mind **5** thorax

It's a full *moon*, a time in which people exhibit odd behaviors. So *wrap* all your *fiendish* emotions in a tight bundle and hide them in your **bosom**.

1984

脑

脳
TRAD SIMPLIFIED

This character with the definition:

brain

Pinyin **nǎo** *and Frequency Rank* **646**

Contains **10 strokes** in the following order:

) 刀 月 月 月` 广 脋 脋 脑 脑

Contains these components:

■ meat 肉 (altered) 753, p.175

□ cover r ⼇ 250, p.66

■ fiendish, ferocious 凶 1982, p.435

With all these meanings & readings:

nǎo [腦] **1** brain

The **brain** is the *body part* in which lies everybody's most *fiendish* and *ferocious* thoughts. We learn to *cover* all this mental ugliness or else no one will ever want to live with anyone else.

Unit 82

1985

恼
惱
TRAD SIMPLIFIED

This character with the definition:

get angry

Pinyin **nǎo** *and Frequency Rank* **1704**

Contains **9 strokes** in the following order:

丶 丶 忄 忄 忙 忉 怊 恼 恼

Contains these components:

heart (skinny) r 忄 1135, p. 256
cover r 冖 250, p. 66
fiendish, ferocious 凶 1982, p. 435

With all these meanings & readings:

nǎo [惱] **1** to get angry

Sometimes things don't go your way. Here's one poor soul whose *heart* is swollen in agitation. He's trying to keep a *cover* on his feelings of *ferocity* which are threatening to overcome him. In short, he's **getting angry**.

1986

文
SIMP & TRAD

This character with the definition:

culture, language

Pinyin **wén** *and Frequency Rank* **148**

Contains **4 strokes** in the following order:

丶 一 ﾅ 文

Contains these components:

cover r 冖 250, p. 66
harmonious crossing c 乂 1837, p. 405

With all these meanings & readings:

wén [文] **1** language **2** culture **3** writing **4** formal **5** literary **6** gentle **7** m for money (archaic) **8** surname Wen

The lid that *covers* the *harmonious cross* strokes of written Chinese creates an appropriate symbol of **culture**—in China's case, one that is more than 4000 years old.

1987

彦
彥
TRAD SIMPLIFIED

This character with the definition:

accomplished, talented

Pinyin **yàn** *and Frequency Rank* **2559**

Contains **9 strokes** in the following order:

丶 一 亠 亠 立 产 产 彦 彦

Contains these components:

culture, language 文 1986, p. 437
cliff r 厂 399, p. 97
feathers r 彡 1611, p. 359

With all these meanings & readings:

yàn [彦] **1** accomplished **2** elegant

Different *cultures* have different ways of recognizing their most **accomplished** members, those that they place up on a pedestal ('*cliff*') of honor. For instance, many Native American tribes recognized superior **talent** by awarding eagle *feathers* to their warriors.

1988

颜
顏
TRAD SIMPLIFIED

This character with the definition:

color

Pinyin **yán** *and Frequency Rank* **1545**

Contains **15 strokes** in the following order:

丶 一 亠 亠 立 产 产 彦 彦 彦 彦 颜 颜 颜 颜

Contains these components:

accomplished, talented 彦 1987, p. 437
page, leaf 页 1408, p. 312

With all these meanings & readings:

yán [颜] **1** color **2** countenance **3** surname Yan

Whenever the *talented* young man received a compliment, his *face* flushed the **color** red with embarrassment.

1989

齐
齊
TRAD SIMPLIFIED

This character with the definition:

neat, even

Pinyin **qí** *and Frequency Rank* **1063**

Contains **6 strokes** in the following order:

丶 一 亠 文 亣 齐

Contains these components:

culture, language 文 1986, p. 437
eight 八 (altered) 1261, p. 282

With all these meanings & readings:

qí [齊] **1** (name of states and dynasties at several different periods) **2** surname Qi
qí [齐] **1** neat **2** even **3** level with **4** identical **5** simultaneous **6** all together **7** to even sth out

He dressed **neatly** to give the impression he possessed *abundant culture*.

1990

TRAD   SIMPLIFIED

This character with the definition:

crowd, jostle

Pinyin **jǐ** *and Frequency Rank* **1661**

Contains **9 strokes** in the following order:

一 丁 扌 扌 扩 护 挤 挤 挤

Contains these components:

☐ hand r 扌 25, p.15
☐ neat, even 齐 1989, p.437

With all these meanings & readings:

jǐ [擠] **1** crowded **2** to squeeze

The waiter places his *hand* under his tray full of dishes strategically in order to keep the tray *even* as the **crowd** in the busy bar **jostles** against him.

1991

TRAD   SIMPLIFIED

This character with the definition:

cross a river

Pinyin **jì** *and Frequency Rank* **360**

Contains **9 strokes** in the following order:

丶 冫 氵 氵 汸 汸 汸 济 济

Contains these components:

☐ water r 氵 314, p.80
☐ neat, even 齐 1989, p.437

With all these meanings & readings:

jì [濟] **1** aid **2** ferry **3** frugal

In order to **cross the river** without losing his gear in the rushing *water*, the hiker bundled his belongings into a *neat*, compact 'package' to balance on his head while he crossed.

1992

TRAD   SIMPLIFIED

This character with the definition:

dose (medical)

Pinyin **jì** *and Frequency Rank* **1546**

Contains **8 strokes** in the following order:

丶 亠 亠 文 齐 齐 剂 剂

Contains these components:

☐ neat, even 齐 1989, p.437
☐ knife r 刂 169, p.46

With all these meanings & readings:

jì [劑] **1** dose

It's time to take your **medical dose**. Unfortunately, each **pill** contains several smaller **doses**. Use a sharp *knife* to carefully cut each **pill** into pieces, and be extra careful to make each piece *even*, or else the **dosage** will vary unacceptably.

1993

TRAD   SIMPLIFIED

This character with the definition:

vein, grain

Pinyin **wén** *and Frequency Rank* **1768**

Contains **7 strokes** in the following order:

纟 纟 纟 纟 纤 纹 纹

Contains these components:

☐ silk r 纟 1037, p.235
☐ culture, language 文 1986, p.437

With all these meanings & readings:

wén [紋] **1** line **2** trace **3** mark **4** decoration **5** decorated with

The *silken* embroidery threads on fine clothing and the patterns of written *language* suggest the patterns formed by **veins** of minerals in stone and the swirls in wood **grain**.

1994

TRAD   SIMPLIFIED

This character with the definition:

slay

Pinyin **liú** *and Frequency Rank* **751**

Contains **6 strokes** in the following order:

丶 亠 文 文 刘 刘

Contains these components:

☐ culture, language 文 1986, p.437
☐ knife r 刂 169, p.46

With all these meanings & readings:

Liú [劉] **1** surname Liu

Slaying members of a *culture* with a *knife* or other weapon sounds like the initial steps of a genocidal massacre.

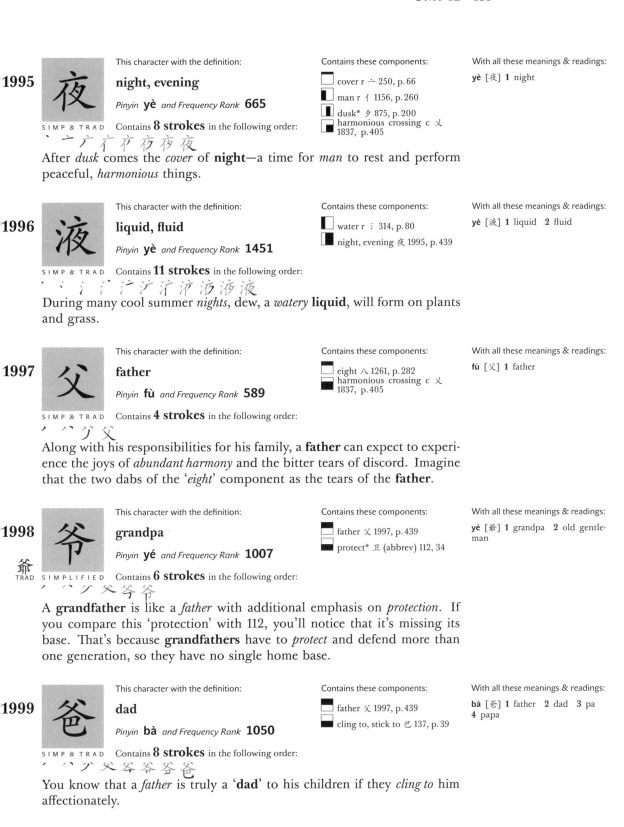

1995

夜

SIMP & TRAD

This character with the definition:

night, evening

Pinyin **yè** *and Frequency Rank* **665**

Contains **8 strokes** in the following order:

丶 一 广 广 疒 疒 夜 夜 夜

Contains these components:

☐ cover r ⼍ 250, p. 66

☐ man r 亻 1156, p. 260

☐ dusk* 夕 875, p. 200

☐ harmonious crossing c 乂 1837, p. 405

With all these meanings & readings:

yè [夜] **1** night

After *dusk* comes the *cover* of **night**—a time for *man* to rest and perform peaceful, *harmonious* things.

1996

液

SIMP & TRAD

This character with the definition:

liquid, fluid

Pinyin **yè** *and Frequency Rank* **1451**

Contains **11 strokes** in the following order:

丶 丶 氵 汋 沪 沪 沪 沪 液 液 液

Contains these components:

☐ water r 氵 314, p. 80

☐ night, evening 夜 1995, p. 439

With all these meanings & readings:

yè [液] **1** liquid **2** fluid

During many cool summer *nights*, dew, a *watery* **liquid**, will form on plants and grass.

1997

父

SIMP & TRAD

This character with the definition:

father

Pinyin **fù** *and Frequency Rank* **589**

Contains **4 strokes** in the following order:

丶 丷 父 父

Contains these components:

☐ eight 八 1261, p. 282

☐ harmonious crossing c 乂 1837, p. 405

With all these meanings & readings:

fù [父] **1** father

Along with his responsibilities for his family, a **father** can expect to experience the joys of *abundant harmony* and the bitter tears of discord. Imagine that the two dabs of the '*eight*' component as the tears of the **father**.

1998

爷

爺
TRAD SIMPLIFIED

This character with the definition:

grandpa

Pinyin **yé** *and Frequency Rank* **1007**

Contains **6 strokes** in the following order:

丶 丷 父 父 爷 爷

Contains these components:

☐ father 父 1997, p. 439

☐ protect* 卫 (abbrev) 112, 34

With all these meanings & readings:

yé [爺] **1** grandpa **2** old gentleman

A **grandfather** is like a *father* with additional emphasis on *protection*. If you compare this 'protection' with 112, you'll notice that it's missing its base. That's because **grandfathers** have to *protect* and defend more than one generation, so they have no single home base.

1999

爸

SIMP & TRAD

This character with the definition:

dad

Pinyin **bà** *and Frequency Rank* **1050**

Contains **8 strokes** in the following order:

丶 丷 父 父 爷 爸 爸 爸

Contains these components:

☐ father 父 1997, p. 439

☐ cling to, stick to 巴 137, p. 39

With all these meanings & readings:

bà [爸] **1** father **2** dad **3** pa **4** papa

You know that a *father* is truly a '**dad**' to his children if they *cling to* him affectionately.

2000 交
SIMP & TRAD

This character with the definition:
meet, intersect
Pinyin **jiāo** *and Frequency Rank* **320**
Contains **6 strokes** in the following order:
丶 亠 亣 六 交 交

Contains these components:
six 六 841, p. 193
harmonious crossing c 乂 1837, p. 405

With all these meanings & readings:
jiāo [交] **1** to deliver **2** to turn over **3** to make friends **4** to intersect (lines) **5** to pay (money)

The place was named 'The *Crossing*' because *six* roads **intersected** there.

2001 咬
SIMP & TRAD

This character with the definition:
bite, nip
Pinyin **yǎo** *and Frequency Rank* **1658**
Contains **9 strokes** in the following order:
丨 口 口 口 口 叶 吖 咗 咬

Contains these components:
mouth 口 37, p. 17
meet, intersect 交 2000, p. 440

With all these meanings & readings:
yǎo [咬] **1** to bite **2** to nip

A dog's **bite** sometimes causes the teeth in its *mouth* to *intersect* with human or animal flesh!

2002 较
較 TRAD
SIMPLIFIED

This character with the definition:
comparatively
Pinyin **jiào** *and Frequency Rank* **491**
Contains **10 strokes** in the following order:
一 七 车 车 车 轧 轩 轩 轳 较

Contains these components:
car 车 1291, p. 289
meet, intersect 交 2000, p. 440

With all these meanings & readings:
jiào [較] **1** comparatively **2** (preposition comparing difference in degree) **3** to contrast **4** to compare **5** rather **6** fairly **7** clearly (different) **8** markedly **9** to haggle over **10** to quibble

Classic *car* owners gather at '*meets*', events which are **comparatively** tamer to those of race *car* owners!

2003 校
SIMP & TRAD

This character with the definition:
school
Pinyin **xiào** *and Frequency Rank* **633**
Contains **10 strokes** in the following order:
一 十 才 木 木 木 村 村 校 校

Contains these components:
tree 木 562, p. 133
meet, intersect 交 2000, p. 440

With all these meanings & readings:
jiào [校] **1** proofread **2** to check **3** to compare
xiào [校] **1** school **2** military officer **3** m 所[suǒ]

The ancient Chinese constructed a **school** by positioning tall *trees* together so that they would *intersect* and support each other; doing so provided the external 'structure' for the **school**.

2004 风
風 TRAD
SIMPLIFIED

This character with the definition:
wind
Pinyin **fēng** *and Frequency Rank* **348**
Contains **4 strokes** in the following order:
丿 几 凡 风

Contains these components:
commonplace 凡 (abbrev) 901, 205
harmonious crossing c 乂 1837, p. 405

With all these meanings & readings:
fēng [風] **1** wind **2** news **3** style **4** custom **5** manner **6** m 阵[陣][zhèn], 丝[絲][sī]

For sailors and mariners, nothing is better than a *commonplace* **wind** that blows the ship quickly from port to port in a *harmonious crossing*.

2005 疯

疯 TRAD · SIMPLIFIED

This character with the definition:

insane

Pinyin **fēng** *and Frequency Rank* **1549**

Contains these components:
- sick r 疒 434, p.104
- wind 风 2004, p.440

With all these meanings & readings:

fēng [瘋] **1** insane **2** mad **3** wild

Contains **9 strokes** in the following order:

丶 一 广 广 广 疒 疒 疯 疯

An **insane** person is mentally *sick* with delusions that are as mysterious and invisible as the *wind*.

2006 飘

飄 TRAD · SIMPLIFIED

This character with the definition:

waft, blow about

Pinyin **piāo** *and Frequency Rank* **1527**

Contains these components:
- ticket 票 1273, p.284
- wind 风 2004, p.440

With all these meanings & readings:

piāo [飄] **1** to float

Contains **15 strokes** in the following order:

一 广 戸 兩 西 西 亜 亜 票 票 票 飘 飘 飘 飘

The blizzard's strong *wind* **blew about** the snow into deep, shifting drifts which forced the airport to shut down—thus making my precious airplane *ticket* worthless.

2007 凤

鳳 TRAD · SIMPLIFIED

This character with the definition:

phoenix

Pinyin **fèng** *and Frequency Rank* **1504**

Contains these components:
- wind 风 (altered) 2004, p.440

With all these meanings & readings:

fèng [鳳] **1** phoenix **2** surname Feng

Contains **4 strokes** in the following order:

丿 几 凤 凤

In mythology, the **phoenix** bird soars like the *wind*, so it makes sense to alter the '*wind*' glyph to represent that. The 'harmonious crossing' innards become the '*simultaneous conditions*' component, which provides a horizontal perch for the **phoenix** when it needs a rest.

2008 杀

殺 TRAD · SIMPLIFIED

This character with the definition:

kill

Pinyin **shā** *and Frequency Rank* **587**

Contains these components:
- harmonious crossing c 乂 1837, p.405
- tree 木 (altered) 562, p.133

With all these meanings & readings:

shā [殺] **1** to kill **2** to murder **3** to slaughter **4** fight

Contains **6 strokes** in the following order:

丿 乂 ㄥ 杀 杀 杀

Our soldiers were camouflaged to hide behind the dense *trees* near the *harmonious crossing* in the forest. As the enemy approached, they suddenly leapt out, and **killed** many enemy soldiers.

2009 刹

剎 TRAD · SIMPLIFIED

This character with the definition:

to brake a car

Pinyin **shā** *and Frequency Rank* **2249**

Contains these components:
- kill 杀 2008, p.441
- knife r 刂 169, p.46

With all these meanings & readings:

chà [剎] **1** Buddhist monastery or temple **2** a brief moment
shā [剎] **1** to brake (car)

Contains **8 strokes** in the following order:

丿 乂 ㄥ 杀 杀 杀 刹 刹

Metaphorically speaking, *killing* the motion of a car is like applying a *knife*'s edge to the car's **brake** mechanism.

Unit 83

2010

區
TRAD SIMPLIFIED

This character with the definition:

administrative division

Pinyin **qū** *and Frequency Rank* **265**

Contains **4 strokes** in the following order:

一 丁 ㄨ 区

Contains these components:

■ basket, box r 匚 152, p.42
☐ harmonious crossing c ㄨ 1837, p.405

With all these meanings & readings:

qū [區] **1** surname Ou
qū [區] **1** area **2** region **3** district **4** small **5** distinguish **6** r
个 [個][gè]

The purpose of dividing a large country such as China into a variety of **administrative districts** is to establish and maintain *harmony* within the *box*-like borders of the region.

2011

歐
TRAD SIMPLIFIED

This character with the definition:

Europe

Pinyin **ōu** *and Frequency Rank* **823**

Contains **8 strokes** in the following order:

一 丁 ㄨ 区 区' 欧' 欧' 欧

Contains these components:

■ administrative division 区 2010, p.442
☐ owe, lack 欠 744, p.173

With all these meanings & readings:

ōu [歐] **1** Europe

A few **European** countries came together and created an *administrative division* called the Euro-zone because they believed their collective powers would be so big that it would not *lack* any resources.

2012

驅
TRAD SIMPLIFIED

This character with the definition:

drive (horse)

Pinyin **qū** *and Frequency Rank* **1511**

Contains **7 strokes** in the following order:

フ 马 马 马' 驱' 驱' 驱

Contains these components:

☐ horse 马 388, p.95
☐ administrative division 区 2010, p.442

With all these meanings & readings:

qū [驅] **1** to expel **2** to urge or
3 to drive **4** to run quickly

To get to *division* headquarters, I must **drive** my *horse*.

2013

網
TRAD SIMPLIFIED

This character with the definition:

net

Pinyin **wǎng** *and Frequency Rank* **605**

Contains **6 strokes** in the following order:

丨 冂 冂 网 网 网

Contains these components:

■ borders r 冂 114, p.34
☐ harmonious crossing c (×2) ㄨ 1837, p.405

With all these meanings & readings:

wǎng [網] **1** net **2** network

An old-fashioned fishing **net** is designed with *borders* that have plenty of *crisscrossing* strands. • 冈 'mountain ridge' and 网 'net' appear similar but remember that the ridge is bigger, while the net is a more complicated structure. That's why 网 is more visually complex than 冈.

2014

趙
TRAD SIMPLIFIED

This character with the definition:

Kingdom of Zhao

Pinyin **zhào** *and Frequency Rank* **1169**

Contains **9 strokes** in the following order:

一 十 土 キ 丰 未 走 赵 赵

Contains these components:

☐ to walk 走 731, p.171
■ harmonious crossing c ㄨ 1837, p.405

With all these meanings & readings:

Zhào [趙] **1** surname Zhao **2** th
Former Zhao 前赵 (304-329) and
Later Zhao 後赵 (319-350) of the
Sixteen Kingdoms

The ancient **kingdom of Zhao** was one of the so-called Warring States that flourished 2200 years ago. As a result of its military prowess, the

Kingdom of Zhao made it possible for people *to walk* around in *harmony* with no fear of personal danger.

2015

義 TRAD   SIMPLIFIED

This character with the definition:

justice

Pinyin **yì** *and Frequency Rank* **208**

Contains **3 strokes** in the following order:

丶 丿 义

Contains these components:

■ harmonious crossing c 乂 1837, p. 405

□ dab r 丶 176, p. 48

With all these meanings & readings:

yì [義] **1** justice **2** righteousness **3** meaning

In three well-placed strokes, you see someone rejoicing—hands raised to give thanks to heaven—as **justice** triumphs over corruption and intolerance.

2016

議 TRAD   SIMPLIFIED

This character with the definition:

discuss, confer

Pinyin **yì** *and Frequency Rank* **368**

Contains **5 strokes** in the following order:

丶 讠 议 议 议

Contains these components:

■ speech r 讠 352, p. 88

■ justice 义 2015, p. 443

With all these meanings & readings:

yì [議] **1** to criticize **2** to discuss

Many legal scholars like to **discuss** and give *speeches* devoted exclusively to the topic of equal *justice*.

2017

儀 TRAD   SIMPLIFIED

This character with the definition:

rites

Pinyin **yí** *and Frequency Rank* **1283**

Contains **5 strokes** in the following order:

丿 亻 亻 仪 仪

Contains these components:

■ man r 亻 1156, p. 260

■ justice 义 2015, p. 443

With all these meanings & readings:

yí [儀] **1** apparatus **2** rites **3** appearance **4** present **5** ceremony

In the early days of *man*, special ceremonial **rites** were performed by people who believed that the ceremonies would ensure *justice* and peace.

2018

岡 TRAD   SIMPLIFIED

This character with the definition:

mountain ridge

Pinyin **gāng** *and Frequency Rank* **2047**

Contains **4 strokes** in the following order:

丨 冂 冈 冈

Contains these components:

□ borders r 冂 114, p. 34

■ harmonious crossing c 乂 1837, p. 405

With all these meanings & readings:

gāng [岡] **1** ridge **2** mound

We're looking down at a topographical map. Within the *borders* of the region are *crossed* strokes representing the spines of intersecting **mountain ridges**.

2019

剛 TRAD   SIMPLIFIED

This character with the definition:

hard, firm, strong

Pinyin **gāng** *and Frequency Rank* **621**

Contains **6 strokes** in the following order:

丨 冂 冈 冈 刚 刚

Contains these components:

■ mountain ridge 冈 2018, p. 443

■ knife r 刂 169, p. 46

With all these meanings & readings:

gāng [剛] **1** hard **2** firm **3** strong **4** just **5** barely **6** exactly

The minerals and the topsoil of the *mountain ridge* are so **firm** and **hard** that you need to use a *knife* to dig into it.

2020

纲

纲 TRAD SIMPLIFIED

This character with the definition:

guiding principle

Pinyin **gāng** *and Frequency Rank* **1934**

Contains **7 strokes** in the following order:

㇆ 乚 纟 纟 纟 纲 纲

Contains these components:

■ silk r 纟 1037, p.235
■ mountain ridge 冈 2018, p.443

With all these meanings & readings:

gāng [纲] **1** head rope of a fishing net **2** guiding principle **3** key link **4** class (taxonomy) **5** outline **6** program

Guiding principles are important in traditional Chinese culture, and here we see two visual references to it. First is the *silk* thread which guides us and pulls us in the proper direction. Next are the *mountain ridges* which serve as paths for an intrepid traveler through life.

2021

钢

鋼 TRAD SIMPLIFIED

This character with the definition:

steel

Pinyin **gāng** *and Frequency Rank* **1609**

Contains **9 strokes** in the following order:

丿 𠂉 午 年 钅 钢 钢 钢 钢

Contains these components:

■ gold 金 1550, p.342
■ mountain ridge 冈 2018, p.443

With all these meanings & readings:

gāng [鋼] **1** steel

Early on, **steel** was regarded as a *precious metal* that was discovered mysteriously near *mountain ridges*.

2022

岗

崗 TRAD SIMPLIFIED

This character with the definition:

mound

Pinyin **gǎng** *and Frequency Rank* **1795**

Contains **7 strokes** in the following order:

丨 ㄓ 山 ㄇ 岗 岗 岗

Contains these components:

□ mountain 山 4, p.10
▤ mountain ridge 冈 2018, p.443

With all these meanings & readings:

gǎng [崗] **1** mound **2** policeman's beat

The squished '*mountain*' on top together with '*ridge*' emphasizes the **mound**-ness of the resulting character.

2023

开

This component has the meaning:

make level c

COMPONENT

And contains these subcomponents:

■ well 井 (altered) 1758, p.388

The ancient scribes must have thought 'reverse psychology' when they designed this component, since none of the strokes used in the altered '*well*' are 'level'—someone needs **to make** them all **level**.

2024

开

開 TRAD SIMPLIFIED

This character with the definition:

operate

Pinyin **kāi** *and Frequency Rank* **94**

Contains **4 strokes** in the following order:

一 二 开 开

Contains these components:

■ make level c 开 2023, p.444

With all these meanings & readings:

kāi [開] **1** to open **2** to start **3** to turn on **4** to write out (a medical prescription) **5** to operate (vehicle) **6** abbr for 开尔文[開爾~] degrees Kelvin

You cannot **operate** machinery unless it is *made level*.

2025

This character with the definition:

shape

Pinyin **xíng** *and Frequency Rank* **269**

SIMP & TRAD   Contains **7 strokes** in the following order:

一 二 于 开 形` 形` 形

Contains these components:

▮ make level c 开 2023, p. 444
▮ feathers r ⺶ 1611, p. 359

With all these meanings & readings:

xíng [形] **1** to appear **2** to look **3** form **4** shape

This character forms a visually interesting **shape** of contrasting parallel lines—the crossed strokes of '*to make level*' on the left, paired with the upward curves of '*feathers r*' on the right.

2026

This character with the definition:

grind

Pinyin **yán** *and Frequency Rank* **447**

SIMP & TRAD   Contains **9 strokes** in the following order:

一 丆 丆 石 石 石¯ 矸 矸 研

Contains these components:

▮ stone, rock 石 522, p. 124
▮ make level c 开 2023, p. 444

With all these meanings & readings:

yán [研] **1** to grind **2** study **3** research

A special *stone* is used **to grind** a surface until it is *made level*.

2027

This character with the definition:

punishment, sentence

Pinyin **xíng** *and Frequency Rank* **1087**

SIMP & TRAD   Contains **6 strokes** in the following order:

一 二 于 开 开ˈ 刑

Contains these components:

▮ make level c 开 2023, p. 444
▮ knife r ⺉ 169, p. 46

With all these meanings & readings:

xíng [刑] **1** punishment

The prisoner's **sentence** was extended as a **punishment** for using a *knife* to *make level* his odds of winning in the gang fight.

2028

This character with the definition:

mold, model, pattern

Pinyin **xíng** *and Frequency Rank* **556**

SIMP & TRAD   Contains **9 strokes** in the following order:

一 二 于 开 开ˈ 刑` 刑 型 型

Contains these components:

▢ punishment, sentence 刑 2027, p. 445
▮ earth, soil 土 9, p. 11

With all these meanings & readings:

xíng [型] **1** model **2** type (e.g. blood type)

Every society sets up a **pattern** of rules that it expects its citizens to abide by. If you violate these and commit a crime such as murder, you could receive a *sentence* that sends you to rest in the *earth*—permanently.

2029
並
并并
TRAD   SIMPLIFIED

This character with the definition:

adjacent

Pinyin **bìng** *and Frequency Rank* **141**

Contains **6 strokes** in the following order:

丶 丷 ꒦ ꒦ 并 并

Contains these components:

▢ eight r ⸺ 1260, p. 282
▮ make level c 开 2023, p. 444

With all these meanings & readings:

bìng [並] **1** and **2** furthermore **3** also **4** together with **5** (not) at all **6** simultaneously **7** to combine **8** to join **9** to merge
bìng [併] **1** to combine **2** to amalgamate
bìng [并] **1** and **2** also **3** together with

When a surface is *made level*, *eight* more things can be placed on it, with each item **adjacent** to the other, without any fear that they will slide off.

2030

This character with the definition:

spell

Pinyin **pīn** *and Frequency Rank* **1820**

SIMP & TRAD Contains **9 strokes** in the following order:

一 寸 扌 扌 扩 扩 拤 拼 拼

Contains these components:

■ hand r 扌 25, p.15
■ adjacent 并 2029, p.445

With all these meanings & readings:

pīn [拼] **1** to piece together **2** to join together **3** to stake all **4** adventurous **5** at the risk of one's life **6** to spell

You "**spell**" Chinese characters by placing movements and strokes *adjacent* to each other and by pretending to draw them on the palm of one *hand*.

2031

This character with the definition:

hold one's breath

Pinyin **bǐng** *and Frequency Rank* **1891**

SIMP & TRAD Contains **9 strokes** in the following order:

一 コ 尸 尸 尸 屏 屏 屏 屏

Contains these components:

■ corpse 尸 499, p.119
■ adjacent 并 2029, p.445

With all these meanings & readings:

bīng [屏] **1** see 屏营 [~营][bing yíng]
bǐng [屏] **1** to get rid of **2** to put aside **3** to reject **4** to keep control **5** to hold (one's breath)
píng [屏] **1** (standing) screen

The unburied *corpse* had begun to smell, so the mourners **held their breath** as they sat *adjacent* to the *corpse* through the burial service.

2032

This character with the definition:

bottle, vase, pitcher

Pinyin **píng** *and Frequency Rank* **1703**

SIMP & TRAD Contains **11 strokes** in the following order:

丶 丷 丷 兰 羊 并 并 并 瓶 瓶 瓶

Contains these components:

■ adjacent 并 2029, p.445
■ tile 瓦 147, p.41

With all these meanings & readings:

píng [瓶] **1** bottle **2** (classifier for wine and liquids) **3** vase **4** pitcher **5** m 个 [個][gè]

Every day, the devoted widow placed a beautiful **vase** of fresh flowers *adjacent* to the framed portrait of her beloved husband on the antique *tile*-topped table.

2033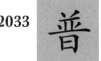

This character with the definition:

general, universal

Pinyin **pǔ** *and Frequency Rank* **630**

SIMP & TRAD Contains **12 strokes** in the following order:

丶 丷 丷 羊 羊 并 并 並 並 普 普 普

Contains these components:

■ adjacent 并 2029, p.445
■ day, sun 日 64, p.24

With all these meanings & readings:

pǔ [普] **1** general **2** popular **3** everywhere **4** universal

Two *adjacent suns* shining together would have a **universal** effect on living conditions. For one thing, this world would be much hotter.

2034

This character with the definition:

bump into, touch

Pinyin **pèng** *and Frequency Rank* **1371**

SIMP & TRAD Contains **13 strokes** in the following order:

一 ノ 丆 石 石 石 石 砃 砃 砃 碰 碰 碰

Contains these components:

■ stone, rock 石 522, p.124
■ adjacent 并 2029, p.445

With all these meanings & readings:

pèng [碰] **1** to touch **2** to meet with **3** to bump

One *stone* can **bump** into another one, butonly if they are *adjacent*.

Unit 84

2035

This character with the definition:

error

Pinyin **chuǎn** *and Frequency Rank* **4694**

SIMP & TRAD Contains **6 strokes** in the following order:

丿 夕 夕 夕 夕 舛

Contains these components:

◪ dusk* 夕 875, p.200
◪ make level c 开 (altered) 2023, p.444

With all these meanings & readings:

chuǎn [舛] **1** mistaken **2** erroneous **3** contradictory

It's easy to make an **error** if you try *to make something level* during the poor light of *dusk*.

2036

This character with the definition:

dance

Pinyin **wǔ** *and Frequency Rank* **1144**

SIMP & TRAD Contains **14 strokes** in the following order:

丿 ㇐ ㇐ ㇐ 征 征 征 無 無 舞 舞 舞 舞 舞

Contains these components:

◻ man 人 (altered) 537, p.127
◼ ten (×4) 十 7, p.11
◻ one 一 1, p.10
◼ error 舛 2035, p.447

With all these meanings & readings:

wǔ [舞] **1** to dance **2** to wield **3** to brandish

Since the young *man's* goal was to **dance**, he practiced *ten* hours every day at the ballet *bar* in the **dance** studio so that his performance would go on without the slightest of *errors* and be perfect.

2037

This component has the meaning:

skull with a brain c

COMPONENT

Imagine this character as if you were looking down at the top of a head and can see the **skull with a brain** inside. The '**x**' is the brain and the single dab-like stroke as the nose.

2038

This component has the meaning:

eat r

COMPONENT

And contains these subcomponents:

◼ eat* 食 1968, p.432

If you scrunch the character 食, '*eat*', you get this radical component, which fits nicely into other characters.

2039 饰

饣 饰

SIMPLIFIED

This character with the definition:

decoration, ornament

Pinyin **shì** *and Frequency Rank* **1604**

Contains **8 strokes** in the following order:

丿 夕 饣 饣 饣 饣 饣 饰

Contains these components:

◪ eat r 饣 2038, p.447
◻ market 市 (altered) 251, p.66

With all these meanings & readings:

shì [饰] **1** decoration **2** ornament **3** to decorate **4** to adorn **5** to hide **6** to conceal (a fault) **7** excuse (to hide a fault) **8** to play a role (in opera) **9** to impersonate

Market days used to be like holidays because vendors would bring out special treats to *eat* and fine **decorations** for all to appreciate.

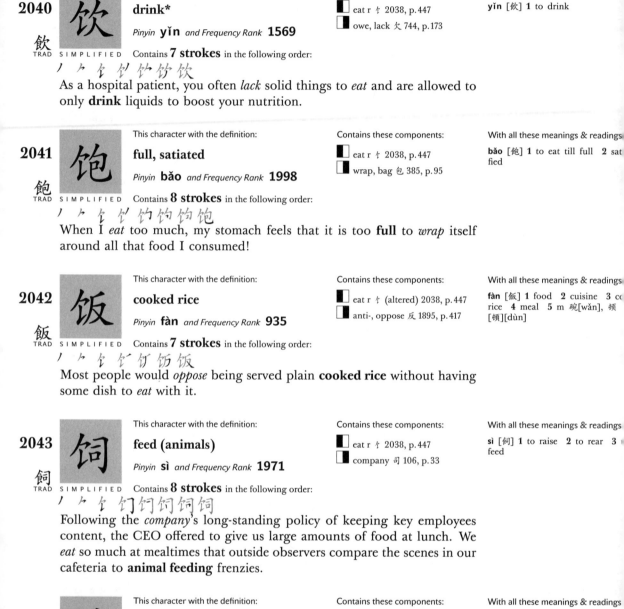

2040

饮

飲
TRAD   SIMPLIFIED

This character with the definition:

drink*

Pinyin **yǐn** *and Frequency Rank* **1569**

Contains **7 strokes** in the following order:

丿 𠂉 𠂉 饣 饣 饮 饮 饮

As a hospital patient, you often *lack* solid things to *eat* and are allowed to only **drink** liquids to boost your nutrition.

Contains these components:

eat r 饣 2038, p. 447

owe, lack 欠 744, p. 173

With all these meanings & readings

yǐn [飲] **1** to drink

2041

饱

飽
TRAD   SIMPLIFIED

This character with the definition:

full, satiated

Pinyin **bǎo** *and Frequency Rank* **1998**

Contains **8 strokes** in the following order:

丿 𠂉 𠂉 饣 饣 饣 饣 饱

When I *eat* too much, my stomach feels that it is too **full** to *wrap* itself around all that food I consumed!

Contains these components:

eat r 饣 2038, p. 447

wrap, bag 包 385, p. 95

With all these meanings & readings

bǎo [飽] **1** to eat till full **2** satisfied

2042

饭

飯
TRAD   SIMPLIFIED

This character with the definition:

cooked rice

Pinyin **fàn** *and Frequency Rank* **935**

Contains **7 strokes** in the following order:

丿 𠂉 𠂉 饣 饣 饭 饭

Most people would *oppose* being served plain **cooked rice** without having some dish to *eat* with it.

Contains these components:

eat r 饣 (altered) 2038, p. 447

anti-, oppose 反 1895, p. 417

With all these meanings & readings

fàn [飯] **1** food **2** cuisine **3** cooked rice **4** meal **5** m 碗[wǎn], 顿[dùn]

2043

饲

飼
TRAD   SIMPLIFIED

This character with the definition:

feed (animals)

Pinyin **sì** *and Frequency Rank* **1971**

Contains **8 strokes** in the following order:

丿 𠂉 𠂉 饣 饣 饲 饲 饲

Following the *company*'s long-standing policy of keeping key employees content, the CEO offered to give us large amounts of food at lunch. We *eat* so much at mealtimes that outside observers compare the scenes in our cafeteria to **animal feeding** frenzies.

Contains these components:

eat r 饣 2038, p. 447

company 司 106, p. 33

With all these meanings & readings

sì [飼] **1** to raise **2** to rear **3** feed

2044

饿

餓
TRAD   SIMPLIFIED

This character with the definition:

hungry

Pinyin **è** *and Frequency Rank* **1911**

Contains **10 strokes** in the following order:

丿 𠂉 𠂉 饣 饣 饣 饿 饿 饿 饿

I eat when I'm **hungry**—how about you?

Contains these components:

eat r 饣 2038, p. 447

I 我 661, p. 156

With all these meanings & readings

è [餓] **1** to be hungry **2** hungry

2045

This component has the meaning:

step forward r
COMPONENT

And contains these subcomponents:

☐ action path c ⼃ 438, p.105
◼ simultaneous action 又 1844, p.406

People striding briskly on an *action path* will often swing their arms *at the same time* as they **step forward**.

2046

This character with the definition:

peak, summit

Pinyin **fēng** *and Frequency Rank* **1473**

SIMP & TRAD   Contains **10 strokes** in the following order:

丨 山 山 屮′ 屮夂 峄 峄 峪 峰 峰

Contains these components:

☐ mountain 山 4, p.10
◼ step forward r 夂 2045, p.449
☐ plentiful 丰 16, p.13

With all these meanings & readings:

fēng [峰] **1** peak **2** summit
3 apex **4** hump of a camel

The *mountain* was popular because of its *plentiful* variety of trails available for hikers to *step forward* toward its **summit**.

2047

This character with the definition:

summer

Pinyin **xià** *and Frequency Rank* **1126**

SIMP & TRAD   Contains **10 strokes** in the following order:

一 厂 丆 丏 百 百 百 頁 夏 夏

Contains these components:

☐ one 一 1, p.10
◼ self 自 232, p.61
◼ step forward r 夂 2045, p.449

With all these meanings & readings:

xià [夏] **1** the Xia or Hsia dynasty c. 2000 BC **2** Xia of the Sixteen Kingdoms (407-432)
3 surname Xia
xià [夏] **1** summer

In the heat and humidity of **summer** I have to force my*self* to take even *one step forward* to do anything!

2048

This character with the definition:

thick ice

Pinyin **líng** *and Frequency Rank* **1731**

SIMP & TRAD   Contains **10 strokes** in the following order:

丶 冫 冫 汢 浐 浐 浐 凌 凌 凌

Contains these components:

☐ ice r 冫 348, p.87
☐ earth, soil 土 9, p.11
◼ eight 八 1261, p.282
◼ step forward r 夂 2045, p.449

With all these meanings & readings:

líng [凌] **1** to encroach **2** to soar
3 thick ice **4** surname Ling

The very cold winter produced two different reactions: the children were delighted they could skate on the pond's *eight*-inch **thick ice**. However, the older people were wary of treading on the *ice*-covered *earth* and sidewalks; as such, they had to *step forward* very carefully to avoid slipping.

2049

酸

This character with the definition:

sour

Pinyin **suān** *and Frequency Rank* **1456**

SIMP & TRAD   Contains **17 strokes** in the following order:

一 丆 丙 西 西 酉 酉 酌′ 酌 酚 酚 酚 酚 酸

Contains these components:

◼ five to seven pm 酉 302, p.77
◼ permit, allow 允 (altered) 995, p.227
◼ step forward r 夂 2045, p.449

With all these meanings & readings:

suān [酸] **1** sour **2** sore **3** ache
4 acid

The vineyard master only *permits* customers to *step forward* and buy wine from *five to seven pm*. He fears any more customer activity will cause his grapes to turn **sour**.

2050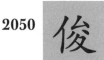

This character with the definition:

handsome, pretty

Pinyin **jùn** *and Frequency Rank* **1847**

SIMP & TRAD   Contains **9 strokes** in the following order:

丿 亻 仁 仵 伫 伀 俊 俊 俊

Contains these components:

■ man r 亻 1156, p. 260
■ permit, allow 允 (altered) 995, p. 227
■ step forward r 夂 2045, p. 449

With all these meanings & readings:

jùn [俊] **1** smart **2** eminent **3** handsome **4** talented

Imagine this character as two views of a **handsome** young *man* prepared to *step forward* for an evening of pleasure. A mirror *allows* him to examine two views of himself: in full length (the left element), and in a closeup profile, showing off his Grecian nose and stylish mustache (the right element).
• Using this image will help you remember that 'nose' is an element of 'permit, allow' (panel 995).

2051

This character with the definition:

window

Pinyin **chuāng** *and Frequency Rank* **1074**

SIMP & TRAD   Contains **12 strokes** in the following order:

丶 冖 宀 宀 穴 穷 窌 窗 窗 窗 窗 窗

Contains these components:

■ cave, den 穴 1347, p. 300
■ dab r 丶 176, p. 48
■ enclosure r 囗 36, p. 17
■ step forward r 夂 2045, p. 449

With all these meanings & readings:

chuāng [窗] **1** shutter **2** window **3** m 扇[shàn]

The skin-diver was trapped in the black *enclosure* of an underwater *cave*. He gingerly used his hands to *step forward* until he spied a *tiny* light-blue glow—the **window** to freedom!—and swam toward it.

2052

This character with the definition:

mausoleum, mound

Pinyin **líng** *and Frequency Rank* **1965**

SIMP & TRAD   Contains **10 strokes** in the following order:

乛 阝 阝 阝 陆 陡 陕 陵 陵 陵

Contains these components:

■ hills r 阝 942, p. 216
■ earth, soil 土 9, p. 11
■ eight 八 1261, p. 282
■ step forward r 夂 2045, p. 449

With all these meanings & readings:

líng [陵] **1** mound **2** tomb **3** hill **4** mountain

To locate the ancient **mausoleum**, which was built for the *eight* corpses of the Imperial Family, you have to *step forward*, and away from the *earth* of the valley and into the rocky *hills*.

2053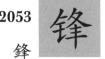

This character with the definition:

sword edge

Pinyin **fēng** *and Frequency Rank* **1671**

TRAD SIMPLIFIED   Contains **12 strokes** in the following order:

丿 𠂉 𠂉 乍 全 钅 钅 锋 锋 锋 锋 锋

Contains these components:

■ gold 金 1550, p. 342
■ step forward r 夂 2045, p. 449
■ plentiful 丰 16, p. 13

With all these meanings & readings:

fēng [鋒] **1** point of a spear **2** edge of a tool **3** vanguard **4** forward (in sports team)

After graduating from college without a job, the young man felt as if he were living on a financial **sword edge**. When he finally found a job, he seized the opportunity to work hard and *step forward* into a prosperous career. He received *plentiful* salary increases and saw his future now paved with *gold*.

054 傻

SIMP & TRAD

This character with the definition:

muddleheaded

Pinyin **shǎ** *and Frequency Rank* **1989**

Contains **13 strokes** in the following order:

ノ 亻 亻 亻 伒 仴 佀 佀 佀 傻 傻 傻 傻

Contains these components:

man r 亻 1156, p. 260
skull with a brain c 囟 2037, p. 447
eight 八 1261, p. 282
step forward r 夊 2045, p. 449

With all these meanings & readings:

shǎ [傻] **1** foolish

Although the old *man* seemed to have a *skull with a brain*, his behavior made him look **muddleheaded**—over and over, he'd take *eight steps forward* and abruptly stop; then take *eight* more *steps forward* and stop abruptly.

055 冬

SIMP & TRAD

This character with the definition:

winter

Pinyin **dōng** *and Frequency Rank* **1384**

Contains **5 strokes** in the following order:

ノ 勹 夂 冬 冬

Contains these components:

step forward r 夊 2045, p. 449
two 二 (altered) 2, p. 10

With all these meanings & readings:

dōng [冬] **1** winter

At the end of **winter** we always move our clocks a *step forward* by an hour—which means an hour less sleep that night. The next morning, I always wake feeling as if I had lost *two* hours of sleep!

056 疼

SIMP & TRAD

This character with the definition:

it hurts!

Pinyin **téng** *and Frequency Rank* **1710**

Contains **10 strokes** in the following order:

丶 亠 广 广 疒 疒 疼 疼 疼 疼

Contains these components:

sick r 疒 434, p. 104
winter 冬 2055, p. 451

With all these meanings & readings:

téng [疼] **1** (it) hurts **2** love fondly **3** ache **4** pain **5** sore

It seems your body feels worse when you get *sick* during the *winter*. Oh, how **it hurts!**

057 终

終 TRAD   SIMPLIFIED

This character with the definition:

end, finish

Pinyin **zhōng** *and Frequency Rank* **558**

Contains **8 strokes** in the following order:

乚 纟 纟 纟 纠 终 终 终

Contains these components:

silk r 纟 (altered) 1037, p. 235
winter 冬 2055, p. 451

With all these meanings & readings:

zhōng [終] **1** end **2** finish

The weavers spin *silk* during the entire *winter* so that they will **finish** the cloth in time for spring.

058 图

圖 TRAD   SIMPLIFIED

This character with the definition:

picture, chart, map

Pinyin **tú** *and Frequency Rank* **476**

Contains **8 strokes** in the following order:

丨 冂 冂 冈 囝 图 图 图

Contains these components:

enclosure r 囗 36, p. 17
winter 冬 2055, p. 451

With all these meanings & readings:

tú [圖] **1** diagram **2** to plan **3** picture **4** drawing **5** chart **6** m 张 [張][zhāng]

In the *winter* time, and the ground is frozen and covered with a permanent layer of snow. We can use this surface to scratch out **pictures** and **maps** and then imagine the *enclosing square* as a *picture frame*.

2059
復
複 复
TRAD

SIMPLIFIED

This character with the definition:

turn around, repeat

Pinyin **fù** *and Frequency Rank* **426**

Contains **9 strokes** in the following order:

ノ 厂 ﾆ 白 白 白 戶 复 复

Contains these components:

☐ man 人 (altered) 537, p.127

☐ speak 日 67, p.24

■ step forward r 夂 2045, p.449

fù [復] **1** to go and return **2** t return **3** to resume **4** to return to a normal or original sta **5** to repeat **6** again **7** to recover **8** to restore **9** to turn over **10** to reply **11** to answer **12** to reply to a letter **13** to retaliate **14** to carry out

fù [複] **1** to repeat **2** to doubl **3** to overlap **4** complex (not simple) **5** compound **6** composite **7** double **8** diplo- **9** d plicate **10** overlapping **11** to duplicate

The *man* was a skilled politician who gave powerful *speeches*. Sometimes he would *step forward* toward his listeners; other times he would **repeat** things he wanted his crowds to remember. • This character very closely resembles the character 夏 ('summer', panel 2047). One way to avoid confusing the two is to note that this character has an altered 'man' element at its top. Use that element to help you remember that only a '*man*' can '**turn around**' or '**repeat**' something.

Unit 85

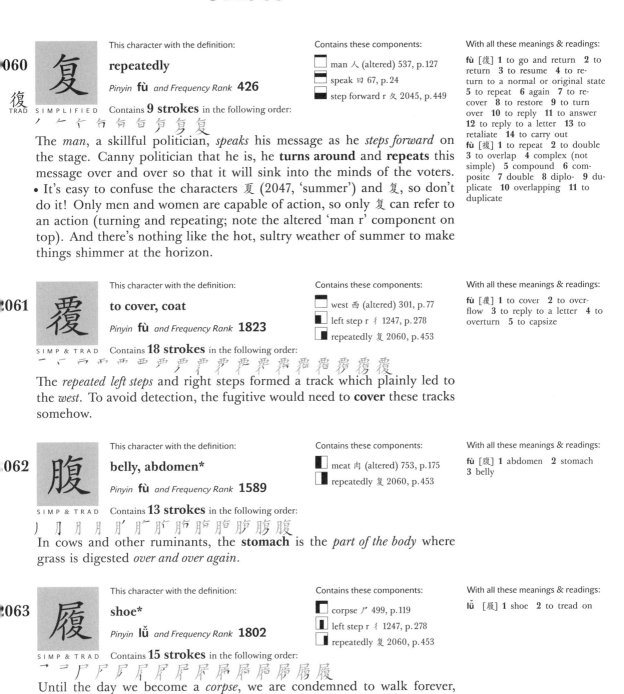

060

復
TRAD · SIMPLIFIED

This character with the definition:

repeatedly

Pinyin **fù** *and Frequency Rank* **426**

Contains **9 strokes** in the following order:

ノ ᄂ ᅩ ㇒ 乍 白 白 复 复

Contains these components:

□ man 人 (altered) 537, p. 127

□ speak 曰 67, p. 24

□ step forward r 夂 2045, p. 449

With all these meanings & readings:

fù [復] **1** to go and return **2** to return **3** to resume **4** to return to a normal or original state **5** to repeat **6** again **7** to recover **8** to restore **9** to turn over **10** to reply **11** to answer **12** to reply to a letter **13** to retaliate **14** to carry out
fù [複] **1** to repeat **2** to double **3** to overlap **4** complex (not simple) **5** compound **6** composite **7** double **8** diplo- **9** duplicate **10** overlapping **11** to duplicate

The *man*, a skillful politician, *speaks* his message as he *steps forward* on the stage. Canny politician that he is, he **turns around** and **repeats** this message over and over so that it will sink into the minds of the voters. • It's easy to confuse the characters 夏 (2047, 'summer') and 复, so don't do it! Only men and women are capable of action, so only 复 can refer to an action (turning and repeating; note the altered 'man r' component on top). And there's nothing like the hot, sultry weather of summer to make things shimmer at the horizon.

061

覆
SIMP & TRAD

This character with the definition:

to cover, coat

Pinyin **fù** *and Frequency Rank* **1823**

Contains **18 strokes** in the following order:

一 厂 一 冂 西 西 襾 覀 覀 覀 覂 覂 覄 覆 覆 覆 覆 覆

Contains these components:

□ west 西 (altered) 301, p. 77

□ left step r 彳 1247, p. 278

□ repeatedly 复 2060, p. 453

With all these meanings & readings:

fù [覆] **1** to cover **2** to overflow **3** to reply to a letter **4** to overturn **5** to capsize

The *repeated left steps* and right steps formed a track which plainly led to the *west*. To avoid detection, the fugitive would need to **cover** these tracks somehow.

062

腹
SIMP & TRAD

This character with the definition:

belly, abdomen*

Pinyin **fù** *and Frequency Rank* **1589**

Contains **13 strokes** in the following order:

丿 刀 月 月 肝 肝 胪 胪 腹 腹 腹 腹 腹

Contains these components:

□ meat 肉 (altered) 753, p. 175

□ repeatedly 复 2060, p. 453

With all these meanings & readings:

fù [腹] **1** abdomen **2** stomach **3** belly

In cows and other ruminants, the **stomach** is the *part of the body* where grass is digested *over and over again*.

063

履
SIMP & TRAD

This character with the definition:

shoe*

Pinyin **lǚ** *and Frequency Rank* **1802**

Contains **15 strokes** in the following order:

一 ㄱ 尸 尸 尸 屄 屄 屄 屄 屄 屦 屦 屦 屦 履

Contains these components:

□ corpse 尸 499, p. 119

□ left step r 彳 1247, p. 278

□ repeatedly 复 2060, p. 453

With all these meanings & readings:

lǚ [履] **1** shoe **2** to tread on

Until the day we become a *corpse*, we are condemned to walk forever, taking *step* after *step*, *repeatedly*, in one pair of **shoes** or another.

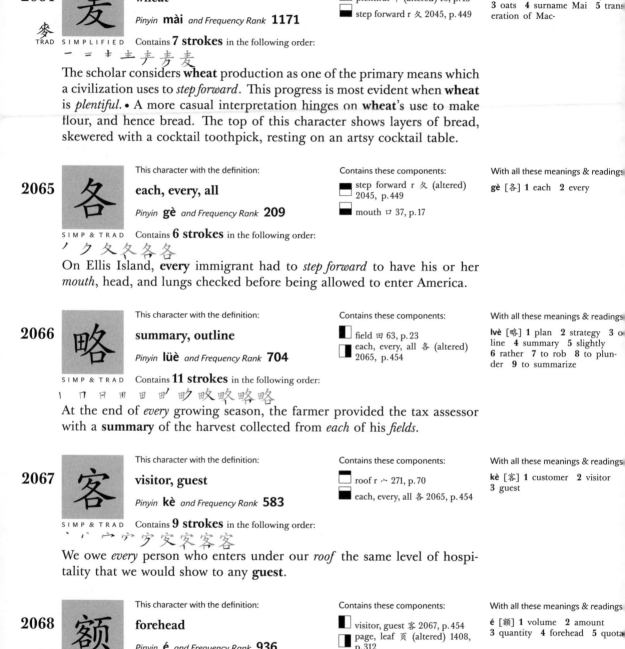

2064

麦

麥
TRAD SIMPLIFIED

This character with the definition:

wheat

Pinyin **mài** *and Frequency Rank* **1171**

Contains **7 strokes** in the following order:

一 二 ‡ 丰 声 麦 麦

Contains these components:

▯ plentiful 丰 (altered) 16, p. 13
▯ step forward r 久 2045, p. 449

With all these meanings & readings

mài [麥] **1** wheat **2** barley **3** oats **4** surname Mai **5** transliteration of Mac-

The scholar considers **wheat** production as one of the primary means which a civilization uses to *step forward*. This progress is most evident when **wheat** is *plentiful*. • A more casual interpretation hinges on **wheat**'s use to make flour, and hence bread. The top of this character shows layers of bread, skewered with a cocktail toothpick, resting on an artsy cocktail table.

2065

各

SIMP & TRAD

This character with the definition:

each, every, all

Pinyin **gè** *and Frequency Rank* **209**

Contains **6 strokes** in the following order:

丿 ク 夂 冬 各 各

Contains these components:

▯ step forward r 久 (altered) 2045, p. 449
▯ mouth 口 37, p. 17

With all these meanings & readings

gè [各] **1** each **2** every

On Ellis Island, **every** immigrant had to *step forward* to have his or her *mouth*, head, and lungs checked before being allowed to enter America.

2066

略

SIMP & TRAD

This character with the definition:

summary, outline

Pinyin **lüè** *and Frequency Rank* **704**

Contains **11 strokes** in the following order:

丨 冂 曰 田 田 田′ 畋 畋 略 略 略

Contains these components:

▯ field 田 63, p. 23
▯ each, every, all 各 (altered) 2065, p. 454

With all these meanings & readings

lüè [略] **1** plan **2** strategy **3** outline **4** summary **5** slightly **6** rather **7** to rob **8** to plunder **9** to summarize

At the end of *every* growing season, the farmer provided the tax assessor with a **summary** of the harvest collected from *each* of his *fields*.

2067

客

SIMP & TRAD

This character with the definition:

visitor, guest

Pinyin **kè** *and Frequency Rank* **583**

Contains **9 strokes** in the following order:

丶 丷 宀 宀 宀 安 客 客 客

Contains these components:

▯ roof r 宀 271, p. 70
▯ each, every, all 各 2065, p. 454

With all these meanings & readings

kè [客] **1** customer **2** visitor **3** guest

We owe *every* person who enters under our *roof* the same level of hospitality that we would show to any **guest**.

2068

额

額
TRAD SIMPLIFIED

This character with the definition:

forehead

Pinyin **é** *and Frequency Rank* **936**

Contains **15 strokes** in the following order:

丶 丷 宀 宀 宀 安 客 客 客′ 客 额 额 额 额 额

Contains these components:

▯ visitor, guest 客 2067, p. 454
▯ page, leaf 页 (altered) 1408, p. 312

With all these meanings & readings

é [額] **1** volume **2** amount **3** quantity **4** forehead **5** quota

The weary traveler entered the small hotel, signed a *page* in the *guest* book, rubbed his **forehead**, then asked if he could have some aspirin before retiring to his room.

069

SIMP & TRAD

This character with the definition:

lattice, grid

Pinyin **gé** *and Frequency Rank* **325**

Contains **10 strokes** in the following order:

一 十 才 木 木 术 杪 杦 枚 格 格 格

Contains these components:

■ tree 木 562, p.133

■ each, every, all 各 2065, p.454

With all these meanings & readings:

gé [格] **1** square **2** frame **3** rule **4** (legal) case **5** style **6** character **7** standard **8** pattern **9** (classical) to obstruct; to hinder **10** (classical) to arrive; to come **11** (classical) to investigate; to study exhaustively

Every one of the **lattices** in our garden is so tall and so thickly covered with flowering vines that, from a distance, *each* one looks like a small *tree*.

2070

阁

TRAD SIMPLIFIED

This character with the definition:

pavilion, chamber

Pinyin **gé** *and Frequency Rank* **1682**

Contains **9 strokes** in the following order:

丶 丨 门 门 闩 闩 阁 阁 阁

Contains these components:

□ doorway 门 243, p.64

■ each, every, all 各 2065, p.454

With all these meanings & readings:

gé [閣] **1** pavilion (usu. two-storied) **2** cabinet (politics) **3** boudoir **4** woman's chamber **5** rack **6** shelf

Each of the king's subjects had to pass through the *Doorway* of the Royal Guards before they were allowed to enter the Royal **Pavilion**.

2071

络

TRAD SIMPLIFIED

This character with the definition:

net-like

Pinyin **luò** *and Frequency Rank* **1118**

Contains **9 strokes** in the following order:

Contains these components:

■ silk r 纟 (altered) 1037, p.235

■ each, every, all 各 2065, p.454

With all these meanings & readings:

lào [絡] **1** small net
luò [絡] **1** net-like

*Every silk*worm spins a **net-like** cocoon around itself; most of these cocoons will then be converted into *silk* thread after the *silk*worms vacate them.

2072

洛

SIMP & TRAD

This character with the definition:

river, Luo

Pinyin **luò** *and Frequency Rank* **978**

Contains **9 strokes** in the following order:

Contains these components:

■ water r 氵 314, p.80

■ each, every, all 各 2065, p.454

With all these meanings & readings:

Luò [洛] **1** surname Luo **2** old name of several rivers (in Henan, Shaanxi, Sichuan and Anhui)

The *water* from nearly *every* stream in Henan province feeds into the **Luo river**, which flows through an area of great archaeological significance in the early history of China.

2073

落

SIMP & TRAD

This character with the definition:

fall, drop

Pinyin **luò** *and Frequency Rank* **496**

Contains **12 strokes** in the following order:

Contains these components:

□ grass r 艹 87, p.29

■ river, Luo 洛 2072, p.455

With all these meanings & readings:

là [落] **1** leave behind
luò [落] **1** alight **2** to fall **3** to drop (behind)

Many farmers with fields along the *Luo river* **drop** *grass* cuttings and other refuse into its flowing waters.

2074

This character with the definition:

road

Pinyin **lù** *and Frequency Rank* **305**

SIMP & TRAD   Contains **13 strokes** in the following order:

丶 丨 口 口 口 口 足 足 星 路 路 路 路

Contains these components:

■ foot r ⻊ 1148, p. 258
■ each, every, all 各 2065, p. 454

With all these meanings & readings

lù [路] **1** road **2** path **3** way **4** surname Lu **5** m 条 [條][tiáo]

To reach your goals in life, you must keep *each* of your *foot*steps on the **road** to success.

2075

This character with the definition:

dew

Pinyin **lù** *and Frequency Rank* **841**

SIMP & TRAD   Contains **21 strokes** in the following order:

一 厂 厂 币 币 雨 雨 雨 雪 雪 雷 雷 雷 雷 雷 霞 霞 露 露 露 露

Contains these components:

■ rain 雨 239, p. 63
■ road 路 2074, p. 456

With all these meanings & readings

lòu [露] **1** to show **2** to reveal **3** to betray **4** to expose
lù [露] **1** dew **2** syrup **3** nectar **4** outdoors (not under cover) **5** to show **6** to reveal **7** to betray **8** to expose

The morning **dew** was so heavy that it looked like *rain* had moistened the *road*.

2076

This character with the definition:

surrender, capitulate

Pinyin **xiáng** *and Frequency Rank* **744**

SIMP & TRAD   Contains **8 strokes** in the following order:

阝 阝 阝' 阝々 降 降 降 降

Contains these components:

■ hills r 阝 942, p. 216
■ step forward r 夂 2045, p. 449
■ make level c 开 (altered) 2023, p. 444

With all these meanings & readings

jiàng [降] **1** to drop **2** to fall **3** to come down **4** to descend
xiáng [降] **1** to surrender **2** to capitulate **3** to subdue **4** to tame

We heard the invading army *step forward* toward our town from the nearby *hills*. Our army refused to **surrender**, so the invaders *made level* our fields by destroying our crops.

2077

This character with the definition:

prosperous, booming

Pinyin **lóng** *and Frequency Rank* **1400**

SIMP & TRAD   Contains **11 strokes** in the following order:

阝 阝 阝' 阝々 降 降 降 隆 隆 隆 隆

Contains these components:

■ surrender, capitulate 降 (altered) 2076, p. 456
■ give birth to 生 210, p. 57

With all these meanings & readings

lōng [隆] **1** sound of drums
lóng [隆] **1** grand **2** intense **3** prosperous **4** start (a fire)

Sometimes, the act of *surrender* can *give birth* to **prosperous** growth for a country, such as that which occurred with Japan after the end of World War II.

2078

This character with the definition:

get along with sb

Pinyin **chǔ** *and Frequency Rank* **206**

TRAD   SIMPLIFIED   Contains **5 strokes** in the following order:

丿 夂 夂 处 处

Contains these components:

■ step forward r 夂 2045, p. 449
■ foretell 卜 187, p. 51

With all these meanings & readings:

chǔ [處] **1** to reside **2** to live **3** to dwell **4** to be in **5** to be situated at **6** to stay **7** to get along with **8** to be in a position of **9** to deal with **10** to discipline **11** to punish
chù [處] **1** place **2** location **3** spot **4** point **5** office **6** department **7** bureau **8** respect **9** m for locations or items of damage: spot, point

There's one reason why this guy always seems to *move forward* in life. It's his ability to *foretell* or "read" personalities which enables him to **get along with everybody**.

079

蜂

SIMP & TRAD

This character with the definition:

bee, wasp

Pinyin **fēng** *and Frequency Rank* **1912**

Contains **13 strokes** in the following order:

丶 ㄧ 口 虫 虫 虫 虫 虫 蚁 蚁 蚁 蜂 蜂

Contains these components:

insect 虫 1016, p. 231

step forward r 夂 2045, p. 449

plentiful 丰 16, p. 13

With all these meanings & readings:

fēng [蜂] **1** bee **2** wasp

Bees and **wasps** exhibit swarming behavior, in which a *plentiful* number of the *insects move forward* collectively as a single entity.

080

戶

COMPONENT

This component has the meaning:

door r

And contains these subcomponents:

corpse ⼫ (altered) 499, p. 119

one 一 1, p. 10

The **doorway** to life is closed forever when *one* becomes a *corpse*. Also, think of the top left corner as a door hinge. The rectangle depicts the **door** itself, and the downward stroke and the top not-quite-horizontal line represent the limits of its swing.

081

后

後
TRAD   SIMPLIFIED

This character with the definition:

behind

Pinyin **hòu** *and Frequency Rank* **48**

Contains **6 strokes** in the following order:

丿 厂 厂 斤 后 后

Contains these components:

door r 戶 (altered) 2080, p. 457

mouth 口 37, p. 17

With all these meanings & readings:

hòu [后] **1** empress **2** queen **3** surname Hou
hòu [後] **1** back **2** behind **3** rear **4** afterwards **5** after **6** later

Here the *mouth* represents a guy on an audition in Hollywood. Oops—he didn't get the part. Let's hope the *door* doesn't bang his **behind** on the way out.

082

户

戶
TRAD   SIMPLIFIED

This character with the definition:

household

Pinyin **hù** *and Frequency Rank* **801**

Contains **4 strokes** in the following order:

丶 ㇇ ㇆ 户

Contains these components:

door r 户 (altered) 2080, p. 457

With all these meanings & readings:

A *door* symbolizes a **household** because a home represents hospitality.

083

扁

扁
萹
SIMPLIFIED
TRAD

This character with the definition:

crushed, flat

Pinyin **biǎn** *and Frequency Rank* **1737**

Contains **9 strokes** in the following order:

丶 ㇇ ㇆ 户 户 肩 扁 扁 扁

Contains these components:

household 户 2082, p. 457

book, booklet 冊 117, p. 35

With all these meanings & readings:

biǎn [扁] **1** flat **2** (old form of character 匾, horizontal tablet with inscription)
piān [扁] **1** surname Pian **2** small boat
piǎn [萹] **1** Polygonum aviculare (knot weed)

The incompetent contractor did such a poor job that one of the entrances to our *household* was as narrow as a *book*. Only really **flat** people could enter comfortably through that doorway.

2084

SIMP & TRAD

This character with the definition:

piece of writing

Pinyin **piān** *and Frequency Rank* **1008**

Contains **15 strokes** in the following order:

丿 𠂉 𠂉 𠂉 𠂉 𠂉 𠂉 竹 竹 𥫗 篁 篇 篇 篇 篇

Contains these components:

⬜ bamboo r ⺮ 264, p. 68

⬛ crushed, flat 扁 2083, p. 457

With all these meanings & readings

piān [篇] **1** sheet **2** piece of writing **3** m for written items chapter, article

'Raw' *bamboo* grows naturally as giant rod-like stems, but modern technology can *crush* and *flatten* it, creating material that's used to make floors and surfaces on which people compose **pieces of writing**.

Unit 86

085

骗
TRAD SIMPLIFIED

This character with the definition:

deceive, cheat

Pinyin **piàn** *and Frequency Rank* **1503**

Contains **12 strokes** in the following order:

フ 马 马 马ˊ 马ˋ 马ˇ 驴 驴 骗 骗 骗 骗

Contains these components:

horse 马 388, p. 95

crushed, flat 扁 2083, p. 457

With all these meanings & readings:

piàn [骗] **1** to cheat **2** to swindle **3** to deceive **4** to fool **5** to hoodwink **6** to trick

The city slicker paid for the *horse* after he examined a photo of it. When he arrived at its 'pasture', he found only an inflatable *horse*, already leaking air. Before his new purchase went completely *flat*, he realized that he had been **deceived**.

086

编
TRAD SIMPLIFIED

This character with the definition:

plait, weave

Pinyin **biān** *and Frequency Rank* **858**

Contains **12 strokes** in the following order:

乚 乚 纟 纟 纩 纩 纩 纩 编 编 编 编

Contains these components:

silk r 纟 1037, p. 235

crushed, flat 扁 2083, p. 457

With all these meanings & readings:

biān [编] **1** weave **2** plait **3** organize **4** group **5** arrange **6** edit **7** compile **8** write **9** compose **10** fabricate

The best use for a bundle of *silk* threads is to **weave** them into a *flat* piece of fabric.

087

偏
SIMP & TRAD

This character with the definition:

inclined to one side

Pinyin **piān** *and Frequency Rank* **1204**

Contains **11 strokes** in the following order:

ノ 亻 亻 亻ˊ 仴 伒 伒 偏 偏 偏 偏

Contains these components:

man r 亻 1156, p. 260

crushed, flat 扁 2083, p. 457

With all these meanings & readings:

piān [偏] **1** one-sided **2** to lean **3** to slant **4** prejudiced **5** inclined to one side **6** the left-hand side of split Chinese character, often the key or radical

The safe fell out of the window and *crushed* the *man* to death. Police discovered that his body had **inclined to one side**—in fact, his head was pointing backwards when they found him.

088

房
SIMP & TRAD

This character with the definition:

house

Pinyin **fáng** *and Frequency Rank* **512**

Contains **8 strokes** in the following order:

丶 一 一 户 户 庐 房 房

Contains these components:

household 户 2082, p. 457

square; direction 方 490, p. 117

With all these meanings & readings:

fáng [房] **1** house **2** room **3** surname Fang **4** m 间 [間][jiān]

The layout of my **house** consists of a *household* placed into a *square* floor plan.

089

雇
TRAD SIMPLIFIED

This character with the definition:

employ

Pinyin **gù** *and Frequency Rank* **1817**

Contains **12 strokes** in the following order:

丶 一 一 户 户 户 庐 庐 庐 雇 雇 雇

Contains these components:

household 户 2082, p. 457

short-tailed bird 隹 1193, p. 267

With all these meanings & readings:

gù [僱] **1** hire

Screens are not installed on *doorways of households* in rural China, so owners need to **employ** creativity to chase out *short-tailed birds* that fly in.

2090

護
TRAD

护
SIMPLIFIED

This character with the definition:

protect

Pinyin **hù** *and Frequency Rank* **529**

Contains **7 strokes** in the following order:

一 丁 才 扩 护 护 护

Contains these components:

■ hand r 扌 25, p.15

■ household 户 2082, p.457

With all these meanings & reading

hù [護] **1** protect

The entrance to our *household* is locked at night to **protect** the family against invaders who use their *hands* to thump and knock on our door.

2091

啟
TRAD

启
SIMPLIFIED

This character with the definition:

inspire, enlighten

Pinyin **qǐ** *and Frequency Rank* **1320**

Contains **7 strokes** in the following order:

、 ㇐ ㇕ 户 户 启 启

Contains these components:

□ household 户 2082, p.457

■ mouth 口 37, p.17

With all these meanings & reading

qǐ [啟] **1** to open **2** to start **3** Qi son of Yu the Great 禹, reported founder of the Xia dynasty 夏朝 (c. 2070-c. 1600 BC

There are so many people in my *household* and they all *mouth* off to me about everything. Not to worry—it **inspires** me to work hard, get a good job, and move out.

2092

爐
TRAD

炉
SIMPLIFIED

This character with the definition:

stove

Pinyin **lú** *and Frequency Rank* **1980**

Contains **8 strokes** in the following order:

丶 丶 丬 火 火 炉 炉 炉

Contains these components:

■ fire 火 1511, p.334

■ household 户 2082, p.457

With all these meanings & readings

lú [爐] **1** a stove **2** a furnace

The *household's fire*, safely contained inside the **stove**, provides toasty warmth on a bitter winter day.

2093

所
SIMP & TRAD

This character with the definition:

a place

Pinyin **suǒ** *and Frequency Rank* **54**

Contains **8 strokes** in the following order:

` 厂 厂 户 户 所 所 所

Contains these components:

■ door r 戶 2080, p.457

□ catty 斤 403, p.98

With all these meanings & readings

suǒ [所] **1** actually **2** place **3** m for houses, small buildings institutions etc **4** that which **5** particle introducing a relative clause or passive **6** m 个 [個][gè]

His **place** is a real *cata*strophe made worse by the *unbalanced door*, which is liable to hit you on the head at any minute.

2094

盾
SIMP & TRAD

This character with the definition:

shield

Pinyin **dùn** *and Frequency Rank* **1395**

Contains **9 strokes** in the following order:

` 厂 厂 尸 斤 盾 盾 盾 盾

Contains these components:

□ door r 戶 (altered) 2080, p.457

■ self 自 232, p.61

With all these meanings & readings

dùn [盾] **1** shield

A *door* painted with a picture of the king him*self* makes for a good **shield**.

095

This character with the definition:

follow, abide by

Pinyin **xún** *and Frequency Rank* **1744**

SIMP & TRAD Contains **12 strokes** in the following order:

Contains these components:

■ left step r 彳 1247, p. 278

■ shield 盾 2094, p. 460

With all these meanings & readings:

xún [循] **1** to follow **2** to adhere to **3** to abide by

丿 彳 彳 彳 彳 彳 彳 彳 循 循 循 循

I am happy to **follow** Hercules into battle. He's got the *shield*, and will bear the brunt of the fighting, while I keep a *step* behind him in the relative calm until he defeats our enemies.

096

This character with the definition:

fan

Pinyin **shàn** *and Frequency Rank* **1993**

SIMP & TRAD Contains **10 strokes** in the following order:

Contains these components:

■ door r 户 2080, p. 457

■ feather, wing 羽 107, p. 33

With all these meanings & readings:

shān [扇] **1** to fan
shàn [扇] **1** fan **2** panel of door or screen **3** wing of screen **4** m for panels, fans, doors, windows etc

丶 丶 亠 户 户 户 户 扇 扇 扇

As you enter through the *door* on this hot day in China, the *feathers* of an old-fashioned hand-held **fan** will provide you with some cooling relief.

097

This character with the definition:

shoulder

Pinyin **jiān** *and Frequency Rank* **1415**

SIMP & TRAD Contains **8 strokes** in the following order:

Contains these components:

■ door r 户 2080, p. 457

■ moon, month 月 1771, p. 391

With all these meanings & readings:

jiān [肩] **1** shoulder

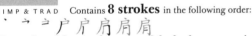

Your **shoulder** is the *part of the body* most suitable for pushing a *door* open when your hands are full.

098

This component has the meaning:

to strike r

COMPONENT

The sharply tipped ends of the crossed strokes of this component suggest a weapon—one that might be used **to strike** a person or animal.

099

This character with the definition:

assault, attack

Pinyin **gōng** *and Frequency Rank* **588**

SIMP & TRAD Contains **7 strokes** in the following order:

Contains these components:

■ labor, work 工 12, p. 12

■ to strike r 攵 2098, p. 461

With all these meanings & readings:

gōng [攻] **1** to attack **2** to accuse **3** to study

一 丁 工 工 工 攻 攻

A thief is both dishonest and lazy: he needs only a few minutes to **assault**, *strike* and steal money from his victim, who *worked* so many hours to earn it.

2100

SIMP & TRAD

This character with the definition:

rose

Pinyin **méi** *and Frequency Rank* **2303**

Contains **8 strokes** in the following order:

一 二 丁 王 王' 玫' 玫 玫

Contains these components:

jade 玉 (altered) 177, p. 48

to strike r 攵 2098, p. 461

With all these meanings & reading

méi [玫] **1** rose

The wealthy couple donated their valuable *jade* stone, which was shaped like a **rose**, to a museum for safekeeping after thieves *struck* their home in an attempt to steal it.

2101

SIMP & TRAD

This character with the definition:

receive, accept

Pinyin **shōu** *and Frequency Rank* **351**

Contains **6 strokes** in the following order:

丨 刂 刂' 刂" 收' 收

Contains these components:

single ear r 卩 (altered) 165, p. 46

to strike r 攵 2098, p. 461

With all these meanings & reading

shōu [收] **1** to receive **2** to accept **3** to collect **4** in care of (used on address line after name)

The old man could only hear through a *single ear*. So the mailman had *to strike* the old man's door repeatedly to get him to open it and **accept** his Special Delivery packages.

2102

SIMP & TRAD

This character with the definition:

herd

Pinyin **mù** *and Frequency Rank* **1580**

Contains **8 strokes** in the following order:

丿 ㇒ 牛 牛 牜' 牜" 牧' 牧

Contains these components:

ox 牛 213, p. 57

to strike r 攵 2098, p. 461

With all these meanings & reading

mù [牧] **1** shepherd **2** surname Mu

Our *ox* was always a quiet animal until we sold him to a farmer with a large **herd**. In those crowded conditions, our quiet *ox* began *to strike* out with his horns at all the animals around him.

2103

SIMP & TRAD

This character with the definition:

government, politics

Pinyin **zhèng** *and Frequency Rank* **150**

Contains **9 strokes** in the following order:

一 丁 下 下 正 正' 正" 政' 政

Contains these components:

to correct, rectify 正 193, p. 52

to strike r 攵 2098, p. 461

With all these meanings & reading

zhèng [政] **1** political **2** politic **3** government

An oppressive **government** does not hesitate *to strike* its own people when it needs '*to correct*' their behavior.

2104

SIMP & TRAD

This character with the definition:

micro, tiny, minute

Pinyin **wēi** *and Frequency Rank* **653**

Contains **13 strokes** in the following order:

丿 彳 彳 彳 彴 彴 彿 微 微 微 微 微

Contains these components:

left step r 彳 1247, p. 278

mountain 山 4, p. 10

dollar 元 (altered) 295, p. 76

to strike r 攵 2098, p. 461

With all these meanings & reading

wēi [微] **1** micro **2** tiny **3** mi ture **4** Taiwan pr wéi

The best way *to strike* at a *mountain*-high challenge is first to take a **tiny** *left step* forward. Sometimes it also helps to imagine *receiving* many *dollars* in reward for your effort.

105

败

败

TRAD   SIMPLIFIED

This character with the definition:

lose, be defeated

Pinyin **bài** *and Frequency Rank* **862**

Contains **8 strokes** in the following order:

丨 冂 贝 贝 贝 贝 贩 败

Contains these components:

cowrie 贝 1394, p. 309

to strike r 攵 2098, p. 461

With all these meanings & readings:

bài [败] **1** be defeated **2** to defeat **3** loss

During a recession, small businesses require large reserves of *money* so that they could *strike* back and not **be defeated** by large corporations.

106

救

救

SIMP & TRAD

This character with the definition:

rescue, save, salvage

Pinyin **jiù** *and Frequency Rank* **872**

Contains **11 strokes** in the following order:

一 十 寸 才 寸 求 求 求 求 救 救

Contains these components:

request, entreat 求 320, p. 81

to strike r 攵 2098, p. 461

With all these meanings & readings:

jiù [救] **1** to save **2** to assist **3** to rescue

The kidnappers refused to release the child despite his parents' tearful *request*. In return, the police decided *to strike* the kidnappers by surprise in order to **rescue** the child.

107

数

数

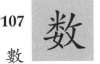

TRAD   SIMPLIFIED

This character with the definition:

number, figure

Pinyin **shù** *and Frequency Rank* **231**

Contains **13 strokes** in the following order:

丶 丷 二 半 米 米 娄 娄 娄 数 数 数 数

Contains these components:

trouble, blunder 娄 1546, p. 341

to strike r 攵 2098, p. 461

With all these meanings & readings:

shǔ [数] **1** to count **2** to enumerate **3** to criticize (i.e. enumerate shortcomings)
shù [数] **1** number **2** figure **3** to count **4** to calculate **5** several **6** m 个 [個][gè]
shuò [数] **1** frequently **2** repeatedly

Because of a communications *blunder*, the army commander was told to expect only half of the **number** of enemy soldiers that actually existed. When he began *to strike* them, his army quickly became overwhelmed.

108

致

致

緻

TRAD   SIMPLIFIED

This character with the definition:

send, deliver

Pinyin **zhì** *and Frequency Rank* **524**

Contains **10 strokes** in the following order:

一 工 工 至 至 至 至 致 致 致

Contains these components:

to, until 至 980, p. 224

to strike r 攵 2098, p. 461

With all these meanings & readings:

zhì [緻] **1** fine and close
zhì [致] **1** to send **2** to devote **3** to deliver **4** to cause **5** to convey

It pained the king *to strike* the enemy one more time, just to **send** the message to "Surrender." He hated prolonging the war *until* this enemy finally accepted defeat but he had to do it.

109

改

SIMP & TRAD

This character with the definition:

transform, change

Pinyin **gǎi** *and Frequency Rank* **350**

Contains **7 strokes** in the following order:

一 コ 己 己 改 改 改

Contains these components:

self* 己 135, p. 39

to strike r 攵 2098, p. 461

With all these meanings & readings:

gǎi [改] **1** to change **2** to alter **3** to transform **4** to correct

My husband's personality **changed** after he lost his job and we were forced to *sell* our house. He used to be a gentle man but now *strikes* out at things in anger.

Unit 87

2110

敵
TRAD 敌
SIMPLIFIED

This character with the definition:

enemy, foe

Pinyin **dí** *and Frequency Rank* **523**

Contains these components:

▪ tongue 舌 770, p.179

▪ to strike r 攵 2098, p.461

With all these meanings & reading

dí [敵] **1** enemy **2** match

Contains **10 strokes** in the following order:

丿 二 千 千 舌 舌 舌 舌' 敌 敌

Irresponsibly spreading rumors with your *tongue* can *strike* someone else with great force and pain. It's easy for gossips and slanderers to make **enemies.**

2111

散
SIMP & TRAD

This character with the definition:

break up, distribute

Pinyin **sàn** *and Frequency Rank* **866**

Contains these components:

▪ contented cows c 芇 1622, p.361

▪ meat 肉 (altered) 753, p.175

▪ to strike r 攵 2098, p.461

With all these meanings & reading

sǎn [散] **1** leisurely **2** loosen **3** powdered medicine **4** to sca ter **5** to come loose
sàn [散] **1** to break up (of cou ples) **2** to distribute **3** to let out **4** to fire or discharge (sb.

Contains **12 strokes** in the following order:

一 十 土 ⺗ 芇 芇 芇 芇 背 背 散 散

The *contented cows* have been sent to the slaughterhouse where they will be *struck* and killed so that the town butcher could have some *meat* to **distribute** to his customers.

2112

撒
SIMP & TRAD

This character with the definition:

scatter, sprinkle

Pinyin **sǎ** *and Frequency Rank* **1445**

Contains these components:

▪ hand r 扌 25, p.15

▪ break up, distribute 散 2111, p.464

With all these meanings & reading

sā [撒] **1** let go
sǎ [撒] **1** to scatter

Contains **15 strokes** in the following order:

一 十 扌 扌 扩 扩 扩 押 捛 捛 捛 捛' 捛 撒 撒

You've *broken up* the stale bread you brought with you to the park and are using your *hand* to **scatter** the pieces so that the ducks that are waiting impatiently will have a tasty snack.

2113

敦
SIMP & TRAD

This character with the definition:

sincere, honest

Pinyin **dūn** *and Frequency Rank* **1722**

Contains these components:

▪ enjoy 享 262, p.68

▪ to strike r 攵 2098, p.461

With all these meanings & reading

dūn [敦] **1** kind-hearted **2** plac name

Contains **12 strokes** in the following order:

丶 二 亠 吉 亩 亨 享 享 敦' 敦 敦 敦

Very good friends can *enjoy* each other's company and be **honest** about difficult issues without *striking* personal attacks at each other.

2114

教
SIMP & TRAD

This character with the definition:

teach

Pinyin **jiāo** *and Frequency Rank* **191**

Contains these components:

▪ filial 孝 498, p.118

▪ to strike r 攵 2098, p.461

With all these meanings & readings

jiāo [教] **1** to teach
jiào [教] **1** religion **2** teaching **3** to make **4** to cause **5** to te

Contains **11 strokes** in the following order:

一 十 土 少 耂 考 孝 孝 敎' 教 教

In many cultures, parents believe they must *strike* their children in order to **teach** them *filial* respect.

2115

效
傚
TRAD   SIMPLIFIED

This character with the definition:

imitate

Pinyin **xiào** *and Frequency Rank* **551**

Contains **10 strokes** in the following order:

丶 一 亠 六 亠 交 交 效 效 效

Contains these components:

meet, intersect 交 2000, p. 440

to strike r 攵 2098, p. 461

With all these meanings & readings:

xiào [傚] **1** imitate
xiào [效] **1** effect   **2** efficacy
3 imitate

At the tennis *meet*, the young player decided to **imitate** his idol by aggressively *striking* the ball from the very start of the game. This helped him win the match.

2116

This character with the definition:

old, former

Pinyin **gù** *and Frequency Rank* **572**

SIMP & TRAD   Contains **9 strokes** in the following order:

一 十 士 古 古 古 扣 故 故

Contains these components:

ancient 古 53, p. 21

to strike r 攵 2098, p. 461

With all these meanings & readings:

gù [故] **1** happening   **2** instance
3 reason   **4** cause   **5** deceased
6 old

The *ancient* monument commemorated the **former** Chinese Imperial Army which expanded the Empire by *striking* and conquering territories.

2117

This character with the definition:

do, make

Pinyin **zuò** *and Frequency Rank* **246**

SIMP & TRAD   Contains **11 strokes** in the following order:

丿 亻 仁 什 什 估 估 估 做 做 做

Contains these components:

man r 亻 1156, p. 260

old, former 故 2116, p. 465

With all these meanings & readings:

zuò [做] **1** to do   **2** to make
3 to produce   **4** to write   **5** to
compose   **6** to act as   **7** to engage in   **8** to hold (a party)
9 to be   **10** to become   **11** to
function (in some capacity)
12 to serve as   **13** to be used
for   **14** to form (a bond or relationship)   **15** to pretend   **16** to
feign   **17** to act a part   **18** to put
on appearance

The young *man's* hobby was to '**make** *old* things new' by skillfully renovating them.

2118

This character with the definition:

imperial edict

Pinyin **chì** *and Frequency Rank* **3435**

SIMP & TRAD   Contains **11 strokes** in the following order:

一 广 亍 亘 束 束 束 敕 敕 敕 敕

Contains these components:

bundle, bunch 束 590, p. 140

to strike r 攵 2098, p. 461

With all these meanings & readings:

chì [敕] **1** imperial orders

The **imperial edict** ordered the emperor's subjects to deliver twenty percent of their goods, wrapped in *bundles*, to the palace. The farmers feared such an **edict** would *strike* down their ability to survive.

2119

This character with the definition:

complete, entire

Pinyin **zhěng** *and Frequency Rank* **416**

SIMP & TRAD   Contains **16 strokes** in the following order:

一 广 亍 亘 束 束 束 敕 敕 敕 敕 敕 敕 整 整 整

Contains these components:

imperial edict 敕 2118, p. 465

to correct, rectify 正 193, p. 52

With all these meanings & readings:

zhěng [整] **1** exactly   **2** in good
order   **3** whole   **4** complete
5 entire   **6** in order   **7** orderly
8 to repair   **9** to mend   **10** to
renovate   **11** to make sb suffer
12 to punish   **13** to fix   **14** to
give sb a hard time

The *imperial edict* was issued to *correct* the 'misbehavior' of the **entire** country.

2120

This character with the definition:

sharp, keen

Pinyin **mǐn** *and Frequency Rank* **1436**

SIMP & TRAD   Contains **11 strokes** in the following order:

丿 𠂉 𠂉 匃 每 每 每 每 每 敏 敏

Contains these components:

☐ every 每 819, p.188

☐ to strike r 攵 2098, p.461

With all these meanings & readings

mǐn [敏] **1** quick **2** nimble
3 agile **4** clever **5** smart

Most experts feel it is not necessary *to strike* a dog in order to teach it to be **sharp** in responding to *every* command.

2121

This character with the definition:

complicated

Pinyin **fán** *and Frequency Rank* **1296**

SIMP & TRAD   Contains **17 strokes** in the following order:

丿 𠂉 𠂉 匃 匃 每 每 敏′ 敏′ 敏′ 敏 敏 繁 繁 繁 繁 繁

Contains these components:

☐ sharp, keen 敏 2120, p.466

☐ silk r 纟 1037, p.235

With all these meanings & readings

fán [繁] **1** complicated **2** many
3 in great numbers **4** abbr for
繁体 [~體][fán tǐ], traditional
form of Chinese characters

The most valuable *silk* embroidery involves **complicated** patterns with *sharp* details.

2122

This character with the definition:

respect, politely offer

Pinyin **jìng** *and Frequency Rank* **1209**

SIMP & TRAD   Contains **12 strokes** in the following order:

一 艹 艹 艹 芍 芍 芍 苟 苟′ 苟′ 敬′ 敬

Contains these components:

☐ thoughtless, careless 苟 370, p.92

☐ to strike r 攵 2098, p.461

With all these meanings & readings

jìng [敬] **1** to respect **2** to venerate **3** to salute **4** to offer

When I saw my child *strike* his playmate, I immediately made him **politely offer** an apology for his aggressive, *thoughtless* behavior.

2123

This character with the definition:

warn, alert

Pinyin **jǐng** *and Frequency Rank* **687**

SIMP & TRAD   Contains **19 strokes** in the following order:

一 艹 艹 艹 芍 芍 苟 苟 苟′ 苟′ 敬′ 敬 敬 敬 警 敬 警 警

Contains these components:

☐ respect, politely offer 敬 2122, p.466

☐ speech 言 256, p.67

With all these meanings & readings

jǐng [警] **1** to alert **2** to warn **3** police

I was new to living in a big city, and my very kind neighbor gave me a *speech* that **warned** me about dangerous areas and *politely offered* to accompany me on any errand after dark.

2124

This character with the definition:

thus, that which

Pinyin **yōu** *and Frequency Rank* **3416**

SIMP & TRAD   Contains **7 strokes** in the following order:

丿 亻 仆 㐹 仲 攸 攸

Contains these components:

☐ man r 亻 1156, p.260

☐ scepter c | 5, p.10

☐ to strike r 攵 2098, p.461

With all these meanings & readings

yōu [攸] **1** distant, far **2** adverbial prefix

The sport of golf requires a *man* or woman to use a long, *scepter*-like 'club' *to strike* a small, hard ball—**thus** causing it to travel a very near (a 'putt') or very far (a 'drive') distance.

125 修 **repair**

Pinyin **xiū** *and Frequency Rank* **740**

SIMP & TRAD

This character with the definition:

Contains these components:
- thus, that which 攸 (altered) 2124, p. 466
- feathers r 彡 1611, p. 359

With all these meanings & readings:

xiū [修] **1** to decorate **2** to embellish **3** to repair **4** to build **5** to study **6** to write **7** to cultivate

Contains **9 strokes** in the following order:

丿 亻 亻 化 攸 攸 修 修 修

Flocks of birds that migrate long distances need to rest and **repair** their damaged *feathers*. *Thus*, they stop for a few days and usually at the same place every year.

126 条 **strip (sth long and narrow)**

Pinyin **tiáo** *and Frequency Rank* **214**

條 TRAD   SIMPLIFIED

This character with the definition:

Contains these components:
- to strike r 攵 (altered) 2098, p. 461
- tree 木 562, p. 133

With all these meanings & readings:

tiáo [条] **1** strip **2** item **3** article **4** clause (of law or treaty) **5** m for long thin things (ribbon, river, road, trousers etc)

Contains **7 strokes** in the following order:

丿 夂 夂 冬 条 条 条

Go ahead—really *strike* that *tree*! A lot of branches—**long and narrow** pieces of the *tree*—will fall all around after you do it.

127 放 **put, place**

Pinyin **fàng** *and Frequency Rank* **291**

SIMP & TRAD

This character with the definition:

Contains these components:
- square; direction 方 490, p. 117
- to strike r 攵 2098, p. 461

With all these meanings & readings:

fàng [放] **1** to release **2** to free **3** to let go **4** to put **5** to place **6** to let out **7** to set off (fireworks)

Contains **8 strokes** in the following order:

丶 亠 方 方 方 放 放 放

A skilled soccer player accurately **places** the ball '*square*' in the goal with only one *strike* of his foot. • On occasion, this character may appear in an abbreviated form: 方 .

128 敖 **ramble**

Pinyin **áo** *and Frequency Rank* **3573**

SIMP & TRAD

This character with the definition:

Contains these components:
- earth, soil 土 (altered) 9, p. 11
- put, place 放 2127, p. 467

With all these meanings & readings:

áo [敖] **1** ramble

Contains **11 strokes** in the following order:

一 二 丰 圭 圭 丰 丰 圹 敖 敖

Because the drought turned his green grass to hard brown *soil*, the farmer must *place* bales of hay out so that his cows will **ramble** over and eat.

129 傲 **proud, haughty**

Pinyin **ào** *and Frequency Rank* **1960**

SIMP & TRAD

This character with the definition:

Contains these components:
- man r 亻 1156, p. 260
- ramble 敖 2128, p. 467

With all these meanings & readings:

ào [傲] **1** proud **2** overbearing **3** insolent **4** arrogant

Contains **12 strokes** in the following order:

丿 亻 亻 亻 伴 住 傲 傲 傲 傲 傲 傲

The **proud** wealthy *man* felt the entire world was his own playground to *ramble* through wherever and whenever he wanted.

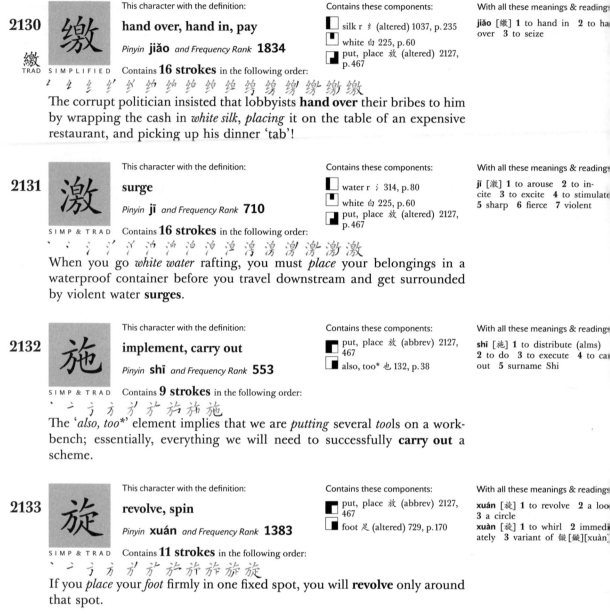

2130

缴

缴
TRAD SIMPLIFIED

This character with the definition:

hand over, hand in, pay

Pinyin **jiǎo** *and Frequency Rank* **1834**

Contains **16 strokes** in the following order:

Contains these components:
- silk r 纟 (altered) 1037, p. 235
- white 白 225, p. 60
- put, place 放 (altered) 2127, p. 467

With all these meanings & readings
jiǎo [缴] **1** to hand in **2** to hand over **3** to seize

The corrupt politician insisted that lobbyists **hand over** their bribes to him by wrapping the cash in *white silk, placing* it on the table of an expensive restaurant, and picking up his dinner 'tab'!

2131

激

SIMP & TRAD

This character with the definition:

surge

Pinyin **jī** *and Frequency Rank* **710**

Contains **16 strokes** in the following order:

Contains these components:
- water r 氵 314, p. 80
- white 白 225, p. 60
- put, place 放 (altered) 2127, p. 467

With all these meanings & readings
jī [激] **1** to arouse **2** to incite **3** to excite **4** to stimulate **5** sharp **6** fierce **7** violent

When you go *white water* rafting, you must *place* your belongings in a waterproof container before you travel downstream and get surrounded by violent water **surges**.

2132

施

SIMP & TRAD

This character with the definition:

implement, carry out

Pinyin **shī** *and Frequency Rank* **553**

Contains **9 strokes** in the following order:

Contains these components:
- put, place 放 (abbrev) 2127, 467
- also, too* 也 132, p. 38

With all these meanings & readings
shī [施] **1** to distribute (alms) **2** to do **3** to execute **4** to carry out **5** surname Shi

The '*also, too**' element implies that we are *putting* several *tool*s on a workbench; essentially, everything we will need to successfully **carry out** a scheme.

2133

旋

SIMP & TRAD

This character with the definition:

revolve, spin

Pinyin **xuán** *and Frequency Rank* **1383**

Contains **11 strokes** in the following order:

Contains these components:
- put, place 放 (abbrev) 2127, 467
- foot 足 (altered) 729, p. 170

With all these meanings & readings
xuán [旋] **1** to revolve **2** a loop **3** a circle
xuàn [旋] **1** to whirl **2** immediately **3** variant of 鏇[鏇][xuàn]

If you *place* your *foot* firmly in one fixed spot, you will **revolve** only around that spot.

2134

族

SIMP & TRAD

This character with the definition:

tribe, clan

Pinyin **zú** *and Frequency Rank* **549**

Contains **11 strokes** in the following order:

Contains these components:
- put, place 放 (abbrev) 2127, 467
- arrow 矢 552, p. 130

With all these meanings & readings
zú [族] **1** race **2** nationality **3** ethnicity **4** clan **5** by extension, social group (e.g. office workers 上班族)

People from the same **tribe** share the same desire in battle: to *put* their *arrows* in the bodies of their mutual enemy.

Unit 88

135

旅
SIMP & TRAD

This character with the definition:

trip, journey

Pinyin **lǚ** *and Frequency Rank* **950**

Contains **10 strokes** in the following order:

Contains these components:

put, place 放 (abbrev) 2127, 467

clothing 衣 (altered) 1068, p.242

With all these meanings & readings:

lǚ [旅] **1** trip **2** travel **3** to travel

丶 一 亍 方 方 方 方 旅 旅 旅

You prepare yourself for a **trip** by carefully selecting and *placing* your *clothing* into a suitcase well before departure.

136

旗
SIMP & TRAD

This character with the definition:

banner, flag

Pinyin **qí** *and Frequency Rank* **1407**

Contains **14 strokes** in the following order:

Contains these components:

put, place 放 (abbrev) 2127, 467

his, hers, its, theirs 其 1341, p.299

With all these meanings & readings:

qí [旗] **1** banner **2** flag **3** (in Qing times) refers to Manchurian ruling class, from 八旗[bā qí] eight banners **4** administrative subdivision in inner Mongolia equivalent to 县[縣][xiàn] county **5** m 面[miàn]

丶 一 亍 方 方 方 � 旃 旃 旃 旃 旗 旗 旗

Designing the new **flag** was a nightmare! Everyone wanted to *put his, her, its,* and *their* favorite symbol on it.

137

游
SIMP & TRAD

This character with the definition:

roam

Pinyin **yóu** *and Frequency Rank* **9999**

Contains **9 strokes** in the following order:

Contains these components:

put, place 放 (abbrev) 2127, 467

son, child 子 24, p.15

With all these meanings & readings:

yóu [斿] **1** scallops along lower edge of flag

丶 一 亍 方 方 方 斿 斿 斿

It's necessary to *place* young *children* in special enclosures called playpens so that they will not **roam** around.

138

游
遊
游
TRAD SIMPLIFIED

This character with the definition:

swim

Pinyin **yóu** *and Frequency Rank* **695**

Contains **12 strokes** in the following order:

Contains these components:

water r 氵 314, p.80

roam 斿 2137, p.469

With all these meanings & readings:

yóu [游] **1** to walk **2** to tour **3** to roam **4** to travel **5** to swim **6** surname You
yóu [遊] **1** to walk **2** to tour **3** to roam **4** to travel **5** surname You

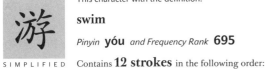

Since I never learned how to **swim**, I can only *roam* along the edge of a deep body of *water*.

139

务
務
TRAD SIMPLIFIED

This character with the definition:

affair, business matter

Pinyin **wù** *and Frequency Rank* **245**

Contains **5 strokes** in the following order:

Contains these components:

to strike r 攵 (altered) 2098, p.461

strength 力 471, p.113

With all these meanings & readings:

wù [務] **1** affair **2** business **3** matter

丿 夂 夂 务 务

Most people do not realize that an important **business matter** can resemble a battle, requiring opponents *to strike* each other. Whoever has the greatest mental *strength* and cleverness will gain the advantage.

2140

This character with the definition:

fog, mist

Pinyin **wù** *and Frequency Rank* **1670**

Contains these components:

▭ rain 雨 239, p. 63
▭ affair, business matter 务 2139, p. 469

With all these meanings & readings:

wù [霧] **1** fog **2** mist **3** m 场 [場][cháng], 阵 [陣][zhèn]

Contains **13 strokes** in the following order:

一 宀 户 币 雨 雷 雷 雷 雰 雰 雾 雺 霧

We were all looking forward to our annual sales meeting, a very special *affair* at a luxury beach resort. On the morning of our meeting, however, a heavy **fog** rolled in and was followed soon after by heavy tropical *rain*! Our 'special *affair*' was memorable but not very enjoyable!

2141

This character with the definition:

dare

Pinyin **gǎn** *and Frequency Rank* **795**

Contains these components:

▭ second (in a series) 乙 (altered) 146, p. 41
▭ ear 耳 76, p. 26
▭ to strike r 攵 2098, p. 461

With all these meanings & readings:

gǎn [敢] **1** dare

Contains **11 strokes** in the following order:

丁 エ 子 开 耳 耳 耳 耴 敢 敢 敢

After one man decides **to dare** another, one of two body reactions can result. The first requires the other man's *ear* to hear the dare, and the *second* requires his brain to decide whether he should *strike* the man or simply ignore him.

2142

This character with the definition:

m for coins, small objects

Pinyin **méi** *and Frequency Rank* **1884**

Contains these components:

▭ tree 木 562, p. 133
▭ to strike r 攵 2098, p. 461

With all these meanings & readings:

méi [枚] **1** m for coins, rings, badges, pearls, sporting medals, rockets, satellites etc

Contains **8 strokes** in the following order:

一 十 ォ 木 杧 杧 杕 枚

After you *strike* the *tree* hard, a lot of **small objects** (acorns?) will tumble down.

2143

This character with the definition:

prepare, get ready

Pinyin **bèi** *and Frequency Rank* **397**

Contains these components:

▭ to strike r 攵 2098, p. 461
▭ field 田 63, p. 23

With all these meanings & readings:

bèi [備] **1** to prepare **2** get ready **3** to provide or equip

Contains **8 strokes** in the following order:

ノ 夂 夂 冬 各 各 备 备

Everyone loves the spring, except perhaps the farmers who work furiously to **prepare** their *fields* for planting. They must weed, hoe, aerate the soil, and so on. To do all this they must *strike* the *field* and cause great violence to the soil.

2144

This component has the meaning:

move forward r

COMPONENT

If you visualize this component as the side profile of a big human foot and ankle, you may remember the image as the primary body parts that people rely on to **move forward**.

2145

This character with the definition:

enlighten, guide

Pinyin **dí** *and Frequency Rank* **1440**

SIMP & TRAD   Contains **8 strokes** in the following order:

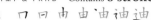

Contains these components:

■ move forward r 辶 2144, p.470
■ reason, by means of 由 58, p.22

With all these meanings & readings:

dí [迪] **1** direct **2** to enlighten **3** to follow

One *reason* that some people *move forward* in life is because they use their learning and experience to **guide** them.

2146

This character with the definition:

suffer (misfortune)

Pinyin **zāo** *and Frequency Rank* **1048**

SIMP & TRAD   Contains **14 strokes** in the following order:

Contains these components:

■ move forward r 辶 2144, p.470
■ medium-sized group of people 曹 97, p.31

With all these meanings & readings:

zāo [遭] **1** meet by chance (usually with misfortune) **2** m for events: time, turn, incident

It is said that people who have a *medium-sized group* of close friends and family are less likely to **suffer** some misfortune and more able to *move forward* in life.

2147

This character with the definition:

near, close to

Pinyin **jìn** *and Frequency Rank* **374**

SIMP & TRAD   Contains **7 strokes** in the following order:

Contains these components:

■ move forward r 辶 2144, p.470
■ catty 斤 403, p.98

With all these meanings & readings:

jìn [近] **1** near **2** close to **3** approximately

Since I wanted to say something *catty* about our boss to my friend, it was 'human nature' for me to *move forward* to be **close to** my friend's ear—even though no one else was **near** us to overhear!

2148

This character with the definition:

escape, flee

Pinyin **táo** *and Frequency Rank* **996**

SIMP & TRAD   Contains **9 strokes** in the following order:

Contains these components:

■ move forward r 辶 2144, p.470
■ omen 兆 236, p.63

With all these meanings & readings:

táo [逃] **1** to escape **2** to run away **3** to flee

Every culture has an ancient myth in which a special *omen* warns a god-like hero to *move forward* quickly in order to **flee** from imminent danger.

2149

This character with the definition:

welcome

Pinyin **yíng** *and Frequency Rank* **1069**

SIMP & TRAD   Contains **7 strokes** in the following order:

Contains these components:

■ move forward r 辶 2144, p.470
■ head held high c 卬 926, p.210

With all these meanings & readings:

yíng [迎] **1** to welcome **2** to meet **3** to face **4** to forge ahead (especially in the face of difficulties)

With his *head held high*, the young man *moved forward* **to welcome** his parents into his first 'home away from home'.

2150

SIMP & TRAD

This character with the definition:

to pressure, force

Pinyin **bī** *and Frequency Rank* **1559**

Contains **12 strokes** in the following order:

一 厂 厂 戸 戸 戸 高 高 畐 畐 逼 逼

Contains these components:

■ move forward r 辶 2144, p. 470

■ size range c 畐 162, p. 45

With all these meanings & readings:

bī [逼] **1** force **2** compel **3** dri **4** press for **5** extort **6** press or towards **7** press up to **8** to close (in on) **9** make (someone do something) **10** vagina (vulgar)

Our growing family **forced** us to *move forward* and into a neighborhood that had a larger *size range* of houses.

2151

SIMP & TRAD

This character with the definition:

compel, force

Pinyin **pò** *and Frequency Rank* **1006**

Contains **8 strokes** in the following order:

丿 亻 白 白 白 迫 迫 迫

Contains these components:

■ move forward r 辶 2144, p. 470

■ white 白 225, p. 60

With all these meanings & readings:

pò [迫] **1** to force **2** to compel **3** pressing **4** urgent

Sometimes people who recover from a coma report seeing a *white* light that **compelled** them to *move forward* towards it.

2152

SIMP & TRAD

This character with the definition:

create, invent

Pinyin **zào** *and Frequency Rank* **354**

Contains **10 strokes** in the following order:

丿 一 牛 牛 生 告 告 告 造 造

Contains these components:

■ move forward r 辶 2144, p. 470

■ tell 告 234, p. 62

With all these meanings & readings:

zào [造] **1** to make **2** to build **3** to invent **4** to manufacture

If you **invent** something special, you should quickly *move forward* to secure a patent before you *tell* anyone about it.

2153

造
TRAD   SIMPLIFIED

This character with the definition:

this, these

Pinyin **zhè** *and Frequency Rank* **11**

Contains **7 strokes** in the following order:

丶 亠 文 文 文 这 这

Contains these components:

■ move forward r 辶 2144, p. 470

■ culture, language 文 1986, p. 437

With all these meanings & readings:

zhè [這] **1** this **2** these **3** (commonly pronounced zhei4 before classifier, especially in Beijing)

'**This**' object can be used during your speech. *Move* this object *forward*, when you mention the important *cultural* artifact.

2154

遠
TRAD   SIMPLIFIED

This character with the definition:

far

Pinyin **yuǎn** *and Frequency Rank* **386**

Contains **7 strokes** in the following order:

一 二 テ 元 元 远 远

Contains these components:

■ move forward r 辶 2144, p. 470

■ dollar 元 295, p. 76

With all these meanings & readings:

yuǎn [遠] **1** far **2** distant **3** remote

The more **distant** are the places that you want to *move forward to* via train, the more *money* the train ticket will cost.

155 过

过
TRAD | SIMPLIFIED

This character with the definition:

cross, go over

Pinyin **guò** *and Frequency Rank* **46**

Contains **6 strokes** in the following order:

一 丁 寸 寸 讨 过

Contains these components:

move forward r 辶 2144, p.470

inch 寸 216, p.58

With all these meanings & readings:

guò [過] **1** (experienced action marker) **2** to cross **3** to go over **4** to pass (time) **5** to celebrate (a holiday) **6** to live **7** to get along **8** excessively **9** too- **10** surname Guo

Crossing a street or **moving forward** over a bridge requires you to *move forward, inch* by *inch.*

---

156 遗

遺
TRAD | SIMPLIFIED

This character with the definition:

leave behind

Pinyin **yí** *and Frequency Rank* **892**

Contains **12 strokes** in the following order:

丶 一 口 中 虫 虫 虫 虫 贵 贵 遗 遗

Contains these components:

move forward r 辶 2144, p.470

expensive 贵 1396, p.310

With all these meanings & readings:

yí [遺] **1** to lose **2** to leave behind

We want to **leave behind** our rundown neighborhood and *move forward* into a better one. But the houses in the new area are so *expensive* that we must wait until we earn more money—or win the lottery—before we can relocate!

---

157 速

速
SIMP & TRAD

This character with the definition:

speed

Pinyin **sù** *and Frequency Rank* **617**

Contains **10 strokes** in the following order:

一 厂 一 口 市 束 束 凍 速 速

Contains these components:

move forward r 辶 2144, p.470

bundle, bunch 束 590, p.140

With all these meanings & readings:

sù [速] **1** fast **2** rapid **3** quick **4** velocity

Even though I enjoy walking to my food store, it is difficult for me to *move forward* at a very fast **speed** on my way home because of the large *bundles* of food that are weighing me down.

---

158 述

述
SIMP & TRAD

This character with the definition:

narrate, relate

Pinyin **shù** *and Frequency Rank* **674**

Contains **8 strokes** in the following order:

一 十 才 木 术 术 讲 述

Contains these components:

move forward r 辶 2144, p.470

tree 木 562, p.133

dab r 丶 176, p.48

With all these meanings & readings:

shù [述] **1** to state **2** to tell **3** to narrate **4** to relate

The rings in a *tree* trunk **narrate** its life history—not only its age but the climate conditions that it grew in—as it *moved forward* toward the sky each year. For instance, if a ring is only a thread-like *dab*, it means that the *tree* suffered from a drought or other severe weather conditions that year.

---

159 迁

遷
TRAD | SIMPLIFIED

This character with the definition:

move*

Pinyin **qiān** *and Frequency Rank* **1630**

Contains **6 strokes** in the following order:

一 二 千 千 讦 迁

Contains these components:

move forward r 辶 2144, p.470

thousand 千 767, p.178

With all these meanings & readings:

qiān [遷] **1** to move **2** to shift

When you **move** to a new house, you are *moving forward* in life a distance that is a *thousand* miles from the old place.

Unit 89

2160

遥

TRAD SIMPLIFIED

This character with the definition:

distant, remote

Pinyin **yáo** *and Frequency Rank* **1715**

Contains **13 strokes** in the following order:

ノ ノ ハ ゥ ゥ 产 乒 乒 乒 乑 乑 遙 遥

Contains these components:

▯ move forward r 辶 2144, p. 470
▯ hands raised high c ⼍ 1657, p. 368
▮ archaeological vessel 缶 181, p. 49

With all these meanings & readings

yáo ［遙］ **1** distant **2** remote **3** far **4** far away

The workers carrying the priceless *archaeological vessel* must make sure to hold it with *hands raised high* as they *move forward*. That way, they can transport it to the **distant** storage facility without breaking it.

2161

迟

TRAD SIMPLIFIED

This character with the definition:

late, tardy

Pinyin **chí** *and Frequency Rank* **1374**

Contains **7 strokes** in the following order:

ᐯ ᒣ 尸 尺 尺 迟 迟

Contains these components:

▯ move forward r 辶 2144, p. 470
▮ ruler (length) 尺 507, p. 120

With all these meanings & readings

chí ［遲］ **1** late **2** delayed **3** slo

I broke my walking stick so I used a *ruler* to *move forward* to my friend's house. The *ruler* was was so short that it caused me to walk slower than normal, and I arrived very **late**.

2162

遍

SIMP & TRAD

This character with the definition:

all over, everywhere

Pinyin **biàn** *and Frequency Rank* **1012**

Contains **12 strokes** in the following order:

丶 ㇇ ㇋ 户 户 启 启 扁 扁 扁 谝 遍

Contains these components:

▯ move forward r 辶 2144, p. 470
▮ crushed, flat 扁 2083, p. 457

With all these meanings & readings

biàn ［遍］ **1** a time **2** everywher **3** turn **4** all over **5** one time

Every boat owner knows to secure all loose items in the cabin or else they will *move forward* with the slightest wave, slide **all over** a surface until they reach the top edge, and then drop onto the hard floor, where the most fragile items will be *crushed* to pieces.

2163

迈

TRAD SIMPLIFIED

迈

This character with the definition:

step, stride

Pinyin **mài** *and Frequency Rank* **1698**

Contains **6 strokes** in the following order:

一 ㇅ 万 万 迈 迈

Contains these components:

▯ move forward r 辶 2144, p. 470
▮ ten thousand 万 917, p. 208

With all these meanings & readings

mài ［邁］ **1** take a step

To complete a journey of *ten thousand* meters, you must first *move forward* with a single **step**.

2164 **运** 運 TRAD SIMPLIFIED

This character with the definition:

move, transport

Pinyin **yùn** *and Frequency Rank* **345**

Contains **7 strokes** in the following order:

Movers—people who **transport** household goods—do a good job when each of them *says* encouraging words to the others as they are *moving forward*, carrying heavy objects.

Contains these components:

- move forward r 辶 2144, p. 470
- say 云 967, p. 221

With all these meanings & readings:

yùn [運] **1** to move **2** to transport **3** to use **4** to apply **5** fortune **6** luck **7** fate

2165 **还** 還 TRAD SIMPLIFIED

This character with the definition:

still more, even more

Pinyin **hái** *and Frequency Rank* **80**

Contains **7 strokes** in the following order:

You tried to *move forward*, but the authorities would *not* allow it. Therefore, you **have yet** to reach your goal.

Contains these components:

- move forward r 辶 2144, p. 470
- no! 不 493, p. 117

With all these meanings & readings:

hái [還] **1** still **2** still in progress **3** still more **4** yet **5** even more **6** in addition **7** fairly **8** passably (good) **9** as early as **10** even **11** also **12** else
huán [還] **1** to pay back **2** to return **3** surname Huan

2166 **进** 進 TRAD SIMPLIFIED

This character with the definition:

move forward, advance

Pinyin **jìn** *and Frequency Rank* **81**

Contains **7 strokes** in the following order:

The enemy **advances** into the cave in which is hidden the *well* that we covered with a grid of sticks. As they *move forward* in the gloom, they step on the sticks, which causes them to break. You can hear the enemy tumbling down, screaming for mercy.

Contains these components:

- move forward r 辶 2144, p. 470
- well 井 1758, p. 388

With all these meanings & readings:

jìn [進] **1** to advance **2** to enter **3** to come in

2167 **逻** 邏 TRAD SIMPLIFIED

This character with the definition:

patrol

Pinyin **luó** *and Frequency Rank* **1591**

Contains **11 strokes** in the following order:

The park manager was assigned a special **patrol**—to catch rare birds so that scientists could place tracking bands on them. He was selected because he could *move forward* so quietly that the birds were not aware of his presence until they were trapped in his *bird net*!

Contains these components:

- move forward r 辶 2144, p. 470
- bird net 罗 894, p. 203

With all these meanings & readings:

luó [邏] **1** logic **2** patrol

2168 **适** 適 TRAD SIMPLIFIED

This character with the definition:

appropriate, suitable

Pinyin **shì** *and Frequency Rank* **663**

Contains **9 strokes** in the following order:

Hansel and Gretel sit blindfolded, hands tied, in the gingerbread house. They *move forward* carefully, using their *tongues* to navigate a **suitable** escape route.

Contains these components:

- move forward r 辶 2144, p. 470
- tongue 舌 770, p. 179

With all these meanings & readings:

shì [適] **1** to fit **2** to suit **3** just now

2169

SIMP & TRAD

This character with the definition:

be fascinated

Pinyin **mí** *and Frequency Rank* **1153**

Contains **9 strokes** in the following order:

丶 丷 丷 半 米 米 㳇 迷 迷

Contains these components:

◻ move forward r 辶 2144, p. 470
◼ rice (food) 米 1535, p. 339

With all these meanings & readings:

mí [迷] **1** bewilder **2** crazy about **3** fan **4** enthusiast **5** lo **6** confused

After the wedding ceremony, the bride and groom *move forward* toward their limousine. The young children **are fascinated** as grains of white *rice* fly through the air toward the couple—snowflakes in June!

2170

SIMP & TRAD

This character with the definition:

route, way, road

Pinyin **tú** *and Frequency Rank* **1085**

Contains **10 strokes** in the following order:

丿 人 亼 仐 仐 余 余 㳇 诠 途

Contains these components:

◻ move forward r 辶 2144, p. 470
◼ surplus, spare 余 1276, p. 285

With all these meanings & readings:

tú [途] **1** way **2** route **3** road

Trade **routes** were established to help merchants *move forward* to distant markets so that they could sell their *surplus* goods for money or barter them for exotic items.

2171

達
TRAD

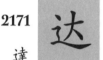

SIMPLIFIED

This character with the definition:

attain, reach

Pinyin **dá** *and Frequency Rank* **289**

Contains **6 strokes** in the following order:

一 ナ 大 㕕 达 达

Contains these components:

◻ move forward r 辶 2144, p. 470
◼ big 大 544, p. 129

With all these meanings & readings:

dá [達] **1** attain **2** pass through **3** achieve **4** reach **5** realize **6** clear **7** inform **8** notify **9** dignity

It's your *big* day. Years of nose to the grindstone and slow but steady *movement forward* through the company are finally paying off. Today you **attain** your goal—a promotion to vice-president in charge of advertising!

2172

選
TRAD

SIMPLIFIED

This character with the definition:

choose, select

Pinyin **xuǎn** *and Frequency Rank* **499**

Contains **9 strokes** in the following order:

丿 ㇠ 屮 㞧 步 先 㳇 选 选

Contains these components:

◻ move forward r 辶 2144, p. 470
◼ first 先 291, p. 75

With all these meanings & readings:

xuǎn [選] **1** to choose **2** to pick **3** to select **4** to elect

As he *moves forward* in life, he always seems to do better than anyone else, as if he is always *first* to receive great opportunities. He claims it's because he always **chooses** the best alternatives.

2173

遜
TRAD

SIMPLIFIED

This character with the definition:

modest, unassuming

Pinyin **xùn** *and Frequency Rank* **1697**

Contains **9 strokes** in the following order:

㇇ 了 孑 孖 孙 孙 㳇 逊 逊

Contains these components:

◻ move forward r 辶 2144, p. 470
◼ grandson 孙 1340, p. 299

With all these meanings & readings:

xùn [遜] **1** to abdicate **2** modest **3** yielding **4** unpretentious **5** inferior to

In societies that value family tradition, a *grandson* may *move forward* in age but he will always remain **modest** and respectful toward his elders.

2174

This character with the definition:

make one's rounds, patrol

Pinyin **xún** *and Frequency Rank* **1544**

SIMP & TRAD Contains **6 strokes** in the following order:

〈 〈〈 〈〈〈 〈〈〈 巡 巡

Contains these components:

■ move forward r ⻌ 2144, p.470
□ river 川 (altered) 444, p.107

With all these meanings & readings:

xún [巡] **1** to patrol **2** to make one's rounds

The night guards were ordered to *move forward* and **make their rounds** along the *river* bank, where smugglers often dropped off their illegal goods.

2175

This character with the definition:

side, edge

Pinyin **biān** *and Frequency Rank* **316**

邊
TRAD SIMPLIFIED Contains **5 strokes** in the following order:

フ 力 ㇆力 边 边

Contains these components:

■ move forward r ⻌ 2144, p.470
□ strength 力 471, p.113

With all these meanings & readings:

biān [邊] **1** side **2** edge **3** margin **4** border **5** boundary **6** m 个 [個][gè]
biān [邊] **1** suffix of a noun of locality

Stranded in the desert, we have no choice but to *move forward*. Using our last reserves of *strength*, we reach the **edge** of the sands just before we give out from dehydration.

2176

This character with the definition:

pursue, chase

Pinyin **zhú** *and Frequency Rank* **954**

SIMP & TRAD Contains **10 strokes** in the following order:

一 ㇆ 丆 万 歺 豸 豖 豖 逐 逐

Contains these components:

■ move forward r ⻌ 2144, p.470
■ pig, boar 豕 1453, p.321

With all these meanings & readings:

zhú [逐] **1** to pursue **2** to chase **3** individually **4** one by one

I saw the angry *boar move forward* rapidly, determined to **pursue** me. All I could do was scramble up the nearest tree.

2177

This character with the definition:

filter, seep through

Pinyin **tòu** *and Frequency Rank* **1077**

SIMP & TRAD Contains **10 strokes** in the following order:

丿 二 千 禾 禾 秀 秀 秀 透 透

Contains these components:

■ move forward r ⻌ 2144, p.470
■ put forth ears of grain 秀 606, p.143

With all these meanings & readings:

tòu [透] **1** to penetrate **2** to pass through **3** thoroughly **4** completely **5** transparent **6** to appear **7** to show

Because our new irrigation system allowed water to **seep through** to our plants even during periods of drought, the plants *put forth ears of grain* that we will soon *move forward* to harvest!

2178

This character with the definition:

disobey, misbehave

Pinyin **nì** *and Frequency Rank* **1975**

SIMP & TRAD Contains **9 strokes** in the following order:

丶 丷 丷 ㇠ 屶 弟 弟 逆 逆

Contains these components:

■ move forward r ⻌ 2144, p.470
■ sheep 羊 (altered) 1486, p.329
■ receptacle r ㇂ 157, p.43

With all these meanings & readings:

nì [逆] **1** contrary **2** opposite **3** backwards **4** to go against **5** to oppose **6** to betray **7** to rebel

As soon as the shepherd's border collie saw the *running sheep* **misbehave**, it quickly *moved forward* to correct their behavior. The shepherd rewarded his alert companion with a treat from the special *receptacle* that he carried precisely for that purpose.

2179

達
TRAD   SIMPLIFIED

This character with the definition:

oppose

Pinyin **wéi** *and Frequency Rank* **1184**

Contains **7 strokes** in the following order:

一 二 三 韦 韦 讳 违

Contains these components:

■ move forward r ⻌ 2144, p. 470
■ leather 韦 109, p. 33

With all these meanings & readings:

wéi [違] **1** to disobey **2** to violate **3** to separate **4** to go against

Since I knew my mother would **oppose** my wearing a short black *leather* skirt to the school dance, I waited for her to become engrossed with her computer and then quickly *moved forward* to the front door. As I escaped from our house, I called out: "See you later!"

2180

SIMP & TRAD

This character with the definition:

go through

Pinyin **tōng** *and Frequency Rank* **190**

Contains **10 strokes** in the following order:

⁊ ⁊ ⁊ 月 用 甬 甬 通 通 通

Contains these components:

■ move forward r ⻌ 2144, p. 470
■ corridor, passageway 甬 1811, p. 400

With all these meanings & readings:

tōng [通] **1** to go through **2** to know well **3** to connect **4** to communicate **5** open **6** to clear
tòng [通] **1** m for actions

When you **go through** a maze, you often become confused as you *move forward* through all the different *passageways*.

2181

隨
TRAD   SIMPLIFIED

This character with the definition:

follow, comply with

Pinyin **suí** *and Frequency Rank* **498**

Contains **11 strokes** in the following order:

⻖ ⻖ ⻖ 阝 阝 阝 陌 陌 陌 随 随

Contains these components:

■ hills r ⻏ 942, p. 216
■ move forward r ⻌ 2144, p. 470
■ have 有 1777, p. 392

With all these meanings & readings:

suí [隨] **1** to follow **2** to comply with **3** varying according to... **4** to allow **5** surname Sui

The troops *move forward*, out from the protection of the *hills*, and **follow** the commander. As soon as all the soldiers are in **compliance**, we'll *have* a superb fighting regiment.

2182

SIMP & TRAD

This character with the definition:

meet by chance

Pinyin **féng** *and Frequency Rank* **2181**

Contains **10 strokes** in the following order:

丿 夕 夂 冬 冬 夆 夆 逢 逢 逢

Contains these components:

■ move forward r ⻌ 2144, p. 470
■ step forward r 夂 2045, p. 449
■ plentiful 丰 16, p. 13

With all these meanings & readings:

féng [逢] **1** to meet by chance **2** to come across **3** to fawn upon

My sister is very shy. She will not take a *step forward* beyond her work and her apartment. I told her that if she will simply *move forward* and become involved in a few activities, she will likely **meet by chance** a *plentiful* number of new friends.

2183

縫
TRAD   SIMPLIFIED

This character with the definition:

sew, stitch

Pinyin **féng** *and Frequency Rank* **1852**

Contains **13 strokes** in the following order:

乚 纟 纟 纟 纠 终 绀 终 终 缝 缝 缝 缝

Contains these components:

■ silk r 纟 1037, p. 235
■ meet by chance 逢 2182, p. 478

With all these meanings & readings:

féng [縫] **1** to sew **2** to stitch
fèng [縫] **1** seam **2** crack **3** narrow slit

People think they *meet other people by chance* but ancient myths teach us that connections are made by means of mystical *silk* thread that special goddesses **stitch** and **sew** together.

184

This character with the definition:

invite, request

Pinyin **yāo** *and Frequency Rank* **1854**

SIMP & TRAD Contains **16 strokes** in the following order:

Contains these components:

◼ move forward r 辶 2144, p. 470

◻ white 白 225, p. 60

◼ put, place 放 (altered) 2127, p. 467

With all these meanings & readings:

yāo [邀] **1** invite to come

How do you **invite** 'failure' to your job interview? Do not *put* on a tie or wear a clean *white* shirt, and *move forward* ever so slowly that you arrive late for the interview.

Unit 90

2185

This character with the definition:

rapid

Pinyin **xùn** *and Frequency Rank* **1090**

SIMP & TRAD Contains **6 strokes** in the following order:

飞 飞 凡 凡 讯 迅

Contains these components:

■ move forward r 辶 2144, p. 470
■ commonplace 凡 (altered) 901, p. 205

With all these meanings & readings

xùn [迅] **1** rapid

Ambitious young people work hard to make a **rapid** *move forward*, away from their *commonplace* past, and toward a bold and more exciting future.

2186

This character with the definition:

possessive marker

Pinyin **zhī** *and Frequency Rank* **44**

SIMP & TRAD Contains **4 strokes** in the following order:

丶 丷 之

Contains these components:

■ move forward r 辶 (altered) 2144, p. 470

With all these meanings & readings

zhī [之] **1** (possessive particle, literary equivalent of 的) **2** him **3** her **4** it

For **my children's** spring vacation, I decided we would rent a 'camper' and use it to *move forward* to Minnesota, the state known as the 'Land **of** Ten Thousand Lakes'. • This character accompanies words indicating possession and phrases that include 'of'.

2187

This character with the definition:

tired, weary

Pinyin **fá** *and Frequency Rank* **1399**

SIMP & TRAD Contains **5 strokes** in the following order:

丿 𠂉 乏 乏

Contains these components:

□ action path c 丿 (altered) 438, p. 105
■ possessive marker 之 2186, p. 480

With all these meanings & readings

fá [乏] **1** short of **2** tired

After spending a long day at work, I was so **tired** that *my* **weary** feet could not bear to walk the short *action path* to the One-Day Sale at the 'House *of* Bargains'.

2188
泛
汛
TRAD SIMPLIFIED

This character with the definition:

float, suffused with

Pinyin **fàn** *and Frequency Rank* **1327**

Contains **7 strokes** in the following order:

丶 丶 氵 氵 泛 泛 泛

Contains these components:

■ water r 氵 314, p. 80
■ tired, weary 乏 2187, p. 480

With all these meanings & readings

fàn [泛] **1** to float **2** to be suffused with **3** general **4** extensive **5** non-specific **6** flood **7** pan- (prefix)

I exercise in the *water* every day, but today I am just so *tired* that I'll just **float** calmly along instead.

2189
連
TRAD SIMPLIFIED

This character with the definition:

join, link

Pinyin **lián** *and Frequency Rank* **399**

Contains **7 strokes** in the following order:

一 𠂇 车 车 车 连 连

Contains these components:

□ move forward r 辶 2144, p. 470
□ car 车 1291, p. 289

With all these meanings & readings

lián [连] **1** surname Lian **2** even **3** as **4** join **5** to link **6** successively

Cars are popular since they give us freedom to *move forward* at any time to any place, often to **join** our friends on vacation.

2190

莲

蓮
TRAD SIMPLIFIED

This character with the definition:

water lily

Pinyin **lián** *and Frequency Rank* **1837**

Contains **10 strokes** in the following order:

一 十 艹 艹 芒 芢 苬 莲 莲 莲

Contains these components:

☐ grass r 艹 87, p. 29

■ join, link 连 2189, p. 480

With all these meanings & readings:

lián [蓮] **1** lotus

A **water lily** looks like an individual flower floating on a pond. But it is really a type of *grass* with a complex root system that *links* its parts together below the water surface.

2191

避

SIMP & TRAD

This character with the definition:

avoid, evade

Pinyin **bì** *and Frequency Rank* **991**

Contains **16 strokes** in the following order:

⁊ ⁊ ⁊ 尸 尸 尺 吊 郤 郤 辟 辟 辟 辟 避 避 避

Contains these components:

☐ move forward r ⻌ 2144, p. 470

☐ penal law 辟 685, p. 161

With all these meanings & readings:

bì [避] **1** to avoid **2** to shun **3** to flee **4** to escape **5** to keep away from **6** to leave **7** to hide from

If you *move forward* in life by striving to avoid the *penal law*, you will not have to worry about trying to **evade** punishment.

2192

道

SIMP & TRAD

This character with the definition:

way, direction

Pinyin **dào** *and Frequency Rank* **52**

Contains **12 strokes** in the following order:

丶 丷 丷 丷 产 芢 首 首 首 首 道 道

Contains these components:

☐ move forward r ⻌ 2144, p. 470

■ head, leader 首 1599, p. 356

With all these meanings & readings:

dào [道] **1** direction **2** way **3** road **4** path **5** principle **6** truth **7** morality **8** reason **9** skill **10** method **11** Dao (of Daoism) **12** to say **13** to speak **14** to talk **15** m for long thin stretches, rivers, roads etc **16** province (of Korea do 및, and formerly Japan dō) **17** m 条 [條][tiáo], 股[gǔ]

A *leader* is one who is willing to *move forward* bravely when others don't know the **way**.

2193

退

SIMP & TRAD

This character with the definition:

retreat, withdraw

Pinyin **tuì** *and Frequency Rank* **723**

Contains **9 strokes** in the following order:

⁊ ⁊ ⁊ 尸 尺 艮 艮 退 退

Contains these components:

☐ move forward r ⻌ 2144, p. 470

☐ tough, chewy 艮 1952, p. 429

With all these meanings & readings:

tuì [退] **1** retreat **2** to decline **3** to move back **4** to withdraw

After the long, hard battle, our army could *move forward* no farther and was forced to **retreat**. Even worse, their food supply had spoiled or was too *tough* to eat.

2194

腿

SIMP & TRAD

This character with the definition:

leg

Pinyin **tuǐ** *and Frequency Rank* **1351**

Contains **13 strokes** in the following order:

丿 几 月 月 月⁷ 月⁷ 月⁷ 胛 胩 腿 腿 腿 腿

Contains these components:

☐ meat 肉 (altered) 753, p. 175

☐ retreat, withdraw 退 (altered) 2193, p. 481

With all these meanings & readings:

tuǐ [腿] **1** leg **2** m 条 [條][tiáo]

Any dog that is lucky enough to receive a **leg** of raw *meat* will quickly *withdraw* to a hiding place to enjoy it out of sight.

2195

This character with the definition:

carry to, deliver

Pinyin **sòng** and Frequency Rank **656**

SIMP & TRAD   Contains **9 strokes** in the following order:

丶 ⸝ 丷 ⸜ 关 关 关 送 送

Contains these components:

■ move forward r ⻍ 2144, p. 470

□ eight r ⸜ 1260, p. 282

■ heaven 天 548, p. 129

With all these meanings & readings:

sòng [送] **1** to deliver **2** to carr
3 to give (as a present) **4** to
present (with) **5** to see off **6** t
send

I forgot that today is our wedding anniversary! Since my wife will surely expect me to **deliver** a surprise to her, I must *move forward* quickly and head to the flower shop. I'm relieved to see the shop still open and happy to find an *abundance* of her favorite flowers for sale.

2196

This character with the definition:

return to

Pinyin **fǎn** and Frequency Rank **1430**

SIMP & TRAD   Contains **7 strokes** in the following order:

⸝ 厂 厃 反 返 返 返

Contains these components:

■ move forward r ⻍ 2144, p. 470

■ anti-, oppose 反 1895, p. 417

With all these meanings & readings:

fǎn [返] **1** to return (to)

After the *opposition* is quashed, the soldiers can *move forward* and **return** home.

2197

遞
TRAD

This character with the definition:

hand over, transmit

Pinyin **dì** and Frequency Rank **1538**

SIMPLIFIED   Contains **10 strokes** in the following order:

丶 ⸝ 丷 ⸜ 쓰 弟 弟 弟 递 递

Contains these components:

■ move forward r ⻍ 2144, p. 470

■ younger brother 弟 1494, p. 330

With all these meanings & readings:

dì [遞] **1** to hand over **2** to pas
on sth. **3** gradually (increase o
decrease) **4** progressively

Since the estate was **handed over** to the oldest son, the *younger brothers* had to learn to *move forward* with their lives and not depend on family money for support.

2198

This character with the definition:

abide by, obey

Pinyin **zūn** and Frequency Rank **1593**

SIMP & TRAD   Contains **15 strokes** in the following order:

丶 ⸝ 丷 ⺆ 뿌 酋 酋 酋 酋 尊 尊 尊 尊 遵 遵

Contains these components:

■ move forward r ⻍ 2144, p. 470

■ honor, venerate 尊 1477, p. 326

With all these meanings & readings:

zūn [遵] **1** to observe **2** to obey
3 to follow **4** to comply with

You **abide by** your professor's rules and you *move forward* with *honor*.

2199

跡
TRAD

This character with the definition:

footprints, mark, trace

Pinyin **jì** and Frequency Rank **1098**

SIMPLIFIED   Contains **9 strokes** in the following order:

丶 ⸠ 亠 亣 亦 亦 亦 迹 迹

Contains these components:

■ move forward r ⻍ 2144, p. 470

■ also, too 亦 842, p. 193

With all these meanings & readings:

jì [跡] **1** footprint **2** mark
3 trace **4** vestige **5** sign **6** ind
cation **7** Taiwan pr jī

Several things happen when you *move forward* on a trip. First, you get closer to your travel goal. But you *also* leave **traces** of yourself—footprints, tire tracks, credit card receipts, and so on—behind.

2200

This component has the meaning:

long stride r

COMPONENT

It may help you to remember this character's meaning if you think of the two sharp vertical curves as short footsteps, and the one horizontal stroke as a **long stride**.

2201

This character with the definition:

establish, set up*

Pinyin **jiàn** *and Frequency Rank* **244**

SIMP & TRAD   Contains **8 strokes** in the following order:

丁 コ ヨ ヨ 글 聿 建 建

Contains these components:

☐ long stride r 廴 2200, p. 483
◼ writing instrument, pen 聿 31, p. 16

With all these meanings & readings:

jiàn [建] **1** to establish **2** to found **3** to set up **4** to build **5** to construct

With the invention of *writing instruments*, primitive peoples were able to advance their cultures in *long strides*—the instruments were used to record historical events, **establish** legal codes, and create art.

2202

This character with the definition:

fortify

Pinyin **jiàn** *and Frequency Rank* **979**

SIMP & TRAD   Contains **10 strokes** in the following order:

丿 亻 亻ᄀ 亻ᄀ 亻ᄅ 倡 倡 律 健 健

Contains these components:

☐ man r 亻 1156, p. 260
◼ establish, set up* 建 2201, p. 483

With all these meanings & readings:

jiàn [健] **1** healthy **2** to invigorate **3** to strengthen **4** to be good at **5** to be strong in

A *man* or woman must **fortify** him- or herself mentally and physically in order to *establish* a successful new business.

2203

This character with the definition:

imperial court

Pinyin **tíng** *and Frequency Rank* **1626**

SIMP & TRAD   Contains **6 strokes** in the following order:

ᄼ 二 千 王 廷 廷

Contains these components:

◻ long stride r 廴 2200, p. 483
☐ action path c 丿 438, p. 105
◼ earth, soil 土 9, p. 11

With all these meanings & readings:

tíng [廷] **1** palace courtyard

Whenever the Emperor was displeased with his **imperial court**, he left the room in brisk, *long strides*, and headed on a direct *path* to the flower-filled *soil* of his peaceful private garden.

2204

This character with the definition:

stand up straight

Pinyin **tǐng** *and Frequency Rank* **1467**

SIMP & TRAD   Contains **9 strokes** in the following order:

一 十 才 扌 扩 扩 挂 挺 挺

Contains these components:

◼ hand r 扌 25, p. 15
◼ imperial court 廷 2203, p. 483

With all these meanings & readings:

tǐng [挺] **1** straight and stiff **2** rather **3** quite **4** very **5** m for guns, machinery, etc.

If anyone in the *imperial court* did not **stand up straight** in the Emperor's presence, he pointed at them with his *hand* and signaled for his guards to arrest the offender.

2205

This character with the definition:

courtyard

Pinyin **tíng** *and Frequency Rank* **931**

Contains these components:

◱ shelter r 广 427, p. 103

◱ imperial court 廷 2203, p. 483

With all these meanings & readings:

tíng [庭] **1** court **2** courtyard

SIMP & TRAD   Contains **9 strokes** in the following order:

丶 一 广 广 庐 庆 庭 庭 庭

The members of the *imperial court* had just gathered in the **courtyard** to celebrate Chinese New Year when a violent thunderstorm suddenly moved in and forced everyone to take *shelter*.

2206

This character with the definition:

dragonfly

Pinyin **tíng** *and Frequency Rank* **4083**

Contains these components:

◱ insect 虫 1016, p. 231

◱ imperial court 廷 2203, p. 483

With all these meanings & readings:

tíng [蜓] **1** see 蜻蜓, dragonfly

SIMP & TRAD   Contains **12 strokes** in the following order:

丶 口 口 中 虫 虫 虫 虫 虫 虫 蜓 蜓

The only *insect* good enough for the *imperial court* is the graceful, beautiful, and eye catching **dragonfly**.

2207

This character with the definition:

small boat

Pinyin **tǐng** *and Frequency Rank* **1372**

Contains these components:

◱ boat 舟 822, p. 189

◱ imperial court 廷 2203, p. 483

With all these meanings & readings:

tǐng [艇] **1** vessel **2** small ship

SIMP & TRAD   Contains **12 strokes** in the following order:

丿 丿 丿 月 舟 舟 舟 舟 舟 艇 艇 艇

Only **small boats** are allowed at the *imperial court*. These *boats* must be smaller than the emperor's.

2208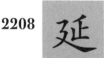

This character with the definition:

prolong, extend

Pinyin **yán** *and Frequency Rank* **1103**

Contains these components:

◱ long stride r 廴 2200, p. 483

◱ action path c ノ 438, p. 105

◱ stop! 止 190, p. 52

With all these meanings & readings:

yán [延] **1** to prolong **2** to extend **3** to delay **4** surname Yan

SIMP & TRAD   Contains **6 strokes** in the following order:

丿 丿 壬 正 延 延

Young adults enjoy taking *long strides* between one *activity* and another and do not like to **prolong** their time performing any particular one. They never like to hear anyone say '*Stop!*' to them.

2209

誔
TRAD   SIMPLIFIED

This character with the definition:

birth, birthday

Pinyin **dàn** *and Frequency Rank* **1997**

Contains these components:

◱ speech r 讠 352, p. 88

◱ prolong, extend 延 2208, p. 484

With all these meanings & readings:

dàn [诞] **1** birth **2** birthday **3** brag **4** boast **5** to increase

Contains **8 strokes** in the following order:

丶 讠 讠 讠 讠 讠 诞 诞

My father did not expect his intoxicated younger brother to *prolong* his fiftieth **birthday** party by giving a long, rambling *speech* in praise of his older brother.

Unit 91

2210

SIMP & TRAD

This character with the definition:

and, in, on

Pinyin **jí** *and Frequency Rank* **198**

Contains **3 strokes** in the following order:

ノ 乃 及

Contains these components:

☐ action path c ノ 438, p.105
☐ long stride r ㇂ 2200, p.483

With all these meanings & readings:

jí [及] **1** and **2** to reach **3** up to **4** in time for

If you want to take *long strides* **in** life, you need to believe you are moving forward **on** an *action path* every day.

2211

吸

SIMP & TRAD

This character with the definition:

suck up, absorb

Pinyin **xī** *and Frequency Rank* **924**

Contains **6 strokes** in the following order:

丨 冂 口 叮 叨 吸

Contains these components:

☐ mouth 口 37, p.17
☐ and, in, on 及 2210, p.485

With all these meanings & readings:

xī [吸] **1** to breathe **2** to suck in **3** to absorb **4** to inhale

The plastic straw is designed to **suck up** cold liquids that are stored *in* containers and transported into your *mouth*.

2212

级
TRAD

SIMPLIFIED

This character with the definition:

level, rank, grade

Pinyin **jí** *and Frequency Rank* **415**

Contains **6 strokes** in the following order:

乙 纟 纟 纟 级 级

Contains these components:

☐ silk r 纟 (altered) 1037, p.235
☐ and, in, on 及 2210, p.485

With all these meanings & readings:

jí [级] **1** level **2** grade **3** rank **4** step **5** m 个[個][gè]

Even early *on*, merchants began to **grade** *silk* fabric based *on* the different **levels** of quality *in* their weave.

2213

極
TRAD

SIMPLIFIED

This character with the definition:

extremely*

Pinyin **jí** *and Frequency Rank* **363**

Contains **7 strokes** in the following order:

一 十 才 木 朽 极 极

Contains these components:

☐ tree 木 562, p.133
☐ and, in, on 及 2210, p.485

With all these meanings & readings:

jí [極] **1** extremely **2** pole (geography, physics) **3** utmost **4** top

That *tree* is perfect for the municipal Christmas *tree*—it's **extremely** tall. We will intensify its festive nature by decorating it with ornaments *in many different positions*.

2214

禸

This component has the meaning:

animal track r

COMPONENT

And contains these subcomponents:

☐ borders r 冂 114, p.34
☐ private r 厶 963, p.220

I was very distressed to discover a trail of very large **animal tracks** emerging from the forest. They crossed over the *borders* of my pasture and went straight into the *private* garden next to my house! • This component is a radical and appears here with four strokes; a five-stroke variant can also appear at the bottom of characters such as 禺.

2215

禺

SIMP & TRAD

This character with the definition:

monkey

Pinyin **yù** *and Frequency Rank* **3056**

Contains these components:

☐ speak 曰 67, p. 24

☐ animal track r 内 2214, p. 485

With all these meanings & readings:

yú [禺] **1** (place) **2** district

Contains **9 strokes** in the following order:

丶 冂 曰 曰 巴 禺 禺 禺 禺

Even though **monkeys** can be taught to '*speak*' to humans with 'hand' gestures, they still leave four-legged *animal tracks* in the soil.

2216

愚

SIMP & TRAD

This character with the definition:

foolish

Pinyin **yú** *and Frequency Rank* **1895**

Contains these components:

☐ monkey 禺 2215, p. 486

☐ heart (fat) r 心 1096, p. 248

With all these meanings & readings:

yú [愚] **1** stupid

Contains **13 strokes** in the following order:

丶 冂 曰 曰 巴 禺 禺 禺 禺 愚 愚 愚

When people *feel* they have been made to look **foolish**, they may exclaim, "You made a *monkey* out of me!"

2217

偶

SIMP & TRAD

This character with the definition:

by chance

Pinyin **ǒu** *and Frequency Rank* **1361**

Contains these components:

☐ man r 亻 1156, p. 260

☐ monkey 禺 2215, p. 486

With all these meanings & readings:

ǒu [偶] **1** accidental   **2** image
3 pair   **4** mate

Contains **11 strokes** in the following order:

丿 亻 individual strokes 偶 偶 偶 偶

People get into heated arguments about whether *man* descended **by chance** from *monkeys*.

2218

遇

SIMP & TRAD

This character with the definition:

encounter

Pinyin **yù** *and Frequency Rank* **899**

Contains these components:

☐ move forward r 辶 2144, p. 470

☐ monkey 禺 2215, p. 486

With all these meanings & readings:

yù [遇] **1** meet with   **2** how
one is treated   **3** an opportunity
4 surname Yu

Contains **12 strokes** in the following order:

丶 冂 曰 曰 巴 禺 禺 禺 禺 遇 遇 遇

Be sure to *move forward* very cautiously if you ever **encounter** a *monkey*.

2219

离

離
TRAD   SIMPLIFIED

This character with the definition:

leave, depart

Pinyin **lí** *and Frequency Rank* **418**

Contains these components:

☐ skull with a brain c 囟
2037, p. 447

☐ animal track r 内 2214, p. 485

With all these meanings & readings:

lí [離] **1** to leave   **2** to depart
3 to go away   **4** from

Contains **10 strokes** in the following order:

丶 亠 文 这 卤 卤 禸 离 离 离

When I saw traces in the snow change to large *animal tracks*, my *skull with a brain* knew that it was time to turn around and **leave** the forest!

2220

SIMP & TRAD

This character with the definition:

glazed tile

Pinyin **lí** *and Frequency Rank* **1894**

Contains **14 strokes** in the following order:

一 二 干 王 王 王⁻ 玙 玙 璃 琍 琍 璃 璃 璃

Contains these components:

☐ jade 玉 177, p. 48
◼ leave, depart 离 2219, p. 486

With all these meanings & readings:

lí [璃] **1** colored glaze **2** glass

Because of the economic downturn, the value of the *jade* business has fallen to nothing. As the taste for *jade left* the buying public, consumers turned to decorative **glazed tile**, which is a cheaper decorative piece.

2221

This component has the meaning:

child c

COMPONENT

And contains these subcomponents:

☐ cover 盖 1592, p. 354
◼ private r 厶 963, p. 220

As a **child**, I hid my toys in a *private* place under a *cover* to protect them from my mischievous younger brother.

2222

SIMP & TRAD

This character with the definition:

flow

Pinyin **liú** *and Frequency Rank* **396**

Contains **9 strokes** in the following order:

丶 亠 氵 氵 汸 浐 浐 浐 流 流

Contains these components:

☐ water r 氵 314, p. 80
☐ child c 云 2221, p. 487
◼ river 川 444, p. 107

With all these meanings & readings:

liú [流] **1** to flow **2** to spread **3** to circulate **4** to move

Because the *river* behind my house **flows** very slowly, I allow my *child* to wade into the shallow *water* along its edge.

2223

SIMP & TRAD

This character with the definition:

sparse, scattered

Pinyin **shū** *and Frequency Rank* **1897**

Contains **11 strokes** in the following order:

一 了 了 正 正 正 近 疋 疏 疏 疏

Contains these components:

◼ to correct, rectify 正 (altered) 193, p. 52
☐ child c 云 2221, p. 487
◼ river 川 444, p. 107

With all these meanings & readings:

shū [疏] **1** to dredge **2** to clear away obstruction **3** thin **4** sparse **5** scanty **6** distant (relation) **7** not close **8** to neglect **9** negligent **10** surname Shu **11** to present a memorial to the Emperor **12** commentary **13** annotation

Every Saturday, my neighbor spends hours teaching his only *child* the *correct* way to fish, even though he knows there are only a **sparse** number of fish in the *river*.

2224

TRAD   SIMPLIFIED

This character with the definition:

discard, abandon, give up

Pinyin **qì** *and Frequency Rank* **1105**

Contains **7 strokes** in the following order:

丶 亠 云 云 亖 弁 弃

Contains these components:

☐ child c 云 2221, p. 487
◼ action scaffolding c 廾 1751, p. 387

With all these meanings & readings:

qì [棄] **1** to abandon **2** to relinquish **3** to discard **4** ot throw away

The drug-addled mother is standing on top of the *scaffolding* and threatening to toss her *child* off of it if she doesn't get drug money. How could anyone **abandon** their children in such a depraved way?

2225

SIMP & TRAD

This character with the definition:

near midnight

Pinyin **hài** *and Frequency Rank* **3179**

Contains **6 strokes** in the following order:

` 一 亠 ナ 亥 亥

Contains these components:

■ child c 亠 2221, p. 487

□ man 人 537, p. 127

With all these meanings & readings:

hài [亥] **1** 12th earthly branch: 9-11 p.m., 10th solar month (7th November-6th December), year of the Boar

A young *man* knows that he is no longer a *child* when he is allowed to go to bed **near midnight**.

2226

刻

SIMP & TRAD

This character with the definition:

engrave, carve

Pinyin **kè** *and Frequency Rank* **618**

Contains **8 strokes** in the following order:

` 一 亠 ナ 亥 亥 刻 刻

Contains these components:

■ near midnight 亥 2225, p. 488

□ knife r 刂 169, p. 46

With all these meanings & readings:

kè [刻] **1** quarter (hour) **2** moment **3** to carve **4** to engrave **5** to cut **6** oppressive **7** (classifier for short time intervals)

As the policeman began his patrol *near midnight*, he found a gang member using a *knife* to **carve** evil symbols into a park bench.

2227

核
覈

TRAD SIMPLIFIED

This character with the definition:

nut, fruit pit

Pinyin **hé** *and Frequency Rank* **828**

Contains **10 strokes** in the following order:

一 十 才 木 木 朾 栌 栌 核 核

Contains these components:

■ tree 木 562, p. 133

■ near midnight 亥 2225, p. 488

With all these meanings & readings:

hé [核] **1** pit **2** stone **3** nucleus

hé [覈] **1** to investigate thoroughly

During the summer solstice every year, the tribe gathered *near midnight* to watch their leader carefully plant a **fruit pit**, hoping that it would grow into a *tree* that would serve to honor the gods of nature.

2228

该
該

TRAD SIMPLIFIED

This character with the definition:

should, ought to*

Pinyin **gāi** *and Frequency Rank* **319**

Contains **8 strokes** in the following order:

` 讠 讠 诤 诤 诼 诼 该

Contains these components:

■ speech r 讠 352, p. 88

■ near midnight 亥 2225, p. 488

With all these meanings & readings:

gāi [該] **1** should **2** ought to **3** most likely **4** to deserve **5** to owe **6** to be sb's turn to do sth **7** that **8** the above-mentioned

Polite people know that they **should** lower the sound of their *speech near midnight*—so as not to disturb those who may already be asleep.

2229

孩
該

TRAD SIMPLIFIED

This character with the definition:

child*

Pinyin **hái** *and Frequency Rank* **533**

Contains **9 strokes** in the following order:

フ 了 孑 孑 孖 孖 孩 孩 孩

Contains these components:

■ child 童 694, p. 162

■ near midnight 亥 2225, p. 488

With all these meanings & readings:

hái [孩] **1** child

When your young *child* wakes you up *near midnight*, you need to respond as an adult parent and restrain your 'inner **child**' from becoming cranky and impatient.

2230

This character with the definition:

rear, raise

Pinyin **yù** *and Frequency Rank* **609**

SIMP & TRAD   Contains **7 strokes** in the following order:

丶 一 亠 云 亠 育 育 育

Contains these components:

☐ child c 𠫓 2221, p.487
■ meat 肉 (altered) 753, p.175

With all these meanings & readings:

yù [育] **1** nourish **2** to rear

Modern parents disagree on the best way to **raise** their children. For instance, the amount of *meat*, if any, to be included in a *child's* diet is often a topic of contention.

2231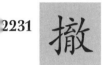

This character with the definition:

remove, take away, withdraw

Pinyin **chè** *and Frequency Rank* **1270**

SIMP & TRAD   Contains **15 strokes** in the following order:

一 亅 扌 扩 护 护 护 护 拹 拹 拹 撝 撤 撤 撤

Contains these components:

▯ hand r 扌 25, p.15
▯ rear, raise 育 2230, p.489
▯ to strike r 攵 2098, p.461

With all these meanings & readings:

chè [撤] **1** to remove **2** to take away **3** to withdraw

The ancient Confucian system of child *raising* advised plenty of *corporal punishment*. But such a system guaranteed the **removal** of any love for one's family.

2232

This component has the meaning:

show r

COMPONENT

And contains these subcomponents:

■ show, indicate 示 (altered) 1265, p.283

This component is notable because none of its strokes **show** any balance or symmetry with the others.

2233

This character with the definition:

ancestor

Pinyin **zǔ** *and Frequency Rank* **1025**

SIMP & TRAD   Contains **10 strokes** in the following order:

丶 ㇇ 衤 礻 礻 礻 袒 祖 祖 祖

Contains these components:

▯ show r 礻 2232, p.489
▯ moreover 且 84, p.28

With all these meanings & readings:

zǔ [祖] **1** ancestor **2** forefather **3** grandparents **4** surname Zu

Many Asians *show* respect to their **ancestors** by visiting their graves on certain holidays. *Moreover*, they keep small shrines in their homes to honor them every day.

2234

This character with the definition:

society, organization

Pinyin **shè** *and Frequency Rank* **270**

SIMP & TRAD   Contains **8 strokes** in the following order:

丶 ㇇ 衤 礻 礻 礻 社 社

Contains these components:

▯ show r 礻 2232, p.489
▯ earth, soil 土 9, p.11

With all these meanings & readings:

shè [社] **1** society **2** group

A mature **society** has cities that are so congested with concrete that the *earth* barely *shows* between the buildings.

Unit 92

2235

SIMP & TRAD

This character with the definition:

god, divinity

Pinyin **shén** *and Frequency Rank* **227**

Contains **10 strokes** in the following order:

丶 ㇇ 礻 礻 礻 衬 神 袖 袖 神

Contains these components:

□ show r 礻 2232, p. 489

□ express 申 57, p. 22

With all these meanings & readings:

shén [神] **1** God **2** unusual **3** mysterious **4** soul **5** spirit **6** divine essence **7** lively **8** spiritual being **9** m 个[個][gè] **10** abbreviation of 神舟[shén zhōu]

Mankind has historically looked to a **divinity** to *show* them how to travel an honorable path through life and to *express* spiritual truths.

2236

SIMP & TRAD

This character with the definition:

good fortune

Pinyin **fú** *and Frequency Rank* **683**

Contains **14 strokes** in the following order:

丶 ㇇ 礻 礻 礻 衬 衬 衬 福 福 福 福

Contains these components:

□ show r 礻 2232, p. 489

□ size range c 畐 162, p. 45

With all these meanings & readings:

fú [福] **1** good fortune **2** happiness **3** luck **4** abbr for Fujian 福建 province **5** surname Fu

The ancient Chinese believed that a man *showed* his **good fortune** by having a wide *size range* of male children.

2237

视

TRAD

SIMPLIFIED

This character with the definition:

regard, look at

Pinyin **shì** *and Frequency Rank* **438**

Contains **8 strokes** in the following order:

丶 ㇇ 礻 礻 礻 衬 视 视

Contains these components:

□ show r 礻 2232, p. 489

□ see 见 307, p. 78

With all these meanings & readings:

shì [视] **1** to look at **2** to regard **3** to inspect

In order to sell your house, you must be prepared to *show* its interior so that potential buyers can **look at** every room and *see* its condition.

2238

SIMP & TRAD

This character with the definition:

express good wishes

Pinyin **zhù** *and Frequency Rank* **1651**

Contains **10 strokes** in the following order:

丶 ㇇ 礻 礻 礻 衬 衬 祝 祝

Contains these components:

□ show r 礻 2232, p. 489

□ elder brother* 兄 293, p. 75

With all these meanings & readings:

zhù [祝] **1** invoke **2** pray to **3** wish **4** to express good wishes **5** surname Zhu

To *show* my deep affection for my *elder brother* at his wedding celebration, I stood up during my speech so that all the guests could hear me **express good wishes** to him and his wife and their future together.

2239

SIMP & TRAD

This character with the definition:

propitious

Pinyin **xiáng** *and Frequency Rank* **1674**

Contains **11 strokes** in the following order:

丶 ㇇ 礻 礻 礻 衤 衤 衬 祥 祥 祥

Contains these components:

□ show r 礻 2232, p. 489

□ sheep 羊 1486, p. 329

With all these meanings & readings:

xiáng [祥] **1** auspicious **2** propitious

After we bought our *sheep* farm, Nature *showed* us a **propitious** sign that our pastures would be covered with lush green grass by sending three days of rain.

2240

祸

TRAD   SIMPLIFIED

This character with the definition:

misfortune, disaster

Pinyin **huò**   *and Frequency Rank* **1870**

Contains **11 strokes** in the following order:

丶 ㇇ 衤 衤 衤 衤 衤 祸 祸 祸 祸

Contains these components:

- show r 衤 2232, p. 489
- mouth 口 37, p. 17
- inside* 内 785, p. 182

With all these meanings & readings:

huò [祸] **1** disaster

The tall stranger looks just like any regular guy. But as you get to know him, he (symbolized by the *mouth*) will *show* you his *inner*, darker self, which has been plagued by **misfortune**.

2241

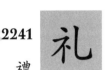

禮

TRAD   SIMPLIFIED

This character with the definition:

ceremony, rite

Pinyin **lǐ**   *and Frequency Rank* **926**

Contains **5 strokes** in the following order:

 丶 ㇇ 衤 礼

Contains these components:

- show r 衤 2232, p. 489
- mineshaft c 乚 122, p. 36

With all these meanings & readings:

lǐ [禮] **1** gift **2** propriety **3** rite **4** m 份[fèn]

In ancient times, recruits to an army were ceremonially led to the edge of a deep *mineshaft* where they **ritually** threw their civilian clothes away to *show* their allegiance to their king and country! This **ceremony**, a rite of passage, marked the transformation from civilian to soldier.

2242

This component has the meaning:

stairs c

COMPONENT

Stairs are formed by vertical steps that resemble the rectangles in this component.

2243

SIMP & TRAD

This character with the definition:

chase, pursue

Pinyin **zhuī**   *and Frequency Rank* **768**

Contains **9 strokes** in the following order:

丿 亻 ㇉ 阝 阝 阝 追 追 追

Contains these components:

- move forward r ⻍ 2144, p. 470
- stairs c 阝 2242, p. 491
- dab r 丶 176, p. 48

With all these meanings & readings:

zhuī [追] **1** to pursue (a problem) **2** to chase

I did not realize that my son had left our back door open until I saw our cat *move forward* toward the *stairs* leading to the open door. It was only a *few* feet from running outside when I **chased** it back inside and closed the door.

2244

SIMP & TRAD

This character with the definition:

government official

Pinyin **guān**   *and Frequency Rank* **432**

Contains **8 strokes** in the following order:

丶 丷 宀 宀 官 官 官 官

Contains these components:

- roof r 宀 271, p. 70
- stairs c 阝 2242, p. 491

With all these meanings & readings:

guān [官] **1** official **2** government **3** organ of body **4** m 个[個][gè]

For security reasons, only a few **government officials** are granted access to the *stairs* that lead to the *roof* of City Hall.

2245

This character with the definition:

manage, control

Pinyin **guǎn** *and Frequency Rank* **252**

SIMP & TRAD   Contains **14 strokes** in the following order:

ノ ゝ ⺀ ⺀' ⺀⺀ ⺀⺀ ⺀⺀ ⺀⺀ 笃 笃 管 管 管 管

Contains these components:

☐ bamboo r ⺮ 264, p.68
☐ government official 官 2244, p.491

With all these meanings & readings:

guǎn [管] **1** to take care (of) **2** to control **3** to manage **4** to be in charge of **5** to look after **6** to run **7** tube **8** pipe **9** surname Guan

To show that he was in complete **control** of our town, the new *government official* ordered a Town Jail to be built out of tall *bamboo* stalks.

2246

館
TRAD SIMPLIFIED

This character with the definition:

guest accommodation

Pinyin **guǎn** *and Frequency Rank* **1011**

Contains **11 strokes** in the following order:

ノ ⺀ ⻡ ⻡ ⻡ ⻡ 饣 饣 馆 馆 馆

Contains these components:

☐ eat r 饣 2038, p.447
☐ government official 官 2244, p.491

With all these meanings & readings:

guǎn [館] **1** building **2** shop **3** term for certain service establishments **4** embassy or consulate **5** m 家[jiā]

When the new *government official* arrived in our town, he ordered us to provide him and his family with **guest accommodations** and food to *eat* while his immense house was being built.

2247

This character with the definition:

marsh grass

Pinyin **xuē** *and Frequency Rank* **1953**

SIMP & TRAD   Contains **16 strokes** in the following order:

一 十 艹 艹 芦 芦 芦 芦 莳 莳 莳 薛 薛 薛 薛 薛

Contains these components:

☐ grass r ⺾ 87, p.29
☐ dab r 丶 176, p.48
☐ stairs c 阝 (altered) 2242, p.491
☐ hardworking 辛 684, p.160

With all these meanings & readings:

xuē [薛] **1** surname Xue **2** wormwood

Marsh grass is collected for the special minerals it contains. It must be stored high up, up a flight of *stairs* so the *little* marsh creatures fall down as the *grass* dries. The high water content makes the **marsh grass** very heavy and ensures that this chore is given only to the most *hardworking* of laborers.

2248

This character with the definition:

send, dispatch

Pinyin **qiǎn** *and Frequency Rank* **1780**

SIMP & TRAD   Contains **13 strokes** in the following order:

丶 ⼀ 口 中 虫 电 串 串 串 串 遣 遣 遣

Contains these components:

☐ move forward r 辶 2144, p.470
☐ middle 中 38, p.18
☐ one 一 1, p.10
☐ stairs c 阝 2242, p.491

With all these meanings & readings:

qiǎn [遣] **1** dispatch

Get out of my way! I need to *move forward* and up the *stair steps* of the *central* post office to **send** *one* letter before it closes.

2249

This component has the meaning:

rundown c

COMPONENT

And contains these subcomponents:

☐ stairs c 阝 (altered) 2242, p.491
☐ ancient bamboo spear 殳 (altered) 1913, p.420

Imagine this character as a **rundown** property: the *stair steps* are missing some parts, and the top of the *ancient bamboo spear* has been turned around.

2250

假

SIMP & TRAD

This character with the definition:

holiday, vacation

Pinyin **jià** *and Frequency Rank* **636**

Contains **11 strokes** in the following order:

ノ 亻 亻 亻 但 俨 俨 假 假 假 假

Contains these components:

■ man r 亻 1156, p. 260
■ rundown c 叚 2249, p. 492

With all these meanings & readings:

jià [假] **1** fake **2** false **3** artificial **4** to borrow **5** if **6** suppose
jià [假] **1** vacation

The *man* was feeling so *rundown* that he knew it was time for a **vacation**.

2251

万

COMPONENT

This component has the meaning:

obstacle c

And contains these subcomponents:

□ one 一 1, p. 10
■ wrap r 勹 (altered) 364, p. 90

If you blow against a *horizontal surface*, the line of breath will *wrap* around itself but the surface acts as an **obstacle** that prevents the air from penetrating through it.

2252

亏

虧
TRAD   SIMPLIFIED

This character with the definition:

unfair treatment

Pinyin **kuī** *and Frequency Rank* **1738**

Contains **3 strokes** in the following order:

一 二 亏

Contains these components:

□ one 一 1, p. 10
■ obstacle c 万 2251, p. 493

With all these meanings & readings:

kuī [虧] **1** deficiency **2** deficit **3** luckily

Tests are the *one obstacle* I can't surmount. I feel that judging me only by my test-taking abilities results in **unfair treatment**.

2253

巧

SIMP & TRAD

This character with the definition:

ingenious

Pinyin **qiǎo** *and Frequency Rank* **1219**

Contains **5 strokes** in the following order:

一 丁 工 工 巧

Contains these components:

■ labor, work 工 12, p. 12
■ obstacle c 万 2251, p. 493

With all these meanings & readings:

qiǎo [巧] **1** opportunely **2** coincidentally **3** as it happens **4** skillful **5** timely

An **ingenious** craftsman *works* hard to design tools to make it easier to overcome *obstacles*.

2254

号

號
TRAD   SIMPLIFIED

This character with the definition:

number (in a series)

Pinyin **hào** *and Frequency Rank* **487**

Contains **5 strokes** in the following order:

丿 口 口 吕 号

Contains these components:

□ mouth 口 37, p. 17
■ obstacle c 万 2251, p. 493

With all these meanings & readings:

háo [號] **1** roar **2** cry **3** m 个 [個][gè]
hào [號] **1** day of a month **2** (suffix used after) name of a ship **3** (ordinal) number

The beast's howl, issuing angrily from its *mouth*, is provoked by the large **number** of *obstacles*, a **series** really, that the villagers have constructed to protect themselves.

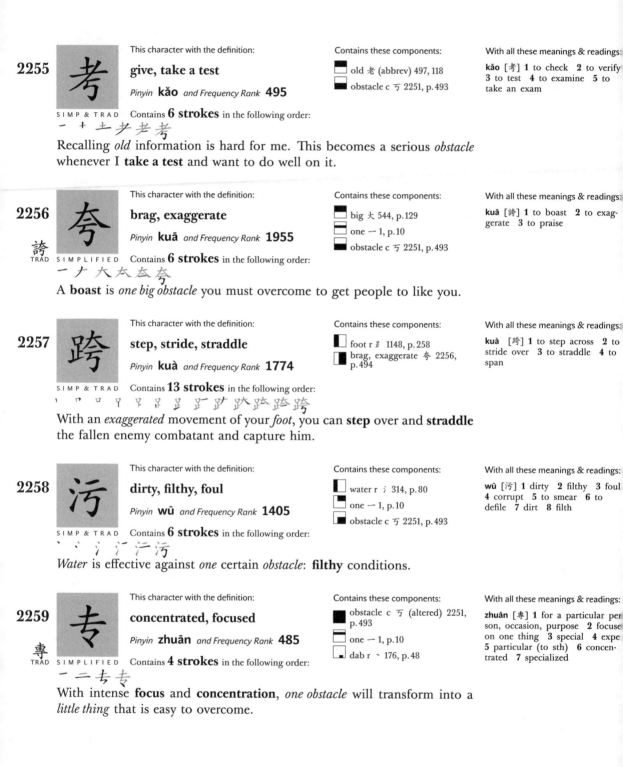

2255

考

SIMP & TRAD

This character with the definition:

give, take a test

Pinyin **kǎo** *and Frequency Rank* **495**

Contains **6 strokes** in the following order:

一 十 土 耂 老 考

Contains these components:

old 老 (abbrev) 497, 118

obstacle c 丂 2251, p.493

With all these meanings & readings:

kǎo [考] **1** to check **2** to verify **3** to test **4** to examine **5** to take an exam

Recalling *old* information is hard for me. This becomes a serious *obstacle* whenever I **take a test** and want to do well on it.

2256

夸

誇
TRAD   SIMPLIFIED

This character with the definition:

brag, exaggerate

Pinyin **kuā** *and Frequency Rank* **1955**

Contains **6 strokes** in the following order:

一 ナ 大 太 夻 夸

Contains these components:

big 大 544, p.129

one 一 1, p.10

obstacle c 丂 2251, p.493

With all these meanings & readings:

kuā [誇] **1** to boast **2** to exaggerate **3** to praise

A **boast** is *one big obstacle* you must overcome to get people to like you.

2257

跨

SIMP & TRAD

This character with the definition:

step, stride, straddle

Pinyin **kuà** *and Frequency Rank* **1774**

Contains **13 strokes** in the following order:

丨 口 口 𝆐 𝆑 𝆒 足 𝆓 𝆔 趵 趺 跨 跨

Contains these components:

foot r ⻊ 1148, p.258

brag, exaggerate 夸 2256, p.494

With all these meanings & readings:

kuà [跨] **1** to step across **2** to stride over **3** to straddle **4** to span

With an *exaggerated* movement of your *foot*, you can **step** over and **straddle** the fallen enemy combatant and capture him.

2258

污

SIMP & TRAD

This character with the definition:

dirty, filthy, foul

Pinyin **wū** *and Frequency Rank* **1405**

Contains **6 strokes** in the following order:

丶 丶 氵 汀 汚 污

Contains these components:

water r 氵 314, p.80

one 一 1, p.10

obstacle c 丂 2251, p.493

With all these meanings & readings:

wū [污] **1** dirty **2** filthy **3** foul **4** corrupt **5** to smear **6** to defile **7** dirt **8** filth

Water is effective against *one* certain *obstacle*: **filthy** conditions.

2259

专

專
TRAD   SIMPLIFIED

This character with the definition:

concentrated, focused

Pinyin **zhuān** *and Frequency Rank* **485**

Contains **4 strokes** in the following order:

一 二 专 专

Contains these components:

obstacle c 丂 (altered) 2251, p.493

one 一 1, p.10

dab r 丶 176, p.48

With all these meanings & readings:

zhuān [專] **1** for a particular person, occasion, purpose **2** focused on one thing **3** special **4** expe 5 particular (to sth) **6** concentrated **7** specialized

With intense **focus** and **concentration**, *one obstacle* will transform into a *little thing* that is easy to overcome.

Unit 93

260

转

转 TRAD SIMPLIFIED

This character with the definition:

turn, shift, change

Pinyin **zhuǎn** *and Frequency Rank* **376**

Contains **8 strokes** in the following order:

一 � 车 车 车 轩 轩 转 转

Contains these components:

■ car 车 1291, p. 289

□ concentrated, focused 专 2259, p. 494

With all these meanings & readings:

zhuǎn [转] **1** to convey **2** to forward (mail) **3** to transfer **4** to turn **5** to shift
zhuàn [转] **1** to revolve **2** to turn **3** to circle about **4** to walk about

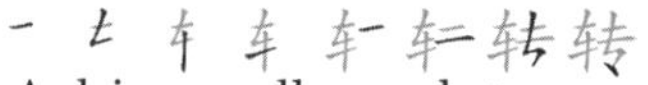

A driver really needs to *concentrate* on controlling the motion of a *car* when making a sharp **turn** on a wet road.

261

传

傳 TRAD SIMPLIFIED

This character with the definition:

pass on, impart

Pinyin **chuán** *and Frequency Rank* **332**

Contains **6 strokes** in the following order:

丿 亻 仁 仨 传 传

Contains these components:

■ man r 亻 1156, p. 260

□ concentrated, focused 专 2259, p. 494

With all these meanings & readings:

chuán [傳] **1** to pass on **2** to spread **3** to transmit **4** to infect **5** to transfer **6** to circulate **7** to conduct (electricity)
zhuàn [傳] **1** biography **2** historical narrative **3** commentaries **4** relay station

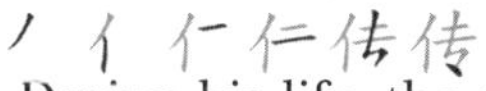

During his life, the *man* was so *focused* on the principles of his craft that he made sure to **impart** them to his children and disciples.

262

This component has the meaning:

plank r

COMPONENT

Visualize the vertical stroke of this character as the trunk of a tree (panel 562) which had half of its branches removed in order to make **planks** of wood. Therefore, only the branches on its left side remain.

263

状

狀 TRAD SIMPLIFIED

This character with the definition:

form, appearance

Pinyin **zhuàng** *and Frequency Rank* **624**

Contains **7 strokes** in the following order:

丶 冫 爿 爿 状 状 状

Contains these components:

■ plank r 爿 2262, p. 495

□ dog 犬 673, p. 158

With all these meanings & readings:

zhuàng [狀] **1** accusation **2** suit **3** state **4** condition **5** strong **6** great **7** -shaped

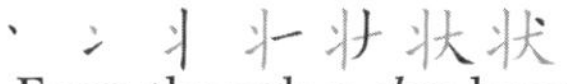

Even though a *dog* house may have the **appearance** of a solid structure, it is usually made from thin *planks* of wood.

264

壮

壯 TRAD SIMPLIFIED

This character with the definition:

strong, powerful

Pinyin **zhuàng** *and Frequency Rank* **1432**

Contains **6 strokes** in the following order:

丶 冫 爿 爿 壮 壮

Contains these components:

■ plank r 爿 2262, p. 495

□ knight 士 8, p. 11

With all these meanings & readings:

zhuàng [壯] **1** to strengthen **2** strong **3** robust **4** Zhuang ethnic group of Guangxi, the PRC's second most numerous ethnic group **5** Zhuang: Bouxcuengh

A *knight* can use a *plank* as a weapon because he's **strong** and **powerful**.

2265

TRAD SIMPLIFIED

This character with the definition:

dress up

Pinyin **zhuāng** *and Frequency Rank* **467**

Contains **12 strokes** in the following order:

丶　亠　丬　丬　壮　壮　壮　壮　娄　娄　装　装

Contains these components:

■ strong, powerful 壮 2264, p. 495

■ clothing 衣 1068, p. 242

With all these meanings & readings:

zhuāng [裝] **1** adornment **2** to adorn **3** dress **4** clothing **5** costume (of an actor in a play) **6** to play a role **7** to pretend **8** to install **9** to fix **10** to wrap (sth in a bag) **11** to load **12** to pack

You **dress up** in fine *clothing* to make a *strong* and *powerful* impression.

2266

This component has the meaning:

back to back r

COMPONENT

And contains these subcomponents:

■ stop! 止 (abbrev) 190, 52

■ stop! 止 (abbrev) 190, 52

Here are two people, resting **back to back** position with one another. It is a particularly comfortable position and *stops* each person from sliding down. A second look at this component shows two curved spines touching in a relaxed **back to back** posture.

2267

SIMP & TRAD

This character with the definition:

scale, climb

Pinyin **dēng** *and Frequency Rank* **817**

Contains **12 strokes** in the following order:

フ　マ　ㄗ　ㄗ　癶　癶　癶　登　登　登　登　登

Contains these components:

■ back to back r 癶 (altered) 2266, p. 496

■ bean 豆 1597, p. 355

With all these meanings & readings:

dēng [登] **1** scale **2** climb **3** ascend **4** mount **5** go up **6** register **7** note **8** to publish **9** to issue **10** to record

It's usually pretty easy to **climb** atop a hill of *beans*, for it fits nicely in the open space and offers a great view for my best friend and I when we sit *back to back*.

2268

This component has the meaning:

speak up! c

COMPONENT

As someone cups his ear to hear what his buddy is saying, he's thinking: "**Speak up**"!

2269

TRAD SIMPLIFIED

This character with the definition:

to fix or make correct

Pinyin **jiū** *and Frequency Rank* **1723**

Contains **5 strokes** in the following order:

乚　幺　纟　纠　纠

Contains these components:

■ silk r 纟 1037, p. 235

■ speak up! c 丩 2268, p. 496

With all these meanings & readings:

jiū [糾] **1** gather together **2** to investigate **3** to entangle **4** to correct, rectify

Fancy officials, all dressed up in their *silk* gowns, can intimidate ordinary citizens. However, one honest soul has discovered an error in the proclamation and decides to *speak up* in an effort to **fix** the situation for everyone.

2270 钅

This component has the meaning:

gold r

COMPONENT

And contains these subcomponents:

gold 金 (altered) 1550, p. 342

Take the '*gold*' character (panel 1550) and squeeze hard to derive this component.

2271 钻 鑽 TRAD SIMPLIFIED

This character with the definition:

drill, bore

Pinyin **zuān** *and Frequency Rank* **1724**

Contains **10 strokes** in the following order:

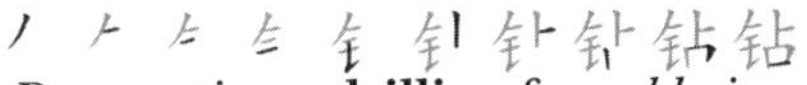

Contains these components:

gold r 钅 2270, p. 497

practice divination 占 188, p. 51

With all these meanings & readings:

zuān [鑽] **1** to drill **2** to bore **3** to get into **4** to make one's way into **5** to enter (a hole) **6** to thread one's way through **7** to study intensively **8** to dig into **9** to curry favor for personal gain

zuàn [鑽] **1** an auger **2** diamond

Prospecting—**drilling** for *gold*—is much like *practicing divination*. You hope for the best, but you never know what you'll find.

2272 铜 銅 TRAD SIMPLIFIED

This character with the definition:

copper

Pinyin **tóng** *and Frequency Rank* **1772**

Contains **11 strokes** in the following order:

Contains these components:

gold r 钅 2270, p. 497

same, similar 同 116, p. 35

With all these meanings & readings:

tóng [銅] **1** copper (chemistry) **2** see also 红铜[紅銅][hóng tóng] **3** m 块[塊][kuài]

Many metals—especially when newly minted and untouched by tarnish—are so bright and shiny that they appear *similar* to *gold*. **Copper**, a prominent metal, takes on this quality.

2273 铺 鋪 舖 TRAD SIMPLIFIED

This character with the definition:

spread, extend

Pinyin **pū** *and Frequency Rank* **1613**

Contains **12 strokes** in the following order:

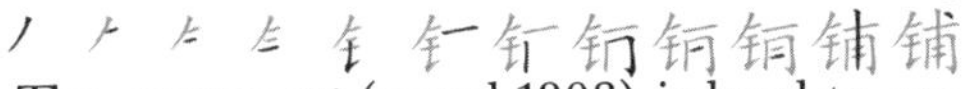

Contains these components:

gold r 钅 2270, p. 497

just now, only 甫 1803, p. 398

With all these meanings & readings:

pù [舖] **1** a store

pū [鋪] **1** to spread

pù [鋪] **1** a bed **2** a store

The *monument* (panel 1803) is hard to see. They *just* covered it in *gold leaf*, which **extends** the area of visibility many times over.

2274 铅 鉛 TRAD SIMPLIFIED

This character with the definition:

lead (metal)

Pinyin **qiān** *and Frequency Rank* **2641**

Contains **10 strokes** in the following order:

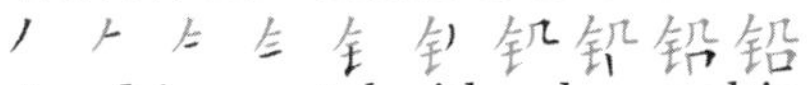

Contains these components:

gold r 钅 2270, p. 497

how much, how many 几 896, p. 204

mouth 口 37, p. 17

With all these meanings & readings:

qiān [鉛] **1** lead (chemistry)

Lead is a *metal* with a low melting point. That's why you get *several* of those *mouth*-shaped lumps when you drop the **lead** solder on a hot stove.

2275

铁

鐵
TRAD   SIMPLIFIED

This character with the definition:

iron

Pinyin **tiě** *and Frequency Rank* **779**

Contains **10 strokes** in the following order:

丿 丿 𠂉 𠂉 钅 钅 钅 钅 铁 铁

Contains these components:

gold r 钅 2270, p.497

lose 失 721, p.169

With all these meanings & readings:

tiě [鐵] **1** iron (chemistry)

The *gold* bars somehow became spoiled, as if they were living things. Gradually, they *lost* their color—and their value depreciated. Now, they're just **iron** ingots.

2276

钟

鐘
TRAD   SIMPLIFIED

This character with the definition:

clock

Pinyin **zhōng** *and Frequency Rank* **905**

Contains **9 strokes** in the following order:

丿 丿 𠂉 𠂉 钅 钅 钟 钟 钟

Contains these components:

gold r 钅 2270, p.497

middle 中 38, p.18

With all these meanings & readings:

zhōng [鐘] **1** clock **2** o'clock **3** time as measured in hours and minutes **4** bell **5** surname Zhong **6** m 架[jià], 座[zuò]

The *metal* item that was of central importance in ancient China was the **bell**, which was located in the *middle* of the town square. It sounded the **time**, tolled for important events, and represented authority and prosperity.

2277

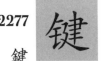

键

鍵
TRAD   SIMPLIFIED

This character with the definition:

key (lock)

Pinyin **jiàn** *and Frequency Rank* **1471**

Contains **13 strokes** in the following order:

丿 丿 𠂉 𠂉 钅 钅 钅 钅 钅 键 键 键 键

Contains these components:

gold r 钅 2270, p.497

establish, set up* 建 2201, p.483

With all these meanings & readings:

jiàn [鍵] **1** (door lock) key **2** ke (on piano or keyboard)

Most banks *set up* complex security procedures that require more than one **key** in order to gain access to the *gold deposit*.

2278

𭥾

This component has the meaning:

great idea! c

COMPONENT

You can always tell when characters in an animated cartoon have a brilliant idea, because a simulated light bulb flashes, showing rays emanating from the top of their head. The short strokes on top are the light rays, and the smooth cover is the top of a cartoon skull.

2279

觉

覺
TRAD   SIMPLIFIED

This character with the definition:

think

Pinyin **jué** *and Frequency Rank* **327**

Contains **9 strokes** in the following order:

丶 丷 丷 𭥾 𭥾 觉 觉 觉 觉

Contains these components:

great idea! c 𭥾 2278, p.498

see 见 307, p.78

With all these meanings & readings:

jiào [覺] **1** a nap **2** a sleep **3** n 场[場][cháng]
jué [覺] **1** feel **2** find that **3** thinking **4** awake **5** aware

The result of hard **thinking** is a *great idea*, which allows us to *see* our way through to a clear solution.

280

學
TRAD SIMPLIFIED

This character with the definition:

to study

Pinyin **xué** *and Frequency Rank* **66**

Contains **8 strokes** in the following order:

丶 ﹀ ﹀ ﹀ ﹀ 学 学 学

Contains these components:

☐ great idea! c ﹀ 2278, p. 498

■ son, child 子 24, p. 15

With all these meanings & readings:

xué [學] **1** learn **2** study **3** science **4** -ology

The *child*'s head is like an open tap from which *great ideas* flow non-stop. That's the fruit of hard **study**.

Character Frequencies *Postlude*

The earliest survey I know of Chinese character frequencies was made in 1928. According to it, 2000 distinct characters accounted for 96.5% of the text selections in this study, which was comprised of over 900,000 characters. Most recently, in an analysis of over 87 million characters of non-technical material, Jun Da basically reproduced this result—he found that 2000 characters continued to account for 96.5% of text drawn from modern fiction and non-fiction. [Please refer to *Proceedings of the Fourth International Conference on New Technologies in Teaching and Learning Chinese* (edited by Pu Zhang *et. al.*), pp. 501-11, 2004. (Beijing: Tsinghua University Press) for further details.] Moreover, there were only 8,435 distinct characters in this large sample—a far cry from the "tens of thousands" that uninformed 'sources' claim need be learned. This scholar has made his list of character frequencies available for downloading (from lingua.mtsu.edu/chinese-computing), and it is the first 2000 or so of these characters with which we concern ourselves in these pages. I am grateful to this researcher for allowing me to use his results.

INDICES

This guide contains three indices. The first, the **Component Index** below, lists all 83 components that we use in the construction of characters. Components are listed alphabetically, with the panel and page number of their first appearance. No component can be used independently, and there are two varieties. Those identified with the suffix 'r' are those called radicals. Those with the 'c' suffix are components identified for the purposes of implementing the method of this book.

The second, the **Definition Index**, is an alphabetical list of all panel headings, which are definitions for their characters. Each entry also provides the character, its pinyin transcription, and the panel and page numbers.

Finally, the third index is the **Pinyin Index**, in which entries are grouped by pinyin pronunciation; the pinyin entry heading tells you how many characters fall under the heading. Each entry contains the character's name, the character itself, and its panel and page numbers.

COMPONENT INDEX

DEFINITION INDEX

PINYIN INDEX

常 often, 1570, p.347
长 long, length, 920, p.209
偿 compensate, repay, 1572, p.347
尝 taste, 1571, p.347
chǎng × 2 entries
  厂 factory, 425, p.103
  场 gathering place, field, 464, p.111
chàng × 1 entry
  唱 sing, 69, p.25
chāo × 1 entry
  超 overtake, surpass, super-, 735, p.172
cháo × 2 entries
  朝 dynasty, 1790, p.396
  潮 tide, current, 1791, p.396
chǎo × 1 entry
  吵 quarrel, make noise, 1325, p.296
chē × 1 entry
  车 car, 1291, p.289
chě × 1 entry
  扯 pull, 192, p.52
chè × 2 entries
  撤 remove, take away, withdraw, 2231, p.489
  彻 thoroughly, complete, 1258, p.280
chén × 7 entries
  晨 morning*, 1976, p.434
  尘 dust, dirt, 1332, p.297
  沉 submerge, lower, 914, p.208
  辰 time, day, occasion, 1972, p.433
  陈 put on display, 1289, p.288
  臣 subject of a ruler, 154, p.43
  沈 to sink, 1726, p.382
chèn × 1 entry
  趁 take advantage of, 1615, p.360
chēng × 1 entry
  称 to nickname, 1338, p.298
chéng × 9 entries
  呈 appear, 48, p.20
  诚 sincere, 660, p.156
  程 rule, order, 596, p.141
  成 become, turn into, 657, p.155
  承 carry, hold, 323, p.82
  惩 punish, discipline, 1253, p.279
  盛 dish out, ladle, 659, p.155
  乘 multiply, ride, 602, p.142
  城 city wall, wall, 658, p.155
chī × 1 entry
  吃 eat, 837, p.192
chí × 3 entries
  持 control, handle (under duress), 221, p.59
  迟 late, tardy, 2161, p.474
  池 pool, pond, 332, p.84
chǐ × 2 entries
  齿 tooth, 543, p.128
  尺 ruler (length), 507, p.120
chì × 4 entries
  敕 imperial edict, 2118, p.465
  斥 scold, reprimand, 408, p.99
  赤 red, be flushed, 843, p.193
  啻 not only, 697, p.163
chōng × 2 entries
  冲 rinse, flush, wash away, 350, p.88
  充 ample, sufficient, 996, p.227
chóng × 2 entries
  崇 sublime, 1270, p.284
  虫 insect, 1016, p.231
chōu × 1 entry
  抽 take out, 59, p.22
chóu × 3 entries
  愁 worry about, 1522, p.336
  筹 tally, counter, 1677, p.372
  仇 hatred, 1233, p.275
chǒu × 1 entry
  丑 clown, 33, p.17
chū × 2 entries
  初 at first, 1080, p.245
  出 exit, 158, p.43
chú × 2 entries
  除 remove, eliminate, 1278, p.285
  刍 hay for fodder, 873, p.199
chǔ × 4 entries
  处 get along with sb, 2078, p.456
  础 base, foundation*, 525, p.125
  储 store up, save, 1245, p.277
  楚 clear, 738, p.172
chù × 2 entries
  畜 livestock, 1006, p.229
  触 touch, contact, 1817, p.401
chuān × 2 entries
  川 river, 444, p.107
  穿 penetrate, pierce, 1355, p.302
chuán × 2 entries
  传 pass on, impart, 2261, p.495

船 nautical vessel, 900, p.205
chuǎn × 2 entries
  舛 error, 2035, p.447
  喘 gasp for breath, 82, p.27
chuàn × 1 entry
  串 strung together, 51, p.21
chuāng × 1 entry
  窗 window, 2051, p.450
chuáng × 1 entry
  床 bed, 619, p.147
chuàng × 1 entry
  创 initiate, inaugurate, 850, p.195
chuī × 1 entry
  吹 blow, puff, 745, p.174
chuí × 1 entry
  垂 droop, 781, p.181
chūn × 1 entry
  春 spring (season), 1672, p.371
chún × 2 entries
  唇 lip, 1977, p.434
  纯 pure, unmixed, 1044, p.237
cí × 5 entries
  茨 thatch, 750, p.175
  磁 magnetism, 1005, p.229
  词 word, term, 356, p.89
  慈 compassionate, kind, 1115, p.252
  辞 diction, 778, p.180
cǐ × 1 entry
  此 this, 196, p.53
cì × 2 entries
  刺 thorn, splinter, 592, p.140
  次 time, occurrence, 748, p.174
cōng × 2 entries
  匆 hasty, 925, p.210
  聪 intelligent, 1582, p.349
cóng × 2 entries
  从 from, 860, p.197
  丛 cluster, 861, p.197
còu × 1 entry
  凑 assemble, 1669, p.370
cū × 1 entry
  粗 coarse, 1536, p.339
cù × 1 entry
  促 promote, urge, 1177, p.264
cuī × 2 entries
  崔 lofty, 1208, p.270
  催 to urge*, 1209, p.270
cuì × 2 entries
  脆 fragile, brittle, 835, p.192
  粹 pure*, unmixed*, 1542, p.340
cūn × 1 entry
  村 hamlet, 577, p.136
cún × 1 entry
  存 store, preserve, 453, p.108
cùn × 1 entry
  寸 inch, 216, p.58
cuò × 2 entries
  措 arrange, 1624, p.361
  错 wrong, mistaken, 1628, p.362
dā × 1 entry
  搭 build, 1686, p.374
dá × 2 entries
  答 answer, 1683, p.373
  达 attain, reach, 2171, p.476
dǎ × 1 entry
  打 hit, 27, p.16
dà × 1 entry
  大 big, 544, p.129
dāi × 2 entries
  呆 dull-witted, 566, p.134
  待 stay, 1254, p.279
dǎi × 1 entry
  歹 evil, vicious, 881, p.201
dài × 5 entries
  带 band, belt, 270, p.70
  袋 pouch, bag, pocket, 1222, p.273
  戴 wear, put on (clothes), 1756, p.388
  代 take the place of, 1221, p.273
  贷 loan, borrow, 1443, p.319
dān × 3 entries
  担 undertake, 73, p.25
  单 single, sole, 1586, p.353
  丹 red, cinnabar, 1770, p.391
dǎn × 1 entry
  胆 bravery, audacity, 1831, p.404
dàn × 5 entries
  旦 dawn, 70, p.25
  诞 birth, birthday, 2209, p.484
  蛋 egg, 1018, p.231
  但 but, 186, p.262
  淡 bland, weak, 1524, p.336
dāng × 1 entry

当 work as, become, 1333, p.297
dǎng × 2 entries
  党 political party, 1574, p.347
  挡 ward off, block, 1334, p.297
dàng × 2 entries
  荡 swing, shake, wash away, 467, p.112
  档 file, archive, 1335, p.298
dāo × 1 entry
  刀 knife, 469, p.112
dǎo × 3 entries
  导 transmit, guide, 224, p.60
  岛 island, 395, p.97
  倒 topple, fall over, 1183, p.265
dào × 3 entries
  到 arrive, 981, p.224
  道 way, direction, 2192, p.481
  盗 steal, burglarize, 749, p.174
de × 2 entries
  得 verbal particle, 1255, p.279
  的 of, 372, p.92
dé × 1 entry
  德 morality, 1257, p.280
dēng × 2 entries
  登 scale, climb, 2267, p.496
  灯 lamp, light, 1530, p.337
děng × 1 entry
  等 wait, 266, p.69
dèng × 1 entry
  邓 surname of Deng Xiaoping, 1927, p.423
dī × 2 entries
  低 low, below average, 1231, p.275
  滴 drip, 698, p.163
dí × 3 entries
  迪 enlighten, guide, 2145, p.471
  敌 enemy, foe, 2110, p.464
  翟 long-tailed pheasant, 1201, p.269
dǐ × 3 entries
  抵 support, sustain, 415, p.101
  氐 basic, 414, p.100
  底 bottom, base, 429, p.103
dì × 6 entries
  递 hand over, transmit, 2197, p.482
  帝 emperor*, 696, p.163
  弟 younger brother, 1494, p.330
  第 prefix for number in series, 1495, p.331
  蒂 base of fruit, 699, p.163
  地 earth, ground, 133, p.38
diǎn × 2 entries
  典 canon, dictionary, 1633, p.363
  点 dot, 1033, p.234
diàn × 3 entries
  电 electric current, 149, p.42
  殿 hall, palace, temple, 1923, p.422
  店 shop, 428, p.103
diāo × 1 entry
  雕 carve, engrave, 1836, p.405
diào × 3 entries
  掉 drop, fall, 203, p.54
  吊 suspend, hang, 119, p.35
  调 tune, 1835, p.405
diē × 1 entry
  跌 fall, tumble, 1151, p.259
dīng × 2 entries
  盯 stare, 86, p.29
  丁 fourth (in a series), 19, p.13
dǐng × 1 entry
  顶 carry on your head, 1410, p.313
dìng × 2 entries
  定 decide*, 783, p.181
  订 draw up, agree on, 354, p.88
diū × 1 entry
  丢 lose, misplace, 975, p.223
dōng × 2 entries
  东 east, 1288, p.288
  冬 winter, 2055, p.451
dǒng × 2 entries
  懂 understand, know, 1137, p.256
  董 director, 769, p.178
dòng × 2 entries
  洞 hole, cavity, 331, p.84
  动 move, 971, p.222
dōu × 1 entry
  都 all, 961, p.220
dǒu × 2 entries
  斗 cup-shaped, 185, p.51
  抖 tremble, 186, p.51
dòu × 1 entry
  豆 bean, 1597, p.355
dū × 1 entry
  督 supervise, 1902, p.418
dú × 3 entries
  毒 poison, 812, p.187

sì × 4 entries
四 four, 300, p.77
寺 Buddhist temple, 220, p.59
似 seem, appear, 1176, p.264
饲 feed (animals), 2043, p.448

sōng × 1 entry
松 pine tree, 1373, p.305

sǒng × 1 entry
竦 to tower, 862, p.197

sòng × 3 entries
讼 litigation, 1376, p.306
送 carry to, deliver, 2195, p.482
宋 Song dynasty, 579, p.137

sōu × 2 entries
搜 search, collect, 1881, p.414
艘 m for ships and vessels, 1883, p.414

sǒu × 1 entry
叟 old gentleman, 1880, p.414

sū × 1 entry
苏 revive*, 1466, p.324

sú × 1 entry
俗 vulgar, 1370, p.305

sù × 5 entries
肃 esteem, respect, 1468, p.324
速 speed, 2157, p.473
诉 speak one's mind, tell, 409, p.99
素 plain, simple, 1040, p.236
宿 stay overnight, 1191, p.267

suān × 1 entry
酸 sour, 2049, p.449

suàn × 1 entry
算 calculate, compute, 1764, p.390

suī × 2 entries
尿 urine, 506, p.120
虽 although, even though, 1019, p.231

suí × 1 entry
随 follow, comply with, 2181, p.478

suì × 2 entries
岁 years old, 895, p.204
碎 to smash, break, 1076, p.244

sūn × 1 entry
孙 grandson, 1340, p.299

sǔn × 1 entry
损 decrease, lose, 1423, p.315

suō × 1 entry
缩 contract, shrink, 1192, p.267

suǒ × 3 entries
锁 lock up, lock, 1558, p.343
索 scout around, look for, 1047, p.237
所 a place, 2093, p.460

tā × 3 entries
他 he, 1168, p.262
她 she, 797, p.184
它 it, 277, p.71

tǎ × 1 entry
塔 pagoda, 1684, p.373

tà × 2 entries
踏 step on, tread, stamp, 1152, p.259
沓 repeat sth numerous times, 316, p.81

tāi × 1 entry
胎 fetus, baby, 1827, p.403

tái × 2 entries
抬 raise, lift, 992, p.226
台 you (literary), 991, p.226

tài × 3 entries
态 attitude, 1130, p.255
太 too (much), 547, p.129
泰 peace, quiet, 1671, p.371

tān × 1 entry
贪 corrupt, 1705, p.378

tán × 3 entries
弹 pluck, play (an instrument), 1587, p.353
坛 altar, 970, p.222
谈 chat, talk, 1525, p.336

tǎn × 1 entry
坦 flat, 71, p.25

tàn × 2 entries
探 look for, explore, 1350, p.301
叹 sigh, exclaim, 1929, p.424

tāng × 1 entry
汤 soup, 466, p.112

táng × 3 entries
唐 Tang dynasty, 725, p.170
糖 sugar, sweets, carbs, 1543, p.340
堂 special room, 1568, p.346

tǎng × 2 entries
倘 if, in case, 1576, p.348
躺 lie down, 1575, p.348

táo × 3 entries
逃 escape, flee, 2148, p.471
桃 peach, 574, p.136
陶 pottery, 954, p.218

tǎo × 1 entry
讨 discourse, discuss, 359, p.89

tào × 1 entry
套 sheath, cover, 922, p.209

tè × 1 entry
特 special, unusual, 222, p.59

téng × 2 entries
疼 it hurts!, 2056, p.451
腾 gallop, prance, 1798, p.397

tī × 1 entry
梯 ladder, 1496, p.331

tí × 2 entries
提 lift, 195, p.53
题 topic, subject, title, 1414, p.313

tǐ × 1 entry
体 body*, 1234, p.275

tì × 1 entry
替 for, on behalf of, 719, p.168

tiān × 2 entries
添 increase, 1339, p.298
天 heaven, 548, p.129

tián × 3 entries
甜 sweetness, 772, p.179
填 fill out (form), 1380, p.307
田 field, 63, p.23

tiáo × 1 entry
条 strip (sth long and narrow), 2126, p.467

tiāo × 1 entry
挑 select, pick, 237, p.63

tiào × 1 entry
跳 jump, 1150, p.259

tiē × 1 entry
贴 paste, stick to, 1402, p.311

tiě × 1 entry
铁 iron, 2275, p.498

tīng × 2 entries
厅 public room, 423, p.102
听 hear, listen, 410, p.100

tíng × 5 entries
廷 imperial court, 2203, p.483
亭 pavilion, kiosk, 255, p.67
庭 courtyard, 2205, p.484
蜓 dragonfly, 2206, p.484
停 stop, pause, 1685, p.374

tǐng × 2 entries
挺 stand up straight, 2204, p.483
艇 small boat, 2207, p.484

tōng × 1 entry
通 go through, 2180, p.478

tóng × 3 entries
同 same, similar, 116, p.35
童 child, 694, p.162
铜 copper, 2272, p.497

tǒng × 1 entry
统 unite, gather, 1054, p.239

tòng × 1 entry
痛 painful, 1812, p.400

tōu × 1 entry
偷 pilfer, 1693, p.375

tóu × 2 entries
投 throw, fling, 1914, p.421
头 head, 708, p.165

tòu × 1 entry
透 filter, seep through, 2177, p.477

tū × 1 entry
突 dash forward, 1349, p.300

tú × 4 entries
涂 smear, apply, 1280, p.286
图 picture, chart, map, 2058, p.451
途 route, way, road, 2170, p.476
徒 disciple, pupil, follower, 1256, p.280

tǔ × 2 entries
土 earth, soil, 9, p.11
吐 spit, 45, p.19

tù × 1 entry
兔 rabbit, 739, p.172

tuán × 1 entry
团 round, circular, 455, p.109

tuàn × 1 entry
彖 determine, make a judgment, 1456, p.322

tuī × 1 entry
推 push, 1195, p.268

tuǐ × 1 entry
腿 leg, 2194, p.481

tuì × 1 entry
退 retreat, withdraw, 2193, p.481

tūn × 1 entry
吞 swallow, gulp down, 561, p.133

tún × 1 entry
屯 stockpile, store up, 159, p.44

tuō × 3 entries
脱 shed, take off, 1362, p.303
拖 pull, drag, haul, 541, p.128
托 hold (in palm), 28, p.16

tuǒ × 1 entry
妥 proper, 1658, p.368

wā × 1 entry
挖 dig, excavate, 1359, p.302

wá × 1 entry
娃 baby, 791, p.183

wǎ × 1 entry
瓦 tile, 147, p.41

wài × 1 entry
外 outside, external, 877, p.200

wān × 2 entries
弯 bent, curved, 845, p.194
湾 gulf, bay, 846, p.194

wán × 4 entries
完 to complete, finish, 297, p.76
顽 stupid, stubborn, 1415, p.314
丸 pill, 533, p.126
玩 have fun, amuse oneself, 296, p.76

wǎn × 4 entries
晚 evening, 741, p.173
碗 bowl, 893, p.203
宛 winding, 892, p.203
挽 draw, pull, 743, p.173

wàn × 1 entry
万 ten thousand, 917, p.208

wāng × 1 entry
汪 expanse of water, 328, p.83

wáng × 2 entries
亡 perish, 259, p.67
王 king, 15, p.12

wǎng × 2 entries
往 direction toward, 1248, p.278
网 net, 2013, p.442

wàng × 2 entries
望 gaze into distance, 1774, p.392
忘 forget, 1111, p.251

wēi × 3 entries
微 micro, tiny, minute, 2104, p.462
危 danger, imperil, 834, p.191
威 power, might, 806, p.186

wéi × 7 entries
惟 way of thought, -ism, 1211, p.271
唯 alone, only, 1196, p.268
为 do, accomplish, 481, p.115
维 hold together, 1200, p.269
韦 leather, 109, p.33
违 oppose, 2179, p.478
围 surround, enclose, 110, p.34

wěi × 4 entries
委 listless, dejected, 803, p.185
尾 tail, 505, p.120
伪 false, fake, bogus, 1246, p.278
伟 great, imposing, 1236, p.276

wèi × 11 entries
畏 fear, dread*, 420, p.102
魏 Wei dynasty, 1013, p.230
慰 console, comfort, 1285, p.288
尉 military official, 1284, p.287
位 m for persons (polite), 1225, p.274
未 have not yet, 582, p.137
谓 say*, 1823, p.402
味 flavor, 583, p.138
卫 protect*, 112, p.34
胃 stomach, 1822, p.402
喂 to feed, 421, p.102

wēn × 1 entry
温 lukewarm, to warm up, 340, p.86

wén × 3 entries
闻 hear, smell, 245, p.65
纹 vein, grain, 1993, p.438
文 culture, language, 1986, p.437

wěn × 2 entries
稳 steady, steadfast, 1127, p.254
吻 kiss, 468, p.112

wèn × 1 entry
问 ask, 244, p.64

wō × 1 entry
窝 nest, lair, 1348, p.300

wǒ × 1 entry
我 I, 661, p.156

wò × 3 entries
卧 lie down, crouch (animals), 205, p.55
沃 fertile, rich, 717, p.168
握 hold tight (in hand), 984, p.224

wū × 4 entries
乌 dark, 398, p.97
巫 wizard, 728, p.170
污 dirty, filthy, foul, 2258, p.494
屋 house*, 983, p.224

wú × 4 entries